AUSTRALIAN BANKING AND FINANCE LAW AND REGULATION

Australia's banking and finance sectors continue to evolve and adapt to technological disruption, product innovation and increasing globalisation while also facing increasing scrutiny from policymakers, regulators and consumers following a series of highly publicised crises and scandals. *Australian Banking and Finance Law and Regulation* provides a comprehensive, up-to-date and accessible introduction to the complexities of contemporary law and regulation of the banking and financial sectors in one volume.

The book provides a detailed analysis of Australia's financial market regulatory framework and the theoretical underpinnings of government intervention in the field. It delves into the legal changes implemented in response to the Global Financial Crisis and recent local scandals, exploring the complexities and subtleties of the 'banker–customer' relationship. Other topics include:

- consumer credit protection
- financial product regulation
- payment methods
- electronic banking
- emerging regulatory challenges
- the advent of central bank digital currencies
- data-sharing initiatives, confidentiality and data protection
- adherence to anti-money laundering and counter-terrorism regulations
- the effects of technological innovation and disruption on traditional banking practices.

Readers will appreciate the clear and concise treatment of key issues, cases and examples that offer an overview of major developments. The questions at the end of each chapter serve as an effective tool for readers to assess and reinforce their grasp of the fundamental principles discussed.

Through their careful selection and examination of crucial issues, Han-Wei Liu and Weiping He offer an essential guide for those aiming to understand and keep pace with the ever-evolving landscape of Australian banking and finance law and regulation.

Han-Wei Liu is Associate Professor of Law at the Yong Pong How School of Law, Singapore Management University, and an Adjunct Senior Research Fellow at Monash Business School.

Weiping He is a lecturer at Monash Law Faculty, Monash University.

AUSTRALIAN BANKING AND FINANCE LAW AND REGULATION

Han-Wei Liu

Weiping He

CAMBRIDGE
UNIVERSITY PRESS

CAMBRIDGE
UNIVERSITY PRESS

Shaftesbury Road, Cambridge CB2 8EA, United Kingdom

One Liberty Plaza, 20th Floor, New York, NY 10006, USA

477 Williamstown Road, Port Melbourne, VIC 3207, Australia

314–321, 3rd Floor, Plot 3, Splendor Forum, Jasola District Centre,
New Delhi – 110025, India

103 Penang Road, #05–06/07, Visioncrest Commercial, Singapore 238467

Cambridge University Press is part of Cambridge University Press & Assessment,
a department of the University of Cambridge.

We share the University's mission to contribute to society through the pursuit of
education, learning and research at the highest international levels of excellence.

www.cambridge.org
Information on this title: www.cambridge.org/highereducation/isbn/9781108999793

First published 2024

Cover designed by Simon Rattray, Squirt Creative
Typeset by Lumina Datamatics Ltd

A catalogue record for this publication is available from the British Library

A catalogue record for this book is available from the National Library of Australia

ISBN 978-1-108-99979-3 Paperback

Additional resources for this publication at www.cambridge.org/highereducation/
isbn/9781108999793/resources

CONTENTS

About the authors *xiii*
Acknowledgements *xiv*
Table of cases *xv*
Table of statutes *xxiii*
List of abbreviations *xxxv*

1 Regulatory theory and framework **1**
1.1 Introduction 2
1.1.1 Public interest theory 8
1.1.2 Private interest theory 9
1.2 Regulatory objectives, institutional structure and strategies 11
1.2.1 Regulatory objectives revisited 11
1.2.1.1 Prudential regulation 11
1.2.1.2 Conduct regulation 13
1.2.2 Institutional structure 13
1.2.3 Strategies of regime design in a nutshell 16
1.2.3.1 Command-and-control versus self-regulation 16
1.2.3.2 Rules-based versus principles-based regulation 17
1.3 Regulators and regulations 18
1.3.1 Regulators at the domestic level 20
1.3.1.1 Reserve Bank of Australia (RBA) 20
1.3.1.2 Australian Prudential Regulation Authority (APRA) 22
1.3.1.3 Australian Securities and Investments Commission (ASIC) 25
1.3.1.4 Council of Financial Regulators (CFR) 26
1.3.1.5 Australian Competition and Consumer Commission (ACCC) 28
1.3.1.6 Australian Transaction Reports and Analysis Centre (AUSTRAC) 29
1.3.1.7 Financial Regulator Assessment Authority (FRAA) 30
1.3.2 Governance of the financial market at the global level 31
1.3.2.1 Financial Stability Board (FSB) 31
1.3.2.2 Bank for International Settlements (BIS) 33
1.3.2.3 Basel Committee on Banking Supervision (BCBS) 34
1.4 Summary 36
Further reading 36
Questions 37

2 Consumer protection and consumer credit **39**
2.1 Introduction 40
2.1.1 Consumer credit protection in Australia 40

2.1.2 Scope of the *NCCPA* 45
2.1.2.1 Key features 45
2.1.2.2 Covered activities 46
2.2 Licence and other obligations under the *NCCPA* and the *NCC* 50
2.2.1 Key categories of credit activity and licensing requirements 50
2.2.2 Primary obligations of the ACL under the *NCCPA* 53
2.2.2.1 Mandatory disclosure requirements 53
2.2.2.2 Responsible lending obligation 54
2.2.2.3 'Best interests' duty 58
2.2.3 Key features of the *NCC* 61
2.2.3.1 Pre-contractual disclosure 61
2.3 Challenges ahead 65
2.3.1 Payday loan: A perennial problem 65
2.3.2 The rise of 'buy now, pay later' 68
2.4 Summary 70
Further reading 71
Questions 71

3 Financial products regulation 73
3.1 Introduction 74
3.1.1 The Wallis Inquiry 74
3.1.2 The Murray Inquiry 75
3.1.3 Emerging reforms: Australian Law Reform Commission's recommendations 76
3.2 Regulatory framework 78
3.2.1 Financial services 78
3.2.2 Financial products 79
3.2.2.1 General definition 80
3.2.2.2 Specific inclusions 80
3.2.2.3 Overriding exclusions 80
3.2.3 The concept of 'clients': Retail versus wholesale 82
3.2.4 AFSL licensee's requirements 83
3.2.4.1 Requirements for application 83
3.2.4.2 Representatives 84
3.2.4.3 General obligations 85
3.2.4.4 Disclosure requirements 85
3.2.4.5 Additional obligations 89
3.3 Product intervention and product design and distribution obligations 99
3.3.1 Product Intervention Power (PIP) 100
3.3.2 Product Design and Distribution Obligation (DDO) 104
3.4 Robo-advice 107
3.4.1 Facts, financial product advice and relevant requirements 107
3.4.2 Resources 108
3.4.3 Adequate risk management systems 109

3.4.3.1 Monitoring and testing algorithms 109
3.4.3.2 Cyber risks and information security 109
3.4.4 Compensation arrangements 110
3.5 Summary 110
Further reading 110
Questions 111

4 New challenges in the data-driven financial markets 113
4.1 Introduction 114
4.2 Regulatory sandbox: Australia and beyond 119
4.2.1 Background 119
4.2.2 Eligibility 121
4.2.2.1 Eligible persons 121
4.2.2.2 Conditions of entry 121
4.2.3 Scope of activities 123
4.2.4 Time frame and exposure limits 124
4.2.5 Other conditions 125
4.2.6 Other jurisdictions: United Kingdom and beyond 126
4.3 Data protection 130
4.3.1 Data protection in Australia: An overview 130
4.3.1.1 Statutes 130
4.3.1.2 Self-regulation 131
4.3.1.3 Equitable duties of confidence 131
4.3.1.4 Common law duties of confidentiality 132
4.3.2 *Privacy Act 1988* (Cth) 132
4.3.2.1 Background 132
4.3.2.2 Scope of application and structure 133
4.3.2.3 Credit reporting 135
4.3.2.4 Australian Privacy Principles (APPs) 136
4.3.3 New developments: European Union's *General Data Protection Regulation* (GDPR) and 'the Brussels Effect' 142
4.4 Summary 145
Further reading 145
Questions 146

5 Banks, banking and the banker–customer relationship 148
5.1 Introduction 149
5.2 Nature of the relationship 149
5.2.1 A debtor–creditor relationship 149
5.2.2 A special kind of debt with special terms 150
5.2.2.1 Bank may refuse to make any payment 151
5.2.2.2 Reasonable notice 151
5.2.2.3 Reasonable care 151
5.2.3 Implied terms 151
5.2.4 Other relationships between banker and customer 152

5.3 Who is the customer? 152
5.4 Terminating the relationship 154
5.5 Altering the relationship 155
5.6 Statutory limitations of actions 157
5.6.1 General rules 157
5.6.2 Limitation and overdrafts 158
5.7 Special customers 159
5.7.1 Unincorporated associations 159
5.7.2 Incorporated associations 160
5.7.3 Partnerships 160
5.7.4 Minors 161
5.7.5 Executors/administrators 162
5.7.6 Companies 163
5.8 Dormant accounts 164
5.9 Summary 165
Further reading 166
Questions 166

6 Accounts **167**
6.1 Introduction 168
6.2 Some types of accounts 168
6.2.1 Current (transaction) accounts 168
6.2.2 Savings accounts 168
6.2.3 Term deposits 169
6.2.3.1 Particular purpose deposits 170
6.2.3.2 Overdrafts 170
6.2.3.3 Trust accounts 171
6.2.3.4 Joint accounts 172
6.2.3.5 Statements and passbooks 174
6.3 Combining accounts 175
6.3.1 General rules 175
6.3.2 The rule in *Clayton's case* (*Devaynes v Noble*) 177
6.3.3 'Exceptions' to the *Clayton* rule 177
6.4 Freezing the account 178
6.4.1 Mental incapacity 178
6.4.2 Death 178
6.4.3 Bankruptcy and winding up 179
6.4.3.1 Basic terminology 179
6.5 Garnishee orders 184
6.6 Tracing orders 187
6.6.1 Example 188
6.7 Summary 188
Further reading 189
Questions 189

7 Duties of the banker and the customer **190**
7.1 Introduction 191
7.2 The *Tournier* duty 191
7.2.1 Legal compulsion 192
7.2.2 Public interest 193
7.2.3 Commercial interest 194
7.2.4 Consent 195
7.3 Duty to the enquirer/third parties 197
7.4 Duty to question a valid mandate 199
7.5 Safe custody 200
7.6 The *Macmillan* duty 202
7.7 The *Greenwood* duty 204
7.8 Other possible duties 205
7.8.1 Duty to discover forgeries 206
7.8.2 Duty to prevent forgeries 206
7.8.3 Duty to organise business 207
7.9 Summary 208
Further reading 208
Questions 208

8 Cheques and bills of exchange **210**
8.1 Introduction 211
8.2 Cheques 211
8.2.1 Definitions 212
8.2.1.1 Cheque 212
8.2.1.2 Financial institution 212
8.2.1.3 No payee 213
8.2.1.4 Sum certain 213
8.2.1.5 Unconditional order 213
8.2.1.6 Note on unconditional order – conditional delivery 214
8.2.1.7 On demand 214
8.2.1.8 Date 215
8.2.1.9 Order and bearer cheques 215
8.2.2 Transfer by negotiation 215
8.2.3 Role of the drawer's signature 215
8.2.4 Crossings 216
8.2.4.1 Definition 216
8.2.4.2 The effect of crossing 216
8.2.4.3 Who may cross 216
8.2.4.4 'Account payee only' 217
8.2.5 Bank cheques 217
8.2.6 Traveller's cheques 217
8.2.7 Payment by cheque 218
8.2.8 The meaning of 'dishonour' 219

8.2.9 The duty to pay 219
8.2.9.1 Proper manner 220
8.2.9.2 Funds available 220
8.2.9.3 Legal impediment 220
8.2.9.4 Proper presentation 221
8.2.10 Prompt payment or dishonour 222
8.2.11 Wrongful dishonour 222
8.2.12 Wrongful payment 224
8.2.12.1 Wrong amount 224
8.2.12.2 Wrong person 224
8.2.13 Defences of the paying bank 224
8.2.13.1 Contractual defences 224
8.2.13.2 The 'equitable defence' 225
8.2.13.3 Statutory defences 226
8.3 Bills of exchange 227
8.3.1 Definition 227
8.3.1.1 Unconditional order 227
8.3.1.2 In writing 227
8.3.1.3 Addressed by one person to another 227
8.3.1.4 Signed by the person giving it 228
8.3.1.5 Requiring the drawee to pay on demand 228
8.3.1.6 Or at a fixed or determinable future time 228
8.3.1.7 A sum certain in money 228
8.3.1.8 To or to the order of a specified person or to bearer 229
8.3.2 Analysis 229
8.3.2.1 Promissory notes 232
8.3.3 Transfer/negotiation 233
8.3.4 Introduction to liability 234
8.3.4.1 Holder for value, and holder in due course 235
8.3.5 Acceptance 237
8.3.5.1 Presentment for acceptance 238
8.3.5.2 Where the bill is not accepted 238
8.3.5.3 Acceptance for honour 239
8.3.6 Payment 239
8.3.7 Liabilities of parties 240
8.3.7.1 Who may be liable 240
8.3.7.2 Extent of liability 240
8.3.7.3 Effect of forgery 241
8.3.7.4 Inchoate instruments 242
8.3.7.5 Circuity of action 242
8.3.7.6 Measure of liability 243
8.3.8 Discharge 243
8.3.8.1 Payment in due course 243
8.3.8.2 Acceptor becoming holder 244

8.3.8.3 Express waiver 244
8.3.8.4 Cancellation 244
8.3.8.5 Material alteration 244
8.4 Summary 245
Further reading 245
Questions 245

9 Electronic banking 246
9.1 Introduction 247
9.1.1 Payment system, regulators and governing legislation/regulations 247
9.1.2 A snapshot of payment systems 249
9.1.3 Main payment instruments 253
9.1.3.1 Credit cards 254
9.1.3.2 Debit cards 255
9.1.3.3 BPAY 256
9.1.3.4 Stored value cards 256
9.2 *ePayments Code* 257
9.2.1 History 257
9.2.2 The legal nature of the *ePayments Code* 257
9.2.3 Key provisions examined 258
9.2.3.1 Types of transactions 258
9.2.3.2 To whom does the *ePayments Code* apply? 259
9.2.3.3 Allocation of liability for unauthorised transactions 259
9.2.3.4 Mistaken internet payments 263
9.2.3.5 Complaint process 266
9.2.3.6 Compliance monitoring and data collection 267
9.2.3.7 Other emerging challenges 267
9.3 New challenges: Open Banking and digital currencies 272
9.3.1 The rise of Open Banking 272
9.3.1.1 Introduction 272
9.3.1.2 Consumer data rights in Australia 274
9.3.2 Digital currencies issued by central banks 279
9.3.2.1 The rise of digital currencies 279
9.3.2.2 Selected cases 280
9.4 Summary 283
Further reading 283
Questions 284

10 Lending, secured lending and guarantees 286
10.1 Introduction 287
10.2 Lending 287
10.2.1 Types of lending 287
10.2.1.1 Secured/unsecured loans 287
10.2.1.2 Overdrafts 287
10.2.1.3 Term loans 289

10.2.1.4 Commercial bills 289
10.2.1.5 Letters of comfort 290
10.2.2 Types of borrowers 291
10.2.2.1 Minors 291
10.2.2.2 Unincorporated businesses 292
10.2.2.3 Companies 292
10.2.2.4 Consumers 293
10.3 Secured lending: Real property 295
10.3.1 Legal and equitable interests 295
10.3.1.1 Introduction 295
10.3.1.2 'Competing interests' – priority rules 295
10.3.1.3 'Legal' mortgage – general law 297
10.3.1.4 Equitable mortgage 297
10.3.1.5 Second and subsequent mortgages 298
10.3.1.6 Remedies on default – general law 298
10.3.1.7 The power of sale 298
10.3.1.8 Equitable charges 299
10.3.2 Torrens system 299
10.3.2.1 Introduction 299
10.3.2.2 Priorities with respect to unregistered interests 300
10.3.2.3 Mortgages under the Torrens system 301
10.4 Guarantees 302
10.4.1 Introduction 302
10.4.1.1 Parties 302
10.4.1.2 Guarantee versus indemnity 303
10.4.1.3 Consideration 303
10.4.1.4 Continuing guarantees 303
10.4.1.5 Guarantee not a contract *uberrimae fidei*, but ... 304
10.4.2 Liabilities 304
10.4.2.1 Rights of guarantors 304
10.4.2.2 Co-guarantors/co-sureties and contribution 305
10.4.2.3 Minors 305
10.4.2.4 *Dobbs* clauses 306
10.4.2.5 Limitation of guarantor's liability 306
10.4.3 Avoidance 306
10.4.3.1 Guarantees by married women 307
10.4.4 Discharge of the surety 308
10.4.5 Statutory provisions affecting guarantees 309
10.5 Summary 309
Further reading 310
Questions 310

Index *311*

ABOUT THE AUTHORS

Dr Han-Wei Liu is Associate Professor of Law at the Yong Pong How School of Law, Singapore Management University, and an Adjunct Senior Research Fellow at Monash Business School. Dr Liu's research interests lie in international economic law and financial regulations, specifically how they interact with emerging technologies and innovation. He investigates various regulatory strategies for new technologies and assesses their effects on domestic markets, both financial and non-financial, employing a comparative legal approach. Additionally, he examines the broader implications of these regulatory strategies in international economic law, providing insightful contributions to this dynamic area.

Dr Weiping He is a lecturer at Monash Law Faculty, Monash University. Her research interests primarily lie in the areas of comparative financial markets regulation (securities markets and banking) and comparative studies in corporate law. She is interested in how regulatory regimes differ in terms of nature and dynamics as a result of varied historical, political and economic circumstances. Her research also incidentally attempts to evaluate the proper role of government vis à vis the market – for example, in assessing the efficiency of various regulatory regimes and the competence and effectiveness of regulators.

ACKNOWLEDGEMENTS

Han-Wei Liu: My heart overflows with gratitude to my former colleagues at Monash – Minu Scaria, Matt Nichol and Toan Le – and to my exceptional research assistants, Amanda Tan (Monash), Derek Zhang, Denise Siah, Jody Chng and Bernadette Teo (Singapore Management University). Thank you, Ange, Carmen and Sharyon, for your support. Thank you also to Michelle Welsh, whose trust brought me to Monash to lead the Banking Law unit. I am profoundly grateful to my family for their steadfast encouragement. This book, a cherished creation, would not have come to fruition without each and every one of you.

Weiping He: To my husband, for his unwavering love and steadfast support.

The authors and Cambridge University Press would like to thank the following for permission to reproduce material in this book.

Figure 9.1: original figure © AUSTRAC for the Commonwealth of Australia 2019, reproduced under Creative Commons Attribution 4.0 International (CC BY 4.0), https://creativecommons.org/licenses/by/4.0/legalcode; graphics used in adaptation © Getty Images/Amin Yusifov (people), © Getty Images/Dedy Setyawan (globe), © Getty Images/Steppeua (bank), © Getty Images/mikroman6 (Australia).

Figure 9.2: © Reserve Bank of Australia. Reproduced under Creative Commons Attribution 4.0 International (CC BY 4.0): https://creativecommons.org/licenses/by/4.0/legalcode.

Table 9.1: © Reserve Bank of Australia. Reproduced under Creative Commons Attribution 4.0 International (CC BY 4.0): https://creativecommons.org/licenses/by/4.0/legalcode.

Extracts from Australian Securities and Investments Commission, *ePayments Code* (2 June 2022) https://download.asic.gov.au/media/lloeicwb/epayments-code-published-02-june-2022.pdf: © Australian Securities and Investments Commission. Reproduced under Creative Commons Attribution 4.0 International (CC BY 4.0): https://creativecommons.org/licenses/by/4.0/legalcode.

Extracts from Law Reports, Queen's Bench (QB) (Third Series): reproduced with permission of the Incorporated Council of Law Reporting for England and Wales.

Extracts from Australian Commonwealth legislation: sourced from the Federal Register of Legislation and reproduced under Creative Commons Attribution 4.0 International (CC BY 4.0). For the latest information on Australian Government law, please go to https://www.legislation.gov.au.

Every effort has been made to trace and acknowledge copyright. The publisher apologises for any accidental infringement and welcomes information that would redress this situation.

TABLE OF CASES

Airservices Australia v Ferrier (1996) 185 CLR 483, 181
Akrokerri (Atlantic) Mines Ltd v Economic Bank [1904] 2 KB 465, 174
Alliance Bank Ltd v Kearsly (1871) LR 6 CP 433, 160
Ambrose v Badcock [2021] FCA 1647, 180
Andrews v Australia and New Zealand Banking Group Ltd (2011) 211 FCR 53, 257
Ansell Rubber Co Pty Ltd v Allied Rubber Industries Pty Ltd [1967] VR 37, 132
Arab Bank Ltd v Ross [1952] 2 QB 216, 236–7
Ardern v Bank of New South Wales [1956] VLR 569, 173
Atkas v Westpac Banking Corporation Ltd (2010) 241 CLR 79, 223
Australia Bank Ltd v Hokit Pty Ltd (1996) 39 NSWLR 377, 174
Australian Competition and Consumer Commission v Sony Interactive Entertainment Network Europe Ltd (2020) 381 ALR 531, 270
Australian Mutual Provident Society v Derham (1979) 39 FLR 165, 226
Australian Securities and Investments Commission v BHF Solutions Pty Ltd (2022) 293 FCR 330, 49–50
Australian Securities and Investments Commission v Channic Pty Ltd (No 4) [2016] FCA 1174, 55–6
Australian Securities and Investments Commission v Commonwealth Bank of Australia (2023) 412 ALR 536, 98–9
Australian Securities and Investments Commission v Fast Access Finance [2015] FCA 1055, 47
Australian Securities and Investments Commission v Financial Circle Pty Ltd (2018) 353 ALR 137, 94–5
Australian Securities and Investments Commission v Golden Financial Group Pty Ltd (No 2) [2017] FCA 1267, 94
Australian Securities and Investments Commission v Mayfair Wealth Partners Pty Ltd (No 2) [2021] FCA 247, 67
Australian Securities and Investments Commission v NSG Services Pty Ltd (2017) 122 ACSR 47, 94
Australian Securities and Investments Commission v The Cash Store Pty Ltd (in liq) [2014] FCA 926, 55
Australian Securities and Investments Commission v Wealth & Risk Management Pty Ltd (No 2) (2018) 124 ACSR 351, 94
Australian Securities and Investments Commission v Westpac Banking Corporation (2019) 139 ACSR 25, 57

B Liggett (Liverpool) Ltd v Barclays Bank Ltd [1928] 1 KB 48, 225
Backhouse v Charlton (1878) 8 Ch D 444, 160
Bagley v Winsome and National Provincial Bank [1952] 2 QB 236, 186
Baker v Australia and New Zealand Bank Ltd [1958] NZLR 907, 223
Baker v Efford (1873) 4 AJR 161, 228
Banbury v Bank of Montreal [1918] AC 626, 199

Bank of England v Vagliano Brothers [1891] AC 107, 224, 229
Bank of Ireland v Evans Charities Trustees in Ireland (1855) 10 ER 950, 206
Bank of New South Wales v Brown (1983) 151 CLR 514, 288
Bank of New South Wales v Laing (1953) 54 SR (NSW) 76, 151
Bank of New South Wales Ltd v Barlex Investments Pty Ltd (1964) 64 SR (NSW) 274, 186
Bank of New South Wales Savings Bank Ltd v Fremantle Auto Centre Pty Ltd [1973] WAR 161, 186
Bank of Queensland Ltd v Dutta [2010] NSWSC 574, 48
Bank of Tokyo Ltd v Karoon [1987] AC 45, 195
Banque Brussels Lambert SA v Australian National Industries Ltd (1989) 21 NSWLR 502, 290–1
Barclays Bank Ltd v Quistclose Investments Ltd [1970] AC 567, 176
Barclays Bank plc v O'Brien [1994] 1 AC 180, 308
Barker v GE Mortgage Solutions Ltd [2013] QCA 137, 63
Barnhart v Greenshields (1853) 14 ER 204, 297
Bavins Jnr & Sims v London & South Western Bank Ltd [1900] 1 QB 270, 214
Berry v Gibbons (1873) 8 Ch App 747, 162
Berwick v Lloyds TSB Bank plc [2007] EW Mis 1, 170
Birch v Treasury Solicitor [1951] Ch 298, 174
Bobbett v Pinkett (1876) 1 Ex D 368, 226
Bodnar v Townsend (2003) 12 Tas R 232, 194
BP Refinery (Westernport) Pty Ltd v Hastings Shire Council (1977) 180 CLR 266, 151
Bradford Old Bank Ltd v Sutcliffe [1918] 2 KB 833, 159, 176
Braidwood v Turner (1908) 10 WALR 105, 223
Breskvar v Wall (1971) 126 CLR 376, 300
Brewer v Westminster Bank Ltd [1952] 2 All ER 650, 173–4
Brown v Westminster Bank Ltd [1964] 2 Lloyd's Rep 187, 205
Burnett v Westminster Bank Ltd [1966] 1 QB 742, 155–6

Catlin v Cyprus Finance Corporation (London) Ltd [1983] QB 759, 173
Charles v Blackwell (1877) 2 CPD 151, 226
Cigno Pty Ltd v Australian Securities and Investments Commission [2020] FCA 479, 102–3
Cinema Plus Ltd (admins apptd) v Australia and New Zealand Banking Group Ltd (2000) 49 NSWLR 513, 176
Clarke v Palmer (1882) 21 Ch D 12, 296
Clayton v Le Roy [1911] 2 KB 1031, 201
Clenae Pty Ltd v Australia & New Zealand Banking Group [1999] 2 VR 573, 43
Codelfa Construction Pty Ltd v State Rail Authority (NSW) (1982) 149 CLR 337, 152
Commercial Bank of Australia Ltd v Amadio (1983) 151 CLR 447, 307
Commercial Banking Co of Sydney Ltd v RH Brown & Co (1972) 126 CLR 337, 197, 198
Commissioner of Taxation v English, Scottish and Australian Bank Ltd [1920] AC 683, 153
Commonwealth Bank of Australia v Cohen (1988) ASC 55-681, 308
Commonwealth Bank of Australia v Smith (1991) 42 FCR 390, 43
Commonwealth Trading Bank of Australia v Reno Auto Sales Pty Ltd [1967] VR 790, 221

Commonwealth Trading Bank of Australia v Sydney Wide Stores Pty Ltd (1981) 148 CLR 304, 202–3
Con-Stan Industries of Australia Pty Ltd v Norwich Winterthur Insurance (Australia) Ltd (1986) 160 CLR 226, 152
Consul Development Pty Ltd v DPC Estates Pty Ltd (1975) 132 CLR 373, 172
Cooper v National Provincial Bank Ltd [1945] 2 All ER 641, 304
Corrs Pavey Whiting & Byrne v Collector of Customs (Vic) (1987) 14 FCR 434, 193–4
Cory Brothers & Co Ltd v Owners of the Turkish Steamship Mecca [1897] AC 286, 169, 177
Coshett v Australian Securities and Investments Commission [2014] AATA 677, 45
Crantrave Ltd (in liq) v Lloyds Bank plc [2000] QB 917, 225
Croton v The Queen (1967) 117 CLR 326, 150
Curtice v London City & Midland Bank Ltd [1908] 1 KB 293, 221
Cuthbert v Robarts, Lubbock & Co [1909] 2 Ch 226, 170, 288

Day & Dent Constructions Pty Ltd (in liq) v North Australian Properties Pty Ltd (1982) 150 CLR 85, 183
De Francesco v Barnum (1890) 45 Ch D 430, 154
Deeley v Lloyds Bank Ltd [1912] AC 756, 169
Dennis v Commonwealth Bank of Australia [2020] FCCA 1313, 42
Derry v Peek (1889) LR 14 App Cas 337, 198
Devans v Noble (1816) 35 ER 781, 182
Devaynes v Noble (1816) 35 ER 781, 177–8, 187, 292
DFC New Zealand Ltd v McKenzie [1993] 2 NZLR 576, 159
Di Cioccio v Official Trustee in Bankruptcy [2015] FCAFC 30, 180
Diamond v Bank of London and Montreal Ltd [1979] QB 333, 199
Dickson v Muckleston (1872) 8 Ch App 155, 296
Direct Acceptance Corporation Ltd v Bank of New South Wales (1968) 88 WN (Pt 1) (NSW) 498, 176
DJ Colburt & Sons Pty Ltd v Ansen [1966] 2 NSWR 289, 187
Dobbs v National Bank of Australasia Ltd (1935) 53 CLR 643, 175, 306
Douglas v Lloyds Bank Ltd (1924) 34 Com Cas 263, 165
Duncan, Fox & Co v North & South Wales Bank (1879) 11 Ch D 88, 305

Ellaw Co Ltd v Lloyds Bank Ltd (1934) 4 LDAB 455, 223
EMU Brewery Mezzanine Ltd (in liq) v Australian Securities and Investments Commission (2006) 32 WAR 204, 228
Ex parte Waring (1815) 34 ER 546, 290

Farrar v Farrars Ltd (1880) 40 Ch D 395, 299
Flach v London & South Western Bank Ltd (1915) 31 TLR 334, 223
Fleming v Bank of New Zealand [1900] AC 577, 220
Foley v Hill (1848) 9 ER 1002, 149–50, 168
Foskett v McKeown [2001] 1 AC 102, 251
Frazer v Walker [1967] 1 AC 569, 300
Freeman & Lockyer v Buckhurst Park Properties (Mangal) Ltd [1964] 2 QB 480, 164
Fried v National Australia Bank Ltd (2001) 111 FCR 322, 171

Garcia v National Australia Bank Ltd (1998) 194 CLR 395, 43, 308
Garnett v M'Kewan (1872) LR 8 Ex 10, 176
Gartside and Outram [1857] 26 LJ CH 113, 193
Gibbons v Westminster Bank Ltd [1939] 2 KB 882, 222
Goodwin v National Bank of Australasia Ltd (1968) 117 CLR 173, 304
Great Western Railway Co v London & County Banking Co Ltd [1901] AC 414, 153
Greenwood v Martins Bank Ltd [1933] AC 51, 151, 204–5
Gye v McIntyre (1991) 171 CLR 609, 183

Hamilton v Watson (1845) ER 1139, 304
Harrods v Tester [1937] 2 All ER 236, 186
Hassneh Insurance Co of Israel v Mew [1993] 2 Lloyd's Rep 243, 194
Hawkins v Clayton (1988) 164 CLR 539, 208
Healey v Commonwealth Bank of Australia [1998] NSWCA 103, 169
Hedley Byrne & Co Ltd v Heller & Partners Ltd [1964] AC 465, 197
Heller Factors Pty Ltd v Toy Corporation Pty Ltd [1984] 1 NSWLR 121, 236
Heppenstall v Jackson [1939] 1 KB 585, 186
HH Dimond (Rotorua 1966) Ltd v Australia and New Zealand Banking Group Ltd [1979] 2 NZLR 739, 222
Hill v National Bank of New Zealand Ltd [1985] 1 NZLR 736, 223
Hirschorn v Evans (Barclays Bank Ltd, Garnishees) [1938] 2 KB 801, 186
Hodgson & Lee Pty Ltd v Mardonius Pty Ltd (1986) 5 NSWLR 496, 215
Hoon v Maloff; Jarvis Construction Co Ltd (Garnishees) (1964) 42 DLR (2d) 770, 186
Hopkinson v Rolt (1861) 11 ER 829, 302
Huenerbein v Federal Bank of Australia (1892) 9 WN 65, 170
Husband v Davis (1851) 138 ER 256, 221

Inflatable Toy Co Pty Ltd v State Bank of New South Wales Ltd (1994) 34 NSWLR 243, 235
Initial Services Ltd v Putterill [1968] 1 QB 396, 193
Ireland v Livingston (1872) LR 5 HL 395, 220

Jackson v White [1967] 2 Lloyd's Rep 68, 173
Jade International Steel Stahl und Eisen GmbH & Co KG v Robert Nicholas (Steels) Ltd [1978] QB 917, 235
Jayson v Midland Bank Ltd [1968] 1 Lloyd's Rep 409, 223
Joachimson v Swiss Bank Corporation [1921] 3 KB 110, 150–1, 154, 158, 185
Jones v Gordon (1877) 2 App Cas 616, 236

Karak Rubber Co Ltd v Burden (No 2) [1972] 1 WLR 602, 199
Kepitigalla Rubber Estates Ltd v National Bank of India Ltd [1909] 2 KB 1010, 206
Kpohraror v Woolwich Building Society [1996] 4 All ER 119, 222

L Shaddock & Associates Pty Ltd v Parramatta City Council (1981) 150 CLR 225, 197
Ladbroke & Co v Todd [1914] 30 TLR 433, 153
Laney v Gates (1935) 35 SR (NSW) 372, 233

Lauvan Pty Ltd v Bega (No 2) [2018] NSWSC 155, 48
Lee Gleeson Pty Ltd v Sterling Estates Pty Ltd (1991) 23 NSWLR 571, 195–6
Libyan Arab Foreign Bank v Bankers Trust Co. [1989] QB 728, 251
Linkenholt Pty Ltd v Quirk (2000) ASC 155-040, 48
Lipkin Gorman v Karpnale Ltd [1992] 4 All ER 409, 199–200
Little v Slackford (1828) 1 Mood & M 171, 227
London Joint Stock Bank Ltd v Macmillan & Arthur [1918] AC 777, 151, 202–4, 205, 220
Lubbock v Tribe (1838) 3 M & W 607, 218
Lumley General Insurance Ltd v Oceanfast Marine Pty Ltd [2001] NSWCA 479, 306
Lyritzis v Westpac Banking Corporation (1994) ATPR 41-360, 217

Mackenzie v Albany Finance Ltd [2004] WASCA 301, 164, 165
Macquarie Bank Ltd v Sixty-Fourth Throne Pty Ltd [1998] 3 VR 133, 300
MAG Financial and Investment Ventures Pty Ltd v El-Saafin [2022] VSCA 286, 49
Mahoney v McManus (1981) 180 CLR 370, 305
Makower, McBeth & Co Ltd v Dalgety & Co Ltd [1921] VLR 365, 201
Marfani & Co Ltd v Midland Bank Ltd [1968] 1 WLR 956, 154
Marshall v Colonial Bank of Australasia (1904) 1 CLR 632, 202, 203
Marzetti v Williams (1830) 109 ER 842, 220
Matthews v Williams-Brown & Co (1894) 10 TLR 386, 153
Matzner v Clyde Securities Ltd [1975] 2 NSWLR 293, 302
Mercantile Credits Ltd v Australia and New Zealand Banking Group Ltd (1988) 48 SASR 407, 302
Miller Associates (Australia) Pty Ltd v Bennington Pty Ltd [1975] 2 NSWLR 506, 234
Music Masters Pty Ltd v Minelle [1968] Qd R 326, 186
Mutual Life & Citizens' Assurance Co Ltd v Evatt (1968) 122 CLR 556, 196, 198

Narni Pty Ltd v National Australia Bank Ltd [1998] VSC 146, 288
Nathan v Ogdens Ltd (1905) 93 LT 553, 214
National Australia Bank Ltd v Dionys [2016] NSWCA 242, 175
National Australia Bank Ltd v Hokit Pty Ltd (1996) 39 NSWLR 377, 207–8
National Australia Bank Ltd v KDS Construction Services Pty Ltd (in liq) (1987) 163 CLR 668, 181
National Australia Bank Ltd v Nemur Varity Pty Ltd (2002) 4 VR 252, 204
National Australia Bank Ltd v Swed (No 2) [2015] NSWSC 1322, 257
National Bank of Australasia v United Hand-in-Hand and Band of Hope Co (1879) 4 App Cas 391, 289
National Bank of Greece SA v Pinios Shipping Co No 1 [1990] 1 AC 637, 170, 288
National Bank of New Zealand Ltd v Walpole and Patterson Ltd [1975] 2 NZLR 7, 206
National Provincial Bank of England Ltd v Glanusk [1913] 3 KB 335, 304
National Westminster Bank Ltd v Barclays Bank International Ltd [1975] QB 654, 206
Naumoski v NCR Australia Pty Ltd [2004] NSWCA 310, 172
NCR Australia Pty Ltd v Credit Connection Pty Ltd [2004] NSWSC 1, 172
Neonbrook Pty Ltd v Thusi Pty Ltd [1999] 1 Qd R 429, 214
Northside Developments Pty Ltd v Registrar-General (1990) 170 CLR 146, 206

Ogilvie v Adams [1981] VR 1041, 158
Oliver v Davis [1949] 2 KB 727, 236
Oliver v Hinton [1899] 2 Ch 264, 296

Paciocco v Australia and New Zealand Banking Group Ltd (2014) 309 ALR 249, 171
Paciocco v Australia and New Zealand Banking Group Ltd (2016) 258 CLR 525, 42
Park Ave Nominees Pty Ltd v Boon (2001) ASC 155-052, 48
Parr's Banking Co Ltd v Yates [1898] 2 QB 460, 158
Paul Gooley v NSW Rural Assistance Authority [2020] NSWCA 156, 48, 63
Peacocke & Co v Williams (1909) 28 NZLR 354, 227
Pendlebury v Colonial Mutual Life Assurance Society Ltd (1912) 13 CLR 676, 299
Perry-Herrick v Attwood (1857) 44 ER 895, 296
Philipp v Barclays Bank UK plc [2023] 3 WLE 284, 200
Pitt Son & Badgery Ltd v Proulefco SA (1984) 153 CLR 644, 201
Port Swettenham Authority v TW Wu and Co Sdn Bhd [1979] AC 580, 201
Privacy Commissioner v Telstra Corporation Ltd (2017) 249 FCR 24, 276
Prosperity Ltd v Lloyds Bank Ltd (1923) 39 TLR 372, 154

Queensland Bacon Pty Ltd v Rees (1966) 115 CLR 266, 182

Re Australia & New Zealand Savings Bank Ltd; Mellas v Evriniadis [1972] VR 690, 186
Re Bourne [1906] 2 Ch 427, 161
Re City and Country Property Bank (in liq) (1896) 22 VLR 235, 288
Re Diplock's Estate [1948] Ch 465, 178, 187
Re EJ Morel (1934) Ltd [1962] Ch 21, 176
Re Gross; Ex parte Kingston (1871) 6 Ch App 632, 176
Re Hallett's Estate (1879) 13 Ch D 696, 178, 188
RE Jones Ltd v Waring and Gillow Ltd [1925] 2 KB 612, 235
Re Keever; Ex parte Trustee of Property of Bankrupt v Midland Bank Ltd [1967] Ch 182, 181
Re Laughton [1962] Tas SR 300, 177, 188
Re MacDonald [1975] Qd R 255, 178
Re McHenry [1894] 3 Ch 290, 158
Re Sass: Ex parte National Provincial Bank of England Ltd [1896] 2 QB 12, 306
Re Tarrant and Australian Securities and Investments Commission (2013) 62 AAR 192, 45
Re Tawil v Public Trustee of New South Wales (2009) 2 ASTLR 317, 174
Re York Street Mezzanine Pty Ltd (in liq) (2007) 162 FCR 358, 228
Rees v Bank of New South Wales (1964) 111 CLR 210, 182
RHG Mortgage Corporation Ltd v Saunders [2016] NSWSC 929, 62
Rice v Rice (1853) 61 ER 646, 296
Richardson v Commercial Banking Co of Sydney Ltd (1952) 85 CLR 110, 181
Rimmer v Webster [1902] 2 Ch 163, 296
Ringrow Pty Ltd v BP Australia Pty Ltd (2005) 224 CLR 656, 288
RnD Funding Pty Ltd v Roncane Pty Ltd (2023) 297 FCR 91, 187
Robertson v Canadian Imperial Bank of Commerce [1995] 1 All ER 824, 192
Robinson v Midland Bank Ltd (1925) 41 TLR 402, 154

Rogers v Whitely [1892] AC 118, 185
Rolin v Steward (1854) 14 CB 595, 222
Rosenhain v Commonwealth Bank of Australia (1922) 31 CLR 46, 228
Rouse v Bradford Banking Co Ltd [1894] AC 586, 288
Royal Bank of Canada v Inland Revenue Commissioners [1972] Ch 665, 191
Royal Bank of Scotland v Greenshields [1914] SC 259, 304
Ruff v Webb (1794) 1 Esp 129, 227
Russell v Scott (1936) 55 CLR 440, 173
Russian Commercial and Industrial Bank v Comptoir dÉscompte de Mulhouse [1925] AC 112, 155
Russo v Bendigo Bank Ltd [1999] 3 VR 376, 300

Saltman Engineering Co Ltd v Campbell Engineering Co Ltd [1963] 3 All ER 413, 131
San Sebastian Pty Ltd v Minister Administering Environmental Planning and Assessment Act 1979 (NSW) (1986) 162 CLR 340, 208
Schofield v Earl of Londesborough [1896] AC 514, 202
Scholefield Goodman & Sons Ltd v Zyngier [1986] VR 311, 290
Selangor United Rubber Estates Ltd v Craddock (No 3) [1968] 1 WLR 1555, 199, 221
Shannon v Permanent Custodians Ltd (No 3) [2022] WASCA 112, 64
Simonovski v Bendigo Bank Ltd [2005] VSCA 125, 174
Sinclair v Brougham [1914] AC 398, 163
Slingsby v District Bank Ltd [1932] 1 KB 544, 204
Société Eram Shipping v Compagnie Internationale de Navigation [2004] 1 AC 260, 187
South Australian Banking Co v Horner (1868) 2 SALR 109, 288
Spalla v St George Wholesale Finance Pty Ltd (1999) 93 FCR 359, 214
Standard Bank of Canada v Wiley (1919) 19 SR (NSW) 384, 213
State Bank of New South Wales Ltd v Currabubula Holdings Pty Ltd (2001) 51 NSWLR 399, 178
State Bank of New South Wales Ltd v Hibbert (2000) 9 BPR 17,543, 308
Stoney Stanton Supplies (Coventry) Ltd v Midland Bank Ltd [1966] 2 Lloyd's Rep 373, 154
Sunderland v Barclay's Bank Ltd (1938) 5 LDAB 163, 195
Sutherland Shire Council v Heyman [1982] 2 NSWLR 618, 208
Swiss Bank Corporation Ltd v Lloyds Bank Ltd [1982] AC 584, 297

Tai Hing Cotton Mill Ltd v Liu Chong Hing Bank Ltd [1985] 3 WLR 333, 195
Tai Hing Cotton Mill Ltd v Liu Chong Hing Bank Ltd [1986] AC 80, 157, 174, 175, 204, 206
Taylor v Johnson (1983) 151 CLR 422, 304
Territory Sheet Metal Pty Ltd v Australia and New Zealand Banking Group Ltd [2009] NTSC 31, 43
Thomas Cook (New Zealand) v Inland Revenue Commissioner [2004] UKPC 53, 165
Thorpe v Jackson (1837) 160 ER 515, 173
Tilley v Official Receiver in Bankruptcy (1960) 103 CLR 529, 219
Tina Motors Pty Ltd v Australia and New Zealand Banking Group Ltd [1977] VR 205, 205
Tournier v National Provincial & Union Bank of England [1924] 1 KB 461, 132, 191–2, 191–7
Turner v Royal Bank of Scotland plc [1999] 2 All ER (Comm) 664, 196

Union Bank of Australia Ltd v Murray-Aynsley [1898] AC 693, 177
Universal Guarantee Pty Ltd v Derefink [1958] VR 51, 186
Universal Guarantee Pty Ltd v National Bank of Australasia Ltd [1965] 1 WLR 691, 217

Vissenjoux v Australian Securities and Investments Commission [2015] AATA 98, 45

Walker v Linom [1907] 2 Ch 104, 296
Walker v Manchester and Liverpool District Banking Ltd (1913) 29 TLR 492, 206
Walsh v Lonsdale (1882) 21 Ch D 9, 297
Watt v State Bank of New South Wales [2002] FCA 1184, 308
Watts v Public Trustee [1949] 50 SR (NSW) 130, 174
West v Commercial Bank of Australia Ltd (1935) 55 CLR 315, 205
West v Williams [1899] 1 Ch 132, 302
Westminster Bank Ltd v Zang [1966] AC 182, 220
Westpac Banking Corporation v Diagne (2014) 17 BPR 33,551, 43
Westpac Banking Corporation v Metlej (1987) Aust Tort Rep 80-102, 206
Westpac Banking Corporation v Savin [1984] 2 NZLR 41, 171–2
Westpac Securities Administration Ltd v Australian Securities and Investments Commission (2021) 270 CLR 118, 90
Wingecarribee Shire Council v Lehman Brothers Australia Ltd (in liq) (2012) 301 ALR 1, 76
Woods v Martins Bank Ltd [1959] 1 QB 55, 153
WP Greenhalgh and Sons v Union Bank of Manchester [1924] 2 KB 153, 170

Yerkey v Jones (1939) 63 CLR 649, 307
Young v Grote (1827) 130 ER 764, 202
Young v Queensland Trustees Ltd (1956) 99 CLR 560, 159, 165

Zreika v Royal (2019) 271 FCR 65, 187

TABLE OF STATUTES

AUSTRALIA

Amending Acts 1…0 to 1999 Repeal Act

…ing and Counter-
…cing Act 2006,

TABLE OF STATUTES

AUSTRALIA

Amending Acts 1990 to 1999 Repeal Act 2016, 132
Anti-Money Laundering and Counter-Terrorism Financing Act 2006, 29–30, 193
s 5, 30, 252
s 6, 30
s 41, 193
s 41(1), 30
s 41(2), 30
s 43, 30, 193
s 45, 30
s 46, 30
s 84(2), 30
s 84(3), 30
s 212, 30
Australian Consumer Law, 28, 40, 157, 202, 247, 270, 302, 309
s 18, 217
s 23(3), 175
s 60, 201
s 64, 201
Australian Information Commissioner Act 2010, 132
Australian Prudential Regulation Authority Act 1998, 22, 24
s 8(2), 23
s 9, 23
s 91, 23
Australian Prudential Regulation Authority Regulations 2018, 24
Australian Securities and Investments Commission Act 2001, 25, 26, 40, 67, 94, 100, 152, 157, 302
pt 2 div 2, 100, 104
s 1, 26
s 12BAA, 79
s 12CB, 67
s 12CB(1), 63
s 12DA(1), 67
s 12DB, 67
Australian Securities Commission Act 1989, 25
Banking Act 1959, 7, 20, 24, 25
div 2A, 155
s 2A(3), 6
s 5, 149
s 7, 149
s 8, 149
s 9, 149
s 9(3A), 4
s 9D, 3
s 11AA(1), 4
s 17, 25
s 69, 164
s 69(1), 164
s 69(4)–(5), 164
s 69(7), 165
s 69(9), 165
s 69AA, 179
Banking Act 1966
s 69, 165
Bankruptcy Act 1966, 180
s 40, 183
s 58, 182
s 58(1)(a), 179
s 58(5), 181
s 58(6), 180
s 115, 180
s 116(1)(b), 180
ss 120–122, 180
s 120(1), 181
s 121(1), 181
s 121(2), 181
s 122, 181
s 122(1), 181
s 122(4), 182
s 122(4)(c), 182
s 123, 180

Bankruptcy Act 1966 (cont.)
s 124, 180
s 124(1)(a), 180
s 124(1)(b), 180
s 125(1), 183
s 125(2), 183
s 126, 182
s 126(1), 182
s 126(2), 182
s 134(1)(ma), 182
ss 139ZIA–139ZIT, 183
Bankruptcy Regulations 2021
reg 27(1), 124
Bills of Exchange Act 1909, 212, 217, 218, 227, 231, 239
pt 3, 212
s 4, 229, 233
s 6(2), 212
s 8, 212
s 8(1), 227
s 8(4), 228
s 10, 229
s 11, 228
s 12, 229
s 13(3), 234
s 14, 228, 229
s 15, 228
s 16, 228
s 18(1), 228
s 18(2), 228
s 19(1), 236
s 20, 239
s 21, 241
s 23, 237
s 24, 237
s 25(1)–(2), 242
s 25(3), 242
s 29, 241
s 30, 240
s 31, 240
s 32, 236
s 32(2), 236
s 33, 243
s 34, 235
s 34(2), 237
s 34(3), 235, 236
s 35(1), 236
s 35(2), 235
s 37, 233
s 37(a), 233
s 37(c), 233
s 37(d), 237
s 38, 233
s 39, 234
s 39(4), 234
s 40, 234
s 40(1), 234
s 40(2), 234
s 41(3), 236
s 42, 242
s 43(1)(a), 235
s 43(1)(b), 235
s 44, 238
s 45(1), 238
s 45(2), 238
s 46, 238
s 47, 238
s 48, 238
s 49(1), 237
s 49(2), 237
s 49(3), 238
s 51, 240
s 52, 240
s 53, 238, 240
s 56, 238
s 57, 239
s 59, 240
s 60, 241
s 61, 241
s 62, 243
s 63, 241
s 64, 243
s 64(1), 243
s 64(3), 243, 289
s 65, 242
s 66, 243, 244
s 67, 243
s 67(1), 244
s 67(2), 244
s 68, 243, 244

s 69, 243
s 69(1), 244
s 69(2), 244
s 70, 239
s 72, 239
s 73, 239
s 89, 232–3
s 95, 229, 233
Cheques Act 1986, 155, 211, 212, 216, 217, 218, 224
s 3(5), 221
s 4, 213
s 5, 217
s 10, 212, 213, 215
s 14, 214
s 14(1), 214
s 15(1), 213
s 15(2), 213
s 16, 215
s 19, 224
s 20, 213
s 21, 215
s 22, 213, 215
s 27, 214
s 28, 214
s 31, 215
s 32, 206, 216
s 32(1), 224, 226
s 39, 215, 216, 217
s 40, 215
s 42, 212
s 53, 216
s 54, 216
s 55, 216
s 56, 216
s 57, 216
s 60, 162
s 61(2), 215
s 63, 221
s 64(b), 222
s 66(1), 218
s 67, 218, 219, 222
s 68, 221
s 69, 219
s 70A, 219
s 78(2), 224
s 79, 226
s 82, 226
s 88, 219
s 90(1)(a), 221
s 90(1)(b), 178
s 90(1)(b)–(c), 221
s 90(1)(c), 178
s 90(2)(a), 178
s 90(2)(b), 178
s 91, 224
s 92, 226
s 93(1), 226
s 93(2), 226
s 94(1), 226
s 94(2), 226
s 95, 217, 227
s 113, 219
Commonwealth Bank Act 1911, 20
s 5, 20
Competition and Consumer Act 2010, 28, 175
pt IVB, 28
pt IVD, 275, 276
s 29B, 28
s 51(1), 28
s 56AC(3), 276
s 56AI, 451, 276
s 56BD(1)(b), 276
s 131A, 40
sch 2, 40, 157, 247, 302
Competition and Consumer (Consumer Data Right) Rules 2020, 275
div 4.2.1, 275
div 4.3.2B, 275
r 4.5, 275
r 4.6A, 275
r 4.7, 275
r 6.6, 274
s 6.2 item 2(b)(iii), 275
sch 2, 278
sch 3 s 1.2, 275
sch 4, 275

Consumer Data Right (Authorised Deposit-Taking Institutions) Designation 2019, 276
ss 5–8, 276
ss 6–8, 276
s 9, 276
Consumer Data Right (Energy Sector) Designation 2020, 275
Corporations Act 2001, 26, 40, 81, 100, 101, 104, 125, 163, 183, 184, 231, 257
ch 2J, 293
ch 7, 44, 74, 76, 77, 78, 80, 82, 97, 110
div 4, 78
pt 5B.2, 121
pt 5.7B, 183
pt 6D.2, 104
pt 7.3, 22, 248
pt 7.7, 82, 86, 90
pt 7.7(2)(A), 86
pt 7.7(3)(C), 86
pt 7.7A, 82, 90, 92, 98, 99
pt 7.7A div 2, 92
pt 7.7A div 3, 99
pt 7.7A div 4, 98
pt 7.7A div 5(A), 98
pt 7.7A div 5(B), 98
pt 7.8A, 104
pt 7.9, 104
pt 7.9(2)(B), 86
pt 7.9A, 100
reg 7.9.07FA, 89
s 9, 79
s 9(a), 79
ss 124–130, 163
s 128, 163, 292, 293
s 129, 292, 293
s 129(3), 163
s 301E(1), 101
s 420, 184
s 468, 184
s 588FG(2), 184
s 760A, 6
s 761A, 75, 78, 84
s 761G(5), 82
s 761G(6), 82
s 761G(6A), 82
s 761G(7), 82
s 761G(7)(a), 82
s 761G(7)(b), 44, 82
s 761G(7)(c), 82
s 761G(7)(d), 82
s 761G(10), 82
s 761G(12), 82
s 761GA, 82
s 761GA(d), 83
s 762A, 79, 80
s 763A, 80, 100
s 763B, 80
s 763C, 80
s 763D, 80
s 763E, 80
s 764A, 80, 100
s 764A(1)(l), 40
s 764A(1)(m), 80
s 765(1)(h)(i), 40
s 765A, 80, 81
s 765A(y), 81
s 765A(z), 81
s 766A, 78
s 766A(1), 78
s 766A(1)(b), 79
s 766A(1)(c), 79
s 766A(1)(d), 79
s 766B, 78
s 766B(1), 89
s 766B(2), 89
s 766B(3), 90
s 766B(3)(b), 90
s 766B(3A), 90
s 766B(4), 90
s 766B(5), 89
s 766C, 78
s 766C(1), 79
s 766C(1)(c), 79
s 766C(2), 79
s 766C(3), 79
s 766C(4), 79
s 766D, 78, 79
s 766E, 78
s 766F, 78

s 766G, 78
s 766H, 78
s 823CA, 22
s 910A, 84
s 911A, 75, 83
s 911A(2)(a), 84
s 911B, 84
s 912A, 83, 85
s 912A(1)(a), 85
s 912A(1)(aa), 85
s 912A(1)(b), 85
s 912A(1)(c), 85
s 912A(1)(ca), 85
s 912A(1)(cb), 85
s 912A(1)(cc), 85
s 912A(1)(d), 85
s 912A(1)(e), 85
s 912A(1)(f), 85
s 912A(1)(g), 85
s 912A(1)(h), 85, 109
s 912A(1)(j), 85
s 912A(2)–(2A), 85
s 912A(3A)–(3G), 85
s 912B, 110
s 913A, 83
s 913B, 75, 83
s 913B(1), 83
s 913B(2), 83
s 913BA, 83
s 913BA(1), 83
s 916A, 84
s 916A(1), 84
s 916A(4), 84
s 916B, 84
s 916B(3), 84
s 916D(1), 84
s 916E(1), 84
s 916F(1), 84
s 916F(3), 85
s 923A(1), 87
s 923A(5), 87
s 923A(5)(a)(ii), 87
s 923A(7A), 87
s 941C, 87
s 941C(6)–(7), 89
s 941D(1), 87
s 942B(1), 86
s 942B(2), 86
s 942B(2)(a), 86
s 942B(2)(b), 87
s 942B(2)(c), 87
s 942B(2)(d), 87
s 942B(2)(e), 87
s 942B(2)(f), 87
s 942B(2)(fa), 87
s 942B(2)(g), 87
s 942B(2)(h), 87
s 942B(2)(i), 87
s 942B(2)(j), 87
s 942B(2)(k), 87
s 945A, 91
ss 946A–947E, 88, 108
s 946AA, 88
s 946AA(1)(b), 88
s 946AA(5), 88
s 946AA(6), 88
s 946B, 88
s 946B(5)–(6), 89
s 946B(7), 87, 88
s 947B(2), 88
s 961(1), 90
s 961(6), 92
s 961B, 92, 94, 95
s 961B(1), 92, 108
s 961B(2), 92, 93, 96
s 961B(2)(a), 93
s 961B(2)(a)–(f), 92
s 961B(2)(b), 93
s 961B(2)(c), 93
s 961B(2)(d), 93
s 961B(2)(e), 93
s 961B(2)(f), 93
s 961B(2)(g), 93, 96
s 961G, 92, 94, 95
s 961H(1), 92
s 961J, 60, 95
s 961J(1), 92
s 961J(1)(a)–(f), 92
s 961J(2)–(3), 92
s 961K, 93

Corporations Act 2001 (cont.)
s 961K(2), 94
s 961K(2)(b), 94
s 961L, 94, 95
s 961Q, 93
s 962A(1), 99
s 962G, 99
s 962R, 99
s 962S, 99
s 963A, 98
s 994A(1), 104
s 994AA, 104
s 994AA(1), 104
s 994B, 105, 106
s 994B(1), 104
s 994B(1)(a), 104
s 994B(1)(b), 104
s 994B(1)(ba), 104
s 994B(1)(c), 104
s 994B(2), 104
s 994B(3), 104
s 994B(8), 105
s 994B(8)(b), 106
s 994B(9), 105
s 994C, 106
s 994D, 105
s 994E(1), 105
s 994E(3), 105
s 994F(1), 105
s 994F(3), 105
s 994F(6), 105
s 994G, 105
ss 1012A–1012C, 88
s 1012D(2), 89
s 1012D(2A), 89
s 1013D(g), 88
s 1013D(h), 88
s 1013D(i), 88
s 1023B, 100
s 1023C(1), 101
s 1023D, 69
s 1023D(1), 101, 103
s 1023D(1)(a), 100
s 1023D(1)(b), 101
s 1023D(3), 101, 103
s 1023D(3)(a), 100
s 1023D(4), 101
s 1023D(5), 101
s 1023E, 103
s 1023E(1), 101
s 1023F(1), 102
s 1023F(2), 102
s 1023G(2), 102
s 1023H, 102
s 1023J, 102
s 1023L(1), 102
s 1023L(3), 102
s 1023L(6)–(7), 102
sch 1, 76
sch 10BA, 89
Corporations (FinTech Sandbox Australian Financial Services Licence Exemption) Regulations 2020, 119, 123
reg 5, 121
reg 6(1) note 2, 124
reg 6(2), 123
reg 8, 126
reg 8(b)–(c), 122
reg 8(h), 126
reg 8(i), 122
reg 10, 123
reg 11, 123
reg 12(1), 124
reg 13(1), 124
reg 17, 126
reg 18, 125
reg 19, 125
reg 20, 125
reg 21, 125
reg 23, 125
reg 24, 125
Corporations Regulations 2001, 104
reg 1.0.02, 123
reg 7.1.06, 40
regs 7.1.18–7.1.24, 82
reg 7.1.28, 82
reg 7.7.09A, 88
reg 7.8A.02(4), 104
reg 7.8A.05, 104
reg 7.8A.07, 104

reg 7.9.61AA, 89
Disability Discrimination and Other Human Rights Legislation Amendment Act 2009, 132
Do Not Call Register Act 2006, 130–1, 140
s 5, 131
s 14, 130
Electronic Transactions Act 1999, 294
Financial Regulator Assessment Authority Act 2021, 30
s 12(1)(a)–(d), 31
s 12(3), 31
s 14(1), 31
Financial Sector Reform Act 2022
sch 4 item 6, 68
sch 4 item 12, 67
sch 4 item 14, 68
sch 4 item 22, 68
sch 4 item 26, 67
sch 4 item 49, 68
sch 4 item 50, 67
Financial Sector Reform Bill 2022, 67, 68
Financial Sector Reform (Hayne Royal Commission Response) Protecting Consumers (2019 Measures) Act 2020, 59
Financial Services Authority Act 2021, 30
s 12(2), 31
Financial Services Reform Act 2001, 75
Financial Transaction Reports Act 1988, 29
First Home Saver Accounts Act 2008, 80
Freedom of Information Act 1982, 141
Insurance Act 1973, 25
s 55, 25
Insurance Contracts Act 1984, 26
Life Insurance Act 1995, 26
Medical Indemnity (Prudential Supervision and Product Standards) Act 2003, 26
Minors (Property and Contracts) Act 1970
s 47, 291
National Consumer Credit Protection Act 2009, 40, 41–2, 44, 47–8, 51, 54, 58, 59, 67, 69, 70, 74, 101, 104, 125, 136, 254, 257, 287
ch 2, 45
ch 2 pt 2-2 div 5, 45
ch 3, 45
ch 3 div 2, 45
div 3, 46
form 5, 61
pt 2-2 div 3, 50
pt 3, 53
pt 3-1, 45, 53, 54
pt 3-2, 45, 53, 54
pt 3-5 div 2, 53
pt 6-7A, 100
s 5, 51, 64, 65
s 6, 46
s 6(1), 46, 47
s 6 item 1, 46
s 6 item 2, 46
s 6 item 3, 46
s 6 item 4, 46
s 6 item 5, 47
s 6 item 6, 47
s 7, 50
s 8, 50
s 9, 51
s 29, 50
ss 45–46, 50
s 47, 52
s 113, 53
s 114, 53
s 115, 54, 56
s 116, 56
s 117, 55
s 118, 56
s 118(4), 56
s 119, 56
s 119(2), 57
s 119(4), 56
s 120, 55, 57
s 121, 53
s 124B, 68
s 126, 53
s 126(2), 53
s 128, 54, 56
s 130, 55
s 130(1), 57
s 130(2), 57
s 131, 56

National Consumer Credit Protection Act 2009 (cont.)
s 131(2), 56–7
s 131(4), 56
s 132, 55, 57
s 133BA(1), 254
s 133BB, 254
s 133BC, 254
s 133BD, 254
s 133BH, 254
s 133BI(1)(a), 254
s 133BI(1)(b), 254
s 133BI(1)(c), 254
s 133CB, 66
s 133CF, 68
s 137, 53, 54
s 140, 55
s 140(1A), 68
s 141, 56
s 142, 56
s 143, 55
s 144, 53
s 151, 54
s 153, 55
s 155, 55
s 158, 53
s 158LA, 59, 60, 61
s 158LB, 60
s 158LE, 59, 60
s 158LF, 60
s 158N, 60–1
s 158NB, 60
s 158ND, 60
s 158NE, 60
s 158NF, 60
s 199, 42
s 301C(1), 101
s 301D, 100
s 301D(1), 101
s 301D(1)(b), 101
s 301D(3), 101
s 301D(4), 101
s 301D(5), 101
s 301F(1), 102
s 301J, 102
s 301L(1), 102
s 310D(1), 101
s 310F(2), 102
s 310G(2), 102
s 310H, 102
s 310L(3), 102
s 310L(6)–(7), 102
sch 1, 40, 41, 293
National Consumer Credit Protection Amendment (Supporting Economic Recovery) Bill 2020, 57–8
sch 1, 57
National Consumer Credit Protection (FinTech Sandbox Australian Credit Licence Exemption) Regulations 2020, 120, 123, 124
reg 5(c), 124
reg 5(d), 124
reg 5(e), 124
reg 5(f), 124
reg 6 note 2, 124
reg 10(1), 124
reg 15, 125
reg 16, 125
reg 18, 125
National Consumer Credit Protection Regulations 2010, 40, 254
pt 2-4 div 1 sub-div 1.1, 51
pt 7-3, 294
reg 24(6), 51
reg 24(7), 51
reg 24(8), 51
reg 25(2), 51
reg 25(2A), 51
reg 25(5), 51
reg 28J, 56
reg 28LCA, 67
reg 28LCB, 67
reg 110, 61
sch 6, 254
National Credit Code, 40, 41, 44, 53, 67, 70, 298, 302, 309
div 2, 303
pt 2-3, 46
pt 4 div 1, 46

pt 4 div 2, 46
pt 5, 46
pt 7, 46
pt 8, 46
s 3(1), 47
s 3(2), 47
s 4, 46, 48
s 5(1), 293
s 5(1)(b)(i), 48
s 5(1)(b)(ii), 48
s 5(1)(c), 49
s 5(4)(a), 48
s 5(4)(b), 48
s 6, 69, 293
s 6(1), 47
s 6(4), 47, 293
s 6(5), 47, 49
s 6(7)(a), 293
s 7, 50
s 8, 50
s 9, 50
s 16, 294
ss 16–18, 45
s 16(1)(a)–(b), 61
s 17, 61, 294
s 20, 294
s 31A, 64, 67
s 31A(2), 64
s 31A(3), 64
s 32A(1), 64
s 32A(4), 64
s 32B, 46
s 39B, 46, 64
s 43, 45, 294
s 55, 294
s 56, 45, 294
s 57, 294
s 58, 295
s 60, 295
s 60(3), 291
s 60(4), 295
ss 64–66, 62
s 64(1)–(2), 62
s 64(4), 62
s 64(5), 62
s 72, 62
ss 72–75, 46
s 72(1), 62
s 72(2), 62
s 72(3), 62
s 74(2), 62
s 76, 42, 46, 62–3, 294
s 76(2), 63, 294
s 76(4), 63
s 77, 64
s 78, 46
s 88, 302
s 88(2), 298
s 111, 294
s 174(1A), 68
s 175AA, 67
s 184(1), 61
s 204, 50
s 204(1), 64
Payment Systems and Netting Act 1998, 247, 249, 251
Payment Systems (Regulation) Act 1998, 247, 249
pt 3, 248
pt 3 div 3, 248
pt 3 div 4, 248
pt 3 div 5, 248
pt 3 div 6, 248
s 7, 247
s 8, 248
s 10, 248
s 10(2), 248
s 18, 248
Privacy Act 1988, 67, 130, 131, 132, 145, 192, 277, 278
pt III, 145
pt III div 2, 136
pt IIIA, 135, 136, 144
pt IIIC, 133
s 2A, 134
s 5B(2), 133
s 5B(3), 133
s 6, 133, 134, 135, 145
s 6(1), 134
s 6C, 134

Privacy Act 1988 (cont.)
s 6D, 134, 276
s 6G, 135
s 6QA, 136
s 7B(3), 133
s 13(1), 134
s 13(4A), 133
s 13G(3), 133
s 15, 134
s 16A, 137
s 20, 136
s 20A, 136
s 20A(2), 136
s 20E, 136
s 20N, 136
s 20R, 136
s 21D, 136
s 26WA, 133
s 26WE, 133
s 26WE(1)(a), 133
s 36, 135
s 40, 134, 135
s 40A, 135
s 40A(1), 135
s 49(1), 135
s 52, 135
sch 1 pt 1 cl 1.1, 136
sch 1 pt 1 cl 1.2, 136
sch 1 pt 1 cl 1.4, 137
sch 1 pt 1 cl 1.5, 137
sch 1 pt 1 cl 1.6, 137
sch 1 pt 1 cl 2.1, 137
sch 1 pt 1 cl 2.2(a), 137
sch 1 pt 1 cl 2.2(b), 137
sch 1 pt 2 cls 3.1–3.2, 137
sch 1 pt 2 cl 3.3, 137
sch 1 pt 2 cl 3.4(a), 137
sch 1 pt 2 cl 3.4(c), 137
sch 1 pt 2 cl 3.4(d), 138
sch 1 pt 2 cl 3.4(e), 138
sch 1 pt 2 cl 3.5, 138
sch 1 pt 2 cl 3.6, 138
sch 1 pt 2 cl 4.1, 138
sch 1 pt 2 cl 4.3, 138
sch 1 pt 2 cl 4.4, 138
sch 1 pt 2 cl 5.1, 138
sch 1 pt 2 cl 5.2, 138
sch 1 pt 3 cl 6.1, 139
sch 1 pt 3 cl 6.2, 139
sch 1 pt 3 cl 6.3, 139
sch 1 pt 3 cl 7.1, 139
sch 1 pt 3 cl 7.2, 139
sch 1 pt 3 cl 7.3, 140
sch 1 pt 3 cl 7.8, 140
sch 1 pt 3 cl 8.1, 140
sch 1 pt 3 cl 8.2, 140
sch 1 pt 3 cl 9.1, 140
sch 1 pt 3 cl 9.2, 140
sch 1 pt 4 cl 10.1, 141
sch 1 pt 4 cl 10.2, 141
sch 1 pt 4 cl 11.1, 141
sch 1 pt 4 cl 11.2, 141
sch 1 pt 5 cl 12.1, 141
sch 1 pt 5 cl 12.2, 141
sch 1 pt 5 cl 12.3, 141
sch 1 pt 5 cl 12.4, 142
sch 1 pt 5 cl 12.9, 142
sch 1 pt 5 cl 13.1, 142
sch 1 pt 5 cl 13.2, 142
sch 1 pt 5 cl 13.3, 142
sch 1 pt 5 cl 13.4, 142
Privacy Amendment Act 1990, 132
Privacy Amendment (Enhancing Privacy Protection) Act 2012, 136
Privacy Amendment (Notifiable Data Breaches) Act 2017, 133
Privacy Amendment (Office of the Privacy Commissioner) Act 2000, 132
Privacy Amendment (Private Sector) Act 2000, 132
Privacy (Credit Reporting) Code 2014, 136
Privacy Legislation Amendment (Enforcement and Other Measures) Act 2022, 133
Privacy Regulations 2013, 136
Reserve Bank Act 1959, 20, 247
s 5, 22
s 8, 20
s 8A(1)–(2), 21
s 10, 20
s 10(2), 20, 21

s 10B(3), 22
s 10B(3)(a), 247
s 10B(3)(b), 248
s 10B(3)(c), 248
s 10C(1), 22
s 10C(2), 22
s 10C(3), 22
s 11(1), 21
s 12, 22
s 14, 22
s 25, 22
s 26(a), 20
s 27, 22
Retirement Savings Accounts Act 1997, 26, 80
Spam Act 2003, 131, 140
s 16, 131
Superannuation Industry (Supervision) Act 1993, 25, 26, 80
s 10, 25
s 29E(1)(a), 25
Superannuation (Resolution of Complaints) Act 1993, 26
Trade Practices Act 1974, 28
Treasury Laws Amendment (2018 Measures No 2) Act 2020, 119
Treasury Laws Amendment (Consumer Data Right) Act 2019, 275
Treasury Laws Amendment (Design and Distribution Obligations and Product Intervention Powers) Act 2019, 26, 100
Treasury Laws Amendment (Ending Grandfathered Conflicted Remuneration) Act 2019, 99
Treasury Laws Amendment (Strengthening Corporate and Financial Sector Penalties) Act 2019, 26
Uniform Consumer Credit Code, 41, 61, 74, 293

Australian Capital Territory

Health Records (Privacy and Access) Act 1997, 130
Information Privacy Act 2014, 130

New South Wales

Contracts Review Act 1980, 62, 309
Health Records and Information Privacy Act 2002, 130
Limitation Act 1969, 157
ss 63–65, 159
Minors (Property and Contracts) Act 1970, 291
s 47, 305
Partnership Act 1892
s 1(1), 160
s 5, 161
Privacy and Personal Information Protection Act 1998, 130
Real Property Act 1900, 302

Northern Territory

Information Act 2002, 130

Queensland

Information Privacy Act 2009, 130
Partnership Act 1891
s 5(1), 160
s 8(1), 161

South Australia

Minors Contracts (Miscellaneous Provisions) Act 1979
s 5, 306
Partnership Act 1891
s 1(1), 160
s 5, 161
Real Property Act 1886, 302

Tasmania

Partnership Act 1891
s 6(1), 160
s 10, 161
Personal Information Protection Act 2004, 130

Victoria

Associations Incorporation Reform Act 2012, 160
Consumer Credit (Victoria) Act 1995
s 39, 294
s 40, 294

Health Records Act 2001, 130
Instruments Act 1958
s 126, 303
Limitation of Action Act 1958
s 5(1), 158
Partnership Act 1958
s 5(1), 160
s 9, 161
Privacy and Data Protection Act 2014, 130
Supreme Court (General Civil Procedure) Rules 2015
r 71.02, 186
r 71.03, 186
r 71.03(1), 186
Transfer of Land Act 1958, 299, 301

Western Australia

Limitation Act 2005
s 59, 159
Partnership Act 1895
s 7(1), 160
26, 161

EUROPEAN UNION

Commission Delegated Regulation 2018/389 of 27 November 2017 Supplementing Directive 2015/2366 of the European Parliament and of the Council with Regard to Regulatory Technical Standards for Strong Customer Authentication and Common and Secure Open Standards of Communication, 273
Council Directive 2015/2366 on Payment Services in the Internal Market, 272, 278
art 7, 273
art 109, 272
European Data Act, 273
General Data Protection Regulation, 145
art 3(1), 143
art 3(2), 143
art 17, 143
recital 71, 143

NEW ZEALAND

Credit Contracts and Consumer Finance (Buy Now, Pay Later) Amendment Regulations 2023, 70
cl 2, 70

SINGAPORE

Personal Data Protection Act 2012, 273

UNITED KINGDOM

Bills of Exchange Act 1882, 231
Partnership Act 1890, 160
s 1(1), 160
s 5, 161
Payment Services Regulations 2017, 278
Sale of Goods Act 1893, 231
Statute of Frauds (Amendment) Act 1828, 199
s 6, 199

UNITED STATES

Bank Secrecy Act 1970, 268
Dodd-Frank Act 2010
s 1033, 268
Electronic Fund Transfer Act 1978, 268, 269
Gramm-Leach-Bliley Act 1999, 268
Truth in Lending Act 1968, 268

INTERNATIONAL INSTRUMENTS

International Covenant on Civil and Political Rights
art 17, 132

ABBREVIATIONS

AAC	APRA–ASIC Committee
ABA	Australian Banking Association
ACCC	Australian Competition and Consumer Commission
ACL	Australian credit licence
ADI	authorised deposit-taking institution
AEMO	Australian Energy Market Operator
AFCA	Australian Financial Complaints Authority
AFSL	Australian Financial Services Licence
AI	artificial intelligence
ALRC	Australian Law Reform Commission
AML/CTF Act	*Anti-Money Laundering and Counter-Terrorism Financing Act 2006* (Cth)
ANZ	Australia and New Zealand Banking Group
APCA	Australian Payments Clearing Association Limited
APCS	Australian Paper Clearing System
API	application programming interface
APPs	Australian Privacy Principles
APRA	Australian Prudential Regulation Authority
APRA Act	*Australian Prudential Regulation Authority Act 1998* (Cth)
APS 110	Prudential Standard APS 110 Capital Adequacy
ASC	Australian Securities Commission
ASIC	Australian Securities and Investments Commission
ASIC Act	*Australian Securities and Investments Commission Act 2001* (Cth)
ATM	automated teller machine
ATO	Australian Taxation Office
AUSTRAC	Australian Transaction Reports and Analysis Centre
BAS	business activity statement
BCBS	Basel Committee on Banking Supervision
BCCC	Banking Code Compliance Committee
BIS	Bank for International Settlements
BNM	Bank Negara Malaysia
BNPL	buy now, pay later
CBA	Commonwealth Bank of Australia
CBDC	central bank digital currency
CBT	cross-border testing
CCA	*Competition and Consumer Act 2010* (Cth)
CDR	Consumer Data Right
CFPB	Consumer Financial Protection Bureau (United States)
CFR	Council of Financial Regulators
CLERP	Corporate Law Economic Reform Program
COAG	Council of Australian Governments
COIN	Community of Interest Network

CP	credit provider
CR Code	*Privacy (Credit Reporting) Code 2012* (Cth)
CRB	credit reporting bodies
CS	clearing and settlement
CT	certificate of title
Cth	Commonwealth of Australia
DDO	Design and Distribution Obligation
DNDC	dual-network debit card
DSB	Data Standards Body
ECB	European Central Bank
ECMH	efficient capital markets hypothesis
EDR	external dispute resolution
EFT	electronic funds transfer
EFTPOS	electronic funds transfer at point of sale
ERS	Enhanced Regulatory Sandbox
ESA	Exchange Settlement Account
EU	European Union
FATF	Financial Action Task Force
FCA	Financial Conduct Authority (UK)
FHSA	first home saver account
FOFA	Future of Financial Advice
FOS	Financial Ombudsman Services
FRAA	Financial Regulator Assessment Authority
FSB	Financial Stability Board
FSF	Financial Stability Forum
FSG	Financial Services Guide
FSR	Financial Sector Reform
FSR Act	*Financial Sector Reform Act 2022* (Cth)
FSR Bill	Financial Sector Reform Bill 2022 (Cth)
FTR Act	*Financial Transaction Reports Act 1988* (Cth)
GDP	gross domestic product
GDPR	General Data Protection Regulation
GFC	Global Financial Crisis
GFIN	Global Financial Innovation Network
HCA	High Court of Australia
ICCPR	International Covenant on Civil and Political Rights
ICO	initial coin offering
IFTI	international funds transfer instruction
IMF	International Monetary Fund
LCR	least-cost routing
LOLR	lender of last resort
MAS	Monetary Authority of Singapore
MoU	Memorandum of Understanding
NAB	National Australia Bank

NCC	National Competition Council
NCC	*National Credit Code*
NCCPA	*National Consumer Credit Protection Act 2009* (Cth)
NCCPR	*National Consumer Credit Protection Regulations 2010* (Cth)
NCPA	National Credit Providers Association
NDB	Notifiable Data Breaches
NEM	National Energy Market
NFC	near-field communication
NOHC	non-operating holding company
NPP	New Payments Platform
OAIC	Office of the Australian Information Commissioner
OECD	Organisation for Economic Co-operation and Development
PDS	Product Disclosure Statement
PI	professional indemnity
PIN	personal identification number
PIO	product intervention order
PIP	Product Intervention Power
PISP	Payment Initiator Service Provider
PSB	Payments System Board
PSP	payment services provider
RB Act	*Reserve Bank Act 1959* (Cth)
RBA	Reserve Bank of Australia
RITS	Reserve Bank Information and Transfer System
RSA	retirement savings account
RSE	registrable superannuation entity
RTGS	Real-Time Gross Settlement System
SACC	small-amount credit contract
SARB	South African Reserve Bank
SMR	suspicious matter report
SMSF	self-managed superannuation fund
SOA	Statement of Advice
SWIFT	Society for Worldwide Interbank Financial Telecommunications
TMD	target market determination
TPP	third-party provider
TTR	threshold transaction report
UAE	United Arab Emirates
UCCC	*Uniform Consumer Credit Code*
UK	United Kingdom
US	United States
Westpac	Westpac Banking Corporation

CHAPTER 1

REGULATORY THEORY AND FRAMEWORK

1.1 Introduction

The financial system fulfils several quintessential roles within the economic framework.[1] For instance, it expedites transactions by administering a secure and robust payment system. This mechanism not only assures the secure transference of financial assets but also accommodates transactions across borders, thus facilitating arm's-length commercial interactions on a macro-economic scale.[2] The financial system is also instrumental in mobilising savings from households that possess financial resources surplus to their immediate consumption needs.[3] In doing so, it enables these households to accrue returns on their capital, thereby enhancing their consumption possibilities in subsequent periods.

To put this in a broader context, the financial system acts as the intermediary apparatus responsible for the judicious allocation of financial resources.[4] It serves to channel these resources between individuals and institutions in possession of surplus capital and those in need of such capital for investment purposes. For instance, corporations require financial resources in order to acquire and maintain their physical infrastructure and human capital, and to incubate innovative ventures. Conversely, individuals accumulate savings with various objectives in mind, such as retirement, unforeseen medical exigencies, or substantial expenditures such as real estate or automotive purchases. It is crucial to note, however, that the practical landscape is considerably more complex than this theoretical construct. Individuals may find it necessary to incur debt to fulfil their immediate obligations or to facilitate property acquisition; and companies could generate profits in excess of their operational and investment needs, thus becoming lenders within the financial ecosystem. The financial system could both channel capital from savers to projects and selectively allocate it to those with the potential for returns, ensuring efficient and profitable use of capital.[5]

There are myriad institutions within the financial system offering a comprehensive suite of products and services aimed at generating profits, mitigating risks, and so on. These include traditional financial products (eg managed funds),[6] risk-management solutions (eg life and travel insurance),[7] and payment and settlement methods

1 See generally Robert C Merton, 'The Financial System and Economic Performance' (1990) 4(4) *Journal of Financial Services Research* 263. See also John Armour et al, *Principles of Financial Regulation* (Oxford University Press, 2016) 2.2; Martin Neil Baily and Douglas J Elliott, *The Role of Finance in the Economy: Implications for Structural Reform of the Financial Sector* (The Brookings Institution, 2013).

2 See, eg, 'Payment Systems', *The World Bank* (Web Page) <https://www.worldbank.org/en/topic/paymentsystemsremittances>; Alberto Bucci and Simone Marsiglio, 'Financial Development and Economic Growth: Long-Run Equilibrium and Transitional Dynamics' (2019) 66(3) *Scottish Journal of Political Economy* 331, 335.

3 See, eg, Bucci and Marsiglio (n 2) 334.

4 See, eg, Rene M Stulz et al, *Handbook of the Economics of Finance: Corporate Finance* (Elsevier Science, 2013). See also Armour et al (n 1) 2.3.

5 See S Gurusamy, *Financial Services and Systems* (McGraw Hill Education, 2nd ed, 2009). See also Armour et al (n 1) 2.2.

6 Top-performing large funds such as Merlon Concentrated Australian Share Fund are prime examples. The concept of 'financial product' will be discussed in Chapter 3.

7 The largest life insurance companies in Australia are TAL Life (owned by Dai-ichi Life) and AIA Australia (owned by AIA Group).

(eg cash, cheques, credit cards, digital wallets and digital currencies)[8] that facilitate transactions between various parties. Some institutions may go beyond these basics to offer specialised services such as trade financing.[9] These functions enable the smooth flow of funds between a variety of entities, such as individuals, businesses and governments.

Among other intermediaries, banks – known as 'authorised deposit-taking institutions' (ADIs) in the *Banking Act 1959* (Cth) – are central to the financial system.[10] By and large, as per Cranston et al, banks have three main functions: saving mobilisation, maturity transformation, and management of liquidity risks.[11] Their profound impact on economic stability and growth is underscored by events such as the collapse of major banks, including Lehman Brothers, during the Global Financial Crisis (GFC),[12] and the more recent failures of Silicon Valley Bank and First Republic Bank, also in the United States.[13] Australia's banking industry is dominated by four major banks – namely, Commonwealth Bank of Australia (CBA), Westpac Banking Corporation (Westpac), National Australia Bank (NAB), and Australia and New Zealand Banking Group (ANZ) – which collectively accounted for over 75 per cent of the households lending market as of April 2022.[14]

8 Payment systems are examined in Chapter 9.

9 JP Morgan, for instance, offers comprehensive wealth management solutions for ultra-high net-worth individuals across Asia through its Hong Kong and Singapore offices. See 'Our Office', *JPMorgan Private Bank* (Web Page) <https://privatebank.jpmorgan.com/apac/en/locations/asia?y_source=1_MzMzMjE5MC00ODMtbG9jYXRpb24ud2Vic2l0ZQ%3D%3D>.

10 ADIs include not only banks but also credit unions, building societies, etc. More recently, the 2018 amendments to the *Banking Act 1959* (Cth) (*'Banking Act'*), under s 9D, allow the Australian Prudential Regulation Authority (APRA) to issue restricted banking licences for a two-year period. These licences aim to foster competition by enabling startups, particularly digital 'neo banks', to offer limited services as 'restricted ADs' while securing the capital for a full licence. Among other requirements, restricted ADIs must maintain A$3 million in liquid assets and submit an 'exit plan' during their application. Under the restricted ADI regime, a licensee is granted a maximum of two years to transition to a full ADI licence. Failure to meet these criteria within the two-year time frame necessitates an exit from the banking industry. See, eg, *APRA, ADI: New Entrants – A Pathway to Sustainability* (Information Paper, August 2021) 14–23 <https://www.apra.gov.au/sites/default/files/2021-08/Information%20paper%20-%20ADIs%20New%20entrants%20-%20a%20pathway%20to%20sustainability_0.pdf>; APRA, *Guidelines: Restricted Words under the Banking Act 1959* (20 August 2018) <https://www.apra.gov.au/sites/default/files/apra-guidelines-restricted-words-under-the-banking-act-august-2018.pdf>.

11 Mobilising savings entails gathering deposits from individuals and businesses and channelling them into loans for enterprises at market-driven interest rates. Through the process of maturity transformation, banks can provide long-term financing options such as mortgages, even while relying on short-term deposits. Additionally, effective liquidity risk management ensures that banks keep enough liquid assets on hand to meet their immediate financial commitments, a crucial function especially in times of financial crisis. Collectively, these roles underscore the vital function banks serve within the financial ecosystem: they act as intermediaries that streamline the flow of capital, support long-term investment opportunities and contribute to overall financial stability. For an overview, see generally Ross Cranston et al, *Principles of Banking Law* (Oxford University Press, 2018) 6–8.

12 See generally Grant Wyn and Graham K Wilson, 'Conclusion' in Grant Wyn and Graham K Wilson (eds), *The Consequences of the Global Financial Crisis: The Rhetoric of Reform and Regulation* (Oxford University Press, 2012) 247.

13 Amit Seru, 'How Worried Should We Be about a Financial Crisis?', *New York Times* (4 May 2023).

14 'Banking Industry in Australia', *Statista* (Web Page) <https://www-statista-com.libproxy.smu.edu.sg/study/68793/banking-industry-in-australia/>.

Other non-ADI financial institutions in Australia[15] include superannuation funds,[16] general insurance companies[17] and asset management companies.[18] Typically, these financial institutions exhibit interconnectivity within the financial ecosystem. An ADI, for example, may constitute a subsidiary within a broader financial conglomerate, wherein a holding company exercises control over diverse business entities operating across multiple segments of the financial market.[19] Together, these financial intermediaries form a primary pillar of the Australian economy. In 2015, for example, this sector contributed approximately A$140 billion to Australia's gross domestic product (GDP), with around 450 000 people employed.[20] Given the pivotal role of these financial institutions, they operate under a comprehensive and increasingly complex regulatory framework. As elaborated in this chapter and throughout this book, these regulations are designed to ensure the integrity, stability and efficiency of the financial system, while also safeguarding consumers and fostering competition.

This chapter aims to introduce the banking and finance industry from a regulatory perspective. It begins by exploring the underlying rationales that may justify regulatory intervention in this sector. It then offers an overview of the industry's regulatory framework, equipping readers with the knowledge required to navigate the complexities of the financial world. The chapter is guided by three sets of perennial issues facing policymakers, industry stakeholders and academics: *Should we regulate? If so, why (or why not)? Who regulates, and how do we regulate?* We commence with an investigation of the concept of regulation, elucidating the fundamental rationales that necessitate its application within this multifaceted industry.

15 For an overview of Australia's financial system, see, eg, 'The Structure of the Australian Financial System (2006) (March) *Financial Stability Review* <https://www.rba.gov.au/publications/fsr/2006/mar/struct-aus-fin-sys.html>.

16 See, eg, 'About Us', *UniSuper* (Web Page) <https://www.unisuper.com.au/about-us>; 'About Us', *Australian Super* (Web Page) <https://www.australiansuper.com/about-us>.

17 See, eg, QBE Insurance Group Limited <https://www.qbe.com/>; Suncorp Group Limited <https://www.suncorpgroup.com.au/>.

18 See, eg, Wilson Asset Management <https://wilsonassetmanagement.com.au/lic/wam-capital/>; Macquarie Asset Management <https://www.macquarie.com/au/en/about/company/macquarie-asset-management.html>.

19 It is not uncommon to see conglomerates in financial markets. In Australia, the *Banking Act* establishes the framework for 'non-operating holding companies' (NOHCs) under s 5 of the Act. These NOHCs are listed in the Register of Non-Operating Holding Companies and are authorised by APRA under the *Banking Act* s 11AA(1). The framework under this section enables APRA to effectively supervise financial conglomerates by granting them certain authorities. The NOHC ensures a centralised point of regulatory oversight for its subsidiaries, as indicated in s 9(3A). The overarching aim of the Act is to foster a more organised financial system by clearly defining the roles and responsibilities of NOHCs. ANZ Group Holding Limited, AMP Limited and Macquarie Group Limited are prime examples. See 'Register of Non-Operating Holding Companies', *Australian Prudential Regulation Authority* (Web Page) <https://www.apra.gov.au/register-of-non-operating-holding-companies>.

20 'The Strength of Australia's Financial Sector', *The Treasury* (Web Page, 18 March 2016) <https://treasury.gov.au/publication/backing-australian-fintech/the-strength-of-australias-financial-sector>. See also Fariborz Moshirian and Eliza Wu, 'Banking in Australia and New Zealand – Geographic Proximity, Market Concentration, and Banking Integration' in Allen N Berger, Philip Molyneux and John OS Wilson (eds), *The Oxford Handbook of Banking* (Oxford University Press, 3rd ed, 2019) 1190–3. (Note that the Australian banking industry is not just highly concentrated but also deeply interconnected, with the Big Four banks commanding a dominant market share. This represents an exceptionally high concentration of market power in a developed banking system, more than doubling the banking concentration in both the United States and the United Kingdom.)

It is challenging to distil the term 'regulation' into a single, universally accepted definition. As Baldwin et al remark, it encompasses 'a variety of definitions in usage which are not reducible to some platonic essence or single concept'.[21] Julia Black likewise points out that the definition one adopts often hinges on the specific problem or issue under investigation.[22] Echoing Black's pluralist view, Levi-Faur argued for a more nuanced approach, stating that 'we should recognize the many meanings of regulation and devote our attention to understanding each other's terms'.[23]

For the purposes of this book, 'regulation' is loosely understood in two interrelated ways. First, although some interpretations of the term capture 'all mechanisms of social control – including unintentional and non-state processes',[24] we focus more narrowly on the set of rules endorsed by governmental bodies to govern the behaviour of entities subject to regulation.[25] This endorsement naturally leads us to the second aspect, often characterised by a 'command-and-control' or 'interventionist' approach.[26] In this framework, the State takes the lead in formulating and enforcing regulations. Typically, it is an ongoing process, otherwise referred to as 'supervision'.[27]

Traditionally, the efficient capital markets hypothesis (ECMH), a tenet of economic liberalism, posits that in an efficient market, asset prices fully incorporate all accessible information; market participants hence make rational decisions, thereby leading the market to an optimal condition.[28] There are, however, instances where the ECMH falls short, particularly in the presence of information asymmetry or dishonest and fraudulent activities.[29] Insights from behavioural economics challenge traditional finance principles, highlighting that market anomalies and investor behaviours often stem

21 Robert Baldwin et al, 'Introduction' in Robert Baldwin et al (eds), *A Reader on Regulation* (Oxford University Press, 1998) 2.

22 Julia Black, 'Critical Reflections on Regulation' (2002) 27 *Australian Journal of Legal Philosophy* 1, 36: 'Regulation is not a concept that travels well, in either a centred or "decentred" form.'

23 David Levi-Faur, 'Regulation and Regulatory Governance' in David Levi-Faur et al (eds), *Handbook on the Politics of Regulation* (Edward Elgar, 2011) 5.

24 Baldwin et al (n 21) 5; Julia Black, 'Decentring Regulation: Understanding the Role of Regulation and Self-Regulation in a "Post-Regulatory" World' (2001) 54(1) *Current Legal Problems* 112.

25 Two caveats are needed. Although some differentiate between 'legislation' and 'regulation' based on their origins – legislation being the product of legislature and regulation emanating from the executive branch – we adopt a more inclusive definition. In our usage, the term 'regulation' also encompasses legislation, indicating that regulation can be established through various mechanisms, including legislation. Second, we will discuss the role of 'soft law', such as the *Banking Code of Practice,* wherever relevant, in this book. See Nir Kosti et al, 'Legislation and Regulation: Three Analytical Distinctions' (2019) 7(3) *Theory and Practice of Legislation* 169.

26 Ian Bartle, 'Regulatory Approaches to Climate Change Mitigation' in David Levi-Faur et al (eds), *Handbook on the Politics of Regulation* (Edward Elgar, 2011) 629.

27 For the purpose of our book, we use 'regulation' and 'supervision' interchangeably. When differentiation is needed, we follow the World Bank's definitions by understanding 'regulation' as referring to financial sector laws and rules, while 'supervision' means the oversight of these regulations, including off-site analysis and on-site inspections. In addition, for a detailed account of public and private interest theories in the banking sector, see Weiping He, *Banking Regulation in China* (Palgrave Macmillan, 2014).

28 Eugene F Fama, *Foundations of Finance: Portfolio Decisions and Securities Prices* (Basic Books, 1977) 132; see also Armour et al (n 1) 102–3.

29 André Prüm, 'The European Union Crisis and the Efficient Capital Markets Hypothesis' (2013) 20(1) *Columbia Journal of European Law* 1 (using the financial and sovereign debt crises in the European Union context to demonstrate the limitation of the ECMH).

from human decision-making biases.[30] Government intervention may be necessary to correct 'market failure', as an uncontrolled market has the potential to create economic inefficiency.[31]

Regulatory intervention would be deemed essential when there is a potential for market failure resulting from information asymmetry, fraudulent actions, misconduct or other similar reasons. This perspective is supported by the objectives of relevant regulation in Australia, which are: to make markets for financial products 'fair, orderly and transparent'; to ensure financial services providers' 'fairness, honesty and professionalism'; and to help consumers make 'confident and informed decisions' while facilitating 'efficiency, flexibility and innovation' of financial products and services[32] and addressing 'systemic risks'.[33]

Others have underscored the multifaceted purposes of financial regulation, ranging from ensuring safety and soundness, to promoting competitiveness, advocating for fairness and disclosure, optimising resource allocations, preventing abuses and managing monetary policy.[34] These objectives may not necessarily align and could change as circumstances evolve.[35] Therefore, it is imperative to contextualise them and to address the inherent conflicts through the lens of regulatory activities. For instance, unequal resources possessed by different groups of stakeholders within a society could drive the State to enact regulations to redistribute resources. Considering the constrained resources at governments' disposal, if the legislature does not clearly prioritise regulatory objectives, it could grant regulators discretion to determine these priorities on their own.[36] Meanwhile, self-interested industry stakeholders could lobby a government for or against particular regulatory approaches to benefit themselves.[37] The complexity and significance of financial regulation are evidenced by the GFC and the findings of the Royal Commission into Misconduct in the Banking, Superannuation and Financial Services Industry ('Banking Royal Commission').[38]

30 See, eg, Azizah Abu Bakar et al, 'Does Mood Explain the Monday Effect?' (2014) 33(6) *Journal of Forecasting* 40; Emilios Avgouleas, 'Reforming Investor Protection Regulation: The Impact of Cognitive Biases' in M Faure and F Stephen (eds), *Essays in the Law and Economics of Regulation in Honour of Anthony Ogus* (Intersentia Uitgevers NV, 2008) 143. On behavioural economics and regulation in general, see Cass R Sunstein, 'Nedge.gov: Behaviorally Informed Regulation' in Eyal Zamir and Doron Teichman (eds), *The Oxford Handbook of Behavioral Economics and the Law* (Oxford University Press, 2014) 719.

31 Robert Baldwin et al, *Understanding Regulation: Theory, Strategy, and Practice* (Oxford University Press, 2nd ed, 2013) 18–19.

32 See generally the *Corporations Act 2001* (Cth) ('*Corporations Act*') s 760A.

33 See, eg, *Banking Act* s 2A(3) ('It is intended that APRA, in taking actions to address risks to financial system stability in Australia, may consider specific sources of systemic risks, whether geographic, sectoral or otherwise.')

34 See, eg, Richard Aspinwall, 'Conflicting Objectives of Financial Regulation' (1993) 36(6) *Challenge* 53.

35 See, eg, Charles Goodhart et al, *Financial Regulation: Why, How and Where Now?* (Routledge, 1998) 4 (arguing that the primary purposes for public sector regulation are to safeguard consumers from monopolistic practices, offer protection to smaller, less-informed retail clients, and maintain systemic stability).

36 See Aspinwall (n 34) 3–4.

37 Natasha Tusikov, 'Transnational Non-State Regulatory Regimes' in Peter Drahos (ed), *Regulatory Theory: Foundations and Applications* (Australian National University Press, 2017) 339, 339–42.

38 See *Royal Commission into Misconduct in the Banking, Superannuation and Financial Services Industry* (Final Report, 1 February 2019) vol 1 ('*Banking Royal Commission Final Report*').

Andenas and Chiu have noted that following the GFC, policymakers put safeguarding taxpayers and mitigating systemic risk at the forefront of their agenda.[39] Frank Partnoy also argued that financial crises could result in allocative inefficiency; insofar as financial assets do not reflect their fundamental values, and resources are misallocated as parties deal based on incorrect pricing information, it could add uncertainty for investors, thus harming the economy in the long run.[40] To the extent that regulation can improve financial stability and reduce the effects of financial crises, per Partnoy, government intervention is worth pursuing.[41] Put differently, financial stability could be considered a 'public good',[42] as it is neither depletable nor excludable.[43] A regulatory regime, if ill-designed, could exacerbate market failure and deepen the crises. Some policies could facilitate moral hazard and lead financial intermediaries to behave in ways that 'widen information asymmetry', thus increasing agency costs.[44] Therefore, contrary to the popular belief that markets are autonomous and self-regulating entities are guided by an 'invisible hand', it is increasingly recognised that they are actually shaped by political processes, social structures and networks, with law serving as a key component.[45] 'It is no longer accurate to say', Kingsford-Smith and Dixon maintain, that 'the state is involved in markets only in the defence of property and enforcement of contracts'. Thus, even the scholars who strongly advocate for the theory of an efficient market still agree that the financial market serves as 'the infrastructure of the infrastructure' that enables the rest of the economy to function.[46]

To delve deeper into the nuances of regulation, we explore two primary viewpoints on governmental intervention: public interest theory and private interest theory. We do so using the banking sector to illustrate the debates around regulation.[47] While it is true that the financial market is so complicated that it goes beyond banking activities and protecting depositors (eg protection of insurance policyholders and investors), and that certain factors are context-specific, some considerations are nonetheless central to the bigger picture and could shed light on the fundamental functioning of financial markets and help us to situate laws in financial markets. Following the introduction of the

39 Mads Andenas and Iris H-Y Chiu, *The Foundations and Future of Financial Regulation: Governance for Responsibility* (Routledge, 2013) 16.

40 Frank Partnoy, 'Financial Systems, Crises, and Regulation' in Niamh Moloney, Eilís Ferran and Jennifer Payne (eds), *The Oxford Handbook of Financial Regulation* (Oxford University Press, 2015) 70.

41 Ibid.

42 See Andenas and Chiu (n 39) 18. As Andenas and Chiu pointed out, there are two potential interpretations of the term 'public good'. One is rooted in economic theory, while the other is a more flexible rhetorical usage, often found in policy discussions, that actually pertains to 'public interest' within a socio-political context.

43 For a literature review of financial stability as a public good, see Faruk Ülgen, 'Public Good, Collective Action and Financial Regulation' (2021) 92(1) *Annals of Public and Cooperative Economics* 147.

44 Partnoy (n 40) 70.

45 Dimity Kingsford-Smith and Olivia Dixon, 'The Consumer Interest and the Financial Markets' in Niamh Moloney, Eilís Ferran and Jennifer Payne (eds), *The Oxford Handbook of Financial Regulation* (Oxford University Press, 2015) 701.

46 Ibid.

47 The terms 'bank', 'banking' and 'banking activities', referred to in this chapter, are understood to have the same meaning in Chapter 5. The use of these terms is restricted, subject to the licence requirements under the *Banking Act*.

regulatory theories, Section 1.2 examines the issues around the institutional arrangements and strategies facing policymakers. Section 1.3 discusses the regulatory framework of Australia's financial market in a globalised context. Section 1.4 summarises the key points of this chapter.

1.1.1 Public interest theory

The public interest theory of regulation is based on the idea that regulatory authorities are guided by the concept of the public interest – which is intrinsically linked to how it is identified or constructed across different economic, social and political contexts.[48] The theory identifies two sets of key components of the public interest: (a) objectives and outcomes; and (b) process and procedure. 'Objectives and outcomes' refers to the shared values, common good and collective interests of the public. This aspect often represents a compromise, aiming to balance various conflicting interests within society. 'Process and procedure', on the other hand, focuses on achieving objectives and outcomes through fair, inclusive and transparent methods.[49] Regulation, in terms of public interest, should embody both appropriate processes and outcomes. It should adhere to standards of due process, including fairness, transparency and equity, while also fulfilling public ends and reflecting shared values.[50]

The public interest theory identifies that the goal of banking regulation is to reflect the shared values of the public.[51] This theory positively maps appropriate regulatory processes for realising this goal. For instance, the meaning of the 'public' in the banking sector can be loosely conceived to include various stakeholders – individual depositors, wholesale customers, and banks.[52] Such a broad range indicates that banking regulation is becoming increasingly complicated in serving multiple objectives, as already noted above.

The justifications for banking regulation are predominantly economically driven. The public interest theory presumes that markets for goods and services are imperfect. Thus, regulatory intervention could avoid or mitigate the adverse outcomes of market imperfection and seek to remedy private enterprises' market failures.[53]

There are several economic grounds that exist for government intervention in the banking sector. This chapter will briefly outline four such grounds. The first is to ensure fair and open competition. This view is consistent with the public interest, because the fundamental function of banks is to soundly allocate credit supply to creditworthy borrowers, as this preserves a level playing field among banking institutions.[54] The second is to impose entry barriers to foreign banks and their ongoing operation. This occurred

48 See, eg, Weiping He, *Banking Regulation in China* (Palgrave Macmillan, 2014) 29; see also Andenas and Chiu (n 39) 17.
49 He (n 48) 29.
50 Ibid.
51 Ibid.
52 Ibid.
53 Ibid 33.
54 Ibid 34. See also Geoff Edward and Leonard Waverman, 'The Effects of Public Ownership and Regulatory Independence on Regulatory Outcomes' (2008) 29(1) *Journal of Regulatory Economics* 23.

as the GFC underscored the concerns that foreign banks may be a source of instability.[55] The third ground is to protect individual depositors. This is because information asymmetry leads to banks being more knowledgeable about business risks than their depositors; consequently, banking staff may engage in actions to divert resources for their gain.[56] The fourth ground is to protect wholesale customers. This concern became salient following the extension of the traditional bases for banking regulation, as the GFC saw wholesale customers also becoming vulnerable.[57]

Other considerations for banking regulation should also be underscored. First, a robust banking system is crucial for the economic wellbeing of a nation. Bank deposits serve as a foundational element of the country's credit infrastructure. Hence, any systemic failure in the banking sector can lead to severe economic downturns and abrupt shifts in the nation's balance of payments, thus affecting its trade capabilities with other countries.[58] Second, it is in the public interest that banking regulatory measures are designed to restore market stability and market confidence. Further, some crises have even exhibited contagious effects, swiftly affecting other seemingly stable countries.[59] Thus, banking regulation must aim to prevent or mitigate crises that might cause the systemic collapse of banks and the economy.

1.1.2 Private interest theory

The private interest theory hypothesises that regulation is driven by the private interests of the government, the regulators and the regulated. Broadly, the private interest theory believes that as the government attempts to regulate, it will increasingly become influenced by actors pursuing their own interests.[60] According to this view, a captured regulator is likely to exhibit reduced vigilance in overseeing the industry. Instead of fulfilling its primary mandate of promoting public welfare, the regulator would act in a manner that aligns more closely with the interests of the firms it is supposed to regulate.[61] Thus, the private interest theory can be used to support the argument that government intervention is inefficient.[62]

55 He (n 48) 31. See also Ernesto Dal Bo, 'Regulatory Capture: A Review' (2006) 22(2) *Oxford Review of Economic Policy* 203.

56 He (n 48). See also David S Hoelscher et al, 'The Design and Implementation of Deposit Insurance Systems' (Occasional Paper No 251, International Monetary Fund, December 2006).

57 He (n 48) 31.

58 'Banking Crisis', *The World Bank* (Web Page, 2016) <https://www.worldbank.org/en/publication/gfdr/gfdr-2016/background/banking-crisis>.

59 Rudiger Dornbusch et al, 'Contagion: Understanding How it Spreads' (2000) 15(2) *The World Bank Research Observer* 177 <https://documents1.worldbank.org/curated/en/769291468180276956/pdf/766460JRN0WBRO00Box374385B00PUBLIC0.pdf>. (The article uses the Asian Financial Crisis as a case study to illustrate contagion effects. It demonstrates how vulnerabilities in one economy quickly spread to others, exacerbated by globalisation and interconnected financial markets. It emphasises speculative attacks, capital flow reversals and the lack of adequate regulatory frameworks as key factors contributing to the crisis.)

60 He (n 48) 34–5. See also Katharina Pistor, 'Banking Reform in the Chinese Mirror' (Working Paper No 354, Columbia Law School, August 2009) 19–20.

61 Hadar Y Jabotinsky, 'Revolving Doors: We Got It Backwards' (2021) 89(2) *University of Cincinnati Law Review* 432, 436.

62 He (n 48) 35. See also Fred S McChesney, 'Rent Extraction and Rent Creation in the Economic Theory of Regulation' (1987) 16(1) *Journal of Legal Studies* 101.

One can further break down the private interest theory of regulation into two distinct versions, each having its own focus. The first version emphasises the interests of politicians, suggesting that regulation is a tool for them to impose their own demands on private industries.[63] Here, the primary drivers are the interests of the politicians and bureaucrats, rather than the public good.[64] This view contends that historical banking regulations have often been tailored to facilitate government spending, to endorse politically favourable actions, and to enhance the welfare and influence of politicians and bureaucrats. Thus, in this context, banks essentially serve as a financial resource for government needs. Additionally, this variation posits that private industries, including banks, could potentially 'capture' the regulatory process to primarily serve their own interests.[65]

The second version argues that the main purpose of regulation is to benefit banks themselves, as they are the entities being regulated. This view holds that since banks are commercial, profit-driven entities, effective regulation must consider the banks' private interests. It suggests that the focus of policymakers and regulators should be on ensuring the overall effectiveness and efficiency of the banking system, rather than on micromanaging banking operations.[66] This version also identifies several factors that could contribute to corruption and inefficiency in the banking system, such as restricted market access, limitations on business operations, high levels of government ownership and arbitrary regulatory discretion.[67]

The private interest theory of regulation has faced several criticisms. One key critique is that it overlooks the common interests shared by the public and regulated banks – specifically, the mutual desire for a secure banking environment. Another point of criticism is its emphasis on the inefficiency of government regulation,[68] a stance that contrasts sharply with public interest theory, which gains relevance in economies experiencing bank failures. For instance, public confidence in government waned following the GFC.[69] Finally, the two guises of private interest theory have been criticised because they converge at the point of corruption, where regulation is distorted for the regulator and the banks. Such corruption indicates that banking regulation is captured by the interests of the government and banks.

63 He (n 48) 34.
64 Ibid.
65 Ibid 34–5. The term 'regulatory capture' can be defined as a situation where 'an agency set up to regulate a group of firms or other organizations ends up coming under the control of the group(s) whose actions they were intended to control'. On this score, see, eg, George Norman and Darlene C Chisholm, *Dictionary of Industrial Organization* (Edward Elgar, 2014). The risks of regulatory capture may occur at not only the domestic level but also at the international level – the drafting of the Basel Capital Accords is a prime example. See Maurizia De Bellis, 'The Legitimacy of Banking and Financial Standards: Representation, Due Process and Regulatory Capture' in Mariolina Eliantonio and Caroline Cauffman (eds), *The Legitimacy of Standardisation as a Regulatory Technique* (Edward Elgar, 2020) 197. Notably, although regulatory capture typically involves negative images, in some cases, according to David Thaw, it can enable regulators to harness private expertise to advance public interests. See David Thaw, 'Enlightened Regulatory Capture' (2014) 89(2) *Washington Law Review* 329.
66 He (n 48) 34.
67 Ibid.
68 Ibid 38.
69 Ibid.

1.2 Regulatory objectives, institutional structure and strategies

The primary aim of financial regulation is to maintain the stability and integrity of the financial system. This can be achieved through two main pillars: prudential regulation and conduct regulation. In terms of crafting an optimal regulatory framework to meet these goals, various options exist within the context of institutional structure. For our purpose, we refer to 'institutional structure' as the arrangement of agencies responsible for the regulation and oversight of financial institutions and markets.[70] Among these options, the Twin Peaks model, as implemented in Australia, stands out as a prominent choice.

After exploring regulatory objectives and institutional structure, we then examine the challenge of regime design. Key questions include whether to rely on government-led or market-based self-regulation, and whether to use prescriptive rules or high-level principles. With the rise of data-driven technologies, the complexity of financial markets has significantly increased, leading to the development of a wide variety of regulatory strategies, which will be addressed in Section 1.2.3. These strategies are tailored to the specific demands and intricacies of different situations and are aimed at effectively managing and influencing market behaviour.

Against the backdrop of these evolving regulatory strategies in increasingly complex financial markets, we pivot to a deeper examination of our next set of issues – reassessing the foundational goals driving these frameworks.

1.2.1 Regulatory objectives revisited

1.2.1.1 Prudential regulation

Prudential regulation is a type of regulation focused on enhancing financial safety, soundness and stability, with the goal of ensuring that financial intermediaries fulfil their commitments. This form of regulation has dual emphases. On the one hand, from a micro-prudential perspective, it targets the 'risks to the soundness of individual financial firms'; on the other hand, when viewed from a macro-prudential perspective, the focus shifts to addressing the 'systemic risks to the stability of the financial system as a whole'.[71]

More specifically, from a micro-level viewpoint, obligations are imposed on individual firms to ensure that they operate safely and soundly, irrespective of the actions of other firms.[72] Such firm-level rules should be best understood as being 'concerned with the protection of users, such as investors and consumers'.[73]

Before the GFC, prudential regulation was thought to provide sufficient protection to banks' depositors and the broader financial system.[74] However, the GFC demonstrated

70 David Llewellyn, 'Institutional Structure of Financial Regulation and Supervision: The Basic Issues' (Seminar Paper, World Bank, 6–7 June 2006).
71 Peter O Mülbert, 'Managing Risk in the Financial System' in Niamh Moloney, Eilís Ferran and Jennifer Payne (eds), *The Oxford Handbook of Financial Regulation* (Oxford University Press, 2015) 365.
72 Armour et al (n 1) 76.
73 Ibid.
74 Ibid 68.

that prudential regulation was inadequate for preserving financial stability. As a result, new measures were introduced to increase the impact of financial regulation. Namely, special regulations were imposed on those institutions that were considered 'systemically important', and there was an increased focus on regulations known as 'macro-prudential regulation'.[75] Macro-prudential regulation, at that time, had been an approach to safeguarding financial stability that had received little attention from regulators.[76] Although the idea that underlay the macro-prudential perspective – namely, the linkage between prudential regulation and macro-economic concerns – had been present even prior to the GFC,[77] this approach rose to great prominence only following the GFC. Unlike the previous singularly dominant approach of micro-prudential regulation, which focused on safeguarding financial firms, macro-prudential regulation focused on stabilising the financial system.

Macro-prudential regulation is now the preferred approach because it facilitates the connection between firms' assets, liabilities and investment strategies, which significantly affects the overall system's stability; and because it instils portfolio restrictions on firms, classes of firms or whole sectors in a way that reflects how investment strategies interrelate.[78] Macro-prudential regulation encompasses two perspectives. The first of these is the 'cross-sectional' perspective, which is concerned with ensuring the financial system's overall reliance if a shock to the system occurs. The second is the 'time-series' perspective, which is concerned with the overall build-up of risk in the financial system over time. The idea is that insights from the lead-up to the GFC may facilitate the identification of cycles that involve the aggregate build-up and consequential wind-down of risk.

Although prudential regulation, in theory, has two distinct perspectives, the regulatory tools are sometimes less clear-cut. Some policy tools – for instance, deposit insurance schemes – could have dual functions by reducing or mitigating the risks to

75 Ibid 69; Steve Kourabas, 'Trends and Theory in Financial Regulation and Regulatory Design after the Global Financial Crisis' in Douglas W Arner et al (eds), *Research Handbook on Asian Financial Law* (Edward Elgar, 2020) 30 (noting: 'Owing to the special role of finance within the economy, most jurisdictions have specific regulations in place to ensure the safety and soundness of a limited category of financial institutions. Before the GFC, most prudential regulation was "microprudential" in nature, meaning that it addressed the safety and soundness of individual financial institutions': 32). Cf Mülbert (n 71) 366 (arguing that '[e]ven before the GFC, though, prudential regulation of financial institutions was not limited to a purely micro-economic perspective'). Cf also Domenica Tropeano, 'The Interplay of Macro-Prudential Regulation and Microeconomic Financial Regulation in the European Union 2011–2014' (2022) 51(3) *International Journal of Political Economy* 229. (Tropeano notes that macro-prudential regulation came into prominence as a reaction to the GFC, with the expectation of outperforming traditional micro-economic-level prudential regulation. However, she also contends that the application of macro-prudential policies in the European Union during the crisis failed to effectively mitigate financial instability. This ineffectiveness may have been due to large systemic banks employing financial techniques to circumvent increased costs.)

76 Mülbert (n 71) 409, citing Andrew Crockett, 'Marrying the Micro- and Macro-Prudential Dimensions of Financial Stability' (Speech, Financial Stability Forum, 21 September 2000); C Borio, 'Towards a Macroprudential Framework for Financial Supervision and Regulation?' (2003) 49(2) *CESifo Economic Studies* 181; SG Hanson, AK Kashyap and JC Stein, 'A Macroprudential Approach to Financial Regulation' (2011) 25(1) *Journal of Economic Perspectives* 3; G Galati and R Moessner, 'Macroprudential Policy – A Literature Review' (Working Paper No 337, Bank for International Settlements, February 2011).

77 Piet Clement, 'The Term "Macroprudential": Origins and Evolution' (2010) *BIS Quarterly Review* 60.

78 Armour et al (n 1) 77.

the soundness of individual firms and financial stability.[79] In other contexts, the goals of these tools are not always aligned – as Peter Mülbert points out, for instance. While funding diversification would make individual financial intermediaries more resilient, it could create additional systemic risks.[80]

1.2.1.2 Conduct regulation

'Conduct regulation' refers to the regulation of business conduct. It focuses primarily on bank business practices relating to consumers, to ensure that they have appropriate information and that banks comply with proper industry practices.[81] Conduct regulation focuses on mandatory information disclosure, because this highlights the importance of having a disciplined market that provides market signals that come from risk monitors, as this pressures banks to amend their risk-taking behaviours and enables market participants to react. Conduct regulation also focuses on banks and their employees' honesty and integrity, the level of banks' competence in supplying financial products and services, and fair business practices in general.[82]

Market discipline and corporate governance are central to conducting regulation. Market discipline allows market participants to assess critical information regarding the capital of banks, risk exposure, risk-assessment processes and the overall capital adequacy of banks.[83] This encourages banks to maintain strong risk-management profiles in order to stand out from those with weaker profiles. Further, market discipline requires incentive structures to monitor and discipline banks' risk-taking.[84]

Corporate governance plays a crucial role in conduct regulation because it relates to how individual banks respond to risks identified in the process of risk monitoring and risk management. A sufficiently robust corporate governance structure within banks minimises the inherent asymmetries of information and the potential for market failure within the overall banking system.[85]

1.2.2 Institutional structure

There are at least three main types of institutional structure when it comes to regime design – namely, the Twin Peaks model, the institutional model and the integrated model. The Twin Peaks model – a term coined by Michael Taylor in the 1990s – refers to institutional structures where prudential and conduct regulation and supervision are separated.[86] Its defining feature is that regulatory responsibilities are divided according to the entity's purpose, rather than its type. Under this model, there are two broad

79 'Financial Claims Scheme', *Australian Prudential Regulation Authority* (Web Page) <https://www.apra.gov.au/financial-claims-scheme-0>.
80 Mülbert (n 71) 366.
81 He (n 48) 41.
82 Ibid 42.
83 Ibid 42–3.
84 Ibid 42.
85 See Basel Committee on Banking Supervision, *Guidelines: Corporate Governance Principles for Banks* (July 2015) <https://www.bis.org/bcbs/publ/d328.pdf>.
86 Michael Taylor, *Peak Practice: How to Reform the UK's Regulatory System* (Centre for Study of Financial Innovation, October 1996).

regulatory functions being pursued: (1) market conduct integrity and consumer protection; and (2) prudential regulation and financial system stability.[87] The roles of conduct and prudential regulators can be, as Jeffrey Carmichael argues, analogised to those of law enforcement agencies and medical practitioners, respectively. Conduct regulators function primarily as enforcers, scrutinising the interactions between financial institutions and their clients to ensure transparency, fairness, and the appropriateness of offered products. On the other hand, prudential regulators act more like healthcare providers for financial institutions, focusing on their overall wellbeing and ability to fulfil their commitments.[88]

The Twin Peaks model first gained traction in the United Kingdom in the mid-1990s as a response to an increasingly complex financial regulatory system that struggled to keep pace with the fast-evolving financial sector after the structural deregulation of the 1980s.[89] However, Australia was the first jurisdiction to implement this model, following the recommendations of the Wallis Inquiry.

The Wallis Inquiry concluded that the justification for financial regulation largely stems from the need to address market failures.[90] The overall cost of implementing such regulation, which includes both direct and indirect expenses, should not exceed the societal costs incurred as a consequence of ignoring these market failures. In the realm of prudential regulation, the primary market failure identified is the informational imbalance between the buyers and sellers of financial products. This imbalance becomes more pronounced when dealing with complex, hard-to-understand financial products that have significant societal implications if they fail. Thus, the Wallis Inquiry recommended that certain areas such as banking, insurance and superannuation are especially deserving of prudential oversight.[91] On the other hand, conduct regulation requires a more expansive approach due to the elevated risks of fraud and misrepresentation in the financial sector.[92] These risks are further magnified by the intricate nature of financial products and the time gap between what is promised and what is ultimately delivered.[93] Following the recommendations of the Wallis Inquiry, Australia restructured its regulatory framework to what is now known as the Twin Peaks model.

87 Andrew Godwin, 'Financial Regulatory Models in the Asia-Pacific: A Case Study in Diversity' in Douglas W Arner et al (eds), *Research Handbook on Asian Financial Law* (Edward Elgar, 2020) 51.

88 Jeffrey Carmichael, 'Reflections on Twenty Years of Regulation under Twin Peaks' in Andrew Godwin and Andrew Schmulow (eds), *The Cambridge Handbook of Twin Peaks Financial Regulation* (Cambridge University Press, 2021) 32, 33–4. ('It has also generated the view that conduct regulators are primarily "regulators", while prudential regulators are primarily "supervisors".')

89 Initially, the concept piqued the interest of the UK Labour Party, which was then in opposition but would come to power in 1997, as well as some UK regulatory professionals. However, the Bank of England opposed the model, as it threatened to strip the bank of its supervisory role over the banking sector. For a history, see generally Michael W Taylor, 'The Three Episodes of Twin Peaks' in Andrew Godwin and Andrew Schmulow (eds), *The Cambridge Handbook of Twin Peaks Financial Regulation* (Cambridge University Press, 2021) 17.

90 *Financial System Inquiry Final Report: Overview* (AGPS, 1997) 19–20 <https://treasury.gov.au/sites/default/files/2019-03/02-fsi-fr-overview.pdf>.

91 Ibid 21.

92 Ibid 1–2.

93 *Financial System Inquiry Final Report* (AGPS, 1997) ch 7, 237–8 <https://treasury.gov.au/sites/default/files/2019-03/11-fsi-fr-chapt07.pdf>.

There are two other options: the 'institutional' model and the 'integrated' model. The former – also referred to as a subset of the broader 'sectoral' approach – assigns a specialised regulator to each type of financial institution, such as a bank or insurer, and oversees all their regulated activities across various markets and sectors. Typically, each institution is regulated by a single authority.[94] However, as financial products and institutions grow more complex, including the rise of financial conglomerates, such a sectoral model faces challenges, and the level of complexity can lead to coordination issues and overlapping jurisdictions among the relevant regulatory bodies.[95]

The latter – otherwise known as the 'unified' or 'super-regulator model' – aims to create a single regulator that monitors both the conduct of market participants and the prudential soundness of financial institutions.[96] This approach was initially favoured by the United Kingdom before it transitioned to the Twin Peaks model. However, the integrated model has its drawbacks. One major concern is that prudential and conduct regulations require distinct approaches and organisational cultures, casting doubt on a single regulator's ability to manage both effectively. Another issue is the potential lack of focus on the diverse objectives and rationales for regulation and supervision, which could result in inadequate differentiation between various types of institutions and businesses.

The advantages of the Twin Peaks model are that having two regulators means that each regulator can have more distinct objectives and mandates, allowing them to focus on a specific area of regulation.[97] Because of this, each regulator is also able to create and foster its own culture that best suits its objectives, instead of having many cultures under one roof. In the same way, having two separate regulators minimises the danger of one aspect of regulation dominating the regulatory landscape and ensures that both objectives are adequately seen. Compared to other models such as the institutional model, the Twin Peaks model is better equipped to regulate under such evolving circumstances, as there would be fewer problems of coordination and regulatory overlap.[98] Moreover, this model minimises the inherent risks of conflicts of interest that arise in a system that is reliant on a single super-regulator.

However, the Twin Peaks model has several disadvantages. First, having two regulators may result in an overlap in the regulation of dual-regulated entities, meaning that some entities would have to adhere to two sets of regulatory rules and systems.[99] Second, there is a more general risk that regulators will insufficiently cooperate with regulation and that coordination will prove difficult. Further, where the level of involvement of central banks is not clearly defined, or the central bank retains a level of involvement in

94 Godwin (n 87) 53.
95 Ibid 50–1.
96 Ibid 51.
97 Ibid.
98 Andrew Godwin, Timothy Howse and Ian Ramsay, 'A Jurisdictional Comparison of the Twin Peaks Model of Financial Regulation' (2017) 18(2) *Journal of Banking Regulation* 103, 105.
99 Godwin (n 87) 52, citing Joint Committee on the draft Financial Services Bill, Draft Financial Services Bill – Report, together with formal minutes and appendices. HL 2010–12, 236, HC 2010–12, 1447, 73 [83]. See also Andrew Godwin, 'Introduction to Special Issue – The Twin Peaks Model of Financial Regulation and Reform in South Africa' (2017) 11(4) *Law and Financial Markets Review* 151, 151–2.

the supervisory system, this model may create conflicts of interest with the central bank through its implementation.[100]

Presently in Australia, functions are divided between the Australian Securities and Investments Commission (ASIC) and the Australian Prudential Regulation Authority (APRA), with ASIC responsible for regulating companies, market conduct and consumer protection; and APRA responsible for prudential regulation.[101] The Reserve Bank of Australia, thus, remains responsible for monetary policy and financial stability. Countries other than Australia that have adopted the Twin Peak model include the Netherlands, Belgium, New Zealand, the United Kingdom and South Africa, while the United States has considered it.[102]

1.2.3 Strategies of regime design in a nutshell

Having examined the regulatory theories, regulators and regulatory models, we now consider another challenge facing policymakers: formulating strategies to design the regime. For instance, should governments take the lead in developing and enforcing various types of regulations or allow the regulatees to play a role through market-based, self-regulation in responses to new challenges? Should we regulate by a set of prescriptive rules or high-level principles? As the level of complexity has continued to increase in the financial market, especially as we embrace data-driven technologies, a multifaceted and multilayered matrix of regulatory strategies has emerged for controlling entities' behaviour. These strategies may vary depending on the nature and complexity involved across different contexts. For our present purposes, we briefly consider these strategies along the following dimensions – *command-and-control/self-regulation* and the *rules-based/principles-based approach* – to achieve the optimal institutional design and ensure an orderly market.

1.2.3.1 Command-and-control versus self-regulation

State regulatory power enforces financial regulations upon entities; it is dependent upon the government, as well as any economic, social and cultural circumstances that may affect it. Such power may be exercised via the regulatory approaches of command-and-control or self-regulation.[103]

The command-and-control regulatory approach assigns the government the task of prescribing mandatory rules that encourage, permit and prohibit the behaviour exhibited by regulated entities.[104] By contrast, under the self-regulation approach, private entities have responsibility for developing rules that govern their behaviour.[105] Self-regulation

100 Godwin (n 87) 52. (Godwin notes that, depending on the Twin Peaks model's design, the central bank could face conflicts of interest if it oversees both prudential regulation and monetary policy. Citing Llewellyn (n 70), Godwin suggests that such a central bank might ease monetary policy during challenging times. But this dual role could also create synergies due to the central bank's expertise in monetary policy and financial markets.)

101 Ibid.

102 Ibid 58.

103 He (n 48) 45.

104 Ibid.

105 Darren Sinclair, 'Self-Regulation versus Command and Control? Beyond False Dichotomies' (1997) 19(4) *Law & Policy* 529, 534 (describing self-regulation as 'characterized as relying substantially on

may be viewed through the lens of a contractual relationship between the delegator and delegatee of the powers of regulation; the government essentially delegates state regulatory power upon the private entities, who, as delegatees, exercise such powers upon themselves.[106]

1.2.3.2 Rules-based versus principles-based regulation

There is a choice between the different regulatory models: either rules-based or principles-based approaches.[107] The rules-based approach produces a set of regulatory standards in the form of rules by which the entity will abide.[108] This approach addresses compliance responsibilities with more precision, provides regulatory certainty, and ensures that entities are acting within their legal scope. Yet, due to its rigidity, entities adopting such an approach may fail to adapt to the innovative and ever-changing landscape of the banking sector.[109] Furthermore, entities may potentially incur unnecessary implementation and compliance costs due to their inflexible rules.

The principles-based approach, which is the preferred approach in many jurisdictions, including the United Kingdom, stands in sharp contrast to the rules-based approach by imposing broad, principles-based standards to achieve the desired outcomes.[110] Principles-based regulation can generally be understood as 'moving away from reliance on detailed, prescriptive rules and relying more on high-level, broadly stated rules or

the goodwill and cooperation of individual firms for their compliance. The emphasis is upon gaining a moral commitment from participants, upon using information, education, technology sharing, and perhaps peer group pressure ...').

106 He (n 48) 46. For a reflection of the role of self-regulation in the Australian banking sector, see Nicola Howell, 'Revisiting the Australian Code of Banking Practice: Is Self-regulation Still Relevant for Improving Consumer Protection Standards?' (2015) 38(2) *University of New South Wales Law Journal* 544.

107 Julia Black, Martyn Hopper and Christa Band, 'Marking a Success of Principles-Based Regulation' (2007) 1(3) *Law & Financial Markets Review* 191.

108 He (n 48) 45.

109 From a law and economics perspective, as noted by some American scholars, the financial implications of rules-based and principles-based regulations differ significantly. In a rules-based framework, the economic onus of crafting, researching and enforcing specific regulations is shouldered by the regulatory authority. For instance, establishing a 55 km/hr speed limit involves conducting studies and evaluations, and setting up enforcement mechanisms, all of which are funded by the regulator. This model provides clear guidelines and simplifies enforcement but may be rigid and less adaptable to unique circumstances. Conversely, principles-based regulation redistributes the economic burden to the individual who is subject to the rule. For instance, a principle like 'drive safely' necessitates that the driver invests their own resources to interpret what constitutes a 'safe' speed under varying conditions. This might include evaluating road conditions, the capabilities of their vehicle and their own driving skills. While this model offers flexibility and is more adaptable to specific situations, it also elevates the individual's cost of compliance, as they are responsible for their own risk assessments to meet the regulatory standard. See Eric J Pan, 'Understanding Financial Regulation' (2012) (4) *Utah Law Review* 1897, 1919. See also Vincent Di Lorenzo, 'Principles-Based Regulation and Legislative Congruence' (2012) 15(1) *New York University Journal of Legislation and Public Policy* 45, 47 (distinguishing between principles-based and rules-based regulation). According to Lorenzo, principles-based regulation sets broad standards or objectives that industry members must meet to fulfil legislative goals. It provides a general guideline for behaviour, allowing regulators the discretion to determine if specific actions warrant penalties. Conversely, rules-based regulation is characterised by detailed, prescriptive criteria that explicitly outline which actions will incur penalties.

110 Black et al (n 107) 191.

[p]rinciples to set the standards by which regulated firms must conduct business'.[111] In the banking sector, for instance, this approach is designed to withstand its rapidly changing environment and to align the entity's initiatives with regulation as per good business practice. The Australian Government, as reflected in the relevant documents by Treasury and the Australian Law Reform Commission,[112] also recognises the limitations of a highly prescriptive legislative approach in financial services, which contributes to unnecessary complexity. There is a shift towards a more principles- and outcomes-based approach, drawing inspiration from international developments such as in the United Kingdom.

However, this approach has its shortcomings, too: it runs the risks of uncertain regulation, the proliferation of guidance, regulatory creep, issues surrounding accountability and unpredictability, hindsight-driven enforcement of regulations, and inappropriate skills and mindsets of both the regulators and the regulated.[113]

1.3 Regulators and regulations

Generally, the Australian financial system's contour is shaped by domestic regulators and global actors. As part of the globalised process, international organisations and networks – of which Australia is a member – develop international standards for countries to implement domestically. The Basel Committee on Banking Supervision (as detailed below) is a case in point. Before we consider each of these actors in turn, it is helpful to start with the Wallis Inquiry, which generally set out Australia's regulatory approach in financial markets.

Conducted between 1996 and 1997, the Wallis Inquiry was a seminal investigation into the Australian financial system.[114] Its primary goal was to provide recommendations for regulatory frameworks that would promote greater efficiency and further competition, and to create a flexible structure to enable the financial system to maintain cost-effectiveness in the face of changing circumstances.[115] There were 115 recommendations from the Wallis Inquiry, which were largely adopted by the Australian Government and have formed the cornerstone of the country's current financial regulatory structure.

The regulatory philosophy outlined in the Wallis Inquiry emphasises that regulation is essential for addressing market failures that generate inefficiency.[116] In the complex landscape of the financial sector, specialised regulation is crucial for ensuring market integrity and consumer protection. Certain segments of the financial system necessitate safety regulations, typically manifesting as prudential regulation, as elaborated further below.[117] The Inquiry proposed that the rigour of this regulation should be most pronounced in areas with significant financial commitments and where the potential for

111 Ibid.

112 See Australian Law Reform Commission, *Final Report: Confronting Complexity: Reforming Corporations and Financial Services Legislation* ('ALRC Report 141') (November 2023) 252, 258.

113 See generally Julia Black, 'Principles Based Regulations: Risks, Challenges and Opportunities' (Speech, Sydney, 27 March 2007) <https://eprints.lse.ac.uk/62814/>.

114 *Financial System Inquiry: Final Report* (AGPS, 1997) <https://treasury.gov.au/publication/p1996-fsi-fr>.

115 *Financial System Inquiry: Final Report* (AGPS, 1997) Overview <https://treasury.gov.au/sites/default/files/2019-03/02-fsi-fr-overview.pdf>.

116 *Financial System Inquiry Final Report* (AGPS, 1997) ch 5 <https://treasury.gov.au/sites/default/files/2019-03/09-fsi-fr-chapt05.pdf>.

117 Ibid.

market failure is highest. Yet, it recommended that governments should exercise caution in applying safety regulations universally across the entire financial system. The protections afforded by prudential regulation should not be misconstrued as government guarantees for all financial commitments. At the same time, the Inquiry noted that mandating that financial institutions support certain activities via 'community service obligations' could adversely impact their operational efficiency and may not be sustainable in a competitive marketplace.[118] Therefore, given that regulation incurs costs, both direct and indirect, a balanced approach is necessary that weighs prudential concerns against efficiency. The Inquiry's guiding principles for effective regulation include competitive neutrality, cost-effectiveness, transparency, flexibility and accountability.[119]

One of the key outcomes of the Wallis Inquiry was the proposal for a unified prudential regulator that would consolidate the prudential regulation activities previously carried out by multiple government agencies.[120] This led to the creation of the Australian Prudential Regulation Authority. Additionally, the Inquiry recommended the creation of a new market-conduct and consumer-protection regulator for the financial market, which led to the establishment of the Australian Securities and Investments Commission.[121] Decades later, in December 2017, the Australian Government established the Banking Royal Commission, led by former High Court Justice Kenneth Hayne, to investigate misconduct in the country's banking and financial services sectors.[122]

Concluding in February 2019, the Commission's final report offered 76 recommendations aimed at enhancing ethics, governance and consumer protections within the industry.[123] Of these recommendations, some actions are required to improve the coordination between regulators. For instance, following the Banking Royal Commission's report, there has been a concerted effort to formalise and strengthen the collaboration between APRA and ASIC. An updated Memorandum of Understanding (MoU) has been established, in line with Commissioner Hayne's Recommendation 6.10,[124] to foster a proactive and collaborative relationship between the two agencies. This MoU is supported by a new engagement structure, led by the APRA–ASIC Committee (AAC), which focuses

118 Ibid.

119 Ibid.

120 Ibid.

121 Ibid.

122 The Australian Government under former Prime Minister Malcolm Turnbull announced the Royal Commission into Misconduct in the Banking, Superannuation and Financial Services Industry on 30 November 2017, appointing Kenneth Hayne as the commissioner. The Commission held public hearings from March to November 2018, covering various financial sectors and their regulators, APRA and ASIC. The final report, released in February 2019, included 76 recommendations and 24 referrals for potential criminal prosecution. The Government committed to implementing most of these recommendations, except for some concerning remuneration practices in the mortgage broking industry. For background, see, eg, Phillip Hawkins, 'Financial Services Royal Commission', *Parliament of Australia* (Web Page) <https://www.aph.gov.au/About_Parliament/Parliamentary_Departments/Parliamentary_Library/pubs/BriefingBook46p/FinancialServicesRC>.

123 *Banking Royal Commission Final Report* (n 38) 1–2.

124 Ibid. Recommendation 6.10 ('ASIC and APRA should prepare and maintain a joint memorandum setting out how they intend to comply with their statutory obligation to co-operate. The memorandum should be reviewed biennially and each of ASIC and APRA should report each year on the operation of and steps taken under it in its annual report.')

on various issue areas such as credit, banking, insurance and enforcement activities.[125] Such a structure aims to eliminate duplicative or contradictory actions by promoting day-to-day engagement in areas of joint responsibility. The increased inter-agency collaboration has led to more effective discussions on key risks, better information sharing, and coordinated enforcement activities, which would help to enhance collaborative efforts, optimising outcomes in both prudential and conduct regulation.[126] Likewise, the Financial Regulator Assessment Authority (FRAA), an independent statutory body, was established following the Banking Royal Commission's Recommendations 6.13 and 6.14 to evaluate and report on the performance and capabilities of ASIC and APRA.[127] The role of FRAA will be further elaborated below.

1.3.1 Regulators at the domestic level

1.3.1.1 Reserve Bank of Australia (RBA)

The RBA is Australia's central bank and was established on 14 January 1960 through the *Reserve Bank Act 1959* (Cth) ('*RB Act*').[128] The predecessor of the RBA was the Commonwealth Bank of Australia, which was statutorily established in 1911 under the *Commonwealth Bank Act 1911* (Cth).[129] The CBA did not commence as a central bank; instead, it gradually acquired powers and responsibilities over time. It was not until 1945 that the role of the CBA as a central banking entity was formalised. At that time, it functioned as both a central bank and a commercial bank, which raised questions about potential conflicts of interest. Ultimately, in 1959, the CBA's central banking functions were removed, and the RBA was established as Australia's central bank.[130]

Broadly, the RBA plays a regulatory role in the banking sector and carries out regular banking functions – subject to the restrictions under the *RB Act* and the *Banking Act 1959*.[131] As a central bank, the RBA is responsible for ensuring the fundamental stability of Australia's financial systems via interest rates and regulating payment systems.[132] The RBA defines a financially stable system as one that promotes economic growth through economic activity.[133] Put differently, a financially stable system is one in which financial institutions, markets and market infrastructure work together to facilitate the steady flow of funds between savers and investors.

In accordance with the *RB Act* s 8, the RBA is, furthermore, endowed with a range of powers under the *RB Act* and any other applicable laws. These powers include the

125 'APRA and ASIC: A New Era in Cooperation', *Australian Prudential Regulation Authority* (Web Page) <https://www.apra.gov.au/apra-and-asic-a-new-era-cooperation#Milestones%20Since%20The%20Royal%20Commission>.

126 Ibid. The APRA–ASIC Committee (AAC), supported by five standing committees, would help ensure that 'the actions of each agency are coordinated and not duplicative or contradictory'.

127 *Banking Royal Commission Final Report* (n 38) Recommendations 6.13–6.14.

128 *Reserve Bank Act 1959* (Cth) ('*RB Act*') s 26(a).

129 *Commonwealth Bank Act 1911* (Cth) s 5.

130 'Our History', *Reserve Bank of Australia* (Web Page) <https://www.rba.gov.au/about-rba/history/>.

131 *RB Act* s 10.

132 Ibid s 10(2).

133 'About Financial Stability', *Reserve Bank of Australia* (Web Page) <https://www.rba.gov.au/fin-stability/>.

management of deposits, borrowing and lending of funds, and participation in financial market activities such as the purchase and sale of securities; additionally, the RBA is authorised to conduct transactions in foreign currencies and precious metals.[134] It is also empowered to set up credit lines, to issue guarantees and to underwrite loans, among other financial activities.[135] Prior to 1998, the RBA held the responsibility for prudential supervision. This role was subsequently transferred to APRA in that year.[136]

Of these functions, it is crucial to underscore the 'lender of last resort' (LOLR) role.[137] An LOLR facility serves as a form of insurance for both banks and their depositors, offering a safety net in times of financial distress.[138] While the RBA is not obligated to act as an LOLR, it does possess the authority to receive deposits, as well as to borrow and lend money, as part of its central banking functions.[139] This gives the RBA the capability to step in as an LOLR if it chooses to do so.

More specifically, under the *RB Act*, the RBA's function is carried out through two boards: the Reserve Bank Board and the Payments System Board. The Reserve Bank Board's duties concern monetary policy, which is specified in the *RB Act* ss 10(2) and 11(1). Section 10(2) mandates that the Reserve Bank Board must aim to benefit the Australian people by focusing on currency stability, full employment and overall economic well-being.[140] Section 11(1) underscores the Reserve Bank Board's obligation to keep the government informed about the RBA's monetary and banking policies.[141] The Reserve Bank Board is responsible for the RBA's monetary and banking policy, and for its policy on all other matters other than its payments system policy, and has the power to take such action as is necessary to ensure that effect is given by the RBA to the policy so determined.[142]

134 *RB Act* s 8.

135 Ibid.

136 Graeme Thompson, 'Prudential Supervision and the Changing Financial System' (Speech, Monash University Law School Foundation, 28 March 1996).

137 Simply put, a lender of last resort (LOLR) is a financial institution to which banks turn for emergency funding when all other options have been exhausted. This is particularly crucial during periods of financial instability, when interbank lending may be compromised and there is a surge in withdrawals from bank accounts. Central banks traditionally assume the role of LOLR, as they bear the primary responsibility for maintaining the smooth functioning of financial markets and the stability of the financial system. By doing so, central banks aim to shield individuals and businesses from the adverse effects that may occur when banks face financial difficulties. Freixas and Parigi (2014) contend that the scope of the LOLR function has expanded in the post-GFC era. Xavier Freixas and Bruno M Parigi, 'Lender of Last Resort: A New Role for the Old Instrument' in Allen N Berger, Philip Molyneux and John OS Wilson (eds), *The Oxford Handbook of Banking* (Oxford University Press, 3rd ed, 2019) 602.

138 Bryan Fitz-Gibbon and Marianne Gizycki, 'A History of Last-Resort Lending and Other Support for Troubled Financial Institutions in Australia' (Research Discussion Paper 2001–07, Reserve Bank of Australia, October 2001) <https://www.rba.gov.au/publications/rdp/2001/pdf/rdp2001-07.pdf>.

139 See Gail Pearson, *Financial Services Law and Compliance in Australia* (Cambridge University Press, 2009) 26.

140 *RB Act* s 10(2) (which states: 'It is the duty of the Reserve Bank Board, within the limits of its powers, to ensure that the monetary and banking policy of the Bank is directed to the greatest advantage of the people of Australia and that the powers of the Bank ... are exercised in such a manner as, in the opinion of the Reserve Bank Board, will best contribute to: (a) the stability of the currency of Australia; (b) the maintenance of full employment in Australia; and (c) the economic prosperity and welfare of the people of Australia.')

141 Ibid s 11(1) ('The Reserve Bank Board is to inform the Government, from time to time, of the Bank's monetary and banking policy.')

142 Ibid ss 8A(1)–(2), 9, 10.

Similarly, the 'charter' for the Payments System Board is set forth under the *RB Act* s 10B(3). This section obliges this Board to direct the RBA's payment system policy for the benefit of the Australian people.[143] It also outlines how the RBA's powers under various Acts should be exercised to control financial system risks, enhance payment system efficiency, and foster market competition for payment services, all while maintaining financial stability.

In cases where there are conflicting policies between the two Boards, the Reserve Bank Board's policy takes precedence, effectively modifying the Payments System Board's policy to eliminate the inconsistency.[144] In case of a dispute about whether such an inconsistency exists, or about the impact of the modification on the Payments System Board's policy, the Governor of the Reserve Bank is tasked with resolving the disagreement.[145] If, moreover, there is uncertainty about which Board is responsible for setting a particular policy, the Governor also has the authority to make the final determination.[146] The Governor of the RBA plays a pivotal role in resolving internal policy conflicts to maintain financial stability.[147]

Lastly, the RBA functions to provide banking services to the Australian Government and its agencies, as well as to some overseas central banks and official institutions.[148] Part 7.3 of the *Corporations Act 2001* (Cth) forms part of the 'payments system policy',[149] thus falling under the mandate of the RBA.[150]

1.3.1.2 Australian Prudential Regulation Authority (APRA)

Established on 1 July 1998, under the *Australian Prudential Regulation Authority Act 1998* (Cth), APRA took over the role of prudential regulation from the RBA.[151] This transfer of responsibilities was a result of the Wallis Inquiry, which recommended the creation of a single Commonwealth agency to oversee prudential regulation within Australia's financial system. Prior to these reforms, the RBA had been responsible for this regulatory function.

On its establishment, APRA provided neutral regulation across sectors where regulation was previously performed by the RBA, the Insurance and Superannuation Commission, the Australian Financial Institutions Commission and the Australian Securities Commission.[152] In Australia, APRA holds the role of prudential regulator,

143 Ibid s 10B(3).
144 Ibid s 10C(1).
145 Ibid s 10C(2).
146 Ibid s 10C(3).
147 See also ibid ss 12, 14 (Governor and Deputy Governor should form part of the Reserve Bank Board's membership) and 25 (Governor and Deputy Governor should form part of the Payments System Board's membership).
148 Ibid s 27.
149 Ibid s 5.
150 Also, the RBA 'may do an assessment of how well a CS [clearing and settlement] facility licensee is complying with its obligation' under the *Corporations Act*. See *Corporations Act* s 823CA.
151 *Australian Prudential Regulation Authority Act 1998* (Cth) ('*APRA Act*'); 'About APRA', *Australian Prudential Regulation Authority* (Web Page) <https://www.apra.gov.au/about-apra>.
152 'About APRA' (n 151). Despite such reform, the payment system was separated from the prudential regulation of banks due to the growing involvement of non-bank entities. Recognising the critical role that payment systems play in maintaining overall financial stability, the RBA has retained its regulatory authority in this domain. For an account, see Pearson (n 139) 26–7.

while ASIC takes on the role of conduct regulator. This structure, with one regulator whose main objective is financial system stability and the other whose main objective is consumer protection,[153] is a distinct characteristic of the Twin Peaks model that will be elaborated on below.

APRA's mandate, stated in the *Australian Prudential Regulation Authority Act 1988* (Cth) s 8(2), is to 'balance the objectives of financial safety and efficiency, competition, contestability and competitive neutrality and, in balancing these objectives, ... promote financial system stability in Australia'.[154] Within Australia's financial system, APRA has the role of a *prudential regulator* (the concept of prudential regulation will be elaborated on later in Section 1.3), where its overarching goal is to supervise bodies in the financial sector to promote financial system stability.[155] APRA takes a *risk-based* regulatory approach, meaning it allocates limited resources to where they are most required.[156] In determining where resources are most needed, APRA consults with industries where appropriate.[157] To achieve its mandate, APRA primarily follows a principles-based approach, setting general standards and providing guidance on them, rather than specifically prescribing conduct.[158]

APRA's key function is to regulate financial-sector bodies in compliance with Commonwealth laws that provide for prudential regulation or retirement income standards.[159] It does this through formulating and amending the prudential framework, which encompasses setting out prudential standards and guidance. Further, it oversees the compliance of entities that it regulates – for example, by taking enforcement measures where entities fail to meet regulatory requirements. A final core function of APRA – albeit one that is rarely invoked – is to limit the financial impact of entity failures and minimise the disruptions caused by their exits from the financial system.[160]

APRA's primary responsibility is to ensure that organisations within Australia's financial services industry manage their risks appropriately to ensure that their financial commitments are met, in turn limiting disruption to the economy and community.[161] The organisations that APRA monitors include banks, credit unions, mutual societies and other authorised deposit-taking institutions; insurance companies; friendly societies; and most superannuation companies (excluding self-managed superannuation funds).[162]

153 Group of Thirty, *The Structure of Financial Supervision: Approaches and Challenges in a Global Marketplace* (2008) 24 <https://group30.org/images/uploads/publications/G30_Structure FinancialSupervision2008.pdf>.

154 *APRA Act* s 8(2).

155 Ibid.

156 Australian Prudential Regulation Authority, *The APRA Supervision Blue Print* (2015) <https://www .apra.gov.au/sites/default/files/APRA-Supervision-Blueprint-FINAL_0.pdf>.

157 'APRA's Objectives', *Australian Prudential Regulation Authority* (Web Page) <https://www.apra.gov.au/ apras-objectives>; see also ibid.

158 Australian Prudential Regulation Authority (n 156).

159 *APRA Act* ss 9, 9A.

160 'What We Do', *Australian Prudential Regulation Authority* (Web Page) <https://www.apra.gov.au/what-we-do>.

161 G North and T Wilson, 'Has the Australian Prudential Regulation Authority Done Enough to Meet its Legislated Objectives and Prepare Australia for the Next Financial Crisis?' (2020) 43(2) *University of New South Wales Law Journal* 478.

162 See, eg, Australian Prudential Regulation Authority, *Corporate Plan 2022–23* <https://www.apra.gov .au/sites/default/files/2022-08/APRA%20Corporate%20Plan%202022-23.pdf>.

To achieve its objectives, APRA focuses on several specific areas of the operations of financial institutions. These areas can be seen across the prudential and reporting standards published by APRA, which cover governance matters such as audit and disclosure,[163] risk management for credit risk,[164] large exposures and associations with related entities,[165] financial resilience measures such as capital adequacy and liquidity requirements,[166] outsourcing guidelines,[167] and standards for securitisation and covered bonds.[168] APRA provides financial institutions with practical supervision to ensure that such institutions conduct business in a way that is sound, profitable and with integrity. Specifically, APRA does so by creating and enforcing industry standards; by advising the Commonwealth Government on regulatory policy; and by maintaining the stability of Australia's financial system through protecting the system from financial services companies behaving in a manner that is risky, illadvised, fraudulent or negligent.[169] Concerning prudential matters, APRA is responsible for collecting and analysing information and for the evaluation and promotion of sound practices.

The legislation that enables APRA to carry out its roles as outlined above are the *Australian Prudential Regulation Authority Act 1998* (Cth) ('*APRA Act*'), the *Australian Prudential Regulation Authority Regulations 2018*, the *Banking Act 1959* (Cth), the *Insurance*

163 See, eg, Australian Prudential Regulation Authority, *Prudential Standard 3PS 310: Audit and Related Matters* (2017) <https://www.apra.gov.au/sites/default/files/Prudential-Standard-3PS-310-Audit-and-Related-Matters-%28July-2017%29_0.pdf>. (Requires a Level 3 Head to ensure that APRA has access to independent advice from an auditor relating to the operations, internal controls and information provided to APRA in respect of the Level 3 group. In addition, the standard sets out requirements for the roles and responsibilities of the appointed auditor.)

164 See, eg, Australian Prudential Regulation Authority, *Prudential Standard CPS 220: Risk Management* (2017) <https://www.apra.gov.au/sites/default/files/Prudential-Standard-CPS-220-Risk-Management-%28July-2017%29.pdf>. (Requires an APRA-regulated institution and a Head of a group to have systems for identifying, measuring, evaluating, monitoring, reporting, and controlling or mitigating material risks that may affect its ability, or the ability of the group it heads, to meet its obligations to depositors and/or policyholders. These systems, together with the structures, policies, processes and people supporting them, comprise an institution's or group's risk management framework.)

165 See, eg, Australian Prudential Regulation Authority, *Prudential Standard APS 221: Large Exposures* (2019) <https://www.apra.gov.au/sites/default/files/final_prudential_standard_-_aps_221_large_exposures.pdf>. (Requires authorised deposit-taking institutions [ADIs] to implement prudent measures and to set prudent limits to monitor and control their large exposures and risk concentrations.)

166 See, eg, Australian Prudential Regulation Authority, *Prudential Standard: APS 210: Liquidity* (2018) <https://www.apra.gov.au/sites/default/files/APS%2520210%2520FINAL.pdf>. (Requires an ADI to adopt prudent practices in managing its liquidity risks and to maintain an adequate level of liquidity to meet its obligation as they fall due across a wide range of operating circumstances.

167 See, eg, Australian Prudential Regulation Authority, *Prudential Standard CPS 231: Outsourcing* (2017) <https://www.apra.gov.au/sites/default/files/Prudential-Standard-CPS-231-Outsourcing-(July-2017).pdf>. (Requires that all outsourcing arrangements involving material business activities entered into by an APRA-regulated institution and a Head of a group be subject to appropriate due diligence, approval and ongoing monitoring. All risks arising from outsourcing material business activities must be appropriately managed to ensure that the APRA-regulated institution, or the group it heads, is able to meet its financial and service obligations to its depositors and/or policyholders.)

168 See, eg, Australian Prudential Regulation Authority, *Prudential Standard: APS 120 Securitisation* (2018) <https://www.apra.gov.au/sites/default/files/aps_120_securitisation.pdf>. (Aims to ensure that an ADI adopts prudent practices to manage the risks associated with securitisation and that sufficient regulatory capital is held against the associated credit risk.)

169 'Industry Supervision', *Australian Prudential Regulation Authority* (Web Page) <https://www.apra.gov.au/industry-supervision>.

Act 1973 (Cth) and the *Superannuation Industry (Supervision) Act 1993* (Cth),[170] among others.[171] These instruments collectively confer on APRA a broad set of powers that it can take in connection with the performance of its functions. For instance, APRA has the authority under the *Banking Act 1959* (Cth) to remove an auditor from an ADI if the auditor fails to meet specific criteria, such as if its performance is inadequate, it fails to meet fitness and propriety standards, or it is a disqualified person.[172] Under the *Insurance Act 1973* (Cth) s 55, APRA or an inspector is empowered to issue a written notice to a prescribed person associated with a general insurer or related body corporate, and such a notice can require the person to produce relevant books, assist in an investigation or appear for an examination.[173]

1.3.1.3 Australian Securities and Investments Commission (ASIC)

ASIC regulates the conduct of Australia's financial services, markets, companies and professionals. Its aim is to regulate consumer protection and build consumer confidence in companies both within the financial sector and within the overall financial system.[174]

ASIC was established under the *Australian Securities and Investments Commission Act 2001* (Cth) ('*ASIC Act*'), which came into effect on 15 July 2001 as the successor to the *Australian Securities Commission Act 1989* (Cth). The earlier Act established Australia's first federal securities commission, the Australian Securities Commission (ASC).[175] The ASC was established as a consolidation of its predecessors, the National Companies and Securities Commission, and the various Corporate Affairs officers of the states and territories. ASIC carried on the functions of the ASC, as well as expanding consumer protection mandates, including superannuation, insurance and deposit taking, and credit, as added in 2002.[176]

Under the *ASIC Act*, ASIC's central role is to maintain, facilitate and improve the performance of entities within the financial system.[177] More specifically, it is responsible

170 Registrable superannuation entities' (RSEs') licence holders must adhere to APRA prudential standards, which are legally binding regulations setting forth minimum capital, governance and risk management requirements. These standards were established following the Super System Review in 2012 and are an integral part of the 'RSE licensee law' as defined under the *Superannuation Industry (Supervision) Act 1993* (Cth) s 10. Compliance with these standards is a prerequisite for maintaining their RSE licence, as mandated by the same Act under s 29E(1)(a). See, eg, Australian Prudential Regulation Authority, *Instruction Guide: Approval to Own or Control an RSE Licensee* (2020) <https://www.apra.gov.au/sites/default/files/2020-10/Instruction%20Guide%20-%20Approval%20to%20own%20or%20control%20an%20RSE%20licensee.pdf>. For a detailed account of the regulatory development in the superannuation sector, see Pamela Hanrahan, 'Legal Framework Governing Aspects of the Australian Superannuation System' (Background Paper 25, Royal Commission into Misconduct in the Banking, Superannuation and Financial Services Industry, July 2018).

171 For a list of APRA's enabling legislation, see, eg, 'Enabling Legislation', *Australian Prudential Regulation Authority* (Web Page) <https://www.apra.gov.au/enabling-legislation>.

172 *Banking Act* s 17.

173 *Insurance Act 1973* (Cth) s 55.

174 'Our Role', *Australian Securities and Investments Commission* (Web Page) <https://asic.gov.au/about-asic/what-we-do/our-role/>.

175 'History', *Australian Securities and Investments Commission* (Web Page) <https://asic.gov.au/about-asic/what-we-do/our-role/history/>.

176 Ibid.

177 Ibid.

for administering relevant laws effectively and with minimal procedural requirements; for receiving, processing and storing information received efficiently and quickly; and for ensuring that information about companies and other bodies is made available to the public as soon as practicable.[178] ASIC carries out these responsibilities to promote confident and informed participation within Australia's financial system, both by investors and consumers.[179]

ASIC carries out consumer protection responsibilities under various Acts, namely:[180] the *Corporations Act 2001* (Cth); the *ASIC Act 2001* (Cth); the *Insurance Contracts Act 1984* (Cth); the *Superannuation (Resolution of Complaints) Act 1993* (Cth); the *Superannuation Industry (Supervision) Act 1993* (Cth); the *Retirement Savings Accounts Act 1997* (Cth); the *Life Insurance Act 1995* (Cth); and the *Medical Indemnity (Prudential Supervision and Product Standards) Act 2003* (Cth). Central to ASIC's role is the enforcement of the *Corporations Act*. In 2019, significant additions were made to ASIC's portfolio through legislation introducing a design and distribution obligations regime for financial services firms and granting ASIC product intervention powers.[181]

1.3.1.4 Council of Financial Regulators (CFR)

The CFR is a non-statutory vehicle that serves as the coordinating body for Australia's main financial regulatory agencies, APRA, ASIC, the RBA and the Treasury. The CFR was established in 1998 as the successor to the Council of Financial Supervisors, which had operated since 1992.[182] The CFR was implemented following a recommendation from the Wallis Inquiry that recommended not implementing a statutory charter, as this could suggest that the CFR had regulatory functions separate from those of the members it coordinates. As a result, instead of being a separate body with any formal decision-making powers, the CFR was implemented as a body to facilitate cooperation between its members. Upon its establishment, the CFR comprised APRA, ASIC and the RBA, and in 2001 the Treasury joined as a member following the HIH Royal Commission.[183]

During the Murray Inquiry, there was debate over whether the CFR should expand its membership to include other regulatory bodies such as the Australian Competition and Consumer Commission, the Australian Transaction Reports and Analysis Centre and the Australian Taxation Office. Ultimately, the final report of the Financial System Inquiry

178 *Australian Securities and Investments Commission Act 2001* (Cth) s 1 ('*ASIC Act*').

179 According to ASIC, it operates by exercising three major powers: (1) registration and licensing (eg registering financial service providers, maintaining public registers, and issuing Australian financial services and credit licenses); (2) regulating (eg the power to ban defective products, create legislative rules for financial market integrity, and grant relief from legislation); and (3) enforcement (eg where ASIC has the authority to investigate suspected violations, issue infringement notices, seek civil penalties, ban specific activities and prosecute offenders). 'Powers', *Australian Securities and Investments Commission* (Web Page) <https://asic.gov.au/about-asic/what-we-do/our-role/powers/>.

180 'Laws We Administer', *Australian Securities and Investments Commission* (Web Page) <https://asic.gov.au/about-asic/what-we-do/our-role/laws-we-administer/>.

181 These amendments were made via the *Treasury Laws Amendment (Strengthening Corporate and Financial Sector Penalties) Act 2019* (Cth) and the *Treasury Laws Amendment (Design and Distribution Obligations and Product Intervention Powers) Act 2019* (Cth).

182 'History', *Council of Financial Regulators* (Web Page) <https://www.cfr.gov.au/about/history.html>.

183 Ibid.

concluded that such an extension was not necessary. Instead, it was noted that these regulators could attend CFR meetings as required. The report, however, did emphasise the need for increased transparency in the CFR's deliberations, particularly in relation to the assessment and mitigation of financial stability risks.[184]

The unique feature of the CFR is that it operates as a non-statutory entity, lacking formal legislative support. It has no official regulatory or policy-making authority; instead, these powers are vested in its individual members in accordance with their respective legislative powers. The process of coordination between regulators relies on 'soft law' mechanisms that are not directly legally enforceable,[185] such as memoranda of understanding and informal protocols between regulators.[186] These MoUs address key issues such as sharing information, immediate notification of regulatory decisions affecting other members, and consultation protocols during financial crises. As an illustration, the CFR members signed a specialised MoU in 2008 as a response to the GFC.[187]

This approach was supported by the Murray Inquiry, which stated: 'Legislation cannot be relied on to promote a culture of cooperation, trust and mutual support between domestic regulatory agencies. These have been highlighted as essential elements of an effective financial stability framework, especially during a crisis.'[188] This demonstrates the belief that utilising non-statutorily binding instruments such as MoUs aids in cultivating an overall culture of cooperation.

The CFR functions to ensure cooperation and coordination among its four member agencies.[189] The RBA provides the CFR with secretariat support, and the CFR is chaired by the RBA governor. The CFR's overarching objective is to promote the stability of the Australian financial system.[190] It does this by supporting effective and efficient regulation by Australia's financial regulatory agencies. In pursuing this objective, the CFR recognises the benefits of having a financial system that is competitive, efficient and fair.[191]

184 The Treasury, *Financial System Inquiry Final Report* (November 2014) 234 <https://treasury.gov.au/sites/default/files/2019-03/p2014-FSI-01Final-Report.pdf>. ('The Inquiry does not see a need to expand the permanent membership of the CFR to include the Australian Competition and Consumer Commission (ACCC), the Australian Transaction Reports and Analysis Centre (AUSTRAC) or the Australian Taxation Office (ATO), as these agencies can already attend meetings as necessary. However, there would be benefit in increasing the transparency of the CFR's deliberations, including its assessment of financial stability risks and how these are being addressed.')

185 Andrew Godwin et al, 'Twin Peaks in Australia: The Never-Ending Trek?' in Andrew Godwin and Andrew Schmulow (eds), *The Cambridge Handbook of Twin Peaks Financial Regulation* (Cambridge University Press, 2021) 77.

186 Andrew Godwin, 'Australia's Trek towards Twin Peaks – Comparisons with South Africa' (2017) 11(4) *Law and Financial Markets Review* 183, 186.

187 'Memorandum of Understanding on Financial Distress Management Between the Members of the Council of Financial Regulators', *Council of Financial Regulators* (Web Page) <https://www.cfr.gov.au/financial-institutions/crisis-management-arrangements/memorandum-of-understanding-on-financial-distress-management.html>.

188 The Treasury, *Financial System Inquiry Interim Report* (2014) 3-119 <https://treasury.gov.au/sites/default/files/2019-03/p2014-fsi-interim-report.pdf>.

189 'Charter', *Council of Financial Regulators* (Web Page) <https://www.cfr.gov.au/about/charter.html>.

190 Ibid.

191 Ibid.

1.3.1.5 Australian Competition and Consumer Commission (ACCC)

Created in 1995, the ACCC is an independent statutory body whose role is to ensure competition in Australian markets and to regulate anti-competitive behaviour in general.[192] It does this through education, investigation and enforcement. The reason for ensuring competition is to maintain informed and well-regulated markets, which leads to lower prices, an increase in product and service quality, and more choice, all of which increase the welfare and prosperity of Australia and its people.[193]

The primary roles of the ACCC include promoting and preserving competition, protecting consumer rights and welfare, and endorsing fair market practices, especially concerning consumers and small businesses. Additionally, the ACCC undertakes market studies and probes to bolster competition, consumer and regulatory results. It also pinpoints market inefficiencies and advocates for enhanced cost-effectiveness in infrastructure management, usage and investment.[194] The ACCC also provides secretariat support to the National Competition Council (NCC).[195]

The ACCC's functions differ from those of ASIC in that the ACCC does not have a general consumer protection role in the financial sector; ASIC does this exclusively.[196] Through the *Australian Consumer Law*, the ACCC is responsible for setting out the rights and obligations of consumers and businesses in Australia. However, it is important to note that the *Australian Consumer Law* does not apply to financial products and services; instead, it directs such concerns to ASIC's jurisdiction – namely, the *ASIC Act*.[197] The ACCC is also responsible for administering the *Competition and Consumer Act 2010* (Cth) (the '*CCA*') (previously the *Trade Practices Act 1974* (Cth)), which covers product safety and labelling; unfair market practices; price monitoring; industry codes; industry regulation, including airports, electricity, gas and telecommunications; and mergers and acquisitions. Some other Acts allow the ACCC to engage in conduct that would otherwise contravene the *CCA*, as authorised by the *CCA* s 51(1).[198] Although the ACCC is not a primary

192 'About the ACCC', *Australian Competition and Consumer Commission* (Web Page) <https://www.accc.gov.au/about-us/australian-competition-consumer-commission/about-the-accc#accc-purpose>.

193 Ibid.

194 Ibid.

195 The National Competition Council (NCC), established in 1995, is an advisory body that focuses on the regulation of third-party access to services offered by monopoly infrastructure. Governed by the *Competition and Consumer Act 2010* (Cth) s 29B, the NCC advises ministers on applications for service declarations and certifications of state or territory access regimes. Since July 2014, the ACCC has been providing secretarial services to the NCC, although the NCC remains an independent entity. See generally 'About Us', *National Competition Council* (Web Page) <https://ncc.gov.au/about/about_us>.

196 'What We Can and Can't Do for Consumers', *Australian Competition and Consumer Commission* (Web Page) <https://www.accc.gov.au/about-us/australian-competition-consumer-commission/service-charter/what-we-can-cant-do-for-consumers#what-we-can-t-help-you-with>. Before the Wallis reforms, the ACCC was primarily responsible for consumer protection. However, the oversight of financial services consumers has shifted since 1998 from the ACCC to ASIC following the Wallis Inquiry. See ASIC, *Annual Report 1998/99* (Report, 18 October 1999) <https://download.asic.gov.au/media/1327346/complete_edited200612-1998-99.pdf>.

197 'Advertising and Selling Guide', *Australian Competition and Consumer Commission* (Web Page) <https://www.accc.gov.au/publications/advertising-selling/advertising-and-selling-guide/introduction/who-is-this-guide-for>.

198 *Competition and Consumer Act 2010* (Cth) s 51(1) states that in deciding whether a person contravenes pt IVB, anything specified and specifically authorised by an Act or regulations made under an Act must be disregarded.

regulatory in the financial market, two of its functions are still relevant to financial institutions. First, it is required to obtain approval of the ACCC for mergers or acquisitions of financial intermediaries.[199] A notable case is the ACCC's denial of ANZ's attempt to acquire Suncorp Bank by purchasing 100 per cent of SBGH Limited.[200] Second, it is in charge of the implementation of the Open Banking regime – 'Consumer Data Right' – which will be discussed further in Chapter 9.[201]

1.3.1.6 Australian Transaction Reports and Analysis Centre (AUSTRAC)

AUSTRAC is the Australian government agency responsible for protecting the community against criminal abuse of the financial system in the form of serious and organised crime.[202] In pursuit of this goal, AUSTRAC works closely with intelligence partners and federal law enforcement to produce financial intelligence and information that assists government partners in detecting, deterring and disrupting criminal activities within the financial sector.[203] AUSTRAC serves two main functions in Australia: it oversees compliance with anti-money laundering and counter-terrorism financing regulations; and it operates as the national financial intelligence unit. This dual capacity strengthens the financial system's resilience and allows AUSTRAC to employ financial intelligence and regulations to thwart money laundering, financing of terrorism and other grave criminal activities.[204]

AUSTRAC imposes strong regulations on more than 17000 individuals, businesses and organisations in the nation and ensures that these regulated persons and bodies comply with their obligations under the *Anti-Money Laundering and Counter-Terrorism Financing Act 2006* ('*AML/CTF Act*')[205] and the *Financial Transaction Reports Act 1988* ('*FTR Act*'). The *AML/CTF Act* aims to meet Australia's international obligations as part of the Financial Action Task Force (FATF).[206] The Act adopts a 'risk-based' approach,[207] tailoring procedures to different customers and services. The *AML/CTF Act* is supplemented by

199 'Merger Authorisations', *Australian Competition and Consumer Commission* (Web Page) <https://www.accc.gov.au/business/mergers/merger-authorisations>.

200 ANZ sought to acquire 100 per cent of SBGH Limited, which owns Suncorp Bank, but the ACCC denied authorisation on 4 August 2023. Both banks offer similar retail and business banking services in Australia. Suncorp's insurance businesses were not part of the deal. The ACCC had initially released a Statement of Preliminary Views and later received multiple submissions from ANZ and Suncorp. After extending the decision time frame, the ACCC ultimately rejected the acquisition. ANZ and Suncorp have since applied for a review of this decision by the Australian Competition Tribunal. 'ACCC Begins ANZ, Suncorp Merger Authorisation Review', *Australian Competition and Consumer Commission* (Web Page, 12 December 2022) <https://www.accc.gov.au/media-release/accc-begins-anz-suncorp-merger-authorisation-review>.

201 'The Consumer Data Right', *Australian Competition and Consumer Commission* (Web Page) <https://www.accc.gov.au/by-industry/banking-and-finance/the-consumer-data-right>.

202 'AUSTRAC Overview', *Australian Transaction Reports and Analysis Centre* (Web Page) <https://www.austrac.gov.au/about-us/austrac-overview>.

203 'Government Partners', *Australian Transaction Reports and Analysis Centre* (Web Page) <https://www.austrac.gov.au/about-us/our-partners/government-partners>.

204 'What We Do', *Australian Transaction Reports and Analysis Centre* (Web Page) <https://www.austrac.gov.au/about-us/what-we-do>.

205 *Anti-Money Laundering and Counter-Terrorism Financing Act 2006* (Cth) ('*AML/CTF Act*').

206 'What We Do', *Financial Action Task Force* (Web Page) <https://www.fatf-gafi.org/en/the-fatf/what-we-do.html>.

207 'Regulations', *Australian Transaction Reports and Analysis Centre* (Web Page) <https://www.austrac.gov.au/about-us/what-we-do/regulation>.

detailed requirements in the *AML/CTF Rules*. AUSTRAC's chief executive officer formulates these rules after consulting with government agencies and industry stakeholders.[208] The *AML/CTF Act* is applicable to 'reporting entities'[209] providing 'designated services', which encompasses a broad spectrum of activities, including most financial services.[210] Reporting entities are obligated to establish and maintain their own anti-money laundering and counter-terrorism financing programs. These programs are generally divided into two parts. Part A (General) focuses on identifying, mitigating and managing the risks that the services offered by the reporting entity could be used for money laundering or terrorism financing;[211] while Part B (Customer Identification) outlines the procedures for customer identification and verification.[212]

Reporting entities are required to report certain transactions to AUSTRAC under the *AML/CTF Act*. For instance, reporting entities must lodge a 'suspicious matter report' (SMR) to AUSTRAC if they have suspicions that a person or transaction is involved in criminal activities.[213] These suspicions could range from involvement in a crime, to identity misrepresentation, to being a victim of a crime. SMRs related to terrorism financing must be submitted within 24 hours, while those related to other matters such as money laundering have a submission window of three business days.[214] Another type of report is a 'threshold transaction report' (TTR), where transactions involving the transfer of A$10 000 or more, or its foreign currency equivalent, are required to be reported to AUSTRAC within 10 business days following the transaction.[215] Finally, reporting entities must report to AUSTRAC in the case of an 'international funds transfer instruction' (IFTI). Reporting entities are obligated to submit IFTI reports for any funds transferred into or out of Australia, irrespective of the amount. These reports apply to both electronic transfers and those made under designated remittance arrangements.[216] IFTI reports must be submitted within 10 business days after the transfer instruction has been sent or received.[217]

1.3.1.7 Financial Regulator Assessment Authority (FRAA)

The FRAA is an independent body established on 29 June 2021 by the *Financial Regulator Assessment Authority Act 2021* (Cth).[218] It was established on the recommendations of the Banking Royal Commission to create a new authority meant to assess the effectiveness and capabilities of APRA and ASIC.[219] Although both APRA and ASIC had previously been

208 *AML/CTF Act* s 212.
209 Ibid s 5.
210 Ibid s 6. Table I, 'Financial services', features a list of activities in the financial market (eg providing an account of ADI).
211 Ibid s 84(2).
212 Ibid s 84(3).
213 Ibid s 41(1).
214 Ibid s 41(2).
215 Ibid s 43.
216 Ibid s 46.
217 Ibid s 45.
218 'About FRAA', *Financial Regulator Assessment Authority* (Web Page) <https://fraa.gov.au/about-fraa#:~:text=The%20FRAA%20was%20established%20on,on%20the%20Australian%20Parliamentary%20website.>; see also *Financial Services Authority Act 2021* (Cth).
219 Explanatory Memorandum, Financial Regulator Assessment Authority Bill 2021 (Cth) [1.1].

subject to external assessment, review and oversight, and reporting on their activities, there was a lack of regular and systematic reviews of the two regulators, and there were limitations to their existing accountability mechanisms. For instance, parliamentary scrutiny was encumbered by the limited time and resources available for Parliament to undertake detailed reviews of the regulators' performance, especially given the two bodies' broad mandate and scope of functions. Further, the Murray Inquiry noted that parliamentary scrutiny tended to be 'episodic and [to] focus on particular issues or decisions'.[220] While the Murray Inquiry's recommendation for a new oversight body was rejected, the 2019 final report of the Banking Royal Commission raised issues of significant misconduct by stakeholders in the financial services industry and failures by the two regulators.[221] This eventually led the government to accept the Commission's recommendation to establish an oversight body.

The key functions of the FRAA are to biennially assess and report on APRA and ASIC's effectiveness and capabilities,[222] although there is no statutory guidance on how 'effectiveness and capability' should be defined.[223] The FRAA also lacks the power to direct APRA and ASIC to implement its recommendations, with the two regulators remaining responsible only to Parliament.[224] The FRAA's functions do not extend to assessing single cases.[225]

1.3.2 Governance of the financial market at the global level

In the context of globalisation, the governance of financial intermediaries extends beyond individual jurisdictions and becomes a matter of global concern. For our discussion, 'governance' refers to a fluid process encompassing engagement, coordination and negotiation, making it an essential framework for managing international or cross-border issues.[226] This section of the chapter introduces three main bodies that operate on a supra-national and international level. While they are unable to set out 'binding' requirements applicable to all countries in the form of a 'treaty', these bodies serve as platforms for regulatory cooperation and dialogue.[227] Further, they set out regulatory best practices and codes that have been endorsed and followed by several countries globally.

1.3.2.1 Financial Stability Board (FSB)

The FSB is an international body that monitors the global financial system. The FSB was established in April 2009 as the successor to the Financial Stability Forum (FSF).[228]

220 The Treasury (n 184) 241.

221 *Banking Royal Commission Final Report* 476, 480 (Recommendation 6.14 – A New Oversight Body).

222 *Financial Regulator Assessment Authority Act 2021* (Cth) ss 12(1)(a)–(d), 12(3), 14(1).

223 L Freeburn and I Ramsay, 'Accountability of the Australian Securities and Investment Commission and the Establishment of the Financial Regulator Assessment Authority – An Evaluation' (2002) 50(1) *Australian Business Law Review* 6, 22.

224 The Treasury (n 184) [1.30].

225 *Financial Services Authority Act 2021* (Cth) s 12(2).

226 Xenia Roduner, 'Governance in International Financial Institutions: The Case of IMF' in Kern Alexander and Rahul Dhumale (eds), *Research Handbook on International Financial Regulation* (Edward Elgar, 2012) 349–50.

227 See generally Anne Marie Slaughter, *A New World Order* (Princeton University Press, 2005).

228 'History of the FSB', *Financial Stability Board* (Web Page) <https://www.fsb.org/about/history-of-the-fsb/>.

The FSF was founded in 1999 by the G7 Finance Ministers and Central Bank Governors. Before the establishment of the FSF, the President of the Deutsche Bundesbank, Dr Hans Tietmeyer, was commissioned by the G7 Ministers and Governors to recommend a new structure for enhancing cooperation between international financial institutions and national and international supervisory bodies to promote stability within the international financial system. Dr Tietmeyer made a series of recommendations, including a recommendation to create the FSF, the creation of which was then endorsed by the G7 Ministers and Governors.[229]

The FSF first convened in April 1999 and brought together a group of authorities, regulators, supervisors, institutions and committees. Specifically, it included representatives from major economies, such as relevant national authorities including treasuries, central banks and finance ministries. It also included international organisations involved in standard-setting and the implementation of said standards.[230]

In 2008, G20 leaders advocated for the expansion of the FSF. A year later, during the 2009 G20 London Summit, the Financial Stability Board was inaugurated as the FSF's successor. At the subsequent 2009 Pittsburgh G20 Summit, the G20 Heads of State and Government ratified the FSB's initial charter, dated 25 September 2009, which delineated its objectives, mandate and organisational structure.[231] In the 2011 Cannes G20 Summit, the G20 urged the continuous fortification of the FSB's organisational resources and governance. The FSB responded in 2012 by submitting a report at the G20 Los Cabos Summit, outlining its ongoing efforts to bolster its capacity and governance.[232] This summit also saw the G20 leaders endorse an updated FSB charter, which emphasised its role in standard-setting and policy implementation. Finally, in January 2013, the FSB formally registered as a non-profit association under Swiss law, headquartered in Basel, Switzerland.[233]

The FSB's overarching goal is to foster global financial stability by collaborating with its members.[234] This collaboration involves uniting domestic financial authorities from different jurisdictions with international organisations that set standards. The collective effort focuses on fortifying the worldwide financial infrastructure. Furthermore, the FSB strives to create a level playing field across diverse jurisdictions and sectors by advocating for the uniform adoption of best practices and recommendations.

The FSB was established with the main goal of risk identification and assessment – which involves picking out and reviewing potential vulnerabilities and risks to the global financial system. It is also responsible for subsequent follow-up actions – namely,

229 Ibid.

230 Ibid.

231 Financial Stability Board, *Financial Stability Board Charter* (25 September 2009) <https://www.fsb.org/wp-content/uploads/r_090925d.pdf?page_moved=1#:~:text=The%20Financial%20Stability%20Board%20(FSB,and%20other%20financial%20sector%20policies>.

232 Financial Stability Board, *Report to the G20 Los Cabos Summit on Strengthening FSB Capacity, Resources and Governance* (Report, 12 June 2012) <https://www.fsb.org/wp-content/uploads/r_120619c.pdf>.

233 'History of the FSB' (n 228). See 'Members of the FSB', *Financial Stability Board* (Web Page) <https://www.fsb.org/about/organisation-and-governance/members-of-the-financial-stability-board/> for the list of member countries and member organisations of the FSB.

234 'About the FSB', *Financial Stability Board* (Web Page) <https://www.fsb.org/about/#mandate>.

recommending the necessary regulatory, supervisory and related measures to tackle these concerns and their consequences.[235] Further, the FSB promotes coordination and information exchange among various stakeholders such as member jurisdictions, international organisations and standard-setting bodies. In doing so, it undertakes joint strategic reviews of relevant international standard-setting bodies, and of their work on policy development, to ensure that the work is timely, coordinated, sufficiently focused on their objectives and addresses relevant gaps.[236] Moreover, the FSB must support contingency planning for cross-border crisis management and facilitate the implementation of agreed-upon commitments, standards and policy recommendations among its members. This is done by overseeing the progress of implementation, conducting peer reviews and monitoring reporting by members. The FSB is also entrusted with analysing reports to evaluate the extent of adherence of member states to their obligations and the level of compliance by non-members.[237]

Apart from the above, the FSB serves in a consultative and oversight capacity. It provides guidance on compliance requirements, market trends and regulatory policies, as well as formulating criteria for the creation and maintenance of supervisory colleges. Additionally, the FSB partners with the International Monetary Fund (IMF) to carry out Early Warning Exercises.[238]

1.3.2.2 Bank for International Settlements (BIS)

The BIS is an international organisation with an international legal personality and is owned by its shareholding members.[239] Its mission is to 'support central banks' pursuit of financial stability through international cooperation, and to act as a bank for central banks'.[240] In pursuit of its mandate, the BIS provides central banks with a forum for dialogue, broad international cooperation, responsible innovation and knowledge-sharing, as well as in-depth analysis of and insights on core policy issues, and sound and competitive financial services.[241]

Established in 1930, the BIS holds the distinction of being the world's oldest international financial institution. It was originally created to manage Germany's reparation payments following World War I.[242] The foundational treaty for the BIS, known as its 'Convention', was signed on 20 January 1930 in the Hague and involved the governments of Belgium, France, Germany, Italy, Japan, the Swiss Confederation and the United Kingdom. In 1997, the BIS solidified its legal status in Switzerland through the

235 Ibid.
236 Ibid.
237 Ibid.
238 Ibid.
239 See, eg, Mario Giovanoli, 'The Role of the BIS in International Monetary Cooperation and Its Tasks Relating to the ECU' in Robert C Effros (ed) *Current Legal Issues Affecting Central Banks, Volume 1* (International Monetary Fund, 1992) 39.
240 'About', *Bank for International Settlements* (Web Page) <https://www.bis.org/about/index.htm?m=1001>.
241 Ibid.
242 'History – Foundation and Crisis (1930–39)', *Bank for International Settlements* (Web Page) <https://www.bis.org/about/history_1foundation.htm>.

Headquarters Agreement with the Swiss Federal Council. Today, the BIS comprises 63 central banks and monetary authorities from various countries globally.[243]

1.3.2.3 Basel Committee on Banking Supervision (BCBS)

The BCBS, originally known as the Committee on Banking Regulations and Supervisory Practices, was founded in late 1974.[244] It functions as a supra-national international organisation that effectively sets the de facto standards for global banking, proposing prudential regulations for banks around the world. A series of significant disruptions in international banking and currency markets, including the collapse of West Germany's Bankhaus Herstatt, prompted the formation of the BCBS to enhance international financial stability and improve the quality of banking supervision.[245]

In 1975, the BCBS introduced a document called the *Concordat*,[246] which set out guidelines to enable local regulatory bodies to collaborate and share oversight responsibilities for the foreign branches, subsidiaries and joint ventures of banks in host countries.[247] This report underwent several amendments and reissues by the BCBS. In 1983, it was updated and renamed the Principles for the Supervision of Banks' Foreign Establishments.[248] A supplement to the *Concordat* was titled 'Exchanges of Information Between Supervisors of Participants in the Financial Markets'. Then, in 1992, the BCBS chose specific principles for modification and released them as the Minimum Standards for the Supervision of International Banking Groups and Their Cross-Border Establishments.[249]

In 1996, the BCBS published a report titled *The Supervision of Cross-Border Banking*, which received endorsement from 140 countries.[250] The report outlined suggested approaches for addressing the challenges in effectively supervising the cross-border activities of international banks.[251] The following year, in 1997, the BCBS introduced a

243 The BIS currently boasts a membership of 63 central banks and monetary authorities, all of which have voting rights and representation at General Meetings. It includes among its diverse members the Bank of Algeria, the Central Bank of Argentina, the Reserve Bank of Australia, and European institutions such as the European Central Bank, Bank of France and Deutsche Bundesbank. It also includes Asian financial authorities such as the People's Bank of China, Reserve Bank of India and Bank of Japan, as well as American entities such as the Bank of Canada and the Board of Governors of the Federal Reserve System in the United States. Other notable members are the Central Bank of Brazil, the Bank of Mexico, the Saudi Central Bank, and the Bank of England. Each of these institutions is entitled to participate in decision-making processes and has representation at the BIS's General Meetings. See, eg, 'BIS Member Central Banks', *Bank for International Settlements* (Web Page) <https://www.bis.org/about/member_cb.htm> for the full list of countries.

244 'History of the Basel Committee', *Bank for International Settlements* (Web Page) <https://www.bis.org/bcbs/history.htm?m=3076>.

245 Ibid.

246 See Basel Committee on Banking Supervision, *Report to the Governors on the Supervision of Banks' Foreign Establishments* (26 September 1975) <https://www.bis.org/publ/bcbs00a.htm>.

247 Ibid.

248 Basel Committee on Banking Supervision, *Principles for the Supervision of Banks' Foreign Establishments (Concordat)* (28 May 1983) <https://www.bis.org/publ/bcbsc312.htm>.

249 Basel Committee on Banking Supervision, *Minimum Standards for the Supervision of International Banking Groups and Their Cross-Border Establishments* (28 July 1992) <https://www.bis.org/publ/bcbsc314.htm>.

250 'History', *Bank for International Settlements* (Web Page) <https://www.bis.org/bcbs/history.htm?m=3076>.

251 Basel Committee on Banking Supervision, *The Supervision of Cross-Border Banking* (4 October 1995) <https://www.bis.org/publ/bcbs27.htm>.

set of 25 guidelines widely known as the *Core Principles for Effective Banking Supervision*.[252] These principles, as updated in 2012, serve as recommended guidelines for local regulatory bodies to adopt and put into practice.[253]

More recently, in April 2022, the BCBS initiated a review of its Core Principles, aiming to adapt them to the evolving financial landscapes and emerging risks, including climate-related financial risks.[254] The recent Consultative Document outlines the proposed changes, such as requiring supervisors and banks to consider climate-related risks in their methodologies and reporting. Other amendments focus on comprehensive risk management policies, internal control frameworks, corporate governance emphasising diversity and inclusion, and operational resilience against events such as pandemics and natural disasters.[255] With the feedback period concluding on 6 October 2023, the BCBS has moved forward in reviewing stakeholder inputs on these critical revisions.[256]

The BCBS works to fortify global banking regulations, supervision and practices with the goal of boosting financial stability worldwide.[257] It also serves as a platform for collaboration on matters related to banking supervision. Although the standards set by the BCBS are not legally binding, countries often adopt them due to concerns that failing to comply could limit their access to international financial markets. The responsibility for compliance rests with the individual member states.

To fulfil its mission, the BCBS engages in several key activities. It primarily formulates and advocates for global standards, guidelines and best practices in the regulation and supervision of banks.[258] In crafting these standards, the BCBS collaborates with central banks and supervisory authorities to incorporate their insights into policy development and to encourage the adoption of its recommendations. Furthermore, the BCBS monitors how its standards are implemented, both within its member countries and more broadly, aiming for a timely, consistent and effective application that levels the playing field for banks operating internationally.[259]

In addition to its core mission of enhancing global financial stability, the BCBS takes on multiple other responsibilities. It works to fill regulatory and supervisory voids that could jeopardise financial stability, partners with other financial industry standard-setters, scrutinises trends in the global banking sector and financial markets to spot existing or emerging risks, and promotes international collaboration by exchanging insights on supervisory challenges and best practices.[260]

252 Basel Committee on Banking Supervision, *Core Principles for Effective Banking Supervision* (14 September 2012) <https://www.bis.org/publ/bcbs230.htm>.

253 'History' (n 250).

254 Basel Committee on Banking Supervision, *Consultative Document: Core Principles for Effective Banking Supervision* (July 2023) <https://www.bis.org/bcbs/publ/d551.pdf>.

255 The proposed changes are shaped by various thematic areas that mirror recent developments in regulatory and supervisory practices. These themes include financial risks, operational resilience, systemic risk and macroprudential supervision, emerging risks such as climate-related financial risks and digital finance, non-bank financial intermediation, and risk management practices.

256 Basel Committee on Banking Supervision (n 254).

257 'Basel Committee Charter', *Bank for International Settlements* (Web Page, 5 June 2018) s 1 <https://www.bis.org/bcbs/charter.htm?m=3070>.

258 Ibid s 2.

259 Ibid.

260 Ibid.

The BCBS has broadened its membership base from the original G10 countries to include 45 institutions across 28 jurisdictions.[261] Member states collaborate to fulfil the BCBS's objectives by adopting its standards within their own legal frameworks within specified time frames. They also engage in reviews to evaluate the uniformity and efficacy of their domestic regulations and supervisory methods in relation to these standards. Additionally, they actively participate in shaping new standards, guidelines and best practices.[262]

1.4 Summary

This chapter provides a conceptual overview of the regulatory framework of the Australian financial system. Using the banking sector as an example, we illustrate public and private interest theories, and unpack the contextual background for government intervention in this complex market. Regulation in the financial market aims to achieve a balance between different stakeholders and to serve a myriad of economic, social and political goals. Such a balance – as reflected in the regulatory approach adopted by a particular jurisdiction – could vary across jurisdictions. The history of the Global Financial Crisis helps us to reflect upon the role of regulation; and the rise of Fintech, as illustrated in Chapter 4, again prompts us to consider these debates.

This chapter also identifies major actors at the domestic and global levels that affect the Australian financial system. At the domestic level, the RBA, ASIC and APRA play a key role; other regulatory bodies, such as AUSTRAC and the ACCC, also form part of the landscape. Of these regulatory bodies, ASIC is the conduct regulator, while APRA is in charge of prudential regulation. Together, these two bodies comprise Australia's Twin Peaks regulatory model.

FURTHER READING

Armour, John, et al, *Principles of Financial Regulation* (Oxford University Press, 2016).

Berger, Allen N, Philip Molyneux and John OS Wilson (eds), *The Oxford Handbook of Banking* (Oxford University Press, 3rd ed, 2019).

Godwin, Andrew, 'Financial Regulatory Models in the Asia-Pacific – A Case Study in Diversity' in Douglas W Arner et al (eds), *Research Handbook on Asian Financial Law* (Edward Elgar, 2020).

Godwin, Andrew and Andrew Schmulow (eds), *The Cambridge Handbook of Twin Peaks Financial Regulation* (Cambridge University Press, 2021).

Godwin, Andrew, Steve Kourabas and Ian Ramsay, 'Twin Peaks and Financial Regulation: The Challenges of Increasingly Regulatory Overlap and Expanding Responsibilities' (2016) 49(3) *The International Lawyer* 273.

He, Weiping, *Banking Regulation in China* (Palgrave Macmillan, 2015).

Howell, Nicola, 'Revisiting the Australian Code of Banking Practice: Is Self-Regulation Still Relevant for Improving Consumer Protection Standards?' (2015) 38(2) *University of New South Wales Law Journal* 544.

261 See 'Membership', *Bank for International Settlements* (Web Page) <https://www.bis.org/bcbs/membership.htm?m=3071> for the full list of member countries and organisations.

262 'Basel Committee Charter' (n 257) s 5.

McCracken, Sheelagh, et al, *Everett & McCracken's Banking and Financial Institutions Law* (Thomas Reuters, 9th ed, 2017).

Moloney, Niamh, Eilís Ferran and Jennifer Payne (eds), *The Oxford Handbook of Financial Regulation* (Oxford University Press, 2015).

QUESTIONS

(1) You have been tasked to write a guidance note for the compliance division of a foreign bank seeking to understand more about the Australian banking regulatory landscape. As the first step, you are expected to give a broad overview of the current regulatory framework, including the major regulators, and their responsibilities and powers. Further, the foreign bank would also like an explanation of the functions and roles in the Australian regulatory scene of key international organisations, such as the Financial Stability Board and the Basel Committee on Banking Supervision.

(2) At lunch, one of your colleagues mentioned that she believes the market will 'take care of itself' and that regulation is only the 'second-best' option for fixing market failure. You recall that you learnt from your Banking and Finance Law unit about regulatory theories applicable to this complicated market. To what extent do you see the need for regulation in the financial market? What are the relevant laws in Australia that provide justification for government regulation of this market?

(3) Minister James, serving as the Minister of Finance for the Republic of Veridia, has been entrusted with the monumental task of revamping the nation's financial regulatory framework. The objective is to construct a system that is not only robust and transparent but also agile enough to adapt to rapid changes in the financial sector. This new framework must prioritise both consumer protection and the overall stability of the financial system. As Minister James navigates this complex undertaking, several pivotal questions arise, each of which will significantly influence Veridia's financial landscape for years to come. You are asked to help the Minister to consider the following issues:

   (a) *Choice of Institutional Structure*: What options does Veridia have in selecting an institutional structure for its regulatory framework, considering models such as the Twin Peaks model, the institutional model and the integrated model? What are the pros and cons associated with each of these options, particularly in terms of regulatory focus, effectiveness and the potential for conflicts of interest?

   (b) *Regulatory Strategies*: Will the new framework be predominantly rules-based, offering clear and detailed guidelines; or principles-based, allowing for greater flexibility? How will this decision align with broader strategies for regime design, such as a command-and-control approach versus self-regulation? What are the trade-offs in terms of compliance costs, adaptability and enforcement capabilities?

(4) Dive into the following content and critically reflect upon how the current Australian regulatory framework equips itself with effective tools for safeguarding consumers. To what extent do you agree or disagree with Commissioner Hayne's view that we should not create another regulator focusing specifically on consumer protection – as Pamela Hanrahan has suggested?

(a) The Banking Royal Commission reaffirmed in Recommendation 6.1 that 'The "twin peaks" model of financial regulation should be retained'[263] despite notable deficiencies in the regulatory performance of both regulators. For Commissioner Hayne, the focus should be on ASIC's enforcement culture, rather than its scope of responsibilities.[264] The increase in civil penalty provisions and related procedural complexity, combined with ASIC's ineffective enforcement culture, prompts consideration of radical change. For Commissioner Hayne, one option – apart from transferring responsibilities to the ACCC, which option has been ruled out – is to create a specialised civil enforcement agency, mirroring existing criminal breach prosecution agencies.[265] This new agency would retain ASIC's regulatory tools but delegate the authority to initiate civil penalty proceedings based on an evidentiary threshold. ASIC would function as investigators, with the enforcement agency making the ultimate decision to commence proceedings. This setup offers advantages; for instance, a specialised litigation agency would develop essential skills in this specialised legal field, while retaining the Twin Peaks model.[266] 'Notwithstanding the prospect of those benefits,' Commissioner Hayne said, 'I do not recommend such a radical change.'[267] However, he added, 'If, over the coming years, it becomes apparent that ASIC is not sufficiently enforcing the laws within its remit, or if the size of its remit comes at the expense of its litigation capability, further consideration should be given to developing a specialist agency of the type I have described.'[268]

(b) Commenting on Hayne's report, Pamela Hanrahan has argued for the creation of another regulator dedicated to consumer protection in the financial market. 'A market regulator is not, by its nature, a consumer protection regulator, and a prudential regulator is not, by its nature, a consumer protection regulator. Allocating responsibility for oversight of the conduct of superannuation trustees towards members to APRA is inapt. In the quarter-century since the Twin Peaks model was proposed, a third regulatory objective – consumer protection – has emerged.'[269] The new regulatory body would, as Hanrahan described, 'champion consumer protection', ensuring fair treatment for consumers in the financial marketplace, much like the Consumer Financial Protection Bureau in the United States. Its primary focus would revolve around the licensed provider–consumer relationship, fostering a strong working relationship with the consumer complaints handling system, including the newly established Australian Financial Complaints Authority (AFCA).

263 *Banking Royal Commission Final Report* 37 (Recommendation 6.1).
264 Ibid 466.
265 Ibid 430.
266 Ibid 431.
267 Ibid.
268 Ibid.
269 Pamela Hanrahan, 'Twin Peaks after Hayne: Tensions and Trade-offs in Regulatory Architecture', (2019) 13(2–3) *Law and Financial Markets Review* 124, 124–5, 128.

CHAPTER 2

CONSUMER PROTECTION AND CONSUMER CREDIT

2.1 Introduction

This chapter will commence with a comprehensive overview of Australia's legal framework on consumer credit. Subsequently, it will consider the major obligations applied to Australian credit licence holders in this context, with a particular focus on licensing requirements, disclosure, responsible lending, best interest obligations and various consumer rights. Additionally, given the increased consumer access to high-cost payday loans facilitated by digitalisation, this chapter will discuss the relevant issues and proposals for reform.

2.1.1 Consumer credit protection in Australia

Australian consumer credit law is a complex and evolving body of law, but its overarching purpose is to protect consumers who borrow money. The primary legislation in this area is the *National Consumer Credit Protection Act 2009* (Cth) (the '*NCCPA*'), which incorporates the *National Credit Code* (the '*NCC*') (as sch 1 to the *NCCPA*) and the *National Consumer Credit Protection Regulations 2010* (Cth) (the '*NCCPR*'). Consumer credit is also subject to general consumer protection provisions under the *Australian Securities and Investments Commission Act 2001* (Cth) ('*ASIC Act*'). Together, these set up a nationwide consumer credit protection framework in Australia, applicable to all lenders and borrowers regardless of their location. This regime is overseen by ASIC, which possesses various enforcement powers such as the power to investigate complaints, carry out audits, and levy fines and other penalties. As mentioned briefly in Chapter 1, although Australian consumers are generally protected by the *Australian Consumer Law* administered by the Australian Competition and Consumer Commission (ACCC), as set out in sch 2 to the *Competition and Consumer Act 2010* (Cth), the Law does not apply to consumer credit.[1] Meanwhile, the *Corporations Act 2001* (Cth) applies to financial products other than credit.[2]

Consumer protection law is designed to regulate the conduct of businesses in their dealings with consumers.[3] It aims to protect consumers from unfair or deceptive practices and to ensure that they have access to the information they need to

1 *Competition and Consumer Act 2010* (Cth) s 131A.

2 *Corporations Act 2001* (Cth) ('*Corporations Act*') s 765(1)(h)(i) and *Corporations Regulations 2001* (Cth) reg 7.1.06 exempt margin lending from the general consumer credit protection regime under the *National Consumer Credit Protection Act 2009* (Cth) (the '*NCCPA*'). Margin lending is regulated under, among other sections, *Corporations Act* s 764A(1)(l). Margin lending is a sophisticated financial structure that enables individuals to obtain a loan for investment activities, using their existing assets as collateral to secure the borrowed funds. See 'What is Margin Lending?', *Commonwealth Bank of Australia* (Web Page) <https://www.commbank.com.au/articles/investing/what-is-margin-lending.html>.

3 See generally Jeannie Paterson and Nicola Howell, *Everyday Consumer Credit Overview of Australian Law Regulating Consumer Home Loans, Credit Cards and Car Loans* (Background Paper No 4, Royal Commission into Misconduct in the Banking, Superannuation and Financial Services Industry, 2018) 4. They state: 'Consumer law, unlike the private law of contract, is explicitly instrumental. Its purpose is to achieve specific outcomes in order better to protect consumers. These objectives of consumer law are, in general terms, to promote efficient and fair markets.' See also Gill North, 'Regulation Governing the Provision of Credit Assistance and Financial Advice in Australia: A Consumer's Perspective' (2015) 43(3) *Federal Law Review* 369.

make informed decisions to manage the concerns of market failure.[4] The Productivity Commission's review of the Australian Consumer Policy Framework advised the Australian Government to adopt a unified principal aim for consumer policy. The overarching aim is to 'improve consumer wellbeing by fostering effective competition and enabling the confident participation of consumers in markets in which both consumers and suppliers trade fairly and in good faith'.[5] Towards this aim, the Commission suggested six major objectives:

(1) ensuring consumers are well informed, in order to benefit from and boost effective competition
(2) ensuring that goods and services are safe and fit for their intended use
(3) preventing unfair practices
(4) addressing the needs of the most vulnerable or disadvantaged consumers
(5) providing easily accessible and timely remedies for consumer issues
(6) advocating for balanced, risk-based enforcement measures.[6]

The Council of Australian Governments (COAG) endorsed these objectives in 2009, thereby facilitating the passage of the *NCCPA*.[7]

The regulatory landscape for consumer credit in Australia underwent a major transformation with the enactment of the *NCCPA*. The legislation nationalised consumer credit regulations, aligning with agreements made by COAG to centralise these responsibilities at the Commonwealth level. Before the introduction of the *NCCPA*, the *Uniform Consumer Credit Code* (the '*UCCC*') served as the foundation for state- and territory-specific regulations. The *UCCC* was then incorporated into the *NCCPA* as sch 1 and adapted to the *NCC*.[8] This new code retained the *UCCC*'s original objective of ensuring 'truth in lending' while modernising regulations to better reflect the evolving competition and product innovation landscape. For instance, it encompasses various aspects of credit provision such as disclosure requirements and advertising, as well as covering credit for residential investment properties.[9] (Some of these key features will be considered later.)

4 Paterson and Howell (n 3) 4–5. (Note that some goods are difficult for consumers to evaluate before purchase. Consumers may not know what information they need, or the information may be too expensive or difficult to obtain. Additionally, information may be presented in a way that makes it difficult to compare different products. Competition does not always solve these information asymmetries. Businesses may have little incentive to provide accurate information about their goods or services, as their competitors could benefit from that information. Therefore, in some cases, government regulation may be needed to address the information asymmetry.)

5 Productivity Commission, *Review of Australia's Consumer Policy Framework* (Inquiry Report No 45, 2008) vol 1, 63 (Recommendation 3.1).

6 Ibid.

7 *Council of Australian Governments Intergovernmental Agreement for the Australian Consumer Law* (2 July 2009), recitals C and D. Recital C, for instance, states: 'The objective of the new national consumer policy framework is to improve consumer wellbeing through consumer empowerment and protection, to foster effective competition and to enable the confident participation of consumers in markets in which both consumers and suppliers trade fairly.')

8 Explanatory Memorandum, National Consumer Credit Protection Bill 2009 (Cth) 3 ('*NCCPA Explanatory Memorandum*').

9 Ibid 6.

A unified licensing system, overseen by ASIC, governs entities carrying out activities falling under the *NCCPA* through an Australian credit licence (ACL).[10] One key element introduced by the *NCCPA* is the notion of 'responsible lending'.[11] Essentially, responsible lending requirements mandate how credit licensees must behave when engaging in consumer credit contracts or leases. This includes recommending a credit contract or lease to a consumer or helping a customer apply for one. Central to this duty is ensuring that they do not offer or encourage consumers to enter credit contracts or leases that are unsuited to their needs.

Further, the *NCCPA* adopted robust consumer protections through a civil penalty and remedy framework by granting, for instance, powers to ASIC to seek civil penalties and by enabling courts to provide various remedies to consumers, including contract alterations and monetary compensation.[12] In regards to dispute resolution, these can be resolved under the *NCCPA* in three ways: (a) internal resolution with the credit provider (eg lender) or credit assistance providers (eg mortgage broker); (b) an ASIC-approved external dispute resolution (EDR) scheme; and (c) access to the courts.[13] The EDR scheme is part of the requirements to obtain an ACL, as explained further below.

In addition to the *NCCPA*, a comprehensive understanding of consumer credit necessitates examining its intersection with general law. The relationship between consumers and various entities participating in credit transactions (eg banks and mortgage brokers) is also shaped by contract law.[14] In *Paciocco v Australia and New Zealand Banking Group Ltd*, the High Court considered whether a late payment fee on consumer credit card accounts was an unenforceable penalty under contract law, as well as an 'unjust transaction' under the *NCC* s 76.[15] The *Banking Code of Practice* (or the *Code of Banking Practice*, as it was previously known) may also be incorporated into contracts between consumers and such entities to impose contractual liability.[16]

This legal framework becomes increasingly intricate due to the complex contractual connections among different entities involved in these activities, each of which may act either independently or as an agent for another entity.[17] The law of equity serves as a supplement to contract law, offering remedial avenues for cases where consumer

10 Ibid 4. Notably, in a recently released report, the Australian Law Reform Commission (ALRC), while reviewing regulatory frameworks, has explored the possibility of streamlining overlapping financial and corporate legislation and the potential for merging similar licensing regimes for financial services and consumer credit. Complexities, policy differences and institutional constraints led to no recommendations for consolidation. See Australian Law Rreform Commission, *Confronting Complexity: Reforming Corporations and Financial Services Legislation* (Report No 141, November 2023) ('ALRC Final Report') [8.57]–[8.59] <https://www.alrc.gov.au/wp-content/uploads/2024/01/ALRC-FSL-Final-Report-141.pdf>.

11 *NCCPA Explanatory Memorandum* (n 8) 7.

12 See, eg, ibid 121.

13 Ibid 5. Taking legal action is frequently too costly for individuals, especially when the sums of money being contested are relatively small compared to the legal expenses involved. While the *NCCPA* (n 2) s 199 provides for a low-cost, small claims process for certain issues, its utility is not clear. Paterson and Howell (n 3) 2.

14 For an in-depth examination of consumer credit under Australian legal regulations, see Paterson and Howell (n 3); *Paciocco v Australia and New Zealand Banking Group Ltd* (2016) 258 CLR 525.

15 *Paciocco v Australia and New Zealand Banking Group Ltd* (2016) 258 CLR 525, [2].

16 *Dennis v Commonwealth Bank of Australia* [2020] FCCA 1313.

17 For instance, a consumer applies for a home loan through a mortgage broker. The mortgage broker helps the consumer to submit applications to multiple ACLs, which could be banks and non-bank

consent has been compromised or wherever otherwise justifiable.[18] Torts also plays a role, obligating ACL holders to carry out their activities with reasonable care, while creating the grounds for liability in instances of negligence or fraudulent actions.[19] Case law has stated that where a bank assumes responsibility to alert customers in relation to the risks of foreign currency loans, then they owe a duty of care to warn their customers.[20] Nevertheless, there are limits to tortious liability. For example, banks do not owe a duty of care to customers to investigate their financial circumstances to determine if a loan made is appropriate for them.[21] Further, it is generally accepted that the duties of a banker towards its customers lie in contract and not in tort.[22]

Moreover, fiduciary duties may apply to credit assistance providers - and even, under certain circumstances, to credit providers if they provide advisory services to consumers.[23] A fiduciary relationship arose in the case of *Commonwealth Bank of Australia v Smith* because the bank had acted as the consumer's financial adviser for 24 years, and the consumer, who had limited experience in business and financial matters, had evinced complete faith in the bank's representative.[24] These fiduciary obligations prohibit the parties involved from gaining unauthorised profits and require them to avoid behaviour that could lead to conflicts of interest.[25] There was a clear conflict of interest in *Commonwealth Bank of Australia v Smith* because the bank was acting as the adviser of both the seller and the purchaser of a property.

Various industry codes are applicable, such as the *Banking Code of Practice* ('*Banking Code*'),[26] the *Customer Owned Banking Code of Practice*,[27] and the *Mortgage and Finance Industry Association Code of Practice*.[28] The *Banking Code*, last updated in 2021, is a voluntary yet pivotal component of this intricate landscape,[29] and it has garnered subscriptions

lenders. One of the lenders approves the application and offers the consumer a home loan. The consumer accepts the offer and signs a loan agreement with the lender.

18 See, eg, *Garcia v National Australia Bank Ltd* (1998) 194 CLR 395.

19 *Clenae Pty Ltd v Australia & New Zealand Banking Group* [1999] 2 VR 573.

20 Ibid [74]–[81].

21 *Westpac Banking Corporation v Diagne* (2014) 17 BPR 33,551, [69].

22 *Territory Sheet Metal Pty Ltd v Australia and New Zealand Banking Group Ltd* [2009] NTSC 31, [1198]–[1202].

23 *Commonwealth Bank of Australia v Smith* (1991) 42 FCR 390, 455.

24 Ibid 477.

25 Ibid 478.

26 Australian Banking Association, *Banking Code of Practice: Setting the Standards of Practice for Banks, their Staff and their Representatives* (2021) ('*Banking Code*') <https://www.ausbanking.org.au/wp-content/uploads/2021/10/2021-5-Oct-Banking-Code-WEB.pdf>.

27 Customer Owned Banking Association, *Customer Owned Banking Code of Practice 2022* (2022) <https://www.customerownedbanking.asn.au/how-it-works/code-of-practice>.

28 Mortgage & Finance Association of Australia, *Code of Practice 11 November 2023* (2023) <https://myresources.mfaa.com.au/AboutUs/Governance/Documents/071129_MFAA_Code_Practice.pdf>.

29 The Banking Code Compliance Committee (BCCC) serves an oversight role, ensuring compliance with a self-regulated code and advocating for best practices that help banks to achieve favourable outcomes for their customers. Although not a regulatory body enforcing legal standards, the BCCC is responsible for monitoring how well subscribers adhere to the Code. In exercising its monitoring functions, the BCCC may make reasonable requests for Code subscribers to provide or allow access to relevant information, documents or systems. It may also engage with and seek information from third parties, publish external reports, offer guidance to the banking industry, and make findings as well as recommendations. See generally Australian Banking Association and Banking Code

from the majority of Australian banks that offer retail services.[30] It is applicable to 'banking services',[31] delineated as any financial service or product furnished by subscribing banks within Australia to consumers.[32] The term 'banking services' is further illustrated to include offerings of, among others, home loans, personal loans, credit cards and overdrafts.[33] Therefore, insofar as consumer credits are involved, certain obligations outlined in the *Banking Code* intersect with issue areas addressed by the *NCCPA* and the *NCC*. Notably, while the *NCCPA* and the *NCC* generally apply to natural persons and strata corporations, the *Banking Code* broadens its scope to include both individuals and 'small businesses'.[34]

The Code, administered by the Australian Banking Association (ABA), supplements the law by setting up safeguards and protections that exceed those specified by law in certain areas.[35] Although the *Banking Code*, as self-regulation, relocates some regulatory burdens from government agencies to the industry, purportedly enhancing consumer choice and enabling it to adapt swiftly to evolving consumer needs and to respond quickly to technological and other changes,[36] it has also raised criticisms for its effectiveness in terms of protecting consumers.[37] Consumer groups have expressed criticism of the *Banking Code* for its lack of provisions addressing financial exclusion in consumer credit.[38]

Compliance Committee, *Banking Code Compliance Committee (BCCC) Charter* (2019) <https://www.ausbanking.org.au/wp-content/uploads/2019/08/BCCC-Charter.pdf>.

30 Membership of the Australian Banking Association (ABA) mandates that member banks with a retail presence in Australia must adhere to the Code. For a list of the banks subscribed to it, see 'Code Signatories', *Australian Banking Association* (Web Page) <https://www.ausbanking.org.au/banking-code/code-signatories/>.

31 *Banking Code* (n 26) cl 1.

32 Ibid. Notably, the Code is also applicable to products or services that are provided by a subscribing bank via an intermediary.

33 Ibid. Nonetheless, there are specific categories of banking services to which the Code does not apply. These exclusions include shares, bonds and other securities issued by subscribing banks, as well as financial products and services falling under the *Corporations Act* ch 7, provided that customers are classified as a 'wholesale client' rather than a 'retail client'. An exception to this exclusion exists if a consumer is considered a 'wholesale client' solely because of s 761G(7)(b) of the same Act.

34 *Banking Code* (n 26) cl 1. A 'small business' is defined under the *Banking Code* as one that, at the time of using the banking service, had an annual turnover of less than A$10 million in the prior financial year, employs fewer than 100 full-time equivalent staff, and holds less than A$3 million in total debt to all credit providers. Conversely, a business is not considered a 'small business' if it is a publicly listed company on the Australian Stock Exchange, a government entity, or an entity holding an Australian Financial Services License authorised to operate registered investment schemes or provide custodial services.

35 Ibid 4.

36 Gail Pearson, *Financial Services Law and Compliance in Australia* (Cambridge University Press, 2009) 15 ('*Financial Services Law and Compliance in Australia*'); Taskforce on Industry Self-Regulation, *Industry Self-Regulation in Consumer Markets* (Department of the Treasury, 2000) 1, 36 <https://treasury.gov.au/sites/default/files/2019-03/final_report.pdf> ('*Industry Self-Regulation Report*').

37 Legally, the Financial Ombudsman Services (FOS), now known as 'Australian Financial Complaints Authority' (AFCA), commented on the previous version of the Code that if a bank subscribes to an industry code but fails to comply with that code, this constitutes a contractual breach with the customer. Consequently, the customer may be eligible for compensation for any incurred losses. See Financial Ombudsman Service Australia, *The FOS Approach to 2013 Code of Banking Practice* (2014) 3. For a critical assessment, see generally Nicola J Howell, 'Revisiting the Australian Code of Banking Practice: Is Self-Regulation Still Relevant for Improving Consumer Protection Standards?' (2015) 38(2) *University of New South Wales Law Journal* 544.

38 Howell (n 37) 579–81 (noting that one commentator has suggested that 'the bank industry's inability to address breaches of a code that's been in place for almost 10 years indicates that self-regulation isn't working': 579).

The role of ASIC warrants particular emphasis. This regulatory body provides interpretive guidance on applicable statutes, notably those concerning credit licences[39] and the obligations surrounding responsible lending.[40] While ASIC's regulatory guides do not, strictly speaking, possess formal legal status, they have been considered by the Administrative Appeals Tribunal in its adjudicative review of ASIC's decisions, thereby suggesting that these guides are accorded a certain level of significance in legal practice.[41]

2.1.2 Scope of the *NCCPA*

2.1.2.1 Key features

After delving into the background of the *NCCPA*, we now examine its overarching structure. This will set the stage for a more focused discussion on specific issues it addresses. Broadly, the *NCCPA*'s structure addresses four primary consumer protection provisions: (a) a licensing regime;[42] (b) general conduct obligations;[43] (c) mandatory disclosure requirements;[44] and (d) responsible lending obligations.[45] Moreover, the main text of this vital piece of legislation prescribes obligations for credit licensees, including credit providers (eg banks and non-bank lenders)[46] and credit assistance providers (eg brokers),[47] as detailed below.

While the main part of the *NCCPA* applies to both credit providers and credit assistance providers, the *NCC* is concerned more with credit providers than with those offering credit assistance. The *NCC* deals with, among other matters, pre-contractual disclosure,[48] the requirements for contents of credit contracts and related mortgages

39 Australian Securities and Investments Commission, *Do I Need a Credit License?* (Regulatory Guide 203, October 2017) ('ASIC RG 203').

40 Australian Securities and Investments Commission, *Credit Licensing: Responsible Lending Conduct* (Regulatory Guide 209, December 2019) ('ASIC RG 209').

41 Notwithstanding the fact that ASIC Regulatory Guides are not legally enforceable, they nonetheless play a significant role in the way the law is interpreted and are generally followed when their policies are deemed to be sufficiently sound and lawful. Such was the case in *Re Tarrant and Australian Securities and Investments Commission* (2013) 62 AAR 192, [22], where President Kerr observed at [21]: 'The Regulatory Guides appear to be carefully calibrated documents produced by an agency that has responsibility for prudential regulation of the provision of financial advice. The policy appears sound. That observation is not intended to preclude the possibility of later challenges – it is made merely to indicate that where a policy on its face is uncontentious, the Tribunal is lawfully entitled to have regard to such policy and to apply it subject to the right of an applicant to put the matter in issue and subject to the policy not working unfairness in the particular case'. See also *Vissenjoux v Australian Securities and Investments Commission* [2015] AATA 98, [13]–[14]; *Coshett v Australian Securities and Investments Commission* [2014] AATA 677, [16]. See also Pearson (n 36) 153 (noting that ASIC's Regulatory Guides are perceived to have a 'quasi-legal character'); Nicola J Howell, 'Small Amount Credit Contracts and Payday Loans: The Complementarity of Price Regulation and Responsible Lending Regulation' (2016) 41(3) *Alternative Law Journal* 174, 177 (noting that 'ASIC's regulatory guides are not approved by the Parliament or courts, they are not binding and do not amount to legal advice. However, these regulatory guides are often very influential').

42 *NCCPA* (n 2) ch 2.

43 Ibid ch 2 pt 2-2 div 5 (setting out the general conduct obligations of ACLs).

44 See, eg, ibid, ch 3 div 2 (providing credit guide of credit assistance providers).

45 Ibid ch 3.

46 Ibid pt 3-2.

47 Ibid pt 3-1.

48 *National Credit Code* (the '*NCC*') ss 16–18, 43, 56.

and guarantees,[49] and price regulation.[50] The *NCC* also lays down rules for making unilateral or mutually agreed changes to credit contracts,[51] offers avenues for hardship variations,[52] and sets criteria for identifying unjust transactions[53] and unconscionable fees and charges.[54] It further outlines procedures for the termination and enforcement of credit contracts along with associated mortgages and guarantees[55] and extends to related sales and insurance contracts.[56]

2.1.2.2 Covered activities

To begin with some preliminary clarifications, the *NCCPA* is applicable to persons who are involved in 'credit activity'.[57] This encompasses not only 'credit providers' under 'credit contracts', but also 'lessors' in 'consumer leases' as well as those offering 'credit assistance' or serving as 'intermediaries'. Credit activity regulated by the *NCCPA* encompasses a range of transactions, from home loans and mortgages to insurance contracts. The *NCCPA* s 6(1) stipulates the situations when a person engages in a 'credit activity', as summarised below.

For credit contracts,[58] a person is engaged in a credit activity if they act as a credit provider, conduct a business of offering credit that falls under the *NCC*, or fulfil the obligations or rights of a credit provider in relation to a credit contract.[59] Regarding 'credit services',[60] engagement in credit activity occurs when the person offers a credit service. In the context of consumer leases, a person is engaged in credit activity if they act as a lessor, run a business providing consumer leases, or execute the obligations or rights of a lessor in relation to a consumer lease.[61] For mortgages, on the other hand, a person is considered to be involved in a credit activity if they act as a mortgagee or fulfil the obligations or rights of a mortgagee in relation to a mortgage.[62] In the case of guarantees, a person is engaged in credit activity

49 Ibid pt 2-3.
50 See, eg, ibid ss 32B, 39B.
51 Ibid pt 4 divs 1 and 2.
52 Ibid ss 72–75.
53 Ibid s 76.
54 Ibid s 78.
55 Ibid pt 5.
56 Ibid pts 7 and 8.
57 *NCCPA* (n 2) div 3 and s 6.
58 The expression 'credit contract' is also defined under NCC as a contract under which credit is/may be provided. *NCC* (n 48) s 4.
59 *NCCPA* (n 2) s 6 item 1. (In relation to credit contracts, a person engages in a credit activity if: '(a) The person is a credit provider under a credit contract; or (b) the person carries on a business of providing credit, being credit the provision of which the National Credit Code applies to; or (c) the person performs the obligations, or exercises the rights, of a credit provider in relation to a credit contract or proposed credit contract (whether the person does so as the credit provider or on behalf of the credit provider)).'
60 Ibid s 6 item 2. (In terms of credit service, a person engages in a credit activity if 'the person provides a credit service'.)
61 Ibid s 6 item 3. (In relation to consumer leases, a person engages in a credit activity if: '(a) the person is a lessor under a consumer lease; or (b) the person carries on a business of providing consumer leases; or (c) the person performs the obligations, or exercises the rights, of a lessor in relation to a consumer lease or proposed consumer lease (whether the person does so as the lessor or on behalf of the lessor)'.)
62 Ibid s 6 item 4. (In terms of a mortgage, a person engages in a credit activity if: '(a) the person is a mortgagee under a mortgage; or (b) the person performs the obligations, or exercises the rights, of a mortgagee in relation to a mortgage or proposed mortgage (whether the person does so as the mortgagee or on behalf of the mortgagee)'.)

if they are the beneficiary of a guarantee or fulfil the obligations or rights of another person who is a beneficiary of a guarantee.[63] Lastly, a person is engaged in credit activity if they take part in activities that are prescribed by the regulations in relation to credit, provided that the provision of such credit falls under – or would fall under – the *NCC*.[64]

The term 'credit' is defined under the *NCC* s 3(1), which states that credit is provided if, under a contract, '(a) payment of a debt owed by one person (the debtor) to another (the credit provider) is deferred; or (b) one person (the debtor) incurs a deferred debt to another (the credit provider)'.[65] This means that the provision of credit under s 3(1) is the deferment of payment of an existing debt or the incurrence of a deferred debt.[66] The *NCC* also stipulates that 'the amount of credit' is the amount of the debt actually deferred. This does not include:

(a) any interest charge under the contract; or
(b) any fee or charge:
  (i) that is to be or may be debited after the credit is first provided under the contract; and
  (ii) that is not payable in connection with the making of the contract or the making of a mortgage or guarantee related to the contract.[67]

Notably, the *NCC* is not applicable to 'short-term credit' that meets the following criteria: (i) the credit is provided for a period no longer than 62 days; (ii) any fees and charges associated with the credit do not exceed 5 per cent of the total credit amount; and (iii) the imposed or stipulated interest charges do not surpass what would be calculated at an annual percentage rate of 24 per cent.[68] Moreover, the *NCC* does not cover the provision of credit in cases where there is no prior express agreement between the credit provider and the debtor.[69] For instance, this exclusion would apply when a cheque account becomes overdrawn without a formally agreed-upon overdraft facility, or when a savings account incurs a deficit. Furthermore, if the sole 'charge that is or may be made for providing the credit' is a consistent periodic or fixed fee that does not adjust based on the credit amount, the *NCC* would not apply, provided that the *NCC* becomes relevant if the 'charge' aligns with descriptions set by regulations or surpasses the 'maximum charge' defined by such regulations.[70]

Moreover, it is crucial to clarify that the application of the *NCCPA* is contingent not only on whether a person engages in a 'credit activity' under the *NCCPA* s 6(1) but also on the conditions stipulated under the *NCC*. A regulated 'credit contract', as per both the

63 Ibid s 6 item 5. (In terms of guarantees, a person engages in a credit activity if: '(a) the person is the beneficiary of a guarantee; or (b) the person performs the obligations, or exercises the rights, of another person who is a beneficiary of a guarantee or proposed guarantee, in relation to the guarantee or proposed guarantee (whether the person does so on the person's own behalf or on behalf of the other person)'.)
64 Ibid s 6 item 6. (In terms of prescribed activity, a person engages in a credit activity if: '(a) the person engages in an activity prescribed by the regulations in relation to credit, being credit the provision of which the National Credit Code applies to, or would apply to, if the credit were provided.')
65 *NCC* (n 48) s 3(1).
66 *Australian Securities and Investments Commission v Fast Access Finance* [2015] FCA 1055, [10].
67 *NCC* (n 48) s 3(2).
68 Ibid s 6(1).
69 Ibid s 6(4).
70 Ibid s 6(5).

main text of the *NCCPA* and the *NCC*, refers to a contract where (i) the debtor is a natural person or a strata corporation; (ii) the credit is provided wholly or predominantly for personal, domestic or household purposes, or for the purchase, renovation or improvement of residential property for investment purposes, or to refinance credit used for such aims; and (iii) a charge must or may be made for providing the credit, and the credit provider must either be involved in the business of offering credit within the jurisdiction or offer credit as part of or incidentally to any other business conducted in that jurisdiction.[71] In other words, a person conducting credit activities solely for business purposes will not fall under the purview of 'credit activity' as defined by the *NCCPA*, given that the *NCC* specifically regulates consumer credit rather than business credit.[72]

Further elaboration is merited to clarify these components. A 'predominant purpose' is one for which more than half of the credit is used;[73] or if the credit is used for goods and services that fulfil different purposes, a 'predominant purpose' will be the purpose for which the goods and services are most used.[74] In the case of *Paul Gooley v NSW Rural Assistance Authority*,[75] a loan to fund repairs to farming infrastructure and a residence on farmland that was occupied by the appellant's family (who ran a farming partnership) was not regarded as a consumer credit contract because the funds were predominantly intended to be used by the farming partnership to acquire land and stock, not for residential purposes.

In determining the purpose for which the credit is to be used, there remains a question as to whether the purpose should be considered *subjectively* (ie considering the actual, subjective intentions of the parties) or *objectively* (ie considering the manifested intentions of the parties), or using a combination of the two approaches.[76] This is primarily an issue where a person requests a loan for one purpose, but ultimately, due to certain circumstances, ends up using the money for another purpose. There are two main views: first, that the purpose of the loan is what a reasonable person, in the shoes of the credit provider, understood it was intended for at the time the loan was made;[77] and, second, that to determine the purpose of the loan, one must consider the substance of the transaction in the context of its performance, including what the money was actually used for.[78]

To ascertain the loan's purpose, the courts also distinguish between 'ultimate purpose' and 'immediate purpose'.[79] The Victorian Court of Appeal has distinguished between the language used in s 5(1)(b)(i) and 5(1)(b)(ii) of the *NCC*, finding that the former is expressed in the language of *ultimate purpose*, unlike the latter.[80] Practically, this means that credit will only fall under the scope of the latter section if the relevant loan or facility is used directly by

71 Ibid s 4.
72 See also Paterson and Howell (n 3) 20 (note 110).
73 *NCC* (n 48) s 5(4)(a).
74 Ibid s 5(4)(b).
75 *Paul Gooley v NSW Rural Assistance Authority* [2020] NSWCA 156, [46].
76 *Lauvan Pty Ltd v Bega (No 2)* [2018] NSWSC 155, [251].
77 *Park Ave Nominees Pty Ltd v Boon* (2001) ASC 155-052, [46].
78 *Linkenholt Pty Ltd v Quirk* (2000) ASC 155-040, [98]; approved in *Bank of Queensland Ltd v Dutta* [2010] NSWSC 574, [123].
79 *MAG Financial and Investment Ventures Pty Ltd v El-Saafin* [2022] VSCA 286, [112]–[113].
80 Ibid.

the debtor to purchase, renovate or improve residential property for investment purposes. It is insufficient that the ultimate use of funds by a third party involves the improvement of residential property.[81] To illustrate, in *MAG Financial and Investment Ventures Pty Ltd v El-Saafin*, the Court found that the purpose of the loan made to the borrowers was for them to advance the borrowed funds to a third-party company for that third party to carry out residential property investments. This loan was, therefore, not covered under the *NCC*.[82]

The next criterion is that there must be a 'charge' made, such as payment or the promise of payment, for providing the credit. In *Australian Securities and Investments Commission v BHF Solutions Pty Ltd*, the Federal Court of Australia provided a substantial clarification regarding whether the fees charged in the present case should fall within s 5(1)(c) or s 6(5) to determine whether the *NCC* should apply to this case.[83] BHF Solutions Pty Ltd ('BHFS') and Cigno Pty Ltd ('Cigno') were the primary companies involved in this case. Neither held an ACL; they both had commercial arrangements under a Loan Management Facilitation Agreement.[84] As per this agreement, BHFS would lend money to consumers for a maximum term of 62 days and charge a $15 fee. Cigno, on the other hand, was responsible for marketing, application processing, and collections related to these loans. Consumers who borrowed from BHFS via Cigno were subject to various fees, including a 'Financial Supply Fee' that amounted to $13 plus 60 per cent of the loan amount, an 'Account Keeping Fee' of $5.95 per week, as well as a 'Change of Payment Schedule Fee' of $22 under certain conditions. These fees, when annualised, could amount to an interest rate of approximately 800 per cent.

O'Bryan J supported a broader construction of the term, underscoring that the charges should be considered in their commercial context and in relation to the provision of credit. In deciding if a charge has been made for providing the credit, courts will take a substance-over-form approach,[85] such that even charges formally structured as payments for services and not as contractual consideration under the credit contract

81 Ibid [115].

82 Ibid [139].

83 *Australian Securities and Investments Commission v BHF Solutions Pty Ltd* (2022) 293 FCR 330, [179], [183]. ('For the foregoing reasons, I consider that the expression "charge … made for providing the credit" in s 5(1)(c) should be construed as a charge that is made in exchange for, on account of or by reason of the provision of credit. The same phrase used in s 6(5) should be construed in the same manner. Ultimately, the application of the statutory criterion in both ss 5(1)(c) and 6(5) requires an assessment of all relevant facts. It is an evaluative task that requires the relevant charge to be characterised by reference to the statutory criterion … Those facts provide a sufficient basis on which to conclude that the Financial Supply Fee was a charge that was made for providing the BHFS credit. Having regard to the commercial substance of the arrangements, the Financial Supply Fee was imposed on account of or by reason of the provision of BHFS credit and, in a practical commercial sense, was imposed in exchange for that credit …')

84 Ibid [184]. ('The contractual arrangements between Cigno and BHFS, documented in the Loan Management Facilitation Agreement, provide the commercial background to the credit arrangements offered to consumers. The contractual arrangements explain why Cigno advertised the provision of credit on its website whereas BHFS did not [because, as recited in the agreement, Cigno was in the business of marketing, facilitation, management and collections in relation to loans]. The contractual arrangements also explain why the majority of credit charges are imposed by Cigno and not by BHFS (because, by guaranteeing the repayment of the credit under the agreement, Cigno ultimately bears the credit risk on the loans provided.')

85 Ibid [172].

may fulfil this requirement. This broader interpretation aims to prevent companies from circumventing the consumer protection objectives of the *NCC* through intricate fee arrangements.

Although the *NCC* has carved out several types of transactions, it also clarifies that the following arrangements will still fall within its purview: (a) mortgages securing *NCC* credit contract obligations or related guarantees;[86] (b) guarantees tied to an *NCC* credit contract;[87] and (c) leases and hire purchases for personal, domestic or household purposes where lease charges surpass the cash price of the good and the goods are part of or are incidental to the credit provider's business.[88]

2.2 Licence and other obligations under the *NCCPA* and the *NCC*

2.2.1 Key categories of credit activity and licensing requirements

Under the *NCCPA* s 29, engaging in any of these activities that fall within the scope of 'credit providers' and 'credit assistance providers' places a person under the licensing scheme,[89] subsequently subjecting them to the disclosure, conduct and responsible lending obligations. ASIC assesses applications for licences, and can grant licences with imposed conditions, or vary or revoke licences.[90] The term 'credit provider' is defined under the *NCC* s 204 as a person who provides credit and may include banks, credit unions, building societies, finance companies, small-amount lenders, and vendors offering sales contracts such as hire-purchase agreements.[91] Also, a person must obtain an ACL if they offer a 'credit service' either: (i) by providing a customer credit assistance; or (ii) by acting 'as an intermediary'.[92]

In regards to the former, a person will be considered as providing 'credit assistance' if they suggest that a consumer applies for a credit agreement specific to a given credit provider or enters a lease with a specified lessor, advises a consumer to seek an augmentation of their credit limit for a specific credit contract, or aids the consumer in either initiating a specific credit agreement with a particular credit provider or in seeking an increase to their existing credit contract limit.[93] Typical examples are mortgage brokers and credit advisers.[94] Furthermore, in the context of conducting business in Australia, a person is deemed to act as an intermediary when, as part of or incidental to such business operations: (i) they serve, either directly or indirectly, as an intermediary between a credit provider and a consumer, aiming mainly to secure credit provisions under a said credit contract; or (ii) they engage, directly or indirectly, in facilitating a consumer-lease

86 *NCC* (n 48) s 7.
87 Ibid s 8.
88 Ibid s 9..
89 *NCCPA* (n 2) s 29.
90 Ibid pt 2-2 div 3; ss 45–46.
91 *NCC* (n 48) s 204; ASIC RG 203 (n 39) [34].
92 *NCCPA* (n 2) s 7.
93 Ibid s 8.
94 ASIC RG 203 (n 39) [75].

agreement between a lessor and the respective consumer.[95] The capacity in which this role is performed, whether autonomously or representing another entity, remains inconsequential to their status as an intermediary.

An example provided by ASIC's Regulatory Guide 203 is a website that presents comparisons of rates and features for credit cards and home loans and subsequently directs its users to credit providers through website links and application forms. The website's operator might be classified as an intermediary if the primary intention behind such referrals is to facilitate the consumer's acquisition of credit. The operator's intermediary role is particularly evident if they gain a benefit whenever a consumer applies for a credit card or home loan based on their referrals.[96]

This 'acting as an intermediary' designation seems a 'catch-all category', covering entities that participate in credit transactions as a bridge between the consumer and the credit provider.[97] However, these entities do not necessarily offer advice, recommendations or assistance to consumers related to credit provision in the same manner as credit assistance providers.[98]

Certain persons engaged in credit-related activities are exempt from the licensing requirements under the *NCCPA*.[99] Some of these exemptions merit further discussion. First, persons who only pass information provided by or related to a credit licensee onto consumers, supplemented by advice about the licensee, are not construed as engaging in credit activities that necessitate an ACL.[100] Second, certain referrals can be made without the necessity for the referring party to possess an ACL. These exemptions generally encompass two types: 'downstream' and 'upstream' referrals.[101] The former pertains to persons who guide consumers towards credit licensees; while the latter relates to those who, upon obtaining a consumer's consent, convey the consumer's contact details and specific requirements to an ACL, thus facilitating potential interaction.[102] Yet, this type of exemption is subject to specific conditions. Of paramount importance is the obligation for the referrer to disclose any commissions or benefits derived from such referrals to the consumers.

Moreover, 'credit representatives' and 'representatives' are also exempted from the ACL requirement. 'Credit representatives' refers to persons authorised by an ACL holder to undertake specific credit-related activities on their behalf.[103] Such representatives are not required to have their own licensing; rather, they function under another entity's existing licence – a broker acting as a franchisee under a credit franchisor is a prime example.[104] Meanwhile, an ACL holder may operate through its representatives for which the licensee holds responsibility – such as its employees and directors of the licensee.[105]

95 *NCCPA* (n 2) s 9.
96 ASIC RG 203 (n 39) [Example 10].
97 Paterson and Howell (n 3) 26.
98 Ibid.
99 *National Consumer Credit Protection Regulations 2010* (Cth) (the '*NCCPR*') pt 2-4 div 1 sub-div 1.1.
100 Ibid regs 24(6), (7), (8).
101 Paterson and Howell (n 3) 22.
102 *NCCPR* (n 99) reg 25(2), (2A), (5).
103 ASIC RG 203 (n 39) [83].
104 Ibid 43.
105 *NCCPA* (n 2) s 5.

ACL holders are subject to general conduct obligations under the *NCCPA* s 47, which requires such holders to:

- undertake all actions necessary to ensure that the credit activities authorised by the licence are conducted efficiently, honestly and fairly
- have adequate arrangements to safeguard clients from conflicts of interest possibly emerging from credit activities managed by the licensee or its representatives
- comply strictly with the conditions on the licence and with the prevailing credit legislation
- take reasonable steps to ascertain its representatives' adherence to the credit legislation
- consistently maintain the competence required to carry out the credit activities sanctioned by the licence
- guarantee that representatives are adequately trained and demonstrate competence in the approved credit tasks
- institute an internal dispute resolution procedure
- enrol in an approved EDR scheme (ie a scheme administered by the Australian Financial Complaints Authority [AFCA])
- put in place specific compensation arrangements
- put in place adequate arrangements and systems for unwavering compliance
- provide adequate resources for the licensed activities and have in place risk management systems, unless when overseen by the Australian Prudential Regulation Authority (APRA)
- abide by any other duties prescribed by the regulations.[106]

106 Ibid s 47. ('General conduct obligations: (1) A licensee must: (a) do all things necessary to ensure that the credit activities authorised by the licence are engaged in efficiently, honestly and fairly; and (b) have in place adequate arrangements to ensure that clients of the licensee are not disadvantaged by any conflict of interest that may arise wholly or partly in relation to credit activities engaged in by the licensee or its representatives; and (c) comply with the conditions on the licence; and (d) comply with the credit legislation; and (e) take reasonable steps to ensure that its representatives comply with the credit legislation; and (ea) comply with the Reference Checking and Information Sharing Protocol in relation to: (i) if the licensee is an individual to whom the Protocol applies – the licensee; and (ii) if a former, current or prospective representative of the licensee is an individual to whom the Protocol applies – the representative; and (f) maintain the competence to engage in the credit activities authorised by the licence; and (g) ensure that its representatives are adequately trained, and are competent, to engage in the credit activities authorised by the licence; and (h) have an internal dispute resolution procedure that: (i) complies with standards and requirements made or approved by ASIC in accordance with the regulations; and (ii) covers disputes in relation to the credit activities engaged in by the licensee or its representatives; and (ha) give to ASIC the same information it would be required to give under subparagraph 912A(1)(g)(ii) of the *Corporations Act 2001* if it were a financial services licensee (within the meaning of ch 7 of that Act); and (i) be a member of the AFCA scheme; and (j) have compensation arrangements in accordance with section 48; and (k) have adequate arrangements and systems to ensure compliance with its obligations under this section, and a written plan that documents those arrangements and systems; and (l) unless the licensee is a body regulated by APRA: (i) have available adequate resources (including financial, technological and human resources) to engage in the credit activities authorised by the licence and to carry out supervisory arrangements; and (ii) have adequate risk management systems; and (m) comply with any other obligations that are prescribed by the regulations.'). See also Australian Securities and Investments Commission, *Credit Licensing: General Conduct Obligations* (Regulatory Guide 205, 1 April 2020) ('ASIC RG 205').

Additionally, ACL holders could be subject to responsible lending obligations and a 'best interests' duty. The former is legislated in the *NCCPA* pt 3, which requires ACL holders to assess whether a credit contract is 'not unsuitable' for a particular consumer; the obligation generally applies to both credit providers[107] and credit assistance providers.[108] Credit assistance providers, such as mortgage brokers, are required to act in the 'best interests' of consumers when providing credit assistance.[109] We consider each of these below.

2.2.2 Primary obligations of the ACL under the *NCCPA*

2.2.2.1 Mandatory disclosure requirements

Disclosure requirements are paramount within the realm of credit transactions, as mandated by both the *NCCPA* and the *NCC*. The *NCCPA* focuses more on pre-contractual disclosures, delineating the nature and function of the respective entity or entities with which a consumer engages. In contrast, the *NCC* underscores the specific features of individual credit contracts. In this section, we consider the disclosure requirements under the *NCCPA*, while obligations under the *NCC* are discussed later in the chapter.

One of the pivotal disclosure mandates encapsulated within the *NCCPA* is a 'credit guide'.[110] Its function is to equip consumers with critical information at the preliminary stages of the credit transaction, thereby enabling them to make informed decisions.[111] The licensee is obligated to provide its credit guide to the consumer, in accordance with the prescribed requirements, as soon as practicable after it becomes apparent to the licensee that it is likely to enter a credit contract with a consumer. A credit guide must (i) be in written form, (ii) comply with the format required by the relevant regulations, and (iii) state the licensee's name, contact details and ACL number.[112] Additionally, the guide must provide information about the licensee's approach to resolving consumer disputes, including both internal processes and those set out in the relevant AFCA scheme.[113] The credit guide should also highlight the licensee's responsible lending obligations as laid out in the *NCCPA* ss 132 and 133.[114] The obligation to provide a credit guide applies not only to credit providers, but also to credit assistance providers[115] and credit representatives.[116]

It should be noted that, alongside the credit guide, credit assistance providers are obligated to furnish a 'credit quote' for their offerings,[117] and a credit proposal document[118] that elucidates fees, charges and commissions, and offers an estimation of the potential credit amount to be extended.

107 *NCCPA* (n 2) pt 3-2.
108 Ibid pt 3-1.
109 Ibid s 158.
110 Ibid s 126.
111 *NCCPA Explanatory Memorandum* (n 8) 87.
112 *NCCPA* (n 2) s 126(2).
113 Ibid.
114 Ibid.
115 Ibid s 113.
116 Ibid pt 3-5 div 2 (credit guide of credit representative).
117 Ibid ss 114, 137.
118 Ibid ss 121, 144.

2.2.2.2 Responsible lending obligation

The introduction of the responsible lending regime represents a pivotal modification to the consumer credit system that existed prior to the enactment of the *NCCPA*. This regime emerged as a reaction to the Global Financial Crisis (GFC) and, more precisely, to the practice of approving loans for customers who, under normal circumstances, would not have been deemed capable of repayment but were considered eligible due to the collateral they could provide – often referred to as 'sub-prime loan issues'.[119] The underlying rationale of responsible lending is that credit licensees should not initiate, recommend or help a consumer to obtain a credit contract if that contract is not suitable for the consumer's needs.[120] Responsible lending obligation is further observed in the *Banking Code*, which regulates the conduct of banks to ensure that individuals and small businesses are prudently assessed on their suitability for any loans or increases in loan limit.[121]

The responsible lending obligation places a requirement on credit providers and those who provide assistance with credit products to assess the suitability of a credit contract for a particular consumer.[122] Specifically, the obligation applies in the following circumstances:

- when a credit licensee provides a new credit contract or lease to a consumer[123]
- when a credit licensee increases an existing credit limit[124]
- where a credit licensee provides credit assistance in relation to the aforementioned matters.[125]

However, responsible lending obligation does not apply under specific circumstances. While a loan qualifies as consumer credit, the licensee may not participate in activities that would invoke this obligation; for instance, an entity might operate in the capacity of acting as an intermediary but refrain from offering any credit assistance to the consumers.[126]

Generally, the responsible lending obligation imposes requirements upon ACL holders to undertake suitability assessments. Before proceeding with the suitability assessment,

119 Gail Pearson, 'Reading Suitability Against Fitness for Purpose – The Evolution of a Rule' (2010) 32(2) *Sydney Law Review* 311; Reserve Bank of Australia, 'The Global Financial Crisis' <https://www.rba.gov.au/education/resources/explainers/pdf/the-global-financial-crisis.pdf>. Outside Australia, the notion of responsible lending has also been introduced to strengthen the lending practice in the post-GFC era. See World Bank, *Responsible Lending: Overview of Regulatory Tools* (October 2013) <https://documents1.worldbank.org/curated/en/596151468336064796/pdf/832840WP0GFDR00Box0382083B00PUBLIC0.pdf>; Iain Ramsay, 'Consumer Credit Regulation after the Fall: International Dimensions' (2012) 1(1) *Journal of European Consumer and Market Law* 24. The policy narrative can be framed even more broadly, using the term 'responsible credits' to capture both the obligation of 'responsible lending' and its corresponding duty of 'responsible borrowing'. Noah Vardi, *Creditworthiness and 'Responsible Credit': A Comparative Study of EU and US Law* (Kninklijke Brill NV, 2022).

120 ASIC RG 209 (n 40).

121 *Banking Code* (n 26) cl 49.

122 *NCCPA* (n 2) pts 3-2, 3-1.

123 Ibid s 128.

124 Ibid s 151.

125 Ibid ss 115, 137.

126 ASIC RG 209 (n 40) [33]. An illustration of this scenario is when the licensee informs the consumer of various available options but refrains from offering advice or endorsing a specific product, waiting instead for the consumer to select a preferred lender and product.

a credit licensee must: (i) make reasonable inquiries into the consumer's requirements and objectives concerning the credit products; (ii) make reasonable inquiries regarding the consumer's financial position; and (iii) take reasonable steps to verify the consumer's financial information.[127] In terms of credit providers and credit assistance providers, such obligations are undertaken at their respective stages of assessment. While credit assistance providers undertake a 'preliminary assessment',[128] credit providers are tasked with providing a (final) 'assessment'.[129] The responsible lending obligation imposes similar requirements at both stages of assessment.[130] It is crucial to underscore that the completion of a preliminary assessment by a credit assistance provider does not relieve a credit provider of its obligations to undertake its own assessment or of any liabilities stemming from its failure to do so.[131] ASIC refers to the method of defining what types of inquiries and actions are reasonable as 'scalability'.[132] Factors to be taken into account include the potential ramifications of an unsuitable credit product, the intricacy of the credit product, the capacity of a consumer, and the relationship with the consumer (ie new or existing).[133]

The first obligation for a credit licensee to undertake reasonable inquiries into the customer's objectives and requirements has been elaborated upon by ASIC;[134] case law provides guidance on the extent of the obligations, which will differ on a case-by-case basis. The case of *ASIC v The Cash Store Pty Ltd (in liq)* established that, for the credit licensee to have satisfactorily made reasonable inquiries about the consumer's objectives and requirements in applying for small, short-term loans, there must have been evidence of a stated purpose that was 'specific enough to enable [The Cash Store] reasonably to ascertain what the money was needed for'.[135]

The second duty for a credit licensee to undertake reasonable inquiries into the customer's financial situation has also been elaborated upon via case law. In *ASIC v The Cash Store Pty Ltd (in liq)*, David J stated that this obligation required 'a sufficient understanding of the person's income and expenditure', which required, at a minimum, inquiries into the consumer's living expenses and income by way of inquiries into the consumer's rent or mortgage expenses, other expenses including utility bills and groceries, and any existing debts.[136] In *Australian Securities and Investments Commission v Channic (No 4)*, Greenwood J observed:

> The question of whether there is a real chance that a consumer will be unable to comply with his or her financial obligations is to be answered according to all the circumstances of the particular consumer relevant to his or her ability

127 *NCCPA* (n 2) ss 117, 130, 140, 153; ASCI RG 209 (n 40) [43].
128 *NCCPA* (n 2) ss 117, 120, 140, 143.
129 Ibid ss 130, 132, 153, 155.
130 Ibid ss 117, 140, 130, 153.
131 See *Australian Securities and Investments Commission v The Cash Store Pty Ltd (in liq)* [2014] FCA 926, [68] ('*ASIC v Cash Store*'); *Australian Securities and Investments Commission v Channic Pty Ltd (No 4)* [2016] FCA 1174, [1804] ('*ASIC v Channic*').
132 ASCI RG 209 (n 40) [81].
133 Paterson and Howell (n 3) 48–9.
134 ASCI RG 209 (n 40).
135 *ASIC v Cash Store* (n 131) [34]–[35].
136 Ibid [43].

> (or not) to perform those forward-looking financial obligations. Those circumstances would, no doubt, comprehend, in the main, a proper and accurate understanding of the consumer's income, the sources of income, any existing and continuing deductions from that income and an accurate understanding of the consumer's actual expenses so as to understand the financial capacity of the consumer, out of available net receipts, to comply with the new financial obligations under the proposed credit contract. The consumer's domestic and family circumstances may well be relevant. The consumer's credit history and whether, by and large, a consumer has demonstrated a pattern of meeting like or other financial obligations would, no doubt, also be relevant. Whether the consumer has a partner, family member, parent or friend who is willing to support the consumer financially in a materially legal way might also be relevant to the consumer's ability to comply with his or her financial obligations.[137]

Similarly, in RG 209, ASIC indicates that, at a minimum, inquiries should cover current income and its source;[138] the scale of fixed expenditures (eg housing);[139] and the range of variable expenses, along with the factors influencing those expenses (eg the number of dependants).[140]

After conducting the requisite inquiries and verifying the consumer's financial information, the licensee is then mandated to ascertain whether the proposed credit contract or increase in credit is not unsuitable for the specific consumer in context.[141] It is crucial to note that the assessment is not focused on determining whether the contract is 'best' for the client but is 'not unsuitable' for them.[142] The assessment process ought to be completed within a span of 90 days prior to the licensee entering into the contract or making an unconditional representation of the consumer's eligibility to enter the contract.[143] In the case of home loans, a protracted period – 120 days – is stipulated for the ACL holder's assessment.[144] Crucially, the assessment should be based solely on information related to the consumer's financial standing or their specific needs/objectives.[145]

A credit contract will be deemed 'unsuitable' where it does not meet the consumer's requirements/objectives, or where the consumer will be unable to meet repayments either at all or only with substantial hardship.[146] Specifically, there are three (non-exhaustive) circumstances where a credit contract would definitely be unsuitable. As set out in the *NCCPA* s 131(2), these circumstances are where, at the time of assessment, it is likely that:

137 *ASIC v Channic* (n 131) [1173].
138 ASIC RG 209 (n 40) [61]–[63] and Table 1.
139 Ibid Table 3.
140 Ibid Table 4.
141 *NCCPA* (n 2) ss 116, 128.
142 Pearson (n 119) 333.
143 *NCCPA* (n 2) ss 115, 128.
144 *NCCPR* (n 99) reg 28J.
145 *NCCPA* (n 2) ss 118(4), 119(4), 131(4).
146 Ibid ss 118, 119, 131, 141, 142.

(a) the consumer will be unable to comply with the consumer's financial obligations under the contract, or could only comply with substantial hardship, if the contract is entered or the credit limit is increased in the period covered by the assessment; or

(b) the contract will not meet the consumer's requirements or objectives if the contract is entered or the credit limit is increased in the period covered by the assessment; or

(c) if the regulations prescribe circumstances in which a credit contract is unsuitable – those circumstances will apply to the contract if the contract is entered or the credit limit is increased in the period covered by the assessment.[147]

Case law has stated that the circumstances in the *NCCPA* s 130(2) provide guidance as to the extent of the information that is to be collected under s 130(1).[148] In particular, whatever 'must as a matter of necessity be considered' to decide if a consumer will, inter alia, be unable to comply with their obligations or only be able to comply with substantial hardship, is a mandatory matter that the credit provider must account for.[149] This means that when inquiring into a consumer's financial situation, a credit provider is not required to inquire into all of the consumer's financial circumstances – specifically, the credit provider does not have to consider all declared living expenses.[150] Instead, they must only identify some minimum living expenses that cannot be foregone or reduced beyond a certain point.[151] Borrowing from the apt illustration of Perram J, one 'may eat Wagyu beef everyday washed down with the finest shiraz but, if [they] really want [their] new home, [they] can make do on much more modest fare'.[152]

Additionally, a consumer may request a copy of the preliminary assessment/assessment – as the case may be – setting out why the proposed contract is not unsuitable for them.[153] The introduction of the responsible lending obligation has been met with criticisms that the regime has resulted in overly cautious behaviour from credit licensees and excessively onerous prescriptions on consumers and borrowers looking to access credit, which in turn has affected the efficiency of the economy.[154] In 2020, the then Morrison Government introduced the National Consumer Credit Protection Amendment (Supporting Economic Recovery) Bill 2020 (Cth), which proposed a repeal of the responsible lending in efforts to accelerate Australia's post-pandemic economic recovery. It was submitted that removing the responsible lending obligation from most credit transactions[155] would

147 Ibid s 131(2). See also s 119(2) for the context of preliminary assessment.

148 *Australian Securities and Investments Commission v Westpac Banking Corporation* (2019) 139 ACSR 25, [62]–[70].

149 Ibid [70].

150 Ibid [71].

151 Ibid [76].

152 Ibid.

153 *NCCPA* (n 2) ss 120, 132.

154 Josh Frydenberg, 'Simplifying Access to Credit for Consumers and Small Business' (Media Release, 25 September 2020) <https://ministers.treasury.gov.au/ministers/josh-frydenberg-2018/media-releases/simplifying-access-credit-consumers-and-small>.

155 See National Consumer Credit Protection Amendment (Supporting Economic Recovery) Bill 2020 (Cth) sch 1, where it was proposed that the responsible lending duty applies only to small-amount credit contracts (SACC), small-amount credit contract-equivalent loans by ADIs, and consumer leases.

expedite consumers' access to credit, thus encouraging consumer spending and business investment required to improve the economy.[156]

The Bill faced backlash for attempting to diminish ASIC's regulatory role with respect to credit contracts and consumer protection – the repeal would prevent ASIC from enforcing credit licensee compliance with the *NCCPA* and other codes of conduct, such as the *Banking Code*.[157] Instead, the responsibility of individual consumer protection would fall to APRA, notwithstanding that such responsibilities were outside of its regulatory scope and functions.[158] As such, it was argued that the Bill operated unfairly to financially benefit major banks and lending institutions at the cost of insufficient consumer protection.[159] More recently, Assistant Treasurer and Minister for Financial Services Stephen Jones, in his address to the Responsible Lending and Borrowing Summit, made clear that the Labor Government has no intention to axe the responsible lending obligation, referring to 'low and no-doc loans' and the GFC.[160] Such a decision aligns with Commissioner Hayne's recommendation to maintain the obligation without any modifications.[161]

2.2.2.3 'Best interests' duty

The Banking Royal Commission put forward in its final report two recommendations concerning mortgage brokers.[162] In Recommendation 1.2, Commissioner Hayne suggested that 'the law should be amended to provide that, when acting in connection with home

156 Explanatory Memorandum, National Consumer Credit Protection Amendment (Supporting Economic Recovery) Bill 2020, ch 1, 1.6.

157 Senate Economics Legislation Committee, Parliament of Australia, *National Consumer Credit Protection Amendment (Supporting Economic Recovery) Bill 2020 [Provisions]* Dissenting Report from Labor Senators (2020) <https://parlinfo.aph.gov.au/parlInfo/download/committees/reportsen/024633/toc_pdf/NationalConsumerCreditProtectionAmendment(SupportingEconomicRecovery)Bill2020[Provisions].pdf;fileType=application%2Fpdf>; Senate Economics Legislation Committee, Parliament of Australia, *National Consumer Credit Protection Amendment (Supporting Economic Recovery) Bill 2020 [Provisions]* Dissenting Report from the Australian Greens <https://parlinfo.aph.gov.au/parlInfo/download/committees/reportsen/024633/toc_pdf/NationalConsumerCreditProtectionAmendment(SupportingEconomicRecovery)Bill2020[Provisions].pdf;fileType=application%2Fpdf>.

158 Ibid.

159 Ibid. See also Kevin Rudd, 'Under the Cover of Covid, Morrison Wants to Scrap My Government's Protections against Predatory Lending', *The Guardian* (5 October 2020) <https://www.theguardian.com/commentisfree/2020/oct/05/kevin-rudd-under-the-cover-of-covid-morrison-wants-to-scrap-my-governments-predatory-lending-protections>.

160 Stephen Jones, 'Address to the Responsible Lending and Borrowing Summit, Sydney' (Speech, 12 July 2022) <https://ministers.treasury.gov.au/ministers/stephen-jones-2022/speeches/address-responsible-lending-and-borrowing-summit-sydney>. (He made clear that 'our current responsible lending laws achieve an appropriate balance between facilitating access to credit and protecting consumers – particularly in the current environment of rising interest rates and costs of living.')

161 See *Royal Commission into Misconduct in the Banking, Superannuation and Financial Services Industry* (Final Report, 1 February 2019) vol 1 ('*Banking Royal Commission Final Report*'). Commissioner Hayne states in Recommendation 1.1: 'The NCCP Act should not be amended to alter the obligation to assess unsuitability.')

162 Since the 1990s, the mortgage broking sector in Australia has experienced substantial growth and heightened regulation. Mortgage brokers help consumers by suggesting loan products aligned with their needs, adhering to responsible lending obligations, and ensuring they are not unsuitable. In addition to facilitating loan negotiations, brokers handle necessary documentation. They market their expertise in understanding consumer requirements, presenting diverse options and providing support in the lending arena. The mortgage broking landscape is, as Paterson and Bant noted,

lending, mortgage brokers must act in the best interests of the intending borrower'.[163] Recommendation 1.3 further states that it should be 'the borrower, not the lender' who pays the 'mortgage broker a fee for acting in connection with home lending' and that legislative changes should be made to the way remuneration is paid to mortgage brokers. This gave rise to the passage of the *Financial Sector Reform (Hayne Royal Commission Response) Protecting Consumers (2019 Measures) Act 2020* (Cth), inserted as part of the *NCCPA*. As per the Replacement Explanatory Memorandum to the Financial Sector Reform (Hayne Royal Commission Response) Protecting Consumers (2019 Measures) Bill 2019, this legislative change is intended 'to improve consumer outcomes' by 'requiring mortgage brokers to act in the best interests of their clients' and by 'reducing the potential for conflicts of interests to impact the advice consumers receive from mortgage brokers'.[164]

Under the *NCCPA* ss 158LA and 158LE, mortgage brokers and credit representatives are required to act in the best interests of the consumer when offering credit assistance.[165] In contrast to responsible lending, the 'best interests' duty does not contain prescriptive steps that mortgage brokers must follow; rather, it is principles-based.[166] However, as with the responsible lending obligation, what is required to satisfy the duty depends on the individual consumer's circumstances. To comply with the obligation, mortgage brokers are likely to gather information about the consumer[167] and then use that information to assess what credit assistance would be in the consumer's best interests[168] and suggest options to the consumer.[169]

For example, there might be a scenario where a mortgage broker is assisting a consumer in the purchase of a new property and the consumer has expressed a preference for a home loan that the broker deems unsuitable (eg the consumer prefers a credit card package but, based on the consumer's past credit history, the broker suspects they might have difficulty paying it off). In such a scenario, ASIC would expect the broker to present the consumer with information explaining why their preferred home loan (credit card package) might be unsuitable for their needs, along with information on options that the

structured around three primary relationships: between the consumer and the broker, between the broker and the aggregator, and between the aggregator and the bank. Often, it is the aggregators who possess the credit licence, and under this licence, brokers function as credit representatives for the aggregator. The complexity of these relationships has, over the years, raised concerns such as fraud, conflicted remuneration structures and mismatch of consumer expectations. For a detailed analysis, see Jeannie Paterson and Elise Bant, 'Mortgage Broking, Regulatory Failure and Statutory Design' (2020) 31(1) *Journal of Banking and Finance Law and Practice* 7.

163 *Banking Royal Commission Final Report* (n 161) (Recommendations 1.2 and 1.3). Recommendation 1.3 states: 'The borrower, not the lender, should pay the mortgage broker a fee for acting in connection with home lending. Changes in brokers' remuneration should be made over a period of two or three years, by first prohibiting lenders from paying trail commission to mortgage brokers in respect of new loans, then prohibiting lenders from paying other commissions to mortgage brokers.'

164 Replacement Explanatory Memorandum to the Financial Sector Reform (Hayne Royal Commission Response) Protecting Consumers (2019 Measures) Bill 2019 (Cth) (Replacement Explanatory Memorandum) ('*Replacement Explanatory Memorandum to FSR*').

165 *NCCPA* (n 2) ss 158LA, 158LE.

166 Australian Securities and Investments Commission, *Mortgage Broker: Best Interests Duty* (Regulatory Guide 273, 24 June 2020) ('RG 273') [12].

167 Ibid [30]–[43].

168 Ibid [44]–[86].

169 Ibid [87]–[104].

broker considers are more appropriate to their circumstances (eg a home loan without a credit card package).[170]

To be clear, as ASIC explains, the 'best interests' duty and responsible lending obligation are distinct obligations under the *NCCPA*. 'The best interests obligations apply in addition to other laws – such as the responsible lending obligations – which affect the credit assistance that may be provided to consumers.'[171] There might be, indeed, some overlap in the process of collecting information for these duties. Data acquired to adhere to responsible lending requirements can aid in fulfilling the 'best interests' duty. Nevertheless, if further details are necessary to meet that duty, this information must be procured.[172] The ultimate goal of the responsible lending obligation is to determine if a credit product is 'not unsuitable' for a consumer; the 'best interests' duty, by contrast, 'appl[ies] more broadly to the credit assistance [mortgage brokers] provide, which extends to [mortgage brokers'] conduct and processes as well as the appropriateness of the credit product'.[173]

Closely associated with the 'best interests' duty, yet standing as a separate obligation, is the 'conflict priority rule'.[174] The *NCCPA* ss 158LB and 158LF outline that if the licensee knows, or ought to know, that there is a conflict of interest between the consumer and the licensee or the credit representative, the consumer's interests must take precedence.[175] This new duty, per the Replacement Explanatory Memorandum, mirrors s 961J of the *Corporations Act 2001* (Cth), which applies to financial advisers (discussed in Chapter 3).[176] Under this duty, mortgage brokers 'take active steps to identify all conflicts of interest covered by s 158LB to minimise the risk of a contravention, including obligations that can arise because of their commercial relationships with third parties'.[177] The amendment has also prescribed 'conflicted remuneration' restrictions upon mortgage brokers.[178] The term 'conflicted remuneration' is defined as:

> **(a)** any benefit, whether monetary or non-monetary, that:
>
> **(i)** is given to a licensee, or a representative of a licensee, who provides credit assistance to consumers; and
>
> **(ii)** because of the nature of the benefit or the circumstances in which it is given, could reasonably be expected to influence the credit assistance provided to consumers; or

170 Ibid [93].
171 Ibid [105]–[111].
172 Ibid [108].
173 Ibid [109].
174 Ibid [15]. ('The best interests duty and the conflict priority rule are separate obligations that operate alongside each other and apply each time a mortgage broker provides credit assistance.')
175 *NCCPA* (n 2) ss 158LA, 158LE.
176 *Replacement Explanatory Memorandum to FSR* (n 164) [3.28].
177 Ibid [3.29]. An example given by the Replacement Explanatory Memorandum is that if a mortgage broker has an affiliation with a real estate agent, making them an associate, they must recognise potential conflicts and ensure that the consumer's interests are placed above their own or that of the real estate agent.
178 Banking Royal Commission Recommendation 1.3. See also *NCCPA* (n 2) s 158NB (licensee must not accept conflicted remuneration); s 158NC (credit representative must not accept conflicted remuneration); s 158ND (employer must not give employees conflicted remuneration); s 158NE (credit provider must not give conflicted remuneration); s 158NF (mortgage intermediary must not give conflicted remuneration).

(b) any benefit, whether monetary or non-monetary, that:

  (i) is given to a licensee, or a representative of a licensee, who acts as an intermediary; and

  (ii) because of the nature of the benefit or the circumstances in which it is given, could reasonably be expected to influence whether the licensee or representative acts as an intermediary, or how the licensee or representative acts as an intermediary.[179]

A contravention of each obligation of this amended legislation is a civil penalty. Failure to act in the best interests of the consumer, for instance, could be subject to 5000 penalty units.[180]

2.2.3 Key features of the *NCC*

The *NCC* provides detailed rules about, primarily, the formation, content, performance and ending of credit contracts. Among others, this includes rules concerning 'pre-contractual disclosure; content obligations for credit contracts and related mortgages and guarantees; price regulation; unilateral and agreed changes to credit contracts; hardship variations; unjust transactions and unconscionable interest and charges; [and] ending and enforcement of credit contracts'. We consider some of these in greater detail below.

2.2.3.1 Pre-contractual disclosure

As discussed earlier, the *NCC* preserves the objectives of the *UCCC*, central to which is the notion of 'truth in lending' and the importance of disclosure. It follows that the *NCC* requires pre-contractual disclosure in order to ensure that credit providers disclose all relevant information to a prospective borrower, so that the borrower can make an informed decision prior to entering a contract. The *NCC* stipulates that, before a consumer signs a credit contract, they must be provided with a 'pre-contractual statement' and an 'information statement'.[181]

A 'pre-contractual statement' should encompass prescribed information, including the amount of credit, annual amount of credit, annual percentage rate or rates, method of calculation of interest charges, total amount of interest charges payable, amount and number of repayments, credit fees and charges, how changes affecting interest and credit fees and charges will be effected, default rates, enforcement expenses, any mortgage or guarantee, any commission paid by or to the credit provider, and any insurance financed by the contract.[182]

An 'information statement' should also be provided in a prescribed form, setting out the consumer's legal rights and responsibilities.[183] Under the *NCC*, documents must be legible and easily readable.[184]

179 *NCCPA* (n 2) s 158N
180 Ibid s 158LA.
181 *NCC* (n 48) s 16(1)(a)–(b).
182 Ibid s 17. Furthermore, any written document should have a font size of at least 10 points. *NCCPR* (n 99) reg 110.
183 *NCCPR* (n 99) form 5.
184 *NCC* (n 48) s 184(1), (2).

A consumer also has a right to receive notice of changes to the credit contract.[185] Depending on the type of change to the contract, notice must be provided to the consumer as follows. For changes to annual percentage rates, notice must be given on the same day either in writing or in a newspaper.[186] If there is a change in how interest is calculated, a change in credit fees/charges, or any other modification by the credit provider, a 10-day advance written notice is necessary.[187] However, if customer obligations are reduced, no notice is required.[188]

The *NCC* requires debtors to provide credit providers with notice if the debtor considers that they will be unable to meet their obligations under a credit contract.[189] This process begins when the debtor provides their credit provider with a 'hardship notice',[190] which can be conveyed orally or in writing. Case law suggests that the *NCC* s 72(1) authorises oral notices of hardship in the form of a conversation; however, the applicant must make explicit mention of 'hardship' for the notice to be valid.[191]

Upon receiving a hardship notice, the credit provider has the discretion within 21 days to request additional data from the debtor. This information should be pertinent to determining whether the debtor will be or is unable to meet their obligations, or to decide on how the contract might be adjusted.[192] However, these provisions do not place obligations on credit providers to change contracts in response to hardship notices; instead, the credit provider is able to approve or reject the application.[193]

If the credit provider declines to modify a credit contract after receiving a hardship notice, the debtor has the option to approach the court to alter the contract's terms.[194] After allowing relevant parties a fair chance to present their case, the court can either issue an order to modify the credit contract or decide against it. Notably, the court is restricted from ordering changes that would lower the total amount the debtor owes to the credit provider under the contract. A more frequently adopted approach is for the debtor to file a dispute with the appropriate EDR scheme – that is, the AFCA.

Section 76 of the *NCC* grants courts the authority to 'reopen' any credit transaction deemed unjust.[195] While the *NCC* does not specify what constitutes an 'unjust transaction', it emphasises that courts should consider both the broader public interest and the specific circumstances surrounding the case.

185 Ibid ss 64–66.
186 Ibid s 64(1)–(2).
187 Ibid s 64(4).
188 Ibid s 64(5).
189 Ibid s 72.
190 Ibid s 72(1).
191 *RHG Mortgage Corporation Ltd v Saunders* [2016] NSWSC 929, [23].
192 *NCC* (n 48) s 72(2).
193 Ibid, note to s 72(3).
194 Ibid s 74(2). ('The court may, after allowing the applicant, the credit provider and any guarantor a reasonable opportunity to be heard: (a) by order change the credit contract (*but not so as to reduce the amount ultimately payable by the debtor* to the credit provider under the contract) and make such other orders as it thinks fit; or (b) refuse to change the credit contract. (3) The court may, if it thinks it appropriate in the circumstances, stay any enforcement proceedings under the credit contract, and make such other orders as it thinks fit, until the application has been determined.') (Emphasis added.)
195 This stipulation draws inspiration from the *Contracts Review Act 1980* (NSW). See Paterson and Howell (n 3) 65.

More specifically, under s 76, a debtor, mortgagor or guarantor has the right to approach the court to revisit a credit contract, mortgage or guarantee and to argue its unjust nature.[196] When deciding whether to reopen an unjust credit transaction, the court evaluates a myriad of factors. These encompass the consequences of adhering to or deviating from the provisions of the contract, mortgage or guarantee; the relative negotiating power of the parties involved; the extent of any negotiations at the inception or alteration of the contract, mortgage or guarantee; the feasibility of the applicant changing or rejecting any terms of the deal; and whether certain provisions are excessively stringent or unnecessary in safeguarding the legitimate interests of a party.[197] Moreover, courts take into account the clarity of the contract, the adequacy of its explanations, any undue influence or pressure exerted on the debtor, and the precautions taken by the credit provider to ensure the debtor's understanding, along with the risks assumed by the credit provider, among other pertinent considerations.

It follows from the above that the courts are authorised to exercise discretion in deeming transactions unjust, and the definition will vary on a case-by-case basis. In one case, it was held that a lender's awareness of flooding affecting the appellants' bargaining position, as well as asset lending with alleged disregard of the appellants' likelihood of liquidation due to the knowledge that the lender will nevertheless be repaid in the event of default, was not 'unjust' for the purposes of the *NCC* s 76.[198] The Court held that, notwithstanding these claims, the appellant chose to advance the purchase of the land in spite of the continuous bad weather and financial delays; furthermore, the Court found the lender to be sufficiently prudent with the information provided to him – it had been the appellant's failure in disclosing relevant credit arrangements that affected the lender's conduct.[199]

A contract will not be unjust merely because one of the factors listed above is present. Mirroring this, a contract may be found unjust even though none of the above-listed factors is present.[200] The court merely needs to be satisfied that, considering the public interest and all the circumstances of the case,[201] at the time the relevant contract was entered into or was changed, it was unjust. Circumstances that are not reasonably foreseeable when the contract was entered into will not be considered.[202]

When a court considers reopening an unjust transaction, it has a variety of remedies at its disposal. For instance, it can reopen an account previously settled between the parties, revise or alter an associated agreement or mortgage, relieve the debtor and any guarantor from excessive payment, ensure the necessary steps are taken to discharge

196 *NCC* (n 48) s 76. ('The court may, if satisfied on the application of a debtor, mortgagor or guarantor that, in the circumstances relating to the relevant credit contract, mortgage or guarantee at the time it was entered into or changed (whether or not by agreement), the contract, mortgage or guarantee or change was unjust, reopen the transaction that gave rise to the contract, mortgage or guarantee or change.')

197 Ibid s 76(2).

198 *Paul Gooley v NSW Rural Assistance Authority* [2020] NSWCA 156, [37].

199 Ibid [38]. In the case, the relevant discussion of 'unconscionability' for the purposes of the *ASIC Act* s 12CB(1) was used to inform s 76(2) 'unjustness'.

200 *Barker v GE Mortgage Solutions Ltd* [2013] QCA 137, [64].

201 Ibid [71].

202 *NCC* (n 48) s 76(4).

a mortgage, or provide judgment in favour of a party based on what is justly due under the contract, mortgage or guarantee. These decisions are guided by the *NCC* s 77, which is designed to protect consumers from the repercussions of unjust transactions. The section is interpreted broadly and applied flexibly, and is primarily aimed at rectifying injustice rather than imposing penalties. Section 77 is intended to ensure that consumers are protected from the consequences resulting from unjust transactions and thus is to be construed broadly and applied flexibly.[203] Nevertheless, the purpose of s 77 is principally to remedy injustice and not to punish.[204] Therefore, the relief granted will not overly interfere with the rights of the parties beyond what is necessary to avoid unjust consequences or results.[205]

The *NCC* stipulates price regulations that vary depending on the type of product. Section 31A imposes restrictions on fees and charges for credit contracts involving small amounts. Such restrictions require that a small-amount credit contract (SACC)[206] must not impose or provide for fees and charges if the fees and charges are not: (a) a permitted establishment fee (of not more than 20 per cent of the adjusted credit amount – ie the first amount of credit provided);[207] (b) a fee or charge (a permitted monthly fee of not more than 4 per cent of the adjusted credit amount) that is payable on a monthly basis starting on the day the contract is entered into;[208] (c) a fee or charge that is payable in the event of a default in payment under the contract (of not more than 200 per cent of the adjusted credit amount);[209] or (d) a government fee, charge or duty payable in relation to the contract.[210]

However, providers of SACCs are not subject to the prohibition on entering into credit contracts that have an annual cost rate exceeding 48 per cent.[211] This prohibition applies to other credit providers that are not an authorised deposit-taking institution (ADI), such as medium-amount credit contracts.[212]

203 *Shannon v Permanent Custodians Ltd (No 3)* [2022] WASCA 112, [13].

204 Ibid [15].

205 When determining the appropriate relief, the court considers various considerations. These include the degree to which each party is responsible for the situation and how this responsibility should influence the remedial measures. The court also assesses how much the party seeking relief has gained from the transaction and if any benefits were undue. Additionally, the circumstances and positions of the parties before entering the transaction are evaluated. Ibid [16]–[18].

206 See *NCCPA* (n 2) s 5, which states: 'A credit contract is a small amount credit contract if: (a) the contract is not a continuing credit contract; and (b) the credit provider under the contract is not an ADI; and (c) the credit limit of the contract is $2,000 (or such other amount as is prescribed by the regulations) or less; and (d) the term of the contract is at least 16 days but not longer than 1 year (or such other number of years as is prescribed by the regulations); and (e) the debtor's obligations under the contract are not, and will not be, secured; and (f) the contract meets any other requirements prescribed by the regulations.' Historically, the introduction of national price regulation has sparked intense debate. Critics contended that the proposed price caps on products such as SACCs would render lending non-viable, prompting a departure of lenders from the market. They also argued that introducing responsible lending in 2009 made further price regulation redundant. This issue turns on the payday loan problem, as discussed further below. See Howell (n 41).

207 *NCC* (n 48) s 31A(2).

208 Ibid s 31A(3).

209 Ibid s 39B.

210 Ibid s 31A.

211 Ibid s 32A(1), (4).

212 Ibid s 204(1), which states: 'A credit contract is a medium amount credit contract if: (a) the contract is not a continuing credit contract; and (b) the credit provider under the contract is not an ADI; and

2.3 Challenges ahead

2.3.1 Payday loan: A perennial problem

Generally speaking, a payday loan is a short-term, small-amount loan, usually repaid when consumers receive their subsequent pay cheque within two to four weeks of acquiring the loan, and typically comes with a fixed service fee.[213] In Australia, a payday loan is offered through a SACC – a contract for unsecured credit of $2000 or less for a term of 16 days to a year, which must not be a continuing contract or be provided by an ADI, as noted briefly above.[214]

The inception of the payday lending phenomenon in Australia can be traced back to December 1998 in Queensland, when the first storefront dedicated to such lending opened.[215] Several other lenders soon followed suit and began their operations. Over the past 20 years, the payday lending market has witnessed swift expansion: in 2001 alone, an average of 12 800 payday loans were procured each month.[216] Estimating the exact scale of the payday lending industry is challenging, but around A$736 million worth of payday loans were documented in 2016.[217] Women, particularly those who are single parents, are notably over-represented among payday loan users, often resorting to such loans to meet their household expenses more than the broader populace. This inclination seems to be on the rise. The rapid digitisation of payday loan schemes has increased their accessibility and subsequently introduced far-reaching financial repercussions for

(c) the credit limit of the contract is: (i) at least $2,001 (or such other amount as is prescribed by the regulations); but (ii) not more than $5,000 (or such other amount as is prescribed by the regulations); and (d) the term of the contract is at least 16 days but not longer than 2 years (or such other number of years as is prescribed by the regulations); and (e) the contract meets any other requirements prescribed by the regulations.'

213 Sally Andersen, 'The Phenomenon of Payday Lending' (2013) 21(1) *Australian Journal of Competition and Consumer Law* 20. Because of its nature, payday loans reveal some of the features of predatory lending. Some studies have identified several major characteristics linked with predatory lending practices. Specifically, they include: (1) loans structured in ways that potentially inflict substantial net harm upon borrowers; (2) adverse rent-seeking behaviours; (3) loans tied to deceptive or fraudulent strategies; (4) other types of non-transparent loan dealings that might not be outright fraudulent; and (5) loans that demand borrowers to forgo their rights to significant legal action. Payday loans may not always exhibit all these characteristics; in many scenarios, they may only manifest one or two of these elements. See Kathleen C Engel and Patricia McCoy, 'A Tale of Three Markets: The Law and Economics of Predatory Lending' (2002) 80(6) *Texas Law Review* 1255, 1259; Donald P Morgan, *Defining and Detecting Predatory Lending* (Staff Report No 273, Federal Reserve Bank of New York, January 2007).

214 *NCCPA* (n 2) s 5. See Jasmine Ali and Marcus Banks, 'Into the Mainstream: The Australian Payday Loans Industry on the Move' (2014) (3) *JASSA: The Finsia Journal of Applied Finance* 35.

215 Dean Wilson, *Payday Lending in Victoria – A Research Report* (Consumer Law Centre Victoria, 2002) 34. Payday loans are not unique to Australia. In the United States, the payday loan industry emerged as a prevalent financial solution for borrowers in need of immediate funds in the 1990s. Originally, payday loans were provided via cheque-cashing stores and pawnshops.

216 Ali and Banks (n 214) 36.

217 Digital Finance Analytics, *The Costs of Inaction in Payday Lending* (Report, 18 June 2018) 3 <https://consumeraction.org.au/wp-content/uploads/2018/06/180605-DFA-PayDay-Impact-1.pdf>. ASIC's data shows consistent growth in the payday lending market. As of December 2014, it was reported that around 1136 credit licensees were active in the industry – see Australian Securities and Investment Commission, *Payday Lenders and the New Small Amount Lending Provisions* (Report No 426, March 2015) 4 <https://asic.gov.au/regulatory-resources/find-a-document/reports/rep-426-payday-lenders-and-the-new-small-amount-lending-provisions/>.

those Australian consumers who rely on them, with the existing regulatory framework struggling to contain its effects.[218]

This expansion in the payday lending arena can be traced back to elements such as financial deregulation, escalating household debt, and a surge in individuals with compromised credit scores.[219] As the banking sector became more deregulated, banks became more hesitant to lend to low-income consumers or those with poor credit histories.[220] As a result, these individuals often resort to alternative credit sources, typically at significantly higher rates compared to conventional consumer lending rates.

Payday loan schemes often attract consumers who are subject to financial exclusion by mainstream loan sources such as banks, who are reluctant to offer loans based on low income or poor credit scores. Thus, as a consequence, already financially vulnerable consumers are redirected into engaging in high-cost payday loan schemes and are more susceptible to 'debt spirals',[221] in which repeated use of payday loans results in continuous debt as more income is tied up in repaying loans instead of building credit to improve their living standard.[222] Such effects are not mere speculation: according to Digital Finance Analytics, over a five-year period, 15 per cent of payday lenders are likely to fall into a debt spiral, ultimately resulting in bankruptcy.[223]

Some commentators, such as Vivien Chen, have observed that the exponential growth in payday loan schemes is attributable to the aggressive, predatory marketing and misleading tactics used to advertise to potential consumers, despite the availability of more affordable debt management options.[224] Chen, for instance, argued that payday loan websites failed to display the 'risk of lending' warnings on their page as per the requirements under the *NCCPA* s 133CB, or they hid such warnings among more prominent images or text.[225] The websites had also exhibited a lack of transparency regarding repayment costs by making such statements inconspicuous,[226] by using terminology adopted by mainstream finance such as 'micro-loans' or 'cash advances',[227] by utilising altruistic language and misrepresenting such loans as the cheapest available option to consumers,[228] by expanding their online reach by posting blogs with financial tips

218 Digital Finance Analytics (n 217) 3, 40. (The report notes that the online payday lending segment has seen a significant surge, jumping from 4 per cent in 2008 to a whopping 75 per cent in 2017. One marketing strategy employed promises of quick approvals with electronic fund transfers to consumers, often within hours or a day.)

219 Wilson (n 215) 34–5.

220 When situated within a wider, international context, observations from the United States during the 1980s illustrate that banking deregulation, along with the abolition of interest-rate caps, spurred many traditional lenders to abandon the precarious small-loan sector, steering instead towards seeking more profitable, higher-value loans. See Kelly J Noyes, 'Get Cash Until Payday! The Payday Loan Problem in Wisconsin' (2006) (6) *Wisconsin Law Review* 1627, 1631.

221 Vivien Chen, 'Online Payday Lenders: Trusted Friends or Debt Traps?' (2020) 43(2) *University of New South Wales Law Journal* 678.

222 Ibid 678.

223 Digital Finance Analytics (n 217) 1.

224 Chen (n 221) 681.

225 Ibid 685.

226 Ibid 686.

227 Ibid.

228 Ibid 687. Crucially, as Chen (n 221) points out, payday lenders vary in how they disclose costs. She reports that four websites do not reveal fees, and two seem misleading. Some transparent lenders

targeted at financially vulnerable classes of consumers,[229] by promoting their services on social media platforms and review websites such as Instagram, X (formerly Twitter) and Trustpilot,[230] and by accessing consumers' internet banking details to obtain bank statements.[231] Such practices are in direct contravention of several laws and regulations concerning regulated activities, such as the *NCC*,[232] misleading and deceptive conduct as per the *ASIC Act*[233] and the *Privacy Act 1988* (Cth).[234]

Besides encouraging financial literacy and providing more financial information to consumers, as per Vivien Chen, stronger enforcement of existing regulations against misleading advertising needs to be put in place.[235] In fact, the ASIC has stepped up its enforcement actions in relation to misleading and deceptive advertising in recent years. For instance, in 2021, the Federal Court held that Mayfair Wealth Partners Pty Ltd had made statements that were misleading or deceptive in contravention of *ASIC Act* s 12DA(1) by representing that their promissory notes were of a similar risk profile to bank term deposits, when the notes exposed investors to significantly higher risks.[236]

Payday loan operations have faced extensive criticism. To address these concerns, the *NCCPA* and the *NCC* were revised in 2012 to bolster consumer protection. A pivotal and contentious part of the 2012 changes was the inception of national price regulation. Price regulation, as explained earlier, categorised credit products, instituting distinct price caps for each, including the SACC.

More recently, the Financial Sector Reform Bill 2022 (Cth) ('FSR Bill') has been passed by both Houses of Parliament and has received Royal Assent. The *Financial Sector Reform Act 2022* (Cth) ('*FSR Act*') caps total repayments on SACCs and consumer leases for household goods at 10 per cent of a user's net income, stopping consumers from entering into contracts or leases if the total repayments would exceed 10 per cent of their net income in the *NCCPR*.[237] In addition, several key changes are introduced to strengthen the protection of consumer leases, such as caps on indefinite and fixed-term consumer leases, which prohibit lessors from entering into or varying leases to exceed the imposed limits,[238] requiring

display clear tables or calculators with borrowing amounts, fees and repayment sums. But few embrace this level of clarity. Eight hide their fees subtly or use less noticeable fonts, and three sites make users click multiple links to view costs. By and large, borrowers must deduce the real cost of loans themselves, as many calculators do not provide full breakdowns of fees. Clear depictions of the total fee amount in dollar terms are rare. There is, moreover, inconsistency and opacity in displaying borrowing costs. For instance, a lender targeting those with poor credit does not detail small loan costs but lists home loan rates at around 5 per cent – misleadingly lower than typical payday loan rates, potentially giving a false impression of lower costs.

229 Ibid 688, 690.

230 Ibid 688.

231 Ibid 689, 705.

232 For example, lack of transparency regarding loan fees is in breach of the *NCC* s 31A.

233 *Australian Securities and Investments Commission Act 2001* (Cth) ('*ASIC Act*') ss 12CB, 12DB.

234 By requesting Internet banking usernames and passcodes, payday loan schemes may be in contravention of the Australian Privacy Principles 3.2 and 3.5.

235 Chen (n 221) 694.

236 *Australian Securities and Investments Commission v Mayfair Wealth Partners Pty Ltd (No 2)* [2021] FCA 247, [1].

237 *Financial Sector Reform Act 2022* (Cth) ('*FSR Act*') sch 4 items 12 and 26; see also *NCCPR* (n 99) regs 28LCA, 28LCB.

238 *FSR Act* (n 237) sch 4 item 50; see also *NCC* (n 48) s 175AA.

lessors and brokers to consider consumers' information for 90 days before entering into consumer leases with them,[239] and making transparent disclosures regarding the base price of goods under consumer leases.[240]

The *FSR Act* also imposes stronger regulations on SACCs, thus enhancing consumer protection. The most significant of the changes is that lenders will be prohibited from making unsolicited communications to consumers who have ever applied for or borrowed money under a SACC (and the lender ought to have known this). This prohibition effectively prevents lenders such as payday lenders from inviting existing SACC borrowers to take out further credit after entering a SACC loan.[241]

General advertising is still allowed. Yet, limits are placed on payday lenders specifically targeting consumers. Among other changes that ensure transparent and fair repayment practices, providers of SACCs are also required to enhance warning statements per the ASIC guidelines.[242]

Consumer advocacy groups welcomed the introduction of the FSR Bill, as it enhances 'long overdue consumer protections for high-cost payday loans and consumer leases'.[243] However, SACC lenders criticised some provisions in the Bill for being overly restrictive. In its submission, the National Credit Providers Association (NCPA) criticised the reduction of the cap on the total amount of all SACC repayments to 10 per cent of the consumer's net income, as it is a regulatory overreach by taking away a consumer's right to personal choice.[244] The NCPA also submits that this reduction will have several unintended consequences of making the loan more expensive given that extending the loan term is the only way to reduce the repayments.[245]

2.3.2 The rise of 'buy now, pay later'

In recent years, buy-now-pay-later (BNPL) services have risen in popularity as a convenient alternative to traditional credit forms. BNPL providers typically provide consumers with immediate interest-free credit, which they can use to pay for purchases of goods and services, and then collect repayments from these consumers in instalments.[246] Australia's BNPL industry has over six million active accounts, representing up to 30 per cent of the Australian adult population, which resulted in transaction valued at A$5.6 million in 2018–19.[247] Notably, Australia's biggest BNPL companies – Afterpay, Certegy and ZipMoney Payments – account for 96 per cent of that total.[248]

239 *FSR Act* (n 237) sch 4 item 22; see also *NCCPA* (n 2) s 140(1A).
240 *FSR Act* (n 237) sch 4 item 49; see also *NCC* (n 48) s 174(1A).
241 *FSR Act* (n 237) sch 4 item 14; see also *NCCPA* (n 2) s 133CF.
242 *FSR Act* (n 237) sch 4 item 6; see also *NCCPA* (n 2) s 124B.
243 Financial Counselling Australia, 'Bill to Crack Down on Payday Lending and Consumer Leases Welcomed by Consumer Advocates' (Media Release, 9 September 2022).
244 NCPA, Submission No 33 to Senate Standing Committees on Economics, *Inquiry into the National Consumer Credit Protection Amendment (Small Amount Credit Contract and Consumer Lease Reforms) Bill 2019 (No 2)* (February 2020) 13.
245 Ibid 8.
246 The Treasury, *Regulating Buy Now, Pay Later in Australia* (Options Paper, November 2022) ('Treasury, *2022 Options Paper on BNPL*') 7.
247 Australian Securities and Investment Commission, *Buy Now Pay Later: An Industry Update* (Report 672, November 2020) 3, 7.
248 Ibid 7.

This significant growth of the BNPL industry has led to growing calls to regulate BNPL services, as BNPL products are not regulated under the *NCCPA*; they generally fall under the exemptions available to some types of credit in the *NCC* – notably, the 'short-term credit' exemption under the *NCC* s 6.[249] Therefore, BNPL products that operate within these exemptions are not subject to the requirements of the *NCCPA*, such as the responsible lending obligations, and BNPL providers do not need to hold an ACL.[250]

In response to this regulatory gap, there has been heated debate among various stakeholders on the future regulatory framework for BNPL products. Currently, BNPL products are subject to ASIC's product intervention power under the *Corporations Act 2001* (Cth) s 1023D.[251] The use of tailored BNPL legislation has been proposed by Australia's biggest BNPL company, Afterpay, but some commentators argue that an *NCCPA* regulation is preferable given that issues relating to BNPL risks require direct intervention as supplied by the *NCCPA*.[252]

In its options paper published in November 2022, the Treasury set out three alternatives for a new regulatory framework for BNPL with varying degrees of intervention.[253] The first option proposes strengthening the *BNPL Industry Code* and supplementing it with an affordability test under the *NCCPA*.[254] The second option involves limited BNPL regulation under the *NCCPA*, including the requirement for BNPL providers to hold an ACL and a scalable unsuitability test.[255] The third option proposes the regulation of BNPL under the *NCCPA* such that BNPL products are treated similarly to other credit products.[256]

Importantly, in May 2023, Assistant Treasurer and Minister for Financial Services Stephen Jones announced that BNPL products would be regulated as credit products and be enforced by ASIC.[257] The announcement specified that the government would implement the second option presented by the Treasury, as discussed above, and that a Bill would be introduced into Parliament by the end of 2023.[258] This should put Australia behind only the

249 Treasury, *2022 Options Paper on BNPL* (n 246) 4. See also the 'short term credit' exemption in the *NCC* s 6, which states that the NCC 'does not apply to the provision of credit if, under the contract: (a) the provision of credit is limited to a total period that does not exceed 62 days, (b) the maximum amount of credit fees and charges that may be imposed or provided for does not exceed 5% of the amount of credit, and (c) the maximum amount of interest charges that may be imposed or provided for does not exceed an amount (calculated as if the Code applied to the contract) equal to the amount payable if the annual percentage rate were 24% per annum'.

250 Ibid.

251 Australian Securities and Investments Commission, *Regulating Buy Now, Pay Later in Australia: Submission by the Australian Securities and Investments Commission* (January 2023) 7, 22, 34. (Generally, this intervention power allows ASIC to make certain orders if it is satisfied that a credit product has resulted in, or will or is likely to result in, significant detriment to consumers.)

252 afterpaytouch, Submission No 26 to Senate Economics Reference Committee, *Credit and Financial Services Targeted at Australians at Risk of Financial Hardship* (November 2018) 23–4; Daniel Beratis, 'Regulating Buy-Now, Pay-Later Products under the *National Consumer Credit Protection Act 2009* (Cth)' (2023) 33(3) *Journal of Banking and Finance Law and Practice* 107, 132.

253 Treasury, *2022 Options Paper on BNPL* (n 246).

254 Ibid 20.

255 Ibid 21.

256 Ibid 22.

257 Jones (n 160).

258 Ibid.

United Kingdom among countries that have sought to regulate BNPL as credit products.[259] However, the legislative drafting process experienced delays by the Government, resulting in the absence of a draft Bill for Parliament as of February 2024.[260] Consequently, Australia will lag behind New Zealand, which is implementing the *Credit Contracts and Consumer Finance (Buy Now, Pay Later) Amendment Regulations 2023* (NZ), set to be enforced from 2 September 2024.[261] In its final report released in January 2024, the ALRC suggested that implementing the recommendations could help address BNPL issues.[262]

2.4 Summary

In this chapter, we examine the *NCCPA* and the *NCC* and outline the licensing requirements for credit providers and credit assistance providers. ASIC oversees licensing, disclosure and responsible lending requirements, among others. A role for intermediaries and credit assistance providers is highlighted, and licensing exemptions, general conduct obligations of an ACL holder, and responsible lending obligations are explained using case law examples. Following the Banking Royal Commission recommendations, the 'best interests' duty has been introduced to mandate credit assistance providers to prioritise consumer interests, distinguishing it from the responsible lending obligation. Additionally, this chapter discusses proposed legislation to repeal responsible lending obligations for post-pandemic economic recovery, which, amid criticism, has not yet been passed. A hardship variation mechanism for debtors in financial distress is discussed, as well as key *NCC* features governing credit contract dynamics. In addition, the chapter identifies price regulations on various credit products, notably capping fees and charges on small-amount credit contracts to protect consumers from exorbitant fees and costs. Finally, the chapter examines the payday loan landscape in Australia, emphasising the financial vulnerability it poses, especially to certain groups of consumers. It briefly evaluates regulatory initiatives, including the *Financial Sector Reform Act 2022* (Cth), which targets repayment caps and enhanced consumer protection despite opposition

259 Byron Kaye and Renju Jose, 'Australia Hits Buy-Now-Pay-Later Sector with Consumer Credit Law', *Reuters* (22 May 2023) <https://www.reuters.com/technology/australia-regulate-buy-now-pay-later-sector-2023-05-21/>; HM Treasury, *Regulation of Buy-Now Pay-Later: Consultation on Draft Legislation* (February 2023) 1.4. (On 2 February 2021, the UK Government announced its intention to regulate BNPL and in February 2023, the Treasury published its draft regulation on the regulation of BNPL lending.)

260 James Eyers, 'BNPL Laws Delayed until New Year Amid Legislative Drafting Constraints', *Financial Review* (online, 27 November 2023 <https://www.afr.com/companies/financial-services/bnpl-laws-delayed-until-new-year-amid-legislative-drafting-constraints-20231124-p5emmy>.

261 *Credit Contracts and Consumer Finance (Buy Now, Pay Later) Amendment Regulations 2023* (NZ) cl 2.

262 ALRC Final Report (n 10) [9.61]: 'ALRC's recommendations may be applied to credit legislation to make it more adaptive and therefore amenable to policy change. For example, BNPL arrangements are a diverse and evolving area, so it may prove challenging to insert a definition of BNPL arrangements to bring them within the scope of the NCCP Act. A definition that is too narrow and detailed may be unsuitable, causing evolving BNPL service providers to fall outside of the NCCP Act. A wide definition would allow flexibility, but if exclusions and exemptions were to be introduced without a coherent legislative hierarchy, then unnecessary complexity may accrue over time. This is where the ALRC's recommended legislative model could provide the requisite flexibility while minimising unnecessary legislative complexity.'

from payday lending organisations. BNPL is a burgeoning issue whose regulatory lacunas are examined, along with proposed consumer protection frameworks and the Australian Government's shift towards recognising BNPL products as credit products, in order to create a consumer-protective credit environment.

FURTHER READING

Australian Securities and Investments Commission, *Buy Now Pay Later: An Industry Update* (REP 672, November 2020).

Australian Securities and Investments Commission, *Regulating Buy Now, Pay Later in Australia: Submission by the Australian Securities and Investments Commission* (January 2023).

Beratis, Daniel, 'Regulating Buy-Now, Pay-Later Products under the *National Consumer Credit Protection Act 2009* (Cth)' (2023) 33(3) *Journal of Banking and Finance Law and Practice* 107.

Brown, Christine Ann, Kevin Davis and David Mayes, 'Regulatory Change in Australia and New Zealand Following the Global Financial Crisis' (2015) 7(11) *Journal and Financial Economic Policy* 8.

Chen, Vivien, 'Online Payday Lenders: Trusted Friends or Debt Traps?' (2020) 43(2) *University of New South Wales Law Journal* 674.

Howell, Nicola J, 'Revisiting the Australian Code of Banking Practice: Is Self-Regulation Still Relevant for Improving Consumer Protection Standards?' (2015) 38(2) *University of New South Wales Law Journal* 544, 557–62.

Howell, Nicola J, 'Small Amount Credit Contracts and Payday Loans: The Complementarity of Price Regulation and Responsible Lending Regulation' (2016) 41(3) *Alternative Law Journal* 174.

O'Brien, Lucinda, Ian Ramsay and Paul Ali, 'Innovation, Disruption and Consumer Harm in the Buy Now Pay Later Industry: An Empirical Study' (2024) 47(2) *University of New South Wales Law Journal* (forthcoming).

Paterson, Jeannie and Elise Bant, 'Mortgage Broking, Regulatory Failure and Statutory Design' (2020) 31(7) *Journal of Banking and Finance Law and Practice* 7.

Paterson, Jeannie and Nicola Howell, *Everyday Consumer Credit: Overview of Australian Law Regulating Consumer Home Loans, Credit Cards and Car Loans* (Background Paper 4, Royal Commission into Misconduct in the Banking, Superannuation and Financial Services Industry, 2018).

Pearson, Gail, 'Reading Suitability Against Fitness for Purpose – The Evolution of a Rule' (2010) 32(2) *Sydney Law Review* 311.

Ramsay, Iain, 'From Truth in Lending to Responsible Lending' in Geraint Howells, André Janssen and Reiner Schulze (eds), *Information Rights and Obligations* (Ashgate, 2005) 47.

The Treasury, *Regulating Buy Now, Pay Later in Australia* (Options Paper, November 2022) <https://treasury.gov.au/sites/default/files/2022-11/c2022-338372-op.pdf>.

The Treasury, *Review of the Small Amount of Credit Contract Laws* (Final Report, March 2016) <https://treasury.gov.au/sites/default/files/2019-03/C2016-016_SACC-Final-Report.pdf>.

QUESTIONS

(1) Edward, who owns a winery, is planning on acquiring a new plot of land in the countryside to serve as an additional vineyard to supply his winery business. To do this, he took a $1 million loan from a licensed moneylender. In the loan agreement, the purpose of the loan is stipulated as 'to be used for the acquisition and development

of a plot of land for the production of wine'. However, when he inspected the land later, Edward learnt that it included a villa. He planned to refurbish and renovate the building so that he and his family could stay there during the children's school holidays. These renovations were partially financed by the loan. When the COVID pandemic hit, Edward received a call from the moneylender, who stated that the annual interest rate on his loan would be increased from 15 per cent to 33 per cent, in light of the 'change in global circumstances'. Edward was shocked, even though he knew that the interest rate was subject to variations as determined by the moneylender. Advise Edward.

(2) Kevin owns a very successful personal fitness training business, HealthyLife. He is keen to buy a large apartment. To secure a loan of $500 000, Kevin had a meeting in June 2019 with his best high-school mate, Gary, now a senior loan officer at Mega Bank.

(a) During the meeting, Gary gave Kevin a document called 'Mega's Pre-Contractual Disclosure'. Kevin noticed that some information was missing from the document (eg it didn't specify when loan repayments should be made, and the interest rate wasn't set out clearly), but he didn't mention this to Gary.

(b) Gary asked Kevin a few simple questions about the purpose of the loan and his financial position. Kevin said he planned to use $400 000 to purchase an apartment in the Melbourne CBD. He would use the remaining $100 000 to buy furniture and new equipment to expand his fitness business. He told Gary that he would provide more information upon request, but Gary didn't bother to ask for anything more. He was already satisfied with the information Kevin had given him and took him out for dinner. Not long after the contract was signed, Kevin's business declined dramatically due to the COVID pandemic. He sold his luxury cars to make several of the loan repayments and stopped eating out at expensive restaurants. Later, as the pandemic continued and his business declined further, he found it a challenge just to meet his essential daily needs. Eventually, Kevin defaulted on his loan in June 2021. Please advise Cindy, a junior compliance officer with Mega Bank, about the breach of the *NCCPA* in this case.

(3) Kevin was frustrated with the failure of his business and with the fact that he had entered into a loan agreement that was unsuitable for him. He approached his college friend, Harvey, a solicitor who specialises in banking and financial regulations, for advice. Harvey mentioned the hardship variation and unjust transactions under the *NCC*, but he was too busy to give Kevin more details. Help Kevin by discussing whether these two options might be applicable.

CHAPTER 3

FINANCIAL PRODUCTS REGULATION

3.1 Introduction

In Australia, the regulatory oversight of credit and financial products is primarily vested at the federal level. As discussed in Chapter 2, credit products are regulated by the *National Consumer Credit Protection Act 2009* (Cth) (the '*NCCPA*'). This Act replaced the prior state-based system, notably the *Uniform Consumer Credit Code*. In this chapter, we aim to expound upon the regulatory architecture governing financial products, chiefly regulated under ch 7 of the *Corporations Act 2001* (Cth) ('*Corporations Act*'). It is paramount to acknowledge that additional regulations, regulatory guides and sector-specific codes are crucial to the comprehensive Australian regulatory matrix concerning financial affairs. Before embarking on a detailed analysis, a brief overview of the historical context leading to the present regulatory system for financial products in Australia is warranted. Pivotal moments in this narrative are the Wallis Inquiry, the Murray Inquiry and, more recently, the Banking Royal Commission, which largely shaped financial regulation as it is today. With this foundational understanding established, we will then turn our focus to the requisite licensing conditions and the salient duties incumbent upon licensees. The most recently introduced product design and distribution obligations and product intervention orders will also be discussed.

3.1.1 The Wallis Inquiry

In 1996, the Commonwealth Government Treasurer, Peter Costello, initiated the Wallis Inquiry. Under its terms of reference, the task of the Wallis Inquiry was to examine the effects of the deregulation of the Australian financial system since the early 1980s and to analyse the forces driving further change, with a focus on technological development.[1] The terms of reference also required the Wallis Inquiry to recommend regulatory arrangements that would 'best ensure an efficient, responsive, competitive and flexible financial system to underpin stronger economic performance, consistent with financial stability, prudence, integrity and fairness'.[2] The Wallis Inquiry produced a number of recommendations that subsequently catalysed the promulgation of multiple legislative enactments.

In 1997, the Commonwealth Government initiated the Corporate Law Economic Reform Program (CLERP) with the aim of reforming corporations legislation. The objectives were to promote 'business and market activity leading to important economic outcomes including increased employment, by enhancing market efficiency and integrity and investor confidence. Corporate regulation will be revamped to provide a clear and consistent framework which reflects the contemporary business [environment] and encourages businesses to create wealth, prosperity, and jobs.'[3] These principles were the same as those underlying the Wallis Inquiry, and the reforms from the CLERP resulted

1 *Financial System Inquiry: Final Report* (AGPS, 1 March 1997) app A ('Wallis Inquiry') <https://treasury.gov.au/sites/default/files/2019-03/23-fsi-fr-appenda.pdf>.
2 Ibid 707.
3 'Corporate law Economic Reform Program – Policy Framework', *The Treasury* (Web Page, 1 May 1998) <https://treasury.gov.au/publication/clerp-policy-framework/corporate-law-economic-reform-program-policy-framework>.

in the enactment of the *Financial Services Reform Act 2001* (Cth).[4] The Australian Financial Services Licence (AFSL) was introduced under that Act and in conjunction with significant amendments to the *Corporations Act*. Individuals or entities that hold such a licence will henceforth be addressed herein as 'AFS licensees' or 'AFSL holders'.

Under the *Corporations Act* s 911A, an AFSL is generally required if a person 'carries on a financial services business' in Australia.[5] The terms 'financial services business' and 'financial services' are defined in the *Corporations Act*, as explained further below. More specifically, an AFSL is granted under s 913B, which 'authorises a person who carries on a financial services business to provide financial services'.[6] Section 913B will be discussed further below.[7]

3.1.2 The Murray Inquiry

On 20 December 2013, 17 years after the Wallis Inquiry in 1996, the Murray Inquiry into Australia's financial system was announced by the Commonwealth Government Treasurer, Joe Hockey.[8] The Murray Inquiry aimed to provide insights into how to adapt the regulatory framework that was based on the recommendations of the Wallis Inquiry to the significant changes that had occurred in the domestic and global financial environment.[9] The Murray Inquiry offered a range of suggestions to enhance the efficiency, resilience and fairness of Australia's financial system. In the process, it pinpointed two major areas for improvement: financing of the Australian economy and the fostering of competition.[10]

The Murray Inquiry recommended narrowing the scope of the AFSL regime by limiting the requirement for an AFSL to service providers of 'large, widely used payment systems', instead of the then current approach of implementing various exceptions for small payment systems.[11] This change would increase the simplicity and clarity of the current retail payments system regulation. Another recommendation by the Inquiry was to implement an industry funding model for the Australian Securities and Investments Commission (ASIC) to strengthen its enforcement of the current AFSL regime, such as its AFSL licensing powers.[12] For example, there should be a requirement to gain approval from ASIC in the event of a change in ownership or control of licensees.[13] ASIC should also have the power to consider 'previous conduct in other businesses' for the purposes of determining whether to grant a licence to an applicant and to impose conditions on firms that had engaged in systemic misconduct.[14]

4 Department of Parliamentary Services (Cth), *Bills Digest* (Digest No 26 of 2001–02, 21 August 2001) 2–3.
5 *Corporations Act 2001* (Cth) ('*Corporations Act*') s 911A.
6 Ibid s 761A. ('"Australian financial services licence" means a licence under s 913B that authorises a person who carries on a financial services business to provide financial services.')
7 Ibid s 913B.
8 The Treasury, *Financial System Inquiry: Final Report* (November 2014) ('Murray Inquiry') vii <https://treasury.gov.au/sites/default/files/2019-03/p2014-FSI-01Final-Report.pdf>.
9 Nicholas Simoes da Silva and Dr William Isdale, 'Risk and Reform in Australian Financial Services Law' (2022) 96(6) *Australian Law Journal* 408, 420.
10 Murray Inquiry (n 8) vii.
11 Ibid 161.
12 Ibid 250.
13 Ibid.
14 Ibid.

In short, financial services regulation in Australia, as Gail Pearson noted, has two primary goals: to create informed, risk-taking citizens and an efficient, innovative market that benefits everyone.[15] The focus is thus on empowering consumers to make informed decisions through strategies such as risk disclosure and financial literacy. This is reflected in ch 7 of the *Corporations Act*, which standardises the rules across various financial activities via product-neutral regulation. This not only simplifies compliance for providers, who all need an AFSL, but also fosters market efficiency and innovation.

3.1.3 Emerging reforms: Australian Law Reform Commission's recommendations

Notwithstanding various reforms, the current framework governing Australia's financial services industry was found by the Australian Law Reform Commission (ALRC) to be 'unnecessarily complex' and 'no longer for purpose'.[16] The ALRC's findings echo those made by Commissioner Kenneth Hayne, underscoring that 'fundamental norms of behaviour are unclear, and the law should be simplified so that its intent can be met'.[17] In its Final Report, titled *Confronting Complexity: Reforming Corporations and Financial Services Legislation* and released on 18 January 2024, the ALRC presented 58 recommendations, aiming at 'transforming corporations and financial services legislation from what one judge has described as "porridge," to a more adaptive, efficient, and navigable legislative framework'.[18]

This initiative stems from a detailed analysis aiming for legislative simplification, with 23 of these recommendations previously highlighted in Interim Reports A, B and C, and 13 already enacted into law by 1 October 2023.[19] Central to the report's proposals is the transformation of the current legal structure into a 'Financial Services Law' within the *Corporations Act*'s sch 1.[20]

15 See generally Gail Pearson, *Financial Services Law and Compliance in Australia* (Cambridge University Press, 2012) 7–9.

16 Australian Law Reform Commission (ALRC), *Confronting Complexity: Reforming Corporations and Financial Services Legislation* (Final Report No 141, November 2023) [2.1]–[2.2] ('*Confronting Complexity*') <https://www.alrc.gov.au/wp-content/uploads/2024/01/ALRC-FSL-Final-Report-141.pdf>.

17 Ibid.

18 Ibid [2.30] (citing Justiçe Rares, who, in *Wingecarribee Shire Council v Lehman Brothers Australia Ltd (in liq)* (2012) 301 ALR 1 ['*Wingecarribee*'], referred to the complexity as 'labyrinth' and 'legislative porridge'). See also *Wingecarribee* [948].

19 *Confronting Complexity* (n 16) [1.17]–[1.18].

20 See generally *Confronting Complexity* (n 16) [5.66]–[5.74], Recommendations 41–2. For some, the idea of integrating financial services–related provisions within a schedule to the *Corporations Act* is appealing. They believe it would establish a 'prominent home' for the Financial Services Law, thus amplifying its identity, broadening awareness, and bolstering its ability to communicate its principles effectively. Others, such as Professor Marina Nehme, cautioned that situating the legislation in a schedule might create a perception among industry and market participants of the laws being considered secondary due to their placement at the end of the *Corporations Act* – see *Confronting Complexity* (n 16) [5.71]. Thus, an ideal option would be the creation of a standalone financial services Act. The ALRC recommends that the envisaged Financial Services Law should be enacted within the *Corporations Act* sch 1.

The reform aims to streamline the definitions of 'financial product' and 'financial service',[21] tackle the complexities of delegated legislation, and unify offence and penalty regulations to clarify the repercussions of breaches. This envisaged 'Financial Services Law' framework is structured to include primary legislation,[22] a Scoping Order for defining its scope, and thematic rulebooks that provide detailed guidance for compliance.[23] Among others,[24] the ALRC identified four major reform pillars: consumer protection,[25] disclosure,[26] financial advice[27] and general regulatory obligations.[28] The first three pillars aim to simplify areas for substantial benefits, while the fourth pillar reforms the Australian financial services licensing regime's general regulatory obligations.[29]

The next steps depend on the Government's review of the Final Report's recommendations. The ALRC suggests a phased implementation, considering stakeholder feedback on the need for the industry to prepare adequately for legal modifications. The Government must also assess how these changes would align with other reforms, such as the Quality of Advice Review and updates to the regulatory framework for managed investment schemes, including legislation affecting foreign financial services providers.

21 The complexity of the current regime can be seen by reference to the broader definition of the terms 'financial product' and 'financial service' as compared to the ones under the *Corporations Act* ch 7. On the proposed reforms around 'financial product' and 'financial service', see *Confronting Complexity* (n 16) [5.14]–[5.40], Recommendations 31–2.

22 *Confronting Complexity* (n 16) Recommendations 41–2.

23 Given that the present 'legislative hierarchy of *Corporations Act* ch 7 is neither principled nor coherent', the ALRC suggests a major reform of the legislative hierarchy, as outlined under Recommendation 43. This model advocates for a 'vertical' structuring of legislation in the reformed framework, aimed at providing a clear and logical placement for various aspects of the regulatory regime. It proposed a staged amendment to introduce primary legislation (which includes key obligations and prohibitions enacted directly by Parliament, ensuring that fundamental regulatory principles are established at the highest legislative level), a Scoping Order (which is a single, consolidated legislative instrument designed to handle inclusions, exclusions, class exemptions, and other details vital for defining the scope of the primary legislation), and thematic rulebooks (which are consolidated legislative instruments containing specific rules that operationalise the primary legislation across different regulatory contexts, tailored to the unique needs of each area). See, eg, *Corporations Act* (n 5) [6.4]–[6.15], Recommendation 43.

24 *Confronting Complexity* (n 16) [7.55]–[7.74]. In addition to these four pillars, there are another two. Pillars Five (Miscellaneous) and Six (Policy-evolving provisions) aim to refine and evolve the *Corporations Act's* framework. Pillar Five addresses reforms not covered by other pillars, focusing on specific provisions requiring further consideration, such as advertising and cooling-off rules. Its scope is flexible, determined by the extent of reforms in other areas. Pillar Six emphasises applying legislative models and design principles for new policies, ensuring reforms remain dynamic and responsive. These pillars highlight the importance of adaptable and thematic legislative approaches in financial regulation reform.

25 *Confronting Complexity* (n 16) Recommendation 33. This pillar also enforces the above-mentioned Recommendation 31 by adopting a unified and simplified definition for both 'financial product' and 'financial service', in addition to implementing Recommendation 32 concerning provisions for consumer protection.

26 This pillar underscores streamlining the disclosure requirements for financial products and services as delineated in *Corporations Act* ch 7, aligning with the ALRC's Recommendation 36. It aims to simplify the extensive and complex disclosure regulations, particularly in pts 7.7 and 7.9, which involve numerous ASIC legislative instruments and a significant portion of ch 7's text and regulations. Reforming these disclosure provisions can create substantial legal clarity and reduce complexity for regulated entities, consumers and the government. *Confronting Complexity* (n 16) Recommendation 36.

27 *Confronting Complexity* (n 16) Recommendation 38.

28 Ibid Recommendations 39–40.

29 Ibid [7.10].

Implementing these recommendations will profoundly transform Australia's regulatory landscape for financial services. Expected consultations on legislative changes suggest an era of dynamic reform and stakeholder engagement. Reflecting on the philosophical evolution within Australia's financial services over recent years underscores the significance of these developments. Consequently, while this book captures the present legal structure, one should prepare for forthcoming revisions. With this context in mind, we proceed to examine the definitions of financial services and financial products as outlined in the *Corporations Act.*

3.2 Regulatory framework

3.2.1 Financial services

The *Corporations Act* defines 'financial services business' as the 'business of providing financial services'.[30] 'Financial service' is defined in div 4 of the same Act, which forms a core part of Australia's 'financial services law',[31] with ch 7 playing a pivotal role in overseeing 'financial services'.[32] According to s 766A of the Act, a person provides a 'financial service' if they:[33]

(a) provide financial product advice [see s 766B]; or
(b) deal in a financial product [see s 766C]; or
(c) make a market for a financial product [see s 766D]; or
(d) operate a registered scheme; or
(da) operate the business and conduct the affairs of a CCIV [corporate collective investment vehicle]; or
(e) provide a custodial or depository service [see s 766E]; or
(ea) provide a crowd-funding service [see s 766F]; or
(eb) provide a claims handling and settling service [see s 766G]; or
(ec) provide a superannuation trustee service [see s 766H]; or
(f) engage in conduct of a kind prescribed by regulations made for the purposes of this paragraph.

The term 'dealing' in relation to financial products is expansive, encompassing a wide range of activities. These activities include not only issuing, applying for, acquiring and

30 *Corporations Act* (n 5) s 761A.
31 Ibid. The term 'financial services law' is defined under s 761A to mean: '(a) a provision of this Chapter or of Chapter 5C, 5D, 6, 6A, 6B, 6C, 6D, 8A or 8B; or (b) a provision of Chapter 9 as it applies in relation to a provision referred to in paragraph (a); or (ba) a provision of the Passport Rules for this jurisdiction; or (c) a provision of Division 2 of Part 2 of the ASIC Act; or (d) any other Commonwealth, State or Territory legislation that covers conduct relating to the provision of financial services (whether or not it also covers other conduct), but only in so far as it covers conduct relating to the provision of financial services; or (e) in relation to a financial services licensee that is a licensed trustee company (in addition to paragraphs (a) to (d)) – any rule of common law or equity that covers conduct relating to the provision of financial services that are traditional trustee company services (whether or not it also covers other conduct), but only in so far as it covers conduct relating to the provision of such services'.)
32 Ibid ch 7.
33 Ibid s 766A(1).

varying a financial product but also disposing of it.[34] When it comes to securities or interests in managed investment schemes, the definition extends to include underwriting those securities or interests.[35] Moreover, if a person arranges for another individual to engage in any of these activities, that person is also considered to be 'dealing' in the financial product; this does not apply if the person's activities are more appropriately categorised as providing financial product advice rather than dealing.[36]

In s 766A(1)(d), 'registered schemes' refers to managed investment schemes, which are outlined in s 9 of the Act. Managed investment schemes are characterised as a scheme where people contribute money to acquire rights to or interests in benefits produced by the scheme.[37] Within such schemes, any of the contributions are meant to be pooled or used in a common enterprise to yield financial benefits for the members holding interests; crucially, the members do not maintain day-to-day control over the scheme's operation. Registered schemes include cash management and property trusts, Australian and international equity schemes, mortgage schemes, time-sharing schemes and serviced strata schemes.[38] Additionally, the phrase 'make a market for a financial product', as outlined in s 766A(1)(c), is clarified in s 766D. It refers to a person who regularly states prices at which they intend to buy or sell financial products for themselves.[39] This is notably different from operating a financial market, where prices for a financial product are quoted on behalf of others.[40]

3.2.2 Financial products

To 'deal in a financial product' constitutes a financial service.[41] The definition of 'financial product' in the *Corporations Act* is complex and includes a general definition and specific inclusions and overriding exclusions.[42]

34 Ibid s 766C(1). There are several exceptions to this broad definition. For instance, according to s 766C(3), an entity that deals in a financial product solely on its own behalf is generally exempt from being considered as providing a financial service. This exemption is particularly relevant for product issuers dealing in their own financial products. Similarly, under s 766C(4), a corporate body that deals in its own securities, such as issuing its own debentures, is usually not considered to be 'dealing' in a financial product.

35 Ibid s 766C(1)(c).

36 Ibid s 766C(2).

37 Ibid s 9(a). ('Managed investment scheme' means: '(a) a scheme that has the following features: (i) people contribute money or money's worth as consideration to acquire rights (interests) to benefits produced by the scheme (whether the rights are actual, prospective or contingent and whether they are enforceable or not); (ii) any of the contributions are to be pooled, or used in a common enterprise, to produce financial benefits, or benefits consisting of rights or interests in property, for the people (the members) who hold interests in the scheme (whether as contributors to the scheme or as people who have acquired interests from holders); (iii) the members do not have day-to-day control over the operation of the scheme (whether or not they have the right to be consulted or to give directions)...')

38 Australian Securities and Investments Commission, *Doing Financial Services Business in Australia* (Regulatory Guide 121, July 2013) ('*RG 121*') [34].

39 *Corporations Act* (n 5) s 766D.

40 ASIC, *RG 121* (n 38) [32].

41 *Corporations Act* (n 5) s 766A(1)(b).

42 Ibid s 762A. 'Financial product' is also defined in the *Australian Securities and Investments Commission Act 2001* (Cth) ('*ASIC Act*') s 12BAA. The definition is similar to that in the *Corporations Act*, with specific inclusions and exclusions. However, the definition is broader in the *ASIC Act*, as the specific inclusions and exclusions in that Act are less exhaustively prescribed than those in the *Corporations Act*. For example, the *Corporations Act* specifically excludes reinsurance, while the *ASIC Act* does not. However, in its Final Report, the ALRC has recently made recommendations to amend the definition

3.2.2.1 General definition

The general definition of 'financial product' is:[43]

> (1) ... a facility through which, or through the acquisition of which, a person does one or more of the following:
> (a) makes a financial investment [see s 763B];
> (b) manages financial risk [see s 763C];
> (c) makes non-cash payments [see s 763D].

This broad definition is subject to specific exemptions. As outlined in s 763E of the Act, a product is not considered a financial product if it is 'an incidental component of a facility that also has other components' or 'a facility that is incidental to one or more other facilities' and its primary purpose is not for 'making a financial investment; managing financial risk; or making non-cash payments'.[44] However, the product may still qualify as a financial product if it meets the criteria for a 'specific inclusion'.[45]

3.2.2.2 Specific inclusions

Section 764A of the *Corporations Act* enumerates items that qualify as financial products, irrespective of whether they fit the general definition mentioned earlier. These specific inclusions include interests in registered schemes and select managed investment schemes; particular life insurance policies; superannuation interests as defined by the *Superannuation Industry (Supervision) Act 1993* (Cth); retirement savings accounts (RSAs) as per the *Retirement Savings Accounts Act 1997* (Cth); first home saver accounts (FHSAs) according to the *First Home Saver Accounts Act 2008* (Cth); deposit-taking facilities made available by authorised deposit-taking institutions (ADIs); government-issued or proposed debentures, stocks or bonds; certain foreign exchange contracts; and margin lending facilities. Furthermore, s 764A(1)(m) of the *Corporations Act* includes a catch-all clause that allows for items to be declared as financial products through regulations.[46]

3.2.2.3 Overriding exclusions

Section 765A of the *Corporations Act* provides a list of products specifically excluded from the definition of 'financial product'; thus, the ch 7 regime is not applicable. These products are excluded, even if they satisfy the general definition or are covered by a

of 'financial product' in the *Corporations Act* to cover the broader definition currently found in s 12BAA of the *ASIC Act*. Other legislations, such as the *ASIC Act*, should adopt the same definitions by reference to the *Corporations Act* in order to simplify the legislative framework. See *Confronting Complexity* (n 16) [5.14]–[5.20].

43 *Corporations Act* (n 5) s 763A. 'Making a financial investment' under s 763B pertains to situations where the client contributes money or something of monetary value for the recipient to use in generating a financial gain or other advantage for the client. 'Managing a financial risk' under s 763C refers to the client taking steps to mitigate the financial impact of certain events occurring to them or to minimise the financial effects of variations in income or expenses. Lastly, under s 763D, 'making non-cash transactions' concerns cases where the client settles payments to third parties through methods other than using physical cash.

44 Ibid s 763E.

45 Ibid s 762A.

46 Ibid s 764A(1)(m).

specific inclusion.[47] In addition to certain insurance policies (including reinsurance policies, which are taken out by insurance providers to protect themselves against large-scale claims), certain facilities (including credit facilities other than margin lending facilities), certain superannuation interests, immediately settled foreign exchange contracts, interests in certain schemes and deposit-taking facilities connected with state banking, specific exclusions also cover benefits provided by employee associations, contracts of insurance, funeral benefits, physical equipment or infrastructure provided by something other than a financial product, among others.[48] Section 765A(y) and (z) excludes facilities, interests and other products declared by regulations or ASIC as not being a financial product. There has been debate as to whether digital currencies or crypto-assets should be recognised as financial products.[49] ASIC, in its initial 2014 submission to the Senate's investigation into digital currencies, stated that such currencies did not meet the existing legal criteria for being classified as a 'financial product' under either the *Corporations Act* or ASIC. ASIC's initial stance was that, for several reasons, 'digital currencies themselves do not fall within the current legal definition of a financial product'.[50] For instance, digital currencies, similar to real property and bullion, are not considered to be facilities for making a financial investment.[51] Nor do they function as facilities for managing financial risk, unlike insurance contracts.[52] Moreover, they are not designed to facilitate non-cash payments, as such payments rely on separate agreements with accepting parties.[53]

Yet, with the rise of initial coin offerings (ICOs) and the diverse uses of coins or tokens, ASIC later revised its stance. While specific pure digital currencies such as Bitcoin continue to fall outside the legal definition of a financial product, certain crypto-assets and ICOs may now be categorised as financial products, depending on their intrinsic features or organisational structure.[54]

47 Ibid s 765A.

48 Ibid.

49 Paul Latimer and Michael Duffy, 'Deconstructing Digital Currency and Its Risks: Why ASIC Must Rise to the Regulatory Challenge' (2019) 47(1) *Federal Law Review* 126; Senate Economics References Committee, Parliament of Australia, *Digital Currency: Game Changer or Bit Player* (Report, August 2015) <https://www.aph.gov.au/parliamentary_business/committees/senate/economics/digital_currency/~/media/Committees/economics_ctte/Digital_currency/report.pdf>.

50 Australian Securities and Investments Commission, Submission No 44 to Senate Standing Committee on Economics, *Digital Currency Inquiry* (December 2014) [45].

51 Ibid [47].

52 Ibid [48].

53 Ibid [49].

54 Australian Securities and Investments Commission, *Crypto-assets* (Information Sheet 225, October 2021) ('INFO 225') pt C <https://asic.gov.au/regulatory-resources/digital-transformation/crypto-assets>. ASIC's INFO 225 seeks to guide various stakeholders in the crypto-asset industry, from issuers to consumers, on the regulatory landscape. It acknowledges that crypto-assets and ICOs could be classified as financial products under the *Corporations Act* while outlining relevant activities that may be caught under the AFSL. Crypto-assets could be considered as managed investment schemes, securities, derivatives, or non-cash payment facilities, each with its own set of regulatory requirements. For instance, if a crypto-asset or ICO involves pooling of funds to produce financial benefits and the contributors do not have day-to-day control, it is likely to be categorised as a managed investment scheme. In such cases, issuers are required to register the scheme, making it subject to the AFSL and relevant requirements. Similarly, if the value of a crypto-asset is based on another asset or financial product, it may be classified as a derivative. Issuers offering such products

3.2.3 The concept of 'clients': Retail versus wholesale

Chapter 7 of the *Corporations Act* distinguishes between 'retail' and 'wholesale' clients.[55] One critical difference between them is that some specific requirements under ch 7 – for instance, disclosure concerning financial products and services, the 'best interests' duty and related obligations – generally only apply to retail clients, as wholesale clients are considered to be better informed and so do not require the same level of protection as retail clients.[56]

As a starting point, whether a client is classified as a retail or a wholesale client depends on the type of financial product or service provided. For instance, superannuation products, RSA products and traditional trustee company services are always provided to persons as retail clients.[57] Certain specified general insurance products, such as motor vehicle and travel insurance, are also provided to individuals or small businesses as retail clients.[58] For all other financial products and services, clients are retail clients unless the client satisfies one of the following tests:

- A *'price or value' test* is satisfied when the price or value of the provision of a financial product equals or exceeds A$500 000, the amount specified in regulations made for the purposes of s 761G(7)(a).[59] Such regulations also set out how a price or value is to be calculated for the purposes of the test concerning a specified class of financial products.[60]
- A *'business use' test* is satisfied when the financial product or service is provided for use in connection with a business other than a small business (ie a business employing fewer than 100 people if it is involved in the manufacture of goods, or fewer than 20 people otherwise).[61]
- A *'client wealth' test* is satisfied if the person acquiring the product or service gives the provider a copy of a certificate issued within the past six months by a qualified accountant stating that the person has net assets of at least A$2.5 million or a gross income (for each of the last two financial years) of at least $250 000 as specified in the *Corporations Regulations 2001* (Cth).[62]
- A *'professional investor' test* is satisfied if the person is a professional investor.[63]

Where a client satisfies one of these tests, they are deemed to be a wholesale client.[64] An exception also exists for 'sophisticated investors'.[65] Under this exception, a client can be

to retail investors would need to obtain an AFSL and comply with relevant requirements. Notably, INFO 225 stops short of offering exhaustive guidelines. It is a daunting task for regulators to offer definitive guidance, given the rapidly evolving nature of the crypto-asset industry.

55 *Corporations Act* (n 5) ch 7.
56 Ibid pts 7.7 and 7.7A; *The Treasury, Wholesale and Retail Clients: Future of Financial Advice* (Options Paper, January 2011) 4–5.
57 *Corporations Act* (n 5) s 761G(6) and (6A).
58 Ibid s 761G(5).
59 *Corporations Regulations 2001* (Cth) ('*Corporations Regulations*') regs 7.1.18–7.1.24.
60 *Corporations Act* (n 5) s 761G(7)(a) and (10); see also *Corporations Regulations* (n 59) regs 7.1.18–7.1.24.
61 *Corporations Act* (n 5) s 761G(7)(b) and (12).
62 Ibid s 761G(7)(c); *Corporations Regulations* (n 59) reg 7.1.28.
63 *Corporations Act* (n 5) s 761G(7)(d).
64 Ibid s 761G(7).
65 Ibid s 761GA.

categorised as a wholesale client if the financial service licensee reasonably believes that the client has sufficient prior experience with financial services and products. This experience should be such as to enable the client to evaluate the product or service's worth, merits and associated risks and to determine their own informational needs and the sufficiency of the information provided by both the licensee and the issuer of the product.[66]

3.2.4 AFSL licensee's requirements

3.2.4.1 Requirements for application

As already noted, a person must hold an AFSL to conduct a financial services business in Australia. Section 913B of the *Corporations Act* sets out when an AFSL may be granted.[67] Under that section, ASIC is obligated to grant an AFSL to an applicant if:

(a) the application is made in line with s 913A
(b) there is no reason to believe the applicant would breach the obligations of s 912A once licensed
(c) the applicant passes the 'fit and proper person test' under s 913BA for the specific licence they are applying for
(d) the applicant fulfils any additional requirements as determined by related regulations.[68]

Conversely, if these conditions are not met, ASIC should not grant the licence.[69]

In short, an application for an ASFL is made to ASIC,[70] which either grants or rejects the application.[71] As s 913B of the *Corporations Act* directs ASIC on when it must grant or deny applications, ASIC must assess whether the application meets the requirements set out in the legislation. Specifically, ASIC must be satisfied that it has no reason to believe that the applicant is likely to contravene the obligations that will apply under s 912A if the AFSL is granted.[72] It must also be satisfied that the following persons comply with the 'fit and proper person' test: the applicant; officers of a body corporate applicant; partners, trustees or senior managers of a partnership or trust applicant; and controllers of the applicant.[73]

66 Ibid s 761GA(d) ('... if the licensee is satisfied on reasonable grounds that the client has previous experience in using financial services and investing in financial products that allow the client to assess: (i) the merits of the product or service; and (ii) the value of the product or service; and (iii) the risks associated with holding the product; and (iv) the client's own information needs; and (v) the adequacy of the information given by the licensee and product issuer').

67 Ibid ss 911A and 913B.

68 Ibid s 913B(1).

69 Moreover, ASIC is obliged to deny the AFSL if they determine that either the application for the licence, or any information, audit report or statement submitted to ASIC, contained materially false or misleading details, or if a significant matter was omitted from the application, information, audit report or statement: ibid s 913B(2).

70 Ibid s 913A. ('A person may apply for an Australian financial services licence by lodging an application with ASIC that: (a) includes the information required by regulations made for the purposes of this paragraph, and (b) is accompanied by the documents (if any) required by regulations made for the purposes of this paragraph.')

71 See generally ibid s 913B.

72 Ibid s 913B(1).

73 Ibid s 913BA(1).

3.2.4.2 Representatives

Employees or directors of the AFS licensee or third-party representatives of an AFS licensee are 'representatives' of AFS licensees to provide financial services (ie 'authorised representatives').[74] The term 'representatives' in the context of financial services is defined as covering 'an authorised representative of the licensee', 'an employee or director of the licensee', 'an employee or director of a related body corporate of the licensee', or 'any other person acting on behalf of the licensee'.[75] More specifically, an 'authorised representative' of an AFS licensee refers to 'a person authorised in accordance with s 916A or s 916B to provide a financial service or financial services on behalf of the licensee'.[76] Authorised representatives may be individuals, bodies corporate, partnerships, or trustees of a trust.[77]

Section 916A of the *Corporations Act* provides that an AFS licensee may provide a person with written notice authorising them to act as an authorised representative.[78] The authorisation can be revoked at any time by the AFS licensee giving written notice to the authorised representative.[79] Under s 916B, an authorised representative may sub-authorise individuals to provide financial services on behalf of the licensee, but only where the licensee consents in writing to the sub-authorisation.[80] Generally, an AFSL holder cannot be the authorised representative of another AFS licensee.[81] The only exception is where an AFS licensee is authorised by another AFS licensee who is an insurer and acts under a binder given by the insurer.[82]

Essentially, authorised representatives are not licensed themselves but provide financial services under the licensee's licence.[83] However, an authorised representative must still comply with the provisions stipulated under s 911B of the *Corporations Act*.[84] Also, upon issuing an authorisation or a sub-authorisation, an AFS licensee or an authorised representative who sub-authorises must notify ASIC in the prescribed written form within 15 business days of issuing the authorising written notice.[85] If there are any

74 Ibid s 910A (definition of 'representative').

75 Ibid.

76 Ibid s 761A.

77 Australian Securities and Investments Commission, *Who Can Be an Authorised Representative of an AFS Licensee* (Information Sheet 91, November 2016) ('INFO 91') <https://asic.gov.au/for-finance-professionals/afs-licensees/appointing-and-ceasing-an-afs-authorised-representative/who-can-be-an-authorised-representative-of-an-afs-licensee/>.

78 *Corporations Act* (n 5) s 916A(1). ('A financial services licensee may give a person (the authorised representative) a written notice authorising the person, for the purposes of this Chapter, to provide a specified financial service or financial services on behalf of the licensee.')

79 Ibid s 916A(4). ('An authorisation may be revoked at any time by the licensee giving written notice to the authorised representative.')

80 Ibid s 916B(3). ('An authorised representative (an authoriser) of a financial services licensee may, in that capacity, give an individual a written notice authorising that individual, for the purposes of this Chapter, to provide a specified financial service or financial services on behalf of the licensee, but only if the licensee consents in writing given to the authoriser.')

81 Ibid s 916D(1).

82 Ibid s 916E(1).

83 Ibid s 911A(2)(a).

84 Ibid s 911B.

85 Ibid s 916F(1).

changes in the authorised representative's details or revocation of an authorisation, the authoriser must lodge a written notice to ASIC within 10 business days.[86]

3.2.4.3 General obligations

Under the *Corporations Act* s 912A, AFS licensees must:

- do all things necessary to ensure that the financial services covered by the licence are provided efficiently, honestly and fairly[87]
- have in place adequate arrangements for the management of conflicts of interest that may arise[88]
- comply with the conditions on the licence[89]
- comply with the financial services laws, and take reasonable steps to ensure that its representatives do so too[90]
- have available adequate resources to provide the financial services covered by the licence and to carry out supervisory arrangements[91]
- maintain the competence to provide those financial services[92]
- ensure that its representatives are adequately trained and are competent to provide those financial services[93]
- have adequate risk management systems[94]
- if financial services are provided to retail clients, have a dispute resolution system in place and give ASIC the information specified in any instrument[95]
- if applicable, comply with the law of a host economy or the Reference Checking and Information Sharing Protocol[96]
- comply with any other obligations that are prescribed by regulations.[97]

3.2.4.4 Disclosure requirements

In the realm of financial market regulation, disclosure mechanisms serve as an essential safeguard, particularly vital in markets replete with complex and often enigmatic products. The utilisation of disclosure-based approaches by policymakers is, according to Enriques and Gilotta, driven by multiple factors.[98] Primarily, disclosure is a cost-effective tool that does not necessitate direct governmental expenditure.[99] It is more likely to

86 Ibid s 916F(3).
87 Ibid s 912A(1)(a).
88 Ibid s 912A(1)(aa).
89 Ibid s 912A(1)(b).
90 Ibid s 912A(1)(c), (ca).
91 Ibid s 912A(1)(d).
92 Ibid s 912A(1)(e).
93 Ibid s 912A(1)(f).
94 Ibid s 912A(1)(h).
95 Ibid s 912A(1)(g), (2)–(2A).
96 Ibid s 912A(1)(cb), (cc), (3A)–(3G).
97 Ibid s 912A(1)(j).
98 Luca Enriques and Sergio Gilotta, 'Disclosure and Financial Market Regulation' in Niamh Moloney, Ellis Ferran and Jennifer Payne (eds), *The Oxford Handbook of Financial Regulation* (Oxford University Press, 2015) 511, 512.
99 Ibid 513.

garner bipartisan support, offering a measured response to calls for more stringent regulation, especially in the aftermath of financial crises.[100] Moreover, disclosure usually encounters less resistance from the interest groups it affects, who often favour the transparency it provides over more intrusive, behaviour-limiting measures.[101]

Consumer engagement with unsuitable or complex financial products carries significant risks, including potential financial losses. These risks, such as fraud and intentional mis-selling, can be mitigated through a robust disclosure regime. A well-designed disclosure framework guides consumers by answering key questions about the transaction, the product and its implications. This improves transparency and allows for comparability between similar financial services and products.

The potential for consumers to engage, inadvertently or intentionally, with unsuitable or overly complex financial products poses a significant risk. Such engagement could lead to substantial financial losses, as demonstrated by historical financial crises and the collapse of various investment schemes. These risks, which include fraudulent activities and intentional mis-selling, can be substantially mitigated through a comprehensive disclosure regime. In jurisdictions such as Australia, regulatory frameworks aim to keep consumers adequately informed about their interactions with financial intermediaries, emphasising the importance of timely and transparent information exchange. Enhancing these disclosure requirements with financial literacy initiatives could further empower consumers to make informed decisions.[102]

In this context, it is pertinent to examine three major disclosure documents for an AFSL: (1) the Financial Services Guide,[103] (2) the Statement of Advice,[104] and (3) the Product Disclosure Statement.[105]

Financial Services Guide

A Financial Services Guide (FSG) is a disclosure document crafted to ensure that retail clients receive enough information to help them determine whether to engage in financial services with the providing entity,[106] by way of offering relevant information as per the *Corporations Act* pt 7.7. The main requirements of an FSG are set out in s 942B of the Act, and the requirements in this section apply to any providing entity that is an AFSL holder.[107] As set out in s 942B(2), the FSG must include the statements and information set out below.[108]

An FSG must include the name and contact details of the entity providing the service.[109] It should also have a statement detailing instructions on how the client can

100 Ibid.

101 Ibid.

102 'Educating Clients is Good for Business', *Australian Securities and Investments Commission* (Web Page, 10 August 2011) <https://asic.gov.au/regulatory-resources/markets/resources/markets-articles-by-asic/educating-clients-is-good-for-business/>.

103 *Corporations Act* (n 5) pt 7.7(2)(A).

104 Ibid pt 7.7(3)(C).

105 Ibid pt 7.9(2)(B).

106 Australian Securities and Investments Commission, *Licensing: Financial Product Advisers – Conduct and Disclosure* (Regulatory Guide 175, 15 June 2021) ('*RG 175*') [97].

107 *Corporations Act* (n 5) s 942B(1).

108 Ibid s 942B(2).

109 Ibid s 942B(2)(a).

communicate with the providing entity,[110] and details about the financial services that the entity is licensed to offer.[111] Information on whose behalf the providing entity is acting when offering authorised services is also necessary,[112] as well as details on compensation, commissions and benefits received by the providing entity and related parties.[113]

Disclosure about any relationships that could influence the provision of authorised services is also mandated.[114] If authorised services include personal advice to retail clients, and if using restricted terms would violate s 923A(1) of the Act, the provider must disclose that the provider is not 'independent, impartial, or unbiased' as per s 923A(5), and explain why. Further, if regulations specify additional restricted words or expressions under s 923A(5)(a)(ii), the provider must state that they cannot use these terms in the context of providing personal advice and must explain the reasons for this limitation. Finally, the provider must meet other requirements under s 923A(7A).[115] Where the authorised services include the provision of market-related advice, or advice to which s 946B(7) applies, a statement that sets out the client's ability to request a record of such advice, along with particulars of how the client may request the record, is necessary. Any limitations concerning the time within which a client may request a record must comply with any applicable requirements in regulations made for the purposes of s 942B(2)(g). If none apply, time-based limitations must be such as to allow the client a reasonable opportunity to request a record.[116]

Information is also required about the system for resolving disputes, which covers complaints from individuals receiving financial services from the providing entity, and about how to access this system.[117] In cases where the providing entity is acting under a binder, a statement indicating that the entity is acting under a binder, identifying the services provided under the binder, and explaining the significance of the services provided under a binder, is necessary.[118] On the other hand, if the providing entity is a participant in a licensed market or licensed clearing and settlement (CS) facility, a statement indicating such information should be included.[119] Lastly, the FSG should encompass any other statements or information the regulations require.[120]

The FSG must be given to a client as soon as practicable, and before the provision of the financial service.[121] An FSG is not required in some situations, as listed in s 941C.[122]

Statement of Advice

A Statement of Advice (SOA) is a document intended to assist retail clients in understanding and deciding whether to act on personal financial advice.[123] Unlike the FSG, the

110 Ibid s 942B(2)(b).
111 Ibid s 942B(2)(c).
112 Ibid s 942B(2)(d).
113 Ibid s 942B(2)(e).
114 Ibid s 942B(2)(f).
115 Ibid s 942B(2)(fa).
116 Ibid s 942B(2)(g).
117 Ibid s 942B(2)(h).
118 Ibid s 942B(2)(i).
119 Ibid s 942B(2)(j).
120 Ibid s 942B(2)(k).
121 Ibid s 941D(1).
122 Ibid s 941C.
123 *RG 175* (n 106) [167].

obligation to issue an SOA, as per ss 946A–947E of the *Corporations Act*, typically arises only when personal financial product advice is given to a retail client.[124]

The SOA must contain specific content as mandated by the *Corporations Act*, including the basis on which the advice was given, contact details of the providing entity, and information about remuneration and other interests.[125]

The *Corporations Act* s 946B outlines exceptions to the SOA requirement. For instance, an SOA is not needed if the advice pertains to neither the acquisition or disposal of any specific financial product, nor to modifications to an investment strategy or a contribution level regarding the financial product, and remuneration is not received for the advice.[126]

Additionally, an SOA is not mandatory if the total value of the financial investments related to the advice does not exceed A$15 000 (known as 'small investment advice').[127] In such cases, the providing entity must document the advice in a Record of Advice and deliver it to the client as soon as possible, and certainly before offering any additional financial service related to that advice.[128] This exception is not applicable if the advice involves a derivative, a general insurance product, a life risk insurance product, a superannuation product, or a retirement savings account product (unless the client already holds an interest in the product).[129]

Product Disclosure Statement

A Product Disclosure Statement (PDS) is a disclosure document designed to help retail clients make informed decisions about acquiring financial products.[130] The PDS provides essential details, including the fees associated with the product, its key features, and the risks and benefits of holding it.[131] Additionally, it outlines the system for resolving disputes related to complaints from product holders,[132] any tax implications,[133] and any applicable cooling-off periods.[134] A PDS must generally be given to the prospective client either at or before the time that the issuer or seller provides any recommendations to acquire a financial product or when the financial product is offered or issued.[135]

It is not required to provide a PDS if the client already possesses a similar type of financial product and the regulated person has reasonable grounds to believe that the client has either received or had access to all the information that would have been included

124 *Corporations Act* (n 5) s 944A; Australian Securities and Investments Commission, *Disclosure: Product Disclosure Statements (and other Disclosure Obligations)* (Regulatory Guide 168, 6 July 2022) ('*RG 168*') [28].
125 *Corporations Act* (n 5) s 947B(2).
126 Ibid s 946B(7).
127 Ibid s 946AA; *Corporations Regulations* (n 59) reg 7.7.09A.
128 *Corporations Act* (n 5) s 946AA(5), (6).
129 Ibid s 946AA(1)(b).
130 *RG 168* (n 124) [39].
131 Ibid [40].
132 *Corporations Act* (n 5) s 1013D(g).
133 Ibid s 1013D(h).
134 Ibid s 1013D(i).
135 Ibid ss 1012A–1012C. As explained further by ASIC, typically, a regulated person is required to provide a retail client with a PDS either at the time or before they make (a) a suggestion to purchase a financial product; (b) a proposal to issue or facilitate the issuance of a financial product; or (c) a proposal to sell the product, provided that such a sale necessitates disclosure. *RG 168* (n 124) [13].

in the PDS, as per s 1012D(2).[136] If the financial product is an interest in a self-managed superannuation fund (SMSF), and the issuer or adviser has reasonable grounds to believe that the joining member has received or has access to all the information that would be in a PDS, then the issuer or adviser is not obligated to provide a PDS.[137]

Instead of providing a full PDS, a short-form PDS may be given as an alternative for most financial products, with the exception of general insurance products.[138] This abbreviated document summarises essential information such as issuer details, benefits, risks, costs, returns, dispute resolution and cooling-off periods. In doing so, it aims to 'help product issuers avoid the problem of lengthy and complex product disclosure documents by allowing them to present a summary document rather than a full-length PDS'.[139] However, a full PDS must be given upon a client's request.

3.2.4.5 Additional obligations

Other than the three disclosure documents discussed above, additional conduct and disclosure obligations may come into play depending on the nature of the financial product advice and the type of clients.

As a starting point, financial product advice is generally defined as a recommendation or statement of opinion that aims, or could reasonably be seen as aiming, to 'influence a person or persons in making a decision regarding a specific financial product or category of financial products, or an interest in a specific financial product or category of financial products'.[140]

However, the term does not include advice offered by a lawyer in their professional role concerning legal matters, legal interpretation, or the application of law to specific facts; or, except as specified by regulations, any other counsel provided by a lawyer as part of their standard legal activities and that is considered a necessary component of those activities; or, except as specified by regulations, guidance offered by a registered tax agent or business activity statement (BAS) agent given as part of their regular duties as such an agent and considered a necessary component of those activities.[141]

'General advice' versus 'personal advice'

Financial product advice can be either personal advice or general advice.[142] 'Personal advice' refers to 'financial product advice that is given or directed to a person ... in circumstances where: the provider of the advice has considered one or more of the person's objectives, financial situation and needs ... or a reasonable person might expect

136 *Corporations Act* (n 5) s 1012D(2).

137 Ibid s 1012D(2A). Moreover, if the financial product is a basic deposit product or a related non-cash payment facility, the provider is not required to offer an FSG, PDS or SOA. Instead of these standard disclosure documents, the provider must supply the client with specific alternative information. For instance, instead of an SOA, the provider should offer a brief statement outlining remuneration, affiliations and interests that could potentially affect the quality or content of the advice given. See ibid ss 941C(6)–(7), 946B(5)–(6); *Corporations Regulations* (n 59) reg 7.9.07FA.

138 *Corporations Regulations* (n 59) reg 7.9.61AA; *Corporations Act* (n 5) sch 10BA.

139 *RG 168* (n 124) [112].

140 *Corporations Act* (n 5) s 766B(1).

141 Ibid s 766B(5).

142 Ibid s 766B(2).

the provider to have considered one or more of those matters',[143] but it does not include 'the acts of asking for information solely to determine whether a person is in a target market ... for a financial product, and of informing the person of the result of that determination'.[144] On the other hand, 'general advice' refers to financial product advice that is not personal.[145]

In 2021, the High Court of Australia clarified the distinction between general and personal advice in the case of *Westpac Securities Administration Ltd v Australian Securities and Investments Commission*.[146] The test of whether the financial product advice is personal advice within the meaning of s 766B(3)(b) is an objective one that is assessed at the time in which the advice was given and in light of all the circumstances, including the nature of the relationship between the provider and client, the form, content and context of the advice given.[147] Where a reasonable person standing in the position of the client might expect the provider to 'have taken into account, had regard to, or given attention to, one or more of the person's objectives, financial situation and needs', the advice will be considered personal advice with more onerous obligations being imposed on the adviser.[148] Notably, given the phrase 'might expect' in s 766B(3)(b), the standard to be applied here is a lower one of reasonable possibility and not reasonable probability.[149]

In this case, the Court held that Westpac gave personal advice within the meaning of s 766B(3)(b) in light of all the circumstances.[150] While the consumers were given a general advice warning once at the beginning of the call, they were subsequently asked directly about their personal objectives and, having been told what they were, the adviser then confirmed those stated objectives were relevant and common objectives.[151] Coupled with the fact that there was a pre-existing relationship of dependence between the members of the adviser, a reasonable person might expect that the advice would be given taking into account the member's objectives and, thus, personal advice was given.[152]

The distinction made between personal and general advice is particularly crucial, as the conduct and disclosure obligations under pts 7.7 and 7.7A of the *Corporations Act* vary depending on whether the advice provided is personal or general. As discussed below, 'best interests' duty and related obligations only apply to advice providers providing personal advice to retail clients.[153]

'Best interests' duty and related obligations

Before the 'best interests' duty and related obligations introduced by the Future of Financial Advice (FOFA) reforms, the suitability rule, also known as the 'know your

143 Ibid s 766B(3).
144 Ibid s 766B(3A).
145 Ibid s 766B(4).
146 *Westpac Securities Administration Ltd v Australian Securities and Investments Commission* (2021) 270 CLR 118 ('*Westpac v ASIC*').
147 Ibid [57], [72].
148 Ibid [2], [59].
149 Ibid [58].
150 Ibid.
151 Ibid [80].
152 Ibid [81], [82].
153 *Corporations Act* (n 5) s 961(1).

client' or 'appropriate advice' rule, governed the regulation of financial adviser conduct.[154] Under the rule, AFSL holders or authorised representatives (known as 'providing entities') were required to comply with three separate but interrelated obligations under the then s 945A of the *Corporations Act*: (1) the obligation to assess the client's relevant personal circumstances before giving advice; (2) the obligation to consider and investigate the subject matter of the advice; and (3) the obligation to ensure that the client receives appropriate advice based on that consideration and investigation.[155]

The basis of the FOFA reforms may be best illustrated by the *Ripoll Report*, which was conducted in response to various financial product and services provider collapses at the time[156] and sought to address declining investor confidence in financial advisers.[157] The report established the need for the following:

- 'to improve the standard of advice offered to consumers, whether that be through enhanced legislative requirements about the standard of advice required or enhanced enforcement of existing standards, or both, so that consumers can be confident about the advice received'
- 'to better inform customers about the products signed up for' so that consumers would only buy products that 'entail a comfortable level of risk'
- 'to ensure that advisers are better informed about the products being sold'.[158]

Moreover, there were calls to bridge the gap between clients' expectations and adviser duties under the existing suitability rule: while clients held the view that financial advisers were providing a professional service, which meant they would provide advice in the client's best interests, the *Corporations Act* merely imposed upon advisers the duty to provide advice that was appropriate and suitable for managing existing conflicts.[159]

With these objectives in mind, the *Ripoll Report* recommended the creation of a statutory fiduciary duty for financial advisers that would require them to prioritise their clients' interests over their own.[160] However, following criticisms that a statutory fiduciary duty would destroy the 'balance between appropriate levels of consumer protection and ... the availability, accessibility and affordability of high quality financial advice',[161] the 'best interests' duty and related obligations were introduced to replace the suitability rule to hold financial advisers to a higher standard with regards to the provision of advice.[162]

154 Han-Wei Liu et al, 'In Whose Best Interests? Regulating Financial Advisers, The Royal Commission and the Dilemma of Reform' (2020) 42(1) *Sydney Law Review* 42.

155 Weiping He and Han-Wei Liu, 'Regulating Financial Advisers in the UK: Lessons for Australia' (2021) 44(1) *University of New South Wales Law Journal* 445.

156 Evidence to Parliamentary Joint Committee (PJC) on Corporations and Financial Services, Parliament of Australia, Melbourne, 26 August 2009, 62 (Michael Davison, CPA Australia Ltd), quoted in PJC on Corporations and Financial Services, Parliament of Australia, *Inquiry into Financial Products and Services in Australia* (Report, November 2009) ('*Ripoll Report*') vii.

157 Liu et al (n 154) 38.

158 *Ripoll Report* (n 156) 86 [5.69].

159 Ibid 86 [5.69].

160 Ibid 150 [7.10].

161 Mathias Cormann, 'The Way Forward on Financial Advice Laws' (Media Release, Treasury (Cth), 20 June 2014) <https://ministers.treasury.gov.au/ministers/mathias-cormann-2014/media-releases/way-forward-financial-advice-laws>.

162 Liu et al (n 154) 42.

Division 2 of pt 7.7A of ch 7 of the *Corporations Act* sets out the 'best interests' duty, which requires financial advisers to 'act in the best interests of the client in relation to the advice',[163] and its related obligations. Importantly, such obligations are imposed only in cases where personal advice is provided to retail clients;[164] as such, advice providers, which include AFS licensees, authorised representatives or other representatives of an AFS licensee, are required to comply with the 'best interests' duty and related obligations.[165] If, however, the advice is not provided by an individual but is provided instead by an entity such as a computer program, the obligations will apply to the legal person who provides the advice (ie a corporate licensee or authorised representative).[166] Advice providers who provide personal advice to retail clients have the following obligations:

- To 'act in the best interests of the client in relation to the advice',[167] which is satisfied if the provider proves that they have taken the steps set out in s 961B(2) [*'best interests' duty*].[168]
- To 'only provide the advice to the client if it would be reasonable to conclude that the advice is appropriate to the client, had the provider satisfied the duty under s 961B to act in the best interests of the client' [*'appropriate advice' duty*].[169]
- '[I]f it is reasonably apparent that information relating to the objectives, financial situation and needs of the client on which the advice is based is incomplete or inaccurate, the provider must ... warn the client that: the advice is, or may be, based on incomplete or inaccurate information relating to the client's relevant personal circumstances; and because of that, the client should, before acting on the advice, consider the appropriateness of the advice, having regard to the client's objectives, financial situations and needs' [*duty to warn the client if the advice is based on incomplete or inaccurate information*].[170]
- If the provider knows, or reasonably ought to know, that there is a conflict between the interests of the client and the interests of the provider or an entity specified in s 961B(2)(a)–(f), 'the provider must give priority to the client's interests when giving the advice' [*duty of priority*].[171] However, this obligation does not apply to advice in relation to a basic banking product, a general insurance product or a consumer credit insurance.[172]

Failure to comply with the above obligations amounts to a breach of the provisions in div 2 of pt 7.7A of the *Corporations Act*.[173] An AFS licensee will be liable for a civil penalty

163 *Corporations Act* (n 5) s 961B(1).
164 Ibid.
165 *RG 175* (n 106) [33].
166 Ibid [34]; *Corporations Act* (n 5) s 961(6).
167 Ibid s 961B(1).
168 Ibid s 961B(2).
169 Ibid s 961G.
170 Ibid s 961H(1).
171 Ibid s 961J(1).
172 Ibid s 961J(2)–(3).
173 *RG 175* (n 106) [34] (note).

if it breaches, or its unauthorised representatives breach, these provisions.[174] Authorised representatives who breach the provisions will be similarly subject to civil liabilities,[175] whereas unauthorised representatives who breach the provisions will be subject to administrative sanctions.[176]

Although the term 'best interests' is not defined, s 961B(2) of the *Corporations Act* sets out 'safe harbour' conditions, which, if complied with, signal that an advice provider satisfies the 'best interests' duty.[177] These 'safe harbour' conditions are met in the following circumstances:

- The advice provider has identified the objectives, financial situation and needs of the client that were disclosed to the provider by the client through instructions.[178]
- The advice provider has identified the subject matter of the advice that has been sought by the client (whether explicitly or implicitly) and the objectives, financial situation and needs of the client that would reasonably be considered as relevant to advice sought on that subject matter (the client's relevant circumstances).[179]
- Where it was reasonably apparent that information relating to the client's relevant circumstances was incomplete or inaccurate, the advice provider made reasonable inquiries to obtain complete and accurate information.[180]
- The advice provider assessed whether the provider has the expertise required to provide the client advice on the subject matter sought and, if not, declined to provide the advice.[181]
- If, in considering the subject matter of the advice sought, it would be reasonable for the advice provider to consider recommending a financial product: the advice provider conducted a reasonable investigation into the financial products that might achieve those of the objectives and meet those of the needs of the client that would reasonably be considered as relevant to advice on that subject matter; and assessed the information gathered in the investigation.[182]
- The advice provider based all judgements in advising the client on the client's relevant circumstances.[183]
- The advice provider took any other step that, at the time the advice is provided, would reasonably be regarded as being in the best interests of the client, given the client's relevant circumstances.[184]

The lack of definition afforded to 'best interests' and the qualifications set out by s 961B(2) have attracted criticisms that the 'safe harbour' clause directs financial advisers to focus on the process required to achieve 'best interests', rather than the substance or principles of the advice given.[185] In particular, s 961B(2)(g) was criticised for the likelihood it

174 Ibid [35]; *Corporations Act* (n 5) s 961K.
175 *RG 175* (n 106) [36]; *Corporations Act* (n 5) s 961Q.
176 *RG 175* (n 106) [37].
177 Liu et al (n 154) 43; *Corporations Act* (n 5) s 961B(2).
178 *Corporations Act* (n 5) s 961B(2)(a).
179 Ibid s 961B(2)(b).
180 Ibid s 961B(2)(c).
181 Ibid s 961B(2)(d).
182 Ibid s 961B(2)(e).
183 Ibid s 961B(2)(f).
184 Ibid s 961B(2)(g).
185 Liu et al (n 154) 44.

would introduce uncertainty in norms of behaviour required by the law,[186] although its inclusion sought to discourage the 'tick-a-box' approach that the 'safe harbour' clause would promote.[187] The Federal Court of Australia's interpretation and application of the 'best interests' duty was highly anticipated given the somewhat controversial way in which this law was developed.[188] Relevant court decisions are summarised below.

- *Australian Securities and Investments Commission v NSG Services Pty Ltd* (2017) 122 ACSR 47: This case marked the first finding of civil liability against an AFS licensee for breaches of the 'best interests' duty.[189] In this case, Moshinsky J held that the defendant, NSG Services Pty Ltd, breached s 961B (and, relatedly, s 961G) of the *Corporations Act* as NSG Services representatives provided the following advice to clients: recommended a superannuation fund for which the client was not eligible; failed to disclose fees adequately; rolled over a client's superannuation to other firms without permission; and failed to provide a statement of advice.[190] Accordingly, NSG Services was 'automatically' liable under s 961K(2)(b) for the violations by its employee representatives.[191] Further, NSG Services breached s 961L for failing to take reasonable steps to ensure its representatives complied with the requirements.[192] The Court ordered the defendant to pay penalties of A$250 000 and A$750 000 due to its contravention of ss 961K(2) and 961L.[193]
- *Australian Securities and Investments Commission v Wealth & Risk Management Pty Ltd (No 2)* (2018) 124 ACSR 351: This case concerned a complex cash rebate scheme operated by JECA Holdings Pty Ltd (JECA) that ASIC alleged breached various provisions of the *Corporations Act* and the *Australian Securities and Investments Commission Act 2001* (Cth) ('*ASIC Act*'). Essentially, this scheme was found to breach the 'best interests' duty because the scheme incentivised Wealth & Risk Management Pty Ltd (WRM) advisers to give advice that was not appropriate and to not prioritise their clients' interests.[194] Instead of their clients' best interests driving their advice, it was driven by commissions and fees. Accordingly, each of the defendant entities was subject to an 18-year ban restraining them from providing financial services, and all defendants were ordered to pay penalties, with values ranging from A$650 000 to A$1.8 million.[195]

186 *Ripoll Report* (n 156) 49 [4.23].
187 Ibid 50 [4.28].
188 Liu et al (n 154) 45.
189 Australian Securities and Investments Commission, 'Financial Advice Firm to Pay $1 million Penalty for Breach of Best Interests Duty' (Media Release 17-365MR, 30 October 2017) 1 <https://asic.gov.au/about-asic/news-centre/find-a-media-release/2017-releases/17-365mr-financial-advice-firm-to-pay-1-million-penalty-for-breach-of-best-interests-duty/>.
190 Liu et al (n 154) 45; *Australian Securities and Investments Commission v NSG Services Pty Ltd* (2017) 122 ACSR 47, 80 [112], 85 [142] ('*ASIC v NSG*').
191 Liu et al (n 154) 45; *ASIC v NSG* (n 190) 55 [32].
192 Liu et al (n 154) 45; *ASIC v NSG* (n 190) 60–2 [75]–[76].
193 Liu et al (n 154) 45; *Australian Securities and Investments Commission v Golden Financial Group Pty Ltd (No 2)* [2017] FCA 1267 [9], [35] ('*ASIC v GFG (No 2)*').
194 Liu et al (n 154) 45; *Australian Securities and Investments Commission v Wealth & Risk Management Pty Ltd (No 2)* (2018) 124 ACSR 351, 366 [63], 379 [150] ('*ASIC v WRM*').
195 Liu et al (n 154) 45; *ASIC v WRM* (n 194) 356–7 [8], 381 [161], 383 [175].

- *Australian Securities and Investments Commission v Financial Circle Pty Ltd* (2018) 353 ALR 137: This case served as a follow-up to the WRM proceedings mentioned above.[196] In this instance, Mr Fuoco, who had been an owner and director of the firms involved in the prior case, founded new companies that subsequently acquired Financial Circle Pty Ltd. Although Financial Circle was an AFS licensee with a business model resembling that of the defendants in the earlier case, it diverged by tying loans to the provision of financial advice, as opposed to a cash rebate scheme.[197] Notably, loan applicants were subject to undisclosed conditions, including a significant advice fee taken from the client's superannuation.[198] As a result, clients found themselves in a less favourable financial position after participating in Financial Circle's loan and advice programs.
- Moshinsky J granted an interim injunction restraining Financial Circle from engaging in the relevant businesses.[199] O'Callaghan J found that in providing its clients with advice regarding insurance and superannuation, Financial Circle failed to prioritise the clients' interests, but otherwise enabled itself and/or its employees to receive commissions and advice fees. Accordingly, it was held that Financial Circle contravened its duties under the *Corporations Act* s 961L, which is to take reasonable steps to ensure its representatives complied with ss 961B, 961G and 961J.[200] Financial Circle was fined A$1 million and was permanently disqualified from carrying on financial services.[201]

In 2019, the Banking Royal Commission, in its final report, discussed the possibility of amending s 961B of the *Corporations Act* in order to better manage conflicts between duties owed by advisers and their own financial interests.[202] The final report proposed two options that could be taken to amend the provision: to amend it 'to be more prescriptive about how an adviser must pursue the client's best interests'; or 'to remove the safe harbour provision entirely'.[203] The former option was rejected as it would be a 'significant expansion' of the 'safe harbour' model.[204] In regard to the latter option, the Commissioner acknowledged the possible ground for removal of the provision, with the report stating:[205]

> The safe harbour provision currently has the effect that, in practice, an adviser is required to make little or no independent inquiry into, or assessment of, products. By prescribing particular steps that must be taken, and allowing

196 Liu et al (n 154) 47; *Australian Securities and Investments Commission v Financial Circle Pty Ltd* (2018) 353 ALR 137, 138 [2] ('*ASIC v Financial Circle*').
197 Liu et al (n 154) 47; *ASIC v Financial Circle* (n 196) 137, 138 [2].
198 Liu et al (n 154) 47; *ASIC v Financial Circle* (n 196), 484, 488 [9], 490–2 [22]–[33], 505 [107].
199 *ASIC v Financial Circle* (n 196), 137, 139 [4]–[5], 159 [99].
200 Ibid 484, 508–9 [122]–[135].
201 Ibid 484, 527 [236], 529–30 [236].
202 *Royal Commission into Misconduct in the Banking, Superannuation and Financial Services Industry* (Final Report, 1 February 2019) ('*Banking Royal Commission Final Report*') vol 1, 170, 177.
203 Ibid 177.
204 Ibid.
205 Ibid.

> advisers to adopt a 'tick a box' approach to compliance, the safe harbour provision has the potential to undermine the broader obligation for advisers to act in the best interests of their clients.

The report questions: 'Is enough attention being given to compliance? Is it working in practice? Or is it just box-ticking?'[206] As a result, Recommendation 2.3 of the final report states that a review should be conducted to enhance the quality of advice, and this review should assess the need to maintain the 'safe harbour' provision in s 961B(2) of the *Corporations Act*.[207] Unless there is a clear justification for retaining that provision, this clause, as per the Commissioner, should be repealed.[208]

Scholars have reacted to the 'box-ticking' critique by arguing that it is still necessary to provide some form of instructions to financial advisers and that the value of the catch-all provision in s 961B(2)(g) should not be overlooked.[209] Notably, the reading of s 961B(2)(g) has been left open to judicial interpretation by the court, as exemplified by the three cases summarised above.[210] As such, advisers are unlikely to just merely adopt a 'box-ticking' approach to ensure their compliance with the 'best interests' duty and this critique does not justify the removal of the whole provision. Further, it is argued that removing the 'safe harbour' provision would result in there being less context for the court to interpret the meaning of financial advisers acting 'in the best interests of the client' under the 'best interests' duty, and thus issues may arise with the judges' interpretation of the duty in the above three cases.[211] While removing the 'safe harbour' provisions would respond to criticisms of the 'box-ticking' nature of the provisions, it would have an adverse effect on the interpretation of the 'best interests' duty.[212]

In 2021, the Australian Law Reform Commission published an interim report in relation to the reform of corporations and financial services legislation.[213] In the report, the ALRC suggests reforming the 'best interests' obligation so that the currently prescriptive 'safe harbour' provisions 'are re-cast as indicative behaviours of compliance, to which a court must have regard when assessing compliance with the duty'.[214] This amendment would not only 'promote more meaningful – rather than "tick a box" – compliance' but also ensure clarity for advisers by providing useful guidance on how to comply with the 'best interests' obligation.[215] In doing so, it would help 'achieve a more principled and simple legislative regime'.[216]

In response to Recommendation 2.3 of the Banking Royal Commission's final report as discussed above, the Australian Treasury published the *Quality of Advice Review* in

206 Ibid 334.
207 Ibid 178.
208 Ibid.
209 Liu et al (n 154) 56.
210 Ibid 56.
211 Ibid 57.
212 Ibid 59.
213 Australian Law Reform Commission, *Financial Services Legislation: Interim Report A* (Report 137, 30 November 2021) ('*ALRC Interim Report*').
214 Ibid 500, 534.
215 Ibid 534, 538.
216 Ibid 534.

December 2022. In the review, the Australian Treasury recommended replacing the 'best interests' duty and related obligations in ch 7 of the *Corporations Act* with a 'good advice' duty.[217] The 'good advice' duty requires a person who provides personal advice to a retail client to provide 'advice that, at the time the advice is provided, is fit for purpose having regard to the scope, content and nature of the advice, the client's relevant circumstances and is, in all the circumstances, good'.[218] This good advice duty focuses attention on the wants and needs of consumers and requires the advice provider to genuinely consider whether the advice provided is 'sound, fit for purpose and good' instead of the current checklist-based approach of the 'best interests' duty.[219]

However, in joint submissions to the Australian Treasurer, consumer advocate groups have criticised this proposed 'good advice' duty as vague and poorly defined as it could permit the provision of advice that is 'good' by the client's standards but may not be in the consumer's best interests.[220] Also, introduction of this 'good advice' duty might not only result in an expansive transition process for companies in terms of amendment of their compliance practices, but also lead to uncertainty until a comprehensive test on what constitutes 'good advice' is clarified by the courts.[221] As such, consumer groups argue that the 'best interests' duty incorporates good advice and hence should remain in place.[222]

Most recently, the ALRC, in its final report released in January 2024, did not formalise the proposed amendments to the 'best interests' duty in the 2021 interim report.[223] This is in light of the recommendations made by the *Quality of Advice Review* as discussed above, the ongoing consultation relating to financial advice provisions, and the improvements that would be effected by implementing Recommendation 38 in the final report, which seeks to restructure and reframe provisions relating to financial advice by grouping them together.[224] As such provisions are currently dispersed throughout ch 7 of the *Corporations Act*, Recommendation 38 is said to make the Act more amenable to implementing recommendations concerning the provision of good advice.[225] Crucially, shifts in the regulatory philosophies have been and continue to be drivers of policy change in the financial services sector.[226] For instance, the 2012 FOFA reforms that introduced the 'best interests' obligations were in light of a shift in regulatory philosophy away from disclosure of conflicts of interest by financial advisers and towards the reduction of such conflicts.[227]

217 The Treasury, *Quality of Advice Review* (Final Report, December 2022) ('*Quality of Advice Review*') 92.
218 Ibid 8, 89.
219 Ibid 89.
220 Aleks Vickovich and Lucy Dean, 'Push to Save "Best Interests" Duty in Financial Advice', *Australian Financial Review* (26 September 2022) <https://www.afr.com/companies/financial-services/industry-body-backs-consumer-groups-on-good-advice-duty-20220923-p5bkhl>.
221 'Proposed Good Advice Duty "Vague, Poorly Defined": Consumer Groups', *Insurance News* (Web Page, 10 March 2023) <https://www.insurancenews.com.au/daily/proposed-good-advice-duty-vague-poorly-defined-consumer-groups>.
222 Vickovich and Dean (n 220).
223 *Confronting Complexity* (n 16) [9.55].
224 Ibid [9.56].
225 Ibid.
226 Ibid [9.16].
227 Ibid.

Part 7.7A of the *Corporations Act* bans various conflicted payments in the advice industry and is separated into three parts:[228]

(1) Division 4 stipulates a ban on conflicted remuneration given to AFS licensees and representatives who provide financial product advice to retail clients in relation to personal and general advice.
(2) Division 5(A) stipulates a ban on volume-based shelf-space fees paid to platform operators.
(3) Division 5(B) stipulates a ban on charging retail clients asset-based advice fees on borrowed funds.

As set out in the *Corporations Act* s 963A, 'conflicted remuneration' refers to any benefit given to an AFS licensee or its representative who provides financial advice to retail clients that '(a) could reasonably be expected to influence the choice of financial product recommended by the licensee or representative to retail clients; or (b) could reasonably be expected to influence the financial product advice given to retail clients by the licensee or representative'.[229]

In the 2023 case of the *Australian Securities and Investments Commission v Commonwealth Bank of Australia,* the Full Federal Court clarified the meaning and scope of the conflicted remuneration provisions. First, the term 'benefit' in the *Corporations Act* s 963A refers to 'any advantage, monetary or non-monetary, including a reduction of detriment' and not a 'net benefit'.[230] Second, the prohibition on conflicted remuneration within the meaning of s 963A can apply where the AFS licensee only offers a single financial product.[231] It is not limited to circumstances where the AFS licensee is confronted with making a choice between two or more different financial products when making a recommendation to the client.[232] Third, a necessary element of the definition of conflicted remuneration in s 963A is that the AFS licensee provides financial product advice and the burden of proving this lies on ASIC.[233] Lastly, the prospect of conflicted remuneration in s 963A can arise in circumstances where benefits are given by one legal entity to another within the same group of companies and is not limited to 'benefits that exist between arms-length entities that are not part of a single consolidated group'.[234]

In this case, the Full Federal Court dismissed ASIC's appeal against an earlier Federal Court decision to dismiss ASIC's case against the CBA for allegedly breaching conflicted remuneration regulations. While the contractual promises and cash transfers received by CBA constituted benefits for the purposes of s 963A,[235] the Court held that ASIC had failed to prove that CBA provided financial product advice to persons as retail clients in respect of Essential Super.[236] The statements contained in the relevant sales 'scripts' for

228 *Corporations Act* (n 5) pt 7.7A.
229 Ibid s 963A.
230 *Australian Securities and Investments Commission v Commonwealth Bank of Australia* (2023) 412 ALR 536, [146]–[154] ('*ASIC v CBA*').
231 Ibid [167].
232 Ibid.
233 Ibid [175].
234 Ibid [181].
235 Ibid [187].
236 Ibid [217].

Essential Super were merely simple statements of facts on the features of Essential Super and did not constitute recommendations.[237] Given that no financial product advice was given, the benefits given did not constitute conflicted remuneration and the appeal was dismissed.[238]

In its final report, the Banking Royal Commission recommended that 'grandfathering provisions for conflicted remuneration should be repealed as soon as is reasonably practicable'.[239] Following this recommendation, the *Treasury Laws Amendment (Ending Grandfathered Conflicted Remuneration) Act 2019* (Cth) amended the *Corporations Act* to prohibit the grandfathering of conflicted remuneration paid to financial advisers from 1 January 2021.[240]

Division 3 of pt 7.7A of the *Corporations Act* stipulates two further obligations on those who have ongoing fee arrangements with clients who receive personal advice.[241] These obligations are: providing a fee disclosure statement annually;[242] and obtaining the client's consent before deducting, accepting deductions, or arranging to deduct ongoing fees.[243] 'Ongoing fee arrangements' exist when an AFS licensee or its representative gives personal advice to a retail client and enters into an arrangement with that retail client whereby a fee must be paid during a period of more than 12 months.[244]

3.3 Product intervention and product design and distribution obligations

In 2019, with implementation set for 2021, the Australian Government sought to introduce two key reforms: (1) a provision giving ASIC the power to intervene temporarily in product designs when there is a significant risk of consumer detriment – known as 'product intervention power'; and (2) a new governance regime for design and distribution obligation, which includes obligations such as a requirement to consider various factors when designing such financial products or distribution strategies.[245] The purpose of these obligations is, in line with the Murray Inquiry's Recommendations 21 and 22,[246] to benefit consumers by facilitating the creation of consumer-centric product offerings.[247] We examine them briefly below.

---

237 Ibid [219].

238 Ibid [221].

239 *Banking Royal Commission Final Report* (n 202) 26.

240 *Treasury Laws Amendment (Ending Grandfathered Conflicted Remuneration) Act 2019* (Cth).

241 *Corporations Act* (n 5) pt 7.7A.

242 Ibid s 962G.

243 Ibid ss 962R, 962S.

244 Ibid s 962A(1).

245 Australian Securities and Investements Commission, *Product Design and Distribution Obligations* (Consultation Paper No 325, 19 December 2019) ('*CP 325*') 6 <https://download.asic.gov.au/media/5423121/cp325-published-19-december-2019.pdf>.

246 Murray Inquiry (n 8) 198, 206. Recommendation 22 urged the Government to introduce 'a proactive product intervention power that would enhance the regulatory toolkit available where there is risk of significant consumer detriment', while Recommendation 21 called for the creation of 'a targeted and principles-based product design and distribution obligation'. See also Nehme (n 20) (noting also that '[t]hese powers have been on the horizon since the Financial System Inquiry (FSI) in 2014, which hoped that product intervention powers (PIPs) might help to "build consumer confidence and trust in the financial system"': 88).

247 *CP 325* (n 245) 6.

3.3.1 Product Intervention Power (PIP)

As indicated earlier, the 2014 Murray Report advised the Australian Government to augment ASIC's regulatory toolkits with intervention powers for scenarios posing significant consumer detriment risks. This recommendation was crystallised through the *Treasury Laws Amendment (Design and Distribution Obligations and Product Intervention Powers) Act 2019* (Cth) following the Banking Royal Commission. One of the underlying rationales for introducing the PIP is, as per the Explanatory Memorandum, the limitations of the disclosure requirement.[248] Despite available disclosures in the *Corporations Act*, many retail clients incurred unexpected losses from misunderstood investments, showcasing that even compliant disclosures did not clarify product risks to consumers. Disclosure may fall short because of factors such as consumer disengagement, complex documents, behavioural biases, misaligned interests and low financial literacy. Even available financial advice might not mitigate these issues.

The PIP was thus introduced as a response to the 2014 Inquiry. The PIP is seen as 'a last resort or pre-emptive measure where there is [a] risk of significant detriment to a class of consumers'.[249] The PIP does not aim to 'address problems with pricing of retail financial products, where consumers might be paying more than expected for a particular product or where a large number of consumers have incurred a small detriment'.[250] This power is intended to serve as a proactive regulatory measure for minimising consumer harm through early, targeted intervention, as opposed to reacting post-detriment. By having the ability to halt sales or address issues post-sale, ASIC could avert broader consumer detriment.[251]

ASIC is empowered to issue a PIP if a 'financial product' or 'credit product' (or a class of such products) has caused, is causing, or is likely to cause significant consumer detriment, under pt 7.9A of the *Corporations Act* and pt 6-7A of the *NCCPA*. Generally, there are three types of products that could fall within the scope of the PIP: 'financial products' regulated by the *Corporations Act*[252] (as explained earlier in this chapter); 'credit products' under the *NCCPA*;[253] and 'financial products' as defined by the *ASIC Act*.[254] Given the broader remit of the *ASIC Act*, the concept of 'financial product' is much broader

248 Exposure Draft Explanatory Memorandum, Treasury Laws Amendment (Design and Distribution Obligations and Product Intervention Powers) Bill 2018 (Cth) [1.2]–[1.3].

249 Ibid [3.37].

250 Ibid [3.38].

251 Ibid [3.38]–[3.39]. See also Australian Securities and Investments Commission, *Product Intervention Power* (June 2020) ('*RG 272*') [2]. The PIP, as ASIC explains, enables it to proactively regulate the market and mitigate significant consumer detriment. This power facilitates a 'flexible, targeted, effective and timely' response to issues, enables market-wide action, and can be exercised without a demonstrated or suspected legal breach, allowing pre-emptive action to prevent or halt significant detriment to consumers, thus better aligning with community expectations regarding the conduct of firms issuing or distributing products.

252 The PIP under the *Corporations Act* (n 5) applies to financial products available, or likely available, for retail clients by issue, and regulated sales of such products per ss 1023D(1)(a) and (3)(a) and 1023B. These products include, among other products, securities, managed investment scheme interests, derivatives, insurance, superannuation products and deposit-taking facilities. For a comprehensive list of 'financial products' under the *Corporations Act*, refer to ss 763A and 764A of the Act. *RG 272* (n 251) [17].

253 *National Consumer Credit Protection Act 2009* (Cth) ('*NCCPA*') s 301D; *RG 272* (n 251) [18].

254 Under s 1023B of the *Corporations Act* (n 5), the term 'ASIC Act financial product' refers to a financial product as defined in the *ASIC Act* pt 2 div 2. Whereas 'financial product' encompasses an *ASIC Act* financial product, it excludes: (i) financial products issued or offered for regulated sale by an exempt body or exempt public authority; and (ii) financial products specified in regulations made for this clause.

and includes some types of extended warranties, some types of short-term credit and certain buy-now-pay-later arrangements that are not covered by, or are exempt from, the *Corporations Act* and the *NCCPA*.

Generally, ASIC can make two types of product intervention order (PIO), according to the PIP:

(1) an individual PIO, applying specifically to specified person(s) not to engage in specified conduct in relation to a product[255]

(2) a market-wide PIO, applying to a person not to engage in specified conduct in relation to a class of products.[256]

Some examples of interventions that ASIC can make include:[257] ordering that the product be offered to specific consumers or in specific circumstances; ordering the amendment, restriction or banning of marketing or promotional activities relating to a product; and banning a feature or even the issue of the product. However, the PIO cannot order a person to satisfy a standard of training, or require a person who is not required to hold an AFS or credit licence to join an external dispute resolution scheme and impose requirements on a person's remuneration other than the remuneration that is conditional to the financial product's performance.[258] The interventions must be prospective,[259] and the conduct covered by the PIO can only relate to consumer conduct.[260]

ASIC can exercise its PIP when it is satisfied that the product will, or likely will, result in significant consumer detriment.[261] The term 'detriment' should be given its ordinary meaning, but it is intended to cover a wide range of damage caused by the product, including harm arising from the product's characteristics, inadequate disclosures, poor design and inappropriate distribution.[262] The detriment can be financial in nature, including actual or financial detriment, or non-financial in nature, such as affecting one's credit rating.[263] The detriment must also be 'significant', which may refer to the detriment being 'sufficiently great to justify an intervention', given the context and object of the intervention.[264]

The factors that ASIC will consider include:[265]

(a) the nature and extent of the detriment, with considerations such as the number or proportion of individuals affected, the amount of detriment incurred or likely to incur at both the individual and market level

255 *Corporations Act* (n 5) s 1023D(1); *NCCPA* (n 253) s 301D(1); *RG 272* (n 251) [21].
256 *Corporations Act* (n 5) s 1023D(3); *NCCPA* (n 253) s 301D(3); *RG 272* (n 251) [21].
257 *Corporations Act* (n 5) s 1023D(1); *NCCPA* (n 253) s 301D(1); *RG 272* (n 251) [26].
258 *Corporations Act* (n 5) s 1023D(4); *NCCPA* (n 253) s 301D(4), which additionally states that the PIO cannot impose conditions on a person's remuneration, other than conditions relating to the fees or other consideration paid by the consumer to the person; *RG 272* (n 251) [31].
259 *Corporations Act* (n 5) s 1023C(1); *NCCPA* (n 253) s 301C(1); *RG 272* (n 251) [33].
260 *Corporations Act* (n 5) s 1023D(5); *NCCPA* (n 253) s 301D(5); *RG 272* (n 251) [34].
261 *Corporations Act* (n 5) s 1023D(1)(b); *NCCPA* (n 253) s 301D(1)(b); *RG 272* (n 251) [38].
262 Revised Explanatory Memorandum to the Treasury Laws Amendment (Design and Distribution Obligations and Product Intervention Powers) Bill 2019 (Cth) ('*Revised Explanatory Memorandum*'); *RG 272* (n 251) [40].
263 *RG 272* (n 251) [41].
264 *Revised Explanatory Memorandum* (n 262); *RG 272* (n 251) [46].
265 *Corporations Act* (n 5) s 1023E(1); *NCCPA* (n 253) s 301E(1); *RG 272* (n 251) [52], Table 1.

(b) the actual or potential losses incurred or expected to incur, such as cost of product or losses incurred by consumers from the product
(c) the impact that the detriment likely has or will have on consumers, which would vary between demographics - for example, whether the impact would be greater on a socio-economic disadvantaged population
(d) other factors prescribed by regulations.

Before making the PIO, ASIC must consult the persons who are reasonably likely to be affected[266] and propose a range of intervention options.[267] This consultation would generally be a public one, where the consultation document - containing the proposed order, or a description of the proposed order - will be published on the ASIC website and the public is invited to comment on it.[268]

Subsequently, ASIC must also make public its decision to exercise the PIP by publishing the PIO on its website and must describe the significant detriment to consumers and why the order would reduce that detriment, the consultation taken by ASIC, and the commencement date.[269] This is in addition to serving the order to any persons whom ASIC considers the order to apply to.[270]

ASIC may make a PIO of up to 18 months initially, and an extension would require the approval of the Minister.[271] ASIC can also amend or revoke the PIO anytime if it has not been extended. If it has been extended, the amendment or revocation would require the Minister's approval.[272] All amendments must be published on ASIC's website with a notice describing the reasons for such amendments and the consultation process in arriving at the amendments.[273]

A further example of ASIC's PIP, and of how the courts have interpreted this power, is the case of *Cigno Pty Ltd v Australian Securities and Investments Commission*.[274] In this case, the applicant Cigno applied for judicial review of ASIC's purported exercise of the PIP through a PIO regarding short-term credit.[275] The short-term lending model in question was essentially as follows:[276] the credit offered to consumers consisted mainly of small amounts (up to A$1000), and the application process was advertised to take up to two weeks. An associate of the short-term credit provider would provide separate services to speed up the process if the consumer wanted the money immediately, and the fees for such collateral services might amount to 990 per cent of the loan amount. The money then had to be repaid within 62 days or less, leading to a high risk of defaults. Cigno essentially argued that: (1) ASIC had wrongly focused on the detriment caused by the

266 *Corporations Act* (n 5) s 1023F(1); *NCCPA* (n 253) s 301F(1); *RG 272* (n 251) [61].
267 *RG 272* (n 251) [62].
268 *Corporations Act* (n 5) s 1023F(2); *NCCPA* (n 253) s 301F(2); *RG 272* (n 251) [64].
269 *Corporations Act* (n 5) s 1023L(3); *NCCPA* (n 253) s 301L(3); *RG 272* (n 251) [74].
270 *Corporations Act* (n 5) s 1023L(1); *NCCPA* (n 253) s 301L(1); *RG 272* (n 251) [78].
271 *Corporations Act* (n 5) ss 1023H, 1023G(2); *NCCPA* (n 253) ss 301H, 301G(2); *RG 272* (n 251) [79].
272 *Corporations Act* (n 5) s 1023J; *NCCPA* (n 253) s 301J; *RG 272* (n 251) [83].
273 *Corporations Act* (n 5) s 1023L(6)–(7); *NCCPA* (n 253) s 301L(6)–(7); *RG 272* (n 251) [84].
274 *Cigno Pty Ltd v Australian Securities and Investments Commission* [2020] FCA 479 ('*Cigno v ASIC*').
275 Ibid [1], [3].
276 Ibid [13].

'short-term lending model', rather than the required detriment in respect of the 'financial product'; and hence (2) ASIC was wrongly satisfied about the 'significant detriment to retail clients' caused as it had considered the detriment to be caused by the 'short-term lending model' and the 'collateral fees and charges'.[277]

The first question that the Court posed was: 'Must the financial product or the class of financial products directly cause the significant consumer detriment, or is indirect causation sufficient?'[278] The Court was of the latter view, and concluded that 'the causal requirement is satisfied if the detriment would not have occurred but for the financial product or the class of financial products being made available in those circumstances'.[279] The reasons that led to that conclusion include:

(1) The power in the *Corporations Act* s 1023D(1) and (3) is nuanced, and the prohibition or conditions need not relate to a feature of the product or class of product themselves, and can relate to 'conduct in relation to' the product or product class.[280]
(2) The detriment can arise from circumstances in which the product or product class is issued, as supported by s 1023D(1) and (3).[281]
(3) The Revised Explanatory Memorandum for the Treasury Laws Amendment (Design and Distribution Obligations and Product Intervention Powers) Bill 2019 (Cth) similarly suggests that the PIP contemplates the circumstances in which the product or product class is issued or offered, causing significant detriment, and not something inherent in the product or product class, and hence significant detriment indirectly caused by the product is sufficient.[282]
(4) Section 1023E does not indicate there that there must be a direct causal relationship between the product and the detriment.[283]

Here, the provision of short-term credit in conjunction with collateral contracts constitutes a class of financial products in which a PIO can be made if ASIC is satisfied that the class of financial products has resulted in, or would or was likely to result in, significant detriment to retail clients.[284] Therefore, while ASIC was not satisfied about the fees charged for the short-term credit product resulting in detriment, it was satisfied that the class of financial products – the combination of those fees and the collateral fees – led to significant detriment.[285] Hence, in conclusion, the grounds of review failed.[286]

277 Ibid [18]–[22].
278 Ibid [38].
279 Ibid [42].
280 Ibid [43]–[44]; *Corporations Act* (n 5) s 1023D(1) and (3).
281 *Cigno v ASIC* (n 274) [45]; *Corporations Act* (n 5) s 1023D(1) and (3).
282 *Cigno v ASIC* (n 274) [46]–[52].
283 Ibid [55]; *Corporations Act* (n 5) s 1023E.
284 *Cigno v ASIC* (n 274) [64]; ASIC, *Product Intervention Orders: Short Term Credit Facilities and Continuing Credit Contracts* (Consultation Paper 371, 10 August 2023) ('*CP 371*') 16 <https://download.asic.gov.au/media/51sfg5b5/cp371-published-10-august-2023.pdf>.
285 Ibid [65].
286 Ibid [76].

3.3.2 Product Design and Distribution Obligation (DDO)

The obligations are found under the *Corporations Act* pt 7.8A. The products that are subject to these obligations include:[287]

(a) products that are required to prepare a PDS under the *Corporations Act* pt 7.9 (eg general insurance)

(b) securities that are required to prepare disclosure documents under the *Corporations Act* pt 6D.2, with the exception of ordinary shares, unless the shares are to be converted to preference shares

(c) products that fall outside the purview of pts 6D.2 or 7.9, but which are identified as 'financial products' under div 2 of pt 2 of the *ASIC Act* (as per s 994AA(1)), such as credit facilities defined by the *ASIC Act*. This category comprises credit contracts regulated by the *NCCPA*, such as credit cards and home loans, along with short-term credit not governed by the *NCCPA*

(d) products prescribed under the *Corporations Regulations* (eg depository interests in simple corporate bonds and basic banking products).[288] Products that are new or continuing products are subject to these obligations, but closed products, also known as 'legacy products', that have ceased to offer or issue further post-commencement are not subject to the design and distribution obligations.[289]

The obligations are applicable to the 'issuers'[290] and 'distributors'[291] of financial products that can be acquired either by issue or through regulated sale in Australia.[292] Generally,

287 *Corporations Act* (n 5) ss 994AA, 994B(1); Australian Securities and Investments Commission, *Product Design and Distribution Obligations* (Regulatory Guide 274, 11 December 2020) ('*RG 274*') [20].

288 *Corporations Regulations* (n 59) regs 7.8A.05, 7.8A.07. Certain financial products are exempt from the design and distribution obligations according to *Corporations Act* (n 5) s 994B(3), such as MySuper products, margin lending facilities, fully paid ordinary shares in a company, securities from employee share schemes, and specific products outlined by the *Corporations Regulations* as not requiring a target market determination (TMD), such as medical indemnity insurance. *See RG 274* (n 287) [21].

289 *CP 325* (n 245) 7–8; *Corporations Act* (n 5) s 994B(2).

290 The DDO extends to issuers who fall under several categories: first, those who are required to prepare a disclosure document under the *Corporations Act* (n 5), including entities such as managed investment scheme responsible entities and superannuation trustees, as detailed in the *Corporations Act* s 994B(1)(a) and (b); and, second, if falling outside the first category, those who engage in the regulated sale of financial products as defined in the *ASIC Act* pt 2 div 2, per s 994B(1)(ba). Finally, those who are required by the *Corporations Regulations* (n 59) to make a TMD – such as those issuing, or proposing to issue, basic banking products (as outlined in reg 7.8A.07) – are included under the design and distribution obligations per the *Corporations Act* s 994B(1)(c). See also *RG 274* (n 287) [26].

291 For distributors, the DDO applies to regulated persons as defined in the *Corporations Act* (n 5) s 994A(1), including AFS licensees, authorised representatives and those exempt from holding an AFS licence. As extended by the *Corporations Regulations* (n 59), the definition of 'regulated persons' also extends to cover, among others, credit licensees and credit representatives as per the *NCCPA* (n 253) – including those who are exempt from holding a credit licence (the *Corporations Regulations* (n 59) reg. 7.8A.02(4)). Also, the meaning of 'distribution' is defined under the *Corporations Act* (n 5) s 994A(1) as including: (i) 'dealing in the financial product'; (ii) 'giving a disclosure document in relation to offering a financial product'; (iii) 'providing a PDS'; and (iv) 'providing financial product advice'. For the interpretation of 'distributor' and 'distribution', see *RG 274* (n 287) [27]–[30].

292 *Corporations Act* (n 5) s 994B(1), (2).

the key obligations of an issuer are: (i) to identify an appropriate target market determination (TMD) that describes the target market and distribution conditions and restrictions;[293] (ii) to make that TMD accessible to the public for free;[294] (iii) to take reasonable steps to ensure that distribution will be consistent with that TMD;[295] and (iv) to notify ASIC of any 'significant dealings' that are not consistent with the target market determination.[296] A TMD is 'appropriate' if it would be reasonable to conclude that, if the product is issued or sold in a regulated sale, the retail client would likely be in the target market; and the product would likely be consistent with the likely objectives, financial situation and needs of the retail client.[297] Also, a record-keeping obligation applies to an issuer.[298]

Similarly, the distributor is not permitted to distribute the product unless an appropriate target determination has been made.[299] It is required to take reasonable steps to ensure that distribution is consistent with the TMD,[300] and to notify the issuer of any inconsistent 'significant dealings'.[301] Distributors are also subject to record-keeping duty.[302]

In other words, the DDO mandates issuers and distributors to adopt a consumer-centric approach – prioritising consumer outcomes throughout the product cycle.[303] The DDO sets up requirements at each stage of the process of designing and distributing a financial product, which includes product design,[304] product distribution,[305] and monitoring and review.[306] During the product design phase, per ASIC it is crucial that product governance arrangements encompass a product design and approval mechanism, which should have 'an initial assessment of whether a financial product has been designed in a way that is likely to be consistent with the likely objectives, financial situation and needs of the class of consumers for whom the product is intended'.[307] Within this assessment, issuers ought to contemplate information within reasonable reach regarding consumer outcomes from preceding or similar products.[308] The DDO means that a product development procedure neglecting consumer outcomes 'will not be feasible'.[309] ASIC has explained how this obligation could apply to new financial products

293 *RG 274* (n 287) [8], [59]–[135]; *Corporations Act* (n 5) s 994B.
294 *RG 274* (n 287) [136]–[138]; *Corporations Act* (n 5) s 994B(9).
295 *RG 274* (n 287) [139]–[147]; *Corporations Act* (n 5) s 994E(1).
296 *RG 274* (n 287) [157]–[162]; *Corporations Act* (n 5) s 994G.
297 *Corporations Act* (n 5) s 994B(8); *RG 274* (n 287) [64]–[66].
298 *Corporations Act* (n 5) s 994F(1), (3); *RG 274* (n 287) [164]–[165]
299 *RG 274* (n 287) [168]; *Corporations Act* (n 5) s 994D.
300 *RG 274* (n 287) [166]–[210]; *Corporations Act* (n 5) s 994E(3).
301 *RG 274* (n 287) [211]–[215]; *Corporations Act* (n 5) s 994F(6).
302 *RG 274* (n 287) [216]–[223]; *Corporations Act* (n 5) s 994F(3).
303 See *Revised Explanatory Memorandum* (n 262) [1.7].
304 See, eg, *Corporations Act* (n 5) s 994B.
305 See, eg, ibid s 994E(3).
306 See, eg, ibid s 994C.
307 *RG 274* (n 287) [39].
308 Ibid.
309 Ibid.

and continuing products[310] while underscoring the 'consumer-centric approach' in designing a product.[311]

Issuers and distributors are required to take reasonable steps to fulfil their DDO by putting in place product governance arrangements at the distribution stage. These arrangements must be 'designed to reduce the risk that financial products will not be consistent with the likely objectives, financial situation and needs of the consumers who acquire them'.[312] Moreover, such arrangements must encompass a mechanism for efficient communication between those tasked with designing the financial product and those in charge of marketing and distributing it, especially concerning the intended consumer outcomes associated with the product.[313] Finally, product governance arrangements should enable a continuous design and distribution process with regular monitoring and review of product performance to address issues.[314]

In December 2022, ASIC issued interim stop orders against Australian Fiduciaries Limited for three funds due to deficiencies in their TMD, halting certain activities to protect retail investors per the requirements under the DDO.[315] Notwithstanding these developments, a recent review by ASIC of the reforms has shown that there is 'considerable room for improvement'.[316] The key issue was found in determining an appropriate target market. There were cases where the target market was defined too broadly, or

310 The product design stage for new financial products entails identifying a target consumer group, defining the product based on this group's likely objectives, and ensuring the product aligns with their needs. It also involves analysing expected distribution methods to ensure the product reaches its target market, conducting thorough testing of the product, and establishing a framework for measuring and monitoring consumer outcomes during distribution, adhering to the monitoring obligation specified in *Corporations Act* (n 5) ss 994B and 994C and in *RG 274* (n 287) [42]. On the other hand, the product design stage for continuing products involves establishing a target market, reviewing current distribution arrangements, possibly redesigning the product or distribution if misalignment occurs, and setting up a system to measure and monitor consumer outcomes over time, in line with the obligation for periodic reviews under the *Corporations Act* ss 994B and 994C and *RG 274* (n 287) [43].

311 As ASIC explains, when designing a financial product and delivering it to the target market, taking a 'consumer-centric' approach is crucial. Issuers should use their existing knowledge and experience of consumer behaviour to align with the DDO, ensuring that their tactics do not hinder consumers from accessing 'products that are consistent with their likely objectives, financial situation and needs or that will result in consumers receiving unsuitable products'. *RG 274* (n 287) [47].

312 Ibid [48].

313 Ibid [49].

314 *Corporations Act* (n 5) ss 994B(8)(b) and 994C. Also, it is crucial that, post-launch, an issuer should utilise reasonably available information regarding how consumers in the target market are engaging with its product or comparable products in the market and the actual consumer outcomes from these products. ASIC, *RG 274* (n 287) [51], [151]–[153].

315 Australian Securities and Investments Commission, 'Interim Stop Orders Placed on Three Funds from Australian Fiduciaries Limited' (Media Release, 2 December 2022) <https://asic.gov.au/about-asic/news-centre/find-a-media-release/2022-releases/22-335mr-interim-stop-orders-placed-on-three-funds-from-australian-fiduciaries-limited/>. ASIC expressed concern that the Australian Fiduciaries Limited inadequately assessed risks while defining target markets for the three funds. It found that the inclusion of investors needing liquidity, those tolerating medium to high risk, and those with an undefined higher net worth was inappropriate due to the funds' liquidity features and investment risks.

316 Australian Securities and Investments Commission, *Design and Distribution Obligations: Investment Products* (Report No REP 762, 3 May 2023) 2 <https://download.asic.gov.au/media/llbdpf5b/rep762-published-03-may-2023.pdf>.

where distribution conditions were not made or were made inappropriately, or where inappropriate levels of risks or portfolio allocation were used in the target market.[317] ASIC continues to monitor the industry and will take action for any breaches.[318]

3.4 Robo-advice

Digital advice, otherwise known as 'robo-advice' or 'automated advice', is defined by ASIC as the 'provision of automated financial product advice using algorithms and technology and without the direct involvement of a human adviser'.[319]

Robo-advice has gained significant attention and investment within the financial and credit services sector, driven by its stringent regulations and the appeal of reducing costs while ensuring compliance.[320] The systematic, statistics-based nature of advisory services lends itself well to automation, drawing investments from both established and emerging financial entities into digital solutions for operations and client engagements.[321] In practice, in the financial sector, robo-advice spans insurance, credit, budgeting and investment, with the latter two being the most prevalent.[322] Investment robo-advice typically involves consumers completing a questionnaire to establish their financial goals, expectations and risk tolerance, leading to personalised investment recommendations based on matched profiles and pre-set portfolios.[323] In Australia, the digital advice landscape has evolved rapidly since its notable growth inception in 2014. This evolution is characterised by the emergence of new AFS licensees focused on startup digital advice ventures, alongside the strategic pivot of existing AFS licensees to integrate digital advice solutions into their service offerings.[324] This trend reflects a robust growth trajectory within the digital advice sector, signalling a transformative shift in the financial services industry.

Regulatory Guide 255 ('*RG 255*') offers hands-on advice to digital advisers in Australia, covering everything from obtaining a licence to the delivery of advice. While *RG 255* does not deviate from ASIC's current policy directions, it does delve deeper into a few aspects especially relevant to digital advice, offering detailed practical guidance.

3.4.1 Facts, financial product advice and relevant requirements

In determining the necessity for an AFSL, the distinction between providing 'facts' and 'financial product advice' plays a critical role. If the robo-advice solely dispenses 'factual'

317 Ibid 3.
318 Ibid 4.
319 Australian Securities and Investments Commission, *Providing Digital Financial Product Advice to Retail Clients* (Regulatory Guide 255, 30 August 2016) ('*RG 255*').
320 Jeannie Marie Paterson, 'Making Robo-Advisers Careful? Duties of Care in Providing Automated Financial Advice to Consumers' (2021) 15(3–4) *Law and Financial Markets Review* 278, 281.
321 Ibid.
322 Ibid. See also Donatella Porrini, 'The Effects of Innovation on Market Competition: The Case of the Insurance Comparison Websites' (2018) 29(3) *Marketing and Management of Innovations* 324; Daphne Foreman, 'Best Budgeting Apps of 2022' (*Forbes*, 2 September 2022); Taylor Tepper, '5 Best Robo Advisors of September 2022' (*Forbes*, 1 September 2022).
323 Paterson (n 320); Daniel Belanche, Luis V Casaló and Carlos Flavián, 'Artificial Intelligence in FinTech: Understanding Robo-Advisors Adoption among Customers' (2019) 119(7) *Industrial Management & Data Systems* 1411, 1411–13.
324 *RG 255* (n 319).

information, obtaining an AFSL is unnecessary as communications that consist only of factual information will not constitute financial product advice.[325] Per ASIC, 'factual information' refers to objectively ascertainable information whose truth or accuracy cannot be reasonably questioned.[326] Examples typically include online calculators or websites that set out information about features of various financial products which do not endorse any specific product, investment strategy or action plan but, rather, offer fact-based data that might benefit the customer.[327] Such factual advice constitutes objectively verifiable details about financial products, whose truth or accuracy is beyond reasonable dispute.[328]

Conversely, providing 'financial product advice' necessitates holding an AFSL or qualifying for an exemption.[329] The provision of 'financial product advice' includes both 'general advice' and 'personal advice'.[330] When delivering general advice, advisers must issue a caution to their clients, indicating that the advice does not take into consideration the client's personal objectives, financial situation or needs.[331] Clients are advised to assess the relevance of the advice given their own circumstances before acting on it.[332] Moreover, if the advice pertains to acquiring a specific financial product, clients are encouraged to review the PDS for the product, if applicable, before making any purchase decisions.[333]

Similarly, in the case of 'personal advice', which is defined as financial product advice given where the provider has considered the client's objectives, financial situation and needs, or a reasonable person might expect the provider to do so, an AFSL is required unless an applicable exemption applies.[334] However, there are additional obligations to issue an SOA and to comply with the 'best interests' duty and related obligations, as noted earlier in this chapter, when personal financial product advice is given to a retail client.[335]

3.4.2 Resources

Digital advice licensees must possess adequate resources in two main areas, as specified by ASIC: human resources and technological resources.[336] For human resources, digital advice licensees must have people within their business who understand the technology and algorithms used for providing digital advice and are capable of reviewing the advice generated by algorithms to ensure compliance.[337] This mitigates the risk of poor-quality

325 Ibid [20].
326 Ibid [21].
327 Ibid [22]–[30].
328 Ibid [21].
329 Ibid [23].
330 Ibid [25].
331 Australian Securities and Investments Commission, *Giving Information, General Advice and Scaled Advice* (Regulatory Guide 244, December 2012) [38].
332 Ibid.
333 Ibid.
334 ASIC, *RG 255* (n 319) [26]; *Corporations Act* (n 5) s 766B(3).
335 *Corporations Act* (n 5) ss 946A–947E, s 961B(1).
336 *RG 255* (n 319) [59].
337 Ibid [60].

advice or system issues.[338] The adequacy of human resources required to meet these regulatory guidelines may vary depending on the size and complexity of the business.[339]

Furthermore, a digital advice licensee must ensure adequate technological resources for maintaining client records, protecting confidential information, meeting operational needs, and complying with legal obligations.[340] Crucially, if there is outsourcing of functions related to the digital advice business, measures should be in place to select suitable outsourced service providers and to monitor their ongoing performance, as digital advice licensees remain responsible for the financial services provided to clients despite outsourcing.[341]

3.4.3 Adequate risk management systems

As per the *Corporations Act* s 912A(1)(h), digital advice licensees have an obligation to establish and maintain adequate risk management systems; this remains consistent regardless of whether they provide traditional financial product advice or digital advice, except for APRA-regulated bodies.[342] An adequate risk management system will require the regular monitoring and testing of algorithms that underpin the advice, as well as the management of cyber risks and assessment of information security arrangements.[343]

3.4.3.1 Monitoring and testing algorithms

Digital advice licensees are expected to monitor and test the algorithms that underpin their advice regularly, with the extent of these arrangements depending on the nature, scale and complexity of their business.[344] This involves various measures such as having system design documentation, documented test strategies, processes for managing algorithm changes, and controls for error detection and resolution, among others.[345] Furthermore, there should be robust compliance arrangements to monitor and test the quality of advice provided to clients.[346]

3.4.3.2 Cyber risks and information security

In addition, digital advice licensees must be aware of the heightened risk of cyber threats, including malicious cyber activities, as they are more likely to be targeted by hackers.[347] As such, digital advice licensees are expected to evaluate their cybersecurity using established frameworks and standards, such as those provided by the National Institute of Standards and Technology or the Australian Signals Directorate, and to ensure that their information security arrangements comply with recognised security standards, particularly in the context of cloud technology adoption.[348]

338 Ibid [62].
339 Ibid [64].
340 Ibid [65].
341 Ibid [67].
342 Ibid [70].
343 Ibid [70]–[79].
344 Ibid [72].
345 Ibid [73].
346 Ibid [74].
347 Ibid [75]–[76].
348 Ibid [77]–[79].

3.4.4 Compensation arrangements

Under the *Corporations Act* s 912B, AFS licensees serving retail clients must establish compensation arrangements to reimburse clients for losses incurred due to breaches by the licensee or its representatives of their obligations in ch 7.[349] These arrangements must generally either obtain adequate professional indemnity (PI) insurance as required in the *Corporations Regulations* or receive ASIC approval as alternative arrangements.[350] While the adequacy of a PI insurance depends on the nature, scale and complexity of the business, and its potential liability for compensation claims, Regulatory Guide 126 provides guidance on ASIC's minimum criteria for adequate PI insurance as well as requirements for alternative arrangements approval.[351]

In assessing the adequacy of the compensation arrangements, the following factors should be considered: client growth trends, potential widespread losses from flawed algorithms, and the implications of claims aggregation clauses and sub-limits.[352] Additionally, digital advice providers are advised to review their PI policy features regularly to address any gaps or changes in business operations, to notify PI insurers of significant business changes, and to ensure sufficient financial resources to cover any insurance gaps if renegotiation is not feasible.[353]

3.5 Summary

This chapter provides the historical background against which the current Australian regime governing financial services was created. It is a requirement to hold an Australian Financial Services Licence to provide financial services unless permitted otherwise (eg the sandbox exemption detailed in Chapter 4). This chapter introduces various disclosure and conduct duties applied to an AFS licensee. The 'best interests' duty and related obligations created by the FOFA reform are of particular significance. These duties have received criticism from the Banking Royal Commission; currently, the Government is considering a new proposal to overhaul the regime. In this chapter, we also delve into recent reforms. First, the Product Intervention Power enables ASIC to pre-emptively address consumer risks in financial product designs. Second, the Design and Distribution Obligation mandates a consumer-centric approach in financial product design and distribution, ensuring that products meet the needs and financial conditions of the target market. These reforms, aimed at enhancing consumer protection, reflect proactive regulatory measures.

FURTHER READING

Byrne, Corey, 'The Liability of Directors and Officers When AFS Licensees Provide Defective Financial Product Advice' (2022) 39(1) *Company and Securities Law Journal* 19.

349 Ibid [80].
350 Ibid [81].
351 Ibid [83].
352 Ibid [85].
353 Ibid.

Hanrahan, Pamela, 'Legal Framework for the Provision of Financial Advice and Sale of Financial Products to Australian Households' (Background Paper 7, Royal Commission into Misconduct in the Banking, Superannuation and Financial Services Industry, 2018) <https://financialservices.royalcommission.gov.au/publications/Documents/legal-framework-for-the-provision-of-financial-advice-background-paper-7.pdf>.

He, Weiping and Han-Wei Liu, 'Rebuilding Trust: Regulation of Financial Advisers in the UK' (2021) 16(4) *Capital Markets Law Journal* 393.

He, Weiping and Han-Wei Liu, 'Regulating Financial Advisers in the UK: Lessons for Australia' (2021) 44(1) *University of New South Wales Law Journal* 424.

Latimer, Paul and Michael Duffy, 'Deconstructing Digital Currency and Its Risks: Why ASIC Must Rise to the Regulatory Challenge' (2019) 47(1) *Federal Law Review* 126.

Liu, Han-Wei et al, 'In Whose Best Interests? Regulating Financial Advisers, the Royal Commission and the Dilemma of Reform' (2020) 42(1) *The Sydney Law Review* 37.

Nehme, Marina, 'Product Intervention Power: An Extra Layer of Protection to Consumers' (2020) 31(1) *Journal of Banking and Finance Law and Practice* 88.

Paterson, Jeannie, 'Making Robo-Advisers Careful? Duties of Care in Providing Automated Financial Advice to Consumers' (2021) 15(3–4) *Law and Financial Markets Review* 278.

Peckham, Matthew, 'From the Wallis Report to the Murray Report: A Critical Analysis of the Financial Services Regime between Two Financial System Inquiries' (2015) 33(7) *Company and Securities Law Journal* 478.

Tarr, Julie-Anne, 'Financial Advisers – New Remuneration Constraints and Competency Requirements Addressing Perverse Incentives and Poor Advice' (2017) 35(8) *Company and Securities Law Journal* 561.

Thomas, Rosie, 'Regulating Financial Product Design in Australia: An Analysis of the UK Approach' (2017) 28(2) *Journal of Banking and Finance Law and Practice* 95.

QUESTIONS

(1) Alex oversees the development of a compliance training program for a financial advisory firm. The aim is to ensure that all employees are well versed in the latest financial regulations. By the end of the course, Alex expects participants to understand what constitutes 'financial services' and 'financial products'.

   (a) Would crypto-assets be considered as 'financial products'?
   (b) Differentiate between 'retail' and 'wholesale' clients.
   (c) Identify the three main disclosure documents required for financial advisory firms.
   (d) Explain what 'FSG', 'SOA' and 'PDS' are. When are they required (and not required)?
   (e) Explain the 'best interests' duty and related obligations under the *Corporations Act 2001* (Cth).
   (f) To what extent would you agree with the critique from the Banking Royal Commission about the 'best interests' duty and the 'safe harbour' provision?

(2) Ben is having difficulty paying his rent, as he spent his rent money on a new smartphone. In need of cash urgently, he responded to an advertisement he saw on Facebook by XYZ Pty Ltd, which offered 'fast cash' within 48 hours with 'no credit check required'. Ben immediately registered on XYZ's website for the $2000 cash rebate promotion.

The next morning, Ben received a phone call from Alex, an employee of XYZ. Alex asked Ben a few questions about himself, such as his age, occupation and income. Ben gave vague responses to the questions, saying that he was unsure about his income, as it fluctuated. As Alex had to rush to another important work meeting, he didn't have time to probe further and proceeded to give Ben financial advice. Specifically, Alex advised him to switch his life insurance and superannuation policies to a new provider in order to receive the cash rebate. Although Ben hasn't heard of this before, as it isn't mentioned on XYZ's website, he accepts Alex's advice so as to get the cash rebate.

Subsequently, advice fees are charged out of Ben's superannuation funds, and Ben receives his $2000 cash rebate from XYZ, which is a small portion of the commission XYZ gained from the insurer. Ben is shocked when he notices that his superannuation balance has dropped by 35 per cent. For context, XYZ holds an Australian Financial Services Licence, which allows it to advise its retail clients about life insurance and superannuation products. XYZ's internal policies require its employees to switch their clients' insurance and superannuation policies to a company called 'Insurance & Super'. Since the start of this year, XYZ has conducted two compliance training courses for its employees regarding their regulatory obligations as financial advisers.

Ben asks his friend Cindy for advice on whether she thinks Alex has breached the 'best interests' duty and related obligations under the *Corporations Act 2001* (Cth).

CHAPTER 4

NEW CHALLENGES IN THE DATA-DRIVEN FINANCIAL MARKETS

4.1 Introduction

In recent times, banks, financial organisations and technology companies have leveraged emerging technologies such as artificial intelligence (AI), big data and blockchain to transform the global financial market at an unparalleled pace. The term 'Fintech', a blend of 'financial' and 'technology', has become a part of common vocabulary. Generally speaking, 'Fintech' refers to the application of technology in providing financial services.[1] The Financial Stability Board (FSB) describes Fintech as 'technologically enabled innovation in financial services that could result in new business models, applications, processes or products with an associated material effect on financial markets and institutions and the provision of financial services'.[2]

While the term 'Fintech' gained popularity towards the end of the twentieth century, the integration of technology into the financial sector has a much longer history. Researchers have pointed to the commercial use of the telegraph and the establishment of the first successful transatlantic cable by the Atlantic Telegraph Company as foundational elements for the initial wave of financial globalisation in the late 1800s.[3] The introduction of the automated teller machine (ATM) by Barclays Bank in 1967,[4] the launch of online banking by Wells Fargo in the United States in 1995[5] and of direct banks without branches in the United Kingdom in 2005,[6] are all prime examples.[7] Fintech activities can now be seen elsewhere in the financial market. According to the FSB, there are five major categories:

(1) payment, clearing and settlement
(2) deposits, lending and capital raising
(3) insurance
(4) investment management
(5) market support.[8]

While it is true that Fintech has been around for decades, it is equally valid that various factors have facilitated the adoption of new technologies, making Fintech today a

1 According to Arner et al, the origin of the term 'Fintech' can be traced to the early 1990s and the Financial Services Technology Consortium, a Citigroup-led project to foster technological cooperation efforts. See Douglas W Arner, Janos Barberis and Ross P Buckley, 'The Evolution of FinTech: A New Post-Crisis Paradigm' (2016) 47(4) *Georgetown Journal of International Law* 1271, 2172; see also Stephanie Walden, 'What is Fintech', *Forbes Advisor* (25 July 2022) <https://www.forbes.com/advisor/banking/what-is-fintech/> (which defines 'Fintech' as a catch-all phrase for technology related to the provision of financial services).

2 'FinTech', *Financial Stability Board (FSB)* (Web Page, 4 December 2023) <https://www.fsb.org/work-of-the-fsb/financial-innovation-and-structural-change/fintech/>.

3 Arner et al (n 1) 1274.

4 'From the Archives: The ATM is 50', *Barclays* (Web Page, 27 June 2017) <https://home.barclays/news/2017/06/from-the-archives-the-atm-is-50>.

5 Alyssa Bentz, 'First in Online Banking', *Wells Fargo* (14 March 2019) <https://www.wellsfargohistory.com/first-in-online-banking/>.

6 For instance, First Direct was launched by Midland Bank more than 30 years ago. See, eg, Nicholas Megaw, 'HSBC Plans First Direct Relaunch to Compete with Digital Rivals', *Financial Times* (14 October 2019).

7 Arner et al (n 1) 1283.

8 Financial Stability Board, *Financial Stability Implications from FinTech: Supervisory and Regulatory Issues that Merit Authorities' Attention* (27 June 2017) ('*FinTech Supervisory and Regulatory Issues*') 8 <https://www.fsb.org/wp-content/uploads/R270617.pdf>.

'phenomenon distinct from earlier eras of innovation'.[9] Among other factors, the Global Financial Crisis (GFC) played a decisive role. The collapse of major investment banks such as Lehman Brothers severely shattered the financial sector's brand image. For instance, a 2009 survey showed that only 22 per cent of Americans expressed trust in banks – down from 53 per cent just five years before the crisis.[10] In contrast, high-tech companies such as Google, Amazon and Apple gained a higher level of public confidence (above 50 per cent).[11] High-tech firms were able to take advantage of this shift in public perception to offer new solutions to clients who previously considered the incumbent financial institutions as the only potential handlers of their money. Digital wallet providers such as Apple Pay and Google Pay, as discussed in Chapter 9, are notable examples of these alternatives to traditional banks.

The GFC not only changed the public's perception of the financial sector but also led to labour market shifts. As the post-crisis reforms (eg Basel III's more onerous rules relating to the extension of credit[12]) were gradually put in place, the increased compliance costs damaged financial institutions' profitability.[13] The ensuing large-scale redundancies left many professionals seeking jobs elsewhere.[14] As the prestige of working with Wall Street financial institutions declined, Silicon Valley high-tech firms – which often offered considerable revenue sharing among employees through stock-based compensation schemes – emerged as a popular alternative.[15] Such structural shifts coincided with the rapid development of new technologies such as AI, big data and blockchain, aided by high-level penetration of smart devices and sophisticated application programming interfaces (API) that bring together applications that usually would not be able to communicate.[16] There is therefore a growing demand to meet a variety of customers' expectations amid the widespread adoption of new technologies and mobile devices.

As new technologies redefine business models by removing the middleman in many sectors (eg Airbnb and Uber),[17] Fintech also leads to a new phenomenon known as

9 Jelena Madir, 'Introduction' in Jelena Madir (ed), *Fintech: Law and Regulation* (Edgar Elgar Publishing, 2019) 1, 2.

10 Andrew Dugan, 'Confidence in U.S. Banks Low but Rising', *Gallup* (22 June 2015) <https://news.gallup.com/poll/183749/confidence-banks-low-rising.aspx>.

11 'Survey Shows Americans Trust Technology Firms More Than Banks and Retailers', *MEDICI* (25 June 2015) <https://gomedici.com/survey-shows-americans-trust-technology-firms-more-than-banks-and-retailers/>.

12 See BIS, 'Basel III: International Regulatory Framework for Banks' (Web Page) <https://www.bis.org/bcbs/basel3.htm>.

13 Arner et al (n 1) 1302.

14 David Ellis, 'Citigroup to Cut More Than 50,000 Jobs', *CNNMoney* (17 November 2008) <https://money.cnn.com/2008/11/17/news/companies/citigroup/>.

15 Olivia Oran and Heather Somerville, 'Exclusive: Three Goldman Bankers Leave for Uber as Tech World Raids Wall Street Talent', *Reuters* (25 November 2015) <https://www.reuters.com/article/us-goldman-uber/exclusive-three-goldman-bankers-leave-for-uber-as-tech-world-raids-wall-street-talent-idUSKBN0TE0E820151125>; Trusha Chokshi, 'Why Silicon Valley Wants Wall Street's Best', *CNBC* (30 July 2014), <https://www.cnbc.com/2014/07/30/careers-bankers-leave-wall-street-for-technology-industry.html>; Aaron CF Salerno, 'Regulating the Fintech Revolution: How Regulators Can Adapt to Twenty-First Century Financial Technology' (2020) 75 *New York University Annual Survey of American Law* 365, 372.

16 Madir (n 9) 2.

17 Nick Hoffman, 'The Gatekepers Must Go: How Disintermediation is Changing Business Models', *Medium* (9 January 2018) <https://medium.com/@nickhoffman/the-gatekeepers-must-go-how-disintermediation-is-changing-business-models-a37bdddde6a3>.

'financial disintermediation'.[18] While, as Tom Lin observed, the fundamental goals of financial intermediation have remained consistent, technological advancements and market evolutions have significantly altered the methodologies and agents employed to achieve them.[19] Data analytics has emerged as the preferred analytical tool, and automated computer programs have supplanted traditional human-led initiatives.[20] The necessity for physical branches has been largely obviated by the advent of digital platforms, such as websites and mobile applications.[21] Various financial intermediaries, separate from traditional banking entities, have risen to prominence. Hedge funds, private equity firms and other capital market entities have seen an increase in their influence, particularly with the rise of shadow banking systems.[22] High-speed electronic communication networks and alternative trading platforms now present viable alternatives to traditional stock exchanges,[23] while online banking institutions (eg Ally in the United States)[24] and automated wealth management services (eg Vanguard) are providing formidable competition to traditional solutions.[25] Peer-to-peer lending platforms[26] and innovative payment systems such as Apple Pay and Google Pay have further disrupted traditional financial intermediation mechanisms.[27] In short, while the core objectives of financial intermediation remain unaltered, the methods and agents employed in achieving them have undergone substantial transformation.

Despite the rise of disintermediation and the significant impact of high-tech companies in the evolving financial landscape, the role of traditional banks and legacy financial institutions remains important. In certain situations, these incumbent banks can engage in the Fintech revolution by integrating new technologies or by partnering with Fintech firms.[28] The use of technology is crucial for banks to survive a significant expansion in the regulatory environment and to react to the challenges of newcomers in the post-GFC era. In other situations, banks and financial institutions take stakes in Fintech firms or acquire them outright: in Australia, for instance, the Big Four banks have invested in over 50 Fintech companies, local and overseas, in the past few years.[29] In still other contexts,

18 Tom CW Lin, 'Infinite Financial Intermediation' (2015) 50(3) *Wake Forest Law Review* 643.

19 Ibid 652.

20 'Ask the Algorithm: Human Wealth Advisers are Going Out of Fashion', *Economist* (7 May 2015).

21 Jonathan Pearlman, 'Australia's Post-Covid-19 Endangered Species: ATMs and Bank Branches', *Straits Times* (29 January 2023) <https://www.straitstimes.com/asia/australianz/australia-s-post-covid-endangered-species-atms-and-bank-branches>.

22 Lin (n 18) 653.

23 Jason Fink, Kristin E Fink and James P Weston, 'Competition on the Nasdaq and the Growth of Electronic Communication Networks' (2006) 30(9) *Journal of Banking & Finance* 2537.

24 'About Us: Committed Beyond Banking', *Ally* (Web Page), <https://www.ally.com/about/>; Estelle Liu, *Stay Competitive in the Digital Age: The Future of* Banks (IMF Working Paper No. 2021/046, 1 February 2021) <https://ssrn.com/abstract=3852774>.

25 'Vanguard's Big Push Into Financial Advice', *Economist* (13 January 2022).

26 Mark Cummins et al, 'Addressing Information Asymmetries in Online Peer-to-Peer Lending' in Theo Lynn et al (eds), *Disrupting Finance: FinTech and Strategy in the 21st Century* (Palgrave, 2019) 15.

27 Adam J Levitin, 'Pandora's Digital Box: The Promise and Perils of Digital Wallets' (2018) 166(2) *University of Pennsylvania Law Review* 305.

28 Sarah Simpkins, 'Big Banks Well-Placed Against Fintech Rivals', *Momentum Media* (22 May 2019) <https://www.fintechbusiness.com/industry/1397-big-banks-well-placed-against-fintech-rivals>.

29 Clancy Yeates, 'ACCC's Sims Warns on Big Banks Fintech Takeovers' *Sydney Morning Herald* (26 January 2021).

incumbent banks may engage in anti-competitive conduct[30] or lobby against market entry. In terms of the latter, banks have traditionally had comparative advantages compared to high-tech companies in leveraging their influence in the law-making process, domestic or international, to drive policies in their favour;[31] such 'regulatory capture', as noted in Chapter 1, is still evident even following the GFC.[32] Admittedly, though, some of these tech companies – especially Big Techs – have emerged as active players in influencing government policies.[33] It is also the case that policymakers may see the rise of Fintech as new opportunities to fill gaps in the availability of local financial services and therefore roll out policies that are friendly to startups.

A pressing inquiry that naturally arises from these evolving trends is the appropriate regulatory response to rapidly advancing technologies within this stringently regulated sector: *Should governments adopt a more laissez-faire stance towards Fintech activities? If so, why, and through what mechanisms? Conversely, if not, what might the limitations or regulations look like?* This presents a formidable challenge for policymakers – balancing the promise of innovation against potential risks. While Fintech appears promising, the GFC's history has revealed that innovation is not always a good thing and may come hand in hand with risks.[34]

Navigating the appropriate regulatory framework for Fintech activities is fraught with complexities, not least of which is the 'pacing problem' – the inherent lag in the legal system's ability to adapt to rapidly evolving technologies.[35] In the post-GFC era, policymakers confront what Brummer and Yadav have termed the 'Innovation Trilemma', which compels regulators to strike a delicate balance among three competing policy objectives: maintaining market integrity, fostering financial innovation, and ensuring that the rules are both simple and transparent. This conundrum makes the task of regulation not just

30 Sarah Simpkins, 'Regulation, Major Banks Killing Competition: Fintech Inquiry', *Investor Daily* (28 January 2020).

31 Kathryn Petralia et al, *Banking Disrupted? Financial Intermediation in an Era of Transformational Technology* (Geneva Reports on the World Economy 22, 2019).

32 Huw Macartney, David Howarth and Scott James, 'Bank Power and Public Policy Since the Financial Crisis' (2020) 22(1) *Business and Politics* 1.

33 The term 'Big Tech' often refers to four major technology firms in the United States, which may include Facebook, Apple, Google and Amazon (FAGA). Occasionally, Microsoft is added to the list. See, eg, Richard Waters, 'Move Over Faangs, Make Way for Maga', *Financial Times* (28 July 2018) (referring to 'Maga' as including Microsoft, Apple, Google and Amazon).

34 Manuel Sánchez, 'Financial Innovation and the Global Crisis' (2010) 11(5) *International Journal of Business and Management* 26.

35 The interplay between law and technology over time is a common topic in legal and policy discussions, often emphasising outdated legislation. In these dialogues, law is frequently seen as lagging behind technological development. While this view might oversimplify their dynamics, it underscores the difficulty in maintaining laws that are relevant and adaptable in a continuously changing socio-technical setting. This dilemma is sometimes termed the pacing problem or the challenge of regulatory coherence. See generally Braden R Allenby, 'Governance and Technology Systems: The Challenge of Emerging Technologies' in Gary E Marchant et al (eds), *The Growing Gap Between Emerging Technologies and Legal-Ethical Oversight: The Pacing Problem* (Springer, 2011) 3; Lyria Bennett Moses and Monika Zalnieriute, 'Law and Technology in the Dimension of Time' in Sofia Ranchordás and Yaniv Roznai (eds), *Time, Law and Change: An Interdisciplinary Study* (Hart Publishing, 2020) 303; and Lyria Bennett Moses, 'Recurring Dilemmas: The Law's Race to Keep Up with Technological Change' (2007) (2) *University of Illinois Journal of Law, Technology and Policy* 239.

challenging, but a critical endeavour that requires thoughtful deliberation and agile policymaking.[36]

Various regulatory approaches have evolved in response to such a trilemma. Some countries opt for a 'do nothing' approach – this can be permissive to highly restrictive, depending on the current state of play of the relevant laws.[37] Others use case-by-case exemptions – such as 'no-action' letters in the United States.[38] Still others adopt a more structured experimental approach by creating the regulatory sandbox to test their business concepts in a controlled environment, as seen in Australia.

Of relevance to our purpose is the sandbox approach. Under this model, innovators are offered an environment with fewer regulatory constraints in which to conduct limited tests in the real world. In doing so, regulators can control and manage the associated risks while supporting innovation and, hence, economic growth. In a way, therefore, regulatory sandboxes can serve as a 'forum for educating regulators on new technologies' and for 'lowering regulatory barriers to entry to allow new tech firms to compete with the largest financial institutions'.[39] In short, as per the FSB, the regulatory sandbox can help to meet policy objectives such as consumer and investor protection, market integrity, financial inclusion, and the promotion of innovation and competition.[40] The regulatory sandbox was first introduced in the United Kingdom as part of its Project Innovate; it was then gradually diffused to Australia, Canada, Hong Kong, Malaysia, Singapore, Taiwan, Thailand, the Netherlands and Switzerland, among other jurisdictions.[41] However, the design of each of these sandboxes may vary. Some are open to *both* existing licence holders and startups, while others are restricted to one or the other. In some jurisdictions, admission into the sandbox is subject to *ex ante* regulatory approval; in others, it is sufficient to notify regulators. Some jurisdictions allow the testing period to continue for up to two years, while others limit it to no more than six months.

This chapter examines Australia's adoption of regulatory sandboxes and contextualises this within the wider ambit of comparative law. Additionally, we shall explore a subject intrinsically connected to the data-driven financial market: data protection. The escalation of data sharing will be addressed in Chapter 9, alongside other emerging trends, given that the Australian Government is presently assessing its payments ecosystem. The ensuing discourse will elucidate the nuances of these topics, integrating them into the broader context of financial regulatory frameworks.

To be sure, the applications of Fintech and their ramifications go beyond the scope of this book, as do issues such as cybersecurity, digital disclosure and 'RegTech' – that

36 Chris Brummer and Yesha Yadav, 'Fintech and the Innovation Trilemma' (2019) 107(2) *Georgetown Law Journal* 235, 237–42.

37 Dirk A Zetzsche et al, 'Regulating a Revolution: From Regulatory Sandboxes to Smart Regulation' (2017) 23(1) *Fordham Journal of Corporate and Financial Law* 31, 50.

38 Ibid 59.

39 Hilary J Allen, 'Regulatory Sandboxes' (2019) 87(3) *George Washington Law Review* 579, 580.

40 *FinTech Supervisory and Regulatory Issues* (n 8) 5.

41 Chang-Hsien Tsai, Ching-Fu Lin and Han-Wei Liu, 'Sandbox Regulatory Strategy and Its Limitations' (2020) 53(3) *Cornell International Law Journal* 261; Baker McKenzie, *A Guide to Regulatory Fintech Sandboxes Internationally* (2020) <https://www.bakermckenzie.com/-/media/files/insight/guides/2020/baker-mckenzie--a-guide-to-regulatory-fintech-sandboxes-internationally.pdf>.

is, using technologies in response to the ever-growing demands of compliance within the financial industry.[42] Data-driven challenges are prevalent across the banking and financial sectors. Among others, we delve into robo-advice (digital advice) in Chapter 3 ('Financial Products Regulation') and digital currencies and data sharing further in Chapter 9 ('Electronic Banking').

4.2 Regulatory sandbox: Australia and beyond

4.2.1 Background

In 2015, the Australian Securities and Investments Commission (ASIC) launched its innovation hub designed to help businesses work through the regulatory regime. Building upon this, in 2016 ASIC launched the first iteration of the regulatory sandbox framework by releasing Regulatory Guide 257: *Testing Fintech Products and Services Without Holding an AFS or Credit Licence* ('*RG 257*').[43] Inspired by a similar regulatory initiative in the United Kingdom,[44] the 'fintech industry licensing exemption', provided under *ASIC Corporations (Concept Validation Licensing Exemption) Instrument 2016/1175* and *ASIC Credit (Concept Validation Licensing Exemption) Instrument 2016/1176*, was intended to allow businesses to test their technology.[45] While these instruments appeared promising, the sandbox has been far from successful in attracting Fintech businesses, for there have been only seven applications since its establishment.

February 2020 saw the passage of the *Treasury Laws Amendment (2018 Measures No 2) Act 2020* (Cth), implemented through the *Corporations (FinTech Sandbox Australian Financial Services Licence Exemption) Regulations 2020* (Cth) ('*AFSL Exemption Regulations*') and the *National Consumer Credit Protection (FinTech Sandbox Australian Credit Licence*

42 FSB refers to 'RegTech' as 'any range of applications of FinTech for regulatory and compliance requirements and reporting by regulated financial institutions'. The Basel Committee on Banking Supervision (BCBS) also coined another concept – namely, Supervisory Technology (SupTech), which pertains to the use of Fintech by supervisory authorities. See generally Financial Stability Board, *Artificial Intelligence and Machine Learning in Financial Services – Market Developments and Financial Stability Implications* (Report, 1 November 2017) <http://www.fsb.org/wp-content/uploads/P011117.pdf>; Basel Committee on Banking Supervision, *Sound Practices – Implications of Fintech Developments for Banks and Bank Supervisors* (Report, February 2018) 4 <https://www.bis.org/bcbs/publ/d431.pdf.>. Some commentators argue that RegTech has then evolved through various iterations – from RegTech 1.0 and 2.0 to, now, the beginning of 3.0. RegTech 1.0, which is primarily focused on basic data gathering prior to the onset of the GFC in 2008. RegTech 2.0, spanning from 2008 to approximately 2018, emphasised utilising data for regulatory and supervisory reporting, while RegTech 3.0 introduces an innovative phase, characterised by the dynamic and inventive application of data, leveraging machine learning and artificial intelligence (AI). See, eg, George Walker, 'Regulatory Technology (RegTech) – Construction of a New Regulatory Policy and Model' (2021) 54(1) *International Lawyer* 1, 2; see also Douglas W Arner, Jànos Barberis and Ross P Buckley, 'FinTech, RegTech and the Reconceptualization of Financial Regulation' (2017) 37(3) *Northwestern Journal of International Law and Business* 371. In the Australian context, see, eg, Productivity Commission, 'Regulatory Technology' (Information Paper, 9 October 2020) <https://www.pc.gov.au/research/completed/regulatory-technology/regulatory-technology.pdf>.

43 Lev Bromberg et al, 'Fintech Sandboxes: Achieving a Balance between Regulation and Innovation' (2017) 28(4) *Journal of Banking and Finance Law and Practice* 314, 318.

44 Ibid.

45 Australian Securities and Investments Commission, *Testing Fintech Products and Services without Holding an AFS or Credit Licence* ('*RG 257*') (withdrawn).

Exemption) Regulations 2020 (Cth) ('*ACL Exemption Regulations*'). These amendments have given rise to the so-called Enhanced Regulatory Sandbox (ERS), effective from 1 September 2020 and superseding the old regime under *RG 257*.[46]

ERS is created on the premise that it can 'further promote Australia's FinTech capability', 'strike a better balance in encouraging innovation that delivers choice for consumers and minimising risks to consumers and the integrity of the financial system', and 'allow businesses to confirm their concept through initial market testing prior to seeking the appropriate licence from ASIC'.[47] In addition, ERS recognises that 'innovation is not limited to new offerings previously unseen in the market, but may encompass improvements to specific elements of a product or service, drawing on practices from other industries, or combining elements together in new ways to deliver benefits for consumers'.[48]

Accordingly, as with its previous iteration, the ERS permits individuals and businesses to trial specific financial services or credit activities without the requirement to secure an Australian Financial Services Licence (AFSL) or an Australian credit licence (ACL). Unlike *RG 257*, however, the ERS improves the testing environments on various fronts – for instance, by increasing the testing period from 12 to 24 months, broadening the range of financial services for testing, and empowering ASIC to place qualifications on testing. A unique feature under the old regime (*RG 257*) was the automatic right of eligible persons to be admitted into the sandbox if they notified the regulator. ASIC did not have to consider each individual application and whether it was innovative, thus decreasing the regulatory burden.[49] Like *RG 257*, the ERS requires eligible persons to notify ASIC. In contrast to *RG 257*, the ERS requires that the notification should include information regarding, inter alia, the 'net public benefit test' and the 'innovation test' (as detailed below) and that the exemption will start after the end of the 30-day notification period.

The ERS sets out various testing parameters. For instance, there are limitations on the types of financial and credit products that an eligible person may offer, along with caps on exposure to retail clients and an aggregate exposure limit set at A$5 million. Should any of these prescribed conditions be violated, the exemption will automatically cease to apply.[50] An eligible person's exemption can also be terminated if that person notifies ASIC that they are no longer relying on the exemption, or if ASIC notifies the person that the exemption is no longer applicable either in respect of a specific financial service or credit activity or to the person more generally.[51]

A licence requires a significant investment to be made upfront. The government can help businesses to accelerate their innovation by overcoming these hurdles through a regulatory sandbox. The Australian model is situated against the backdrop of the ongoing

46 'Enhanced Regulatory Sandbox', *Australian Securities and Investments Commission* (Web Page) ('ERS Website') <https://asic.gov.au/for-business/innovation-hub/enhanced-regulatory-sandbox/>.

47 Explanatory Memorandum, Treasury Laws Amendments (2018 Measures No 2) Bill 2019 (Cth) 5–6.

48 Explanatory Statement, *Corporations (FinTech Sandbox Australian Financial Services Licence Exemption) Regulations 2020* (Cth) 1 ('*AFSL Exemption Regulation Explanatory Statement*').

49 Bromberg et al (n 43) 327.

50 *AFSL Exemption Regulation Explanatory Statement* (n 48) 2–3.

51 Ibid 6.

tension in balancing the potential benefits of Fintech innovation against the risks to consumers, investors and financial systems. The following sections outline the key requirements of the ERS against this backdrop.

4.2.2 Eligibility

4.2.2.1 Eligible persons

To be eligible for the ERS under *AFSL Exemption Regulations* reg 5, an applicant must not already be either an AFSL holder providing financial services concerning that kind of financial product, or an authorised representative of an AFSL holder providing financial services concerning that kind of financial product.[52] This is the key change of eligibility from the previous iteration, as it permits already licensed businesses to test new services *they are currently not authorised to provide*.[53] Further prohibitions on eligibility relate to:

- persons who are an operator of a financial market or a clearing and settlement facility; and
- a related body corporate of a person who is:
  (i) authorised by an AFSL to provide the financial service in relation to that kind of financial product; or
  (ii) an authorised representative of an AFSL holder for the provision of the financial service in relation to that type of financial product.[54]

A parallel can be found in *ACL Exemption Regulations* reg 5, which states that an eligible person must not be authorised by an ACL to conduct the credit activity, or a credit representative given authorisation to engage in said activity on behalf of an ACL holder; and a related body corporate of a person who is authorised by an ACL to undertake the credit activity, or a credit representative permitted to perform the activity on behalf of an ACL holder.[55]

There are also specific requirements applicable to natural persons and foreign companies. To be an eligible person, a natural person must be an Australian citizen or permanent resident.[56] If the person is a foreign company, they must be registered pursuant to the *Corporations Act 2001* (Cth) pt 5B.2.

4.2.2.2 Conditions of entry

Under the ERS, eligible persons are required to notify ASIC, using prescribed forms, in respect of financial services or credit activities.[57] ERS applicants must submit details

52 *Corporations (FinTech Sandbox Australian Financial Services Licence Exemption) Regulations 2020* (Cth) ('*AFSL Exemption Regulations*') s 6(1), drawn from the definition of 'eligible person' under reg 5.

53 Ibid. See also Australian Securities and Investments Commission, *Comparison of Key Features of the ASIC Sandbox and the Australian Government's Enhanced Regulatory Sandbox* (August 2020) ('*Comparison of Key Features of ERS and RG 257*') <https://download.asic.gov.au/media/5763623/comparison-asic-sandbox-enhanced-regulatory-sandbox-published-25-august-2020.pdf>.

54 *AFSL Exemption Regulations* (n 52) reg 5.

55 *National Consumer Credit Protection (FinTech Sandbox Australian Credit Licence Exemption) Regulations 2020* (Cth) reg 5 ('*ACL Exemption Regulations*').

56 *AFSL Exemption Regulations* (n 52).

57 Australian Securities and Investments Commission, 'Notification to Use the Enhanced Regulatory Sandbox Exemption to Test Eligible Financial Services' (1 September 2020) ('Notification to Use

about officers if the applicant is a body corporate, about partners or senior managers if the applicant is a partnership, about trustees or senior managers if applying as a multiple trustee of a trust, or about key decision-makers who may not be employees or directors but are responsible for making significant choices about the continuous provision of each eligible financial service.[58] Such submissions are necessary for ASIC to consider whether the eligible persons and the people involved are fit and proper to perform their functions. Likely, this is mirrored in pt 6 of the 'Notification to Use ERS Exemption' for credit activities.[59]

More crucially, the ERS features a more rigorous notification scheme by requiring ASIC to review two new tests – the net public benefit test and the innovation test. To satisfy the net public, as per ASIC, the eligible person must 'adequately explain why exempting each eligible financial service, financial product or credit activity will result, or be likely to result, in a benefit to the public' and the benefit 'must outweigh any detriment to the public that will result, or be likely to result, from exempting that service'.[60] For the innovation test, it is required to 'adequately explain why each eligible financial service, financial product or credit activity is considered either new or a new adaptation or improvement of another service'.[61]

ASIC may find grounds to refuse an application where it is not satisfied that the potential provider passes either the innovation test or the public benefit test.[62] ASIC may also refuse an application where there is reasonable belief that the provision of the financial service is likely to result in significant detriment to one or more persons as retail or wholesale clients.[63] There are further grounds for refusal where ASIC reasonably believes that the purpose for seeking the exemption is simply to continue the trial for another person who previously held an exemption. ASIC may also refuse where there is a reasonable belief that the provider failed to act fairly, efficiently and honestly in providing financial services or engaging in credit activities. While some stakeholders expressed concerns that adding such requirements to ASIC's assessment could introduce more restrictions to the ERS than those outlined in the exemption, these new tests reflect that the Australian Government aimed to rebalance the broader interests while pursuing economic development through Fintech innovation.

Although the ERS has made the notification process more demanding, it is still different from the UK sandbox under which the applicant cannot test their products or

AFSL Exemption') <https://download.asic.gov.au/media/5772220/20200826_notification-to-use-the-enhanced-regulatory-sandbox-exemption-financial-services.pdf>; Australian Securities and Investments Commission, 'Notification to Use the Enhanced Regulatory Sandbox Exemption to Test Eligible Credit Activities' (1 September 2020) ('Notification to Use ACL Exemption') <https://download.asic.gov.au/media/5772214/20200826_notification-to-use-the-enhanced-regulatory-sandbox-exemption-credit.pdf>.

58 'Notification to Use AFSL Exemption' (n 57).

59 Ibid.

60 Australian Securities and Investments Commission, *Enhanced Regulatory Sandbox* (Information Sheet 248, August 2020) ('INFO 248') <https://asic.gov.au/for-business/innovation-hub/enhanced-regulatory-sandbox/info-248-enhanced-regulatory-sandbox/>.

61 Ibid.

62 *AFSL Exemption Regulations* (n 52) reg 8(b)–(c).

63 Ibid reg 8(i).

services unless they are granted permission. By contrast, in Australia, so long as the regulator does not communicate with the eligible person that it is not able to rely on the ERS exemption, the intending ERS user may start their testing when the 30-day period ends (ie testing is permitted on the 31st day after lodgement of the notification). Thus, the default settings differ in these two jurisdictions, as further elaborated below.

4.2.3 Scope of activities

Intending ERS users can test 'eligible financial services' in relation to 'eligible financial products'. Regulation 5 of the *AFSL Exemption Regulations* defines an 'eligible financial service' as one that does one of the following:

(a) provides financial product advice in relation to a particular kind of financial product
(b) applies for or acquires a particular kind of financial product
(c) issues, varies or disposes of a non-cash payment facility
(d) arranges for the issuing, varying or disposing of a particular kind of financial product
(e) provides a crowdfunding service.

More specifically, the range of services and related products provided under the ERS varies depending upon the type of client – be it wholesale or retail, as explained in Chapter 3. For wholesale clients, the provision of financial services is permitted for almost all financial products, save for derivatives and margin lending facilities.[64] In contrast, for retail clients, the options available to prospective users of the ERS are more limited. These include:

(a) deposit-taking facilities issued by an authorised deposit-taking institution (ADI) regulated by the Australian Prudential Regulation Authority (APRA)
(b) non-cash payment facilities, also under the purview of an APRA-regulated ADI
(c) general insurance products issued by an APRA-authorised general insurer, with consumer credit insurance products being the exception
(d) life insurance products distributed by an APRA-authorised life insurer
(e) superannuation products managed by an APRA-regulated superannuation fund
(f) interests in simple managed investment schemes.[65]

Also, in terms of insurance products, an eligible person can act as an agent or a principal.[66] Parallel provisions can be seen in the *ACL Exemption Regulations*. Without going

64 *AFSL Exemption Regulations* (n 52) reg 10.

65 Ibid reg 11. Also, a simple managed investment scheme is defined under *Corporations Regulations 2001* (Cth) reg 1.0.02 as a registered scheme (other than a passport fund) that invests at least 80 per cent of its assets with a bank on the basis that the money is available for withdrawal under certain conditions (eg immediately during the bank's normal business hours; at the end of a fixed-term period that does not exceed three months; or in arrangements where the investments can be realised at market value within 10 days).

66 *AFSL Exemption Regulations* (n 52) reg 6(2).

into exhaustive detail, the ERS enables eligible persons to conduct eligible credit activities, including providing credit contracts, and credit services relating to a credit contract (or a proposed one), provided the following conditions are met:[67] (i) the contract duration is no longer than four years;[68] (ii) the contract's credit limit is above A$2000 but below A$25 000;[69] (iii) the agreement is neither a reverse mortgage nor a small-amount credit contract;[70] and (iv) the agreement is not backed by a charge or lien on a consumer's residential property under reg 27(1) of the *Bankruptcy Regulations 2021* (Cth).[71]

4.2.4 Time frame and exposure limits

The ERS exemption is granted to an eligible individual for up to 24 months for each eligible financial service, whether it pertains to a specific type of financial product or an eligible credit activity.[72] As previously mentioned, the exemption period commences on the 31st day following the notification's submission to ASIC. Furthermore, this 24-month duration is fixed and cannot be extended, halted or reset.[73] It is crucial to highlight that the provider's exemption status terminates automatically if the provider obtains a licence to offer the eligible financial service or engage in credit activity.[74]

Under the ERS, there exists a cumulative exposure limit for all eligible financial services and credit activities undertaken by an eligible person and their related body corporates. Specifically, the aggregate client investment cap stipulates that the sum of all relevant amounts cannot exceed A$5 million and includes:[75]

- all amounts committed by all clients in relation to all kinds of financial products for which the person provides financial services
- all amounts of the gross premiums that all clients have committed to in relation to general insurance and life risk insurance products for which the person provides financial services
- all amounts that all clients contribute to superannuation products for which the person provides financial services
- all amounts of credit activity under the *ACL Exemption Regulations*.

Individual exposure limits are also in place for each retail client. Specifically, retail clients can invest up to A$10 000 in financial services related to certain financial products. These products include interests in simple managed investment schemes, Commonwealth debentures, stocks, bonds, securities listed on approved domestic or overseas markets, and securities offered via a crowdfunding service.[76] Yet, there is no individual cap applicable to eligible general insurance products, life risk insurance products, superannuation

67 *AFSL Exemption Regulation Explanatory Statement* (n 48) 6, 15.
68 *ACL Exemption Regulations* (n 55) reg 5(f).
69 Ibid reg 5(e).
70 Ibid reg 5(c).
71 Ibid reg 5(d).
72 *AFSL Exemption Regulation Explanatory Statement* (n 48) 7, 15.
73 Ibid.
74 *AFSL Exemption Regulations* (n 52) reg 6(1) note 2; *ACL Exemption Regulations* (n 55) reg 6 note 2.
75 *AFSL Exemption Regulations* (n 52) reg 13(1); see also *ACL Exemption Regulations* (n 55) reg 10(1).
76 *AFSL Exemption Regulations* (n 52) reg 12(1); *Comparison of Key Features of ERS and RG 257* (n 53) 2.

products, deposit products, and non-cash payment products offered by an ADI.[77] As noted earlier, the *ACL Exemption Regulations* likewise impose a cap for credit contracts: a credit contract must be between A$2000 and A$25 000.[78]

4.2.5 Other conditions

ERS users are under an ongoing obligation to monitor all limits that are applicable under the ERS exemption. Where any of these limits are breached, the provider cannot rely on the ERS exemption. Of particular note are those conditions relating to consumer protection. First, an ERS user must notify clients that they are operating under the exemption scheme without a licence.[79] ERS users must also provide to clients and potential clients, if applicable, the disclosure documents mentioned earlier, such as a Financial Services Guide, a Statement of Advice, and a Product Disclosure Statement.[80] Additionally, they must notify clients if the test financial service, product or credit activity changes significantly or is no longer offered.[81] This includes where the business ceases to operate, becomes bankrupt, compounds with creditors, ceases testing in the ERS, or the business has obtained a licence for the service or product being tested.

Retail customers must receive details about any compensation, such as commissions, that the provider may earn from offering the financial service.[82] They must also be informed of any connections or affiliations between the provider and related bodies corporate. Additionally, information on available dispute resolution mechanisms, including how to access them and their duration of availability, must be provided. This requirement does not extend to individuals involved in an exempt credit activity.[83]

Notably, there must be adequate compensation arrangements and internal and external dispute resolution processes.[84] Compensation arrangements must be in place for any breaches of the *Corporations Act*, the *National Consumer Credit Protection Act 2009* (Cth) (the '*NCCPA*') or the conditions of the ERS. The compensation arrangement must have a limit of at least A$1 million for any one claim and in the aggregate. This must be approved by ASIC in writing as adequate.[85] For at least 12 months following the end of the exemption period, providers must continue their Australian Financial Complaints Authority membership and any compensation arrangements.

ASIC also has the power to issue a make-good order to eligible persons, requiring compliance within 30 days.[86] Prior to issuing a make-good order, ASIC will consult with all parties, including the provider. The Administrative Appeals Tribunal will review any decision to issue such an order.

77 *AFSL Exemption Regulations* (n 52) s 12(2).
78 *ACL Exemption Regulations* (n 55) s 5(e); *AFSL Exemption Regulations Explanatory Statement* (n 48) 6, 15.
79 *AFSL Exemption Regulations* (n 52) s 17. See also *ACL Exemption Regulations* (n 55) s 14.
80 *Comparison of Key Features of ERS and RG 257* (n 53) 2. See, eg, *AFSL Exemption Regulations* (n 52) regs 18, 21, 23.
81 *AFSL Exemption Regulations* (n 52) reg 19; *ACL Exemption Regulations* (n 55) reg 15.
82 *AFSL Exemption Regulations* (n 52) reg 18. See also *ACL Exemption Regulations* (n 55) reg 15.
83 INFO 248 (n 60).
84 *AFSL Exemption Regulations* (n 52) reg 20; *ACL Exemption Regulations* (n 55) reg 16.
85 INFO 248 (n 60).
86 *AFSL Exemption Regulations* (n 52) reg 24; *ACL Exemption Regulations* (n 55) reg 18.

Protection is also available under the 'best interests' duty to provide financial advice,[87] as well as under responsible lending obligations,[88] the consumer credit law's unfair contract terms, and crowdsourced funding obligations, including gatekeeper and the abovementioned disclosure obligations.[89] ERS users are also under existing obligations related to misleading, deceptive or unconscionable conduct, anti-money laundering or privacy requirements, as well as design and distribution obligations if they issue financial products, credit facilities, or make sale offers that require them to give a disclosure document.[90]

4.2.6 Other jurisdictions: United Kingdom and beyond

As mentioned, the United Kingdom was the first country to launch the sandbox approach, which aims to provide firms with 'the ability to test products and services in a controlled environment', 'reduced time-to-market at potentially lower cost', 'support in identifying appropriate consumer protection safeguards to build into new products and services' and 'better access to finance'.[91] Many others followed suit by rolling out their sandboxes. The design of each sandbox varies, however, depending upon the different social, economic and political contexts.

In contrast with Australia, for instance, the regulatory sandbox in the United Kingdom, administered by the Financial Conduct Authority (FCA), is open to both high-tech firms without licences and incumbents with licences.[92] Further, admission into the sandbox in the United Kingdom is not granted automatically but is subject to the FCA's approval as per the criteria detailed in Table 4.1. Previously, there were two cohorts admitted into the sandbox each year – and from August 2021, the regulatory sandbox accepts applications on a rolling basis throughout the year.[93] The testing period is six months – shorter than what is permitted under the ERS. There are various other requirements under the UK sandbox; for instance, firms are required to have a certain level of staff presence and a head office located in the United Kingdom, and a local bank account is often needed to carry out testing.[94] Once admitted, non-authorised firms in the FCA sandbox would receive a restricted form of authorisation specifically relating to the testing products.

The FCA sandbox has proven popular since its inception in 2016. For instance, the FCA received 24 applications, and 18 firms were admitted to test as part of the first cohort

87 *AFSL Exemption Regulations* (n 52) reg 8(h). Under reg 8, for instance, ASIC may decide that the exemption is not eligible, if the provider 'has failed to comply with Division 2 of Part 7.7A of the [Corporations] Act (about best interests obligations) in relation to the provision of another eligible financial service'.

88 *ACL Exemption Regulations* (n 55) reg 17.

89 See generally INFO 248 (n 60).

90 Ibid.

91 'Regulatory Sandbox', *Financial Conduct Authority* (Web Page, 1 August 2023) <https://www.fca.org.uk/firms/innovation/regulatory-sandbox>.

92 ASIC, ERS Website (n 46).

93 'Applying to the Regulatory Sandbox', *Financial Conduct Authority* (Web Page, 14 April 2023) <https://www.fca.org.uk/firms/innovation/regulatory-sandbox-prepare-application>. ('In August 2021, the Regulatory Sandbox moved to an always open model, allowing firms to submit their applications throughout the year.')

94 Ibid.

Table 4.1 UK FCA's sandbox eligibility criteria

Criteria	Key questions	Positive indicators	Negative indicators
In Scope	• Are you doing something that is within our remit? Will your customers be in the UK?	• Your innovation is intended for the UK market. • The relevant activity is regulated by us or may be used by firms we regulate.	• Your innovation doesn't appear to be intended for use in the UK.
Genuine Innovation	• Are you doing something that's ground-breaking or significantly different? This could be something completely new, or it could be a new market or a new version of an existing model.	• Desk research produces few or no comparable examples of innovation in the market. • Your innovation is a clear step-change in scale.	• There are numerous examples of similar innovations to yours. • Your innovations appear to be a superficial variation of an existing model.
Consumer Benefit	• How does your proposal help consumers (either individuals or businesses)? • How is it an improvement on existing services? • How will you protect them from any risks your model poses?	• Your innovation is likely to lead to a better deal for consumers (eg through lower prices, higher quality, better security etc). • You have considered possible consumer risks and how to address them. • Your innovation will make market entry or compliance with FCA rules easier.	• Potential detrimental impact on consumers, markets or the financial system. • Facilitates circumvention of regulatory or fiscal obligations.

Table 4.1 (cont.)

Criteria	Key questions	Positive indicators	Negative indicators
Readiness	• Have you thought about how your model works with our rules? Have you carried out any background research into the regulations that might apply to your business? • Can you explain how your business will work? • Are you ready to test the innovation in the real market with real consumers?	• You have clearly done background research, have sought to understand obligations, and have a clear, defined business proposal. • You have a well-developed testing plan with clear objectives, parameters and success criteria. • You have already undertaken testing. • You have the resources to test in the Sandbox. • You have sufficient safeguards in place to protect consumers and can provide appropriate redress if required. • Any testing partners are in place, or soon will be. • If authorisation is required for a test, you are ready to apply in the near future.	• You have made little or no effort to understand relevant regulations. • There are unclear testing objectives and/or your plans for testing are underdeveloped. • You don't have the resources for the test. • Your proposed customer safeguards are inadequate and/or appropriate redress can't be provided.
Need for Support	• Do you have a genuine need to test in our Sandbox?	• You have no alternative means of engaging with the FCA. • The innovation doesn't easily fit our existing regulatory framework. • You will benefit from using a Sandbox tool to test in a live environment. • The full authorisation process would be too costly/difficult for a viable and short test.	• You already have a dedicated supervisor who could answer the query. • You have a significant regulatory compliance resource. • Your business model easily fits the existing regulatory framework with no particularly difficult questions. • Live testing is not necessary to answer your question or achieve your goal.

Source: Financial Conduct Authority, 'Regulatory Sandbox Eligibility Criteria' (Web Page, 28 March 2022) <https://www.fca.org.uk/firms/innovation/regulatory-sandbox/eligibility-criteria>.

in 2016.[95] In cohort 2 in the same year, the number of applications rose to 77, of which 24 firms tested their businesses.[96] In the sixth cohort during the COVID pandemic, there were still 68 applications coming from the United Kingdom and overseas; of these, 22 firms were admitted into the sandbox.[97]

Beyond the United Kingdom, the eligibility and regulatory parameters vary across jurisdictions. Some allow only the existing licence holders to use the sandbox (eg Hong Kong),[98] while others emphasise innovation (eg Australia).[99] Some allow testing for up to 24 months (eg Australia and Abu Dhabi),[100] while the testing period in some jurisdictions is as short as three to six months (eg the United Kingdom and Indonesia).[101] Despite such differences, many of these jurisdictions do set up dedicated points of contact, providing services to intended users of the sandbox. The FCA's Innovation Hub[102] and ASIC's Innovation Hub[103] are prime examples, though their eligibility criteria vary. Together with mechanisms such as innovation hubs, the regulatory sandbox presents an opportunity for '*participant–regulator dialogue*' in relation to 'the innovative product, developments in the product's industry generally, and the state of the regulatory landscape from the participant's perspective', among other matters.[104]

More recently, in 2019, the Global Financial Innovation Network (GFIN) was formally launched by an international group of financial regulators and related organisations. Built upon the FCA's 2018 proposal to establish a global sandbox,[105] the GFIN brings together regulators 'to cooperate and share experience of innovation in respective markets, including emerging technologies and business models, and to provide accessible regulatory

95 'Regulatory Sandbox – Cohort 1', *Financial Conduct Authority* (Web Page, 20 September 2023) <https://www.fca.org.uk/firms/regulatory-sandbox/cohort-1>.

96 'Regulatory Sandbox – Cohort 2' *Financial Conduct Authority* (Web Page, 20 September 2023) <https://www.fca.org.uk/firms/regulatory-sandbox/cohort-2>.

97 'Regulatory Sandbox – Cohort 6', *Financial Conduct Authority* (Web Page, 20 September 2023) <https://www.fca.org.uk/firms/regulatory-sandbox/cohort-6>.

98 Hong Kong, for instance, allows financial institutions to partner up with technology firms. See 'Fintech Supervisory Sandbox (FSS)', *Hong Kong Monetary Authority* (Web Page, 22 November 2023) <https://www.hkma.gov.hk/eng/key-functions/international-financial-centre/fintech/fintech-supervisory-sandbox-fss/>.

99 Australia requires the applicant to be 'innovative'. See details in INFO 248 (n 60). For a comparative view, see, eg, Baker McKenzie (n 41). For a recount of the sandbox approach in Asia, see Lev Bromberg, Andrew Godwin and Ian Ramsay, 'Sandboxes and Bridges: The Impact of Fintech on Regulatory Convergence and Coordination in Asia' in Douglas W Arner et al (eds), *Research Handbook on Asian Financial Law* (Edward Elgar Publishing, 2020) 547.

100 'The ADGM RegLab', *ADGM* (Web Page) <https://www.adgm.com/setting-up/reglab/overview>.

101 The UK considers from three to six months as an appropriate duration for testing. See details in Financial Conduct Authority, 'Default Standards for Sandbox Testing Parameters' <https://www.fca.org.uk/publication/policy/default-standards-for-sandbox-testing-parameters.pdf>. In Indonesia, the duration of the testing can be up to one year if operated under the sandbox of the Financial Services Authority (Otoritas Jasa Keuangan) (OJK) or six months if under the regime managed by Bank Indonesia (BI): Baker McKenzie (n 41) 16.

102 'Innovate and Innovation Hub', *Financial Conduct Authority* (Web Page) <https://www.fca.org.uk/firms/innovate-innovation-hub>.

103 'Innovation Hub', *Australian Securities and Investments Commission* (Web Page, 11 July 2023) <https://asic.gov.au/for-business/innovation-hub/>.

104 Byungkwon Lim and Charles Low, 'Regulatory Sandboxes' in Jelena Madir (ed), *Fintech: Law and Regulation* (Edward Elgar, 2019) 307.

105 'Global Financial Innovation Network (GFIN)', *Financial Conduct Authoirty* (Web Page, 15 February 2023) <https://www.fca.org.uk/firms/innovation/global-financial-innovation-network>.

contact information for firms', 'provide[s] a forum for joint RegTech work and collaborative knowledge sharing/lessons learned', and offers firms 'an environment in which to trial cross-border solutions'.[106] Among other initiatives, GFIN has rolled out its cross-border testing (CBT) – 'an environment that allows firms to consecutively or concurrently trial and scale new technologies, products or business models in multiple jurisdictions, gaining real-time insight into how a product or service might operate in multiple markets'.[107] Not all GFIN members participate in the CBT initiative, although ASIC is part of it.[108]

4.3 Data protection

Privacy is a crucial area that merits attention for banks and financial institutions in the data-driven era. In this next section, we first outline the regulatory landscape of data protection in Australia – which is, by and large, governed through a series of statutes, self-regulatory codes of conduct, and duties at common law and equity. We will then move on to consider specific aspects of the major instrument – the *Privacy Act 1988* (Cth) ('*Privacy Act*').

4.3.1 Data protection in Australia: An overview

4.3.1.1 Statutes

The *Privacy Act* contains data protection provisions regulating the collection, use, disclosure and management of personal information by private sector and federal public sector organisations.[109] Additionally, the Act protects personal information related to credit or credit reporting systems, as well as the collection, use, disclosure and management of tax file numbers.[110] The various states and territories have additional regulations dealing with financial services to public sector bodies.[111] Besides the *Privacy Act*, Victoria, New South Wales and the Australian Capital Territory all have in place health records Acts.[112] The purpose of these Acts is to provide specific privacy protection for personal health information.

Additionally, the *Do Not Call Register Act 2006* (Cth) protects individuals from receiving unsolicited telemarketing calls by providing a register for consumers to opt into.[113]

---

106 Global Financial Innovation Network, *Terms of Reference for Membership and Governance of the Global Financial Innovation Network* (August 2019) <https://static1.squarespace.com/static/5db7cdf53d173c0e010e8f68/t/5db92a0d519a7150a9072bc6/1572416023693/gfin-terms-of-reference.pdf>.

107 Global Financial Innovation Network, 'Cross-Border Testing Frequently Asked Questions (FAQs)' <https://static1.squarespace.com/static/5db7cdf53d173c0e010e8f68/t/5fa14d55698ad91a1acc68e3/1604406619143/20201028_GFIN_CBT_FAQs.pdf>.

108 Global Financial Innovation Network, 'The GFIN Cross Border Testing Lessons Learned (Cohort 1.0), *Cross-Border Testing* (Web Page) <https://www.thegfin.com/crossborder-testing>.

109 *Privacy Act 1988* (Cth).

110 Ibid pt IIIA; *Privacy (Tax File Number) Rule 2015* (Cth).

111 *Privacy and Personal Information Protection Act 1998* (NSW); *Privacy and Data Protection Act 2014* (Vic); *Personal Information Protection Act 2004* (Tas); *Information Privacy Act 2009* (Qld); *Information Privacy Act 2014* (ACT); *Information Act 2002* (NT). Western Australia and South Australia do not have any specific privacy legislation.

112 *Health Records Act 2001* (Vic); *Health Records (Privacy and Access) Act 1997* (ACT); *Health Records and Information Privacy Act 2002* (NSW).

113 *Do Not Call Register Act 2006* (Cth) s 14.

A consumer who has opted into the Register may receive telemarketing calls only from specified organisations.[114] Electronic spam messaging is regulated through the *Spam Act 2003* (Cth).[115] Under the Act, a person or organisation can send a commercial electronic message only to those recipients who have consented to receive such messages; there is an electronic means of unsubscribing to them; and the messages identify the sender and their contact details.[116]

4.3.1.2 Self-regulation

The *Banking Code of Practice* is a voluntary code shared between Australian banks.[117] It includes obligations to comply with the *Privacy Act*, as well as restating the common law and equitable duties of confidentiality.[118] The *ePayments Code*, as discussed further in Chapter 9, regulates consumers' electronic payments through technologies such as ATMs, EFTPOS, credit card transactions, online payments, internet and mobile banking, and BPAY.[119] The Code provides guidelines on the application of the Australian Privacy Principles (APPs) of the *Privacy Act* by making individuals aware of transaction monitoring, preventing unauthorised access to personal information and ensuring that transaction receipts do not unnecessarily disclose personal details.[120]

4.3.1.3 Equitable duties of confidence

Facets of privacy and data protection also enliven the equitable duty of confidence. This arises where information of a confidential nature (it must merit equities protection and is to some extent a secret)[121] comes to be known by someone (the confidant) in circumstances where they agreed or had notice, or a reasonable expectation, that the information had the quality of confidence. The unauthorised use or disclosure of this information then amounts to a breach of confidence in equity, or a breach of a contractual obligation

114 Ibid s 5.
115 *Spam Act 2003* (Cth).
116 Ibid s 16.
117 Australian Banking Association, *Banking Code of Practice: Setting the Standards of Practice for Banks, their Staff and their Representatives* ('*Banking Code of Practice*'; 1 March 2020) <https://www.ausbanking.org.au/wp-content/uploads/2020/06/2020-Code-A4-Booklet-with-July-1-COVID-19-Special-Note-WEB.pdf>.
118 Ibid. Chapter 5 of the *Banking Code of Practice* states: 'We will protect your confidentiality ... We will meet our general duties under law to protect your confidentiality ... We will also have our own privacy policies available on our website.' Chapter 6 also makes clear that '[i]f the Code imposes an obligation on us that is in addition to obligations applying under a relevant law, then we will comply with the Code unless doing so would lead us to breach the law'.
119 Australian Securities and Investments Commission, *ePayments Code* (2 June 2022) <https://download.asic.gov.au/media/lloeicwb/epayments-code-published-02-june-2022.pdf>.
120 Ibid ch D cl 24. The *ePayments Code* sheds light on how subscribers comply with the *Privacy Act* as follows. If a subscriber uses surveillance methods (eg video or sound recording) to observe transactions, they must inform users before the transaction begins about the surveillance type. Subscribers are responsible for ensuring that unauthorised individuals cannot access information about a facility they operate. Furthermore, transaction receipts should not reveal complete identifiers or the user's name or address. If a subscriber has an electronic address through which users can access or conduct transactions, they need to offer a transparent privacy policy through that address and provide it to users when asked. By way of illustration, subscribers might meet these requirements by having their privacy policy available on their website.
121 *Saltman Engineering Co Ltd v Campbell Engineering Co Ltd* [1963] 3 All ER 413.

of confidence where a contract includes a confidentiality obligation.[122] Hence, privacy concerns around data protection may fall into the scope of this duty.

4.3.1.4 Common law duties of confidentiality

As with equitable duties, common law duties of confidentiality may also apply. As discussed in Chapter 5, there is a duty of confidentiality that arises by virtue of the relationship between banker and customer.[123] There are several prominent exceptions to this duty: where it is overridden by specific legislation (typically relating to criminal or evidence matters), where there is a duty to the public to disclose, where it is in the banks' interest to disclose, or where the disclosure is made with the express or implied consent of the customer. We will consider this aspect in further detail later in this book.

4.3.2 *Privacy Act 1988* (Cth)

4.3.2.1 Background

Australia's *Privacy Act 1988* (Cth), which became effective in 1989, marked a significant step in harmonising Australia's practices with global norms.[124] The enactment honoured Australia's commitment to adopt the Organisation for Economic Co-operation and Development (OECD) Guidelines on the Protection of Privacy and Transborder Flows of Personal Data[125] and responsibilities under art 17 of the *International Covenant on Civil and Political Rights* (ICCPR).[126] The Act was amended various times – for instance, in 1991, it incorporated provisions on consumer credit reports through the *Privacy Amendment Act 1990* (Cth).[127] In 2000, the independent Office of the Privacy Commissioner was established; later, in 2001, the Act was expanded to include some private sector organisations via the *Privacy Amendment (Private Sector) Act 2000* (Cth).[128] In 2010, the *Australian Information Commissioner Act 2010* (Cth) facilitated the creation of the Office of the Australian Information Commissioner (OAIC).[129] This new entity integrated the

122 *Ansell Rubber Co Pty Ltd v Allied Rubber Industries Pty Ltd* [1967] VR 37.

123 *Tournier v National Provincial & Union Bank of England* [1924] 1 KB 461.

124 'History of Privacy Act', *Office of the Australian Information Commissioner* (Web Page) <https://www.oaic.gov.au/privacy/privacy-legislation/the-privacy-act/history-of-the-privacy-act>.

125 Organisation for Economic Cooperation and Development, *OECD Guidelines on the Protection of Privacy and Transborder Flow of Personal Data* (2001) <https://www.oecd-ilibrary.org/docserver/9789264196391-en.pdf?expires=1701843180&id=id&accname=guest&checksum=DD982ADB47923669FE08989728BF988A>. In 1978, the OECD established a Group of Experts on Transborder Data Barriers and Privacy Protection to develop guidelines for the flow and protection of personal data. The aim was to harmonise national legislation, leaving room for a future international convention. The work, in collaboration with the Council of Europe and the European Community, was targeted for completion by 1 July 1979. Notably, this expert group was chaired by Mr Justice Kirby of Australia.

126 Article 17 of the *International Covenant on Civil and Political Rights* states: '1. No one shall be subjected to arbitrary or unlawful interference with his privacy, family, home or correspondence, nor to unlawful attacks on his honour and reputation. 2. Everyone has the right to the protection of the law against such interference or attacks.'

127 *Privacy Amendment Act 1990* (Cth) (repealed by *Amending Acts 1990 to 1999 Repeal Act 2016* (Cth)).

128 *Privacy Amendment (Office of the Privacy Commissioner) Act 2000* (Cth) (as amended by the *Disability Discrimination and Other Human Rights Legislation Amendment Act 2009* (Cth)).

129 *Australian Information Commissioner Act 2010* (Cth).

previously established Office of the Privacy Commissioner and introduced supplementary statutory roles to support the Commissioner.

The *Privacy Amendment (Notifiable Data Breaches) Act 2017* (Cth) amended the *Privacy Act* by including a new pt IIIC concerning notification of eligible data breaches – known as the Notifiable Data Breaches (NDB) scheme. A data breach is considered 'eligible' in cases where unauthorised access, disclosure or loss of personal information can potentially cause 'serious harm' to individuals involved.[130] If an eligible breach occurs, the affected entity must inform both the OAIC and the impacted individuals, unless exceptions apply.[131] A failure to comply with the reporting requirements is deemed to be an 'interference with privacy' under the *Privacy Act* s 13(4A), attracting the full range of sanctions available to the Commissioner under the Act.

More recently, the *Privacy Legislation Amendment (Enforcement and Other Measures) Act 2022* (Cth) was passed. This amendment increases penalties for breaches: companies can face up to A$50 million, three times the benefit derived from the breach, or 30 per cent of their turnover.[132] Moreover, it grants the OAIC more power to gather information regarding confirmed or potentially eligible data breaches. This enhancement was seen as vital to allow the Commissioner to fully understand the extent of data exposed in a verified or suspected breach, thereby facilitating a more accurate assessment of potential harm to individuals. The law also broadens its reach to foreign entities doing business in Australia, regardless of data collection within the country.[133]

4.3.2.2 Scope of application and structure

The *Privacy Act* defines 'personal information' as data or opinions about an individual who is either specifically identified or can reasonably be identifiable. This holds true regardless of the accuracy of the information or opinion, and irrespective of whether it is recorded in a physical form or not.[134] Also, information will be considered as 'sensitive

130 *Privacy Act* (n 109) ss 26WA and 26WE (detailing what falls within the scope of 'eligible data breach').

131 The NDB scheme is generally applicable to entities – known as 'APP entities' – bound by APP 11 of the *Privacy Act* (n 109) to safeguard personal information in their possession, as per s 26WE(1)(a) of the Act. Therefore, APPs that receive exemptions under the Act are similarly exempt from the NDB scheme. To illustrate, under certain conditions, private sector employers are exempt from complying with the APPs regarding employee records linked to current and past employment relationships (*Privacy Act* s 7B(3)).

132 Ibid s 13G(3). ('The amount of the penalty for a contravention of subsection (1) [interference with the privacy of an individual] by a body corporate is an amount not more than the greater of the following: (a) $50,000,000; (b) if the court can determine the value of the benefit that the body corporate, and any related body corporate, have obtained directly or indirectly and that is reasonably to the conduct constituting the contravention – 3 times the value of that benefit; (c) if the court cannot determine the value of that benefit – 30% of the adjusted turnover of the body corporate during the breach turnover period for the contravention.')

133 The *Privacy Act* (n 109) has provisions that extended its application beyond Australia's borders, but only for entities with 'Australian links'. As per s 5B(2) of the Act, this connection could be established if, for instance, the foreign entity was an Australian citizen, had formed a partnership in Australia, or was a company incorporated within Australia. A broader definition of this connection was found in s 5B(3) of the Act, which states: '[A]n organisation or small business operator has an Australian link if the following conditions are met: the organisation or operator is not described in subsection (2); and the organisation or operator carries on business in Australia or an external Territory.' Ibid s 5B(2) and (3).

134 Ibid s 6.

information' where it contains or refers to information about an individual's racial or ethnic origin, political opinion, membership of a political association, religious beliefs or affiliations, philosophical beliefs, membership of a professional or trade association, membership of a trade union, sexual orientation or practices, or criminal record.[135] Furthermore, information may be sensitive when it refers to the health, genetic or biometric information of an individual.[136]

An 'APP entity' is defined under s 6 of the Act as an agency or organisation.[137] An 'organisation' is an individual, body corporate, partnership, any other unincorporated association, or a trust, unless it is a small business operator, registered political party, state or territory authority, or a prescribed instrumentality of the State.[138] A 'small business operator' will be excluded where there is an annual turnover of A$3 million or less for a financial year unless an exception applies.[139] The exceptions where a small business operator will be liable under the Act include businesses that provide a health service and hold health information other than in employee records, businesses that disclose personal information about another individual for a benefit, service or advantage unless they do so with consent, or businesses that are a contracted service provider for a Commonwealth contract.[140] Instances of the second type of exception might include scenarios where an entity sells a list containing personal information to other organisations for direct marketing purposes, or when an entity gathers information to support a lobbying group.

Under s 15 of the Act, an APP entity must not do an act, or engage in a practice, that breaches the APPs.[141] The APPs are divided into five parts, containing 13 principles in total. They are legally binding and set out the standards, rights and obligations of APP entities in Australia in managing, accessing and holding personal information. The APPs are principle-based. Thus, entities affected by the principles have a degree of flexibility in tailoring their business practice to meet the obligations. These objectives align with the core purpose of the *Privacy Act*, which is to enhance the privacy protection of individuals. They aim to balance this protection with the operational interests of APP entities, to standardise privacy regulation across the nation, to encourage responsible and transparent handling of personal information, and to streamline an effective credit reporting system. Additionally, they aim to enable the smooth exchange of information across international borders, to offer a channel for individuals to file complaints about privacy infringements, and to fulfil Australia's international privacy commitments.[142] It is crucial to note that these APPs are designed to be 'technology-neutral', and hence have equal application between digital and hardcopy filing

As noted above, the OAIC is responsible for enforcing the *Privacy Act*. Any act or practice by an APP entity that violates an APP is considered an 'interference with the privacy' of an individual.[143] Under s 40 of the Act, the Commissioner has the power to investigate an act or

135 Ibid.
136 Ibid.
137 Ibid s 6(1).
138 Ibid s 6C.
139 Ibid s 6D.
140 Ibid.
141 Ibid s 15.
142 Ibid s 2A.
143 Ibid s 13(1).

practice if a complaint has been made under s 36 and there has been an interference.[144] If the Commissioner believes that a criminal offence has occurred in the course of this investigation, they must inform the Commissioner of Police or the Director of Public Prosecutions.[145]

After the investigation, if the Commissioner determines that the complaint is valid, they have the authority to declare that the respondent has violated an individual's privacy. They can also mandate specific actions to cease the misconduct, require reasonable measures to remedy any harm done to the complainant, or indicate that the respondent may be responsible for a certain amount of compensation for any loss or damage. Alternatively, the Commissioner can declare that further action would be inappropriate.[146] If the Commissioner believes it is reasonably possible to conciliate a complaint, then, under s 40A of the Act, they must make a reasonable attempt to conciliate the complaint.[147]

4.3.2.3 Credit reporting

Privacy concerns are a key issue in the lending practice, where various actors play a role. Consumers provide personal information to credit providers (CPs) such as banks or non-ADI lenders[148] when applying for credit. Their credit reports include details such as credit cards, loans, mobile contracts and credit ratings that signify their financial standing. There are middlemen – otherwise known as 'access seekers' – who obtain consumers' permission and help them to liaise with CPs or credit reporting bodies (CRBs).[149] Mortgage brokers or debt management companies are prime examples. CPs relay client credit data to CRBs such as Equifax, Experian and Illion in Australia. These CRBs assess the data to establish a consumer's creditworthiness. Based on these evaluations, CPs can then determine the credit risk associated with an individual.[150]

These processes surrounding credit reporting are regulated under pt IIIA of the *Privacy Act*. The framework governs the way personal data is disclosed by intermediaries, including CPs and CRBs in Australia. While the APPs, along with various industry codes, detail how such personal information should be managed, the fact that consumer credit reporting could be shared with external parties still raises concerns. As a result, ensuring the correctness of this data, how it is accessed, and its specifics, have become focal points.

144 Ibid s 40.
145 Ibid s 49(1).
146 Ibid s 52.
147 Ibid s 40A(1).
148 Ibid s 6G. The term 'credit provider' is defined broadly under the *Privacy Act* (n 109). Naturally, banks are deemed credit providers. Additionally, organisations or small business operators will be considered as 'credit providers' if a substantial part of their business involves the provision of credit. Organisations or small businesses that issue credit cards to customers in connection with the sale of goods or services are likewise recognised as credit providers. In specific scenarios, other entities might qualify as credit providers. For instance, if an organisation or small business provides credit associated with the sale of its goods or services and the repayment is deferred for at least a week, then it could be considered a credit provider within that context, provided it does not already qualify under the primary definitions.
149 'Credit reporting body' is defined under the *Privacy Act* (n 109) s 6 as '(a) an organisation; or (b) an agency prescribed by the regulations; that carries on a credit reporting business'.
150 Office of the Australian Information Commissioner, *2021 Independent Review of the Privacy (Credit Reporting) Code* (September 2022) [1.3.1] <https://www.oaic.gov.au/__data/assets/pdf_file/0016/26251/oaic_2021_independent_review_cr_code_final.pdf>.

In 2012, the *Privacy Amendment (Enhancing Privacy Protection) Act 2012* (Cth) was enacted, overhauling pt IIIA and introducing an enhanced credit reporting system. This shift aimed to bring about 'greater logical consistency, simplicity, and clarity within the Privacy Act'.[151] Part IIIA governs consumer credit reporting and is complemented by the *Privacy Regulations 2013* (Cth)[152] and the *Privacy (Credit Reporting) Code 2014* (Cth) ('*CR Code*').[153]

The *Privacy Act* aims to facilitate a credit reporting system that is both efficient and respectful of individual privacy, all the while ensuring that credit providers can comply with their responsible lending obligations under the *NCCPA*.[154] To this end, pt IIIA of the Act is concerned with the handling of personal information about individuals' activities as it relates to consumer credit. Notably, under s 20A, the APPs do not apply to a CRB concerning personal information that encompasses 'credit reporting information', 'CP-derived information' or a 'pre-screening assessment'.[155] Such information is subject to the rules set out under pt III div 2 of the Act.[156]

For instance, a CRB holding credit reporting data about an individual is typically restricted from using or disclosing it.[157] However, there are exceptions. A CRB may use this information as part of its credit reporting activities or when authorised by laws (excluding consumer data rules), court or tribunal orders, or specific regulations.[158] A CRB is also required to ensure that collected credit information is accurate, up to date and complete.[159] They must also establish agreements with CPs to uphold these standards. Regular independent audits are required to check compliance, and any suspected breaches must be addressed promptly.

4.3.2.4 Australian Privacy Principles (APPs)

Australian Privacy Principle 1: Open and Transparent Management of Personal Information

Principle 1 aims to ensure that APP entities manage personal information openly and transparently.[160] Intrinsic to this is taking reasonable steps to implement practices, procedures and systems that ensure the entity's compliance with the APP.[161] Furthermore,

151 Explanatory Memorandum, Privacy Amendment (Enhancing Privacy Protection) Bill 2012 (Cth) 2.

152 *Privacy Act* (n 109) s 20E. For instance, s 20E refers to the regulations on the meaning of the words 'use', 'disclosure' and 'credit provider'. Another provision that refers to the regulations is s 21D, which provides for the permitted disclosures of credit information to a credit provider.

153 For instance, the *Privacy Act* (n 109) s 20R refers to the manner as prescribed in the *Credit Reporting Code* in which a credit reporting body may give access to the credit reporting information.

154 See, eg, *Privacy Act* (n 109) s 6QA.

155 Ibid s 20A(2). ('The Australian Privacy Principles do not apply to a credit reporting body in relation to personal information that is: (a) credit reporting information; or (b) CP [credit provider] derived information; or (c) a pre-screening assessment.')

156 Ibid s 20. ('This Division sets out rules that apply to credit reporting bodies in relation to their handling of the following: (a) credit reporting information; (b) CP derived information; (c) credit reporting information that is de-identified; (d) a pre-screening assessment. The rules apply in relation to that kind of information or assessment instead of the Australian Privacy Principles.')

157 Ibid s 20E.

158 Ibid s 20E(2)(b).

159 Ibid s 20N.

160 Ibid sch 1 pt 1 cl 1.1.

161 Ibid sch 1 pt 1 cl 1.2.

an APP entity is required to have a clearly expressed and up-to-date policy about the entity's management of personal information, as well as:

- how the entity collects this information
- the purposes for which the entity collects, holds, uses or discloses this information
- how an individual may access personal information about the individual held by the entity
- how an individual may correct such information
- how an individual can escalate and complain about a breach of the APP
- how the entity would deal with the complaint
- whether the entity discloses or is likely to disclose personal information to overseas recipients (and, if so, the countries where the recipients are likely located).[162]

The privacy policy must be accessible at no cost and in a suitable format, usually via the entity's website.[163] Additionally, if an individual requests the privacy policy to be in a specific format, the entity is obligated to make reasonable efforts to provide it in that format.[164]

Australian Privacy Principle 2: Anonymity and Pseudonymity

Principle 2 states that individuals must have the choice to remain anonymous or to use a pseudonym when interacting with an APP entity concerning specific issues.[165] However, this does not apply if the entity is mandated or authorised by Australian law, or a court or tribunal order, to engage with individuals who have provided their identity.[166] Furthermore, the principle will not apply where it is impracticable for the entity to deal with individuals who have not identified themselves or are operating under a pseudonym.[167]

Australian Privacy Principle 3: Collection of Solicited Personal Information

Principle 3 stipulates that an entity should not collect personal information unless it is reasonably essential for, or directly linked to, the entity's operations or functions.[168] In other words, to gather sensitive information from an individual, the entity is required first to secure the individual's consent. Further, the information must be either reasonably essential for, or directly related to, the entity's functions or activities.[169] Conversely, the entity may collect sensitive information about an individual without consent if one of the following applies:

- The collection of the information is required or authorised by an Australian law or a court or tribunal order.[170]
- A permitted general or health situation exists.[171]

162 Ibid sch 1 pt 1 cl 1.4.
163 Ibid sch 1 pt 1 cl 1.5.
164 Ibid sch 1 pt 1 cl 1.6.
165 Ibid sch 1 pt 1 cl 2.1.
166 Ibid sch 1 pt 1 cl 2.2(a).
167 Ibid sch 1 pt 1 cl 2.2(b).
168 Ibid sch 1 pt 2 cls 3.1–3.2.
169 Ibid sch 1 pt 2 cl 3.3.
170 Ibid sch 1 pt 2 cl 3.4(a).
171 Ibid. sch 1 pt 2 cl 3.4(c). Defined under *Privacy Act* (n 109) s 16A, this encompasses a broad range of circumstances such as where it is unreasonable or impracticable to obtain consent and there is

- The entity is an enforcement body and reasonably believes the collection of information is necessary to its function or activities.[172]
- The entity is a non-profit organisation and the information relates to its activities or solely to the members of the organisation or to individuals who have regular contact with it.[173]

The entity must collect such personal information only by lawful and fair means.[174] It must be collected solely from the individual unless one of the following conditions applies:

- The individual consents to the collection of the information from someone else.
- The entity is required or authorised by or under an Australian law, or a court or tribunal order, to collect the information from someone other than the individual.
- It is unreasonable or impracticable to collect the information from the individual.[175]

Australian Privacy Principle 4: Dealing with Unsolicited Personal Information

Principle 4 addresses situations where an entity receives unsolicited personal information.[176] If the information could have been acquired by the entity in compliance with Principle 3, then Principles 5–13 apply as if the entity had collected the information under Principle 3.[177] If, on the other hand, the entity concludes that it could not have collected the information and it is not part of a Commonwealth record, then the entity is obligated either to destroy the information or to de-identify it as soon as it is practical, and only if it is lawful and reasonable to do so.[178]

Australian Privacy Principle 5: Notification of the Collection of Personal Information

Principle 5 applies where an entity has collected personal information about an individual. In these circumstances, an entity must take steps that are reasonable in the circumstances to notify the individual of the matters outlined under sch 1 pt 2 cl 5 of the *Privacy Act* or to ensure otherwise that the individual is aware of these matters.[179]

The matters under this clause outline elements such as the purpose, consequences and scope of information collected by the entity.[180] The individual must also be notified

---

a reasonable belief that disclosure is necessary to prevent a serious threat to life, health, or public health or safety. Additionally, circumstances include where there is suspicion of unlawful activity or misconduct, or where collection is necessary for the establishment of a legal or equitable claim, or for the purposes of an alternative dispute resolution process, or, finally, where there is reasonable belief it is necessary for war operations, peacekeeping, civil aid, humanitarian assistance, medical or civil emergencies, or disaster relief.

172 Ibid sch 1 pt 2 cl 3.4(d).
173 Ibid sch 1 pt 2 cl 3.4(e).
174 Ibid sch 1 pt 2 cl 3.5.
175 Ibid sch 1 pt 2 cl 3.6.
176 Ibid sch 1 pt 2 cl 4.1.
177 Ibid sch 1 pt 2 cl 4.4.
178 Ibid sch 1 pt 2 cl 4.3.
179 Ibid sch 1 pt 2 cl 5.1.
180 Ibid sch 1 pt 2 cl 5.2.

if other persons have had their information collected by the entity and be advised of ways they can access the collected information.[181] The entity must also provide individuals with information detailing avenues of redress.[182]

Australian Privacy Principle 6: Use or Disclosure of Personal Information

Principle 6 specifies that if an entity possesses personal information about an individual, collected for a specific reason (the 'primary purpose'), the entity must not use or disclose that information for a different, secondary purpose.[183] There are exceptions to this, such as where the individual has consented to the use or disclosure of the information or where sch 1 pt 3 cl 6.2 or 6.3 applies.[184]

Under sch 1 pt 3 cl 6.2, disclosure may be allowed without consent if the individual would reasonably anticipate the APP entity to use or disclose the information for the secondary purpose. This is contingent on the secondary purpose being directly related to the primary purpose in the case of sensitive information (or merely related to the primary purpose for non-sensitive information).[185] Disclosure may also be permitted if the following conditions apply:

- It is required under an Australian law or court or tribunal order.
- A permitted general situation exists concerning the use or disclosure of the information.
- The entity is an organisation, and a permitted health situation exists.
- The entity reasonably believes that the use or disclosure of the information is reasonably necessary for the enforcement-related activities of an enforcement body.[186]

Australian Privacy Principle 7: Direct Marketing

An organisation in possession of an individual's personal information is prohibited from using or disclosing such information for the purpose of direct marketing.[187] Notwithstanding this, under sch 1 pt 3 cl 7.2, personal information (except for sensitive information) may be disclosed for the purposes of direct marketing if all of the following conditions are satisfied:

- The information was collected from the individual.
- That individual would reasonably expect the organisation to use or disclose the information for that purpose.
- The organisation provides a simple means by which the individual can easily request not to receive direct marketing communications from the organisation, and they have not done so already.[188]

181 Ibid.
182 Ibid.
183 Ibid sch 1 pt 3 cl 6.1.
184 Ibid.
185 Ibid sch 1 pt 3 cl 6.2.
186 Ibid.
187 Ibid sch 1 pt 3 cl 7.1.
188 Ibid sch 1 pt 3 cl 7.2.

Furthermore, under sch 1 pt 3 cl 7.3, an organisation may use or disclose personal information obtained directly from the individual, even if the individual would not reasonably anticipate such use or disclosure, as long as consent has been given or it is not practical to obtain such consent. The organisation must also provide a simple means by which the individual can then request not to receive direct marketing communication from it.[189] This principle does not apply to the extent that the *Spam Act 2003* (Cth) or the *Do Not Call Register Act 2006* (Cth) applies.[190]

Australian Privacy Principle 8: Cross-border Disclosure of Personal Information

Under Principle 8, an entity is required to take care to ensure that, before sharing personal information about an individual with an overseas recipient, the recipient complies with the APPs regarding that information.[191]

This principle does not apply if the entity reasonably believes that the recipient of the information is subject to a law or a binding scheme that has the effect of protecting the information in a similar way to the protection provided by the APPs, and there are mechanisms for the individual to take action to enforce that protection of the law.[192] Additionally, sch 1 pt 3 cl 8.1 will not apply if the individual has provided informed consent to the disclosure[193] or where the disclosure is required or authorised by Australian law.[194]

Australian Privacy Principle 9: Adoption, Use or Disclosure of Government Related Identifiers

The object of Principle 9 is to discourage the adoption of a government-related identifier for an individual unless an exception applies.[195] The adoption of a government identifier may be permitted when it is required or authorised by or under an Australian law or a court/tribunal order.[196] Additionally, under sch 1 pt 3 cl 9.2, an organisation may use a government-related identifier if:

- it is reasonably necessary in order for the organisation to verify the identity of the individual for the purposes of the organisation's activities or functions
- it is reasonably necessary in order for the organisation to fulfil its obligations to an agency of a state or territory authority
- a permitted general situation exists in relation to the disclosure of the identifier
- the organisation reasonably believes that the use or disclosure of the identifier is reasonably necessary for an enforcement activity conducted by an enforcement body.[197]

189 Ibid sch 1 pt 3 cl 7.3.
190 Ibid sch 1 pt 3 cl 7.8.
191 Ibid sch 1 pt 3 cl 8.1.
192 Ibid sch 1 pt 3 cl 8.2.
193 Ibid.
194 Ibid.
195 Ibid sch 1 pt 3 cl 9.1.
196 Ibid.
197 Ibid sch 1 pt 3 cl 9.2.

Australian Privacy Principle 10: Quality of Personal Information

Entities that have collected personal information must take reasonable steps to ensure that the information is accurate, up to date and complete.[198] The entity must also ensure that the personal information is relevant for the use or disclosure.[199]

Australian Privacy Principle 11: Security of Personal Information

According to Principle 11, entities are obligated to take reasonable steps to safeguard personal information from unauthorised access, misuse, interference, loss, alteration or disclosure.[200] Additionally, if the entity no longer needs the information for any purpose and the information is not contained in a Commonwealth record, and the entity is not required by Australian law to retain the information, then the entity must take reasonable steps to destroy the information or ensure it is de-identified.[201]

Australian Privacy Principle 12: Access to Personal Information

Principle 12 stipulates that if an entity possesses personal information about an individual, the entity is required to, upon the individual's request, provide access to that information.[202] There is an exception to this principle for agencies, which may refuse access if they are required or authorised under the *Freedom of Information Act 1982* (Cth) or under any other Acts that authorise access by persons to documents.[203] If the entity is an organisation, the entity can, under sch 1 pt 5 cl 12.3, refuse to give individuals access to personal information where the entity believes that:

- access to information would pose a serious threat to the life, health or safety of any individual, or to public health or public safety
- access to information would have an unreasonable impact on the privacy of others
- the request is frivolous or vexatious
- the information relates to anticipated legal proceedings/negotiations
- giving access would be unlawful
- denying access is required by an Australian law
- the entity reasonably suspects that unlawful activity or serious misconduct may be engaged in and that giving access would be likely to prejudice the taking of appropriate action in relation to the matter.

Moreover, the entity may decline access if it believes that doing so could likely prejudice the enforcement activities of an enforcement body, or if revealing the information would disclose evaluative data related to a commercially sensitive decision.[204] When a request is made, an entity must comply with specific timelines for disclosure: If the entity is an agency, a response is required within 30 days of the request. Alternatively, if the entity is an organisation, a response must be provided within a reasonable period

198 Ibid sch 1 pt 4 cl 10.1.
199 Ibid sch 1 pt 4 cl 10.2.
200 Ibid sch 1 pt 4 cl 11.1.
201 Ibid sch 1 pt 4 cl 11.2.
202 Ibid sch 1 pt 5 cl 12.1.
203 Ibid sch 1 pt 5 cl 12.2.
204 Ibid sch 1 pt 5 cl 12.3.

following the request. In either case, the entity is obliged to grant access to the requested information in the manner specified by the individual, provided it is reasonable and practicable to do so.[205]

If, however, an entity declines to provide access due to any of the circumstances mentioned above, it is required to issue a written notice to the individual. This notice must outline the reasons for the refusal, describe the available avenues for lodging a complaint against the decision, and include any additional information as mandated by relevant regulations.[206]

Australian Privacy Principle 13: Correction of Personal Information

In accordance with the final principle, if the entity is satisfied that the information it holds is inaccurate or outdated, or if the individual requests a correction, the entity is obligated to take reasonable measures to update the information so that it is accurate.[207] This should be done in consideration of the purpose for which the information is held. Moreover, if the corrected information about an individual has previously been disclosed to a third party, the entity must inform the third party of the corrections, but only if the individual specifically requests such notification.[208] If the entity refuses to issue a correction, the entity must then provide a written notice to the individual of its reasons for refusal.[209] Where an entity refuses to correct information, an individual has the right to request the entity to make a statement and to associate that statement with the information, taking reasonable steps to ensure this statement is apparent to users.[210]

4.3.3 New developments: European Union's *General Data Protection Regulation* (GDPR) and 'the Brussels Effect'

The advent of digital platforms has revolutionised the way we communicate and conduct business, but it has also raised significant concerns about data privacy and security. These platforms often collect, process and store vast amounts of personal information, prompting governments worldwide to take action to protect individuals' data rights.

One of the most significant efforts in this regard is the European Union's (EU) *General Data Protection Regulation*, which came into effect on 25 May 2018. The GDPR is considered a landmark change in European data protection laws, representing the most substantial overhaul in this area in over two decades. As a 'regulation' replacing the EU Data Protection Directive (also known as 'Directive 95/46/EC'), the GDPR will be directly applicable in all EU Member States without the need for implementing legislation at the national level. It sets stringent standards for data collection, storage and processing, and imposes severe penalties for non-compliance.

205 Ibid sch 1 pt 5 cl 12.4.
206 Ibid sch 1 pt 5 cl 12.9.
207 Ibid sch 1 pt 5 cl 13.1.
208 Ibid sch 1 pt 5 cl 13.2.
209 Ibid sch 1 pt 5 cl 13.3.
210 Ibid sch 1 pt 5 cl 13.4.

Although the GDPR originates from the EU, it may have extraterritorial implications – a phenomenon that Anu Bradford termed 'the Brussels Effect'.[211] This means that businesses located in other regions, including Australia, could be impacted by the regulation if they have an establishment in the EU, monitor behaviour within the EU, or offer goods and services to the EU.[212] The GDPR and the *Privacy Act* share something in common: for instance, they both implement a privacy-by-design approach to compliance and require information-handling practices to be transparent.[213] However, there are some notable differences between the two regimes; for instance, the 'right to be forgotten'[214] and the 'right to explanation'[215] under arts 17 and 22 have no equivalent in Australia's *Privacy Act*.[216]

Given the evolving landscape in the era of big data, the Federal Government issued the terms of reference and an issues paper for a review of the *Privacy Act* in October 2020. The review aimed to assess whether the *Privacy Act*'s scope and enforcement mechanisms were still fit for their intended purpose.[217] It came on the heels of the final report by the Australian Competition and Consumer Commission (ACCC) on the Digital Platforms Inquiry and the Government's subsequent response. In the report, the Australian Treasurer concurred with the ACCC's primary conclusion, which emphasised the need for reforms to better safeguard consumers, enhance transparency, address power

211 Anu Bradford, 'The Brussels Effect' (2012) 107(1) *Northwestern University Law Review* 1, 22–5.

212 *General Data Protection Regulation* (EU) 2016/679 (GDPR), art 3(1), (2). Article 3(2) of the GDPR sets out its extraterritorial scope and provides: 'This Regulation applies to the processing of personal data of data subjects who are in the Union by a controller or processor not established in the Union, where the processing activities are related to: the offering of goods or services, irrespective of whether a payment of the data subject is required, to such data subjects in the Union; or the monitoring of their behaviour as far as their behaviour takes place within the Union.'

213 'Australian Entities and the European Union General Data Protection Regulation', *Office of the Australian Information Commissioner* (Web Page, 8 June 2018) <https://www.oaic.gov.au/privacy/guidance-and-advice/australian-entities-and-the-eu-general-data-protection-regulation/>.

214 GDPR (n 212) art 17.

215 Ibid recital 71. ('The data subject should have the right not to be subject to a decision, which may include a measure, evaluating personal aspects relating to him or her which is based solely on automated processing and which produces legal effects concerning him or her or similarly significantly affects him or her, such as automatic refusal of an online credit application or e-recruiting practices without any human intervention. Such processing includes "profiling" that consists of any form of automated processing of personal data evaluating the personal aspects relating to a natural person, in particular to analyse or predict aspects concerning the data subject's performance at work, economic situation, health, personal preferences or interests, reliability or behaviour, location or movements, where it produces legal effects concerning him or her or similarly significantly affects him or her ... *In any case, such processing should be subject to suitable safeguards, which should include specific information to the data subject and the right to obtain human intervention, to express his or her point of view, to obtain an explanation of the decision reached after such assessment and to challenge the decision* ...' [emphasis added].)

216 The Australian Government is considering introducing a 'right to de-index online search results containing personal information', where the search engine may refer to the OAIC for a fee, and this right is limited to the Australian jurisdiction. This is to address the 'right to be forgotten'. It is also considering introducing a 'right for individuals to request meaningful information about how substantially automated decisions with legal or similarly significant effect are made', as a solution to address other concerns including the right to explanation. See generally Attorney-General's Department, *Privacy Act Review: Report 2022* (2022) ('Report, 2022') <https://www.ag.gov.au/sites/default/files/2023-02/privacy-act-review-report_0.pdf>.

217 Attorney-General's Department, *Review of the Privacy Act 1988 – Terms of Reference* (30 October 2020) ('*Privacy Act Review – TOR*') <https://www.ag.gov.au/integrity/publications/review-privacy-act-1988-terms-reference>.

imbalances, and prevent the misuse of significant market power in media and advertising services markets.[218]

The *Privacy Act Review* report was published on 16 February 2023.[219] While it remains to be seen how the *Privacy Act* will be amended, the report has underscored a number of key issues for reform. The report is focused on dealing with an increasingly digitalised economy, especially with respect to data protection. Some key issues in the report include removing or narrowing some exemptions in the *Privacy Act* that have led to Australia's data protection laws being more lax compared to other countries' laws; introducing additional protections regarding the means by which entities can collect individuals' data and the length of time they may keep such data; and streamlining processes for enforcement and for individuals to seek redress should breaches of the *Privacy Act* occur. Notably, however, credit reporting under pt IIIA of the *Privacy Act* is not considered by this review.[220]

The Australian Government subsequently released its response to the *Privacy Act Review Report* on 28 September 2023, agreeing to 38 proposals and agreeing in principle to 68 proposals.[221]

The Government agreed in principle to the imposition of a new test relating to the collection of personal information. Collections, uses and disclosures of personal information must be fair and reasonable in the circumstances, regardless of whether an individual has consented. This objective test is meant to protect the individual's and the public's interest in protecting one's privacy. It would mark a shift away from the current approach of notice and consent to a more substantive approach that considers whether information is actually handled in a fair and reasonable manner. Another obligation to be imposed on entities would be the mandatory privacy impact assessment, which must be completed prior to undertaking a 'high privacy risk activity'.

With respect to the duration for which an entity can hold personal information, the Government also agreed in principle to the proposal that entities must establish maximum and minimum retention periods for personal information they hold and specify these periods in their privacy policies. These retention periods should take into account the type, sensitivity and purpose of the information being retained. Individuals would also have a newly introduced right to erasure – which requires an entity to delete or de-identify their personal information. In line with the general sentiment of granting individuals stronger rights, individuals would also be granted the right to access and receive an explanation about their personal information upon request, and to object to the collection, use or disclosure of their personal information.

Bringing the Australian position closer to other regulations such as the GDPR, the Government also agreed in principle to amend the definition of 'personal information'

218 Josh Frydenberg, 'Release of the ACCC Digital Platforms Report' (Media Release, Treasury Portfolio, 26 July 2019) <https://ministers.treasury.gov.au/ministers/josh-frydenberg-2018/media-releases/release-accc-digital-platforms-report>

219 Report, 2022 (n 216).

220 *Privacy Act Review – TOR* (n 217).

221 Attorney-General's Department, *Government Reponse: Privacy Act Review Report* (2023) <https://www.ag.gov.au/sites/default/files/2023-09/government-response-privacy-act-review-report.PDF>.

in s 6 of the *Privacy Act* to include technical and inferred information that can be used to identify individuals, such as IP addresses and device identifiers.

Another major change would be the removal or narrowing of the small business exception. In particular, small businesses that collect biometric information and trade in personal information should no longer be allowed to rely on the small business exemption, given the sensitivity of the information handled on a regular basis. Nevertheless, recognising the disproportionate burden this could impose on small businesses, the Government stated that any changes would be subject to consultation and would include an appropriate transition period.

As to individuals' recourse to redress, the Government agreed in principle to two proposals. First, individuals should be able to have a direct right of action to the courts. Second, for invasions of privacy which fall outside the *Privacy Act*, individuals should have recourse to a statutory tort for serious invasions of privacy. Presently, there is no tortious right of action for individuals who have suffered harm due to invasions of privacy; hence, this welcome introduction would allow individuals to pursue remedies such as compensation or injunctions in response to such invasions.

Overall, the Government's response to the proposals signals a paradigm shift in Australia's privacy laws towards a greater focus on protecting the individual and placing the onus on entities and organisations to properly collect, use and disclose information.

4.4 Summary

Many jurisdictions have adopted a regulatory sandbox as a policy tool for accommodating the rise of Fintech businesses. However, the sandbox approach may vary from one country to another, depending on its social, economic and political underpinnings. Australia has rolled out its sandbox under Regulatory Guide 257, later amended and upgraded as the 'Enhanced Regulatory Sandbox'. The ERS could help reduce startups' barriers to entry into the financial market or credit market by relaxing the licensing requirements. Based on the idea of experimentalism, the ERS sets out specific parameters for eligible entities to validate their business concepts for up to 24 months. In doing so, policymakers seek to balance competing interests, as they embrace the mixed opportunities brought about by new technologies. Data protection is a paramount concern for virtually every sector, including banks and financial institutions. It is particularly crucial in the context of consumer credit, which is governed by pt III of the *Privacy Act 1988*. This Act, and its APPs, are the main legal instruments regulating data protection in Australia. Globally, the GDPR in the EU can also affect Australians, given its 'Brussels Effect'. Likewise, the *Privacy Act* may affect other jurisdictions because of the 'Australian link' requirement.

FURTHER READING

Allen, Hilary J, 'Regulatory Sandbox' (2019) 87(3) *George Washington Law Review* 579.

Arner, Douglas W, Jànos Barberis and Ross P Buckley, 'FinTech, RegTech and the Reconceptualization of Financial Regulation' (2016) 37(3) *Northwestern Journal of International Law and Business* 371.

Arner, Douglas W, Jànos Barberis and Ross P Buckley, 'The Evolution of Fintech: A New Post-Crisis Paradigm?' (2016) 47(4) *Georgetown Journal of International Law* 1271.

'Australian Entities and the EU General Data Protection Regulation', *Office of the Australian Information Commissioner* (Web Page, 8 June 2018) <https://www.oaic.gov.au/privacy/guidance-and-advice/australian-entities-and-the-eu-general-data-protection-regulation>.

Bennett Moses, Lyria, 'Recurring Dilemmas: The Law's Race to Keep Up with Technological Change' (2007) (2) *University of Illinois Journal of Law, Technology and Policy* 239.

Bennett Moses, Lyria and Monika Zalnieriute, 'Law and Technology in the Dimension of Time' in Sofia Ranchordás and Yaniv Roznai (eds), *Time, Law and Change: An Interdisciplinary Study* (Hart Publishing, 2020).

Bradford, Anu, 'The Brussels Effect' (2012) 107(1) *Northwestern University Law Review* 1.

Bromberg, Lev, Andrew Godwin and Ian Ramsay, 'Fintech Sandboxes: Achieving a Balance between Regulation and Innovation' (2017) 28(4) *Journal of Banking and Finance Law and Practice* 314.

Buckley, Ross, Natalia Jevglevskaja and Scott Farrell, 'Australia's Data-Sharing Regime: Six Lessons for the World' (2022) 33(1) *King's Law Journal* 61.

Didenko, Anton N, 'A Better Model for Australia's Enhanced Fintech Sandbox' (2021) 44(3) *University of New South Wales Law Journal* 1078.

Didenko, Anton N, 'Regulating FinTech: Lessons from Africa' (2018) 19(2) *San Diego International Law Journal* 311.

Office of the Australian Information Commissioner, *Australian Privacy Principles Guidelines* (December 2022) <https://www.oaic.gov.au/privacy/australian-privacy-principles-guidelines>.

Omarova, Saule T, 'Technology v Technocracy: Fintech as a Regulatory Challenge' (2020) 6(1) *Journal of Financial Regulation* 75.

Ranchordas, Sofia, 'Experimental Regulations and Regulatory Sandboxes: Law without Order?' (Research Paper No 10/2021, University of Groningen, 1 December 2021).

Tsang, Cheng-Yun, 'From Industry Sandbox to Supervisory Control Box: Rethinking the Role of Regulators in the Era of FinTech' (2019) (2) *Journal of Law, Technology and Policy* 355.

Walker, George, 'Regulatory Technology (RegTech) – Construction of a New Regulatory Policy and Model' (2021) 54(1) *International Lawyer* 1.

Zetzsche, Dirk A, Douglas W Arner and Ross P Buckley, 'Decentralized Finance' (2020) 6(2) *Journal of Financial Regulation* 172.

Zetzsche, Dirk A et al., 'Regulating a Revolution: From Regulatory Sandboxes to Smart Regulation' (2017) 23(1) *Fordham Journal of Corporate and Financial Law* 31.

QUESTIONS

(1) It is argued that regulatory sandboxes in some jurisdictions such as the United Kingdom would involve 'pre-judging innovative value', a task that is not appropriate for the regulators. To what extent would you agree with what Lim and Low have suggested below:

> Given the wide range and complexity of technologies being developed in the FinTech sector, it is unlikely that regulatory sandbox administrators would have expertise on all products being tested. This means that additional resources will be necessary to hire experts to ensure that the appropriate expertise is available to the regulatory sandbox administrator throughout testing. The reality of resource scarcity imposes upon the

> regulator the duty to choose, amongst many candidates, a few lucky participants for the regulatory sandbox ... These criteria inadvertently force regulators to prematurely decide whether a new FinTech product is technologically innovative and meets a market need. Are the regulators even qualified to have such discretion?[222]

(2) After finishing her academic journey, Olivia is excited to dive into entrepreneurship by establishing a Fintech venture with her associates. She understands that a licence is commonly needed for offering financial services within Australia. She also notices that various countries, including Australia, have been inspired by the United Kingdom's sandbox model, which offers a more lenient regulatory environment for Fintech startups. Based on relevant Australian laws and regulations, how can Olivia evaluate her business idea without first obtaining an Australian Financial Services Licence?
   (a) Who is eligible to participate in the Enhanced Regulatory Sandbox?
   (b) What actions must Olivia take to commence the testing phase? Is a formal submission to ASIC mandated, or will a notification suffice?
   (c) What specific activities are permitted for testing within this sandbox framework?
   (d) What is the time limit for conducting tests in this sandbox?
   (e) Specify the conditions under which the sandbox privilege will expire automatically.

(3) In addition to the Australian market, Henry is also interested in setting up his Fintech business in the United Kingdom. Help him by briefly contrasting the sandbox approaches adopted by the United Kingdom and Australia. The focus should be on three issues:
   (a) who can apply
   (b) whether prior approval is required
   (c) the criteria for being admitted into a sandbox.

   Include a critical assessment of which model you prefer, and why.

222 Lim and Low (n 104).

CHAPTER 5

BANKS, BANKING AND THE BANKER–CUSTOMER RELATIONSHIP

5.1 Introduction

Section 5 of the *Banking Act 1959* (Cth) ('*Banking Act*') defines the 'business of banking' as encompassing activities such as accepting deposits and extending loans. To undertake these activities, entities must obtain an authorised deposit-taking institution (ADI) licence, as stipulated in s 9 of the Act. This licence authorises corporate entities - banks, building societies and credit unions - to operate within Australia's banking sector, all subject to regulatory oversight.

Section 7 of the Act specifies that only corporate bodies, excluding natural persons, are permitted to conduct banking business. Additionally, s 8 restricts banking operations to the Reserve Bank of Australia (RBA) and ADIs. The pathway to acquiring ADI status involves an application process with the Australian Prudential Regulation Authority (APRA), outlined in s 9. This ensures that only entities meeting stringent prudential standards can engage in banking activities.

The regulatory framework, expounded on in Chapter 1, is reinforced by APRA, a prudential regulator that establishes various standards such as Prudential Standard APS 110 Capital Adequacy ('APS 110'). These standards play a crucial role in upholding the stability and integrity of the financial system. They mandate that ADIs maintain sufficient financial resources to manage risks and absorb losses, safeguarding depositors and instilling confidence in the Australian financial system. It is important to note that while the term 'banks' is used in this book, banks represent just one category of ADIs.

By and large, the relationship between a bank and its customers is contractual and governed by the usual contract rules. Such a relationship is also regulated by various statutes. Still, it is a contract in a specialised market with a long history and, consequently, it has acquired a large raft of terms implied by custom and usage. These terms may, of course, always be ousted by express terms, but clear and unequivocal words are required for the effect.

5.2 Nature of the relationship

5.2.1 A debtor-creditor relationship

We start with a fundamental legal question: In what capacity does the bank hold the deposits of its customers? There might be several views: bailee, trustee, agent and debtor. We examine each of them in turn.

It cannot be as a bailee. The bank is not required to return the exact coins and notes the customer deposited with it; in any event, many deposits do not involve cash.

It cannot be as a trustee or an agent, because there is no fiduciary duty when dealing with the deposit to put the interests of the customer ahead of the bank's interests. Such an obligation, even if it existed, could be ousted by an express term to the contrary. However, for centuries, bankers have taken deposits and used them without heed to their customers' interests and without being held to account for the absence of such an ouster.

The bank holds the deposit as a debtor, and the customer deposits it as a creditor. The deposit is a debt owed by the bank to the customer. It was not until the mid-nineteenth century that this view achieved undisputed judicial approval in *Foley v Hill*, a case that turned on the statute of limitations.[1] If the deposit were a mere debt, then the plaintiff's action was statute barred. If it involved a fiduciary obligation, a longer limitation applied and the action could proceed. Lord Cottenham explained, with some repetition for the sake of emphasis, what should be rather obvious:

> Money, when paid into a bank, ceases altogether to be the money of the [customer]; it is by then the money of the banker, who is bound to return an equivalent by paying a similar sum to that deposited ... when he is asked for it. [The money] is known ... to be placed there for the purpose of being under the control of the banker; it is then the banker's money; he is known to deal with it as his own; he makes what profit he can, which profit he retains to himself ... [He] has contracted, having received that money, to repay to the [customer], when demanded, a sum equivalent to that paid into his hands.[2]

A debt is, of course, not a chattel, as it cannot be actually physically owned by the person (unlike, for instance, cars, houses or shoes).[3] It is a chose in action, in that it instead gives a legal right to enforce repayment (in certain circumstances) and thus to have the chose in action converted into chattel – cash. The distinction is important because the law treats a chose in action differently from a chattel. By way of example, consider *Croton v The Queen*.[4]

A man and a woman opened a joint bank account. The pair would periodically deposit money into the account, a substantial part of which was comprised of the woman's earnings. Unbeknown to the woman, and without her authority, the man would later withdraw the entire balance and deposit it into his separate, personal bank account. When the woman learnt of the man's act, she reported him to the police, who charged him with larceny. He was convicted. On appeal to the High Court of Australia, the conviction was overturned (by a majority of 2–1). The common law crime of larceny only exists regarding chattels personal because of the asportation requirement. That is, a right to sue cannot be subject to a physical action, such as being transported from one place to another, because it is not a physical object. You cannot pick up a right to sue and put it in the back of a truck and drive off with it. The correct charge in criminal law would have been something called 'fraudulent misappropriation'.

One of the critical consequences of the relationship between the debtor and the creditor is that (subject to legislative protection) the customer ranks as an unsecured creditor in the event of bank insolvency.

5.2.2 A special kind of debt with special terms

There are additional implied terms, some of which were enumerated in *Joachimson v Swiss Bank Corporation*.[5]

1 *Foley v Hill* (1848) 2 HLC 28; 9 ER 1002.
2 Ibid 1005.
3 LexisNexis, *Halsbury's Laws of Australia* (online at 3 July 2023) Introduction – Meaning and Classification of Personal Property, 'Classification of Chattels Personal' [315-15].
4 *Croton v The Queen* (1967) 117 CLR 326.
5 *Joachimson v Swiss Bank Corporation* [1921] 3 KB 110.

- The bank undertakes to receive money (ie accept deposits) and collect cheques for its customers' accounts.
- The debt does not become due until repayment is demanded.
- Demand is to be made during normal business hours at the branch at which the account is kept.

Ordinarily, it is for a debtor to seek out the creditor and make repayment when it is due without request. However, bank deposits are at call unless otherwise agreed. When *Joachimson* was decided (1921), accounts were maintained by hand in ledger books, so it made sense that the demand should be made at the branch where the account was kept. Today accounts are maintained by electronically linked computers and the status of the account is available even at the most remote branch. As it is the custom of Australian banks to permit withdrawals from any branch, so it is probable that the third term has now been modified by custom and usage to omit the same branch requirement.

5.2.2.1 Bank may refuse to make any payment

On demand to pay more than the due amount, the bank may refuse to pay anything. This idea was expressed by Lord Asquith in *Bank of New South Wales v Laing*: 'If the balance fails short of [the demanded amount] even by a penny, [the customer] fails altogether.'[6] It distinguishes the creditor–debtor relationship in the case of a customer and the banker from that relationship in other cases. Therefore, if the customer writes a cheque for more than the balance in their account, the bank is entitled to refuse any payment at all on the cheque.

5.2.2.2 Reasonable notice

The bank must give reasonable notice if it wishes to cease to do business with the customer. The customer may demand payment to themselves, but they may equally demand payment be made to third parties - for example, by writing a cheque or requesting an electronic funds transfer (EFT). The requirement of notice operates so that the customer will not be embarrassed by writing cheques that will be dishonoured. What constitutes reasonable notice will be discussed below.

5.2.2.3 Reasonable care

The customer must exercise reasonable care when drawing cheques and disclose to the bank any knowledge of forgery so as to prevent fraud. These are called the *MacMillan* and *Greenwood* duties, respectively, from the cases that define their extent (which will be examined when we introduce cheques in Chapter 8).[7]

5.2.3 Implied terms

Some implied terms are found by 'fact'; that is, they must satisfy the requirements of *BP Refinery (Westernport) Pty Ltd v Hastings Shire Council*[8] and *Codelfa Construction Pty Ltd v State*

6 *Bank of New South Wales v Laing* (1953) 54 SR (NSW) 76, 86.
7 *London Joint Stock Bank v Macmillan* [1918] AC 777; *Greenwood v Martins Bank Ltd* [1933] AC 51.
8 *BP Refinery (Westernport) Pty Ltd v Hastings Shire Council* (1977) 180 CLR 266.

Rail Authority (NSW)[9] that they be reasonable and equitable, necessary to give business efficacy to the contract (ie be of such a nature that the contract will not 'work' without them,) and so apparent that they go without saying (ie satisfy the 'officious bystander' test).

The custom and usage of the market in question may imply terms. Essentially, the parties are taken to have contracted on the basis of: 'This is just the way we do these things around here. It's how we have always done them – ask anyone. And if you don't like how we do things here, then you can sod off and try somewhere else – and good luck to you.' Implied terms of this kind must be notorious (in the sense that anyone who deals in the market could reasonably be expected to be aware of them), reasonable, legal and usual practice, but they do *not* have to be *never* deviated from or be efficacious or obvious to someone not in the market. (See, eg, *Con-Stan Industries of Australia Pty Ltd v Norwich Winterthur Insurance (Australia) Ltd* for an explanation.[10]) Notwithstanding that some implied terms might also qualify as being implied by fact, the implied terms of the customer–banker relationship are of this kind.

Occasionally, there are attempts to have new terms implied into the customer–banker relationship. These are almost always termed 'allegedly implied by fact', with no custom in the matter alleged. This does require the criteria in *Codelfa* to be satisfied. Any such attempt seems to have been unsuccessful so far.

However, one must also be aware of terms implied by common law or by statute. For example, the extent of the bank's duties is also governed by various codes of practice that may or may not have the force of law, such as the:

- *ePayments Code*
- *Banking Code of Practice* (concerning 'consumers' and 'small business')
- *Australian Securities and Investments Commission Act 2001* (Cth) ('*ASIC Act*') (which imposes non-excludable warranties as to services provided to 'consumers').

5.2.4 Other relationships between banker and customer

There are other relationships that can be created between customer and banker, either supplementary to the debtor–creditor contract or by entering contracts for other services, with other obligations arising from them. For example, a banker acts as an agent of the customer for the purpose of paying and collecting cheques and with respect to other third-party payments with corresponding obligations. Also, banks may, for instance, offer safe deposit services, under which they will become bailees with respect to the goods deposited. Furthermore, they may offer financial advice, which potentially makes them liable for negligent misrepresentation and brings them within the financial services licensing regime.

5.3 Who is the customer?

It is sometimes necessary to determine whether certain statutory protections are available to the bank in relation to payment on negotiable instruments such as cheques, or

9 *Codelfa Construction Pty Ltd v State Rail Authority (NSW)* (1982) 149 CLR 337.
10 *Con-Stan Industries of Australia Pty Ltd v Norwich Winterthur Insurance (Australia) Ltd* (1986) 160 CLR 226.

whether someone is a customer of the bank. It would seem from the above discussion that a customer is anyone who holds an account with the bank. However, it was previously accepted that a customer was anyone with whom the bank maintained a course of dealing (see, eg, *Matthews v Williams Brown & Co*).[11] But that view was rejected in *Great Western Railway v London & County Banking Co Ltd*.[12]

A rates collector had habitually, for 20 years, presented cheques from ratepayers for collection and payment at the bank where his employer held its account. The cheques were made out to him in his name, but he acted as an agent in collection for his employer. On each occasion, he asked for part of the amount in cash and part to be paid into his employer's account. He misappropriated the cash payments for himself. On discovering this, the employer sued the bank for conversion. The bank relied on a statutory defence that depended on whether the cheque had been collected by the bank for a customer. The House of Lords held that although the bank had regularly collected on cheques at the rate collector's request, he was not a customer of the bank as he held no account with it, and there was no intention by either party that he should.

That an account will be sufficient, whether or not there is a course of dealing associated with it, is established by *Commissioners of Taxation v English, Scottish & Australian Bank Ltd*, where Lord Dunedin held:

> A person whose money has been accepted by a bank on the footing that they undertake to honour cheques up to the amount standing to his credit is ... a customer of the bank ... irrespective of whether his connection is one of short or long standing. The contrast [sic] is not between a habitué and a newcomer but between a person for whom the bank performs a casual service, as for example cashing a cheque for a person introduced by one of their customers, and a person who has an account of their own at the bank.[13]

Ladbroke & Co v Todd also sheds light on this.[14] In that case, a thief stole a cheque and presented it to a bank for collection. The proceeds were used to open an account. It was held that this was enough to constitute the thief as a customer, even though there was no other transaction on the account.

In fact, as the relationship is a contractual one, it is possible to make an argument that the actual opening of an account should not be necessary to establish the relationship. All that should be required is a contractual obligation to open one – that is, to provide those services usually provided by a banker to a customer. There may be some judicial support for this in *Woods v Martins Bank*, although arguably the decision in that case does not turn on whether the person in question was a customer or merely in a contractual relationship with the bank.[15] What needs to be decided is whether the person becomes a customer of the bank on the making of the contract (the undertaking to open an account) or on its performance (the opening of the account).

11 *Matthews v Williams-Brown & Co* (1894) 10 TLR 386.
12 *Great Western Railway Co v London & County Banking Co Ltd* [1901] AC 414.
13 *Commissioners of Taxation v English, Scottish and Australian Bank Ltd* [1920] AC 683.
14 *Ladbroke & Co v Todd* [1914] 30 TLR 433.
15 *Woods v Martins Bank Ltd* [1959] 1 QB 55.

Sometimes a person will open an account in a 'false' name. Generally speaking, people are entitled to call themselves by whatever name they choose. If you choose to call yourself 'Tomato' on certain occasions, then so be it. Your legal identity has not changed. The account is with the person, not with their name. Opening an account in a 'false' name is a rare occurrence these days, due to the *Anti-Money Laundering/Counter-Terrorism Financing Act 2006* (Cth).

Likewise, where the person represents themselves to be someone else – that is, the person impersonates someone – the account is with the rogue, not with the person who is impersonated (*Marfani & Co Ltd v Midland Bank Ltd*).[16] Such contracts are, of course, subject to the usual principles of contractual mistake.

Nor can a person claim to be a customer of the bank when an account is opened in their name but without their authority.[17] See *Stoney Stanton Supplies (Coventry) Ltd v Midland Bank Ltd*,[18] per Lord Denning relying on *Robinson v Midland Bank Ltd.*[19] Therefore, if someone opens an account 'for you' with the bank, without your consent, there is no customer–banker relationship between you and the bank. Sometimes, however, implicit consent is readily found – for example, where a grandparent opens an account in the name of a grandchild without the consent of a parent/guardian. Standard agency law applies.

5.4 Terminating the relationship

A bank cannot terminate the relationship without reasonable notice (*Joachimson v Swiss Bank Corporation*).[20] The rationale is that the customer may, from time to time, write cheques in the expectation that these will be met when presented, and sufficient time ought to be allowed for the presentation of outstanding cheques and for the customer to make alternative arrangements with respect to their business. What is reasonable depends on the individual facts of the case. See, for example, *Prosperity v Lloyd's Bank* where, due to the nature of the business involved, one month's notice was held to be insufficient.[21]

The appropriate remedy would usually be an award of damages. An injunction is not unlikely to be available. It is a discretionary remedy that is generally not awarded if it essentially requires the performance of a contract, that being one for personal services (*Prosperity Ltd v Lloyd's Bank Ltd*).[22] The court is concerned that such performance, as Fry LJ states in *De Francesco v Barnum*, 'is not in the interest of mankind ... [and] turn[s] contracts of service into contracts of slavery'.[23]

16 *Marfani & Co Ltd v Midland Bank Ltd* [1968] 1 WLR 956.

17 RJA Hooley, 'Bills of Exchange and Banking' in Hugh Beale (ed), *Chitty on Contracts* (Thomson Reuters, 34th ed, 2021) 299 [36-257]; Andrew Burrows, *Principles of English Commercial Law* (Oxford University Press, 2015) 195 [6.13]; Alan Tyree, *Banking Law in Australia* (LexisNexis Butterworths, 10th ed, 2021) 53 [3.3.5].

18 *Stoney Stanton Supplies (Coventry) Ltd v Midland Bank Ltd* [1966] 2 Lloyd's Rep 373.

19 *Robinson v Midland Bank Ltd* (1925) 41 TLR 402.

20 *Joachimson v Swiss Bank Corporation* [1921] 3 KB 110.

21 *Prosperity Ltd v Lloyds Bank Ltd* (1923) 39 TLR 372.

22 Ibid.

23 *De Francesco v Barnum* (1890) 45 Ch D 430, 438. See also Prince Saprai, 'The Principle Against Self-Enslavement in Contract Law' (2009) 26(1) *Journal of Contract Law* 25, 35–6.

If the account is in overdraft, the matter may be different. Most overdrafts are granted on the basis that they are repayable on demand, so arguably, no notice is necessary. There is, however, no authority on the matter.

As the banker–customer relationship is a personal one, it terminates automatically once the bank has notice of the customer's death or bankruptcy. However, the *Cheques Act 1986* (Cth) has certain provisions relating to the payment of cheques drawn by a person who, to the bank's knowledge, later died. Likewise, where the customer is other than a natural person, the relationship ceases when, to the bank's knowledge, the entity in question ceases to exist (eg through dissolution of a partnership or deregistration of a company).

There are circumstances in which a bank may 'stop' an account. This is a distinct matter, and 'stopping' does not terminate the relationship. The nature and effect of a 'stop' will be discussed in more detail in the context of the operation of accounts.

The relationship also ceases if the bank ceases to exist. Any amount standing to the credit of a customer becomes immediately due and payable as a debt. Absent any statutory protection, such a customer must prove the amount of the debt and will rank as an ordinary unsecured creditor (*Russian Commercial and Industrial Bank v Comptoir déscompte de Mulhouse*).[24] Note that the *Banking Act* div 2AA protects certain deposits.

5.5 Altering the relationship

As the relationship is contractual, the normal contractual rules regarding variation apply. One way of 'modifying' the relationship is to claim that the contract is subject to some (previously undetected) implied term. Refer to the previous discussion concerning implied terms.

Notice by the bank of a new or modified term may also alter the bank–customer relationship, provided the customer was made aware of and agreed to (by their conduct or words) the aforementioned term. Obviously, unilateral alteration is not possible.

Consider *Burnett v Westminster Bank Ltd.*[25] B kept accounts at two branches of the bank. After B opened his accounts, one only of the branches adopted computerised accounting methods and issued chequebooks with certain features compatible with the new system. The inside cover of the chequebooks contained a notice to the effect that the cheque forms it contained could only be used to draw on accounts at this branch. B used one of the forms to draw on his account at the non-computerised branch. (He struck out the name of the branch printed on the form and replaced it with the name of the non-computerised branch. As we will see later, in usual circumstances this would be a perfectly valid cheque. Cheques, as long as they satisfy the statutory requirements and any express terms agreed between the bank and customer, do not have to be in any particular form, and chequebooks are conventionally provided as an item of convenience only.) He subsequently wished to stop payment on

24 *Russian Commercial and Industrial Bank v Comptoir dÉscompte de Mulhouse* [1925] AC 112.
25 *Burnett v Westminster Bank Ltd* [1966] 1 QB 742.

this cheque and gave notice to the non-computerised branch – the branch on which he believed he had drawn the cheque. The cheque was paid in the ordinary course of the computer processing at the bank (because the form contained a computer readable code that indicated it should be debited to the computerised branch, and this had not been crossed out). The court held that the bank was unable to show that the notice in the chequebook had been brought to B's (actual or constructive) attention, and that therefore they were also unable to show that his use of the book amounted to consent that form was usable (and in fact used) only in relation to the computerised account. The attempt to alter the terms had not been effective and so B was able to alter the form and use it to give instructions to the non-computerised branch. Consequently, his stop order had been directed to the correct branch and should have been acted on by the bank to stop payment on the cheque. Note that had the bank been able to show that B was aware – or constructively aware – of the notice when he wrote the cheque, the bank would have succeeded.

Bear in mind that the *ePayments Code*, as further elaborated upon in Chapter 9, permits certain contractual modifications to be made without showing that the customer was aware of or agreed to the change. For present purposes, it is crucial to note that the *ePayments Code* regulates various electronic transactions that do not require a signature, including those involving bank cards, telephones, the internet, mobile phones and mail contactless transactions.[26] The *ePayments Code* makes special provisions for variation of the 'terms and conditions of use' of these features. It requires written notification for 'important' changes, but only 'mass notification' for others. Subsequent use of the feature will then denote agreement. Moreover, no notification at all is required where the variation is necessary to restore or maintain the security of the system or of individual accounts (cl 4.17).

Otherwise, 'important' changes can only be made after the written notice is given at least 20 days before the change (cl 4.12). 'Important' changes include those imposing or increasing charges, increasing customer liability in relation to losses, or varying periodic transaction limits. Other changes must be notified 'before the change takes effect ... in a way that is likely to come to the attention of as many holders as practicable'.[27]

Furthermore, the institution wishing to implement significant or numerous changes should compile all terms and conditions into a single, consolidated document.[28]

Where the *Banking Code of Practice* applies, there are also rules governing changes by notice. The scheme is very similar to that of the *ePayments Code*. If entered into, 30 days' written notice would have to be provided for important changes, such as:

- new fees or charges (other than government charges)
- variations to minimum balance conditions affecting account-keeping fees
- interest calculation changes
- variation of balance ranges relevant to the application of interest rates
- changes to the frequency of interest payments or debits.

26 Australian Securities and Investments Commission, *ePayments Code* cll 2.4–5.
27 Ibid cl 14.14.
28 Ibid cl 14.15.

Government charges may be notified by public notice, but this is only necessary if the government fails to make such an announcement. In relation to other changes, media advertisement is sufficient, no later than the day on which the change is to come into effect.

Of course, express written agreements can be used to alter the terms of the implied relationship. These are becoming more common, and indeed, are the norm in many overseas jurisdictions (eg the United States). In general, the rule is that there is no duty on the part of the customer to examine the periodic statements provided by the banker and that the risk of forgery prima facie lies with the banker. A common express term in US contracts would require the customer to read their statements and report any irregularity. In default, the customer is stopped from denying the correctness of the statement. Another common term attempts to throw the risk of forgery onto the customer. It was held in *Tai Hing Cotton Mill Ltd v Liu Chong Hing Bank Ltd* that clauses such as these, which attempt to alter the 'traditional' rules, will only be effective if they, and their significance, have been specifically brought to the attention of the customer.[29] In particular, such devices as incorporation by reference will be ineffective. Apparently, it was determined that the implied contractual terms of an ordinary banker–customer relationship are in the nature of common law rights. As Lord Scarman said:

> The burden of the obligation and of the sanction imposed must be brought home to the customer ... [The] test [of this] is rigorous because the bankers would have their terms of business so construed as to exclude the rights which the customer would enjoy if they were not excluded by the express agreement.[30]

Other restraints on the contractual terms can be imposed on customers. For example, the *ASIC Act* contains non-excludable warranties in relation to the provision of financial services that are equivalent to those contained in sch 2 of the *Competition and Consumer Act 2010* (Cth) ('*Australian Consumer Law*') for other types of services, and the *Australian Consumer Law* itself places restrictions on 'unfair terms' in standard-form contracts.

5.6 Statutory limitations of actions

5.6.1 General rules

As the banker–customer relationship is a debtor–creditor relationship founded in contract, rights of recovery are subject to the various state limitation of action Acts. The *Limitation Act 1969* (NSW) ('NSW *Limitation Act*') apart, these Acts impose temporal procedural bars to court recovery. That is to say, once the limitation period has passed, no help is available via court action to recover the debt. The debt itself, however, continues to exist, and if other procedures are available for recovery, then they can be utilised. For example, suppose the creditor has some security. This is typically in the form of a lien. Further suppose that this creditor lives in Victoria and did not take action to recover the debt for six years

29 *Tai Hing Cotton Mill Ltd v Liu Chong Hing Bank Ltd* [1986] AC 80.
30 Ibid 110.

(thus barring itself under the *Limitation of Action Act*).[31] In that case, it can recover the debt via lien, even though a right of action in relation to the debt is not available. More generally, security such as a lien is a separate interest that entitles the creditor to recover upon default, which may operate independently of the bank–customer contract.

Note that the NSW *Limitation Act* is different in this respect in that it not only provides a procedural bar, but also extinguishes the cause of action.

For the purpose of the Acts, time begins to run from the time when the debt becomes due for payment. However, it will restart if the debtor makes a new promise to pay. This new promise may not be express; it can be implied from a new acknowledgement of the debt or from a partial repayment. There is a large amount of case law on what constitutes an implied promise for this purpose. It is important to note that there is no need to show any consideration in exchange for the new promise. We are not trying here to construct a new contract, but rather to revive a procedural right according to a statutory provision.

The clock begins to run when the cause of action arises. In the case of a simple loan repayable on demand, the debt and the associated cause of action arise immediately on the advance of the money (*Ogilvie v Adams*).[32] If the loan contract specifies that the loan is for a particular term, the cause of action does not arise until the term is fulfilled. In other cases, there are implied conditions, one of which is where money is loaned to a banker. A debt owed by a banker to a customer does not become due until such time as the customer makes demand for payment (*Joachimson v Swiss Bank*).[33] There may also be other requirements that must be met in particular cases. For example, in the case of a term deposit, the deposit must also have matured. But in any event, time does not start to run against a customer *before* such time as the customer asks for their deposit.

Where the banker is the creditor who seeks to recover from the customer, the situation is otherwise. In the case of a loan becoming repayable on a specified date, that date is when time begins to run for the purposes of the Limitation Acts (*Re McHenry*).[34] In the case of a loan repayable by instalment, without express terms and conditions to the contrary, each instalment is treated as repayment of a separate loan. However, usually such contracts do contain a contrary term: to the effect that default on a single instalment makes the whole debt due and payable immediately. If that is the case, time starts to run with respect to the entire loan from the time of the default.

5.6.2 Limitation and overdrafts

What rule applies when a bank is attempting to reclaim an overdrawn account? Does the overdraft become due at the time when the advance is made as per the general *Ogilvie v Adams* rule, or only when the bank makes a demand?

According to *Parr's Banking Co Ltd v Yates*,[35] time begins to run, as per *Ogilvie v Adams*, from the date of the advance, and if there are further advances time begins to run on each as it is made. This remains the accepted view. See *Haller v Ayre* and *Young v Queensland*

31 *Limitation of Action Act 1958* (Vic) s 5(1).
32 *Ogilvie v Adams* [1981] VR 1041.
33 *Joachimson v Swiss Bank Corporation* [1921] 3 KB 110.
34 *Re McHenry* [1894] 3 Ch 290.
35 *Parr's Banking Co Ltd v Yates* [1898] 2 QB 460.

Trustees Ltd.[36] Nevertheless, the contrary view has some academic support and has, from time to time, found judicial expression (eg *DFC New Zealand Ltd v McKenzie*).[37] The rationale for the 'demand' view is that it should make no difference to contractual rights as to which side of the ledger happens to be credited at any time and which side is in debit. Insofar as this is not simply an attempt to limit *Ogilvie v Adams* it is an appeal, if you like, to symmetry; however, as such, it is only logical if one is prepared to regard customers and bankers as interchangeable concepts.

The next question arises: What if the bank is trying to recover the overdrawn amount not from the customer but from a guarantor? Essentially, the matter turns on the terms of the guarantee. If the guarantee calls on the guarantor to pay on demand, then time will run from the date of demand (*Bradford Old Bank Ltd v Sutcliffe*).[38] This is logical. The guarantor can hardly be liable to the bank in such a case until the demand is made. The guarantee is not a loan and thus cannot be made subject to the rule in *Ogilvie v Adams*.

On the other hand, if the guarantee requires the surety to pay if the account falls into overdraft or if the overdraft exceeds a certain amount, then the surety surely becomes liable on the occurrence of the relevant event. It is a simple matter of construing the terms of the guarantee as to when the liability of the guarantor arises. Likewise, when the overdraft is secured. Again, the security contract is not the loan, but a contract collateral to it. Regardless of when the cause of action accrues with respect to recovery of the loan money *simpliciter*, the terms of the security need to be construed to determine when the right to enforce the security accrues.

Thus, one can have a situation where the right to proceed against the principal on the loan contract to recover the debt is barred, but the right to proceed to enforce a guarantee with respect to the debt or security concerning it, and to recover that way, is not. Remember that the limitation does not extinguish the debt, but merely bars the right to take certain action with respect to it. (As noted above, the effect of the NSW *Limitation Act* is to extinguish the cause of action, and the situation is otherwise there. See ss 63–65 of the Act.)

A great deal of the difficulty in this area stems from the rule in *Ogilvie v Adams*. Life would be much simpler if the rule were abolished and the cause of action on simple loans payable on demand was held only to arise when demand was made (as the words 'on demand' would indicate and as per bank deposits). The Queensland and NSW Law Reform Commissions have both recommended this. Western Australia has gone a step further: the *Limitation Act 2005* (WA) s 59 provides for the cause of action to accrue on failure to comply with a demand for payment.

5.7 Special customers

5.7.1 Unincorporated associations

An unincorporated association is not a legal entity separate from its members. Unincorporated associations are groups of individuals who form for some

36 *Haller v Ayre* [2005] 2 Qd R 410; *Young v Queensland Trustees Ltd* (1956) 99 CLR 560.
37 *DFC New Zealand Ltd v McKenzie* [1993] 2 NZLR 576.
38 *Bradford Old Bank Ltd v Sutcliffe* [1918] 2 KB 833.

non-profit-making purpose (and so cannot be partnerships) and are bound by some contract as between themselves, which usually amounts to abiding by the association rules. Typically, they are sporting clubs and the like. It is common for them to have bank accounts and for certain of the members to be authorised by the association rules to operate these. As there is no entity that can be sued, prudent banks do not loan money to unincorporated associations or permit their accounts to go into overdraft without security. It is probable that the authorised signatories may be liable, and it is possible under the association rules that the wider membership may also be liable if the signatories can be regarded as their agents – but almost certainly only those who were members at the time the liability was incurred.

5.7.2 Incorporated associations

All jurisdictions have legislation enabling unincorporated associations to incorporate (eg the *Associations Incorporation Reform Act 2012* (Vic)). This means that the association can be essentially regarded as a company with a separate legal identity. However, the legislation is not uniform in its treatment of some matters – for instance, ultra vires actions, the indoor management rule, the doctrine of constructive notice and pre-incorporation contracts. This is not to say that the law is, in any sense, more than usually unclear. If there is no relevant legislative provision, the common law with respect to incorporated bodies applies.

5.7.3 Partnerships

A partnership does not have a separate legal personality. It is a relation 'which subsists between persons carrying on a business in common with a view to profit'.[39] All jurisdictions have Partnership Acts that define a partnership in these terms. Anything which satisfies the definition and is not incorporated is a partnership. The Acts are all substantially identical and are based on the *Partnership Act 1890* (UK). Each partner in a partnership is an agent for each other partner to carry on the business of the partnership. Thus, each partner has the power to open an account in the name of the partnership. Each partner has the power to operate it by means of their own signature (*Backhouse v Charlton*).[40] This authority does not extend to operating a partnership account in the partner's own name (*Alliance Bank Ltd v Kearsley*).[41]

Of course, it is not unknown for a partner to misappropriate partnership funds from the partnership account. In most circumstances, the bank will not be liable to the innocent partners for the loss. The standard rules relating to apparent agency will apply. In particular, the *Partnership Acts* all provide as follows:

> Every partner is an agent of the firm and his other partners for the purpose of the business of the partnership; *and* the acts of every partner who does any

39 *Partnership Act 1890* (UK) s 1(1). See also *Partnership Act 1891* (Qld) s 5(1); *Partnership Act 1891* (SA) s 1(1); *Partnership Act 1891* (Tas) s 6(1); *Partnership Act 1892* (NSW) s 1(1); *Partnership Act 1895* (WA) s 7(1); *Partnership Act 1958* (Vic) s 5(1).

40 *Backhouse v Charlton* (1878) 8 Ch D 444.

41 *Alliance Bank Ltd v Kearsly* (1871) LR 6 CP 433.

> act for *carrying on in the usual way business of the kind* carried on by the firm of which he is a member bind the firm and his partners, *unless* the partner so acting has in fact no authority to act for the firm in the particular matter, *and* the person with whom he is dealing either knows that he has no authority, or does not know or believe him to be a partner [emphasis added].[42]

The bank will be usually unaware of any lack of actual authority and so the usual issue in relation to negligence by the bank regarding fraudulent withdrawals by a partner is whether the bank ought be reasonably aware that the partner is not carrying on the business in the usual way that the partnership carries on business of that kind. There is nothing unusual, in itself, in a partner withdrawing funds from the partnership account. The test is: are the circumstances of the transaction such that a reasonable person in the bank's position should have suspected that something was unusual about this transaction?

Considerations of actual and apparent authority also apply where a partner purports to borrow on behalf of the firm and the bank seeks to recover from the other partners; likewise where a single partner purports to open and operate an account on behalf of a partnership. Generally, most banks will, out of prudence, seek an express mandate from all the partners as to the authority of individual partners to operate accounts, and more especially accounts with overdraft or credit facilities.

Note that since there is no separate legal personality, the liability for partners for debts of the partnership is not limited to their personal contributions or obligations to the partnership or to their share of the partnership assets; it extends to their personal assets.

Of course, partners may no longer act for one another if the partnership is dissolved or no longer exists. Dissolution can occur in a number of ways: by a partner simply indicating that they no longer wish to be a partner and withdrawing from the partnership; by the death of a partner; by the effluxion of time, where the partnership was formed for only a fixed term; by completion of its purpose where it was formed for a specific purpose; or by the bankruptcy of any of the partners. The partnership agreement may, however, provide for the continuation of the partnership by the remaining partners. In the event of dissolution, the only authority that remains is for the operation of the partnership accounts for the purposes of dissolving the partnership. The bank should not *knowingly* permit the operation of the partnership accounts for any other purposes. In the absence of any knowledge to the contrary, however, the bank is entitled to assume that the partners are in fact acting for the purposes of dissolving the partnership (*Re Bourne*).[43]

5.7.4 Minors

At common law, contracts with minors (those under 18 years) are, with a few exceptions that need not concern us here, unenforceable against the minor (but are enforceable *by* them). From a bank's point of view, this only creates problems if the bank lends money to

42 *Partnership Act 1890* (UK) s 5. See also *Partnership Act 1891* (Qld) s 8(1); *Partnership Act 1891* (SA) s 5; *Partnership Act 1891* (Tas) s 10; *Partnership Act 1892* (NSW) s 5; *Partnership Act 1895* (WA) s 26; *Partnership Act 1958* (Vic) s 9.

43 *Re Bourne* [1906] 2 Ch 427.

the minor. Thus, they would likely opt to prevent a minor's account from going into overdraft. Similarly, a minor may draft a cheque which is valid at law, even if the holder of the cheque may not use it against the minor.[44] Where a bank debits the minor's account for the amount of the cheque, the bank is not attempting to enforce the contract against the minor; rather, it is fulfilling its contractual obligation to the minor to pay on the cheque (and indeed, if it did not, it could be sued by the minor for breach of contract). We will address the problems involved in granting a minor credit later in the course, when we deal more specifically with lending.

5.7.5 Executors/administrators

When a person dies, the funeral must be arranged and paid for, outstanding debts owed paid and those owing called in, and the property of the deceased distributed either according to their will or, if there is no will, the law of intestacy. In the case of a will, the person charged with this is the executor. The executor will apply to the appropriate court to prove the will. A grant of probate will be issued which is *evidence* of the executor's powers to deal with the estate. In the case of intestacy, the court will appoint an administrator pursuant to 'letters of administration'. The difference between an executor and an administrator is merely that an executor's power derives from the will, whereas an administrator's power derives from the court. There may be more than one executor/administrator, but if so they hold their powers jointly. That is, together they constitute one legal entity, and generally any one of them is entitled to exercise their powers (although there are exceptions to this latter point in relation to transfer of real property). From a banker's point of view, the absence, death or resignation of one executor/trustee is irrelevant to the administration of the estate, unless the signature of the executor/administrator in question is required to operate an account.

The administration of the estate involves the legal transfer of the net assets to the executor(s)/administrator(s) and then their distribution according to the will/ intestacy provisions.

It may be desirable for the executor/administrator to borrow to facilitate the administration, and since the executor/administrator has power to conduct the estate business for the purpose of administration they have the power to do this. A lending banker does not, however, become a creditor to the estate. They become a creditor to the executor, and are merely entitled to the benefit of the executor's right of indemnity from the estate (*Berry v Gibbons*).[45]

Once the administration of the estate is complete, it is possible that the executor(s) may continue to hold, as directed by the will, part of the assets of the estate as trustee(s) for beneficiaries. At this point, the executor ceases to be an executor and becomes a trustee. The distinction is important, because trustees are not treated collectively as a single legal entity. From a banker's point of view, the operation of any relevant bank accounts proceeds accordingly on this altered basis.

44 *Cheques Act 1986* (Cth) s 60.
45 *Berry v Gibbons* (1873) 8 Ch App 747.

5.7.6 Companies

A company is an artificial legal entity, distinct from the individuals such as its members and directors. A company may sue and be sued in its own right. The formation and operation of a company are governed by the *Corporations Act 2001* (Cth) ('*Corporations Act*'). Although a company is a legal entity, it is an artificial legal person and must act through agents. How a company operates is governed by its rules of governance – that is, its constitution (subject to the provisions of the *Corporations Act*). Generally, the rules of governance of a company vest management of the company in a board of directors, who may in turn delegate various of their powers to individuals among them or to employees.

Historically, anyone dealing with a company potentially faced two problems. The first was one of ultra vires. The company might not have the powers of a natural person. Its rules might restrict the things it could do – specifically, the kinds of activities it could undertake. A transaction that exceeded these powers was void. Thus, for example, a creditor that provided a loan for a company that did not have the capacity to borrow could not successfully claim an action for debt, nor even, potentially, in an action for money had and received (*Sinclair v Brougham*).[46] The second problem was that the company's agents, unknown to those dealing with them, might in fact have limited authority. These problems are addressed by the *Corporations Act* ss 124–130, as follows:

- A company, notwithstanding its rules, has power to do anything that a natural person might do.
- A person dealing with a company is not held to have 'constructive notice' of the company's rules.
- A person dealing with a company is entitled to assume that the company's rules have been complied with.
- A person dealing with a company is entitled to assume that a person who is nominated as an officer of the company in the returns required to be lodged with the Australian Securities and Investments Commission has been duly appointed and has the authority to perform the duties and exercise the powers customarily performed and exercised by such an officer in a similar company.
- A person dealing with the company is entitled to make the assumption that 'anyone who is held out by the company to be an officer or agent of the company: (a) has been duly appointed; and (b) has authority to exercise the powers and perform the duties customarily exercised or performed by that kind of officer or agent of a similar company'.[47]

The assumptions above can be relied on even if 'an officer or agent of the company acts fraudulently or forges a document in relation to the dealings'.[48] However, an assumption cannot be relied on if the person dealing with company knows or suspects that the relevant assumption is incorrect.[49]

46 *Sinclair v Brougham* [1914] AC 398.
47 *Corporations Act 2001* (Cth) s 129(3).
48 Ibid s 128.
49 Ibid.

The rules of apparent authority (eg as applied in *Freeman & Lockyer v Buckhurst Park (Mangal) Ltd*[50]) also apply.

Notwithstanding all this, it is better to prevent issues due to potential lack of authority arising in the first place than to have to rely on legal protection once they do. Thus, bankers dealing with companies should always:

- inspect and retain copies of the company rules
- note the borrowing powers of the company
- note the right to sign cheques and other negotiable instruments and to enter into contracts
- inspect the minutes of any board meetings that authorise bank dealings, such as the opening of accounts, and note the names/positions of those who are authorised to conduct those dealings and operate the relevant accounts.

Various other issues can arise when dealing with companies. They include transactions entered into on behalf of the company by directors who have a conflict of interest; transactions involving a company dealing in its own shares; transactions arising from winding up; and statutory provisions that give regulators the right to examine accounts and override the banker's duty of confidentiality owed to the customer.[51]

5.8 Dormant accounts

The *Banking Act* s 69 deals with 'unclaimed moneys'. 'Unclaimed moneys' is defined as:

> ... all principal, interest, dividends, bonuses, profits and sums of money legally payable by an ADI [authorised deposit-taking institution] but in respect of which the time within which proceedings may be taken for the recovery thereof has expired, and includes moneys to the credit of an account that has not been operated on either by deposit or withdrawal for a period of not less than ... 7 years ... beginning ... at the most recent time when the account was operated on either by deposit or withdrawal.[52]

The subsection also provides that the dormancy period and the date of its commencement may be altered by regulation. The reference to the time for proceedings having expired is obscure given that time only starts to run for the purpose of statutory limitation when a demand is made for payment (*Mackenzie v Albany Finance Ltd*).[53] But in any event, the definition clearly includes accounts that have been dormant for up to three years.

Authorised deposit-taking institutions must pay over such money to the Commonwealth each year, providing a report that would enable the customer or their representative to claim the money (*Banking Act* s 69(4)–(5)). This would then discharge the liability of the ADI to the customer. The money can be claimed from the Commonwealth Treasurer who, if satisfied as to the claim, will pay the funds back

50 *Freeman & Lockyer v Buckhurst Park Properties (Mangal) Ltd* [1964] 2 QB 480.
51 Alan Tyree, *Banking Law in Australia* (LexisNexis, 9th ed, 2017) 80.
52 *Banking Act 1959* (Cth) s 69(1).
53 *Mackenzie v Albany Finance Ltd* [2004] WASCA 301.

to the ADI for the credit of the claimant (*Banking Act* s 69(7)). Details of unclaimed moneys are to be published in the Government Gazette or otherwise made publicly available (*Banking Act* s 69(9)). However, the ADI is not required to make attempts to contact the account holder.

The *Banking Act* s 69 applies to all money 'legally payable' by the ADI. The meaning of this has attracted some judicial attention. 'Payable', in the context of a deposit, would normally indicate that a demand had been made for repayment in accordance with the terms of the deposit. With respect to s 69 of the *Banking Act*, this interpretation would be paradoxical, since the premise of the section is that the money is unclaimed. Evidently, the term means simply that there must be a debt *incurred* by the ADI. The money would be 'legally payable' from the moment of its deposit in the sense that the debt would legally exist from that time. See the Privy Council in *Thomas Cook (New Zealand) v Inland Revenue Commissioner*.[54]

Sometimes money escapes the s 69 mechanism because, although the customer claims the money was deposited long ago, the bank says either that it was not or that it was repaid (and so took no s 69 action). Of course, such situations do not occur only in relation to dormant accounts, but they are more common with respect to them. The burden is on the customer to show that the money was deposited, and is on the bank to show that it was repaid (*Mackenzie v Albany Finance Ltd*; *Young v Queensland Trustees Ltd*).[55] Sometimes in the case of long dormant accounts, evidence can be rather thin on the ground. In that case, the court must do its best on the basis of what is before it: 'by striking a balance of probabilities in the light of all the relevant circumstances of the case', as in *Douglas v Lloyds Bank Ltd*.[56] That case concerned an account that had been dormant from 1868 to 1929. The sum of the evidence was essentially a deposit receipt showing a balance of £3500, the depositor's reputation for being careful with his money, and information that the bank's records for the period had been destroyed, but that those from 1873 showed no sign of the account. The Court found in favour of the bank.

5.9 Summary

The relationship between a bank and its customers is primarily a contractual debtor–creditor relationship. It is governed by the usual rules of contract, and by a large raft of terms and conditions implied by custom and usage, which can be ousted by express terms. When an individual or business opens an account with a bank, they enter into a contract that outlines the terms and conditions governing the use of the bank's services.

Banks in Australia are also guided by industry codes of practice, such as the *Banking Code of Practice* and the *ePayments Code*, which set out the standards of conduct and service that customers can expect from their banks. These codes are voluntary in nature but are expected to be adhered to by major banks.

54 *Thomas Cook (New Zealand) v Inland Revenue Commissioner* [2004] UKPC 53.
55 *Mackenzie v Albury Finance Ltd* [2004] WASCA 301; *Young v Queensland Trustees Ltd* (1956) 99 CLR 560.
56 *Douglas v Lloyds Bank Ltd* (1924) 34 Com Cas 263.

FURTHER READING

Cranston, Ross, *European Banking Law: The Banker–Customer Relationship* (Informa Law, 2020).

Eriksson, Kent, Cecilia Hermansson and Sara Jonsson, 'The Performance Generating Limitations of the Relationship-Banking Model in the Digital Era – Effects of Customers' Trust, Satisfaction, and Loyalty on Client-Level Performance' (2020) 38(4) *International Journal of Bank Marketing* 889.

McIlroy, David and John Freeman, 'The Actionability of Codes of Conduct in English and Irish Law' (2021) 32(2) *Journal of Banking and Finance Law and Practice* 74.

Sandhu, Supreet and Sangeeta Arora, 'Customers' Usage Behaviour of e-Banking Services: Interplay of Electronic Banking and Traditional Banking' (2022) 27(2) *International Journal of Finance and Economics* 2169.

QUESTIONS

(1) What is the nature of the banker–customer relationship? Describe some characteristics of the relationship.

(2) What is 'banking business'? What is a contemporary definition of the 'business of banking'. Are the products and services offered by banks to customers today different from those in 1950?

(3) Alice and Mandy are in a law practice partnership. Both their signatures are required on cheques in the partnership name, and a joint authority has been lodged with the bank. Since Mandy is indisposed, Alice gives a partnership cheque to a supplier who supplied office equipment to the practice. The cheque is only signed by Alice in the name of the partnership. The bank refuses payment on the cheque since the signature does not comply with the authority lodged. Can the supplier enforce payment against the partnership?

CHAPTER 6

ACCOUNTS

6.1 Introduction

Deposits are a loan from the customer to the banker.[1] The terms of that loan are the terms of the 'account'. We refer to 'an account' because the amount deposited is subject to change, and there is a continuous accounting of it as transactions occur so as to show the amount currently on deposit. The terms of the loan are theoretically subject to negotiation between the parties. In practice, they are imposed by the bank. Thus, the number of kinds – the 'types' – of accounts available to customers is generally limited, but terms do vary.

6.2 Some types of accounts

For present purposes, we refer to accounts with certain general (and loose) characteristi by various names. Note, however, that these are not legally defined categories, nor are they terms of bankers' art.

6.2.1 Current (transaction) accounts

Typically, current accounts are drawable on demand, are non-interest bearing or accrue minimal interest, or interest is applicable only on certain balances. Transactions incur fees, and the accounts accommodate third-party payments, traditionally by cheque but now also via electronic funds transfer (EFT). They may also support an overdraft facility. At the time of writing, banks generally offer one type of 'general' everyday account. These accounts have negligible fees attached to them, which are often waived if the customer deposits $2000 monthly.[2] Some banks, however, do not impose fees at all.[3] Banks also offer specialised everyday accounts with varying benefits (commonly the removal of fees) for businesses and pensioners.[4]

6.2.2 Savings accounts

Typically, savings accounts are interest-bearing and drawable on demand, at least up to a specified amount, beyond which some minimal notice may be required. Payments are usually made only to the account holder or to an account of the account holder with the same bank, often the holder's transaction accounts. There are either no fees or minimal fees associated with such accounts. At the time of writing, most banks have one or two types of 'general' savings accounts. These accounts offer interest, generally at 4–5 per cent per annum.[5] These accounts often have an additional introductory interest rate of

1 *Foley v Hill* (1848) 9 ER 1002.

2 'Everyday Account Smart Access', *Commonwealth Bank of Australia* (Web Page) <https://www.commbank.com.au/banking/everyday-account-smart-access.html?ei=tl_smart-access>; 'ANZ Access Advantage', *ANZ* (Web Page) <https://www.anz.com.au/personal/bank-accounts/everyday-accounts/access-advantage/>.

3 'Transaction Account', *Macquarie* (Web Page) <https://www.macquarie.com.au/everyday-banking/transaction-account.html>; 'NAB Classic Banking Account', *NAB* (Web Page) <https://www.nab.com.au/personal/accounts/transaction-accounts/nab-classic-banking>.

4 See, eg,'Business Transaction Account', *Commonwealth Bank of Australia* (Web Page) <https://www.commbank.com.au/business/bank-accounts/business-transaction-account.html?ei=bhp_sixpack_business-transaction-account>.

5 'NetBank Saver', *Commonwealth Bank of Australia* (Web Page) <https://www.commbank.com.au/banking/netbank-saver.html?ei=prod_NBsaver>; 'ANZ Plus', *ANZ* (Web Page) <https://www.anz.com

about 1–3 per cent per annum for the first four or five months, which is added alongside the normal interest the account would ordinarily accrue.[6]

6.2.3 Term deposits

Typically, term deposits are interest-bearing at higher rates that vary with the term and maturity. They are only drawable without penalty on maturity or with specified notice. Payments are made exclusively to the account holder or to an account of the account holder with the same bank. Each deposit represents a separate account with the bank, and there are no associated fees. At the time of writing, banks offer term deposit accounts with interest. For instance, a deposit of less than $1 million for three months would accrue interest at a rate of 4.7 per cent per annum at Macquarie and 3.5 per cent per annum at CBA.[7]

Formerly, current accounts would be operated only by businesses or professionals or the otherwise well-to-do. Ordinary people would make do with 'passbook' savings accounts and cash drawings from these.

The customer kept the passbook and a copy of the customer's account as kept by the bank. The customer made a withdrawal or a deposit by presenting the passbook with a signed withdrawal or deposit slip, and the transaction was then recorded in the passbook and the bank's ledger.[8] Exceptional cases apart, most banks no longer offer new passbook accounts: savings account customers receive periodic paper or e-statements instead, as per a current account. However, they continue to support existing passbook accounts on a 'grandfathering' or 'legacy' basis.

Today, most people maintain a current account with the minimum balance necessary to meet their immediate demands and a savings account that they use to top it up as required. If the bank fees are sufficiently minimal for them or for convenience's sake, they may choose to maintain only a current account.

Which account to credit where there is more than one? Suppose the customer has more than one account to which money can be paid. It is the customer's right to stipulate which account the money should be paid to. If the customer fails to do so, then the bank has discretion as to which account to credit.[9] The issue arises only rarely, as physical deposits are normally subject to a requirement to complete a deposit slip identifying the account to be credited, while e-payments and telephone transfers simply do not function without identification of the account to be credited.

.au/plus/interest-fees/>; 'NAB Reward Saver', *NAB* (Web Page) <https://www.nab.com.au/personal/accounts/savings-accounts/nab-reward-saver>; 'Savings Account', *Macquarie* (Web Page) <https://www.macquarie.com.au/everyday-banking/campaign/savings-account.html>.

6 'NetBank Saver', *Commonwealth Bank of Australia* (Web Page) <https://www.commbank.com.au/banking/netbank-saver.html?ei=prod_NBsaver>; 'ANZ Plus', *ANZ* (Web Page) <https://www.anz.com.au/plus/interest-fees/>; 'NAB Reward Saver', *NAB* (Web Page) <https://www.nab.com.au/personal/accounts/savings-accounts/nab-reward-saver>; 'Savings Account', *Macquarie* (Web Page) <https://www.macquarie.com.au/everyday-banking/campaign/savings-account.html>.

7 'Term Deposits', *Commonwealth Bank of Australia* (Web Page) <https://www.commbank.com.au/banking/term-deposits.html>; 'Term Deposit', *Macquarie* (Web Page) <https://www.macquarie.com.au/everyday-banking/term-deposits.html>.

8 Third-party deposits were entered in the passbook at the time of its next presentation.

9 *Cory Brothers & Co Ltd v Owners of the Turkish Steamship Mecca* [1897] AC 286 ('*The Mecca*'); *Deeley v Lloyds Bank Ltd* [1912] AC 756; *Healey v Commonwealth Bank of Australia* [1998] NSWCA 103.

Sometimes the deposit is made not by a customer but by a third party. When this happens, the third party has almost always been armed by the customer with the relevant account details and can hardly complain if the bank pays to that account without instructions to the contrary by the customer.

6.2.3.1 Particular purpose deposits

Suppose the customer stipulates that the deposit is to be used only for a particular purpose (eg as in *WP Greenhalgh and Sons v Union Bank of Manchester*,[10] for the purpose of meeting payment of a particular bill of exchange). The bank need not accept the deposit (unless they are obliged by the terms of the account to do so).[11] If the banker accepts the deposit, they are bound by the stipulation. For example, in *Huenerbein v Federal Bank of Australia*, the plaintiff had overdrawn their account.[12] They paid in a sum with instructions that it be used to meet a cheque they knew would be presented. Instead, the money was used to reduce the overdraft because the cheque was dishonoured. The plaintiff successfully sued for damages for wrongful dishonour.

6.2.3.2 Overdrafts

A current account may have a negative balance - an overdraft, in which case the state of the account is that the bank becomes the lender and the customer becomes the borrower. This may be agreed ahead of time as part of the terms of the account, generally as a means of short-term financing, but 'informal' overdrafts also occur, where the customer has not expressly requested the facility.

A bank is not obliged to pay on a cheque or authorised debit if there are insufficient funds in the account to do so, absent a prearranged overdraft agreement. However, the drawing of a cheque (or authorisation of a debit) by a customer when there are insufficient funds in the account to meet it is regarded as a request for an overdraft facility which the bank may then grant.[13]

The bank is generally entitled to charge interest on these 'informal' overdrafts and, indeed, to capitalise the interest by adding it periodically to the overdraft balance - a right based apparently on custom and usage,[14] although the right to charge interest, and how much and in what manner in these circumstances, is usually subject to the express terms of the account.

Unauthorised/informal overdrafts are typically accompanied by fees (otherwise known as 'exception fees'), which are often quite onerous. There are periodic attempts by customers to avoid these as penalties.[15] The usual rules as to contractual penalties apply; however, as a general observation, the courts have not been particularly sympathetic to customers in these endeavours. For instance, in *Berwick v Lloyds TSB Bank plc*[16]

10 *WP Greenhalgh and Sons v Union Bank of Manchester* [1924] 2 KB 153.
11 *Huenerbein v Federal Bank of Australia* (1892) 9 WN 65.
12 Ibid.
13 *Cuthbert v Robarts, Lubbock & Co* [1909] 2 Ch 226.
14 *National Bank of Greece SA v Pinios Shipping Co No 1* [1990] 1 AC 637.
15 Students may be aware of several recent high-profile actions in relation to account fees along these lines.
16 *Berwick v Lloyds TSB Bank plc* [2007] EW Mis 1.

and *Paciocco v Australia and New Zealand Banking Group Ltd*,[17] the courts were content to find that the fees were imposed as consideration for the bank's meeting of the customer's request for an overdraft, rather than as a penalty for breaching the terms of the account by allowing it to fall into debit.

6.2.3.3 Trust accounts

This is an account held by one party (ie the trustee) who is bound to exercise their rights over it for the benefit of others (ie the beneficiary or beneficiaries). The existence of a trust as that concept is usually understood is not strictly necessary. The category encompasses all those situations where the account holder owes a *fiduciary duty* to others concerning the funds – therefore, for example, it includes situations where the account is operated as part of an agency agreement. The practice in banking is to refer to all these accounts as trust accounts.

A beneficiary is entitled to sue a bank that wrongfully allows withdrawals from a trust account pursuant to an invalid 'mandate' (eg a cheque), even if the trustee is unwilling to bring the proceedings.[18]

There are two general situations in which the bank will be liable to beneficiaries whether or not a trust account exists:

(1) where the bank knowingly receives trust money and deals with it in a manner inconsistent with the trust (cases of 'knowing receipt')

(2) where the bank knowingly assists in what is, in fact, the misappropriation of the trust property, whether or not it receives any benefit (cases of 'knowing assistance' or 'accessory liability').

These two scenarios reflect the application of the principles in *Barnes v Addy* to the particular case of banks.[19]

A typical example of 'knowing receipt' is when the trustee transfers funds from an account entitled 'trust account' or similar to their personal account to reduce their overdraft. Let's consider another example, *Westpac Banking Corporation v Savin*, to illustrate more fully these concepts – in particular, the nature of the 'knowledge' that is necessary.[20]

AM carried on business selling boats. In 75% of cases, AM sold boats as an agent on behalf of individual non-commercial sellers. The remainder of the sales were on its own account. The bank knew this, although it had no knowledge of which sales were in which category. One of the boats sold belonged to Savin. Proceeds from the sale were paid by AM into its trading account with the bank at a time when this account was heavily overdrawn. Savin sought to recover the money from the bank.

To succeed as to 'knowing receipt', Savin needed to show two things:

17 *Paciocco v Australia and New Zealand Banking Group Ltd* (2014) 309 ALR 249.
18 *Fried v National Australia Bank Ltd* (2001) 111 FCR 322.
19 *Barnes v Addy* (1874) LR 9 Ch App 244.
20 *Westpac Banking Corporation v Savin* [1985] 2 NZLR 41.

(1) that the bank 'knew' the money it received was held on 'trust' (ie under a fiduciary duty) by AM

(2) that the bank's receipt of the money, in the form of a reduction of AM's personal liability to it via reduction of AM's overdraft, was in fact a breach of the trust.

The second point is hardly at issue. AM's appropriation of the money for their personal purposes was obviously a breach of their fiduciary duty under the agency.

As to the first point, the bank had no *actual knowledge* that the particular money in question was subject to the fiduciary obligation. However, *constructive knowledge* is sufficient. The general rule may be stated that the bank must either have actual knowledge of the breach or that a reasonable and honest person in the bank's position would have actual knowledge of it or would have made enquiries that would have provided them with actual knowledge of it. In this case, while the bank did not actually know that the money in question was trust money, it knew that there was a 75 per cent chance that it was, and therefore it was at least reasonable that it should have made enquiries that would have ascertained that it was. In the case of 'knowing receipt', the banker will be obliged to reimburse the funds they have received.

In the case of 'knowing assistance', the banker may have to account for funds which went to the benefit of someone else. This is more onerous. Hence, the threshold of the knowledge test is higher. Based on the HCA majority in *Consul Development Pty Ltd v DPC Estates Pty Ltd*,[21] 'knowledge' here means actual knowledge of the facts of the misappropriation or a wilful and reckless failure to enquire (a deliberate 'shutting of eyes'), but it does not extend to constructive knowledge in the sense of a duty to enquire in circumstances which would put a reasonable person on notice that a misappropriation was occurring but where in fact the bank was not put on notice. Thus, the bank must have deliberately ignored the behaviour that any reasonable person would regard as a breach of the trustee's duty, rather than merely being negligent or incompetent in failing to make enquiries that a reasonable person would have made.[22]

6.2.3.4 Joint accounts

A joint account is simply one opened in the name of two or more customers. The following are typical questions that arise:

- Are both signatures required in order to operate the account, or is a single signature sufficient?
- What occurs upon the death of one of the customers?
- What are the consequences of a bank honouring a fraudulent cheque?

In the absence of an agreement to the contrary, the debt owed by the bank is owed jointly and severally to the customers. Consequently, cheques should be signed by all the account

21 *Consul Development Pty Ltd v DPV Estates Pty Ltd* (1975) 132 CLR 373.

22 See also *NCR Australia Pty Ltd v Credit Connection Pty Ltd* [2004] NSWSC 1 (Austin J). This decision was partially reversed in *Naumoski v NCR Australia Pty Ltd* [2004] NSWCA 310, but Austin J's statement of the law was upheld.

holders.[23] However, it is common for this to be altered by agreement and an express provision made for which signatures are required. Often this is to the effect that the signature of any of the holders will suffice.

Where one of the holders dies, the rule of survivorship operates; that is, the deceased holder's interest in the account passes to the others (and not under the will of the deceased holder). This presumption is subject to evidence of contrary intention.[24]

The most common arguments arise in cases where all – or almost all – of the funds in the account have been provided for one of the parties. In such cases, a finding may be made of a resulting trust in favour of the deceased party's estate. The matter turns on intention as indicated by the facts of each case. Still, generally speaking, for the presumption of survivorship to be overridden, there must be some indication that a trust was intended beyond the mere contribution of the bulk of the funds.[25]

Where the signature of more than one of the holders is required to operate the account, problems arise where the bank honours cheques on which the signature of one of the required parties is missing or forged.

Consider the 1952 English case of *Brewer v Westminster Bank Ltd*.[26] A joint account was operated on the signatures together of the two parties to it. One drew fraudulently on the account by means of cheques he signed himself and on which he forged the signature of the other party. The other party sued the bank for their loss. The court found in favour of the bank on the grounds that no action could be maintained by the joint account holders unless they were all in a position to sue. This was not so as the fraudulent party was obviously both one of the holders and not capable of suing on a fraud that they themselves committed.

To say that *Brewer* has been much criticised would be an understatement It was not followed in Victoria in *Ardern v Bank of New South Wales*,[27] nor later in England in *Catlin v Cyprus Finance Corporation (London) Ltd*.[28] In those cases, the courts accepted the argument that when the account was opened, the terms were that operation of the account required both signatures and that in agreeing to that, the bank was contracting with each party *severally* that it would not honour drawings otherwise signed. This has appeal. The only way the obligation to require both signatures could be enforced (in the circumstances of fraud by one of the holders) is by allowing the innocent holder to sue severally. On the other hand, strict logic suggests that, as the holders are joint, they are legally one, and the fraud of one is the fraud of the other.

23 *Jackson v White* [1967] 2 Lloyd's Rep 68. The Australian Government's Strategic Plan for Australia's Payments System announced the Government's intention to wind down the cheques system by no later than 2030. See The Treasury, *A Strategic Plan for Australia's Payment System: Building a Modern and Resilient Payments System* (2023) <https://treasury.gov.au/sites/default/files/2023-06/p2023-404960.pdf>.

24 *Thorpe v Jackson* (1837) 2 Y & C 553; 160 ER 515.

25 See, eg, *Russell v Scott* (1936) 55 CLR 440 (Dixon and Evatt JJ).

26 *Brewer v Westminster Bank Ltd* [1952] 2 All ER 650.

27 *Ardern v Bank of New South Wales* [1956] VLR 569.

28 *Catlin v Cyprus Finance Corporation (London) Ltd* [1983] QB 759.

The weight of current opinion is certainly against *Brewer*, and the contrary view can probably safely be considered to represent the present law. If that is the case, the appropriate measure of damages is whatever proportion of the extracted funds was the share of the defrauded parties. Thus, for instance, if the account were a trust account, that would be the full amount paid over. And, if it were an account for a partnership in which the two account co-signatories were equal partners, then it would be half.

6.2.3.5 Statements and passbooks

It was once the case that customers were provided with a 'passbook', which was a written copy of the bank's ledger entries regarding the customer's account. From time to time, typically whenever the customer attended at the bank in person, the passbook would be updated. The customer could inspect the passbook for accuracy against their own records. Passbooks have largely been replaced by periodic account statements posted or emailed to customers. Customers can also access those statements via banking apps.

There is some authority that passbooks are the customer's property.[29] However, it has long been near-universal practice for banks in Australia to expressly reserve property in passbooks to themselves as part of the agreement as to their issue. It would be hard to argue that a statement sent to a customer did not become the customer's property.

Sometimes it is necessary to present a passbook to be able to operate the account. In that case, possession of the passbook is evidence of title for the purpose of establishing *donatio mortis causa* (ie a gift in contemplation of death).[30] Bear in mind that it must also be shown that the passbook was handed over in contemplation of impending death. Perhaps surprisingly, an attempt has been made to suggest that possession of statements of account could serve the same purpose. It is not possible to see how these could operate as indicia of title, and this somewhat desperate attempt was predictably rejected by the court.[31]

Notwithstanding some ancient precedents that might be otherwise interpreted, the courts have long refused to impose a duty on the customer to read their statements/passbooks, discover and report forgeries, or indeed to regard uncontested passbook entries or statements as evidence of mutual agreement as to their accuracy (as an 'account stated', to use the jargon of the trade). That is, passive receipt of the statement is not implied agreement to its accuracy.[32]

On the other hand, the bank has a duty to keep accurate accounts and not to misrepresent these to its customers. If a customer reasonably relies on an inaccurate statement to their detriment, the representation may bind the bank. For instance, if the bank leads the customer to reasonably believe that they have more in their account than they do, in fact, have, and the customer relies on this to draw from the account and spend more than they otherwise would have done, then the bank cannot deny its representation.

29 *Akrokerri (Atlantic) Mines Ltd v Economic Bank* [1904] 2 KB 465.

30 *Birch v Treasury Solicitor* [1951] Ch 298; *Watts v Public Trustee* [1949] 50 SR (NSW) 130.

31 *Re Tawil v Public Trustee of New South Wales* (2009) 2 ASTLR 317.

32 See, eg, *Tai Hing Cotton Mill Ltd v Liu Chong Hing Bank Ltd* [1986] AC 80 (*Tai Hing Cotton Mill*); *National Australia Bank Ltd v Hokit Pty Ltd* (1996) 39 NSWLR 377; *Simonovski v Bendigo Bank Ltd* [2005] VSCA 125.

There are a number of case examples, but they can all be explained by the general principles governing equitable estoppel, and all cases of this kind should be assessed by these principles.

Increasingly, many customers do not receive printed statements but instead elect to receive online statements provided by the bank under internet banking arrangements. There is no reason to regard these as being different from paper statements. However, while a bank can have difficulty showing that a customer has received a paper statement, the bank's computer systems will readily determine whether a customer has accessed an 'e-statement'. If a bank can show that the customer has not accessed a statement, the customer's assertion that they relied on the statement may be proved to be false.

Banks may attempt to impose expressly, when the account is opened, a duty on the customer to 'verify' statements. Typically, these are referred to as 'verification clauses', 'confirmation clauses' or 'conclusive evidence clauses' and are in a form similar to this:

> The accuracy of the bank's statement of the account will be confirmed by me the customer. In the absence of such confirmation within 14 days, the bank may take the accuracy of the statement to have been confirmed by the customer.

From *Tai Hing Cotton Mill* (see Chapter 5), we have already seen that banks may impose additional duties on customers through express contractual terms, but that such terms and their effect must be brought to the customer's attention. Further, obviously, such a clause could only be effective if the statement in question had actually been received by the customer. The High Court of Australia has held in *Dobbs v National Bank of Australasia Ltd* that conclusive evidence clauses in commercial contracts are not invalid nor contrary to public policy.[33] However, they may be void if included in a consumer contract as defined under sch 2 of the *Competition and Consumer Act 2010* (Cth), the *Australian Consumer Law,* and considered an 'unfair contract term'.[34] In *National Australia Bank Ltd v Dionys,* the New South Wales Court of Appeal held that it was not open to the bank to unilaterally introduce new terms and conditions into the agreement despite the respondent having failed to check her statement of account or to notify NAB promptly of the unauthorised withdrawals from the account, since the terms in question were not agreed to explicitly by the respondent nor were they brought to her attention.[35]

6.3 Combining accounts

6.3.1 General rules

The bank has no *obligation* to combine accounts with meeting debits. The problem usually arises when the bank dishonours a cheque drawn on one account or a direct debit on that account because there are insufficient funds in the account to meet it, even though there are sufficient funds in another of the customer's accounts to cover the liability.

33 *Dobbs v National Bank of Australasia Ltd* (1935) 53 CLR 643.
34 *Australian Consumer Law* s 23(3).
35 *National Australia Bank Ltd v Dionys* [2016] NSWCA 242.

On the other hand, in some cases, the bank may have a right of combination (ie to treat various of the customer's accounts as one). This is also called a 'right of set-off' or 'consolidation', or sometimes – in an abuse of the term – the 'exercise of a banker's lien'.

The right will exist in the absence of any express or implied agreement to keep the accounts separate. The idea is illustrated by *Garnett v M'Kewan.*[36] The plaintiff had two accounts with the bank. One (B) was overdrawn by £42 15s 11d. The other (L) had a credit of £42 18s 10d. The plaintiff drew cheques to a total of £23 on the account that was in credit. When the cheques were presented, they were dishonoured by the bank, who transferred the debt from B to L, combining the two accounts, without notice. The Court held the bank's actions to be valid.

However, where one of the accounts is governed by the *Banking Code of Practice,* the bank is obliged to give notice as soon as practicable *after* combining the accounts (cl 186, ch 44). An exception is if an account involves a loan regulated by the *National Credit Code,* where combination is forbidden in certain cases of hardship. Generally, however, as noted, the right of combination exists in the absence of any express or implied agreement to keep the accounts separate. One might have thought that the mere act of requesting a second account would indicate an intention that the accounts be kept separate, but that is not so.[37] However, if the accounts are of a sufficiently 'different nature', this will indicate an intention that they should not be combined without express agreement. Examples include:

- where a current account and a loan account are opened with a view to longer-term finance[38]
- where an account is opened for a specific purpose and the other account does not share that purpose (eg in *Re EJ Morel (1934) Ltd,*[39] where an account was opened with the express purpose of being reserved for sums for the payment of wages to the customer's employees).

Nor can the right be exercised to combine a personal account with an account known to be, or that the bank should have known to be, a trust account.[40] That would be a case of the 'knowing receipt' type that we have already encountered. However, by way of example, consider *Re Gross.*[41] The treasurer of the County Authority had two accounts at the bank. One was a personal account in debit, the other was headed 'Police Account' and was in credit. The Court held that, based on these facts – in particular, the title of the account and the knowledge that the person was a public official – the bank *ought* to have known the 'Police Account' was a trust account and thus, as discussed earlier, cannot be combined with the personal account.

What if the bank does not know the account is a trust account and has no reason to suppose it is, and innocently combines it? There is Privy Council authority that the

36 *Garnett v M'Kewan* (1872) LR 8 Ex 10.
37 See, eg, *Direct Acceptance Corporation Ltd v Bank of New South Wales* (1968) 88 WN (Pt 1) (NSW) 498.
38 *Bradford Old Bank Ltd v Sutcliffe* [1918] 2 KB 833; *Cinema Plus Ltd (admins apptd) v Australia and New Zealand Banking Group Ltd* (2000) 49 NSWLR 513.
39 *Re EJ Morel (1934) Ltd* [1962] Ch 21.
40 *Barclays Bank Ltd v Quistclose Investments Ltd* [1970] AC 567.
41 *Re Gross; Ex parte Kingston* (1871) 6 Ch App 632.

bank can maintain the set-off.[42] However, the case appears to have been argued *on the assumption* that the set-off could be maintained if the bank had no reason to suppose that what was involved was a trust account: the only question in issue was whether the bank did have (or should have had) knowledge. That it, it was decided purely on the basis that if there was no 'knowing receipt', the bank was entitled to exercise its right of combination. Thus, the decision should perhaps be regarded as doubtful, as there seems to be no sound policy ground for favouring the interests of the bank, opportunistically exercised, over those of an innocent beneficiary.

6.3.2 The rule in *Clayton's case* (*Devaynes v Noble*)

Suppose that on day one, I open an account with the bank and deposit $1000 into it. That is, I lend $1000 to the bank. On day two, I deposit another $1000. (Therefore, I lend the bank another $1000.) On day three, I withdraw $1000. In other words, the bank repays $1000 on day three. Which $1000 has the bank repaid? Is it the $1000 I deposited on day one or the $1000 I deposited on day two (or some part of each)?

According to the 'rule', it is the loan/deposit first made that is the first repaid – that is, the loans/deposits are repaid in the order in which they were made. First-in, first-out. In the example above, it was the $1000 that I deposited on day one that was repaid.

Normally, this issue is of no consequence; however, in some cases, it is. For instance, in *Clayton's case*, the customer, Clayton, operated an account with a partnership banking firm.[43] One of the partners in this firm died. At that time, the balance of the account was £1700. Shortly afterwards, the bank failed. Between the two events, Clayton had (in total) made withdrawals exceeding £1700 and made deposits of an even greater amount. If the £1700 on deposit at the time of the partner's death had been repaid by the subsequent withdrawals, then the partner's estate was not liable to contribute to Clayton's loss. The Court held that each payment out went to repay the earliest payment in. Thus, the £1700 on deposit at the time of the partner's death had been repaid, and the dead partner's estate was not liable.

6.3.3 'Exceptions' to the *Clayton* rule

The 'rule' is, in fact, a presumption, subject to an agreement otherwise between the parties or to a contrary implication on the facts. (Consider, for instance, the situation where there has been an express purpose deposit.)

It is sometimes said that the rule does not apply to transactions made on the same day. For instance, Halsbury LC said in *The Mecca* that the rule should not apply to intra-day transactions because the order of entry of transactions in the books was likely random.[44] That view was applied in *Re Laughton*, where intra-day claims for which the insufficient funds were paid were based on proportionality.[45] That rationale may be sound where ledger entries are made once at the end of each day, but it is to be doubted where transactions

42 *Union Bank of Australia Ltd v Murray-Aynsley* [1898] AC 693.
43 *Devaynes v Noble* (1816) 35 ER 781.
44 *The Mecca* (n 9) 290–1.
45 *Re Laughton* [1962] Tas SR 300.

are entered when made, which is usually so in these days of instantaneous fund transfers (or even for passbook accounts).

The rule also does not apply if withdrawal was made out of an account that mixes both trust money and a trustee's personal money. Instead, when the trustee withdraws on the account, it is generally considered that the withdrawal was made against the trustee's money (and not with trust money), regardless of the order of deposits.[46] *Clayton*'s rule, however, will apply if the account mixes the money of two beneficiaries or an innocent volunteer.[47]

The rule in *Clayton* is essentially a convenience based on a fictional intention. It exists because there must be some rule of appropriation where running accounts are kept. The rule will be displaced when there is evidence of some other actual intention.

6.4 Freezing the account

In some cases, the bank may refuse to allow further withdrawals from, or deposits into, an account. This is commonly referred to as 'freezing' or 'stopping' the account. Doing so will have the effect, among others, of causing any outstanding cheques that are presented for payment to be dishonoured, or for any direct debits from the account to be rejected. For that reason, one would think that – as with termination – a bank ought to be required to give notice of its intention to stop an account. Apparently, however, there is no implied term to this effect.[48] This is probably justified by the limited circumstances in which stopping the account is allowed. These circumstances are discussed below.

6.4.1 Mental incapacity

The *Cheques Act 1986* (Cth) ('*Cheques Act*') s 90(1)(b) provides that 'the duty and authority ... to pay a cheque [is] terminated by notice of the drawer's mental incapacity'. The degree of mental incapacity in question is presumably related to the capacity to enter contracts, as per agency law, but there is surprisingly little relevant case law.

6.4.2 Death

Again, the *Cheques Act* provides that the duty and authority to pay the customer's cheques are terminated by notice of the customer's death.[49] Death is a somewhat more certain state than mental incapacity, so one would expect relatively few problems here. Nevertheless, there are some things to note.

- The termination of authority does not apply to cheques presented for payment within ten (10) days of notice of the death.[50] However, payment may be expressly countermanded by a person claiming to have the right to administer the estate or to be a beneficiary of it.[51]

46 *Re Hallett's Estate* (1879) 13 Ch D 696; *Re MacDonald* [1975] Qd R 255.
47 *Re Diplock's Estate* [1948] Ch 465.
48 *State Bank of New South Wales Ltd v Currabubula Holdings Pty Ltd* (2001) 51 NSWLR 399.
49 *Cheques Act 1986* (Cth) s 90(1)(c).
50 Ibid s 90(2)(a).
51 Ibid s 90(2)(b).

- Where the account to be withdrawn against is an overdrawn joint account, death of one of the users may result in the bank 'freezing' the account for all users, including the survivors. The deceased's estate is not liable to pay for cheques paid after the date of death, and any further deposits are used to settle cheques paid before this date.[52]
- Upon a customer's death, the executor administrator of the estate may demand payment of the account balance upon the production of the letters of administrators. Hence, the production of these should be sought. The powers of an executor arise immediately on death. However, the bank cannot part with the balance of an account just because someone comes forward claiming to be executor, even if they come with a will appointing them. The will may not be valid. In practice, banks would usually demand production of probate.[53] The *Banking Act 1959* (Cth) s 69AA provides a limited exception: where a depositor dies, an authorised deposit-taking institution (ADI) can apply up to A$15 000 in payment of funeral expenses to anyone who, in the opinion of the ADI, is entitled to the amount.

6.4.3 Bankruptcy and winding up

6.4.3.1 Basic terminology

We will first delve into the terminology that is essential for understanding bankruptcy and winding up.

- *Insolvency* is when a customer is unable to pay their debts when they become due and payable, taking into account the resources that the debtor might realise if given a reasonable opportunity.
- *Bankruptcy* is the state an individual insolvent debtor may find themselves in under the provisions of the *Bankruptcy Act 1966* (Cth) ('*Bankruptcy Act*') where control of their assets and financial affairs is taken out of their hands and placed for a period in those of a trustee in bankruptcy.
- *Winding up* applies to companies. Control of an insolvent company is taken from its directors and given to a liquidator to realise the assets of the company to satisfy, as far as possible, its creditors and then dissolve the company as a legal entity.

Bankruptcy

What is relevant for our purposes is the fact and effect of bankruptcy concerning the customer's dealings with their bank. When a person becomes bankrupt, all their property (with some exceptions, such as basic domestic amenities and tools up to a certain value used to earn an income) immediately vests in the trustee in bankruptcy.[54] This includes not only property owned at the time of the bankruptcy, but all property acquired after the date of bankruptcy and before discharge from it – the latter is called 'after-acquired

52 See discussion of *Clayton's case* above.

53 See, eg, the practice at the Commonwealth Bank of Australia, *Deceased Estates Support Guide* <https://www.commbank.com.au/content/dam/commbank-assets/support/docs/CBA6239-Deceased-Estates-Guide.pdf>.

54 *Bankruptcy Act 1966* (Cth) ('*Bankruptcy Act*') s 58(1)(a).

property' under the *Bankruptcy Act*.[55] The trustee also acquires 'the capacity to exercise and to take proceedings for exercising all such powers in ... respect of property ... [at] or at any time after the commencement of the bankruptcy'.[56]

Somewhat confusingly, however, the date of the bankruptcy – the date on which it was actually determined that the person was bankrupt – and the date of commencement of bankruptcy are different. It is always necessary to be careful as to which event is being referred to. The date of commencement gives a retrospective operation to the bankruptcy. It is considered necessary so that prospective bankrupts cannot thwart their creditors by planning for bankruptcy in advance by disposing of their property to friends or relations or other preferred creditors, and so on. The principle is that all the bankrupt's property vests in the trustee at the date of commencement, and all subsequent dealing with it is, therefore, potentially voidable by the trustee as the legal owner. This is called the 'doctrine of relation back'.

The method of calculating the commencement date is provided for under the *Bankruptcy Act* s 115. For our purposes, however, the point is that no one, including the debtor's banker, is aware of it at the time of its occurrence. Consider a banker paying on a customer's cheque. The customer later becomes bankrupt. As it happens, the cheque was paid after the commencement of the customer's bankruptcy; therefore, it would seem (having not been made at the direction of the yet-to-be-appointed trustee) the payment is recoverable by the trustee, although this circumstance could not have been known to the bank at the time.

As relation back is only meant to prevent the bankrupt from defeating their creditors, there are exceptions to its operation. Hence, subject to the *Bankruptcy Act* ss 120–122, which we will consider shortly, s 123 excludes from the operation of the doctrine transactions before the date of bankruptcy where the other party had no notice that any bankruptcy petition (ie an action to bankrupt the debtor) had been brought against the debtor, and where that party acted in good faith and in the ordinary course of business and where either market value was given, or the debtor was paying one of their creditors.

Moreover, under s 124(1)(a) of the Act, and notwithstanding any other provision of it, a payment of money or a delivery of property at the direction of the debtor before the date of bankruptcy does not attract the doctrine, provided it was done in good faith and in the ordinary course of business. Thus, a banker acting in the manner described above will generally be protected.

It is worth noting at this point that the *Bankruptcy Act* s 124 generally applies to provide a good discharge to anyone who pays money or delivers property at any time (including a security or a negotiable instrument) at the direction of a person who becomes, or has become, bankrupt. In the case of a transfer that occurs after the date of bankruptcy, however, there is an additional requirement that the transfer is 'without negligence'.[57]

55 Ibid s 58(6). There is debate about whether income earned, and property purchased by a bankrupt using this income, becomes after-acquired property (*Di Cioccio v Official Trustee in Bankruptcy* [2015] FCAFC 30; *Ambrose v Badcock* [2021] FCA 1647).

56 *Bankruptcy Act* (n 54) s 116(1)(b).

57 Ibid s 124(1)(b).

Section 120(1) of the Act provides (again subject to some exceptions and modifications as to the period in special cases) that a 'transfer ... by a person who later becomes a bankrupt is void ... if the transfer took place in the period beginning five (5) years before the commencement of the bankruptcy and ending on the date of the bankruptcy and ... [was at] less value than the market value'.

Section 121(1) provides that where a person who later becomes bankrupt transfers property (no matter when this may occur), the transfer will be voidable by a trustee if the primary purpose was to delay or hinder the rights of creditors and the property would probably have become available to the creditors (or trustee) if the transaction had not occurred. The debtor's main purpose can be one of hindering or delaying their creditors if, at the time of the transaction, it can be reasonably inferred that they were or were about to become insolvent.[58] Again, those who act in good faith in the ordinary course of business and give market value are protected.

Section 122(1) provides that transfers of property made between six months before the date of the petition on which the debtor is made bankrupt and the date of bankruptcy are void as against the trustee if made by a debtor who was insolvent at the time and having the effect of giving a creditor a preference to, priority or advantage over other creditors. The usual exemption in market value and good faith in the ordinary course of business applies. There is no preference, unless the creditor's net position is not improved with respect to the recovery of their debt.

There is no preference where the debtor makes a payment (up to the value of the security) to a secured creditor in exchange for the release of the security.[59] This is because a secured creditor has protection in any bankruptcy up to the value of their security. Their security rights are not affected by bankruptcy.[60]

There is difficulty in determining whether there is a preference for a running account between the parties. However, if a payment is one of some larger set of ongoing transactions, the trustee may recover only the difference (the amount reduced) in debit balance.[61] In determining whether the payment is, in fact, one of a larger set of ongoing transactions, apparently, according to the High Court of Australia, the 'business purpose' of the payment *is* a relevant consideration.[62]

Consider how this works in relation to an overdraft. The customer has an overdraft as part of an ongoing arrangement for short-term finance. The size of the overdraft fluctuates over time. During a period to which the *Bankruptcy Act* s 122 applies, and when the bank knows the customer to be insolvent (so that there is no defence available), a number of drawdowns and repayments occur. The total of the repayments is, say, \$80 000, but they have the net effect, considering the drawdowns in the same period, of reducing the overdraft by only \$10 000. Only \$10 000, and not \$80 000, is recoverable by the trustee.

58 Ibid s 121(2).

59 *Re Keever; Ex parte Trustee of Property of Bankrupt v Midland Bank Ltd* [1967] Ch 182; *National Australia Bank Ltd v KDS Construction Services Pty Ltd (in liq)* (1987) 163 CLR 668.

60 *Bankruptcy Act* (n 54) s 58(5).

61 *Richardson v Commercial Banking Co of Sydney Ltd* (1952) 85 CLR 110.

62 *Airservices Australia v Ferrier* (1996) 185 CLR 483.

Further, suppose a customer has an overdraft with the bank of, say, \$20 000. The bank is worried and, in consideration for forbearing to demand immediate repayment, takes security over the customer's assets against future advances. This cannot be security for the \$20 000 already advanced (past consideration), but only for future advances. Over a subsequent period, the customer withdraws \$20 000 and deposits \$20 000. By *Clayton*, the \$20 000 deposited goes to pay off the pre-security advance. The \$20 000 subsequently advanced is secured. It is hardly remarkable in itself, being the whole purpose of the arrangement. But in the context of bankruptcy, the granting of the security is a preference. It improves the bank's position as a creditor. Before, it was an unsecured creditor for \$20 000; now, it is a secured creditor for the same amount. The bank, however, can potentially avail itself of the 'good faith in the ordinary course of business and market value' exception. The value is provided by the bank meeting the customer's subsequent cheques on the overdrawn account (\$20 000 of security in exchange for an advance of \$20 000).

With respect to the good faith element of the exemption, the *Bankruptcy Act* s 122(4)(c) provides that a creditor is taken to have not acted in good faith if they (i) knew or ought to have known that the debtor is insolvent, and (ii) payment is advantageous to this creditor. This has significance for banks, which might naturally be supposed to have knowledge of the financial state of their customers, and in fact, often do demonstrably have such knowledge.[63] However, the mere knowledge that the debtor has had cheques dishonoured is not itself enough to activate s 122(4).[64]

We have noted that not only all the bankrupt's property at the date of bankruptcy vests in the trustee, but so does all property of the bankrupt acquired after the date of bankrupt and before discharge (after-acquired property).[65] Any dealings by the bankrupt with such property are thus prima facie void. However, some protection is provided by s 126 for those dealing with bankrupts in respect of after-acquired property.

One such protection is for bona fide purchasers for value. The *Bankruptcy Act* s 126(1) provides that 'a transaction by a bankrupt with a person dealing with him or her in good faith and for valuable consideration in respect of [after-acquired] property ... is, if completed before any intervention by the trustee, valid'. Bankers are given special treatment under s 126(2), which says that, for s 126(1), 'the receipt of any money, security or negotiable instrument from, or in accordance with the order or direction of, a bankrupt by his or her banker, and any payment of money or delivery of a security or negotiable instrument made to, or in accordance with the order or direction of, a bankrupt by his or her banker' is deemed to be for valuable consideration.

It should be observed that bankrupts usually have bank accounts that they will operate for their benefit. One of the exceptions to the rule that after-acquired property vests in the trustee is that bankrupts are allowed to earn and retain personal income and to use it for their benefit. Further, the *Bankruptcy Act* s 134(1)(ma) allows the trustee to 'make such allowance out of the estate as he or she thinks just to the bankrupt'. This would

63 *Rees v Bank of New South Wales* (1964) 111 CLR 210.

64 *Queensland Bacon Pty Ltd v Rees* (1966) 115 CLR 266.

65 *Bankruptcy Act* (n 54) s 58.

include ordinary living expenses. However, s 125(1) of the Act provides that where a bank finds that an undischarged bankrupt holds an account with it, it must inform the trustee in writing and make no further payments from the account without the written authorisation of the trustee (or a court order). This prohibition lapses, and the bank may deal with the account without any regard to claims or rights of the trustee, if the bank has received neither authorisation nor a court order within a month of notice.[66]

If the bankrupt's income exceeds a certain (relatively generous) threshold, they will be required to make contributions from it to their creditors. In this case, they may be subject to a 'supervised account regime' under which the bankrupt must deposit all their income into an account with specified features and from which withdrawals are supervised by the trustee.[67]

Bankruptcy and set-off

The *Bankruptcy Act* s 86 provides that the right of set-off is available against the accounts of bankrupts unless the person claiming the set-off was aware of an 'available act of bankruptcy' by the person who became bankrupt at the time they gave credit. There is also a requirement that the dealings sought to be set off be 'mutual'.

In general, 'acts of bankruptcy' are events that can be used to find a petition by a creditor to make a debtor bankrupt. Broadly, they indicate a debtor's inability or unwillingness to pay their debts. There are 21 of them listed in the *Bankruptcy Act* s 40. An 'available' act of bankruptcy is an act of bankruptcy that, at the date when the debtor was, in fact, made bankrupt, was available to use to petition for the bankruptcy of the debtor (whether or not it was the act of bankruptcy relied on).

The 'mutuality' requirement is that the transactions sought to be set off need to have been transactions between the same parties acting in the same capacities. Thus, to give a crude example, if A acts as a trustee in some of the transactions and on their own behalf in others, then those dealings will not be 'mutual' as between A and the bankrupt. The set-off can only be exercised concerning those transactions between A as trustee and the bankrupt, and with respect to those transactions between A in their personal capacity and the bankrupt, separately. Lack of mutuality means they cannot all be lumped together. The application of the section can be difficult because 'mutuality' is not always as easy to determine as might be thought.[68]

Winding up

Winding up of a company is different from bankruptcy in that the company remains owner of its assets. Control of the company, however, passes from its board to a liquidator, who is charged with realising those assets and paying out the creditors to the extent possible. The winding-up provisions of the *Corporations Act 2001* (Cth) ('*Corporations Act*') are extensive. Again, there are relation back provisions, and under pt 5.7B, certain transactions are made voidable on the liquidator's application. A defence comprising good

66 Ibid s 125(2).
67 Ibid ss 139ZIA–139ZIT.
68 See *Gye v McIntyre* (1991) 171 CLR 609; *Day & Dent Constructions Pty Ltd (in liq) v North Australian Properties Pty Ltd* (1982) 150 CLR 85.

faith, absence of actual and constructive knowledge of the insolvency of the company, and valuable consideration or prejudicial reliance (ie not market value) is available.[69]

Any disposition of the company's property made following the commencement of the winding up, other than one exempted by the *Corporations Act*, is void in the absence of a court order (a 'validating' order) to the contrary.[70] The date of commencement of the winding up is usually the date on which the order was made. Still, it may be earlier – for instance, in the case of companies already under administration or provisional liquidation. As it happens, exempt dispositions include payments out of a company bank account, provided it was (1) made on or before the winding-up order, (2) in good faith, and (3) in the 'ordinary' course of the bank's business.

Voluntary administration is an alternative to winding up, which also involves the appointment of someone who takes over a company's management, although in that case, with a view to its rehabilitation. A company's administrators and liquidators are appointed to act in the interests of creditors generally. Receivership also involves control of the company, or at least of some of its assets passing to an external party, but the receiver/controller is appointed in the interest of one creditor – a secured creditor – to realise the security after the company has defaulted in the performance of its obligations to that creditor.

Instruments executed by companies that charge their assets in favour of a lender usually contain a provision authorising the charge-holder, in the event of default, to appoint a receiver to enforce the security by taking control of the charged property. The function of the receiver depends on the range of property charged. Typically, the company will charge all its assets and undertakings. In that case, the receiver will take control of the entire company. The directors will remain but will have no active function. In other cases, only some assets will be charged, and the receiver's task will be merely to realise these without bothering themselves with the conduct of the business. Receivers are given various powers according to the instrument under which they are appointed but also, under the *Corporations Act* s 420, a broad set of default powers that enable them effectively to do whatever is necessary to carry out the purposes for which they were appointed.

While a company is in receivership, creditors holding later-ranking charges and even a liquidator acting for unsecured creditors must bide their time while the receiver works to satisfy the claim of the creditor who appointed them. (A receiver may even be appointed to a company in liquidation.) Sometimes a receiver will be able to satisfy the creditor's claim fully. In that case, they retire, and the company is returned to its directors and own devices or to the tender charms of a new receiver appointed by the holder of a lower-ranking charge. More commonly, however, at the end of the receivership, the company will still be insolvent and go into either administration or liquidation.

6.5 Garnishee orders

We now examine garnishee orders by considering a scenario. Assume that X owes $10 000 to Y but does not pay Y. Y sues and becomes a judgment creditor for the amount. Z owes

69 *Corporations Act 2001* (Cth) s 588FG(2).
70 Ibid s 468.

$10 000 to X. Can Y force Z to pay the $10 000 to Y in satisfaction of the judgment debt, notwithstanding that Z is not a debtor to Y? The answer is affirmative: Y can. The process is called a 'garnishee' or 'garnishment'.

Typically, Z – otherwise called the 'garnishee' – is a bank that owes money to the judgment debtor, X, in the form of a deposit it holds from X. For clarity, let's now dispense with X, Y and Z and refer to the judgment debtor, the judgment creditor and the garnishee, respectively.

The process works as follows. The judgment creditor files an affidavit with the court to the effect that they believe the garnishee owes money to the debtor. On this basis, the judgment creditor obtains a garnishee order *nisi* from the court directed to the garnishee and ordering the garnishee to show cause why the money should not be paid to the judgment creditor, and in the interim, restraining the garnishee from dealing with the money. If no cause is shown, the court will make an order absolutely directing the payment. Otherwise, the order will be discharged.

The order *nisi* is often expressed to 'attach' (ie freeze) 'all debts owing or accruing due to the judgment debtor'. The wording of this would seem straightforward: that it is not only the amount of the judgment debt that is frozen but *all* the money in the hands of the garnishee owed or accruing due to the judgment debtor. The question is whether the power of the court extends this far. In *Rogers v Whiteley*, it was held that it did.[71]

Whiteley was a bank. Rogers had an account in credit to the extent of £6800. A creditor obtained a judgment against Rogers for £6000 and then obtained a garnishee order nisi directed at Whiteley for 'all debts owing or accruing due to' Rogers. Rogers subsequently wrote a number of small cheques totalling less than £800. Whiteley dishonoured these and Rogers sued Whiteley for wrongful dishonour. Rogers was unsuccessful.[72]

It is said that *Joachimson v Swiss Bank Corporation*[73] – which, incidentally, was decided after *Rogers v Whiteley* – presents a theoretical difficulty in regard to orders expressed in terms of amounts owing or accruing due to the judgment debtor and aimed at current accounts because that case holds that no amount is owing due on a current account until the customer makes demand. This is almost certainly correct. The argument that the order *nisi* itself represents a demand (by enforced proxy of the court) to pay is a fiction that does not stand much scrutiny, as the order *nisi* is not an order to pay – at least not until it becomes absolute. The point has not, however, to our knowledge, been tested.

Similar difficulties arise, *a fortiori*, in the case of accounts that expressly provide that some requirement be met, such as the production of a passbook or a signed withdrawal form or notice, before the customer is entitled to withdraw funds. Decisions in England,

71 *Rogers v Whiteley* [1892] AC 118.

72 The outcome would have been otherwise if the order had nominated the sum of £6000 as being attached.

73 *Joachimson v Swiss Bank Corporation* [1921] 3 KB 110.

and of the Full Supreme Courts of Western Australia, Victoria and Queensland, support the view that at common law such accounts cannot be attached unless the requirements are complied with concurrently with the service of the order.[74]

However, the common law position in regard to all types of accounts is potentially subject to statutory modification in all jurisdictions. The relevant legislation is the Acts governing the courts in question and the rules of those courts. In each case, these need to be checked. By way of example, the *Supreme Court (General Civil Procedure) Rules 2015* (Vic) r 71.03(1) provides that:

> ... an amount standing to the credit of a judgment debtor in an account in a bank shall ... be a debt due or accruing to the judgement debtor, notwithstanding that any of the following conditions ... has not been satisfied:
> (a) that a demand or notice is required before money is withdrawn;
> (b) that a personal application must be made before money is withdrawn;
> (c) that a deposit book must be produced before money is withdrawn;
> (d) that a receipt for money deposited in the account must be produced before money is withdrawn.

What of money credited to the account after service of the order? Is that attachable as 'owing or accruing due'? The answer is: 'No, not at common law.'[75] What about money deposited after the order is made but before service? It would appear that the answer is likewise.[76] Again, however, in both cases, the situation is potentially subject to statutory provisions in all jurisdictions. In Victoria, as far as the Supreme Court is concerned, the relevant provisions are the *Supreme Court (General Civil Procedure) Rules 2015* (Vic) rr 71.02 and 71.03, which have the effect of making attachable all deposits made after the making of the order *nisi*. Of course, the bank (as opposed to the funds) can only be made subject to the order once it is served.

It would appear standard practice for banks to exercise their right of combination in the face of attachment, which would seem unobjectionable. However, a variation (or, if appropriate, discharge) of the order *nisi* should be sought. The money attached must belong, legally and equitably, to the judgment creditor before it can be attached. It matters not in whose name the account is held but only who is the legal and equitable owner (*Harrods v Tester*:[77] the account of a married woman not available for garnishment where a resulting trust was found in favour of her husband). Thus, trust accounts are not attachable, nor is a joint account where the judgment debt is not in respect to a debt owed by all the account holders,[78] and nor is a partnership account where the judgment debt is a personal one.[79]

74 *Bagley v Winsome and National Provincial Bank* [1952] 2 QB 236; *Bank of New South Wales Savings Bank Ltd v Fremantle Auto Centre Pty Ltd* [1973] WAR 161; *Music Masters Pty Ltd v Minelle* [1968] Qd R 326; *Re Australia & New Zealand Savings Bank Ltd; Mellas v Evriniadis* [1972] VR 690.

75 See *Heppenstall v Jackson* [1939] 1 KB 585.

76 *Bank of New South Wales Ltd v Barlex Investments Pty Ltd* (1964) 64 SR (NSW) 274; *Universal Guarantee Pty Ltd v Derefink* [1958] VR 51.

77 *Harrods v Tester* [1937] 2 All ER 236.

78 *Hirschorn v Evans (Barclays Bank Ltd, Garnishees)* [1938] 2 KB 801.

79 *Hoon v Maloff; Jarvis Construction Co Ltd (Garnishees)* (1964) 42 DLR (2d) 770.

On the other hand, where there are joint and several judgment debtors – that is, where the judgment debt is enforceable against all or any of them – then money owed by all or any of them is attachable. For example, the judgment is against A, B and C; B's account is attachable.[80]

A garnishee order will not be granted if the payment by the garnishee to the judgment creditor will not discharge the legal obligation of the garnishee to pay the judgment debtor – that is, if the judgment debtor still retains a right to recover their debt from the garnishee notwithstanding that the garnishee has paid the amount to the judgment creditor. Consider, by way of example, *Société Eram Shipping v Compagnie Internationale de Navigation.*[81]

Eram sued a Hong Kong company in the French courts and obtained judgment there. The judgment was registered in England under the relevant recognition of judgments legislation and was recognised in English law. The judgment debtor held an account with a Hong Kong Bank (HBSC). After registration, Eram applied for a garnishee order in the English courts directed to the London branch of HBSC. The application was refused on the grounds that HBSC might be placed in double jeopardy. There had been no registration of the judgment in Hong Kong. Therefore, the judgment might not be recognised there, and so, notwithstanding payment by HBSC to Eram, HBSC might still be held liable in Hong Hong to the judgment debtor if the judgment debtor sought repayment on the account held there.

6.6 Tracing orders

Tracing is a procedure that allows, in certain circumstances, the proper owner of the property the right to 'follow' or 'trace' that property, where it has been mixed with another property or transformed or passed to a third party. Money can be equitably traced into a mixed fund and recovered if three pre-conditions are all met:

(1) There must be a fiduciary relationship between the claimant and the person who received the money in the first instance.[82]
(2) The money must be identifiable.
(3) Recovery would not work an injustice.[83]

Clearly of interest to us are situations where the account holder has received money as a fiduciary and mixed it in the account with their own funds and there have been subsequent transactions on the account. How is a determination made as to whether the funds to be traced remain in the account or have been moved on? Indeed, we already know the answer to this from our discussion of the limits to the rule in *Clayton's case*. Money withdrawn by the fiduciary for their personal benefit is considered to be confined, to

80 See *DJ Colburt & Sons Pty Ltd v Ansen* [1966] 2 NSWR 289.
81 *Société Eram Shipping v Compagnie Internationale de Navigation* [2004] 1 AC 260.
82 The Full Court of the Federal Court in *RnD Funding Pty Ltd v Roncane Pty Ltd* (2023) 297 FCR 91 appears to dispense with that pre-condition.
83 *Re Diplock's Estate* (n 47); *Zreika v Royal* (2019) 271 FCR.

the extent possible, to their personal funds in the account. It would be contrary to the fiduciary's duty as a fiduciary to draw on the other funds for that purpose.[84] What if there is more than one fiduciary with deposits, and the amount remaining in the account is insufficient to meet the sum of their claims? They do not take *pro rata*; rather, the rule in *Clayton's case* is applied to apportion their claims.[85]

6.6.1 Example

F operates an account. He makes certain transactions, as shown in Table 6.1, in the order given there for his personal benefit and as fiduciary for A, B and C.

Table 6.1 Example of a transaction

Deposit	Withdrawal	Nature	Balance
$200		For A	$100
$100		Personal	$300
$150		For B	$450
	$250	Personal	$200
$200		For C	$400
	$100	Personal	$300

F's personal withdrawals amount to $350. These are first offset against his personal deposits according to the rule in *Clayton's case*. Thus, the first personal withdrawal of $250 is offset against the personal deposit to the extent of $100, then against the first 'fiduciary deposit' for the remaining $150. At this point, A has a notional residual balance of $50, B of $150 and C of $200. The second personal withdrawal of $100 is then offset against the balance of the first fiduciary deposit ($50) and against the second fiduciary deposit belonging to B (to the extent of $50). Thus, of the remaining balance of the account, A is entitled to zero, B to $100 and C to $200. A and B may, of course, be able to trace further the funds that F has moved on from the account.

6.7 Summary

This chapter provides a general survey of the law as it relates to the types of accounts and services most commonly provided by banks. We have undertaken an examination of the legal principles governing customer transactions involving the deposit and withdrawal of funds from a bank account. This examination necessitates a holistic assessment of various contextual factors, including, but not limited to: the nature of the account in question, the purpose behind the account, and any contractual agreements associated with the account.

84 *Re Hallett's Estate* (n 46).
85 Ibid; *Re Laughton* (n 45).

Furthermore, we have delved into the bank's prerogatives when it comes to managing customer accounts, encompassing considerations such as the extent of a bank's authority to consolidate and offset a customer's outstanding debts, as well as their capacity to implement freezes on accounts, particularly in the context of a customer's bankruptcy or the dissolution of a company. These rights on the part of the banks are not absolute and may be subject to various exceptions.

FURTHER READING

Jelisejevs, Aleksejs, 'Crucial Issues with Legal Protection of Consumers' Human Rights When Banks Unilaterally Close Accounts' (2021) 7(4) *Athens Journal of Law* 617.
Ridge, Pauline, 'Tracing and Associated Claims in Australian Law' (2020) 14(1) *Journal of Equity* 32.
Roxburgh, Alan, 'Knowing Receipt: A Question of Priorities' (2021) 27(4) *Trusts & Trustees* 344.

QUESTIONS

(1) Consider the facts in *Westpac v Savin* [1985] 2 NZLR 41 and discuss whether the bank would be liable if the issue were 'knowing assistance' instead of 'knowing receipt'.

(2) How does the rule in *Clayton's case* determine how money in a customer's current account is appropriated?

(3) Sometimes the deposit is made not by a customer but by a third party. When this happens, the third party has almost always been armed by the customer with the relevant account details and can hardly complain if the bank pays to that account in the absence of instructions to the contrary by the customer. In the situation/example given in Section 6.6.1, does the bank have the discretion to credit another of the customer's accounts?

CHAPTER 7

DUTIES OF THE BANKER AND THE CUSTOMER

7.1 Introduction

The relationship between the bank and the customer gives rise to several duties on the part of the bank. The most important of these is the duty of confidence, also known as the '*Tournier* duty'. In addition, there are two duties implied into the banker–customer contract that are owed by the customer to the bank:

- the *Macmillan* duty, which is the duty to exercise reasonable care in drawing cheques so as not to facilitate fraud
- the *Greenwood* duty, which is the duty to notify the bank of any forgeries known to the customer.

Neither of these duties is particularly onerous, and each gives rise only to estoppel, which the bank is able to set up to negate any claim for wrongful debiting of the account.

7.2 The *Tournier* duty

This duty is named after the case that first 'explained' it (in 1924): *Tournier v National Provincial & Union Bank* ('*Tournier*').[1] In the case, it was held that a banker owes a duty of confidentiality to clients, not only as to the 'actual state of the account (the amount of money in the account) of the customer' but also as to 'any information derived from the account itself', as well as 'transactions that go through the account'. The duty probably extends to all aspects of the banker–customer relationship, even to transactions that are unusual or even extraordinary in this context (see, eg, *Royal Bank of Canada v Inland Revenue Commissioners*[2]).

The facts in *Tournier* itself were fairly straightforward.

Tournier had banked with National Provincial & Union Bank for some time. He overdrew the account and agreed with the branch manager to pay down the overdraft by £1 a week. His address at that time was recorded as that of his employer. He failed to keep to the agreement. The manager telephoned the employer to obtain, he said, Tournier's home address to discuss the matter with him.[3] In the course of the conversation, the manager informed the employer of his particular reason for wishing to contact Tournier, and also, incidentally, that the bank suspected Tournier of gambling, as some of his cheques were in favour of a bookmaker. As a consequence of this conversation, Tournier was sacked from his job. He succeeded in recovering damages from the bank.

The duty appears not just to apply to banks, but to financial institutions generally. It also extends to the disclosure of the information to a company that is part of a group to which the company belongs (eg a subsidiary or holding company).

The source of the duty was said in *Tournier* to be an implied contractual term. This is not entirely convincing. Attempts have been made to justify it in terms of agency and the fiduciary duty that arises from it, but these explanations are even less convincing.

1 *Tournier v National Provincial and Union Bank* [1924] 1 KB 461.
2 *Royal Bank of Canada v Inland Revenue Commissioners* [1972] Ch 665.
3 Note further, however, that there are suggestions that the call was, in fact, motivated by a desire to make mischief, but that is immaterial.

One would argue it is best explained as a particular example of the general equitable duty of confidentiality, owed where information that is secret is passed on in circumstances where there is an express or implied condition that it will not be revealed to other parties or used without permission. However, there are objections to this view, too. Nevertheless, the existence of the duty has never been questioned, and it is probably best to take on face value, and without too much enquiry, the view stated in *Tournier* that it is an implied contractual duty and for practical purposes, under this general rubric, to treat it as *sui generis*.

In *Tournier*, the Court identified four exceptions to the duty, as examined further below:

- disclosure by compulsion of law
- where disclosure is justified in the public interest
- where disclosure is required to protect the commercial interest of the bank
- where disclosure is with the implied or express consent of the customer.

Before we proceed, bear in mind that the statutory obligations (eg the *Privacy Act 1988* (Cth)) would also play a role in data protection, as explained in Chapter 4.

7.2.1 Legal compulsion

At the abstract level, there is little difficulty in justifying the exception. The banker's duty of confidentiality is no more than a simple private obligation which, like any other private obligation, must be subject to the operation of broader general laws aimed at protecting the public and maintaining civic institutions and rights. No one doubts that public policy interests should be capable of overriding the private law of confidentiality applicable to the banker–customer relationship.

At the time of *Tournier*, the example most obviously in the judges' minds was the production of information at the court's order by, for instance, subpoena or in the course of evidence. Where a court order relates to a criminal prosecution, there is no obligation on the bank to notify the customer of the order. In civil cases, there is some doubt about this. The case of *Robertson v Canadian Imperial Bank of Commerce*[4] suggests that such an obligation does exist and, indeed, that there might even be an obligation on the bank to object to the disclosure of 'irrelevant' information. How the bank is meant to determine the relevance of the information sought to the action is problematic, and this idea has little to recommend it.

If the duty of confidence is inconsistent with the general terms of the statute, then the duty will be negated. The examples are search warrants granted under statute in criminal cases for bank records, and subpoenas that may also be issued to compel banks to produce the banking records of a customer in civil and criminal matters. Yet, these are hardly matters for the bank to contest. Given the private basis of the duty, arguments that the confidential information of third parties will be divulged are not relevant.

The legal compulsion exception now has much broader applicability. Most Australian jurisdictions and foreign jurisdictions have statutes that require banks to disclose

4 *Robertson v Canadian Imperial Bank of Commerce* [1995] 1 All ER 824.

confidential information to courts and tribunals, law enforcement agencies, regulators and other authorities. Examples include legislation relating to the production of evidence, financial services, bankruptcy and insolvency, trade practices, tax and social security, and criminal investigation–related laws.

Under the *Anti-Money Laundering and Counter-Terrorism Financing Act 2006* (Cth), for instance, banks are required to disclose personal information to the Australian Transaction Reports and Analysis Centre (AUSTRAC) if it relates to bank accounts engaging in suspicious activity[5] or unusually large transactions.[6]

7.2.2 Public interest

This exception has the virtue of recognising discretion rather than exercising compulsion. Given the vagueness of the concept of 'public duty', it is the most controversial of the exceptions. In *Tournier's case*, Scrutton and Atkin LJJ considered that there is a qualification to the banker's duty of confidentiality when there is a higher duty to *prevent* fraud or crime.

There is room for debate on whether the public interest qualification is wide enough to permit bankers to act as whistleblowers at large in respect of customers involved in cases of crime and fraud. In *Gartside v Outram*, Page Wood V-C said, when speaking in defence of the qualification in the context of the equitable duty of confidence:

> The true doctrine is, that there is no confidence as to the disclosure of iniquity. You cannot make me a confidant of a crime or a fraud, and be entitled to close my lips upon any secret which you have the audacity to disclose to me relating to any fraudulent intention on your part: such confidence cannot exist.[7]

Furthermore, in *Initial Services v Putterill*, Lord Denning MR stated:

> [Disclosure is permissible if it relates to] any misconduct of such a nature that it ought in the public interest to be disclosed to others ... [including] crimes, frauds and misdeeds, both those actually committed as well as those in contemplation.[8]

Australian courts have tended to construe the exemption more narrowly, refusing to authorise an indiscriminate breach of confidence merely because there is some 'public interest in the truth' or that 'disclosure would possibly benefit the society'. Thus said Gummow J in *Corrs Pavey Whiting & Byrne v Collector of Customs (Vic)*. His Honour continued:

> Finally, if there be some other principle of general application inspired by *Gartside v Outram*, it is in my view of narrower application than the 'public interest defence' expressed in the English cases ... That principle, in my view, is no wider than one that information will lack the necessary attribute of confidence if the subject matter is the existence or real likelihood of the existence

5 *Anti-Money Laundering and Counter-Terrorism Financing Act 2006* (Cth) s 41.
6 Ibid s 43.
7 *Gartside v Outram* [1857] 26 LJ Ch 113, 114.
8 *Initial Services Ltd v Putterill* [1968] 1 QB 396, 405.

> of an iniquity in the sense of a crime, civil wrong or serious misdeed of public importance, and the confidence is relied upon to prevent disclosure to a third party *with a real and direct interest in redressing* such crime, wrong or misdeed.[9]

And, in *Bodnar v Townsend,*[10] Blow J of the Tasmanian Supreme Court held that the exemption only operates in relation to the prevention of crimes, and so on, and does not permit a bank to disclose past crimes committed by its clients. The justification of this view, to the extent that it is not merely based on a literal reading of the judgments in *Tournier,* is that a discretionary public interest exemption is unnecessary in relation to past misdeeds as adequate compulsive means are available for the collection of evidence for the prosecution of these.

Thus, there are at least two axes of uncertainty operating concerning the exemption:

(1) Does it extend to an interest in remedying past iniquities or is it confined to preventing future ones?
(2) What degree of certainty is required as to the existence of the iniquity?

Needless to say, banks are entitled to and ought to take a conservative view of the extent of their operation.

7.2.3 Commercial interest

This exemption is more limited than its casual description suggests. According to *Tournier,* the exemption applies to the extent that it is 'reasonably necessary' to protect the bank's legitimate legal interests as against either the customer or third parties. It does not extend to situations where the bank happens to consider that it may turn out to its commercial advantage to make the disclosure. Examples given in *Tournier* include where a bank issues a writ claiming payment of an overdraft stating on the face of the writ the amount of the overdraft or disclosure reasonable and proper for carrying on the business of the account. It is only reasonable that a bank is allowed to sue a rogue customer to enforce security, for instance, and to be allowed to disclose confidential information related to said security. Similarly, in the event that a bank is the subject of a legal action by a customer, the bank shall be able to reveal the confidential information of that customer to the extent that that is relevant to its defence.

The exemption is not limited to disclosures in the context of customer litigation but also applies to disclosures to third parties in relation to transactions processed by the bank for or with the customer. In *Hassneh Insurance Co of Israel v Mew,* Coleman J held:

> [The] bank should be able to disclose the information if to withhold it would or might prejudice the bank in the establishment or protection of its own legal rights *vis-à-vis* ... third parties. The essence of the matter is that it might need to disclose the information either as the foundation of a defence to a claim by a third party, or as the basis for a cause of action against a third party.[11]

9 *Corrs Pavey Whiting & Byrne v Collector of Customs (Vic)* (1987) 14 FCR 434, 455–6 (emphasis added).
10 *Bodnar v Townsend* (2003) 12 Tas R 232.
11 *Hassneh Insurance Co of Israel v Mew* [1993] 2 Lloyd's Rep 243, 249.

The rationale behind disclosure in third-party litigation lies in the bank's entitlement to defend itself against potential liability to a third party.

The exemption cannot be used to justify the disclosure of confidential information to other members of a banking corporate group. Banks often operate as part of a corporate group with activities, such as mortgage lending, commercial banking, credit cards processing, funds management, and so on, performed by separate corporate entities – although their customers may not be aware of this in their day-to-day dealings with their bank. The disclosure by a bank of confidential customer information to a separate company that is part of the same banking group is a breach of the duty of confidentiality (see, eg, *Bank of Tokyo Ltd v Karoon*[12]). It makes no difference that the customer is a customer of both banks in the same banking group or that the banks share the same management. From the point of view of banks, this is highly inconvenient. It is usually circumvented by the bank obtaining an express waiver of the duty as it relates to disclosure to related corporate entities. This leads to the next exemption – namely, consent.

7.2.4 Consent

Whether a customer has consented to disclosure is a question of fact that is determined by an objective examination of their conduct with regard to all the relevant surrounding circumstances. Subject to the observations in *Tai Hing Cotton Mill v Liu Chong Hing Bank*[13] as to the nature of the notice required, there would seem to be few limits on banks modifying their implied duty of confidentiality by express contractual provision.

In the case of implied consent, questions typically arise as to whether the customer's behaviour was in fact indicative of consent and, if so, whether it covered the information disclosed.

In *Sunderland v Barclay's Bank Ltd*,[14] the bank dishonoured Mrs S's cheques due to insufficient funds in her account. It decided not to allow an overdraft since it was aware that the outgoings were due to gambling losses but gave no reason to her. Mrs S complained to her husband, who encouraged her to telephone the bank and request an explanation. She did so. In the course of the conversation, she handed the telephone to Mr S. The bank told him that most of the cheques drawn on the account were in favour of bookmakers. Mrs S subsequently sued for breach of the duty of confidence. The Court held that by handing the telephone to her husband after seeking an explanation, Mrs S had impliedly authorised disclosure to him.

In *Lee Gleeson Pty Ltd v Sterling Estates Pty Ltd*,[15] a property owner's bank informed the builder that it had authority from its customer to make payments on behalf of that customer to the builder. The notification was with the consent of the property owner. The customer later cancelled the payment instructions. The bank did not notify the builder of this, having no express instructions to do so. It argued that it had no consent to do so. The Court held that, in granting the original consent to divulge the authority,

12 *Bank of Tokyo Ltd v Karoon* [1987] AC 45.
13 *Tai Hing Cotton Mill Ltd v Liu Chong Hing Bank Ltd* [1985] 3 WLR 333.
14 *Sunderland v Barclay's Bank Ltd* (1938) 5 LDAB 163.
15 *Lee Gleeson Pty Ltd v Sterling Estates Pty Ltd* (1991) 23 NSWLR 571.

the property owner had impliedly authorised the bank to notify the builder of any revocation of or change to the authority.

A banker's reference is a communication from one bank to another providing information about a customer. It is almost always sought because a customer of the second bank has requested it as information relevant to some contemplated transaction. It is also often given without notice to the customer whose affairs are being reported. In such cases, bankers' references appear prima facie to violate the duty of confidence. They were considered in passing in *Tournier*, where they were considered as justified where express or implied consent could be shown. For example, where a customer gives the name of their banker in the course of business negotiations, it can readily be implied that they do so for the purpose of providing a reference. Indeed, this will be the usual case.

However, there is no reason why the inquirer must have come across the identity of the customer's bank in this manner, and it is (or was until recently) common practice among bankers not to check with their customers before giving references. That practice can only be justified by implied consent based on banking customs and usage. That, in turn, can only be supported if customers might be supposed to be generally aware of the practice – that is, if it is 'notorious'.

There is no Australian case law on the matter unless one counts the odd off-hand remark. (For example, Kitto J in *Mutual Life & Citizens' Assurance Co Ltd v Evatt*[16] asserted, in an entirely incidental remark, that 'everyone' was aware of the practice.) The issue was, however, traversed in 1999 by the English Court of Appeal in *Turner v Royal Bank of Scotland*, where it was held that the practice was not sufficiently known to constitute an implied term that would override the duty of confidence.[17]

Many breaches of the duty will not give rise to loss, so damages would be nominal if the matter were litigated. The customer proposes to write a cheque to a third party in payment for goods. The third party telephones the bank and asks if there are currently sufficient funds in the customer's account to meet the cheque. The bank, without consent from the customer, provides the information. The provision of the information is a breach. If there are sufficient funds, then the transaction goes through and the customer has no loss. If there are insufficient funds, the matter is conceivably more problematic. The customer is forced to argue that: (a) the transaction would have gone ahead but for the breach; and (b) if it had, this would have resulted in a superior outcome for the customer (taking into account their liability if the cheque were dishonoured) than if it had not. Needless to say, it is unlikely if the bank had refused the information that the transaction would have gone ahead. Option (b) is factually possible, although there is the additional consideration that the customer is attempting to hide behind the duty to profit from writing a cheque for which the customer likely knows there are insufficient funds.

Irrespective of whether a *Tournier* exemption applies, a bank can obviously be liable to the customer in negligence if inaccurate information is provided without reasonable

16 *Mutual Life & Citizens' Assurance Co Ltd v Evatt* (1968) 122 CLR 556, 589.
17 *Turner v Royal Bank of Scotland plc* [1999] 2 All ER (Comm) 664.

care and the customer suffers a loss because of this, or for defamation if the communication is defamatory. The usual general law principles apply, and it is not necessary to discuss them here.

7.3 Duty to the enquirer/third parties

The banker, when providing a reference about a customer's financial matters, also has an obligation to the final requester. Indeed, a banker who provides information at all to anyone may be liable for negligent misstatement. The well-known principles of *Hedley Byrne & Co Ltd v Heller & Partners Ltd* ('Hedley Byrne')[18] and *L Shaddock & Associates Pty Ltd v Parramatta City Council (No 1)*[19] related to negligent misstatement apply. The basic outline is that people who make statements owe a duty of care to those to whom the statement is made as to the correctness of the statement, where:

- (a) the person to whom the statement is made relies on the truth of the statement
- (b) it is reasonable in the circumstances for them to rely on the truth of it
- (c) the person making the statement either knew or should have known that the other person would rely on it.

Whether it is reasonable for the plaintiff to rely on the truth of the defendant's statement will often depend on the relative expertise and knowledge of the parties. The standard of care required is that which would be exercised by a reasonable person in the same circumstances as the defendant. For example, in the case of a banker providing a reference, it would be the standard of competence and care that is generally shown by and expected of bankers who carry out the business of providing banking references.

The usual situation is that a third party asks their bank to ask the customer's bank to provide a reference concerning the customer. The bank providing the reference knows, without being told, that the requesting bank is seeking the reference on behalf of some other party seeking to rely on it simply because this is the normal practice. Thus, (c) above will always be satisfied in the case of bankers' references, notwithstanding that the identity of the plaintiff is, at the time, unknown to the supplying bank (see, eg, *Commercial Banking Co of Sydney Ltd v RH Brown & Co* ('*Brown*'[20]).

Note that the bank that merely passes on the reference will not generally be liable. In normal circumstances, it is not to be supposed that *they* are making any statement about the creditworthiness or otherwise of the other bank's customer or that, if they were, it would be reasonable to rely on it.

References are generally provided to the requesting bank with the proviso that the reference is for the 'private use only' (or similar) of the requesting bank. This will not relieve the providing bank from liability to the ultimate inquirer if (or rather when) the reference is passed on to them (*Brown*). This is because banking practice is such that the requesting bank is seeking the information precisely to pass it on to a customer. This is its exact private use.

18 *Hedley Byrne & Co Ltd v Heller & Partners Ltd* [1964] AC 465.

19 *L Shaddock & Associates Pty Ltd v Parramatta City Council* (1981) 150 CLR 225.

20 *Commercial Banking Co of Sydney Ltd v RH Brown & Co* (1972) 126 CLR 337 ('*Brown*').

References also typically come with disclaimers to the effect that the information is not intended to be and should not be relied on. In *Hedley Byrne*, a disclaimer of that nature was sufficient for the defendant to avoid liability. Prima facie, that appears reasonable: that it is *un*reasonable to rely on a statement when the maker warns against reliance on it. But, at least in the case of banker's references, such disclaimers are disingenuous. The provider knows the reference is being sought to make some decision and that it would not be sought otherwise and provides the reference in the full knowledge that it will be used. It would seem better to regard a disclaimer, and the forcefulness of its warning as wording, as merely one circumstance to be taken into account in deciding whether it is reasonable for the recipient to rely on the reference, as suggested by Barwick CJ in *Mutual Life & Citizens' Assurance Co Ltd v Evatt*.[21]

A disclaimer would be of no avail if the reference were fraudulent. The requirement for liability here is that the representation was false, the maker knew it was false or was reckless as to its truth, it was intended to be relied on by the recipient, and it was relied on by the recipient to their detriment (*Derry v Peek*[22]).

Banks do occasionally supply references in bad faith to misrepresent a customer's bank account in circumstances where it will be beneficial to do so, as illustrated by *Brown*. This case also provides an example of the form that bankers' references typically take.

The plaintiffs had, for a number of years, sold wool to W, a company. They had recently entered into a further contract to supply wool to W. Shortly before they were due to deliver the wool, they were informed by their own banker that there were rumours that W was in financial difficulties. They requested their banker to write to W's banker seeking that bank's opinion on W's financial position. The reference was duly provided by the manager of the branch with which W dealt. It said:

> The Company is capably managed by Directors well experienced in the wool trade. The Company has always met its engagements, is trading satisfactorily and we consider that it would be safe for its trade engagements generally. This opinion is confidential and for your private use and without responsibility on the part of this bank or its officers.[23]

The plaintiff proceeded with the contract and W failed, owing money on it to the plaintiff. The plaintiff sued W's bank for deceit (inter alia).

The judgment of the High Court of Australia made it clear that Australian banking practice was such that when a bank requested information from another bank concerning the credit of a customer, it was understood that the enquiring bank did so for the purpose of communicating the information to one of its own customers and that it was impossible to construe the confidentiality provision to mean that the information was to be used only by the enquiring bank for the purpose of giving its own advice to its customers without divulging the actual information. Further, any disclaimer, even if it were adequate to protect the providing bank against negligence, could not protect the giver

21 *Mutual Life & Citizens' Assurance Co Ltd v Evatt* (1968) 122 CLR 556.
22 *Derry v Peek* (1889) LR 14 App Cas 337.
23 *Brown* (n 20) 341.

of the opinion against an action for deceit. In this case, the reference was given with the knowledge that it was false, was made with the intention that it should be acted on by the ultimate enquirer and was acted on by them to their loss.

At this point, it is pertinent to mention the following. The *Statute of Frauds (Amendment) Act 1828* (Imp) remains in force in Tasmania, Western Australia and Victoria. Known as 'Lord Tenterden's Act', it provides that 'no action shall be brought ... [against] any person upon or by reason of any representation ... made ... concerning or relating to the ... credit ... of any other person ... unless such representation ... be made in writing, signed by the party to be charged therewith'.[24] This section applies only to *fraudulent* representations made to induce the plaintiff to advance credit to a third person.[25]

Because it requires that the representation be signed by the person making it, it is never possible to fix a bank with liability where the representation is made by an agent of the bank - which is almost always the case - because, in making the representation, the agent is acting outside their authority. Only the person actually making and signing the statement can be liable. The Act is, of course, an anachronism and should be repealed. It does not apply if the representation is merely negligent.

7.4 Duty to question a valid mandate

Selangor United Rubber v Cradock (No 3)[26] and *Karak Rubber Co Ltd v Burden (No 2)*[27] suggest that, in some cases, a bank has a duty to question a valid mandate. By 'mandate' is meant a general instruction - for example, to honour cheques drawn by a certain person. What if the bank becomes aware that following the instruction in a particular case might not be in the customer's best interests? Under what circumstances are they bound to make enquiries of the customer?

The following example based on *Lipkin Gorman v Karpnale Ltd*[28] gives the idea.

C, a partner in the plaintiff law firm of solicitors, was not only a compulsive gambler but also possessed complete authorisation to make withdrawals from the solicitors' client bank account, which was held at the defendant bank. The partners did not know of C's gambling habit. C, acting within his authority, wrote a cheque in favour of himself. He endorsed this in favour of a gambling club in exchange for chips. The club presented the cheque to the bank for payment, and it was duly honoured. The solicitors brought an action against the bank to recover the money. The branch manager knew of C's habit. Indeed, following a meeting with C concerning C's personal account, the manager recorded that he did not believe C's assertion that the gambling was a 'controlled activity'. The manager made no enquiries of the other partners as to whether the cheque in question ought to be honoured. The solicitors sought to recover the money from the bank on the basis, inter alia, that the bank ought not to have paid the cheque without enquiry.

24 *Statute of Frauds (Amendment) Act 1828* (Imp) s 6.
25 *Diamond v Bank of London and Montreal Ltd* [1979] QB 333; *Banbury v Bank of Montreal* [1918] AC 626.
26 *Selangor United Rubber Estates Ltd v Craddock (No 3)* [1968] 1 WLR 1555.
27 *Karak Rubber Co Ltd v Burden (No 2)* [1972] 1 WLR 602.
28 *Lipkin Gorman v Karpnale Ltd* [1992] 4 All ER 409.

In *Lipkin Gorman v Karpnale Ltd*, all members of the English Court of Appeal agreed that there was some limit on the bank's entitlement to treat a mandate as absolute. It was argued that the limit should be imposed when the relevant transaction was obviously dishonest. The Court imposed a slightly different – or one would say higher – standard on the bank. May LJ held:

> [It] is ... only when the circumstances are such that any reasonable cashier would hesitate to pay a cheque at once and refer it to his or her superior, and when any reasonable superior would hesitate to authorise payment without inquiry, that a cheque should not be paid immediately on presentation and such inquiry made.[29]

Parker LJ thought that the plaintiff must establish that 'there was a serious or real possibility that C was drawing on the client account and using the funds so obtained for his own and not the solicitors' or beneficiaries' purposes'.[30]

On the facts, the Court found in *Lipkin* that there was no breach of the duty. That finding may provide some comfort to bankers, indicating that they will only be held liable where what is occurring is more or less blatant. Parker LJ notes that the bank manager knew of C's gambling and that the bank manager would not have retained C as a customer but for C's association with the plaintiff firm of solicitors. However, that apparently was not enough, even when coupled with the fact that the cheque was payable to a gambling club, to lead a reasonable bank manager to believe that there was 'a serious or real possibility' that the cheque might be a fraud on the client account. Thus, it is true that a bank must exercise some standard of care in following the mandate of its customer, but the standard required is not very high.[31]

7.5 Safe custody

Banks routinely offer safe custody services for the chattels of their customers. Such arrangements, of course, constitute a bailment of the chattels, and the bank becomes a bailee. The law of bailment has a long and complex history. We will content ourselves with a brief outline of the current position in relation to bankers as bailees.

A bailee owes two duties with respect to bailed goods:

(1) to take such care of the bailed goods as is reasonable to protect them from loss or damage in all the circumstances of the case
(2) to deliver the goods to the bailor or as the bailor directs on termination of the bailment.

---

29 Ibid 421.
30 Ibid 441.
31 In recent times there has been growing concern over online scams or 'authorised push payment' frauds where the victim transfers money to a fraudster's account, erroneously believing the fraudster to be their child in peril or a government authority. In *Philipp v Barclays Bank UK plc* [2023] 3 WLR 284, Philipp was falsely led by a fraudster to believe that her substantial savings in Barclays Bank had to be moved to 'safe accounts'. The fraudster claimed to be 'DC Claridge', a representative of the 'National Crime Agency'. The 'safe accounts' were in fact in the United Arab Emirates (UAE). The Court ruled that Barclays Bank had not breached its duty. Despite the large amounts of money forwarded to the UAE accounts, Philipp had given the instructions and confirmed it in person. The bank thus had no reason to enquire further.

The second duty is a strict duty, and the bailor will be liable in conversion or detinue for misdelivery or failure to deliver, even in the absence of negligence. In case of doubt, the bank may retain the goods for a reasonable period to make enquiries (*Clayton v Le Roy*[32]). If there is a dispute between contending parties regarding rightful possession, the bank should interplead.

As regards the first duty, in our case, as the bailee is a banker, the bank must exercise the same standard of care that a reasonable bank in the same circumstances would exercise with respect to the goods.

Those circumstances include whether the bailee has professed skill in the type of bailment in question, which is presumably the case with banks offering safe deposit services, and more particularly, if the bailment is gratuitous or for reward. A bailee for reward may be expected to exercise a higher standard of care than a gratuitous bailee. This is because in the latter case, only the bailor derives a benefit from the bailment, whereas in the former the bailment is in the interests of both.

The distinction between a gratuitous bailment and one for reward is also pertinent to a bailee's vicarious liability. A gratuitous bailee is liable only for their negligence, but not for that of their employees, unless it can be shown that a reasonable bailee would not, in similar circumstances, have entrusted the goods to the care of their employee. A bailee for reward is vicariously liable for the negligence of their employees, subject to the usual requirements concerning vicarious liability being met (see, eg, *Makower, McBeath & Co v Dalgety & Co Ltd*[33]).

These days, many banks charge a fee for safe deposit services, so the issue is not usually in doubt. Some may still provide a limited 'complimentary' safe deposit service. In such cases, to the extent that it comes as part of the broader banker–customer contract, it is likely to be considered a bailment for reward. That said, however, there exists some old - much criticised - authority to the contrary.

In an action for negligence, it is necessary for the bailor to prove the bailment, but the onus of proof is then on the bailee to show that loss/damage was not due to the want of care (*Port Swettenham Authority v TW Wu and Co (M) Sdn Bhd*;[34] *Pitt Son & Badgery Ltd v Proulefco SA*[35]). The latter is, of course, a reversal of the normal onus. This can be justified, as the goods are in the possession of the bailee, who is much better positioned than the bailor to establish the cause of the loss.

A bailee may seek to limit or exclude liability for negligence using an exclusion clause. The usual principles as to exclusion clauses apply. In the case of a customer who is a consumer, the *Australian Consumer Law* ss 60 and 64 import a non-excludable guarantee into contracts for services that the service will be rendered with due care and skill. The term 'services' encompasses an agreement between a customer and a banker that occurs while the banker is conducting banking business. Since safe custody has long been a part of the business of banking, there is little doubt of the applicability of these

32 *Clayton v Le Roy* [1911] 2 KB 1031.
33 *Makower, McBeth & Co Ltd v Dalgety & Co Ltd* [1921] VLR 365.
34 *Port Swettenham Authority v TW Wu and Co Sdn Bhd* [1979] AC 580.
35 *Pitt Son & Badgery Ltd v Proulefco SA* (1984) 153 CLR 644.

provisions with respect to safe deposit services offered by banks to 'consumers' as that term is defined in the *Australian Consumer Law.*

7.6 The *Macmillan* duty

Customers owe banks the *Macmillan* duty, which is the duty to take reasonable care when drawing cheques to prevent fraud. The duty owes its name to the House of Lords' decision in *London Joint Stock Bank Ltd v Macmillan & Arthur,*[36] although one may track it back to *Young v Grote,*[37] a decision made almost a century earlier.

The duty has had a chequered career in Australia. In 1904, the High Court of Australia held in *Marshall v Colonial Bank of Australasia*[38] that there was no such duty. The Court relied on criticism of *Young v Grote* by Lord Halsbury LC in the 1896 House of Lords decision in *Scholfield v Earl of Londesborough.*[39] *Marshall* went on appeal to the Privy Council in 1906, but the High Court of Australia decision was upheld. *Scholfield* was not a case that involved the customer–banker relationship; it concerned the liability of an acceptor of a bill of exchange to a holder in due course. Subsequently, it was decided in *Macmillan* that *Young v Grote* was correctly decided and supported by a powerful body of authority and by policy considerations, and that its authority was not confined by *Scholfield. Macmillan* was subsequently adopted in New Zealand, India, Canada and South Africa. Nevertheless, *Marshall* remained the law in Australia until it was overruled in 1981, in a 7–0 decision by the High Court of Australia, in *Commonwealth Trading Bank of Australia v Sydney Wide Stores Pty Ltd.*[40] Gibbs CJ and Stephen, Mason, Aicken, Wilson and Brennan JJ delivered a joint judgment. Their Honours, in a detailed, historically oriented judgment, made three points in support of *Macmillan*:

(1) Fairness between a banker and a customer dictates that the customer should assume responsibility for a loss resulting from their negligent issuance of a cheque, particularly when that loss stems from fraud. This places a duty on the drawer, as they are simply expected to exercise reasonable care while drawing the cheque.

(2) The *Marshall* view places a significant weight on bankers, leaving them with limited avenues for safeguarding their interests. In contrast, the *Macmillan* viewpoint enhances the negotiability of cheques by giving banks, who must promptly assess the authenticity of a number of cheques, the confidence that a negligent drawer will not increase the risk of loss due to fraudulent alteration without being held accountable for the resulting outcomes.

(3) A persuasive differentiation cannot be established between a situation where the negligent drawing of a cheque results in loss due to fraudulent alteration of the amount, and one where the customer issues a blank cheque and their agent surpasses the authorised amount when filling it out. In the latter scenario, the law has held the drawer responsible.

36 *London Joint Stock Bank Ltd v Macmillan & Arthur* [1918] AC 777.
37 *Young v Grote* (1827) 4 Bing 253; 130 ER 764.
38 *Marshall v Colonial Bank of Australasia* (1904) 1 CLR 632.
39 *Scholfield v Earl of Londesborough* [1896] AC 514.
40 *Commonwealth Trading Bank of Australia v Sydney Wide Stores Pty Ltd* (1981) 148 CLR 304.

Murphy J delivered a separate three-paragraph judgment that provides an instructive model of his jurisprudential method.

The central question revolves around whether a customer who, albeit innocently, carelessly drafts a cheque, thus enabling forgery, should be held accountable for any bank losses resulting from this forgery. The answer delves into the realms of precedent, contemporary negligence theories, and societal policies. The binding precedent in question is the case of *Marshall v Colonial Bank of Australasia Ltd.*[41] In this case, the Privy Council upheld the ruling of this Court, which determined that the drawer should not be held liable. However, this decision stands apart from modern progress of the duty of care principles in both tort and contract law.

In terms of social policy, a valid question arises regarding whether it would be 'better' to continue placing the burden of loss on the banking industry. While the level of care exhibited by cheque drawers may be described as low, Murphy J was not convinced that the application of the Marshall decision has placed a substantial burden on banks. If, in practice, the losses, while burdensome for individual customers, are comparatively minor for the entire banking system, considering the substantial volume of cheque transactions, it might be sensible to maintain the current system of distributing the losses. Furthermore, if the cumulative losses remain relatively small, it would be unreasonable to impose a standard of care that would require every cheque drawer to view their employees and associates as potential forgers. To avoid undesirable social consequences and align this area of the law with other areas, as well as with the laws in other countries, a standard of care could be adopted that doesn't transform our society into one of suspicion. Therefore, the Marshall view should be overruled, and in accordance with contemporary principles of care, the negligent drawer should assume liability, without necessitating an exceptionally high standard of care.

While one may find so much for the theoretical justification, it also raises questions about its practical implications. Almost all the cases where the duty has been successfully deployed involve the drawer leaving convenient spaces into which the fraudulent party, to whom they freely hand over the cheque, can easily write characters that change the nature of the cheque. *Macmillan* itself provides an example of this.

A clerk was employed by a firm of stockbrokers. As part of his duties, he prepared cheques for the signature by the partners. On instructions, the clerk prepared a cheque payable to the firm itself or bearer. The amount of the cheque was not entered into the place for the amount written in words, but in the place for figures, the clerk entered the instructed amount of £2, thus: £ 2 / 00 / 00. The cheque was duly signed and returned to the clerk. The clerk added the words 'One hundred and twenty pounds' in the space for the amount in words and filled in the space in the amount in figures so that it read '£120 / 00 / 00'. He presented it for payment to the firm's bank, who obliged. The firm sued the bank for £118. Although the firm succeeded at first instance and in the Court of Appeal, the House of Lords held that there had been a breach of the duty.

41 *Marshall v Colonial Bank of Australasia* (1904) 1 CLR 632.

Slingsby v District Bank Ltd[42] is another notable example illustrating this duty.

In this case, the executor of a will instructed his solicitors, 'Messrs C&P', to draw a cheque in favour of a stockbroker. The solicitors did this; the executor signed the cheque. One of the solicitors then utilised the rather large space left between the name of the stockbroker and the words 'or order' to add the words 'per pro Messrs C&P' (ie through the agency of Messrs C&P). The solicitor endorsed the cheque to himself, presented it for payment, and had the proceeds paid into his personal account. The executor successfully sued the bank to recover the money. The bank could not rely on the *Macmillan* duty because the endorsement was irregular (as it was not expressed as being made in the capacity of an agent), and the bank should have realised this. The cheque would not have been paid, but for the subsequent negligence of the bank.

The bank may increase the level of care required by the customer by giving explicit instructions on how cheques should be drawn. However, the usual *Tai Hing* requirements must be met: the instructions and the consequences of failing to heed them must be brought to the customer's attention.

It has been argued that *Macmillan*'s scope is too limited, since it seems that this duty pertains solely to the drafting of cheques.[43] However, recent developments have challenged this view. The *Macmillan* principle has been broadened to encompass telegraphic transfers, which are frequently employed for international payments, as exemplified by the Supreme Court of Victoria in the case of *National Australia Bank Ltd v Nemur Varity Pty Ltd*.[44] Likewise, there have been discussions about extending this duty to encompass automated teller machines (ATMs).[45] Consequently, a customer may be held accountable for unauthorised transactions on a stolen card that they neglected to report to the bank.[46] In the same vein, they are required to exercise due care when conducting electronic transfers. The bank terms and conditions may also stipulate that customers do not share their personal identification number (PIN) with anyone, securely dispose of receipts, and shield their PIN when using ATMs.[47]

7.7 The *Greenwood* duty

This duty is straightforward: the customer is obliged to notify the bank of any forgeries known to them. The justification is also evident. The bank bears the risk of payment on a forged signature. It would be unfair to allow the customer to stand aside and expose the bank to loss when the customer was in a position to prevent any loss

42 *Slingsby v District Bank Ltd* [1932] 1 KB 544.

43 Sandra Booysen, 'The Legacy of Cheques on the Evolution of a Bank Customer's Duties: Enduring Principles regarding Risk Allocation' (2022) 38 *Banking and Finance Law Review* 35.

44 *National Australia Bank Ltd v Nemur Varity Pty Ltd* (2002) 4 VR 252.

45 Bill Davies, 'What is the Extent of the Customer's Duty Not to Facilitate Fraud' (2009) 30(11) *Business Law Review* 238.

46 Alan L Tyree, 'The Legal Nature of Electronic Money' (1999) 10(4) *Journal of Banking and Finance Law and Practice* 273.

47 Davies (n 45).

simply by saying something. The duty extends to notifying the bank of any unauthorised transaction on the account known to the customer (*West v Commercial Bank of Australia Ltd*[48]).

The Court in *Greenwood* attempted to find the duty in estoppel by representation, or so commentators have asserted. *If* there *is* a duty to disclose a known forgery, then failure to disclose one certainly amounts to a misrepresentation that there is no forgery. But that hardly establishes a duty to disclose that there is a known forgery. The duty arises from an implied term of the customer–banker contract.

Brown v Westminster Bank Ltd[49] and *Tina Motors Pty Ltd v Australia and New Zealand Banking Group Ltd*[50] are the cases where the customer knew of the forgeries and did not inform the bank at the time. By application of *Greenwood*, the bank is not liable for payment on the cheques, irrespective of any later representation by the customer that the cheques were fine. If, on the other hand, the customer was unaware of the forgeries until queried by the bank, at which time the customer represents that cheques of this type are fine, then the bank can only claim immunity with respect to cheques paid after the representation was made. There cannot be any reliance on a representation before the representation being made.

By way of illustration, consider the facts adapted from *Brown v Westminster Bank Ltd.*[51]

Mrs B's servant forges Mrs B's signature on cheques. Mrs B is unaware of this. The bank approaches Mrs B, who assures the bank that cheques signed in this manner are fine. The bank can only avoid liability on cheques honoured after the representation. If, on the other hand, Mrs B was aware of the forgeries from the beginning, then the bank can invoke *Greenwood* with respect to all the cheques.

7.8 Other possible duties

From time to time, bankers have attempted to have other customer duties implied in the banker–customer contract. For the present purpose, we consider the following.

- a duty to make reasonable efforts to discover forgeries
- a duty (beyond *Macmillan*) to prevent forgeries, usually in the way of taking reasonable care in keeping chequebooks, passbooks, etc
- a broader duty of care by the customer to take reasonable steps to 'organise' their affairs to avoid a loss to the bank.

The courts have been resistant to these attempts, probably because there is little or no justification for their implication either by fact or by custom or usage, and to a lesser extent because it is always open for banks to attempt to impose them by way of the express contractual agreement should they wish.

48 *West v Commercial Bank of Australia Ltd* (1935) 55 CLR 315.
49 *Brown v Westminster Bank Ltd* [1964] 2 Lloyd's Rep 187.
50 *Tina Motors Pty Ltd v Australia and New Zealand Banking Group Ltd* [1977] VR 205.
51 *Brown v Westminster Bank Ltd* [1964] 2 Lloyd's Rep 187.

7.8.1 Duty to discover forgeries

If there is any such implied duty, then, at the very least, it includes an obligation to examine passbook entries/statements and to notify the bank of irregularities. There is so much authority across various jurisdictions stating that this is not so (eg *Kepitagalla Rubber Estates Ltd v National Bank of India Ltd,*[52] *Walker v Manchester and Liverpool District Banking Ltd,*[53] *National Bank of New Zealand Ltd v Walpole and Patterson Ltd*[54] and *Tai Hing Cotton Mill Ltd v Liu Chong Hing Bank Ltd*[55]) that it is remarkable that banks continue to argue the point.[56]

7.8.2 Duty to prevent forgeries

Attempts to argue that the bank should not be liable where the fraud has resulted from negligence in keeping the company seal have met with no success (see, eg, *Bank of Ireland v Evans Charities Trustees in Ireland*[57] and *Northside Developments Pty Ltd v Registrar-General*[58]). The question of whether a customer had a duty to take care of a printed chequebook issued by the bank was considered by the NSW Court of Appeal in *Westpac Banking Corporation v Metlej.*[59]

A partnership account required the signature of both partners on cheques. A practice was adopted whereby one partner signed cheques in blank and left the book with the other, M, for completion as necessary. M carried the chequebook with him and habitually left it in his lunchbox in his car. Three of the pre-signed forms were stolen from the book. M noticed the fact after hours on 6 December and notified the bank of it on the morning of 7 December. The cheques were presented with M's signature forged and cashed over the counter by the bank on 7, 12 and 23 December. The total amount involved was $62 000.

Even leaving aside the fact that the bank apparently cashed the cheques after it had notice of the theft of the forms, it is hard to understand how the case made it to the Court of Appeal. As it happened, the Court found it unnecessary to decide whether a duty was owed to take reasonable care of the chequebook. Probably, there is a bailee's duty if the chequebook is considered the property of the bank. In any event, if any such duty existed, it could hardly have caused the loss. It was the failure of the bank to recognise the forgery that resulted in the loss. A bank is not authorised to debit a customer's account on the basis of a forged signature, since the banker has no mandate from the customer to do so. On this score, see also the *Cheques Act* s 32 and *National Westminster Bank Ltd v Barclays Bank International Ltd.*[60] A forged cheque is not a cheque – at least, not a cheque of the customer whose signature has been forged. The maxim is that a bank has a duty to know

52 *Kepitigalla Rubber Estates Ltd v National Bank of India Ltd* [1909] 2 KB 1010.
53 *Walker v Manchester and Liverpool District Banking Ltd* (1913) 29 TLR 492.
54 *National Bank of New Zealand Ltd v Walpole and Patterson Ltd* [1975] 2 NZLR 7.
55 *Tai Hing Cotton Mill Ltd v Liu Chong Hing Bank Ltd* [1986] AC 80.
56 In the presence of a verification clause, it is likely that the customer is obliged to verify the bank statement and inform the bank if there is any discrepancy. See ibid.
57 *Bank of Ireland v Evans Charities Trusteed in Ireland* (1855) 10 ER 950.
58 *Northside Developments Pty Ltd v Registrar-General* (1990) 170 CLR 146.
59 *Westpac Banking Corporation v Metlej* (1987) Aust Torts Rep 80-102.
60 *National Westminster Bank Ltd v Barclays Bank International Ltd* [1975] QB 654.

its customer's signature. Moreover, one should bear in mind that there is no requirement that cheques should be drawn on pre-printed bank forms. Any supposed duty of the customer to take any particular step to prevent forgeries runs up against this problem. Even if such a duty exists, it will be the supervening failure of the bank to recognise the forgery that causes the loss. Note that this difficulty does not apply in *Greenwood* cases, because there, the customer is estopped from pleading the forgery.

7.8.3 Duty to organise business

The same difficulty must necessarily arise in relation to a more general duty for the customer to reasonably organise their business to minimise the possibility of forgery. That is, the duty of the bank to know their customer's signature must be excused in the case where the customer does not organise their business practices to reasonably avoid the possibility of forgery, or the customer must be estopped from pleading the forgery in such cases. There is a trade-off being asked for, an adjustment of the balance that appeals to the imposition of a 'fair' burden on both sides. The assumption is that the balance is not currently fair, and that the particular adjustment sought will not only make it so but will also ensure that the two duties can be logically set off one against the other.

National Australia Bank Ltd v Hokit Pty Ltd[61] illustrates these issues clearly. In that case, more than 530 cheques were forged by a bookkeeper, B, over a four-year period. The mandate was that they should be signed by a director of the company (its effective controller). A few of the cheques were forged with the knowledge and approval of the director in question. The company did not claim against the bank concerning these. The bank could clearly avail itself of *Greenwood* regarding them. The other forgeries were without the knowledge or consent of the customer company and for B's benefit. The company's lack of adequate controls and accounting procedures facilitated the fraud. The bank made two arguments:

(1) That had the customer complied with the *Greenwood* duty and notified the bank of the 'authorised' forgeries, the bank would have taken steps that would have avoided the other forgeries being paid.
(2) That the exceptions for bank liability in the event of forged cheques extended, either as a result of an implied contractual term or in tort, to impose on the customer a duty to take reasonable care to prevent forgery and to detect unauthorised cheque transactions.

The Court held as follows:

- The *Greenwood* argument failed because the bank provided no evidence to support it; it was sheer speculation what the bank might have done beyond perhaps instructing the company to prohibit the behaviour, which was unlikely to have any effect on B's behaviour with respect to unauthorised forgeries.
- The implied term argument failed because there was no evidence for such a term implied by custom and usage, and no such term was capable of being implied by

61 *National Australia Bank Ltd v Hokit Pty Ltd* (1996) 39 NSWLR 377.

the fact because it was not so obvious as to go without saying and because it was not necessary to give the contract efficacy.

- The tort argument failed because the Court was unwilling to create (and could see no compelling policy justification for creating) what would be a new duty of care along the suggested lines, and because there was no existing duty of care with which the proposed duty could be reconciled. In particular, the bank was unable to establish pre-conditions for negligence for purely economic loss: for example, reliance by the bank and assumption of responsibility by the company concerning the maintenance of the company's books so as to prevent fraud. (In this regard, see also Clarke JA, who drew on *Sutherland Shire Council v Heyman*,[62] *Hawkins v Clayton*[63] and *San Sebastian Pty Ltd v Minister Administering Environmental Planning and Assessment Act 1979 (NSW)*[64].)

7.9 Summary

The relationship between the bank and the customer gives rise to several duties on the part of the bank as well as the customer. Among others, we have examined in detail the *Tournier* duty (ie the duty to keep the customer's information in confidence save for exceptions); the *Macmillan* duty (ie the duty to exercise reasonable care in drawing cheques so as not to facilitate fraud), and the *Greenwood* duty (ie the duty to notify the bank of any forgeries known to the customer). These duties, as applied in case law, are of both theoretical and practical importance for academics, professionals and practitioners in the field.

FURTHER READING

Aitken, Lee, 'The Banker's Obligation to Pay and the Scope of the Quincecare Duty' (2021) 32(1) *Journal of Banking and Finance Law and Practice* 43.

Busch, Danny, 'The Future of the Special Duty of Care in the Financial Sector – Perspectives from the Netherlands' (2021) 32(3) *European Business Law Review* 473.

Plato-Shinar, Ruth, 'The Right to Financial Privacy in an Era of Mandatory Duties of Disclosure' (2022) 38 *Banking & Finance Law Review* 285.

Santiago, Faisal, 'Banking Responsibility to Customers' (2018) 21(1) *European Research Studies Journal* 321.

QUESTIONS

(1) Katherine and Andrew's daughter, Grace, age 20, disappeared after leaving a brief note that stated: 'I'm going to find my own life.' Over the next few months, Grace made only one brief phone call to her parents to let them know she was safe.

62 *Sutherland Shire Council v Heyman* [1982] 2 NSWLR 618.

63 *Hawkins v Clayton* (1988) 164 CLR 539.

64 *San Sebastian Pty Ltd v Minister Administering Environmental Planning and Assessment Act 1979 (NSW)* (1986) 162 CLR 340.

Katherine and Andrew knew that Grace banked with the ABC Bank. In an attempt to learn the whereabouts of their daughter, they phoned the bank to find out the locations of the ATMs where Grace was making regular withdrawals. Advise the ABC Bank.

(2) Vince had injured his dominant arm in a motor vehicle accident and could write only with difficulty. He had received a large compensation payout. He spoke with the manager of his local bank about managing his finances and using a cheque account. Because of Vince's difficulty with writing and his previous inexperience with cheques, the manager explained the need for care when drawing cheques and how to write one. Vince occasionally drew cheques for four-figure sums. When he did so, he had used the word 'thousand' in describing the amount. He also occasionally drew cheques payable to 'cash or bearer' but had not done so for amounts of more than $200. When the first of these 'cash or bearer' cheques had been presented for payment, the accountant at the bank telephoned Vince to confirm the cheque and to warn Vince that cheques should not be drawn in this manner if they were intended for a specific payee. On the occasion in question, a cheque was written by Vince's brother-in-law on Vince's instructions and signed by Vince. It was payable to 'cash or bearer' and was for the amount of $140.00. It had the amount 'one hundred and forty' in the place where the amount was to be written in words, but there was a space in front of the 'one'. Likewise, in the place for figures, there was a space between the '$' and '140.00'. Having been asked to cash the cheque, Vince's brother-in-law inserted the word 'sixty-' in front of 'one' and the numeral '6' in front of '140.00', thus making out the cheque (apparently) for sixty-one hundred and forty dollars. He deposited the cheque for collection with his own bank, and it was duly paid by Vince's bank. The brother-in-law decamped with the money, and Vince sued his bank to recover $6000.00. Could the bank successfully rely on *Macmillan*?

(3) Discuss the applicability of the *Macmillan* duty in the contemporary banking setting.

CHAPTER 8

CHEQUES AND BILLS OF EXCHANGE

8.1 Introduction

In the intricate tapestry of financial transactions, two instruments play pivotal roles in facilitating trade and commerce: cheques and bills of exchange. As we embark on a journey through the labyrinth of these financial instruments, this chapter aims to provide the foundational principles that underpin their functionality and significance.

Cheques, the stalwart of modern banking, serve as a ubiquitous means of transferring funds and making payments. Understanding the anatomy of a cheque, from its issuance to its negotiation, is imperative for individuals and businesses navigating the intricate landscape of financial transactions. In parallel, the enigmatic world of bills of exchange beckons our attention. Unravelling the complexities of bills of exchange, we will explore their role in facilitating international commerce and the intricate mechanisms governing their acceptance and negotiation. Despite their ancient roots dating back centuries, these instruments continue to exert influence in contemporary trade, albeit with an acknowledgement that their impact is gradually diminishing.

This chapter provides a comprehensive primer on the basics of cheques and bills of exchange. The chapter aims to set a foundation upon which to build a nuanced comprehension of these indispensable components in the realm of finance and commerce.

8.2 Cheques[1]

For a long time, cheques were the main – if not the only – means of third-party payment and deposit from and to bank accounts. The process is simple. A customer provides a third party with a cheque that contains important details such as their account number, the date of issue, a payment amount and an endorsement (their signature). The third party then gives this cheque to a bank. The bank confirms the authenticity of the cheque and processes it. If necessary, this requires communicating with the customer's bank if the third party and the customer bank with different banks. The end result is the transference of money from the customer's bank account to the third party's account.

The use of cheques has long been on the decline, displaced by electronic transfers and card transactions, but the law relating to those is informed to some degree by that relating to cheques, as their historical precursor. Furthermore, cheques are still used in large quantities and continue to account for the majority of legal problems with payment. In fact, although they constitute only about 5 per cent of all non-cash payments, there are still 600 000 cheques written daily in Australia (compared to 3 million in 2000). Cheques remain very convenient because the only information needed to make a payment is the payee's name. Also, the payee does not need to have any special facilities or technology in place to deal with them. At most, they may require only a bank account – and not even that if the payee can negotiate their cheques. However, because cheques need to be handled manually, they are more expensive for banks to process and take longer to process than a card and other electronic payments.

1 Unless otherwise specified, provisions referred to are contained in the *Cheques Act 1986* (Cth) ('*Cheques Act*').

Cheques are negotiable instruments and were formerly regulated by the *Bills of Exchange Act 1909* (Cth) ('*Bills of Exchange Act*'), which defined them as 'a bill of exchange drawn on a banker, payable on demand' (s 8). However, they are now regulated under a separate Act, the *Cheques Act 1986* (Cth). The *Bills of Exchange Act* was amended so that its provisions do not apply to cheques as defined in the *Cheques Act*.[2]

The *Cheques Act* introduced four main changes from the provisions regarding cheques in the *Bills of Exchange Act*:

(1) It is not possible to make a cheque non-transferable.
(2) Endorsement is not required in some instances to transfer an order cheque (a cheque that only a specified individual may use).
(3) Banks have protection against actions for losses suffered by holders or customers due to lack of endorsements.
(4) Presentment for payment may be made without presentation of the instrument itself but 'by particulars'.

We will discuss these, except for the second change,[3] in due course.

8.2.1 Definitions

8.2.1.1 Cheque

The *Cheques Act* also defines a cheque slightly differently from the definition given in the *Bills of Exchange Act*, as follows:

(a) an unconditional order in writing
(b) addressed by a person to another person, being a financial institution
(c) signed by the person giving it
(d) requiring the financial institution to pay on demand a sum certain in money.[4]

There are two notable differences:

(1) The drawee must be a financial institution.
(2) The identity of the payee need not be specified.

8.2.1.2 Financial institution

'Financial institution' is defined in the *Cheques Act* s 3(1) as any of the following: the Reserve Bank of Australia, an authorised deposit-taking institution, a state bank, or a person who carries on the business of banking outside Australia. Section 13 of the Act specifies that the order must be addressed only to one financial institution and no one else. So, an instrument drawn on 'Bank A and Bank B' would not be a cheque within the meaning of the *Cheques Act*. Recall that such a drawing would be acceptable under the *Bills of Exchange Act*. An instrument drawn in this way would thus be governed by the provisions of the *Bills of Exchange Act* governing cheques.[5] We will not discuss those provisions, as they are broadly similar to

2 *Bills of Exchange Act 1909* (Cth) ('*Bills of Exchange Act*') s 6(2).
3 It is the subject of *Cheques Act* (n 1) s 42 and is not of particular interest for our purposes.
4 Ibid s 10.
5 *Bills of Exchange Act* (n 2) pt 3.

those in the *Cheques Act* and because cheques of this nature are likely to be rare. However, the point should be borne in mind that occasionally one might come across instruments that do not fall within the definition of a cheque for the purposes of the *Cheques Act* but which, nevertheless, are a cheque of another stripe, inhabiting a kind of nether world regulated still by the *Bills of Exchange Act*. We will see another possible example shortly.

8.2.1.3 No payee

Cheques need not name a payee. Cheques are and were commonly drawn to 'Cash' or 'Wages', and although usually honoured as bearer cheques, there was potential for difficulties to arise. The courts were unwilling to adopt the obvious solution, which was to treat 'Cash' and 'Wages' as fictitious payees; rather, they took the view that, as these cheques named no payee, they were therefore not cheques.[6] The *Cheques Act* avoids this problem by providing that cheques that do not name a payee are payable to the bearer.[7]

8.2.1.4 Sum certain

As with bills of exchange, if more than one sum is written on the cheque, the cheque is taken to be for the smaller amount.[8] The *Cheques Act* s 15(1) provides that to be a 'sum certain', the sum must be 'specified with reasonable certainty', while s 4 preserves the common law rules concerning cheques (insofar as they are consistent with the express provisions of the Act). Therefore, one can say that probably expressions such as '$300.00 together with interest thereon from the date drawn' are fine. However, in *Standard Bank of Canada v Wiley*,[9] the Full Court of the New South Wales Supreme Court held that a sum expressed as 'with bank charges' was not a sum certain. This led to the amendment of the *Bills of Exchange Act* s 14 so that a 'sum payable ... is a sum certain within the meaning of this Act, although it is required to be paid with ... bank charges'. Notably, the *Cheques Act* contains no such provision. Thus, it would seem that an instrument requiring payment of such a sum expressed in such terms would not be a cheque within the meaning of the *Cheques Act* (because the sum would not be a sum certain within the meaning of that Act), although it would be a cheque within the meaning of the *Bills of Exchange Act* (and so the provisions of that Act in relation to cheques would apply to it).

8.2.1.5 Unconditional order

The order must be unconditional, and the discussion on this point as per bills of exchange applies here. Because cheques are used primarily as a means of payment, sometimes – although rarely these days – they come with a receipt attached which the payee is to sign (indicating that the payee acknowledges that the payment is in respect of the underlying transaction, whatever that may be). If the receipt amounts to an instruction to the payee that the instrument should not be paid unless the receipt

6 See, eg, *Orbit Mining v Westminster Bank* [1963] 1 QB 794.
7 *Cheques Act* (n 1) ss 10, 20, 22.
8 Ibid s 15(2).
9 *Standard Bank of Canada v Wiley* (1919) 19 SR (NSW) 384.

is completed (eg 'Pay X on completion of the attached receipt'), then the order to the payee is conditional and the instrument is not a cheque. If, however, the instruction is not to the drawee, then the order remains unconditional (eg 'the payee should complete the attached receipt').

In *Bavins Jnr & Sims v London & South Western Bank Ltd*,[10] an order which read 'Pay to B Bavins the sum of sixty-nine pounds provided the receipt at the foot hereof is signed' was held to be conditional. On the other hand, in *Nathan v Odgens Ltd*,[11] words at the foot of the cheque that read 'The receipt at the back hereof must be signed' were held as being not conditional as directed to the drawee but to the payee.

Generally speaking, words that come before the drawer's signature are more likely to be considered part of the order. In contrast, those that come beneath it are more likely to be considered purely auxiliary and not as qualifying the order.

8.2.1.6 Note on unconditional order – conditional delivery

A cheque may be *delivered* to the payee conditional on a specific event or for a particular purpose. The instruction is not to the drawee and so does not make the *order to pay* conditional. Rather, it is to the payee that the cheque is *issued* subject to certain conditions. The payee does not receive property in the cheque and has no right to present it for payment until the condition is met. This is recognised in the *Cheques Act* s 27.

In *Spalla v St George Wholesale Finance Pty Ltd*,[12] a cheque was delivered to the payee under the express oral condition that it would not be presented for payment until the payee received advice that there were funds available to meet it. The cheque was presented for payment without the payee having received such advice, and the payment was refused. The drawer was not liable.

In *Neonbrook Pty Ltd v Thusi Pty Ltd*,[13] the cheque had been drawn by a third party as security for a debt on the condition that it only be presented if there were default on the debt. There was no default, but the creditor presented the cheque for payment. This was refused. It was held that the cheque had not been dishonoured, since the condition of delivery was not satisfied.

Note, however, the provision in the *Cheques Act* s 28 that, as regards a holder in due course, the drawer is *conclusively presumed* to have made unconditional delivery. As regards a mere holder, the presumption is rebuttable.

8.2.1.7 On demand

According to the *Cheques Act* s 14, an order is an order to pay on demand if it requires payment 'on demand', 'at sight' or 'on presentation'. In fact, almost all cheques make no stipulation at all. Section 14(1) also provides that a cheque is payable on demand if no time is expressed for payment. This is consistent with bills of exchange.

10 *Bavins Jnr & Sims v London & South Western Bank Ltd* [1900] 1 QB 270.
11 *Nathan v Ogdens Ltd* (1905) 93 LT 553.
12 *Spalla v St George Wholesale Finance Pty Ltd* (1999) 95 FCR 359.
13 *Neonbrook Pty Ltd v Thusi Pty Ltd* [1999] 1 Qd R 429.

8.2.1.8 Date

Just as for a bill of exchange, a date is not necessary for a cheque; however, if it bears one, that is presumed to be the date on which it was drawn.[14] The *Cheques Act* s 16 also recognises the validity of post-dated cheques. The logical difficulty with a post-dated cheque – that it cannot be payable 'on demand' – is obviated by s 61(2), which provides that any attempt to obtain payment on a cheque prior to its date is not a valid presentment for payment. This has consequences for the parties to a post-dated cheque, since the drawer and others cannot be liable on a cheque until such time as it is presented for payment. Case law indicates that a post-dated cheque can be validly negotiated prior to its date.[15]

8.2.1.9 Order and bearer cheques

The *Cheques Act* s 22 says that any cheque is a bearer cheque that is not an order cheque; while s 21 says that a cheque is an order cheque if it is expressed, either originally or by endorsement, to require the drawee institution to pay the cheque to or to the order of a person or persons (jointly or in the alternative) as payee or endorsee.

Taking s 21 at face value would indicate that bearer cheques governed by the *Cheques Act* can be converted by endorsement to order cheques.

8.2.2 Transfer by negotiation

Transfer is as per bills of exchange. Bearer cheques are negotiated by delivery, order cheques by endorsement. Delivery and rules as to endorsement are also generally as per bills of exchange.[16] Note that the *Cheques Act* s 39 provides that every cheque may be transferred by negotiation until it is discharged, *notwithstanding anything written or placed on the cheque*. Thus, it is not possible to limit the transferability of a cheque by means of anything written on it. For example, a cheque expressed as 'Pay X only' will be treated as a regular order cheque transferable by X through endorsement and delivery. We will revert to this point again shortly when we discuss the effect of crossing cheques with the notation 'account payee only'.

8.2.3 Role of the drawer's signature

The drawer's signature has three roles:

(1) As a formality necessary to bring the cheque into being[17] (s 10).

(2) To establish the liability of the drawer in the event of an action by a holder.[18] A forged or unauthorised signature is wholly inoperative as the signature of the person it purports to be, unless the signature is adopted or ratified or there is an estoppel. The situation as to estoppel is the same as for bills of exchange. However, the forged/unauthorised signature operates as the signature of the

14 *Cheques Act* (n 1) s 16.
15 *Hodgson & Lee Pty Ltd v Mardonius Pty Ltd* (1986) 5 NSWLR 496.
16 *Cheques Act* (n 1) s 40.
17 Ibid s 10.
18 Ibid s 31.

person who wrote it in favour of any person who takes or pays on the cheque without notice.[19]

(3) As the authorisation whereby the drawer gives a mandate to their bank to pay on the cheque and debit the customer's account for the amount paid. This is a consequence not of the *Cheques Act* but of the banker–customer contract.

8.2.4 Crossings

8.2.4.1 Definition

The *Cheques Act* s 53 (a model of clarity) provides:

> (1) Where a cheque clearly bears across the front of the cheque the addition of:
>
> (a) 2 parallel transverse lines; or
>
> (b) 2 parallel transverse lines with the words *not negotiable* between, or substantially between, the lines;
>
> the addition is a crossing of the cheque, and the cheque is a crossed cheque.
>
> (2) Nothing written or placed on a cheque, other than an addition of a kind referred to in subsection (1), is effective as a crossing of the cheque.
>
> (3) Without limiting the generality of subsection (2), the addition of the words *not negotiable* to a cheque otherwise than between, or substantially between, 2 parallel transverse lines across the front of the cheque is not effective as a crossing of the cheque.[20]

8.2.4.2 The effect of crossing

Crossing acts as an instruction by the drawer to the drawee not to pay the cheque otherwise than to a financial institution.[21] If the drawee does (ie pays the cheque 'over the counter'), then the customer may resist the debiting of their account. The addition of the words 'not negotiable' subjects the cheque to the *nemo dat* rule.

The *Cheques Act* s 55 provides:

> Where a cheque that bears a crossing of the kind referred to in paragraph 53(1)(b) is transferred by negotiation to a person, the person does not receive, and is not capable of giving, a better title to the cheque than the title that the person from whom the first-mentioned person took the cheque had.

The words do not mean that the cheque cannot be transferred per s 39 of the Act.

8.2.4.3 Who may cross

The drawer or any person in possession of the cheque may cross it.[22] They may add the words 'not negotiable' to a blank crossing, and they may add an entirely new crossing.[23]

19 Ibid s 32.
20 Ibid s 53.
21 Ibid s 54.
22 Ibid s 56.
23 Ibid s 57.

8.2.4.4 'Account payee only'

It is not uncommon for cheques to be annotated in this manner within a crossing. Essentially, the annotation has no effect.

The words cannot affect the ability to transfer the cheque.[24] Typically, as we will discuss later, the holder of a cheque will present it to their bank for collection from the drawer's bank. The annotation is towards the 'collecting bank' as they are the only party capable of knowing who the cheque is for. Consequently, any failure to ensure the cheque is collected for the specified account is beyond the control and liability of the bank.[25] Also, as the collecting bank has no contractual relationship with the drawer, there is no reason why they are bound to take any notice of the direction. The annotation can be no more than a warning to the collecting institution – putting them on notice – that the drawer intended that only the named payee was to collect on it. Thus, a collecting bank that paid on such a cheque without making inquiries that the holder was entitled to be paid would probably be denied the protection of the *Cheques Act* s 95. That section will be discussed further when we talk about misappropriated cheques. Still, essentially it provides that a collecting bank incurs no liability to the valid owner of a cheque if, in good faith and without negligence, it receives payment on a cheque and credits the account of a customer who has no title to the cheque.

8.2.5 Bank cheques

Bank cheques (otherwise referred to as 'bank drafts') are cheques drawn by a bank on itself. The payee will be nominated by the customer, and the cheque will be delivered to the customer. The customer's account will be debited for the amount of the cheque, and the bank will, in addition, charge a fee for the service. Bank cheques are regarded as a convenient alternative to carrying large amounts of cash, but as they are invariably crossed 'not negotiable', and as they may be dishonoured in the same way as any cheque and the drawing bank may raise the same defences as the drawer of any cheque, this is a simplistic view.[26] Their status essentially derives from the creditworthiness of the drawer. Beyond that, they are no different from any other cheque.

Under the *Bills of Exchange Act*, bank cheques were probably not cheques at all, as the Act required a cheque to be 'addressed by one person to *another*' (emphasis added). The *Cheques Act* uses the same phrase; however, s 5 of the Act expressly designates them as cheques, although the requirements as to form and certain requirements as to presentment do not apply to them.

8.2.6 Traveller's cheques

A traveller's cheque is an instrument whereby some entity orders its overseas correspondent entity to pay on the instrument against the customer's countersignature on the

24 Ibid s 39.

25 See, eg, *Universal Guarantee Pty Ltd v National Bank of Australasia Ltd* [1965] 1 WLR 691.

26 Indeed, where a person makes a claim that a bank cheque is 'as good as cash' or 'can be cashed at any bank' or similar and another relies on it to their detriment, as has happened, there is a breach of the *Australian Consumer Law* s 18. See *Lyritzis v Westpac Banking Corporation* (1994) ATPR 41-360.

instrument. (The customer is meant to sign the instrument at the time of its issue. Signing again when the instrument is to be cashed thus identifies them as the person entitled to be paid.) Thomas Cook and American Express were (and remain) the chief purveyors of traveller's cheques. Whether such an instrument is a cheque turns on whether the requirement of the customer's countersignature makes the order conditional. Probably it does, and so these instruments are probably not cheques, either under the *Cheques Act* or the *Bills of Exchange Act*. They may, however, form a separate class of negotiable instruments established by mercantile use. Their use has been in steep decline since the 1990s as alternatives such as credit and debit cards, and ATMs, have become widely available to international travellers. Other factors that have led to their decline include the fees charged by the issuer and agent, and the less favourable foreign exchange rate commonly used, compared to cards and ATMs. Given this instrument's declining role, we do not discuss it further in this book.

8.2.7 Payment by cheque

The routine use of a cheque is as a means of payment. The drawer makes the cheque out to the payee in exchange for some service or other. The cheque may then be negotiated further, but the eventual holder will usually present it to their bank for 'collection'. (This is the only option if the cheque is crossed.) Generally, the amount of the cheque will be credited to the holder's account immediately and interest (if any) will begin to accrue from that time, but the proceeds of the cheque will not become available to the holder until the cheque has been 'cleared'. This process typically takes three business days, but it can be expedited by payment of a fee. The holder's bank, called the 'collecting bank', acting as agent for the holder, will transmit the cheque (in fact, these days an electronic 'image' of it) to the drawer's bank, which will debit the account of the drawer, having conducted whatever checks it sees fit, and pay the proceeds to the collecting bank. The proceeds in the holder's account will then be made available to the holder. If the cheque is dishonoured, the initial credit to the holder's account will be reversed and the holder advised. In fact, the clearing process is not performed directly but via the Australian Paper Clearing System (APCS), run by the Australian Payments Clearing Association Limited (APCA), a company limited by guarantee and jointly owned by 24 of Australia's largest financial institutions. The system collates cheques for collection, processes them in batches, and at the end of each day 'nets out' payments between the financial institutions concerned.

An institution collecting a cheque on behalf of a customer acts as the customer's agent. The usual rules of agency apply. The duty to act in the principal's best interest, as well as the *Cheques Act* s 66(1), requires that the bank must present the cheque for payment promptly and will be liable to the customer for any loss occasioned by failure to do so.[27] Likewise, a drawee bank must either pay or dishonour, as soon as practicable, a cheque duly presented for payment.[28]

Where a payee accepts a cheque as payment, the payment is conditional. There are two implied terms here: (1) that the drawer may draw the cheque; and (2) upon

27 *Lubbock v Tribe* (1838) 3 M & W 607.
28 *Cheques Act* (n 1) s 67.

presenting the cheque, that it is met. If the cheque is paid, then the time of payment is generally when the cheque was delivered.[29] If the cheque is dishonoured, the payee may claim the money from the drawer through the cheque itself or on the original debt.

The former is almost always more advantageous. The obligations on the cheque are independent from those on the underlying transaction, and if one sues on the cheque one is not likely to be met with any counterclaims.

The cheque is not an assignment to the payee of funds held by the banker on behalf of the drawer.[30] That is, the cheque does not assign the funds in the drawer's account to the payee. The cheque operates merely as a mandate to the drawee bank. It does not of itself transfer any rights in the drawer's deposit. Thus, the payee has no right against the drawee bank on the cheque itself. The drawee bank's only obligation to the payee is to deal with the cheque – that is, pay or dishonour – promptly.[31] If the bank dishonours the cheque, the payee has no remedy against it.

An advantage of payment by cheque over payment by cash is that the paid cheque provides evidence of payment, operating as a de facto receipt. In fact, the *Cheques Act* s 113 expressly provides that an order cheque that has not been endorsed by the payee and which appears to have been paid by the drawee is evidence of receipt by the payee of the sum on the cheque.[32]

8.2.8 The meaning of 'dishonour'

A cheque is dishonoured when all of the following occur:

(a) The cheque is duly presented for payment.
(b) The drawee bank refuses payment.
(c) The refusal has been communicated to the holder (or the person presenting the cheque on the holder's behalf).[33]

This includes the case where refusal is due to the failure of the drawee bank, provided that the cheque has been presented through the APCS.[34]

8.2.9 The duty to pay

As part of its contractual relationship with its customer, a bank has a duty to pay its customer's cheques where all of the following occur:

(a) The cheque is a proper mandate – properly drawn and signed.
(b) There are funds to meet the cheque.
(c) There is no legal impediment to paying.
(d) The cheque is properly presented for payment.

29 *Tilley v Official Receiver in Bankruptcy* (1960) 103 CLR 529.
30 *Cheques Act* (n 1) s 88.
31 Ibid s 67.
32 Ibid s 113.
33 Ibid s 69.
34 Ibid s 70A.

8.2.9.1 Proper manner

The bank is acting as agent for their customer in paying and therefore will be liable if it does not follow the customer's mandate. Correspondingly, the customer ought to express the mandate clearly. If the mandate is ambiguous, the bank is not obliged to pay. Lord Haldane in *London Joint Stock Bank Ltd v Macmillan & Arthur*[35] states this principle clearly: 'The banker as a mandatory has a right to insist on having his mandate in a form which does not leave room for misgiving as to what he is called upon to do.'[36]

On the other hand, a reasonable interpretation by the agent of their principal's instructions gives the principal no right of complaint either.[37]

8.2.9.2 Funds available

There is, of course, a duty to pay if the customer has an overdraft arrangement adequate to cover the cheque.[38] The bank should ordinarily pay cheques in the order in which they are presented. What occurs if two or more cheques arrive simultaneously and funds are insufficient to meet them all? This problem has exercised academics without giving rise to any compelling answer. It does not appear to have given rise to any case law.

Another question of academic interest is: If a customer's account is in credit but has an insufficient balance to meet the cheque, may the holder of the cheque pay the difference into the customer's account to obtain, in effect, a part payment? (For instance, the cheque is for $100. The balance in the account is $80. Can the holder pay in $20 and receive payment on the cheque, thus recouping $80?) The practical difficulty here is that the holder of the cheque would need to know the amount of the shortfall, and there would be a breach of the duty of confidentiality for the bank to reveal this.

A more practical problem arises in that there is sometimes argument as to the exact amount of the funds available in the account. Uncleared cheques, though usually credited immediately to the account, are not usually available to the account holder. Bank deposit slips almost invariably include a warning that the proceeds of cheques are not available until the cheques are cleared, and such a notice will negative any implied term that the amount shown as the account balance is necessarily available to the customer.[39] Also, when money is paid into an account, it does not become available until the bank has reasonable opportunity to complete the necessary accounting procedures to post it to the ledger,[40] although this consideration is of less significance in these days of almost instantaneous electronic ledger entry.

8.2.9.3 Legal impediment

Without attempting to be exhaustive, legal impediments arise in the following situations:

- The account is subject to a garnishee order.
- The account is subject to a Mareva injunction.

35 *London Joint Stock Bank Ltd v Macmillan & Arthur* [1918] AC 777.
36 Ibid 816.
37 *Ireland v Livingston* (1872) LR 5 HL 395.
38 *Fleming v Bank of New Zealand* [1900] AC 577.
39 *Westminster Bank Ltd v Zang* [1966] AC 182.
40 *Marzetti v Williams* (1830) 1 B & Ad 415; 109 ER 842.

- The surrounding circumstances are such that the bank is on notice to make inquiries as to the validity of the payment – that is, to question the mandate. In other words, would a reasonable and honest banker in a similar position consider there was a serious possibility of the customer being a victim of fraud?[41]
- The cheque is stale. A stale cheque is one that appears on its face to have been drawn more than 15 months earlier.[42] By the *Cheques Act* s 89, the authority of the bank to pay is terminated when the cheque becomes stale, subject to agreement to the contrary between drawer and bank.
- Likewise, the authority to pay is terminated where the bank has notice of the drawer's mental incapacity or the drawer's death, although this does not apply to cheques presented within 10 days of being notified of the drawer's death.[43]
- Payment is countermanded.[44] In the case of a joint account, payment may be countermanded by any of the account holders, irrespective of whether they signed the cheque.[45] There is no particular form of communication required. It would seem that actual notice is required and that constructive notice is insufficient. (Consider *Curtice v London City & Midland Bank Ltd*,[46] where a countermand was sent by telegram. The telegram was placed in the bank's letterbox and was not seen until after payment. The Court held there was no valid countermand, although it noted that an action in negligence may have succeeded.) Moreover, the countermand must come to the attention of a 'responsible officer' of the bank.[47] If the communication is insufficient to identify the person purporting to give the countermanding order, it is probable that the bank is at least put on notice to make inquiries before making payment. In some rare cases where the bank has debited the customer's account in the face of a countermand, it may be possible for the bank to maintain the debit on equitable grounds under what is sometimes called the *Liggett* principle. This is discussed below.

8.2.9.4 Proper presentation

Presentment for payment is usually done by the collecting bank. Refer to the discussion above. Presentment may, however, be done by an individual. This is done by 'exhibiting' (ie showing) the cheque at 'the proper place' at a reasonable hour on a day on which the drawee bank is open for business at that place.[48] As the paying bank is entitled to possession of the cheque on payment, this involves handing over the cheque to the drawee bank in exchange for payment.[49] The 'proper place' is the place of business of the drawee bank as specified on the cheque or, if none is specified, the place of business of the branch on

41 *Selangor United Rubber Estates Ltd v Craddock (No 3)* [1968] 1 WLR 1555.
42 *Cheques Act* (n 1) s 3(5).
43 Ibid s 90(1)(b)–(c).
44 Ibid s 90(1)(a).
45 *Husband v Davis* (1851) 138 ER 256.
46 *Curtice v London City & Midland Bank Ltd* [1908] 1 KB 293.
47 See *Commonwealth Trading Bank of Australia v Reno Auto Sales Pty Ltd* [1967] VR 790, where a (possibly ambiguous) message to countermand was given by telephone to a junior employee, who misunderstood it, with the consequence that the cheque was paid. The payment was held not to have been countermanded.
48 *Cheques Act* (n 1) s 63.
49 Ibid s 68.

which the drawer's account is maintained.[50] Only uncrossed cheques can be presented for payment in this manner.

8.2.10 Prompt payment or dishonour

As noted above, a drawee bank must either pay or dishonour, as soon as practicable, a cheque duly presented for payment.[51] The consequence of not doing so is to make the bank liable to the holder for the value of the cheque, unless the holder has a defective title. Of relevance as to whether payment/dishonour is effected as soon as is reasonably practicable are the means available to pay, the cost, speed and reliability of those means, and custom. The last of these means that customers cannot complain if the cheque is cleared according to the usual clearing house procedures.[52]

8.2.11 Wrongful dishonour

Other than by being dilatory, a bank may breach its duty to pay in two ways:

(1) by refusing to pay when the preconditions for payment exist (wrongful dishonour)
(2) by paying when it should not (wrongful payment).

Wrongful dishonour most commonly occurs where the customer's account has funds to meet the cheque, but the bank (mistakenly) believes otherwise. Whether the bank is negligent or not is immaterial. The action is for breach of the implied term of the customer–banker contract. Damages are thus assessed according to the usual contractual rules, including those as to loss of bargain and remoteness.

In many cases, the customer will claim general damages due to loss of credit (ie loss due to prejudice to the terms on which they could obtain credit, because of having the cheque dishonoured). This is a slightly vexed area because of the distinction traditionally made between 'traders' (who are entitled to general damages in this respect)[53] and 'non-traders' (who must prove their loss), and because it is not entirely clear why general damages ought to be available in any event.

The rule dates from *Rolin v Steward*,[54] where the plaintiff, a merchant, had a cheque wrongly dishonoured. The cheque was met the next day, and no damage was proved. Nevertheless, damages of £500 (reduced to £200 on appeal) were awarded.

The restriction to traders makes little sense, as other community members are no less obviously damaged when a cheque is dishonoured, especially when almost everyone is subjected to a credit rating. There is little reason to maintain the distinction, and it was abolished in England in 1996 by the Court of Appeal in *Kpohraror v Woolwich Building Society*.[55]

One view could be that there is no real justification here at all for recognising general damages for loss of credit in regard to any class of payee. One would have thought that it was a simple enough matter to demonstrate any actual loss in this respect (eg refusal

50 Ibid s 64(b).
51 Ibid s 67.
52 *HH Dimond (Rotorua 1966) Ltd v Australia and New Zealand Banking Group Ltd* [1979] 2 NZLR 739.
53 See, eg, *Gibbons v Westminster Bank Ltd* [1939] 2 KB 882.
54 *Rolin v Steward* (1854) 14 CB 595.
55 *Kpohraror v Woolwich Building Society* [1996] 4 All ER 119.

of credit or granting of credit only at a higher rate), and once the wrongful dishonour is proved, continuing future loss is unlikely. However, *Rolin v Steward* is so long established there is no possibility of this view being accepted. General damages are, of course, available in actions for defamation via wrongful dishonour, and this perhaps has influenced the view that they ought also to be available for breach of contract.

Where a cheque is dishonoured, it is customary for the drawee bank to write an 'answer' (seldom more than an annotation) on the back indicating the reason. Return of the cheque to the collecting bank has the effect of 'publishing' this reason to a third party and thus potentially exposing the drawee bank to an action in defamation by its customer. The answer must, of course, be capable of carrying a defamatory imputation. Common examples such as 'signature indistinct' or 'amount illegible' are unlikely to qualify. However, anything that indicates there are insufficient funds goes to the creditworthiness – and thus the reputation – of the drawer as 'being likely to lower them in the estimation of right-thinking members of society generally', to use the time-honoured formulation. The most common 'answers' used in this situation are the apparently innocuous ones of 'present again' and 'refer to drawer'. The latter is often abbreviated to 'RD' or 'R/D'. The problem is that 'everyone' knows that these notations convey the meaning that the account has insufficient funds to meet the cheque and are thus potentially defamatory. There is considerable case law to this effect.[56] If one looks hard enough, one can also find some to the contrary. For example, in *Flach v London & South Western Bank Ltd*,[57] Scrutton LJ found that the words 'refer to drawer' conveyed no defamatory meaning, but should be accepted at face value as meaning 'We are not paying. If you want to know why, ask the drawer'. But the weight of expressed judicial opinion is overwhelmingly on the other side.[58]

Naturally, a defamation action can only succeed if the dishonour is wrongful and the reputation of the customer is such that it can be damaged by the bank's words. A customer who is notorious for over-drawing will not be likely to be successful in defamation based on an isolated wrongful label of 'insufficient funds'.[59]

One might have thought that publication to the collecting bank/holder might be justified on the grounds of qualified privilege: that is, on the basis that the drawee bank has a duty to make the statement and the holder/collecting bank an interest in receiving it beyond that of a member of the general public. The High Court of Australia (by a 3–2 majority) appears to have definitively rejected the proposition in *Aktas v Westpac*[60] on the grounds that while the drawee has a duty to notify the dishonour, it has no duty to provide a reason for it. The drawee bank could just as easily say 'payment refused'. In the case in question, it chose a form of words ('refer to drawer') that conveyed the imputation that there were insufficient funds.

56 See, eg, *Braidwood v Turner* (1908) 10 WALR 105; *Baker v Australia and New Zealand Bank Ltd* [1958] NZLR 907; *Jayson v Midland Bank Ltd* [1968] 1 Lloyd's Rep 409; *Hill v National Bank of New Zealand Ltd* [1985] 1 NZLR 736; *Aktas v Westpac Banking Corporation Ltd* (2010) 241 CLR 79 ('*Atkas v Westpac*').

57 *Flach v London & South Western Bank Ltd* (1915) 31 TLR 334, 336.

58 *Aktas v Westpac* (n 56) went to the High Court of Australia (HCA), although not on this point. However, it would seem by the remarks in the judgments that the HCA accepted that 'refer to drawer' carried a defamatory imputation.

59 See, eg, *Ellaw Co Ltd v Lloyds Bank Ltd* (1934) 4 LDAB 455.

60 *Atkas v Westpac banking Corporation Ltd* (2010) 241 CLR 79.

8.2.12 Wrongful payment

The duty to pay requires the payment of the proper amount to the proper party.

8.2.12.1 Wrong amount

It occasionally happens that the paying bank pays the wrong amount in error. If so, the paying bank is in breach of its contractual obligation to its customer. If the payment is too large, the bank will generally be able to recover the over-payment. Where the cheque has been fraudulently and materially altered by the holder, the *Cheques Act* s 78(2) provides that it is discharged. Section 91 states that a drawee may debit a holder's account upon presentation of a 'raised' cheque (a fraudulent modification of a cheque to increase the payment to be made) provided: (1) the drawee acted in good faith and without any negligence; and (2) the fraud is the only significant alteration made on the cheque.[61] This may not be a great deal of comfort to the drawee bank, as most raisings are of an order of magnitude or more. Of course, the bank may be able to rely on the *Macmillan* duty. Note also that where the cheque has been fraudulently and materially altered by the holder, s 78(2) provides that it is discharged.

8.2.12.2 Wrong person

Clearly, if a cheque is payable to or to the order of a person, then the duty of the drawee is to pay to that person or someone specified by them. Note that the *Cheques Act* gives the bank statutory defences – discussed shortly – to actions for breach of contract where the breach results from a forged endorsement. Recall that if a cheque is not payable to order, it is payable to the bearer, and the bank's duty is to pay whoever the bearer may be. Thus, it is difficult for a paying bank to pay a bearer cheque to the wrong person. This is presumably why most pre-printed cheque forms carry the rubric 'Pay ... or bearer'. As per bills of exchange, a cheque made out to a non-existent or fictitious person is regarded as a bearer cheque.[62] Again, as per bills of exchange, a 'fictitious person' is one who was never intended by the drawer to have any rights on the instrument.[63] The intention is that of the drawer – that is, the person who signs the cheque. A forged cheque is the cheque of the person who signs it, irrespective of the name they use.[64]

Where a drawer's signature is forged and the bank pays on the cheque, then, as the bank has no mandate from the customer whose signature has been forged, it is not entitled to debit the customer's account.

8.2.13 Defences of the paying bank

8.2.13.1 Contractual defences

These defences are limited. Where the bank improperly pays, it may, in the appropriate circumstances, be able to invoke the *Greenwood* or *Macmillan* duties to recover from the customer, provided the loss is not due to its own supervening negligence.

61 *Cheques Act* (n 1) s 91.
62 Ibid s 19.
63 *Bank of England v Vagliano Brothers* [1891] AC 107.
64 *Cheques Act* (n 1) s 32(1).

8.2.13.2 The 'equitable defence'

In *B Liggett (Liverpool) Ltd v Barclays Bank Ltd*,[65] the bank paid cheques against Liggett's account to Liggett's trade creditors. These cheques were not signed by the requisite number of directors. Wright J ruled in favour of the bank, as Liggett had not actually incurred any new liability from the bank's actions and thus the bank was entitled to stand in the place of Liggett's creditors and to debit the plaintiff's account for the amount of the cheques. Stated in these bare terms, the case cannot be correct. To see why, consider *Crantrave Ltd (in liq) v Lloyds Bank plc*[66] and the remarks of Pill LJ in that case. The facts of the case were these.

A garnishee order *nisi* was served on the bank with respect to the funds of a customer. A few weeks later the bank paid the judgment creditors a sum of over £13 000 from the account. The garnishee order was never made absolute and proceedings on it were stayed. The customer went into liquidation and the liquidator sought repayment of the amount paid away by the bank. The bank argued *Liggett*. Pill LJ said:

> It is a startling proposition that bankers can pay sums to third parties out of a customer's account because they believe the customer to be indebted to that third party ... [This] would place the bank in a position to act as debt collector for creditors of the customer ... the bank could decide in what priority the claims of creditors were to be met out of ... the account, without the customer having recourse against the bank. A bankruptcy or liquidation may occur shortly after a payment as in this case, with possible effects on the rights of creditors generally.[67]

This assessment somewhat overstates the case in respect of a payment of a cheque made in error, but it is certainly true that the customer may wish to dispute the debt that the bank has paid on its behalf and contrary to its instructions, or to set it off against a counterclaim, or it might prefer to use its available funds for other purposes (and, indeed, the source of the wrongful payment may be that the bank had disregarded a countermand made by the customer for one of those very reasons). The bank has not obeyed its mandate and it is not clear why it should be allowed to proceed as if it has. The proper course here is clearly for the bank to recover, if it can, from the creditor (rather than from the customer) for money paid under mistake of fact and for the creditor to sue the customer. In some cases, that might result in the unjust enrichment of the customer at the expense of the bank, or it might be otherwise unconscionable for the customer not to reimburse the bank. The Court in *Crantrave* recognised that in those cases the defence would succeed. But it is up to the bank to demonstrate that those circumstances exist. This, one would be inclined to say, is the correct view. There has, however, certainly been a degree of judicial disagreement over the issue.

65 *B Liggett (Liverpool) Ltd v Barclays Bank Ltd* [1928] 1 KB 48.
66 *Crantrave Ltd (in liq) v Lloyds Bank plc* [2000] QB 917.
67 Ibid 924.

8.2.13.3 Statutory defences

The various sections of the *Cheques Act* that give defences to a bank for wrongful payment are all subject to s 32(1). That is, they offer no protection in the case where a drawer's signature has been forged, unless an estoppel arises or unless there is an adoption or ratification of the forgery by the purported drawer. Having said that, the defences provided by the Act are discussed next.

Where a bank in good faith and without negligence, pays a crossed cheque drawn upon it to a bank, the drawee bank is deemed to have paid the cheque in due course.[68] Payment in due course discharges the cheque and all rights on it.[69] The consequences are, in such a situation, that the drawer cannot sue the drawee bank for breach of contract, that the drawee bank is not liable in conversion to the true owner, and that as between drawer and payee, the debt owed by the drawer to the payee is discharged.[70]

Where a bank disregards a crossing and pays otherwise than to a bank, the bank is liable to the true holder for any loss the true owner suffers as a result of the cheque being paid other than to a bank (s 93(1)),[71] and the drawer may resist debit of their account.[72] However, s 93(2) provides that if the cheque, at the time of presentment, does not appear, on its face, to be, or at any time to have been, a crossed cheque (ie if it has been altered so that the crossing is not apparent), then payment by the bank is deemed to be in due course, again provided it was made in good faith and without negligence.

Where a bank pays on a cheque in good faith and without negligence in the case where an endorsement is forged or unauthorised, then the bank incurs no liability from any failure to concern itself with the genuineness of the endorsement, and the cheque is again deemed to be paid in due course.[73]

Where a bank pays on a cheque *to another bank* in good faith and without negligence in the case where an endorsement is absent or irregular, then the bank incurs no liability from any failure to concern itself with the genuineness of the endorsement and the cheque is again deemed to be paid in due course.[74]

In *Australian Mutual Provident Society v Derham*, D and his spouse were joint payees of an order cheque drawn in their favour by an insurance company. They instructed the insurance company to mail the cheque to their insurance broker, V. V forged an endorsement to himself, signing D's name. V deposited the cheque with his bank, which collected it for him from the drawee bank. The endorsement was forged, and also irregular because it lacked the signature of D's spouse. D failed in an action for conversion against the drawee bank, which successfully argued defences under the *Cheques Act* s 94(1) and (2).[75]

It is important to appreciate that these defences apply to the paying bank. As a collecting bank acts as agent for its customer, it may be exposed to an action in conversion

68 *Cheques Act* (n 1) s 92.
69 Ibid ss 79, 82.
70 *Charles v Blackwell* (1877) 2 CPD 151.
71 *Cheques Act* (n 1) s 93(1).
72 *Bobbett v Pinkett* (1876) 1 Ex D 368.
73 *Cheques Act* (n 1) s 94(1).
74 Ibid s 94(2).
75 *Australian Mutual Provident Society v Derham* (1979) 39 FLR 165.

by the true owner of the cheque if its customer has no title to the cheque. As we shall see, the collecting bank also has defences.[76]

8.3 Bills of exchange[77]

8.3.1 Definition

A bill of exchange is an unconditional order in writing, addressed by one person to another, signed by the person giving it, requiring the person to whom it is addressed to pay on demand, or at a fixed or determinable future time, a sum certain in money to or to the order of a specified person, or bearer.[78]

8.3.1.1 Unconditional order

There must be something in the nature of a command, more than a mere request or authorisation. Inclusion of words of courtesy such as 'please' will not invalidate the bill as a bill, if omitting them would leave an unequivocal order. Thus, 'Please pay' is an order; but 'I would be pleased if you would pay' is not. Note the 'if' here, which indicates the option of not paying. The case law can be obscure. Thus, 'Mr Little please to let the bearer have £7 and place it to my account and you will oblige' was held not to be an order,[79] whereas '[You] will much oblige [me] by paying ...' has been held to be one.[80]

Moreover, the order must not be qualified. Thus, an order to pay out of a particular fund or from a particular source – for instance, 'To C, pay B $500 out of my No 2 account' – is not unconditional because it can only be followed if the account has sufficient funds. On the other hand, if the order merely indicated a source from which C was to reimburse themself after having paid B (rather than from which B is to be paid), then it is unconditional. Again, this can give rise to some tricky problems of interpretation. Thus, apparently, 'Please pay to X £150 and deduct the same from money coming due to me on account from W' is in the second class.[81]

8.3.1.2 In writing

The whole of the order must be written. There is no restriction as to written with what or on what. Crayon on the side of a house will do (although this would pose certain practical problems in terms of presentation to the drawee), as will pencil on a piece of tissue paper or paint on a hot air balloon, and so on.

8.3.1.3 Addressed by one person to another

The person giving the order is called the 'drawer'. The person ordered to pay is called the 'drawee'. A bill may be addressed to ('drawn on') two or more drawees (X and Y), but it is

76 *Cheques Act* (n 1) s 95.
77 Unless otherwise specified, provisions referred to are contained in the *Bills of Exchange Act* (n 2).
78 Ibid s 8(1).
79 *Little v Slackford* (1828) 1 Mood & M 171.
80 *Ruff v Webb* (1794) 1 Esp 129.
81 See *Peacocke & Co v Williams* (1909) 28 NZLR 354.

not a bill if it is drawn on two or more drawees in the alternative (X or Y) or in succession (X, or if X refuses, then Y).[82]

8.3.1.4 Signed by the person giving it

That is, it must be signed by the drawer. It is enough if the bill is signed by some duly authorised person on behalf of the drawer. However, a bill is not signed by the drawer if their signature is forged or if it is signed on their behalf without authority.

8.3.1.5 Requiring the drawee to pay on demand

This includes a bill on which no time for payment is expressed.[83]

8.3.1.6 Or at a fixed or determinable future time

A 'determinable future time' may be a stated date or a stipulated period after the date of the bill ('x days after date') or after 'sight' (ie the date on which the bill is presented to the payee), or after the occurrence of some event that is certain to occur.[84] However, the time cannot depend on an event that is not certain to happen (even if the event should in fact occur) – that is, on a 'contingency'. For instance, an instrument expressed to be payable 'six days after the ship *Childers* clears the Port Phillip Heads' was not a good bill, because at the time it was drawn there was no certainty the event specified would occur.[85]

Despite some earlier contrary authority, it is now accepted that instruments expressed as being payable 'on [date] or before' or 'by [date]' are payable 'at a fixed ... future time'. This is sensible, although the reasoning is somewhat artificial.[86]

Note that there is no requirement for a bill to be dated;[87] however, if it is, the date given is prima facie deemed to be the actual date on which the bill was drawn.[88] Nor is a bill invalid by virtue of it being post-dated or ante-dated.[89]

8.3.1.7 A sum certain in money

The sum payable must be capable of being calculated at the time fixed for payment. This requirement will be satisfied even if the amount is expressed to be payable with interest and/or bank charges, as long as these are capable of being calculated with certainty at the time for payment, or by stated instalments, or payable according to an indicated or ascertainable rate of exchange.[90]

In *Rosenhain v Commonwealth Bank of Australia*,[91] the High Court of Australia held that a bill payable 'sixty days after sight' for a sum plus 'interest at the rate of eight per

82 *Bills of Exchange Act* (n 2) s 11.
83 Ibid s 15.
84 Ibid s 16.
85 *Baker v Efford* (1873) 4 AJR 161.
86 See *EMU Brewery Mezzanine Ltd (in liq) v Australian Securities and Investments Commission* (2006) 32 WAR 204; *Re York Street Mezzanine Pty Ltd (in liq)* (2007) 162 FCR 358.
87 *Bills of Exchange Act* (n 2) s 8(4).
88 Ibid s 18(1).
89 Ibid s 18(2).
90 Ibid s 14.
91 *Rosenhain v Commonwealth Bank of Australia* (1922) 31 CLR 46.

cent per annum until arrival of payment in London to cover' was not a sum capable of ascertainment at the time fixed for payment (sixty days after sight) because the interest was to run to an indeterminate time ('arrival of payment in London').

There is no requirement to write the sum in more than one way on a bill, but it is customary to record it both in words and figures – for instance, 'five dollars' and '$5.00'. Where there are two differing amounts recorded on the bill, the actual sum is taken to be the smaller of these.[92]

8.3.1.8 To or to the order of a specified person or to bearer

The bill must be payable to one or other of the following:

- a specified person ('Pay X')
- the order of a specified person ('Pay X or order')
- bearer ('Pay bearer' or 'Pay X or bearer').

Of these, (a) and (b) are 'order' bills and (c) is a 'bearer' bill. The person to whom the sum is to be paid is called the 'payee'. 'Person' includes a body of persons, whether incorporated or not (s 4 of the *Bills of Exchange Act*).

A bill may be drawn payable to or to the order of the drawer ('To X, pay [drawer]') or to or at the order of the drawee ('To X, pay X'). These variations are, as we shall see, quite common.

What if the drawer and drawee are the same person (ie the drawer orders him- or herself to pay the money)? In that case, the payee may treat the document either as a bill of exchange or (what it really is) as a promissory note.[93] The law is *mutatis mutandis*, which applies to bills of exchange.[94]

Where the payee is a fictitious or non-existent person, the bill may be payable to the bearer.[95] This is also the case where the person designated as payee actually exists but was never intended to have any rights on the bill – for instance, where their name was entered merely as a fiction.[96]

8.3.2 Analysis

So, here in its most basic form, is a bill of exchange (an order bill payable on demand):

> *To X*
> *Pay Y*
> *The sum of $500.00*
> *Z [signed]*

One might reasonably ask why should X take any notice of this demand?

The answer to this question is that probably there is some collateral agreement whereby Z will put X in funds, or that Z has already put X in funds, or maybe it is that

92 *Bills of Exchange Act* (n 2) s 14.
93 Ibid s 10.
94 Ibid s 95.
95 Ibid s 12.
96 *Bank of England v Vagliano Brothers* [1891] AC 107.

X acts out of the sheer goodness of their heart. It doesn't really matter. What is relevant is that X is under no obligation to pay – pursuant to the bill itself, setting aside any collateral agreement or obligation – unless they 'accept' the bill; that is, unless X signs the bill. It is usual to write 'accepted' and then sign, but the word 'accepted' is in fact superfluous. If X does this, then they accept responsibility to pay on the bill when it is due, and they become known as the 'acceptor'. If the bill is not paid or accepted by X, then the primary responsibility to pay on it is with Z.

What is the purpose of bills of exchange, and how did they originate? They originated as a means of facilitating trade when currency was in the form of gold and silver and it was inconvenient and expensive to transport significant amounts of it over large distances.

Thus:

(a) M is a manufacturer in Manchester who borrows from a bank B in London to finance the manufacture of goods which M sells to a trader T in Calcutta. T thus owes M who owes B. M instructs T to pay B directly: To T, Pay B, etc. Even better, if M has an advance order from T, T can be asked to accept the bill (payable, say, when the goods are due) and hand it to B so M can secure an advance from B. Or ...

(b) Consider yourself as an officer of the NSW Corps in Sydney in 1800. A ship sails into the harbour with a cargo of rum. You would like to buy this so you could sell or barter it at an outrageous profit. But you don't have enough silver and gold and there is no bank in town. So, you say to the ship's master, 'My good man, you can see by my uniform and the way I treat the riff-raff here that I am a respected and upstanding member of the local community. I'll write an order to my bank in London – Flock, Fleece & Co – to pay you £200 on presentation. When you get back to London you can present it to them and they will hand over the money. What do you say?' The master says, 'Not that I don't trust you, but see the risk from my point of view. I don't want to have to come back here to sue you if the bank doesn't pay up. Make it £250.' You say, 'I see you're a businessman like myself. I like that. You've got a deal.' The bill, if it were a bearer bill, might look like this:

Sydney Town, New South Wales, 1 April 1800
To Flock, Fleece & Co, Bankers, of London
Pay Arnold Fairweather ship's master or bearer
The Sum of: £250-00-00 for value received
On Demand
Simon Goodenough (Capt, New South Wales Corps)

Obviously, an accepted bill is worth more than an unaccepted one (at least if the acceptor is known, like a reputable bank, to be creditworthy). Goodenough might have been able to strike a better deal with Fairweather if he (Goodenough) had brought a pile of bills with him to Sydney for various amounts that had already been accepted by his bank.

Bills like (a) and (b) are called 'trade bills', and they are still an important means of payment in international trade. Bills can also be used purely to mobilise capital on a short-term basis. Thus:

(c) E, an entrepreneur, needs $1 million in working capital to finance projects. E goes to their bank, B. B agrees to provide E with a 'commercial bill acceptance facility' for a period of two years for a small(ish) fee. The facility works like this. E draws a bill: 'To B, pay E or bearer the sum of $1,000,000.00 ninety days from date.' B accepts the bill. (Note that B, in fact, advances no money.) E takes the bill. The creditworthiness of B is well known and, as it is B who is promising to pay, the bill's value depends only on B's financial stability and the term to maturity, and hence is fairly easily determined. Thus, there is a market for these things. (Bills accepted by banks are called 'bank bills'. You may have heard of the '90-day bank bill rate', which is the discount applied by the market regarding bills like this one.) E trades the bill in the market to C (the new bearer) for $975 000. (If you want to do the maths, you can work out that the discount in the example here would be 10 per cent per annum. Also, if you happen to have a spare $500 000 or so, you can, like C, enter the bank bill market. You will do better with that than with a term deposit.) E pays this amount into their account with B and draws on it as required. Under the agreement with B, when B honours the bill on maturity by paying the bearer at that time (which may or may not be C, depending on whether C has re-discounted the bill to another party), E must reimburse B with $1 million to be drawn from E's account. What if E does not have $500 000 in their account at that time? No problem. A few days before the maturity date, E draws another bill for $500 000 on B, which B accepts and E then discounts in the market for another $975 000 which E pays into their account. This is called 'rolling over' the bill. At worst, E has to find only $25 000 to make up the difference. The bills can be rolled over up to the two-year limit. At that time, E must either (i) stump up $1 million from elsewhere to reimburse B for payment on the final bill, or (ii) renegotiate the facility.

Note that in (c) there is no underlying supply of goods or services. The bank, which is more creditworthy than E, is 'lending its credit' to E. It is operating as a reliable acceptor whose acceptance of the bill makes it valuable security for financial advances to E from third parties. Without the bill, E would either not be able to raise funds from third parties or would only be able to do it at much higher rates.

The law governing bills of exchange is historically part of the law merchant. This is the body of customary law relating to the practice of merchants. To some degree, it was uniform throughout Europe. In England, it was assimilated into the practice of the common law and the common law courts in the eighteenth century. The *Bills of Exchange Act 1882* (UK) codified this.[97] That Act was copied in all Australian jurisdictions and in particular by the Commonwealth in the *Bills of Exchange Act 1909*.

The key legal characteristic of bills of exchange is that they are *negotiable*. That is, they possess these three qualities:

(1) A bill of exchange is transferable, either by delivery (if a bearer bill) or by endorsement and delivery (if an order bill). (Endorsement is discussed further later.)

97 This and the *Sale of Goods Act 1893* (UK) are models of how to draft legislation. They should be compared to the *Corporations Act 2001* (Cth), which stands as a model of how *not* to do it.

(2) The person entitled to a bill may sue for payment on it in their own name. That is, the person entitled to the bill is entitled to be paid on it on its maturity by the acceptor or drawer. There is no defence of lack of privity of contract. The person entitled to the bill does not need to sue the person from whom they received the bill.

(3) The *nemo dat* rule does not apply. A person who takes a bill bona fide for value takes it 'free of equities'. That is, their title is good, and not impugned by any defect of title in the person from whom they took it. The *nemo dat* rule protects the 'rightful' owner, whereas this aspect of negotiability protects the integrity of the transfer.

A bill of exchange represents a debt that is transferable. Debts can also be transferred by legal or equitable assignment, but assignment is inefficient and unsatisfactory as a payment method and as a financing device, for the following reasons:

- While an assignee may sue in their own name as per the holder of a bill, it is not possible to legally assign a part of a debt. While part of a debt may be equitably assigned, in that case the assignee must join the original debtor in an action to recover. In contrast, a debt may be split over any number of bills.
- The bill itself is evidence of the debt. The debt need not be proved.
- It is not necessary for a subsequent holder of a bill to give notice to the original debtor in order either to make the debtor liable on the bill or to establish priority. On the other hand, notice is essential for a legal assignment and necessary on an equitable one to establish priority.
- An assignee, of course, takes subject to equities and set-offs.

If the assignee of a debt sues for payment, any of the above arguments may be raised. On the other hand, the holder of a bill of exchange need only produce the bill with the defendant's signature.

A bill of exchange is not the only example of a negotiable instrument. Others include:

- cheques
- promissory notes
- negotiable certificates of deposit
- warehouse receipts
- traveller's cheques (possibly).

Traveller's cheques are virtually extinct, although we have discussed them briefly when we dealt with cheques. Warehouse receipts are proof of ownership of (and warrant the existence of) a commodity of a particular quantity, type and quality in a named storage facility. They are typically used to settle contracts in lieu of physical delivery. We will not discuss them. Nor will we discuss certificates of deposit, which are analogous instruments in relation to bank deposits (and carry interest rights).

8.3.2.1 Promissory notes

A bill of exchange requires a drawer, a drawee and a payee. A promissory note has only two parties. Essentially, the drawer and drawee are combined. The *Bills of Exchange Act* s 89 defines a promissory note as:

> ... an unconditional promise in writing made by one person to another, signed by the maker, engaging to pay on demand or at a fixed or determinable time, a sum certain in money, to, or to the order of, a specified person or to bearer.

The 'promise' takes the place of the 'order'. As noted above, the *Bills of Exchange Act* applies the law in relation to bills of exchange to promissory notes *mutatis mutandis*.[98]

8.3.3 Transfer/negotiation

A *holder* of a bill is 'the payee or indorsee of a bill or note who is in possession of it, or the bearer thereof'.[99]

The definition could perhaps be clearer. Anyone in possession of a bearer bill is a holder. Bearer bills are transferred (negotiated) by delivery. They circulate like cash. However, in order to be the holder of a bill not payable to bearer (an order bill), the person in possession must either be the original payee or a person to whom the bill has been endorsed (an endorsee). (Note that the terms 'indorse' and 'endorse' are used interchangeably.) Thus, order bills are transferred by delivery and endorsement. *Endorsement must be by the holder*. Endorsement is the means by which a holder 'orders' payment to another.

Consider an order bill payable to X. X may endorse the bill to Y. Writing on it: 'Pay Y. X [signed]'. X is the *endorser*. Y is the *endorsee*. Y becomes the holder when X delivers the bill to them. Y can then make Z the holder by endorsing the bill to Z ('Pay Z. Y [signed]') and delivering it to Z. And so on.

(1) Suppose a bearer bill is stolen by a thief. The thief is a holder. If the thief delivers the bill to X, then X becomes a holder. On the other hand, suppose an order bill is stolen. The thief is not a holder, being neither payee nor endorsee. If the thief delivers the bill to X, having, say, forged the signature of the true holder, X does not become holder (because the bill has not been endorsed by its holder).

(2) It is not possible to split the sum of the bill into parts by endorsing some part to one endorsee and the remainder to another.[100] Joint endorsees are, however, permissible. Joint endorsees who are not partners must each endorse the bill to transfer it. There is the obvious exception where one of more has authority to sign for the others.[101]

(3) It is customary (but not obligatory) to execute endorsements on the back of the bill. Where there is no room for further endorsements an allonge may be attached.[102]

(4) Endorsements are sometimes made with conditions attached – for instance, 'Pay Z on his marriage'. This is permissible, but s 38 provides that the payer of the bill may disregard the condition (ie pay whether or not Z marries and be discharged by the payment). The endorsee himself is probably bound by the condition. That is, Z holds any proceeds of it on trust for the endorser unless the condition is met.[103]

---

98 *Bills of Exchange Act* (n 2) s 95.
99 Ibid s 4.
100 Ibid s 37.
101 Ibid s 37(c).
102 Ibid s 37(a).
103 See, eg, *Laney v Gates* (1935) 35 SR (NSW) 372, but this cannot be regarded as settled law.

(5) An endorsement may be in blank. That is, no endorsee is named. This has the effect of converting the bill to a bearer bill.[104] A bearer may insert their own name or any other name as endorsee above the blank endorsement (and thereby re-convert the bill to an order bill).[105]

(6) There is no provision in the Act that specifically provides a method to convert a bill that was initially drawn as a bearer bill to an order bill. It is sometimes suggested that a bill payable to 'to X or bearer' can be converted to an order bill by X striking out the words 'or bearer' and endorsing the bill to a named party. Such case law as there is suggests otherwise – born a bearer bill, always a bearer bill – based on interpretation s 13(3) of the Act.[106] And one would be inclined to agree.

(7) A *restrictive endorsement* is allowable under s 40. This prohibits further transfer of the bill or expresses that it is a mere authority to deal with the bill as directed and is not a transfer of ownership.[107] Section 40 gives several examples: 'Pay D only', 'Pay D for the account of X', or 'Pay D or order for collection'. A restrictive endorsement gives the endorsee the right to receive payment of the bill, and to sue any party to the bill that the endorser could have sued, but gives the endorsee no power to transfer their rights as endorsee except as expressly authorised by the endorsement.[108] If the endorsement does authorise further transfer, the transferee takes subject to the same rights and liabilities as the endorsee under the restrictive endorsement.

8.3.4 Introduction to liability

We will discuss the liability of various parties to the bill in detail later. For the moment, note the following:

(1) The acceptor promises all parties to pay on the bill.

(2) The drawer promises all subsequent parties that if the drawee does not pay, then they will compensate the holder or compensate any endorser subsequent to them who may be compelled to pay.

(3) An endorser promises all parties subsequent to them that if the drawee does not pay, then they will compensate the holder, or that if an endorser subsequent to them is forced to pay, then they will compensate that endorser.

Consider the following simplified example.

> D draws a bill on E to pay F. E accepts. F endorses the bill to G. G endorses the bill to H. H endorses the bill to I. On maturity, I presents the bill to E, who does not pay. I takes the bill to G, who is obliged to pay as I is a subsequent holder. G pays. G has recourse against D, E and F (but not against H, as H's promise is only to those subsequent to H and G is prior).

104 *Bills of Exchange Act* (n 2) s 39.
105 Ibid s 39(4).
106 *Miller Associates (Australia) Pty Ltd v Bennington Pty Ltd* [1975] 2 NSWLR 506.
107 *Bills of Exchange Act* (n 2) s 40(1).
108 Ibid s 40(2).

8.3.4.1 Holder for value, and holder in due course

The holder of a bill has the right to sue on the bill in their own name.[109] This is taken to mean that the normal privity requirement does not affect the holder's rights as against those parties liable on the bill, but not as otherwise creating a right where none would exist. So, a holder would normally have to take for value (provide consideration) to enforce payment on a bill. Furthermore, it is only a *holder in due course* who obtains freedom from the *nemo dat* rule. Thus, s 43(1)(b) provides that where a holder is a holder in due course, they hold the bill free from any defect of title of prior parties. A holder in due course has a number of other advantages conferred by the Act, and we will discuss these as we come to them, but this is the chief one.

So, who is a holder in due course and what is value? A holder in due course is defined in the Act s 34 as a holder who takes the bill:

(1) complete and regular on its face
(2) before it was overdue
(3) without notice of dishonour
(4) in good faith
(5) for value
(6) without notice, at the time the bill was negotiated to them, of any defect in title of the person who negotiated it to them.

Before we look at these elements, consider the following two provisions.

Section 35(2) provides a rebuttable presumption that every holder is a holder in due course. (This does not apply to the original payee, who cannot be a holder in due course.[110]) The rationale for this is that there must be a prior negotiation before a holder can be a holder in 'due course'; that is, there must be a course of dealing with the bill. A bill is issued to the original payee rather than 'negotiated' to them. If the payee subsequently becomes an endorsee, then the matter is different.[111] For instance:

> P is the payee. P endorses the bill to Q. Q endorses the bill to R. R endorses the bill to P. P can be a holder in due course.

Also, s 34(3) provides that a holder (whether for value or not) who derives their title to a bill through a holder in due course, and who is not themselves a party to any fraud or illegality affecting it, has all the rights of that holder in due course as regards the acceptor and all parties to the bill before that holder. Consider the following:

> X is a holder in due course. X gifts the bill to Y. Y is not a holder in due course (having not given value). Nevertheless, by s 34(3), even though Y has not given value, Y has the same rights against all previous holders of the bill, and the drawer, and acceptor (if any), that X has.

109 Ibid s 43(1)(a).
110 *RE Jones Ltd v Waring and Gillow Ltd* [1925] 2 KB 612; *Inflatable Toy Co Pty Ltd v State Bank of New South Wales Ltd* (1994) 34 NSWLR 243.
111 *Jade International Steel Stahl und Eisen GmbH & Co KG v Robert Nicholas (Steels) Ltd* [1978] QB 917.

Value

Every party whose signature appears on the bill is presumed to have given value for it.[112]

'Value' has an extended definition under the Act s 32. Thus:

(a) Any consideration sufficient to support a simple contract amounts to value. (This is the normal definition of value.)
(b) Any antecedent debt or liability is deemed value. So, 'past' consideration can be good consideration when it comes to bills of exchange. (There must, of course, be some connection between this and the bill: *Oliver v Davis*.[113])
(c) Where the holder of a bill has a lien on it, arising either from contract or by implication of law, they are deemed to be a holder for value to the extent of the sum for which they have a lien.

Also, by s 32(2), where value has been given at any time for a bill, the holder is deemed to be a holder for value as against the acceptor and all parties to the bill (eg endorsers) who became parties to it prior to the giving of value. The result of this is that a person who has received a bill as a gift may sue certain parties on it if value has at any time been given for it, which is consistent with the approach in s 34(3) discussed above. For instance:

> If A gave B the bill for no value, and B gave it as a gift to C, C could not sue on the bill, as at no stage has value been given. However, suppose that C transfers the bill for value to D. D could sue A, B or C. Further, if D gave it to E as a gift, E could not sue D, but could sue A, B or C.

Good faith

Something is done in good faith if it is done honestly, even if it is done carelessly. But if someone refrains from action that would uncover the truth because they fear it will uncover the truth, then that is dishonest.[114]

Overdue

A bill that is not payable on demand falls due for payment on the last day of the time of payment fixed by the bill.[115] On-demand bills become overdue if they have been in circulation for an 'unreasonable length of time'.[116] What is 'unreasonable' is a question of fact to be determined by the circumstances, including the purpose for which the bill was drawn.

Complete and regular on face

The test of whether a bill is 'complete and regular on the face of it' is whether what appears on the bill (all surfaces), including date, endorsements and so on, would reasonably give rise to objective doubt as to its regularity.[117] Consider *Arab Bank Ltd v Ross*.[118]

112 *Bills of Exchange Act* (n 2) s 35(1).
113 *Oliver v Davis* [1949] 2 KB 727.
114 *Jones v Gordon* (1877) 2 App Cas 616.
115 *Bills of Exchange Act* (n 2) s 19(1).
116 Ibid s 41(3).
117 *Heller Factors Pty Ltd v Toy Corporation Pty Ltd* [1984] 1 NSWLR 121.
118 *Arab Bank Ltd v Ross* [1952] 2 QB 216, 233–4.

A bill was drawn in favour of 'F&FN Company'. It was endorsed 'F&FN'. It was held that while the indorsement was valid in the sense that it was effective to transfer the bill and constitute the endorsee as holder, it was nevertheless 'irregular' as the omission of the word 'company' was sufficient to raise doubt as to whether the payee and endorser were the same person. Because of this the endorsee could not be a holder in due course.

Note, that a person who is misdescribed in a bill may endorse it in accordance with the designation or spelling in the bill and may, if they wish, add their 'correct' signature (s 37(d)).[119] If the misdescribed party merely signs in their 'proper' manner, the endorsee will not take as a holder in due course, because the bill will fail the 'regularity' test.

Notice of defect in title

The title of a person who negotiates a bill is defective if they obtained the bill, or its acceptance, by (common law) fraud, duress, or force and fear, or other unlawful means, or for an illegal consideration, or if they negotiated the bill in breach of faith, or under such circumstances amounting to fraud.[120]

8.3.5 Acceptance

As noted, acceptance amounts to a promise to the payee – and every lawful holder of the bill – to pay it according to the terms of the acceptance. Acceptance can occur at virtually any time: before the bill is signed by the drawer, or while it is otherwise incomplete, or when it is overdue, or after it has been dishonoured.[121]

Acceptance may be *general* or *qualified*.[122] A qualified acceptance purports to place conditions on the acceptor's liability. The Act does not impose any limit on the qualifications but sets out five particular types of qualification. These are:

(1) *Conditional.* For instance: 'Accepted payable when goods are received.'
(2) *Partial.* For instance: a bill for $5000 'accepted for $2000.00 only'.
(3) *Local.* For instance: 'Accepted payable at WhichBank Melbourne only.' (Omission of the word 'only' here would be taken as indicating merely a request/preference and the acceptance would be treated as unqualified.)
(4) *Qualified as to time.* For instance: 'Accepted payable nine months after date.'
(5) *Acceptance by one, or some of two or more drawees.* For instance: a bill drawn on X, Y and Z, accepted by X and Y only.

A holder may refuse to take a qualified acceptance and may treat the bill as dishonoured.[123] If a qualified acceptance is taken by the holder, and the drawer or prior endorser(s) does not consent to this, then the drawer/endorser is discharged from liability on the bill.[124]

119 *Bills of Exchange Act* (n 2) s 37(d).
120 Ibid s 34(2).
121 Ibid s 23.
122 Ibid s 24.
123 Ibid s 49(1).
124 Ibid s 49(2).

There is an exception to this: no consent is necessary to a partial acceptance. Partial acceptance makes the drawee liable for the accepted part of the amount, the drawer/endorser(s) remaining liable for the balance.[125]

8.3.5.1 Presentment for acceptance

In three cases, a bill must be presented to the drawee for their acceptance before any party can be liable on it.

(1) If the bill is expressed to be payable 'after sight' (eg 'seven days after sight'). In that case, presentment for acceptance is necessary to determine the maturity date.
(2) If the bill expressly states it must be presented for acceptance.
(3) If the bill is drawn payable elsewhere than at the residence or place of business of the drawee, it must be presented for acceptance before it can be presented for payment.[126]

In other cases, presentment for acceptance is not necessary in order to render any party liable on the bill. (And it is obviously not necessary if the bill has already been accepted.) But the holder of an unaccepted bill is wise to present it, because if the bill is accepted then obviously the holder obtains the security of the acceptor's promise, and if acceptance is refused, the holder obtains the liability of all previous parties to the bill and relief from the need to present the bill for payment.[127]

If a bill payable 'after sight' is negotiated, the holder must either present it for acceptance or further negotiate it within a 'reasonable' time.[128] If the holder fails to do this, the drawer and all prior endorsers are discharged.[129] Again, what is a 'reasonable time' is a question of fact, but custom in Australia suggests by the same time on the next business day after receipt. Section 46 lays down various requirements for presentation. For example, presentation must be at a reasonable hour on a business day before the bill is overdue and to the drawee or a person authorised by them.

8.3.5.2 Where the bill is not accepted

If, within the 'customary' period (again, usually 24 hours) after presentation for acceptance, the drawee fails to accept, the holder must treat the bill as *dishonoured* by non-acceptance. If the holder fails to do so, they will lose their right of recourse against the drawer and prior endorsers.[130] It is necessary for the holder to give notice of dishonour to the drawer and each endorser. A drawer or endorser to whom notice is not given within a reasonable time will be discharged from liability.[131]

Where a 'foreign' bill is dishonoured by non-acceptance, it must also be 'protested'.[132] A foreign bill is any bill that is not an 'inland' bill. An inland bill is one that is both

125 Ibid s 49(3).
126 Ibid s 44.
127 Ibid s 48.
128 Ibid s 45(1).
129 Ibid s 45(2).
130 Ibid s 47.
131 Ibid s 53.
132 Ibid s 56.

drawn and payable in Australia or drawn in Australia on a person resident in Australia. Protesting is a formal procedure involving a statement witnessed by a notary public and is rather like an affidavit. A foreign bill may also be protested, although this is not obligatory. Protesting makes available the following device.

8.3.5.3 Acceptance for honour

Where a bill is protested for dishonour by non-acceptance and is not overdue, any person who is not already liable on it may, with the consent of the holder, intervene and accept the bill 'supra protest for the honour' of any party on it.[133] The person intervening is called an 'acceptor for honour' and they become liable to the holder and to all parties to the bill subsequent to the party for whose honour they have accepted. But before they are liable to pay, the bill must be presented to the original drawee again, this time for payment; if the drawee refuses, the bill must be protested again, this time for non-payment.[134] In fact, the *Bills of Exchange Act* allows a drawer or endorser to indicate on the bill a person to whom the bill should be referred for this purpose – that is, a 'referee in case of need'.[135]

What is seemingly a slightly odd procedure has a supposedly useful purpose. Consider:

> Y draws a bill on X with A as payee. This is negotiated from A to B to C to D to E to F. F presents it to X for acceptance. X refuses. F may then claim from E who may claim from D who may claim from C, etc, until the drawer pays. This lengthy and inconvenient process can be shortened by someone who accepts for the honour of, say, D. The acceptor for honour (who usually specialises in the practice and is usually put in funds for the purpose by D) is then liable to E and F and stands in D's place for the purpose of a right to re-imbursement from C, B, A, and Y, and by effectively acting as a substitute for D, spares D the grief of all this.[136]

8.3.6 Payment

If the holder of a bill wishes to make the drawer and endorsers liable on it, the holder must present the bill to the drawee/acceptor for payment in accordance with the rules in s 50. Otherwise, the drawer and endorsers are discharged. If the bill is not payable on demand, it must be presented on the due date. If the bill is payable on demand, it must be presented within a reasonable time of drawing/endorsement. This refers to the liability of drawer and endorsers. When a bill is accepted generally, presentment for payment is not necessary to make the acceptor liable.[137] It may not always be possible to effect presentment, as the drawee may be a fictitious person or it may be impossible to find them. In these cases, presentment for payment is excused. Also, if there is a delay in making

133 Ibid s 70.
134 Ibid s 72.
135 Ibid s 20.
136 Ibid s 73 allows 'payment for honour' also. If the bill has been dishonoured by non-payment and protested accordingly, any person may intervene and pay the bill for the honour of the defaulting party. There is no obligation on the holder to accept this payment, but if they do not, they lose their right of recourse against any party who would have been discharged by the payment.
137 Ibid s 57.

presentment due to circumstances beyond the holder's control, that delay is excused.[138] (Note that if no place for payment is stated on the bill, then the place of presentment is the place of business of the drawee if this is known, or their place of residence otherwise.)

If a bill is duly presented and not paid, or if presentment for payment is excused and the bill is overdue and unpaid, the bill is dishonoured by non-payment, and the holder has an immediate right of recourse against the drawer and any endorsers.[139] But just as in the case of dishonour by non-acceptance, notice must be given to the drawer and each endorser.[140] It is not necessary, in order to preserve the liability of an acceptor, to give notice of dishonour to them. The notice of dishonour must be given to the last endorser and to each endorser the holder wished to hold liable. In practice, however, the holder will give notice only to the person who transferred the bill to them, who will then give notice to the previous endorser, and so on. Notice must be given within a reasonable time.

8.3.7 Liabilities of parties

Students by now should have a reasonably good idea of who is liable to whom and when on a bill. But here is a detailed summary (and a couple of new concepts).

8.3.7.1 Who may be liable

Capacity to incur liability on a bill of exchange is co-extensive with the capacity to contract and the same principles apply. If a person without contractual capacity signs a bill, their signature will serve to transfer it. However, if the bill is dishonoured, they cannot be sued. Note that a person of unsound mind or an intoxicated person could not set up their incapacity as a defence against a holder in due course, because it is an essential element that the person's condition was known to the other party at the time of contract. Intoxication or mental incapacity will only be a defence against an immediate party with notice.

Regarding authority to sign, care should be taken by a person signing in a representative capacity to make the capacity in which they sign clear. The mere addition of descriptive words will not free them from personal liability. If X signs 'for and on behalf of Y as agent', X has negatived their personal liability. But if X signs, 'X [signature], agent', the word 'agent' is regarded as descriptive of who X is, and not of the capacity in which they sign and X is personally liable.[141] A signature by procuration ('*per pro* Y, X [signature]') is notice that X's authority is limited and Y is bound only if X in signing was acting within the limits of X's authority.[142]

8.3.7.2 Extent of liability

The extent of liability varies for different parties involved in the transaction.

- *Acceptor (s 59):* The acceptor is liable to pay according to the tenor of their acceptance (ie according to the words on the face of the bill). Acceptance estops them from denying certain matters to a holder in due course: eg the existence of the drawer; the

138 Ibid s 51.
139 Ibid s 52.
140 Ibid s 53.
141 Ibid s 31.
142 Ibid s 30.

drawer's capacity and authority to draw the bill; the genuineness of their own signature. Nor can the acceptor deny the capacity of the drawer if the bill is payable to the drawer's order, or of some third person if the bill is payable to the order of that person, to endorse the bill. An acceptor could not, for example, refuse payment to a holder in due course on the ground that the drawer did not exist, or that the drawer's signature was forged. But an acceptor is not responsible for the genuineness of endorsements.

- *Drawer (s 60):* The drawer engages that the bill will be paid by the drawee, and that (provided requisite procedures as to dishonour are taken) they will compensate the holder if it is not paid or any endorser who is compelled to pay on it. If a holder in due course calls on the drawer to pay, the drawer cannot plead that the payee did not exist or had no capacity to endorse. A drawer may negative liability on the bill by writing the words '*sans recours*' or 'without recourse' above their signature.[143]
- *Endorser (s 60):* Like the drawer, an endorser agrees that should the drawee dishonour the bill, the endorsee will compensate the holder or any later endorser called to pay on it, provided again that the proper procedures in relation to dishonour are followed. An endorser is liable to all parties to the bill subsequent to themself. To a holder in due course, the signature of the endorser is a guarantee that the drawer's signature and all endorsements prior to their own are genuine. To their immediate endorsee, the endorser cannot deny that at the time of endorsement the bill was a valid one to which the endorser had good title. Note that an endorser may endorse a bill with the words '*sans recours*' or 'without recourse' like a drawer and so also avoid any liability on the bill.[144]
- *Strangers (s 61):* If a person signs a bill otherwise than as a drawer or acceptor or endorser, they thereby incur the liability of an endorser to a holder in due course.[145] Bills are often 'backed' in this manner. For example, it may be that goods are being supplied to a company but the sellers are not completely happy with the credit position of the company and will only agree to supply on the basis of payment by a bill of exchange that is 'backed' by the directors of the company.
- *Transferor by delivery (s 63):* A person transferring a bearer bill is a 'transferor by delivery', and since they have not put their signature on the bill they are not liable on it. However, if the immediate transferee is a holder for value, the transferor warrants to them that the bill is what it purports to be, that the transferor has the right to transfer it, and that, at the time of transfer, the transferor is unaware of any fact that would make the bill valueless.

8.3.7.3 Effect of forgery

Where a signature on a bill is forged or placed on it without authority, the forged or unauthorised signature is wholly inoperative, unless the party against whom it is sought to enforce payment is estopped – as discussed above – from setting up the forgery or want of authority.[146]

143 Ibid s 21.
144 Ibid.
145 Ibid s 61.
146 Ibid s 29.

Hence, the rights of a person who otherwise is a holder in due course do not apply in the case of a forged endorsement except as regards those who become party to the bill after the forgery. If a bill has been transferred by means of a forged endorsement, the rights of the present holder against persons who were parties prior to the forgery are lost, as the holder has no title. Those who become parties after the forgery have rights and liabilities *inter se*. Recall again, however, that the party from whom payment is sought may be estopped from setting up the forgery.

A paying banker is protected against forged endorsements if the banker pays, in good faith and in the ordinary course of business, bills payable to order on demand. The banker is deemed to have paid the bill in due course, even though the endorsement was forged or made without authority.[147] The rationale for this is that bankers have to deal with hundreds of bills on a regular basis at short notice, and do not have the opportunity or resources (unlike, supposedly, your garden or domestic everyday acceptor) to check if the person presenting a bill is the true owner.

8.3.7.4 Inchoate instruments

An inchoate instrument is one that is incomplete in one or more essential particulars, but which can be turned into a bill by adding things to it. In its basic form, an inchoate instrument may be just the drawer's signature. If it is delivered to someone in order that it be converted into a bill (by filling in the blanks), prima facie that delivery operates as an authority to fill in the instrument in any way the person to whom it is delivered sees fit.[148] Under s 25(3), 'in order that any such an instrument when completed may be enforceable against any person who became a party thereto *prior to* its completion, it must be filled up within a reasonable time, and strictly in accordance with the authority given'. However, if such an instrument *after* completion is negotiated to a holder in due course, it shall be valid and effectual for all purposes in their hands, and they are able to enforce it as if it had been filled up within a reasonable time and strictly in accordance with the authority given.[149]

8.3.7.5 Circuity of action

Where a bill is negotiated back to a party already liable on it, that party is not entitled to enforce payment of the bill against any intervening party to whom they were previously liable.[150] This prevents circuity of action.

For example:

> A endorses to B, B to C, C to D, and D back to A. B, C and D are not liable to A (as endorsers subsequent to A), as A is liable to them (as an endorser subsequent to them). On the other hand, B, C and D each have rights against A (in A's capacity as subsequent endorser) should any of them be compelled to pay to a holder.

147 Ibid s 65.
148 Ibid s 25(1)–(2).
149 Ibid s 25(3).
150 Ibid s 42.

8.3.7.6 Measure of liability

When a bill is dishonoured, the measure of liability against the parties liable is the total of:

- the amount of the bill
- interest on the bill from time of presentment for payment if a demand bill, or from maturity in other cases
- the expenses of noting and protesting, where these are necessary.[151]

8.3.8 Discharge

'Discharge' essentially means that no one has any further liability on the bill. A bill of exchange may be discharged by any of the following means:

- payment in due course[152]
- acceptor becoming the holder[153]
- waiver[154]
- cancellation[155]
- alteration in a material particular.[156]

8.3.8.1 Payment in due course

When a bill is paid, on behalf of the drawee or acceptor, at or after its maturity to the holder of it in good faith and without notice of any defect in the holder's title, it is discharged.[157] When a bill is not paid on behalf of the drawee/acceptor but by, say, an endorser of the drawer, it will not be discharged in this manner because certain liabilities still exist on it.

For example:

> Suppose a bill is drawn by D on A payable to bearer. X, the bearer, loses it, and it is picked up by Y, who presents it for payment to A. A pays in good faith, knowing nothing of Y's defective title. This is payment in due course and will discharge the bill. X's only remedy is to recover from Y, if Y can be found.

Note that an accommodation bill is not discharged by payment until it is paid by the party accommodated.[158] An accommodation bill is one where one of the parties – the drawer, acceptor or endorser (an 'accommodation party') – has signed a bill as drawer, acceptor or endorser without receiving value, and for the purpose of lending their name to some other person (the 'party accommodated').[159]

151 Ibid s 62.
152 Ibid s 64.
153 Ibid s 66.
154 Ibid s 67.
155 Ibid s 68.
156 Ibid s 69.
157 Ibid s 64(1).
158 Ibid s 64(3).
159 Ibid s 33.

> A is short of funds and arranges with a creditworthy friend, B, that A shall draw a 90-day bill which B will accept. B does so, and although he received no value from A, he is liable on it at maturity. In the meantime, A discounts the bill and obtains funds, through B being 'accommodating'.

Section 64(3) effectively implies into every accommodation bill a term that the person for whose accommodation the bill was made will indemnify the accommodation party should the accommodation party be forced to pay.

8.3.8.2 Acceptor becoming holder

When the acceptor becomes the holder in their own right, the bill is discharged.[160] Typically, the bill is negotiated to the acceptor prior to its maturity.

8.3.8.3 Express waiver

When the holder of the bill at or after its maturity absolutely and unconditionally renounces their rights against the acceptor, the bill is discharged.[161] 'Renunciation must be in writing unless the bill is delivered to the acceptor.'[162]

8.3.8.4 Cancellation

The bill may be discharged by being intentionally cancelled by the holder or their agent. Cancellation must be apparent on the face of the bill.[163] This is usually achieved by writing 'cancelled' across the bill and signing it.

8.3.8.5 Material alteration

If a bill or acceptance is altered in a material particular without the assent of all parties liable on the bill, it is avoided except as against a party who themselves made, authorised or assented to the alteration and against any subsequent endorser.[164] An exception is made in the case in which the alteration is not apparent and which is in the hands of a holder in due course.

Without being exhaustive the Act includes the following as material alterations:

(a) alteration of the date
(b) alteration of the sum payable
(c) alteration of the time of maturity
(d) alteration of the place of payment
(e) addition of the place of payment without the acceptor's consent where the bill has been accepted generally.[165]

The main test of 'materiality' is whether the alteration causes the bill to operate differently.

160 Ibid s 66.
161 Ibid s 67(1).
162 Ibid s 67(2).
163 Ibid s 68.
164 Ibid s 69(1).
165 Ibid s 69(2).

> A draws a bill on X for $10, payable to B. X accepts it, and B negotiates it by endorsement to C. C alters the $10 to $100 and negotiates it to D via endorsement, receiving $75 in exchange. The bill is then endorsed from D to E to F. F presents it for payment to X, who refuses to pay because of the alteration. F's position depends on whether the alteration is apparent or not. If it is apparent, F's only rights are against C, D and E. But if it is not apparent, F can hold C, D and E liable for the $100, and as well can hold A, B and X liable for the original tenor ($10).

8.4 Summary

In the age of technology, cheques, unfortunately and fashionably, are considered to be an outdated instrument. In 2023, in light of a recent Australian Government report entitled *A Strategic Plan for Australia's Payments System*, the Treasurer predicted that 'the cheque system in Australia will wind down no later than 2030'.[166] Unfortunately for students of banking law, one cannot understand banking without understanding cheques, notwithstanding their obsolete nature. Furthermore, one cannot understand cheques (in fact, a type of bill of exchange) without understanding bills of exchange. Bills of exchange are rather like diesel engines. It is amazing that something so simple, crude, cumbersome and old-fashioned works so well, is so widely used and is apparently capable of continually being adapted for new uses.

FURTHER READING

Booysen, Sandra, 'Cheques: To Be or Not to Be?' [2018] 4 *Journal of Business Law* 283.

Tyree, Alan, 'Banking Law and Banking Practice: Is Liggett Dead or Just Feeling Poorly?' (2016) 27(1) *Journal of Banking and Finance Law and Practice* 69.

QUESTIONS

(1) Tony gives his wife, Mary, a cheque for their wedding anniversary on the day. It is for $5000 and is duly signed. Mary puts the cheque aside, without cashing it. When Tony later has some financial difficulties, he instructs his bank not to pay on presentation of the cheque. Can Tony's wife enforce the cheque against him?

(2) Tony gives a law practice a cheque for legal services rendered. It is for $5000 and is duly signed. When Tony finds he has left himself short of money, he instructs his bank not to pay on presentation of the cheque. Can the legal practice enforce the cheque against Tony?

(3) David Singer misplaces a cheque made out to his name or bearer. Richard Dancer finds the cheque and passes it to Mary Rainers, who owns his local grocery store, as payment for his weekly shopping. The cheque is not crossed or marked 'not negotiable'. Does Mary have title to the cheque?

---

166 Jim Chalmers, 'Moderning Payments Infrastructure by Phasing Out Cheques' (Media Release, Treasury Portfolio, 7 June 2023) <https://ministers.treasury.gov.au/ministers/jim-chalmers-2022/media-releases/modernising-payments-infrastructure-phasing-out-cheques>.

CHAPTER 9

ELECTRONIC BANKING

9.1 Introduction

Having examined cheques and bills of exchange in Chapter 8, we now move onto more contemporary methods of payment. In this chapter, we start by introducing the regulatory framework and basic concepts, followed by a discussion of the *ePayments Code.* We then consider two sets of emerging issues: Open Banking and Central Bank Digital Currency.

9.1.1 Payment system, regulators and governing legislation/regulations

The Reserve Bank of Australia (RBA) has a specialised board called the Payments System Board (PSB), which is responsible for regulating the payment system, as outlined in Chapter 1. The PSB is empowered by the *Reserve Bank Act 1959* (Cth) ('*RB Act*') to formulate policies related to the payment system. The term 'payment system' is defined under the *Payment Systems (Regulation) Act 1998* (Cth) ('*Payment Systems (Regulation) Act*') as a 'funds transfer system that facilitates the circulation of money, and includes any instruments and procedures that relate to the system'.[1] While that Act does not expressly define 'funds transfer', its typical interpretation in modern payment systems involves a credit to the payee's account and a debit to the payer's account, usually facilitated by financial institutions. Fund transfer systems are a cornerstone of modern payment systems, consisting of critical elements such as participating financial institutions and authorised customers for both sending and receiving payments.[2]

The payment system, commonly understood as the complex network of methods, rules, procedures, standards and technological infrastructures that facilitate the transfer of monetary value among consumers, businesses and other organisations, is an intricate arrangement.[3] It encompasses not only a messaging system for payment orders but also a clearing mechanism and an agreed-upon settlement procedure. To ensure orderly transactions and compliance, this ecosystem is further governed by various legal agreements, such as scheme rules and the customer terms and conditions.[4] We will delve deeper into the complexities of payment systems at a later point.

Turning our attention to regulatory aspects, the PSB has specific mandates it must fulfil, as noted in Chapter 1. First, one of its main duties is to ensure that the RBA's payment system policy operates 'to the greatest advantage of the people of Australia', within the scope of its authorised powers.[5] Second, the Board is responsible for utilising its powers under the *Payment Systems (Regulation) Act* and the *Payment Systems and Netting Act 1998* (Cth) ('*Payment Systems and Netting Act*') in a manner that it believes will (i) control risk

1 *Payment Systems (Regulation) Act 1998* (Cth) ('*Payment Systems (Regulation) Act*') s 7.

2 See generally Alan Tyree, *Banking Law in Australia* (LexisNexis, 10th ed, 2017) 292.

3 The Treasury, *Payments System Review: From System to Ecosystem* (June 2021) 1 ('Treasury, *Payments System Review 2021*') <https://treasury.gov.au/sites/default/files/2021-08/p2021-198587.pdf>.

4 Notably, these contracts must adhere to existing laws and regulations. For instance, they have to be in line with the *Australian Consumer Law,* as outlined in the *Competition and Consumer Act 2010* (Cth) sch 2, various state laws and common law, all of which place limitations on the freedom to draft contract terms. See Tyree (n 2).

5 *Reserve Bank Act 1959* (Cth) ('*RB Act*') s 10B(3)(a).

in the financial system; (ii) promote the efficiency of the payments system; and (iii) promote competition in the market for payment services, consistent with the overall stability of the financial system.[6] Finally, per the *Corporations Act 2001* (Cth) ('*Corporations Act*') pt 7.3, the PSB must exercise the RBA's powers and functions in a way that it deems will contribute to the overall stability of the financial system.[7]

Under the *Payment Systems (Regulation) Act* pt 3, the RBA is authorised to designate a payment system if it deems such designation to be in the public interest.[8] When determining the public interest, the RBA must consider the desirability of the payment systems. In the RBA's view, the system should be financially safe for users, efficient and competitive. Additionally, it should not, in the RBA's opinion, significantly contribute to or cause increased risk within the financial system.[9] Upon designating a system, the RBA is granted four major powers as specified in the *Payment Systems (Regulation) Act* s 10(2).[10] These are the ability to impose an access regime on participants, to establish compliance standards, to arbitrate related disputes and to issue directions to participants within the system.[11] Moreover, some organisations have provided written commitments to the RBA regarding their adherence to its standards specified by the *Payment Systems (Regulation) Act* s 18.[12]

In 2001, the RBA first exercised this power to designate the three credit card payment systems – MasterCard, Visa and Bankcard – then in operation in the nation.[13] Subsequently, it set out standards lowering interchange fees and removing barriers on merchants charging consumers. It also introduced an access regime to facilitate new participants in the credit market.[14] Later, the debit card systems operated by Visa,[15] EFTPOS[16] and MasterCard[17] were designated in 2004, 2012 and 2015, respectively. The RBA, after extensive consultation,

6 Ibid s 10B(3)(b).

7 Ibid s 10B(3)(c).

8 *Payment Systems (Regulation) Act* (n 1) s 10.

9 Ibid s 8. The Reserve Bank of Australia (RBA) may, but is not obliged to, consider other matters that it considers relevant.

10 Ibid s 10(2) provides specifically that the RBA may: impose an access regime on the participants in the payment system (see pt 3 div 3); make standards to be complied with by participants in the payment system (see pt 3 div 4); arbitrate disputes relating to the payment system (see pt 3 div 5); and give directions to participants in the payment system (see pt 3 div 6).

11 See, eg, Reserve Band of Australia, *The Setting of Interchange Fees in the Designated Credit Card Schemes and Net Payments to Issuers* (Standard No 1, 2016) <https://www.rba.gov.au/payments-and-infrastructure/review-of-card-payments-regulation/pdf/comparison-of-standards-to-version-in-consultation-papers-2019-05-31.pdf>.

12 See, eg, Reserve Bank of Australia, *Merchant Pricing for UnionPay Card Transactions* (Undertaking No 1, 2019) <https://www.rba.gov.au/payments-and-infrastructure/payments-system-regulation/undertakings/pdf/2019-10-01-merchant-pricing-for-unionpay-card-transactions.pdf>.

13 For the list of these designations, see 'Regulations', *Reserve Bank of Australia* (Web Page) <https://www.rba.gov.au/payments-and-infrastructure/payments-system-regulation/regulations.html>.

14 See, eg, Reserve Bank of Australia, *Access Regime for the MasterCard Credit Card System* (Access Regime, 1 January 2015) <https://www.rba.gov.au/media-releases/2014/pdf/mr-14-22-gazette-notice-mastercard.pdf>.

15 IJ Macfarlane, *Designation of Payment Systems* (Reserve Bank of Australia, 18 February 2004) <https://www.rba.gov.au/media-releases/2004/pdf/mr-04-01-designation-1.pdf>.

16 Glenn Stevens, *Designation Under the Payment Systems (Regulation) Act 1998* (Designation No 1 of 2012, Reserve Bank of Australia, 12 June 2012) <https://www.rba.gov.au/media-releases/2012/pdf/mr-12-15-designation.pdf>.

17 Glenn Stevens, *Designation Under the Payment Systems (Regulation) Act 1998* (Designation No 2 of 2015, Reserve Bank of Australia, 5 October 2015) <https://www.rba.gov.au/media-releases/2015/pdf/mr-15-19-designation-2015-02-debit-mastercard.pdf>.

determined standards for the setting of interchange fees for both systems and removed the 'honour all cards' rule in the Visa system.[18] Since then, numerous others have been designated (eg the automatic teller machine [ATM] system in 2008)[19] – or their designation has been revoked (eg when the Bankcard scheme was closed in 2007) – and are now subject to standards set out by the RBA under the *Payment Systems (Regulation) Act*.[20] Furthermore, the *Payment Systems and Netting Act* enables the RBA to exercise its powers if it considers it necessary to do so to prevent systemic disruption of the financial system.

It is important to highlight that the Australian Payment Network, known as 'AusPayNet' and formerly referred to as the 'Australian Payments Clearing Association', has a crucial role in shaping the country's payments landscape. AusPayNet is a self-regulatory body and industry association that coordinates the clearing and settlement of payments by setting out rules for cards, cash, cheques, direct debit/credit, high-value payments and the Community of Interest Network (COIN).[21] AusPayNet divides its membership into four types:

(1) *Participant members* are those engaged in the day-to-day operations of Australia's various payment streams.
(2) *Affiliate members* provide goods and services to card issuers, acquirers and payment schemes.
(3) *Operator members* play a crucial role in driving innovation and in shaping governance structures to improve the payments ecosystem.
(4) *Payment service provider members* are technology companies that facilitate different payment functions.[22]

AusPayNet works with regulators, industry stakeholders and the broader community to 'provide thought leadership and policy development for the payments industry' to facilitate an 'efficient, effective payment system'.[23]

9.1.2 A snapshot of payment systems

The term 'payment system', as per the RBA, could be understood as:

> ... arrangements which allow consumers, businesses and other organisations to transfer funds usually held in an account at a financial institution to one

18 For a historical background, see generally Reserve Bank of Australia, 'Review of Card Payments Regulation' (Issues Paper, March 2015) <https://www.rba.gov.au/payments-and-infrastructure/review-of-card-payments-regulation/pdf/review-of-card-payments-regulation-issues-paper.pdf>.

19 Glenn Stevens, *Designation Under the Payment Systems (Regulation) Act 1998* (Designation No 1 of 2008, Reserve Bank of Australia, 8 December 2008) <https://www.rba.gov.au/media-releases/2008/pdf/mr-08-28-atm-desig.pdf>.

20 See, eg, Reserve Bank of Australia, *The Setting of Interchange Fees in the Designated Credit Card Schemes and Net Payments to Issuers* (Standard No 1, 2016) <https://www.rba.gov.au/payments-and-infrastructure/review-of-card-payments-regulation/pdf/standard-no-1-of-2016-credit-card-interchange-2018-05-31.pdf>. Also, several financial institutions such as American Express and UnionPay signed 'undertakings' with the RBA. See, eg, Reserve Bank of Australia, *Merchant Pricing for UnionPay Card Transactions* (Undertaking No 1, 2019) <https://www.rba.gov.au/payments-and-infrastructure/payments-system-regulation/undertakings/pdf/2019-10-01-merchant-pricing-for-unionpay-card-transactions.pdf>.

21 'Network', *Australian Payments Network* (Web Page) <https://www.auspaynet.com.au/network>.

22 'Membership', *Australian Payments System* (Web Page) <https://www.auspaynet.com.au/join-us>.

23 'Policy', *Australian Payments Network* (Web Page) <https://www.auspaynet.com.au/policy>.

> another. It includes the payment instruments – cash, cards, cheques and electronic funds transfers – which customers use to make payments and the usually unseen arrangements that ensure that funds move from accounts at one financial institution to another.[24]

In a financial transaction, three core elements must align: payment, clearing and settlement.[25] According to the Bank for International Settlements (BIS), 'payment' refers to 'the payer's transfer of a monetary claim on a party acceptable to the payee. Typically, claims take the form of banknotes or deposit balances held at a financial institution or at a central bank.'[26] One could identify 'payment' as comprising two components: a payment order and a fund transfer between accounts. The fund transfer process is initiated by a payment order to the bank.[27] Payment orders are instructions by a payer to its bank to effect payment in favour of a payee/beneficiary. These instructions could include a customer's mandate to its bank to pay, the instruction the bank passes on to another bank, and so on.[28] Payment orders have evolved from paper-based to primarily electronic forms, streamlining the process significantly.[29]

The above discussion sets the stage for the payments landscape in Australia, which relies on a multifaceted system to ensure secure, efficient transactions. Payments clearing, the second element, is orchestrated by the abovementioned AusPayNet for most payment types.[30] Independent platforms such as MasterCard, Visa and BPAY also contribute to this clearing process. The New Payments Platform (NPP), launched in 2018, brought real-time capabilities to retail payments.[31] Transitioning to the final

24 'Payments System', *Reserve Bank of Australia* (Web Page) <https://www.rba.gov.au/payments-and-infrastructure/payments-system.html>. The *Payment Systems (Regulation) Act* (n 1) s 7 defines 'payment system' as 'a funds transfer system that facilitates the circulation of money, and includes any instruments and procedures that relate to the system'.

25 Ross Cranston et al, *Principles of Banking Law* (Oxford University Press, 3rd ed, 2002) 337.

26 Bank for International Settlements Committee on Payment and Settlement Systems, *A Glossary of Terms Used in Payment and Settlement Systems* (March 2003) 37 ('BIS, *Glossary*').

27 Fund transfers could further be divided into three categories, depending on the banks involved: (1) intra-bank transfers (ie the bank maintains an account for both the payer and payee by adjusting its own debt liabilities against both the payer by debit and against the payee by credit); (2) interbank transfers (ie accounts of a payer and payee are maintained by at least two different banks; these two banks may have a correspondent bank account – or may have such accounts with a third bank); and (3) central payment system transfers. See Marek Dubovec, *The Law of Securities, Commodities and Bank Accounts* (Edward Elgar, 2014) 132–3.

28 Cranston et al (n 25) 337.

29 In Australia alone, this digitisation has facilitated approximately 55 million daily transactions, amounting to a staggering value of around A$650 billion. See Treasury, *Payments System Review 2021* (n 3).

30 'About RITS', *Reserve Bank of Australia* (Web Page), <https://www.rba.gov.au/payments-and-infrastructure/rits/about.html>.

31 Ibid. In response to Reserve Bank of Australia, 'Strategic Review of Innovation in the Payments System: Conclusion' (2012), which called for a system that provides real-time payments such as those seen in other countries, the industry stakeholders worked with the regulator in proposing a new, purpose-built payments infrastructure. In 2014, 12 authorised deposit-taking institutions committed to sponsoring the establishment and operation of the new platform, which eventually launched in 2018, known as the 'New Payments Platform' (NPP). The RBA worked closely with the payments industry in shaping the direction of the new platform. In addition to payments, it incorporated the settlement component into the NPP, often known as 'Fast Settlement Service', which enables transactions to be settled individually on a 24/7 basis. 'The New Payments Platforms', *Reserve Bank of Australia* (Web Page) <https://www.rba.gov.au/payments-and-infrastructure/new-payments-platform/>.

element, settlement, financial institutions settle their accrued obligations through the RBA, using their Exchange Settlement Accounts (ESAs).[32] For large transactions, real-time settlement is facilitated by the Real-Time Gross Settlement System (RTGS),[33] while retail transactions are usually net-settled.[34] Collectively, these interconnected platforms, ranging from AusPayNet to credit card networks and specialised services such as the NPP, form the backbone of Australia's efficient and secure payments system. Enhanced by the RBA's RTGS, this intricate network not only expedites large-value transactions but also contributes to the overall liquidity and stability of the nationwide financial system.

From a legal perspective, it is crucial to point out that 'fund transfer' does not involve an actual transfer of property. In *Foskett v McKeown*, for instance, Lord Millett held in the relevant part that:

> We speak of money at the bank, and of money passing into and out of a bank account. But of course the account holder has no money at the bank. Money paid into a bank account belongs legally and beneficially to the bank and not to the account holder. We speak of tracing money into and out of the account, but there is no money in the account. There is merely a single debt of an amount equal to the final balance standing to the credit of the account holder. No money passes from paying bank to receiving bank ... There is simply a series of debits and credits which are causally and transactionally linked.[35]

In domestic payment transactions, both participating banks generally maintain accounts with the central bank. Otherwise, the involvement of a correspondent bank is needed.[36] As for cross-border payments, the settlement would be effected by the correspondence arrangements between banks.[37] Notably, the term 'correspondent banking'

32 'Exchange Settlement Account Policy', *Reserve Bank of Australia* (Web Page) <https://www.rba.gov.au/payments-and-infrastructure/esa/>. The Reserve Bank Information and Transfer System (RITS) is the general system used for the settlement of transactions in Australia, including obligations arising from the Austraclear System, SWIFT Payment Delivery System (PDS) transactions, and RITS cash transfers. Exchange Settlement Accounts (ESAs) are used to settle obligations of payment service providers that accrue during the clearing process. ESAs are operated through the RITS.

33 Reserve Bank of Australia (n 30). 'Real-Time Gross Settlement System' (RTGS) refers to settlement transactions taking place in real time. RITS is an approved RTGS system under the *Payment Systems and Netting Act 1998* (Cth).

34 In net settlement, transactions are grouped over a time period, and then the net amount is settled. See BIS, *Glossary* (n 26) 7.

35 *Foskett v McKeown* [2001] 1 AC 102, [127]–[128]. See also *Libyan Arab Foreign Bank v Bankers Trust Co.* [1989] QB 728. (Staughton J stated [at 750] that the term may be misleading because the original obligation is not assigned; rather, a new obligation by a new debtor is created.)

36 In other words, a bank would need to send the instruction through a bank in which it has an account; the settlement between clearing and non-clearing banks would be as correspondence banks. Cranston et al (n 25) 349.

37 Ibid. At the global level, the Society for Worldwide Interbank Financial Telecommunications (SWIFT) plays a crucial role. Established in 1973, SWIFT is an industry-owned limited liability cooperative society created under Belgian law. It serves as a 'proprietary communications platform' to overcome 'the inefficiencies in, as well as to replace telegram and telex systems for international payments' for the global financial market. For a detailed recount, see Susan V Scott and Markos Zachariadis, *The Society for Worldwide Interbank Financial Telecommunication (SWIFT): Cooperative Governance for Network Innovation, Standards, and Community* (Routledge, 2014).

can be defined as an arrangement where a respondent bank places a deposit into a correspondent bank, and the correspondent bank provides services to the respondent bank.[38] A more expanded definition sees it as 'the provision of a current or other liability account, and related services, to another financial institution, including affiliates, used for the execution of third-party payments and trade finance, as well as its own cash clearing, liquidity management and short-term borrowing or investment needs in a particular currency'.[39] Essentially, there must be an agreement between two banks where the respondent bank opens an account with the correspondent bank, and the correspondent bank provides services in return, with a particular importance placed on payment services.[40]

Some of the identified various risks posed to correspondent banking – in particular, cross-border ones – are market, foreign exchange, credit and counterparty, and regulatory risks (eg anti-money laundering and counter-terrorism financing), cost of liquidity, and challenges associated with new technologies.[41] In recent years, the trend of 'de-risking' in response to increasingly stringent compliance obligations and costs has led to a decline in the number of correspondent banking relationships, affecting international payments.[42]

Figure 9.1 Correspondent banking

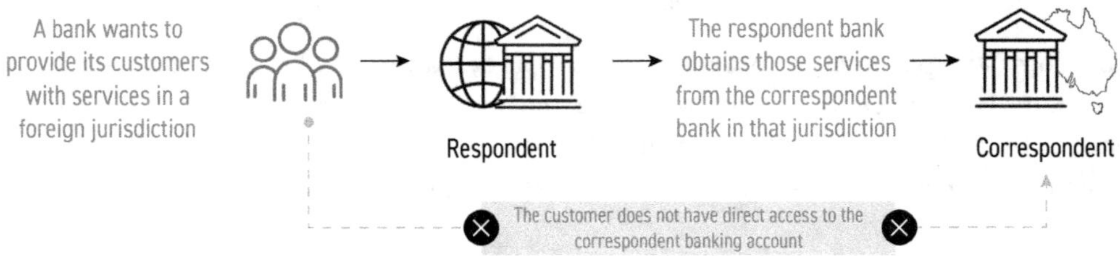

Source: Adapted from 'Correspondent Banking Relationships', *AUSTRAC* (Web Page) <https://www.austrac.gov.au/correspondent-banking-relationships>.

38 Bank for International Settlements Committee on Payments and Market Infrastructure, *Correspondent Banking* (July 2016) 9. In Australia, the *Anti-Money Laundering and Counter-Terrorism Financing Act 2006* (Cth) s 5 ('*AML/CTF Act*') defines a correspondent banking relationship as involving a financial institution (the correspondent) providing banking services to another financial institution (the respondent) in another country.

39 The Wolfsberg Group, *The Wolfsbert Correspondent Banking Due Diligence Questionnaire (CBDDQ): Glossary* (22 February 2018) <https://www.wolfsberg-principles.com/sites/default/files/wb/pdfs/Wolfsberg%27s_CBDDQ_Glossary_220218_v1.0.pdf>

40 Bank for International Settlements Committee on Payments and Market Infrastructure, *Correspondent Banking* (July 2016) 9. In practical terms, the accounts owned in such a relationship are often referred to as 'Nostro' and 'Vostro' accounts – from Italian, meaning 'ours' and 'yours' accounts. A nostro account is an account a bank holds in a foreign bank, while a vostro account means your account with us. Ruth Wandhöfer and Barbara Casu, 'The Future of Correspondent Banking Cross Border Payments' (SWIFT Institute Working Paper No 2017-001, 10 October 2018) 9.

41 Wandhöfer and Casu (n 40) 9.

42 Michaela Erbenová et al, *The Withdrawal of Correspondent Banking Relationships: A Case for Policy Action* (Staff Discussion Note, International Monetary Fund, June 2016).

9.1.3 Main payment instruments

A payment system includes various payment methods such as cash, cards, cheques and electronic funds transfers (EFTs). While cash remains a crucial part of the Australian payment system, the past few years have witnessed its decline. According to the RBA data, non-cash methods are now widespread, with credit and debit cards being the most popular instruments.[43] Chapter 8 has examined the role of the traditional payment method – namely, the cheque. In what follows, we consider some of the more contemporary payment instruments.

Table 9.1 Consumer payment methods[a] (share of number of payments, percent)

	2007	2010	2013	2016	2019
Cash	69	62	47	37	27
Cards	26	31	43	52	63
Debit	15	22	24	30	44
Credit and change cards	11	9	19	22	19
BPAY	2	3	3	2	2
Internet/phone banking	N/A	2	2	1	3
Paypal	N/A	1	3	3	2
Cheque	1	1	0.4	0.2	0.2
Other[b]	1	1	2	4	2

[a] Excluding payments over $9999.
[b] 'Other' methods include prepaid, gift and welfare cards, bank cheques, money orders, 'buy now, pay later' and Cabcharge.
Sources: RBA calculations, based on data from Colmar Brunton, Ipsos and Roy Morgan Research

Source: James Caddy et al, 'Consumer Payment Behaviour in Australia', *RBA Bulletin* (March 2020) 10 <https://www.rba.gov.au/publications/bulletin/2020/mar/pdf/consumer-payment-behaviour-in-australia.pdf>.

43 The Treasury, *A Strategic Plan for Australia's Payments System: Building a Modern and Resilient Payments System* (June 2023) <https://treasury.gov.au/sites/default/files/2023-06/p2023-404960.pdf>. Banks are also gradually phasing out the use of cash and cheques. See, eg, Elena Couper, 'Australia's Big Four Reveal Plans after Major Bank Scraps Cash', *News.com.au* (online, 15 September 2023) <https://www.news.com.au/finance/business/banking/australias-big-four-reveal-plans-after-major-bank-scraps-cash/news-story/50c16292a8abad230b4147b058b4a460>; Joseph Huitson, '"Safer, Faster and Convenient": Macquarie Bank Announces Plan to Phase out Cash and Cheques by End of 2024', *SkyNews Australia* (online, 14 September 2023) <https://www.skynews.com.au/business/finance/safer-faster-and-convenient-macquarie-bank-announces-plan-to-phase-out-cash-and-cheques-by-end-of-2024/news-story/1366ef154f75b4bd73c114d8b3d0092c>; Dannielle Maguire, 'Cheques Will Be Phased out by 2030 as Mobile Wallet Use Sky-rockets', *ABC News* (online, 7 June 2023) <https://www.abc.net.au/news/2023-06-07/australian-government-to-phase-out-cheques-by-2030/102449560>.

9.1.3.1 Credit cards

By and large, card payments include electronic funds transfer at the point of sale (EFTPOS), debit card transactions and credit card transactions. There are two types of card transactions, depending upon their source of funds: debit and credit. Credit card transactions will draw on the financial institution's funds and those funds will be essentially a loan to the cardholder. Debit cards, on the other hand, draw on the cardholder's own funds that are already held in an account with the financial institution. We will discuss debit cards in detail below.

A credit card is issued to a customer following a continuing credit contract[44] between consumers and Australian credit licence (ACL) holders, as regulated by the *National Consumer Credit Protection Act 2009* (Cth) and the *National Consumer Credit Protection Regulations 2010* (Cth). A 'Key Facts Sheet' must be included as part of the application form,[45] which contains relevant information and complies with requirements prescribed by the regulations.[46] Under this contract,[47] consumers have access to credit funds that are made available to the holder of the credit card by the card issuer. Once a consumer uses this credit, it must be paid back to the card issuer. Consumers who exceed their credit card limits will be notified by their credit card provider;[48] however, fees are not to be imposed in light of this unless they have been consented to by the consumer, and such consent has not been withdrawn,[49] and the relevant requirements prescribed by the regulations have been complied with.[50] In Australia, credit card issuers generally belong to either MasterCard or Visa card schemes. A typical credit card transaction, as indicated in Figure 9.2, involves four parties: the cardholder, the cardholder's financial institution (the issuer), the merchant and its financial institution (the acquirer).[51] Issuers often have various ways of charging their customers, or cardholders, such as through annual fees. Similarly, merchants that accept card payments typically face fees from their financial institutions, commonly known as 'merchant service fees'. Additionally, 'interchange fees' may be levied between the issuing and acquiring banks, and the specifics of these fees

44 *National Consumer Credit Protection Act 2009* (Cth) s 133BA(1) ('*NCCPA*').

45 Ibid ss 133BC, 133BD. As an illustration, see, eg, Australia and New Zealand Banking Group Limited, *Key Facts about Our Credit Cards* (8 November 2023) <https://www.anz.com.au/content/dam/anzcomau/documents/pdf/anz-credit-cards-key-facts-sheet.pdf>.

46 *NCCPA* (n 44) s 133BB. The information that must be included in a Key Facts Sheet is defined by the *National Consumer Credit Protection Regulations 2010* (Cth). These guidelines mandate the disclosure of various financial details such as the lowest credit limit, minimum payment obligations, applicable interest rates, as well as annual and late payment charges. *National Consumer Credit Protection Regulations 2010* (Cth) sch 6.

47 See, eg, Westpac Banking Corporation, *Westpac Credit Cards: Terms and Conditions* (7 November 2022), <https://www.westpac.com.au/content/dam/public/wbc/documents/pdf/pb/credit-cards/westpac-credit-card-terms-and-conditions.pdf>.

48 *NCCPA* (n 44) s 133BH.

49 Ibid s 133BI(1)(a), (b).

50 Ibid s 133BI(1)(c).

51 Reserve Bank of Australia, 'Review of Card Payments Regulation' (Issues Paper, March 2015) <https://www.rba.gov.au/payments-and-infrastructure/review-of-card-payments-regulation/pdf/review-of-card-payments-regulation-issues-paper.pdf> ('RBA, Review of Card Payments Regulation: 2015 Issues Paper').

can vary according to different payment schemes.[52] Also, 'three-party' schemes such as American Express and Diners Club serve as both the issuer and acquirer, eliminating the need for interchange fees.[53]

Figure 9.2 The four-party credit card model

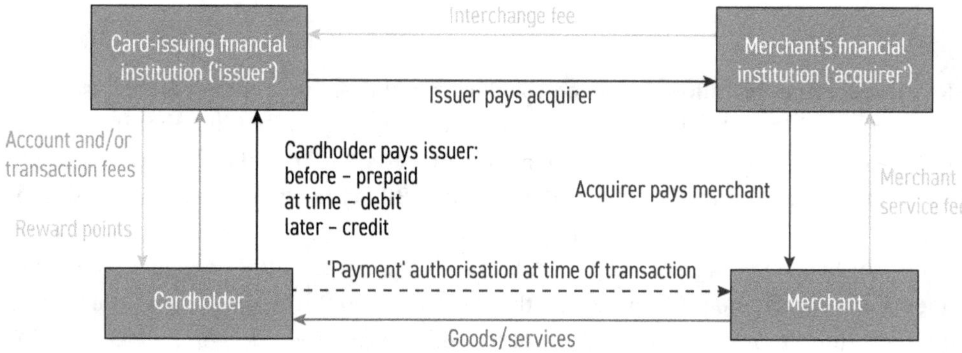

Source: RBA, *Review of Card Payments Regulation* (Issues Paper, March 2015) 6 <https://www.rba.gov.au/payments-and-infrastructure/review-of-card-payments-regulation/pdf/review-of-card-payments-regulation-issues-paper.pdf>.

9.1.3.2 Debit cards

A debit card automatically debits a bank account that has cleared funds (or where there is an agreed overdraft limit). Debit cards are different from credit cards in that debit cards use funds that are already in the nominated account. In Australia, debit cards are the most frequently used payment option; many of those cards are dual-network debit cards (DNDCs).[54] Under a DNDC, a user's domestic point-of-scale transaction will be processed via EFTPOS; alternatively, an online or foreign transaction will be processed through an international scheme such as Debit Mastercard or Visa Debit.[55]

52 'Interchange fee' is defined by MasterCard Australia as a small fee paid by a merchant's bank (acquirer) to a cardholder's bank (issuer) as compensation for the benefits that merchants receive when they accept electronic payments. This allows issuing banks of electronic payments to provide much value to merchants, governments and consumers. See 'Understanding Interchange', *MasterCard Australia* (Web Page) <https://www.mastercard.com.au/en-au/business/overview/support/interchange.html>.

53 RBA, Review of Card Payments Regulation: 2015 Issues Paper (n 51) 36. Thus, as the RBA points out, 'while American Express and Diners Club are subject (by voluntary undertaking) to the Bank's standard on merchant pricing which prevents them from having no-surcharge rules, these schemes have not been subject to the Bank's interchange Standards'.

54 As per the RBA, approximately 90 per cent of debit cards in Australia are dual-network debit cards (DNDCs). A DNDC is a type of card that is compatible with both international networks (such as Visa or MasterCard) and the domestic EFTPOS system, allowing transactions to be routed through either network. Reserve Bank of Australia, 'Review of Retail Payments Regulations' (Conclusions Paper, October 2021) ('RBA, Review of Retail Payments Regulations: 2021 Conclusion Paper') <https://www.rba.gov.au/payments-and-infrastructure/review-of-retail-payments-regulation/conclusions-paper-202110/dual-network-debit-cards-and-least-cost-routing.html>.

55 Reserve Bank of Australia, 'Review of Retail Payments Regulation' (Issues Paper, November 2019) 14. <https://www.rba.gov.au/payments-and-infrastructure/review-of-retail-payments-regulation/pdf/

Regardless of the scheme, a DNDC will withdraw payment money from the same deposit account.[56] Debit cards are regulated by the RBA, which aims to facilitate competition and efficiency within the Australian payments system.[57] In an effort to maximise these results, the RBA has lowered the cap on interchange fees to 10 cents[58] and has imposed an expectation upon debit card issuers with more than 1 per cent value of all debit card transactions to issue DNDCs as part of a least-cost routing (LCR) initiative.[59]

9.1.3.3 BPAY

BPAY is a service that allows service providers to bill their customers where customers have instructed their banks to do so. Bills for services (eg utility bills) that include the BPAY logo can be paid via BPAY, which means that credit to the biller account is instant. The service launched in November 1997. To use BPAY, businesses and organisations must apply for a BPAY scheme membership, of which there are three tiers: participant member, associate member, and payer institution member.[60] BPAY is regulated by ASIC under the *ePayments Code* (discussed further below). In 2021, the Australian Competition and Consumer Commission (ACCC) authorised a proposed merger between BPAY, EFTPOS and NPP Australia to form Australia Payments Plus (AP+), enabling the payment schemes to coordinate investment proposals and encourage shareholders (including major banks) to invest in domestic payment services.[61]

9.1.3.4 Stored value cards

Stored value cards are cards with a monetary value stored on the card itself, rather than in an external credit provider (as with credit cards) or a nominated bank account (as with debit cards). Electronic value can be loaded onto the card and then used with merchants who accept the card. Stored value cards also include gift cards, which may be used when buying goods from one select merchant, known as a 'closed system card'; or a group of merchants authorised by the distributor of the gift card, known as a 'semi-closed system card'.[62]

---

review-of-retail-payments-regulation-issues-paper-nov-2019.pdf> ('RBA, Review of Retail Payments Regulation: 2019 Issue Paper').

56 Ibid.

57 Ibid 20.

58 Reserve Bank of Australia, *The Setting of Interchange Fees in the Designated Debit and Prepaid Card Schemes and Net Payments to Issuers* (Standard No 2, 2016) cl 4.1(a)(i) <https://www.rba.gov.au/payments-and-infrastructure/review-of-card-payments-regulation/pdf/standard-no-2-of-2016-debit-and-prepaid-card-interchange-2021-11-18.pdf>.

59 RBA, Review of Retail Payments Regulations: 2021 Conclusion Paper (n 54) 29.

60 'BPAY', *Australian Payments Network* (Web Page) <https://www.auspaynet.com.au/resources/New-To-Payments-8>.

61 Australian Competition and Consumer Commission, 'ACCC Authorises Payment Systems Merger after Undertaking' (Media Release No 138/21, 9 September 2021). <https://www.accc.gov.au/media-release/accc-authorises-payment-systems-merger-after-undertaking>.

62 An example of a closed-system card is a David Jones gift card, which can only be used for purchases at David Jones stores. In contrast, a semi-closed system card such as a FlyBuys gift card offers more flexibility, allowing you to use it at various merchants, including H&M. See, eg, Australian Institute of Criminology, 'Money Laundering Risks of Prepaid Stored Value Cards', *Trends and Issues in Crime and Criminal Justice* (September 2008) 2 <https://www.aic.gov.au/sites/default/files/2020-05/tandi363.pdf>.

9.2 *ePayments Code*

9.2.1 History

The predecessor to the *ePayments Code* was the *Electronic Funds Transfer Code of Conduct* ('*EFT Code*'), which was implemented in December 1989. It was initially monitored by the Australian Payments System Council but was later supervised by the Australian Securities and Investments Commission (ASIC). The *EFT Code* was essentially an industry code of conduct to which institutions could subscribe. A new version of the Code, the *ePayments Code*, was released in September 2011. Subscribers were required to transition to the updated Code, which commenced on 1 July 2012, by 20 March 2013.[63] The *ePayments Code* has since been updated. The transition period for this new version started from 2 June 2022, and subscribers were required to comply with this Code by 2 June 2023.[64]

9.2.2 The legal nature of the *ePayments Code*

The *ePayments Code* is not legally binding, as it is not a piece of legislation;[65] rather, it is a voluntary code intended to be adopted as a contract between subscribing financial institutions and customers. The Code, alongside the *Corporations Act* and the *National Consumer Credit Protection Act 2009* (Cth), forms the regulatory regime of electronic payment facilities in Australia.[66] It is administered and regularly reviewed by ASIC.[67] For example, in the case of *Andrews v Australia and New Zealand Banking Group*,[68] the Court noted that the *ePayments Code* was a voluntary code of banking practice and lacks statutory force. However, the Court did consider the provisions of the Code, as well as other voluntary codes, when constructing the clauses in contracts in determining the nature of the disputed fees. In another case, *National Australia Bank Ltd v Swed (No 2)*,[69] the Court similarly referred to a previous version of the *ePayments Code* – the *EFT Code* – as they construed terms in the bank's terms and conditions in determining whether there was a breach of contract, as the Code required the bank, as a subscriber, to include a warranty in its terms and conditions that it would comply with the Code. From these cases, it can be seen that the provisions in the *ePayments Code* generally form part of the contract between the bank and the user, and that a breach of such contractual provisions would result in liability.

Notably, in its most recent review of the *ePayments Code*, ASIC has highlighted several key milestones that offer a broader policy context for its ongoing work.[70] Specifically, ASIC pointed to the 2014 Financial System Inquiry, which recommended making Code

63 'ePayments Code', *Australian Securities and Investments Commission* (Web Page) <https://asic.gov.au/regulatory-resources/financial-services/epayments-code/>.

64 *ePayments Code* 4 ('What Does the Code Do?) (as amended 18 March 2022; effective 2 June 2022).

65 Ibid ('Who is Bound by this Code?').

66 Ibid ('What Does this Code Do?').

67 Ibid ('What Is the e-Payments Code?').

68 *Andrews v Australia and New Zealand Banking Group Ltd* (2011) 211 FCR 53.

69 *National Australia Bank Ltd v Swed (No 2)* [2015] NSWSC 1322.

70 Australian Securities and Investments Commission, *Response to Submissions on CP 341 Review of the ePayments Code: Further Consultation* (Report 718, March 2022) 5 ('ASIC, *Report 718*') <https://download.asic.gov.au/media/f0tjuyqt/rep718-published-7-march-2022.pdf>.

protections mandatory.[71] This was followed by a 2019 recommendation from the Council of Financial Regulators (CFR),[72] advocating for legislative authority to be given to ASIC to enforce Code compliance. Adding to this momentum, the Assistant Minister for Superannuation, Financial Services and Financial Technology announced in a November 2020 media release that she had directed the Treasury to collaborate with the Australian Prudential Regulation Authority and ASIC to craft a reform package.[73] Importantly, ASIC has indicated the potential to make the Code mandatory in the future as it continues its efforts to enhance the Code. (This position can also be seen in the Treasury's recent review of the payment system.[74])

9.2.3 Key provisions examined

9.2.3.1 Types of transactions

The *ePayments Code* applies to all electronic transactions, including stored value facilities and transactions. It applies to 'payment, funds transfer and cash withdrawal transactions that are initiated using electronic equipment, and not intended to be authenticated by comparing a manual signature with a specimen signature'.[75] The *ePayments Code* further clarifies that it applies to the following transactions provided by a 'subscriber' – a term discussed further below:[76]

- electronic card transactions (including ATM, EFTPOS, credit card and debit card transactions) that are not intended to be authenticated by comparing a manual signature with a specimen signature
- telephone banking and bill payment transactions
- 'pay anyone' banking facility transactions
- online transactions performed using a card number and expiry date
- online bill payments (including BPAY)
- transactions using facilities with contactless features and prepaid cards, not intended to be authenticated by comparing a manual signature with a specimen signature

71 Ibid 8 (citing Recommendation 16 of The Treasury of Australia, *Financial System Inquiry Final Report* (November 2014) 234 <https://treasury.gov.au/sites/default/files/2019-03/p2014-FSI-01Final-Report.pdf>, which stated: 'Strengthen consumer protection by mandating the ePayments Code. Introduce a separate prudential regime with two tiers for purchased payment facilities.')

72 Ibid 7. (In 2019, the Council of Financial Regulators (CFR) recommended that ASIC be given the power to make compliance with the Code mandatory, such as through a legislative rule-making power.)

73 Ibid (citing Jane Hume, 'Supporting Competition and Innovation in Payment Services' (Media Release, Treasury Portfolio, 6 November 2020): 'Compliance with the ePayments Code should be mandatory for payments product providers').

74 The Treasury, *Payments System Review 2021* (n 3) 71 ('Adherence to standards set by industry bodies is currently not mandatory, which undermines a level playing field for participants within the payments ecosystem. The Review recommends mandating compliance with core industry standards set by authorised standard-setting bodies for holders of the new payments licence. This would ensure consistency and transparency in the application of the standards, such that providers of services that give rise to the same risks would be subject to the same requirements.')

75 *ePayments Code* (n 63) cl 2.4.

76 Ibid cl 2.5.

- direct debits
- transactions using electronic toll devices
- transactions using mobile devices
- transactions using electronic public transport ticketing facilities
- mail order transactions not intended to be authenticated by comparing a manual signature with a specimen signature
- any other transaction specified by ASIC under cl 44 as a transaction to which the Code applies.

ASIC has the discretion to declare that the *ePayments Code* does/does not apply to a type of transaction.[77]

9.2.3.2 To whom does the *ePayments Code* apply?

The *ePayments Code* is currently voluntary; thus, it applies to its 'subscribers', which include most banks, credit unions and building societies, along with a number of non-banking businesses.[78] It applies to both 'holders' (ie the person in whose name the facility has been established/issued) and 'users' (ie the person authorised by the holder to use the facility).[79] It does not, however, apply to:[80]

- a facility designed primarily for use by a business and established primarily for business purposes
- a facility where the holder and the subscriber do not have a contractual relationship
- biller accounts.[81]

Under the Code, exemptions and declarations may apply to select subscribers. ASIC may exempt one or a class of Code subscribers from particular clauses or declare that certain clauses may be modified to apply to a particular transaction or type of transaction, a particular facility or class or facility, or a particular subscriber or class of subscribers.[82] Subscribers may file an application for an exemption or declaration, which will then be assessed by ASIC according to the objectives of the Code, its appropriateness and any potential unreasonable burdens.[83]

9.2.3.3 Allocation of liability for unauthorised transactions

Several updates have been made to the 2022 Code regarding unauthorised transactions. ASIC has introduced a limitation period of six years during which subscribers to the Code must accept a report relating to an unauthorised transaction (beginning from the day

77 Ibid cl 44.

78 Ibid.

79 Ibid Ch A.

80 Ibid cl 2.1(a).

81 'Biller account' is defined under cl 2.6 of the *ePayments Code* as an 'internal account maintained by a business for the purpose of recording amounts owing and paid for goods or services provided by the business'.

82 'Exemptions and declarations under the ePayments Code', *Australian Securities and Investments Commission* (Web Page) <https://asic.gov.au/regulatory-resources/financial-services/epayments-code/exemptions-and-declarations-under-the-epayments-code/>.

83 Ibid.

the user first became aware, or should have reasonably become aware, of the transaction).[84] The period is separate from any limitation periods relating to reports of disputed transactions under a card scheme's chargeback rules. In its report, ASIC acknowledged the separate frameworks underpinning the *Code*'s unauthorised transaction provisions and card chargeback schemes and implemented the update to avoid confusion among subscribers and consumers.[85] A subscriber must not refuse an unauthorised transaction report because the limitation period for chargeback disputes has elapsed.[86]

Another notable update to the 2022 *ePayments Code* pertains to the definition of unauthorised transactions: cl 2.6 defines an 'unauthorised transaction' as 'a transaction that is not authorised by a user'; however, it has been further specified that it does not include self-performed transactions or transactions that the user has consented to being performed by third parties.[87]

More specifically, under ch C of the *ePayments Code*, which sets out the rules for allocating the liability for authorised transactions, cll 9–11 clarify the circumstances where a holder should or should not be liable for relevant loss arising from authorised transactions. In terms of its application, cl 9.1 specifies that the provisions in this chapter are supplementary to any existing processes or rights outlined in a card scheme's chargeback rules.[88] Meanwhile, cl 9.3 states that transactions conducted by a third party, with the user's knowledge and consent, are not deemed unauthorised.[89] It is also worth noting that the chapter is not applicable to low-value facilities, defined as those with a balance limit of up to $500.[90]

There are tailored requirements for a low-value facility – a subscriber offering such a facility must inform users 'whether the subscriber provides a process to report the loss, theft or misuse of a device or breach of passcode security'.[91]

Clause 10.1 lists the cases where a holder is not liable for the loss of an unauthorised transaction if the loss arises from any of the following:[92]

(a) where there is fraud or negligence done by an employee or agent of a subscriber, third party involved in networking arrangements, or by a merchant or their employee or agent
(b) a device, identifier or passcode that is forged, faulty, expired or cancelled
(c) a transaction requiring the use of a device and/or passcode that occurred before the user received the device and/or passcode (including a reissued device and/or passcode)

84 *ePayments Code* (n 63) cl 17.3.
85 ASIC, *Report 718* (n 70) 39–40.
86 *ePayments Code* (n 63) cl 17.3.
87 Ibid cl 2.6. Previously, the *ePayments Code* had defined 'unauthorised transactions' as 'a transaction not authorised by a user'. ASIC has now provided clarification for this ambiguity and excluded from the definition any transactions that were performed by the user or by anyone who performed the transaction with the user's knowledge and consent. Thus, an unauthorised transaction pertains to transactions made by a third party without the user's knowledge or consent.
88 Ibid cl 9.1.
89 Ibid cl 9.3.
90 Ibid cl 2.6.
91 Ibid cl 9.4 (Note).
92 Ibid cl 10.1.

(d) a transaction being incorrectly debited more than once to the same facility
(e) where the subscriber has been informed that the device has been misused, lost or stolen, or the security of a passcode has been breached, and the unauthorised transaction was performed after.

Clause 10.2 of the Code further clarifies that holders are not liable for losses resulting from unauthorised transactions 'made using an identifier without a passcode or device'.[93] If a device, or a device and identifier, was used to make the transaction, but a passcode was not required, holders will only be held liable if the user 'unreasonably delays reporting the loss of theft of the device'.[94]

Moreover, a holder would not be held liable for loss of an authorised transaction where 'it is clear that a user has not contributed to the loss'.[95] Clause 10.4 lays down the rules for a dispute around whether a user received a device or passcode:[96]

(a) There will be a presumption that the user did not receive a device or passcode unless proven otherwise by the subscriber.
(b) An acknowledgement of receipt by the user will aide a subscriber in proving that the user had received the device or passcode.
(c) Proof of delivery to a user's correct mailing or electronic address cannot be relied upon by the subscriber as proof that the user received the device or passcode.

Further, a subscriber is prohibited by cl 10.5 from having 'any term in its terms and conditions that deems a device or passcode sent to a user by mail or electronic communication at the user's correct mailing or electronic address to be received by the user'.[97]

Clause 11 outlines the conditions under which a holder would be responsible for losses due to unauthorised transactions. It emphasises that liability will only be assigned to the holder under the criteria specified in cl 11, when the provisions of cl 10 are not applicable.[98] Clause 11.2 provides the following where it is proven on a balance of probabilities that a user contributed to a loss through fraud or a breach of cl 12 passcode security requirements (the Code has further noted that a breach of passcode security requirements in itself is insufficient for consumer liability – such a breach must be proven to have contributed to the loss):

(a) The holder will be liable for the full actual losses that occur before the loss, theft or misuse of a device or breach of passcode security is reported to the subscriber.
(b) However, the holder is not liable for the portion of losses which
    (i) surpass the daily transaction limit
    (ii) exceed any set periodic transaction limit

93 Ibid cl 10.2.
94 Ibid.
95 Ibid cl 10.3.
96 Ibid cl 10.4.
97 Ibid cl 10.5.
98 Ibid cl 11.1.

(iii) go beyond the existing balance on the facility, including any pre-arranged credit, or

(iv) are incurred on a facility that was not authorised to be accessed using the device or credentials employed for the transaction.[99]

Clause 11.3 then clarifies that, in a scenario where the performance of a transaction requires one or more passcodes[100] and a subscriber is unable to prove a user's breach of cl 12 security passcode requirements for all required passcodes,[101] a holder would be held liable under cl 11.2 if the subscriber proves, on a balance of probability, that when assessed with all contributing causes, the breach of passcode security requirements under cl 12 was the main cause for the loss (more than 50 per cent responsible).[102] A typical unauthorised transaction may occur when a consumer leaves a card in an ATM. In this regard, cl 11.4 stipulates that a holder would be liable for losses arising from unauthorised transactions due to a user leaving a card in an ATM, on the condition that there are reasonable safety measures in place to mitigate the risk of such incidents from happening.[103] Examples of mitigation measures include ATMs which 'capture' cards that are not removed after a reasonable time and those which require users to remove their card after swiping to proceed with a transaction.[104]

Clause 11.5 sets out a holder's liability where a subscriber can prove, on the balance of probabilities, that a user had contributed to the losses arising from an unauthorised transaction by unreasonably delaying the process of reporting the misuse, loss or theft of a device, or that all passcode security had been breached. In the presence of an unreasonable delay, the holder will be liable for all losses that transpire between the time the security breach becomes known to the user, or when the user should have reasonably become aware of it, and when the security breach is reported to the subscriber.[105] However, the holder is not held liable for losses that: (i) surpass the daily transaction limit; (ii) exceed any set periodic transaction limit; (iii) go beyond the existing balance on the facility, including any prearranged credit; or (iv) are incurred on a facility that was not authorised to be accessed using the device or credentials employed for the transaction[106] In any case, a holder may still be liable under cl 11.5 if they are identified as the user who contributed to the loss, or if a different user had contributed to the loss.[107]

To determine whether a user contributed to a loss as specified in cll 11.2 and 11.5, cl 11.8 outlines the key factors to consider. These include: (i) all credible evidence, such as reasonable justifications for why the transaction occurred; (ii) while the fact that a facility has been accessed with the correct device and/or passcode is significant, that fact itself is not proof that a user contributed to losses through fraud or a breach of the

99 Ibid cl 11.2. However, the Code also points out that a breach of the passcode security requirements in itself is insufficient to make a consumer liable for loss from an unauthorised transaction.
100 Ibid cl 11.3(a).
101 Ibid cl 11.3(b).
102 Ibid cl 11.3.
103 Ibid cl 11.4.
104 Ibid (Note).
105 Ibid cl 11.5(a).
106 Ibid cl 11.5(b).
107 Ibid cl 11.5 (Note).

passcode security requirements in cl 12, on a balance of probabilities; and (iii) information not required to be kept confidential by the user will not be relevant when assessing the user's liability.[108] Additionally, the decision as to whether unreasonable delay under cl 11.5 has occurred includes taking into account the effect of any charges imposed by the subscriber associated with making a report or replacing a device or passcode (eg replacement fees for a device).[109]

The *ePayments Code* also sets out situations in which there will be a limited liability: where a passcode was required to perform an authorised transaction, and cll 11.2–11.6 do not apply, the holder is liable for the least of: (a) $150 or lower if determined by the subscriber; (b) the balance of the facility or facilities which the subscriber and holder have agreed on to be accessed with the device and/or passcode, including credit that was prearranged; or (c) the actual loss at the time the security breach is reported to the subscriber, except for the losses that exceed any relevant daily or periodic transaction limit.[110]

A subscriber or an external dispute resolution body may, pursuant to cl 11.9 of the Code, exercise discretion to reduce a holder's liability with regards to unauthorised transactions under cll 11.2–11.7, in circumstances where the subscriber has not applied a reasonable daily (or other periodic) transaction limit. When assessing the circumstances of unauthorised transactions, the subscriber or external body must weigh several key factors.[111] First, they should consider the existing industry norms for setting reasonable transaction limits, as these can serve as a benchmark for assessing the subscriber's practices. Second, the effectiveness of the subscriber's own verification processes should be evaluated. Specifically, the question is whether these security measures offered sufficient protection to the holder against losses, especially when there are no reasonable daily or periodic transaction limits in place. Lastly, in cases where an unauthorised transaction taps into a credit facility, it should be assessed whether the subscriber had initially taken adequate steps to inform the holder of the risks associated with unauthorised transactions, especially when the credit facility can be accessed using a specific device and/or passcode.

Also, cl 11.10 indicates that for reported unauthorised transactions on credit, debit or charge card accounts, a holder's liability will not exceed what it would have been if the subscriber had exercised their rights under the card scheme rules at the time of the report, such as invoking charge-back rights.[112] Notably, it is not required for subscribers to exercise their rights.[113]

9.2.3.4 Mistaken internet payments

One of the oft-seen disputes in the electronic payment context is when a consumer transfers money to the wrong account – the so-called mistaken internet payment. In the most recent update, the Code has changed how subscribers address these issues. ASIC narrowed the definition of 'mistaken internet payment' to explicitly exclude any payment

108 Ibid cl 11.8.
109 Ibid cl 11.6.
110 Ibid cl 11.7.
111 Ibid cl 11.9.
112 Ibid cl 11.10(a).
113 Ibid cl 11.10(b).

made as a result of a scam and was intended to relate only to typographical-type errors.[114] The *ePayments Code* defines the term 'mistaken internet payment' as:

> [P]ayment by a user through a pay anyone banking facility and processed by an ADI [authorised deposit-taking institution] where funds are paid into the account of an unintended recipient because the user enters or selects a BSB number and/or identifier that does not belong to the named and/or intended recipient as a result of: the user's error, or the user being advised of the wrong BSB number and/or identifier.[115]

As per ASIC, the framework for mistaken internet payments is not intended to assign liability for lost funds between the consumer and the subscriber. Instead, it serves as a procedural guide for both the sending and receiving ADIs to help recover funds mistakenly sent to the wrong recipient.[116] The Code lays down, among others, the rules as follows.

Disclosure

Subscribers are required to satisfy certain disclosure requirements. Clause 26 states specifically that the terms and conditions must set out the following prescribed processes, including: (i) circumstances where funds will be recovered from an unintended recipient by the subscriber without the unintended recipient's consent; and (ii) circumstances where a holder will be liable for losses arising from a mistaken internet payment.[117]

On-screen warning

The Code has also developed more comprehensive on-screen warning requirements, ensuring that subscribers notify users to check the accuracy of the BSB number or identifier before performing a transaction,[118] and to warn users that the names and identifiers will not be matched, verified or checked by the subscriber.[119] As per ASIC, such changes will provide greater clarity to the consumer that identity checking is not common practice for most ADIs.[120]

Reporting, investigation and record keeping

As per cl 28, a subscriber is required to maintain an 'effective and convenient' report system for mistaken internet payments that is free of charge or at costs similar to a local call.[121] Moreover, a subscriber must also 'acknowledge the receipt of every report', which, while not needing to be in writing, must allow users to verify the date when the report was made.[122] Where a user makes a report, an investigation must be carried out by

114 Ibid cl 25.2.
115 Ibid cl 2.6.
116 ASIC, *Report 718* (n 70) 20.
117 *ePayments Code* (n 63) cl 26.
118 Ibid cl 27.1.
119 Ibid cl 27.1(b).
120 ASIC, *Report 718* (n 70) 22.
121 *ePayments Code* (n 63) cll 28.1, 28.2.
122 Ibid cl 28.3.

the sending ADI to determine whether a mistaken payment has indeed occurred.[123] If the sending ADI finds that a mistake has occurred, the following steps would apply:

(a) As soon as reasonably possible and within five business days from the time of the report, the sending ADI must send the receiving ADI a request for the return of funds.
(b) After receiving the request, within five business days, the receiving ADI must:
    (i) send the return of funds
    (ii) advise whether the account of the unintended recipient has enough funds to cover the mistaken internet payment.[124]

Notably, the expression 'as soon as reasonably possible' under cl 29.2(a), according to the Code, refers to within two business days.[125] Yet, if the sending ADI is not satisfied that the mistaken internet payment has occurred, no further action is required.[126] Both the sending and receiving ADIs are required to keep records that are 'sufficient to demonstrate the steps they took to comply with the mistaken internet payment obligations' under the Code.[127]

Process for handling cases where there are sufficient funds

Clauses 30–32 set out prescribed processes for handling cases where the funds are sufficient. According to cl 30, in a scenario where the mistaken internet payment report was made within 10 business days from the date of payment, and the sending ADI is satisfied that the mistaken payment occurred and of the availability of sufficient funds in the account of the unintended recipient equal to the value of the mistaken payment, cll 30.2–30.4 would apply.[128] Clause 30.2 states that where the receiving ADI is satisfied that a mistaken payment has occurred, the receiving ADI must return the funds to the sending ADI within five days of the request by the sending ADI being made, or 'if practicable, or such longer period as is reasonably necessary, up to a maximum of 10 business days'.[129]

Clause 31 sets out the procedure if a mistaken internet payment has been reported between 10 business days and 7 months and if there are sufficient funds available. In such a case, the receiving ADI must complete its investigation into the report within 10 days of receiving a request. Upon being satisfied that a mistaken payment has occurred, it is required to: (a) disable the unintended recipient from withdrawing the funds for another 10 business days; and (b) notify the unintended recipient that if they do not prove that they are entitled to the funds within those 10 business days, the funds will be withdrawn from their account.[130]

If the unintended recipient has failed to establish entitlement to the funds within 10 business days, the receiving ADI is required to return the funds to the sending ADI

123 Ibid cl 29.1.
124 Ibid cl 29.2.
125 Ibid.
126 Ibid cl 29.3.
127 Ibid cl 29.4.
128 Ibid cl 30.1.
129 Ibid cl 30.2.
130 Ibid cl 31.3.

within two business days. During this period, the unintended recipient is barred from withdrawing the funds.[131] If, however, a report is made after seven months and sufficient funds are available, cl 32 of the Code applies. If the receiving ADI is satisfied that a mistaken internet payment has occurred, consent must be sought from the unintended user to return the funds to the user.[132] Upon receiving consent, 'the receiving ADI must return the funds to the sending ADI',[133] upon which 'the sending ADI must return the funds to the holder as soon as practicable'.[134]

Process for handling cases where there are insufficient funds

According to cl 34.2, the receiving ADI has the discretion of choosing between complete funds, partial funds or no fund retrieval,[135] taking into account the interest of both parties and a set of non-exhaustive factors under cl 34.5 (eg the financial impacts of a retrieval on the unintended recipient, the desire for all parties to have certainty aboput when the process will reach a conclusion, etc.).[136] The receiving ADI is, however, not allowed to exercise discretion under cl 34.2 if its investigations indicate that the 'total amount of the mistaken internet payment is available at the time in the unintended recipient's account'.[137]

9.2.3.5 Complaint process

Chapter F of the *ePayments Code* sets out the complaints process. It stipulates that a complaint means 'an expression of dissatisfaction made to or about an organisation, related to its products, services, staff, or the handling of a complaint, where a response or resolution is explicitly or implicitly expected or legally required'.[138] It also requires that its subscribers who are Australian financial services licensees, unlicensed product issuers, unlicensed secondary sellers, Australian credit licensees or credit representatives have internal dispute resolution procedures that comply with ASIC Regulatory Guide 271 (internal dispute resolution).[139]

The Code sets out the process for complaints, which includes a limitation period of six years from when the user becomes aware, or reasonably aware, of the circumstances that give rise to the complaint and acceptance by the subscriber of the complaint made within that period.[140]

Where a subscriber or its employee's or agent's non-compliance contributes to a decision about a complaint that is against the user or delays the resolution of a complaint, the subscriber may, or as determined by an external dispute resolution scheme, pay part or the full amount of a disputed transaction as compensation, even if the subscriber is

131 Ibid cl 31.4.
132 Ibid cl 32.2.
133 Ibid cl 32.4(a).
134 Ibid cl 32.4(b).
135 Ibid cl 34.2.
136 Ibid cl 34.5.
137 Ibid cl 34.2.
138 Ibid cl 38.3.
139 Ibid cl 39.1; Australian Securities and Investments Commission, *Internal Dispute Resolution* (Regulatory Guide 271, 2 September 2021).
140 *ePayments Code* (n 63) cl 40.1.

not liable under ch C of the *ePayments Code*.[141] Senior management of the subscriber or the external dispute resolution scheme will determine the compensation amount.[142] The *ePayments Code* also stipulates 'tailored requirements for disputed transactions covered by card scheme rules'.[143]

9.2.3.6 Compliance monitoring and data collection

The Code has removed the requirement that subscribers must report unauthorised transactions annually to ASIC,[144] but has retained ASIC's authority to perform ad hoc compliance monitoring of subscribers' compliance with Code obligations (already present within cl 44.2 of the Code), further extending its authority to monitor subscriber activities to the extent that they are relevant to electronic payments.[145] Such powers will enable ASIC to observe emerging developments in the electronic payments sector and to adapt the Code accordingly.[146]

9.2.3.7 Other emerging challenges

The *ePayments Code* currently does not address certain issues that are emerging as a result of recent technologies such as fingerprint or facial recognition, or other biometric authentication that serves as a password; or Apple Pay or Google Pay; or 'screen scraping'. However, this is an area which ASIC has noted requires further examination before it is introduced as an area of regulation by the Code.[147] Some of these issues are discussed briefly below.

Fingerprint/facial recognition/biometric authentication

In March 2022, ASIC released its Report 718, *Review of the ePayments Code*, for further consultation. In the report, ASIC addresses feedback to accommodate biometric authentication in efforts to modernise the Code. In its earlier consultation paper (CP 341),[148] ASIC proposed to define biometric authentication in the *ePayments Code* and to incorporate biometric authentication into the Code in some specific clauses where required, in recognition of the current market trend where biometric authentication replaces previously used passcodes.[149] Currently, ASIC has declined to move forward with this proposal, citing the complexity and rapidly expanding nature of biometric authentication as reasons to delay regulation until it is 'ensure[d] that the benefits of accommodating biometric

---

141 Ibid cl 40.2.
142 Ibid cl 40.3.
143 Ibid cl 19.
144 ASIC, *Report 718* (n 70) 7.
145 *ePayments Code* (n 63) cl 45.1.
146 ASIC, *Report 718* (n 70) 9.
147 In its consultation report, ASIC noted that while biometric authentication is a key area of development since its previous review of the *Code*, and is an area which the Code does not cover, ASIC agrees that further work is required to 'ensure that the benefits of accommodating biometric authentication within the *Code* are balanced appropriately against implications stemming from consumers' use of such technology'. Ibid 43.
148 Australian Securities and Investments Commission, *Review of the ePayments Code: Further Consultation* (Consultation Paper No 341, 21 May 2021) ('*CP 341*').
149 ASIC, *Report 718* (n 70) 41–3 ('Proposal F1').

authentication within the Code are balanced appropriately against implications stemming from consumers' use of such technology'.[150] ASIC has instead committed itself to engage with stakeholders to examine consumers' use of their personal devices vis a vis biometric access and assess the appropriateness of implementing biometric regulations in the voluntary *ePayments Code*, or, alternatively, to await government mandating of the Code before proceeding with the regulation in this area.[151]

Digital wallets: Apple Pay, Google Pay and beyond

Digital wallets,[152] exemplified by applications such as Apple Pay, Google Pay and WeChat Pay, have become increasingly integral to the modern financial landscape.[153] Broadly, these apps serve multiple functions:

- They enable in-person merchant payments via near-field communication (NFC) or QR codes.
- They facilitate peer-to-peer transfers through the app, text messages or QR codes.
- They allow the storage of funds from linked bank accounts or debit cards.
- Some of them provide a platform for cryptocurrency transactions.[154]

Notwithstanding their convenience, they operate in a regulatory grey area, raising concerns for policymakers at home and abroad.

In the United States, for instance, digital wallet providers, especially Big Tech companies, face increasing scrutiny over privacy and consumer protection. Under the *Gramm-Leach-Bliley Act*, these tech companies are obliged to protect users' non-public personal information; however, the practice indicates that they share data with affiliated companies and even share it with non-affiliates unless consumers opt out.[155]

150 Ibid 43.

151 Ibid.

152 The technology of tokenisation is central to the enhanced security of mobile payment systems such as Apple Pay. Unlike traditional card payments, tokenisation replaces sensitive card information with a unique, encrypted 'device account number' that is stored in a secure chip within the device. Each transaction generates a one-time 'dynamic security code', minimising the risk of unauthorised use. This makes mobile payments generally more secure than traditional methods, as they do not expose the user's name, card number or security code. Legally speaking, however, mobile payments pose new challenges. This raises problems not only in Australia, but elsewhere. In the United States, for instance, it has been argued that the introduction of a third party – mobile system operators such as Apple, Google and Samsung – creates legal uncertainties. Existing laws such as the *Truth in Lending Act* and the *Electronic Fund Transfer Act* may not fully account for this new role in the payment process. This raises questions about liability allocation in cases of fraud or unauthorised transactions. See, eg, Mark Edwin Burge, 'Apple Pay, Bitcoin, and Consumers: The ABCs of Future Public Payments Law' (2016) 67(6) *Hastings Law Journal* 1493, 1526. However, some argue that these 'Pays' platforms are still subject to existing regulatory frameworks. Similar to peer-to-peer entities, most of these 'Pays' should be classified as money service businesses under the *Bank Secrecy Act* in the United States. Hence, they are obligated to adhere to that Act and anti-money laundering regulations. See Elizabeth Boison et al, 'Money Moves: Following the Money Beyond the Banking System' (2019) 67(3) *Department of Justice Journal of Federal Law and Practice* 95, 107.

153 For a detailed analysis, see Adam J Levitin, 'Pandora's Digital Box: The Promise and Perils of Digital Wallets' (2018) 166(2) *University of Pennsylvania Law Review* 305.

154 US Congressional Research Services, *Digital Wallets and Selected Policy Issues* (18 April 2022) 1 ('*US CRS Report on Digital Wallets*').

155 The policy issue concerning digital wallets and consumer data might be addressed through upcoming rulemaking for s 1033 of the *Dodd-Frank Act*. This section mandates that any financial

In 2021, the US Consumer Financial Protection Bureau (CFPB) directed major tech firms such as Amazon, Apple and Google to provide details on their payment products, focusing on the issues around 'invasive financial surveillance' and data misuse.[156] This could lead to further regulatory guidelines. For disputes involving authorised transactions in the context of digital wallets, the *Electronic Fund Transfer Act* (P.L. 95-630), implemented through CFPB Regulation E,[157] could apply if the transaction meets the specific criteria for 'authorized transactions',[158] a term with a definition similar to that in the *ePayments Code.*[159]

The Australian Government is currently reviewing the role of digital wallets in a broader policy context. Concerns exist that digital wallets utilised in Australia, but not managed from within the country, may not be subject to the same local regulatory guidelines as those both operated and used domestically.[160] For instance, it is argued that the RBA's power to designate only 'payment systems' under the existing regulatory framework is too narrow to capture the evolving payments ecosystem, which includes digital wallets and tech firms.[161] This creates 'an uneven playing field' between newcomers and existing players.[162] This regulatory gap has led to calls for reform from various stakeholders. The Commonwealth Bank of Australia, for instance, has urged the Government

---

service provider must share the data it has collected with consumers upon request. While this rule has not yet been implemented, it aims to give consumers greater control over their financial data and the freedom to take their business elsewhere. Yet, it is a matter of debate whether this provision would be applicable to companies offering digital wallets. Ibid 1–2.

156 Rohit Chopra, 'Statement Regarding the CFPB's Inquiry into Big Tech Payment Platforms', *Consumer Financial Protection Bureau* (Web Page, 21 October 2021) <https://www.consumerfinance.gov/about-us/newsroom/statement-regarding-the-cfpbs-inquiry-into-big-tech-payment-platforms/>.

157 Regulation E, issued by the Consumer Financial Protection Bureau under the authority of the *Electronic Fund Transfer Act 1978*, focuses on safeguarding individual consumers involved in electronic fund transfers (EFTs) among its various provisions.

158 *US CRS Report on Digital Wallets* (n 154) 2; see also Matt Goble, 'P2P Payment Transfers: Regulation E Liability', *temenos* (Web Page) <https://www.temenos.com/news/2021/06/30/p2p-payment-transfers-regulation-e-liability/>. (Goble argues that in the rising trend of peer-to-peer payment apps such as Apple Pay, the question of liability for unauthorised electronic fund transfers [EFTs] is rather complex in the US context. If a customer disputes a transaction as unauthorised or fraudulent, such disputes will be handled as per the prescribed procedure under s 1005.11 of reg E, which is governed by the *Electronic Funds Transaction Act*. These laws establish the rules and liabilities for EFTs and define unauthorised transactions as 'an electronic fund transfer from a consumer's account initiated by a person other than the consumer without actual authority to initiate the transfer and from which the consumer receives no benefit'. However, for disputes other than unauthorised or fraudulent activities, the institution need not honour the claim under reg E. Instead, it is argued that the reg E responsibility 'would fall to the third-party peer-to-peer payment app such as PayPal or Venmo as they would be considered a service provider that does not hold the consumer's account as prescribed under s 1005.14(b) and commentary of Regulation E'.)

159 As noted above, the definition of 'authorized transaction' under reg E, similar to Australia's *ePayments Code*, is described as 'an electronic fund transfer from a consumer's account initiated by a person other than the consumer without actual authority to initiate the transfer and from which the consumer receives no benefit'. Notably, however, this term is defined by reg E as excluding any electronic fund transfer (a) 'initiated by a person other than the consumer who was furnished with the card, code, or other means of access to such consumer's account by such consumer, unless the consumer has notified the financial institution involved that transfers by such other person are no longer authorized', (b) 'initiated with fraudulent intent by the consumer or any person acting in concert with the consumer', or (c) 'which constitutes an error committed by a financial institution'. Electronic Fund Transfers (Regulation E) 12 CFR §1005.2.

160 Treasury, *Payments System Review 2021* (n 3) 78.

161 Ibid 21.

162 Ibid.

to incorporate digital wallet services into the *ePayments Code* while underscoring the broader implications for competition.[163] Concerns over market competition are further highlighted by the ACCC's investigation into Apple Pay.[164]

Considering the rapidly growing significance of digital wallets – highlighted by WeChat Pay's 690 000 users in Australia alone – there is an immediate need for a more holistic regulatory approach.[165] One proposal being considered by the Australian Government is a new framework that would formally identify and regulate digital wallets, thereby creating an appropriate standard for all payment service providers.[166] Facing the increasing complexity of the payment ecosystem, the Treasury tends to follow the experience of the United Kingdom and Singapore by taking a streamlined, 'functional' or 'activity-based' licensing approach.[167] The Treasury's *Payments System Review 2021* stated in the relevant part:

> Taking a functional or activity-based approach to regulating payments will ensure that PSPs [payment services providers] are regulated according to what they are doing, rather than how they are doing it. It would help level the playing field by targeting regulation to the risk posed by a particular payment activity. For example, the provision of stored-value services should be regulated in the same way irrespective of whether the service is provided through a card or a digital wallet, or by a bank, retailer, or a utilities company.
>
> This approach to payments regulation would also align Australia's regulatory framework with international regulatory frameworks and reduce barriers to entry for overseas providers seeking to enter the Australian market. Singapore, the United Kingdom and Canada have included or are in the process of implementing functional definitions of payment services in their legislative frameworks.[168]

This approach would clarify which entities – including tech firms offering digital wallets – need a licence, be it an Australian Financial Services Licence (AFSL) or a specialised

163 Janes Eyers, 'Regulate Apple Pay, says CBA', *Financial Review* (online, 27 July 2021) <https://www.afr.com/companies/financial-services/cba-s-comyn-attacks-apple-for-being-anti-competitive-20210727-p58d73>.

164 In the inquiry, debate surrounded whether digital wallet systems such as Apple Pay were deliberately avoiding regulation by refusing to subscribe to the voluntary *ePayments Code*, or, because digital wallets are not technically authorised deposit-taking institutions, are not qualified under the regulations. See Parliamentary Joint Committee on Corporations and Financial Services, *Mobile Payment and Digital Waller Financial Services* (October 2021) <https://parlinfo.aph.gov.au/parlInfo/download/committees/reportjnt/024736/toc_pdf/MobilePaymentandDigitalWalletFinancialServices.pdf;fileType=application%2Fpdf>. In a related but separate context, in *Australian Competition and Consumer Commission v Sony Interactive Entertainment Network Europe Ltd* (2020) 381 ALR 531, the ACCC brought proceedings against Sony for breaching the *Australian Consumer Law* by misrepresenting to consumers that they could not obtain refunds to funds that were added to the PlayStation Network digital wallet, when in fact consumers had a right to refund subject to conditions. While this was a case that fell under consumer law, it illustrates the lack of regulations on such payment methods.

165 Treasury, *Payments System Review 2021* (n 3) 80.

166 Ibid.

167 Ibid 13, 25. ('The Review supports a simpler, functional or activity-based licence for PSPs [payment services providers] that provides clarity over who is required to have a licence (whether an AFSL [Australian Financial Services Licence] or a distinct payments licence), and possibly clarity over services that do not require PSPs to have a licence.')

168 Ibid 59.

payments licence, and possibly identify services that do not require licensing.[169] While digital wallets may currently operate outside of the established regulatory framework, it is anticipated that future revisions could bring them under appropriate regulatory oversight.

Screen scraping

'Screen scraping' is a process by which 'automated scripts extract portions of data from one application for use by another application'.[170] This process allows a third party to access a client's account credentials, meaning the third party can obtain additional data without alerting the bank with whom the account is held.[171] The *ePayments Code* currently does not include anything about screen scraping.[172] In CP 341, ASIC maintained that a consumer was unable to disclose their passcodes to anyone, and would not be qualified for indemnity from the subscriber for any loss arising from an unauthorised transaction to which disclosure of passcodes was a main contributor,[173] concluding that 'a consumer takes particular actions at their own risk'.[174] This position was maintained in the *ePayments Code*, which sets out passcode security liability under cl 11.2.[175] ASIC underscored this as follows:

> Our proposal does not prevent consumers from using screen scraping services. It does aim to clarify the existing position that a consumer does so at their own risk that, should the inputting of their internet banking credentials for this purpose amount to 'disclosure' and contribute to an unauthorised transaction, they may be liable for the resulting financial loss.[176]

Notably, more recently, a joint statement was released by the UK Information Commissioner's Office regarding what social media companies and other websites

169 Ibid 80 (noting that '[t]he functional definition of payments under the proposed licensing framework would clarify the regulatory status of digital wallets and allow them to be regulated appropriately. The tiered licensing requirements should assist in ensuring a level playing field for PSPs.)

170 Basel Committee on Banking Supervision, *Report on Open Banking and Application Programming Interfaces* (November 2019) 19; Han-Wei Liu, 'Shifting Contour of Data Sharing in Financial Market and Regulatory Responses: The UK and Australian Models' (2012) 10(3) *American University Business Law Review* 287, 289.

171 Australian Securities and Investments Commission, 'Account Aggregation in the Financial Services Sector' (Consultation Paper 20, May 2001) 15–16.

172 The legality of screen scraping has been debated across jurisdictions. In the European Union, for instance, while the PSD 2 (as explained further below) aimed to replace traditional screen scraping techniques with more secure application programming interfaces (APIs) for data aggregation, screen scraping is still allowed as a fallback option in specific situations (eg when APIs cannot provide the same level of access that was available before PSD 2). For a comparative analysis of the treatment of screen scraping in the United States, the United Kingdom and Australia, see generally Han-Wei Liu, 'Two Decades of Laws and Practice around Screen Scraping in the Common Law World and Its Open Banking Watershed Moment' (2020) 30(1) *Washington International Law Journal* 28.

173 *CP 341* (n 148) 36.

174 Ibid.

175 *ePayments Code* (n 63) cl 11.2: 'Where: (a) more than one passcode is required to perform a transaction, and (b) a subscriber proves that a user breached the passcode security requirements in clause 12 for one or more of the required passcodes, but not all of the required passcodes, the holder is liable under clause 11.2 only if the subscriber also proves on the balance of probability that the breach of the passcode security requirements under clause 12 was more than 50% responsible for the losses, when assessed together with all the contributing causes.'

176 ASIC, *Report 718* (n 70) 37.

should do with respect to data scrapping.[177] The statement outlines the various data privacy risks associated with screen scraping, including the use of scraped data to carry out identity fraud by impersonating individuals, unauthorised intelligence gathering for political purposes, and sending of unwanted spam messages. These risks raise serious privacy issues and may 'undermine [an] individual's trust' in such websites, leading to a 'potentially detrimental impact on the digital economy'.[178] The statement sets out that these websites should be accountable for ensuring that personal information is protected from unlawful data scraping, and that they should implement 'multi-layered technical and procedural controls to mitigate the risks'.[179] These controls include putting together a team to monitor, identify and respond to potential risks associated with data scraping. Additionally, it sets out what individuals can do to minimise their risk, such as being cautious about the information they post on such websites and, when managing their privacy settings, reading the terms and conditions of each website carefully.

9.3 New challenges: Open Banking and digital currencies

9.3.1 The rise of Open Banking

9.3.1.1 Introduction

Open Banking[180] is a new framework being considered by countries across the world which promotes data sharing among different players in the financial market to encourage banks to share banking data (as consented to by consumers) with third parties in a secure way, in a form that facilitates use.[181] Open Banking originated in the EU via *Directive 2015/2366 on Payment Services in the Internal Market* (PSD 2). PSD 2 required all EU Member States to implement the directive into national law by 13 January 2018,[182] which all EU members have done to date. PSD 2, along with its predecessor, aims to increase

177 Information Commissioner's Office, 'Joint Statement on Data Scraping and the Protection of Privacy' (24 August 2023) <ico.org.uk/media/about-the-ico/documents/4026232/joint-statement-data-scraping-202308.pdf>.

178 Ibid [11].

179 Ibid [14].

180 'Open Banking' has evolved into the newer term 'Open Finance'. The non-bank lending sector was designated as part of the Consumer Data Right (CDR) regime on 21 November 2022 through the *Consumer Data Right (Non-Bank Lenders) Designation 2022*. In December 2022, the Treasury initiated a public consultation on applying the CDR to non-bank lenders, concluding on 31 January 2023. The feedback from stakeholders has informed the development of exposure draft rules. These draft rules, aimed at incorporating non-bank lending into the CDR framework due to its parallels with the banking sector, are outlined in sch 3 of the exposure draft rules. See The Treasury, *Consumer Data Right Open Finance Sectoral Assessment: Non-bank Lending* (March 2022) <https://treasury.gov.au/sites/default/files/2022-03/c2022-253782-cp.pdf>; The Treasury, 'Government Statement in Response to the Statutory Review of the Consumer Data Right' (June 2023) <https://treasury.gov.au/sites/default/files/2023-06/p2023-404730-gs.pdf>; The Treasury, 'Exposure Draft Explanatory Materials: Competition and Consumer Act 2010: Issued by Authority of the Assistant Treasurer and Minister for Financial Services: *Competition and Consumer Act 2010- Competition and Consumer (Consumer Data Right) Amendments Rules (No 2) 2023*' <https://treasury.gov.au/sites/default/files/2023-08/c2023-434434-expansion-em.pdf>.

181 Liu (n 170) 287–8.

182 *Council Directive EU/2015/2366 of 25 November 2015 on Payment Services in the Internal Market* [2015] OJ L 337/35, art 109 ('*PSD 2*').

the safety and innovation of payment services.[183] It applies to all PSPs, which includes banks and third parties that provide selected financial services. Essentially, PSD 2 obliges banks to share customers' data with a third party in specific circumstances.[184] It is the first regime to require banks to do this, and it does so as a way to increase competition within the industry by bringing innovative players into the market.[185]

The UK's model was based on this EU model. The UK was the first nation to develop a government program working towards achieving Open Banking as a way to increase competition opportunities and improve outcomes for customers within the banking industry. In 2018, the Competition and Markets Authority made an order that required the UK's nine largest banks[186] to make certain data available via an application programming interface to authorised third parties, thus achieving implementation. The UK's approach was heavily based on that of the EU. The *European Data Act*, which entered into force on 11 January 2024, serves as yet another cornerstone of European data strategy. The regulation is designed to facilitate broader access to data for businesses, individuals and government agencies through a variety of measures.[187]

Since its implementation in the EU and the UK, governments from across the world have slowly moved towards Open Banking, although in varied measures. Singapore, for example, is a supportive jurisdiction that seeks to facilitate Open Banking without mandating it;[188] instead, third-party access to a customer's banking data is subject to compliance with existing regulations pertaining to personal data protection,[189] which, in Singapore, is primarily coded in the *Personal Data Protection Act 2012*.[190] Such an approach to Open Banking reflects the importance placed upon the historically closed relationship between a bank and its customer, with which third-party access to banking data must comply.[191]

183 Ibid art 7.

184 *Commission Delegated Regulation 2018/389 of 27 November 2017 Supplementing Directive 2015/2366 of the European Parliament and of the Council with Regard to Regulatory Technical Standards for Strong Customer Authentication and Common and Secure Open Standards of Communication* [2018] OJ L 69/ 23, art 33.

185 *PSD 2* (n 182) art 7.

186 The nine largest banks in the United Kingdom, known as the CMA9, comprise AIB Group UK, Bank of Ireland, Barclays Bank, HSBC, Lloyds Banking Group, Nationwide Building Society, NatWest Group, Northern Bank Limited and Santander UK. See 'CMA9', *Open Banking* (Web Page) <https://www.openbanking.org.uk/glossary/cma-9/>.

187 The *European Data Act* establishes a comprehensive legal framework that clarifies ownership and usage terms for data generated by both corporations and consumers. It also addresses the issue of contract disparities that have previously hampered the fair distribution of data. The legislation allows government entities to access privately owned data for specific purposes that serve the public interest. Alongside these provisions, the Act focuses on standardising data access rights, particularly for data generated by Internet of Things (IoT) devices, to promote equitable use. It formulates unified rules for sharing data in contexts such as connected products and services and provides for government use of such data in special cases (eg during public emergencies). See European Parliament, 'Briefing: EU Legislation in Progress, "The Data Act"' (May 2023). For a commentary on the Act, see, eg, Rupprecht Podszun and Philipp Offergeld, 'The EU Data Act and the Access to Secondary Markets' (24 October 2022) <https://papers.ssrn.com/sol3/papers.cfm?abstract_id=4256882>.

188 Emma Leong, 'Open Banking: The Changing Nature of Regulating Banking Data: A Case Study of Australia and Singapore' (2020) 35(3) *Banking and Finance Law Review* 445.

189 Ibid 444.

190 *Personal Data Protection Act 2012* (No 26 of 2021, Singapore).

191 Leong (n 188) 446.

In Australia, an Open Banking regime was rolled out as part of the Consumer Data Right (CDR – see further below) scheme.[192] This contrasts with the EU and UK approaches, as CDR is focused on data policy rather than financial services; it will initially apply only to banks but will eventually be applied to the whole economy. The purpose of this regime is to enhance existing data access rules currently in place in Australia, seeing data sharing as a way of promoting competition, enhancing consumer welfare, reducing switching costs and creating a range of business opportunities. All these schemes follow a prescriptive approach which sees a framework being implemented to achieve Open Banking.

9.3.1.2 Consumer data rights in Australia

Background

Open Banking is being implemented in Australia as part of the Consumer Data Right scheme. The CDR was introduced into the banking sector in July 2020, and it is intended that it will eventually be rolled out across all sectors of the Australian economy.[193] It essentially enables individuals to transfer their 'consumer data' to businesses to find products or services tailored to their individual needs, in an effort to save time and money.[194] For example, individuals may use the CDR to monitor their utilities or other services and to switch between different products and services to obtain those most suited to their needs. The scope of what constitutes CDR data is extensive, including not just the initial data specified but also any data that is wholly or partially derived from those original data sets.[195]

The Treasury's Data Standards Body developed the standards that prescribe how data is shared under the CDR.[196] The Office of the Australian Information Commissioner (OAIC) and the ACCC implement and regulate the CDR. Specifically, the OAIC is responsible for regulating privacy and confidentiality under the CDR,[197] and the ACCC is responsible for accrediting businesses.[198] Presently, only businesses that are accredited by the ACCC can provide services under the CDR – these are known as 'accredited data recipients'.[199]

192 'What is CDR Data?', *Office of the Australian Information Commissioner* (Web Page) <https://www.cdr.gov.au/what-is-cdr>. (Consumer Data Right [CDR] offers a voluntary option for consumers to share their data and gives them full transparency about who will have access to it and for what purpose. Using the CDR can make it easier for consumers to compare products and services, access better deals, and to manage their financial situation more effectively.)

193 *Competition and Consumer (Consumer Data Right) Rules 2020* r 6.6 Commencement Table ('*CDR Rules*').

194 Explanatory Memorandum, Treasury Laws Amendment (Consumer Data Right) Bill 2019 (Cth), General Outline and Financial Impact.

195 *Competition and Consumer Act 2010* (Cth) ('*Competition and Consumer Act*') s 56AI.

196 The Data Standards Body (DSB) – part of the Treasury – creates these standards in two categories: Technical Standards for REST APIs and data security; and CX Standards for consumer interactions such as consent. (A REST API is an interface for secure exchange of information, see Amazon Web Services, 'What is a RESTful API?' (Web Page) <https://aws.amazon.com/what-is/restful-api/>.) The DSB collaborates closely with regulatory bodies such as the ACCC and OAIC. 'About', *Consumer Data Standards* (Web Page) <https://consumerdatastandards.gov.au/about>.

197 'Who is Involved?', *Consumer Data Right* (Web Page) <https://www.cdr.gov.au/about#goto-consumer-data-right-regulators>. For background, see also Senate Select Committee on Financial Technology and Regulatory Technology, *Interim Report* (2020) 132 ('Senate, *Interim Report*') <https://parlinfo.aph.gov.au/parlInfo/download/committees/reportsen/024366/toc_pdf/SelectCommitteeonFinancialTechnologyandRegulatoryTechnology.pdf;fileType=application%2Fpdf>.

198 Senate, *Interim Report* (n 197) 132.

199 Office of the Australian Information Commissioner, *CDR Privacy Safeguard Guidelines* (November 2022) Chapter B <https://www.oaic.gov.au/__data/assets/pdf_file/0027/23985/Chapter-B-Key-concepts-v4-Nov-2022.PDF>.

The CDR is an opt-in system,[200] and once an individual has consented to a business accessing their data, they may withdraw their consent at any time[201] and may ask for data to be deleted. Consumers also control what data is transferred, who it can be transferred to and what it can be used for.[202] Accredited data recipients must comply with privacy safeguards and rules to ensure that privacy and data are protected and managed securely.

The CDR was enacted by the *Treasury Laws Amendment (Consumer Data Right) Act 2019* (Cth), which inserted a new pt IVD into the *Competition and Consumer Act 2010* (Cth) ('*Competition and Consumer Act*'). The *Competition and Consumer (Consumer Data Right) Rules 2020* provide the framework for the CDR's operation. Further, the *Consumer Data Right (Authorised Deposit-Taking Institutions) Designation 2019* designates the banking sector to the CDR and the *Consumer Data Right (Energy Sector) Designation 2020* designates the energy sector to the CDR.[203]

Businesses may be subject to the CDR as accredited data recipients or as data holders. In the financial sector, participants in the CDR scheme comprise most major banks and select credit unions, in addition to businesses that facilitate document and information exchange and the provision of payment solutions.[204]

Who can participate?

The CDR regime applies to all authorised deposit-taking institutions (ADIs), except for foreign banks or foreign branches of domestic banks.[205] The four largest Australian banks, as noted in Chapter 1 – ANZ, Commonwealth Bank of Australia, Westpac and NAB – are listed as major ADIs, and began in July 2020 to provide access to consumer banking data as the first phase of the regime, with other ADIs following suit in July 2021.[206]

200 *CDR Rules* (n 193) div 4.2.1.

201 Ibid div 4.3.2B.

202 Ibid rr 4.5, 4.6A, 4.7.

203 Ibid sch 3 s 1.2; *Consumer Data Right (Authorised Deposit-Taking Institutions) Designation 2019*; *Consumer Data Right (Energy Sector) Designation 2020*; 'Consumer Data Right for Energy', *Department of Climate Change, Energy, and the Environment and Water* (Web Page) <https://www.energy.gov.au/government-priorities/energy-markets/consumer-data-right-energy>. CDR is set to expand into the energy sector, initially focusing on the National Electricity Market (NEM). The sharing of product data within the energy sector began on 1 October 2022, followed by the initiation of consumer data sharing on 15 November 2022 for the first group of energy retailers. For the energy sector, more specifically, data holders are categorised into primary and secondary holders based on their relationship with the consumer and the types of data they manage. A primary data holder is typically an energy retailer that directly interacts with the consumer. This retailer possesses various data sets, including customer data, account data, billing data, and tailored tariff data. On the other hand, the Australian Energy Market Operator (AEMO) functions as a secondary data holder. Unlike primary data holders, AEMO does not have a direct relationship with consumers. However, it maintains essential data sets such as metering data, National Metering Identifier standing data, and distributed energy resources register data. The specifics of these data sets are comprehensively outlined in sch 4 to the CDR Rules, detailing the scope and definitions of data relevant to the energy sector's CDR framework.

204 For a comprehensive list of businesses that are currently data holders or data recipients under, and thus subject to, the CDR, see 'Current Providers', *Consumer Data Right* (Web Page) <https://www.cdr.gov.au/find-a-provider>.

205 *CDR Rules* (n 193) s 6.2 item 2(b)(iii).

206 By 1 July 2021, other banks were required to make available account and transaction information for products classified under 'Phase 1'. Following that, by 1 November 2021, they were obligated to release account and transaction data related to Phase 2 products. Lastly, they were required to furnish data concerning Phase 3 products. 'Open Banking', *Australian Banking Association* (Web Page) <https://www.ausbanking.org.au/priorities/open-banking/>.

Reception of data by third-party providers requires them to fulfil privacy and security criteria in order to be listed as an 'accredited recipient'.[207]

What data should be shared under the CDR regime?

Under pt IVD of the *Competition and Consumer Act*, 'CDR data' includes 'information within a class specified by a designating instrument, extending to those wholly or partly derived from such information'.[208] In the banking sector, CDR data comprises three classes of information:

(1) information about a user of a product (eg information identifying the person)
(2) information about use of a product (eg information about a transaction made by the person)
(3) information about a product (eg price, features, and terms and conditions associated with the product).[209]

In the banking sector, the *Consumer Data Right (Authorised Deposit-Taking Institutions) Designation 2019* defines 'CDR data' to include information about the consumer or their associate (eg contact details), usage information of a product by the consumer or their associate (eg transaction data), and details about the product itself (eg terms and conditions).[210] In the same instrument, however, certain kinds of credit information (eg records of credit inquiries made about an individual by credit providers, updates on severe credit infringements) as described in the *Privacy Act 1988* (Cth) are excluded.[211] Meanwhile, geographical limitations are designated in the *Competition and Consumer Act*.[212] In Australia, data qualifies as CDR data only if it has 'been generated or collected in Australia by an Australian person; or been generated or collected in Australia and related to an Australian person; or been generated or collected outside Australia by an Australian person and related to an Australian person'.[213]

The CDR effectively expands the scope of data access, which had previously been delineated by the Australian Privacy Principle 12 ('*APP 12*'). Data access under APP 12 is qualified as 'personal information', which narrows the scope of its application considerably.[214] Furthermore, businesses must have an annual financial turnover of over A$3 million to fall within APP 12's scope of application.[215] The CDR has the potential

207 *Competition and Consumer Act* (n 195) s 56BD(1)(b).
208 Ibid s 56AI; Liu (n 170) 301.
209 *Consumer Data Right (Authorised Deposit-Taking Institutions) Designation 2019* (Cth) ss 6–8.
210 Ibid ss 5–8. Notably, 'materially enhanced data' is exempted from the scope of data sharing.
211 Ibid s 9.
212 *Competition and Consumer Act* (n 195) s 56AC(3).
213 Ibid; Liu (n 170) 301.
214 In the case of *Privacy Commissioner v Telstra Corporation Ltd* (2017) 249 FCR 24, 30, 63, the Federal Court of Australia found 'personal information' to qualify as such if it satisfied the two following conditions: (1) it must be 'about an individual'; and (2) the identity is 'apparent, or can be reasonably ascertained, from the information or opinion'.
215 *Privacy Act 1988* (Cth) s 6D. The *Privacy Act* encompasses Australian Government agencies as well as organisations with an annual revenue exceeding A$3 million. Moreover, certain other entities are also under its purview. Both the APPs and the APP guidelines are applicable to any agency or organisation that falls under the scope of the *Privacy Act*.

to provide access to a far greater range of information on the basis of 'consumer data' rather than 'personal information'.[216]

Who should bear the losses and risks?

Australia is a mandatory data-sharing jurisdiction.[217] A comprehensive liability framework and an allocation of responsibility on the service provider rather than the consumer is considered 'important for the proper functioning of Open Banking',[218] as the liability of each party would 'build community trust and confidence'.[219] Such a regime would provide certainty to industry participants, such as data holders and recipients, and eliminate bilateral negotiations regarding liability risks associated with Open Banking. However, it is yet to be put in place in Australia.[220] The Australian Treasury's *Review into Open Banking* contrasted the proposed liability framework to a market-driven attribution of liability, which could result in less-informed parties accepting the associated risks as 'buried in a dense set of terms and conditions and therefore not readily understood and genuinely agreed to'.[221]

Data protection/cybersecurity under the CDR

The CDR adopts a distinct method for protecting privacy, where personal information circulated within the system is not governed by the *Privacy Act 1988* (Cth) ('*Privacy Act*'). Rather, an independent set of guidelines known as the 'CDR Privacy Safeguards' is used to regulate personal information and 'CDR data' that are transferred as part of the scheme.[222] There are 13 CDR Privacy Safeguards, as follows:

(1) Businesses must maintain open and transparent management of data.
(2) Businesses must provide consumers with the options of anonymity and pseudonymity.

---

216 James Meese, Punit Jagasia and James Arvanitakis, *Consumer Rights to Personal Data: Data Access in the Communications Sector* (2019) (University of Technology Sydney and Australian Communications Consumer Action Network) 1 <https://researchdirect.westernsydney.edu.au/islandora/object/uws%3A52551>. But CDR has raised privacy concerns. See, eg, Mark Burdon and Tom Mackie, 'Australia's Consumer Data Right and the Uncertain Role of Information Privacy Law' (2020) 10(3) *International Data Privacy Law* 222, 227 (observing that 'The CDR replaces the operation of the Privacy Act with the Privacy Safeguards, and thus obviates the challenges of entity and data categorization arising from the Privacy Act' and arguing that CDR may lead to issues related to defining regulated data, redundant privacy and security measures, and a complex regulatory framework that poses conceptual challenges).

217 The United Kingdom and European Union are further examples of mandatory jurisdictions possessing a dedicated framework to address issues and potentially overcome the difficulties faced by jurisdictions with no specific method of regulatory intervention. For instance, in the absence of a bilateral agreement between the bank and the third party during the course of dispute resolution, a consumer in the United States may only seek recourse in the civil liability framework and, in such circumstances, assume the burden of proof by identifying the faulting party to account for losses. This is in contrast with the EU/UK system, where more protective measures for consumers apply: the burden of proof falls on service providers and, unless under exceptional circumstances, such providers are required to provide refunds to consumers for losses. See Liu (n 170) 289.

218 See The Treasury, *Review into Open Banking: Giving Customers Choice, Convenience and Confidence* (December 2017) 65 <https://treasury.gov.au/sites/default/files/2019-03/Review-into-Open-Banking-_For-web-1.pdf>.

219 Ibid.

220 Ibid. See also Liu (n 170) 305.

221 Treasury, *Review into Open Banking* (n 218).

222 Burdon and Mackie (n 216) 222, 226–7.

(3) Businesses can only collect a consumer's data from another business with the consumer's express consent, and only the data they need in order to provide the product or service.
(4) Businesses must destroy any unsolicited data they receive from participants.
(5) Consumers must be notified of their data being collected.
(6) Data can only be used or disclosed where required or authorised, and only with consent.
(7) Data cannot be used to direct marketing unless the consumer consents.
(8) Businesses must not send data overseas.
(9) Businesses cannot adopt, use or disclose government identifiers unless legally required.
(10) Businesses must notify consumers when data is disclosed to another business.
(11) Businesses must ensure the quality of data.
(12) Businesses must meet strict information security requirements, including de-identification and deletion of data.
(13) Businesses must respond to data correction requests to ensure data is not misinterpreted.

Burdon and Mackie have analysed the differences between the *Privacy Act* and the CDR Privacy Safeguards, highlighting that the former operates on a principles-based regulatory mechanism, whereas the latter takes a more prescriptive stance specific to CDR. The *Privacy Act* offers a degree of flexibility, accommodating broad legislative principles that can adapt to rapid technological changes. On the other hand, the CDR Privacy Safeguards are more rigid, requiring compliance with specific regulatory mandates. These contrasting approaches raise concerns about the feasibility of a seamless 'switching process' as envisioned within the CDR framework.[223]

A data breach occurs when there is unauthorised access to, or unauthorised disclosure of, CDR data, or a loss of CDR data that is likely to seriously harm any consumers to whom the data relates. If there is a data breach under the CDR, data recipients have obligations under the *CDR Rules* sch 2, which includes notifying the Australian Cyber Security Centre.[224]

223 Ibid 233.

224 The current liability framework used in the United Kingdom is Payment Systems Regulator, *Specific Direction 17 on Expanding Confirmation of Payee* (October 2022) ('PSR 17'), which has transposed the European Union's Implementing and Delegated Acts ('PSD 2') to *Council Directive 2015/2366 on Payment Services in the Internal Market*. The PSR 17 generally requires banks – termed 'Account Servicing Payment Service Providers' (ASPSP) – to immediately reimburse the customer for losses arising from an unauthorised transaction, irrespective of whether such loss was a result of third-party access. This is unless the bank 'has reasonable grounds to suspect fraudulent behaviour' by the customer and has fulfilled the relevant notification obligation. Per the *Payment Services Regulations 2017* (UK), where errors in payment transactions are initiated through a third-party provider (TPP) (specifically, a Payment Initiation Service Provider [PISP]), the bank is liable unless the PISP is found to be responsible, in which case it will assume liability and provide recompense to the bank. It is the banks or TPPs, rather than customers, that will generally assume the burden of proof to show that the transaction was validly authenticated. PISPs and Account Information Service Provides are moreover required to have professional indemnity insurance or an equivalent guarantee. See Liu (n 170) 306.

9.3.2 Digital currencies issued by central banks

9.3.2.1 The rise of digital currencies

Digital currencies are currencies that only exist in electronic/digital form. The main varieties of digital currency are cryptocurrency (such as Bitcoin), stablecoins[225] and central bank digital currency (CBDC). Digital currencies can be centralised or decentralised. Cryptocurrency is decentralised – meaning it operates independently of any country's government or central bank, instead relying on peer-to-peer networking, which broadens its accessibility.[226] As a digital currency, cryptocurrency possesses no legal tender status.[227] In contrast, CBDC is a digital version of a country's physical currency and is therefore centralised with its central bank. As such, it is bound to the legal and regulatory framework imposed by the country from which it is distributed.[228]

CBDCs focus on their own country's needs, but also work towards increasing the efficiency of cross-border payments, which are important in terms of economic development in a globalised economy.[229] CBDCs can be divided into retail and wholesale types. Retail CBDCs serve as the digital counterpart to physical cash for consumers and businesses, whereas wholesale CBDCs are restricted to specific financial institutions for large-scale interbank settlements.[230] CBDCs are being increasingly considered by economies around the world because of the way in which they seek to support the policy objectives that are commonly held by central banks, such as safeguarding public trust in money and promoting efficiency and safety in payment systems and financial markets infrastructure.[231] While CBDCs are becoming more popular globally, the only CBDCs to have fully launched presently are the Sand Dollar in the Bahamas and JAM-DEX in Jamaica. Many countries are considering issuing a CBDC.[232] We now consider the development of CBDCs in selected jurisdictions.

---

225 Stablecoins are cryptocurrencies that are backed up by tangible assets, such as the US dollar or gold, where the issuer would hold the assets to back the coins in issue. This makes stablecoins, as noted by Tony Richards, 'The Future of Payments: Cryptocurrencies, Stablecoins or Central Bank Digital Currencies? (Speech, Australian Corporate Treasury Association, 18 November 2021) 3 <https://www.rba.gov.au/speeches/2021/sp-so-2021-11-18.html>, 'more money-like and attractive as a store of value or method of payment', as price volatility is minimised.

226 Marion Laboure et al, 'Cryptocurrencies and CBDC: The Route Ahead' (2021) 12(5) *Global Policy* 663.

227 European Central Bank, *Virtual Currency Schemes* (October 2012) <https://www.ecb.europa.eu/pub/pdf/other/virtualcurrencyschemes201210en.pdf>.

228 Laboure et al (n 226) 664.

229 Bank for International Settlements Committee on Payments and Market Infrastructure, *Central Bank Digital Currencies for Cross-Border Payments: Report to the G20* (2021) <https://www.bis.org/publ/othp38.pdf>.

230 The Treasury, *Payments System Review 2021* (n 3); Codruta Boar and Andreas Wehrli, *Ready, Steady, Go? – Results of the Third BIS Survey on Central Bank Digital Currency* (BIS Paper No 114, Bank of International Settlements, 27 January 2021) <https://www.bis.org/publ/bppdf/bispap114.htm>; Heng Wang and Ross Buckley, 'The Coming Central Bank Digital Currency Revolution and the e-CNY' (2023) (1) *Singapore Journal of Legal Studies* 145, 147.

231 'Central Bank Digital Currency', *Reserve Bank of Australia* (Web Page) <https://www.rba.gov.au/payments-and-infrastructure/central-bank-digital-currency/>.

232 China is one of the leading economies developing a central bank digital currency (CBDC); various other economies are working towards the development of CBDCs, such as Japan, Switzerland, France and the United Arab Emirates. The United States is also considering CDBCs; see, eg, 'Central Bank Digital Currency (CBDC): Frequently Asked Questions', *Board of Governors of the Federal*

9.3.2.2 Selected cases

China

China has been working since 2014 on a digital yuan, currently called 'e-CNY', which is in its pilot phase. This would make China the first major economy to issue a CBDC.[233] Accordingly, if China introduces a CBDC, this could potentially affect the overall international financial system, as CBDCs facilitate the transfer of funds globally via cross-border use.

China proposes a two-tier operational system that would see the first layer – including China's central bank, the People's Bank of China – distributing its CBDC to banks and payment platforms. In the second layer, banks and payment platforms then circulate the CBDC to users.[234] China's CBDC would also be loosely coupled with bank accounts, meaning it may be used without linking it to a bank account in some circumstances to allow individuals who do not have bank accounts to open a CBDC wallet in order to meet their daily payments.[235]

Another feature of China's CBDC is that it would allow managed anonymity, essentially meaning that information is not provided to third parties[236] – which contrasts with how e-payments currently operate, as outlined earlier in this document. However, this feature of China's CBDC is yet to be clearly established and outlined.

European Union

Currently, the European Central Bank (ECB) is in the early stages of a digital Euro project, which runs for two years beginning from November 2023 and does not guarantee the issuance of a digital Euro, but will eventually be prepared to issue one.[237] The effort to develop a CBDC aligns with the objectives related to the 'core central bank functions and the economic policies of the EU'.[238] The report by the ECB on the development of a digital Euro assessed various scenarios in which a digital Euro may replace or enhance the existing payments system. It concluded that it could be issued:

Reserve System (Web Page) <https://www.federalreserve.gov/cbdc-faqs.htm>. There are also private players issuing digital currencies – for instance, Diem (previously known as 'Libra'), as launched by Facebook for international payments using its own global payment network. The value of the Diem is tied to a basket of currencies and other assets. See, eg, Liyang Hou and Wei Shen, 'Digital Currency and Regulatory Responses: A Tale of Two Alternative Money Models' (2022) 37(2) *Banking and Finance Law Review* 305. For an up-to-date survey, see 'Central Bank Digital Currency Tracker', *Atlantic Council* (Web Page) <https://www.atlanticcouncil.org/cbdctracker/>; Boar and Wehrli (n 230). Some of the main motivations for countries considering issuing CBCDs include payment safety and robustness, and payment efficiency.

233 Heng Wang, 'China's Approach to Central Bank Digital Currency: Selectively Reshaping International Financial Order' (2022) 18(1) *University of Pennsylvania Asian Law Review* 77.

234 Ibid 84–8.

235 Ibid 88.

236 Ibid.

237 'A Digital Euro', *European Central Bank* (Web Page) <https://www.ecb.europa.eu/paym/digital_euro/html/index.en.html>.

238 European Central Bank, *Report on a Digital Euro* (Report, October 2020) 9 <https://www.ecb.europa.eu/pub/pdf/other/Report_on_a_digital_euro~4d7268b458.en.pdf>.

(i) to support the digitalisation of the European economy and the strategic independence of the European Union
(ii) in response to a significant decline in the role of cash as a means of payment
(iii) if there is significant potential for foreign CBDCs or private digital payments to become widely used in the Euro area
(iv) as a new monetary policy transmission channel
(v) to mitigate risks to the normal provision of payment services
(vi) to foster the international role of the Euro
(vii) to support improvements in the overall costs and ecological footprint of the monetary and payment systems.[239]

Singapore

The Monetary Authority of Singapore (MAS) has undertaken a multi-year project, entitled 'Project Orchid', to research the potential functionalities and outcomes of a pilot retail CBDC system in the country. The project aims to 'build the foundational technology infrastructure and technical competencies necessary to issue a retail a CBDC'.[240] At the conclusion of the first stage, MAS had concluded that there was no pressing need to develop a retail CBDC in Singapore, citing the plethora of pre-existing electronic payment systems and the relative ease and efficiency with which Singaporean civilians and businesses are able to make electronic transactions as reasons against the urgent implementation of a retail CBDC.[241] This finding, however, does not preclude future developmental efforts towards a retail CBDC, given the rapidly evolving landscape of digital transactions. Through Project Orchid, MAS will continue to explore the viability of a retail CBDC system in Singapore through future trials.[242]

Australia

The RBA, which is responsible for overseeing the development of payment systems in Australia, has been exploring whether a CBDC has a role in the local economy.[243] In conjunction with the Digital Finance Cooperative Research Centre, the RBA has undertaken a joint research project to explore how a CBDC may fit into Australia's economy and to assess whether it ought to be introduced. Australia's CBDC pilot project, aimed at exploring the potential and suitability of a central bank digital currency for the Australian economy, concluded in 2023. The project was conducted to assess how a CBDC could enhance payment systems and the broader financial landscape

239 Ibid.
240 Monetary Authority of Singapore, *Project Orchid: Programmable Digital SGD* (Report, November 2022) 7 <https://www.mas.gov.sg/-/media/mas-media-library/development/fintech/project-orchid/mas-project-orchid-report.pdf>.
241 Ibid.
242 Ibid.
243 RBA and Digital Finance CRC, *Australian CBDC Pilot for Digital Finance Innovation* (White Paper, 26 September 2022) 3 <https://www.rba.gov.au/payments-and-infrastructure/central-bank-digital-currency/pdf/australian-cbdc-pilot-for-digital-finance-innovation-white-paper.pdf> ('RBA/DFCRC, *White Paper: Australian CBDC Pilot for Digital Finance Innovation*').

within the country.[244] The main research questions that the pilot seeks to explore are:[245]

- What, if any, are the emerging business models and use cases that a CBDC would support and that are not effectively supported by existing payments and settlement infrastructures in Australia?
- What might be the potential economic benefits of issuing a CBDC in Australia?
- What operational, technology, policy and regulatory issues might need to be addressed in the operation of a CBDC in Australia?

Moreover, in its *Payments System Review 2021*, the Treasury highlighted that Australia, being an open economy with a wide range of international ties, could face domestic repercussions due to the actions of foreign central banks in the area of CBDCs. The nature and extent of these impacts would vary, depending on which country issues the CBDC and how it is designed. For instance, the introduction of a foreign retail CBDC for domestic use in Australia would require careful evaluation of its potential effects on key areas such as financial stability, monetary policy, privacy, national security, anti-money laundering measures, consumer wellbeing, and data collection by oversight bodies.[246]

The RBA has teamed up with other agencies in the industry, both on the national and international level, to research and conduct pilot projects exploring the feasibility of CBDCs.[247] In 2022, the RBA collaborated with the Bank for International Settlements, Innovation Hub Singapore Centre, the Reserve Bank of Australia, Bank Negara Malaysia (BNM), the Monetary Authority of Singapore and the South African Reserve Bank (SARB), also known as 'Project Dunbar', to explore how having a common platform for multiple CBDCs could facilitate less expensive, swifter and less risky cross-border payments.[248]

244 Notable pilot projects include Project Atom and Project Dunbar. Project Atom was a 2020–1 initiative involving the Reserve Bank of Australia, major Australian banks, and tech firms. It developed a proof of concept for a tokenised CBDC for wholesale market use, focusing on syndicated loans via an Ethereum-based platform. Project Dunbar, active in 2021–2, was a multi-country effort led by the BIS Innovation Hub and included central banks from Australia, Malaysia, Singapore and South Africa. It investigated the potential of a shared digital ledger technology platform for issuing multiple wholesale CBDCs to enhance cross-border payments in terms of efficiency, speed, and transparency. 'Central Bank Digital Currency', *Reserve Bank of Australia* (Web Page), <https://www.rba.gov.au/payments-and-infrastructure/central-bank-digital-currency/> ('RBA, *CBDC*'); *Reserve Bank of Australia*, Australian CBDC Pilot for Digital Finance Innovation Project Report (Report, August 2023) <https://www.rba.gov.au/payments-and-infrastructure/central-bank-digital-currency/pdf/australian-cbdc-pilot-for-digital-finance-innovation-project-report.pdf> The findings of the pilot project revealed both the benefits of a CBDC for the payment system and the need for further research on its legal, regulatory, technical, and operational aspects. Brad Jones of the RBA highlighted the project's insights into the CBDC's potential benefits for the financial system and economy, emphasising the importance of collaboration between the industry and policymakers (Brad Jones, 'The Economics of a Central Bank Digital Currency in Australia', Reserve Bank of Australia (Speech, December 2022) <https://www.rba.gov.au/speeches/2022/sp-ag-2022-12-08.html>). The findings will inform the RBA's continued research into the future of money, focusing on tokenization and programmable payments.

245 RBA/DFCRC, *White Paper: Australian CBDC Pilot for Digital Finance Innovation* (n 243) 5.

246 Treasury, *Payments System Review 2021* (n 3) 82.

247 RBA, *CBDC* (n 244).

248 Bank for International Settlements Innovation Hub, *Project Dunbar: International Settlements Using Multi-CBDCs* (March 2022) <https://www.rba.gov.au/payments-and-infrastructure/central-bank-digital-currency/pdf/project-dunbar-report-2022-03.pdf>.

The project has developed successful working prototypes that demonstrate the feasibility and practicality of the concept of multiple CBDCs, and advocates for further development in this area.[249] While Australia is still exploring the role of CBDCs, the RBA has found no compelling public policy reason to introduce a retail CBDC at this point.[250]

9.4 Summary

This chapter examines the regulatory framework that governs Australia's payment systems, highlighting key players such as the Payment Systems Board as part of the RBA, which plays a key role in ensuring system efficiency, competitiveness and stability. It examines the operational details of payment, clearing and settlement from a legal standpoint, covering popular payment instruments such as credit and debit cards, BPAY and stored value cards before discussing the recently amended *ePayments Code*. Originating from the *Electronic Funds Transfer Code of Conduct*, the *ePayments Code*, under ASIC's purview, governs electronic transactions, addressing critical issues such as unauthorised transactions and mistaken internet payments and outlining issues around liability allocations. Although voluntary, it establishes a contractual foundation between financial institutions and customers; the government has indicated the potential of making it mandatory.

The chapter then discusses emerging financial sector challenges, such as Open Banking and CBDC. Open Banking – or Open Finance, depending on its use case – inspired by the PSD 2 directive in the EU, promotes data sharing, encouraging competition and innovation in the banking and financial market. Several frameworks have been implemented globally, including Australia's CDR regime, where consumer-centric data transfers are facilitated under prescribed requirements. Concurrently, digital currencies, especially CBDCs, are burgeoning. In a rapidly transforming digital transaction environment, pioneering nations such as China, the EU, Singapore and Australia are investigating or piloting CBDCs with distinct objectives.

FURTHER READING

Arner, Douglas W, Giuliano G Castellano and Eriks K Selga, 'Financial Data Governance' (2023) 74(2) *Hastings Law Journal* 235.

Awrey Dan, and Joshua Macey, 'The Promise and Perils of Open Finance' (Coase-Sandor Working Paper Series in Law and Economics No 956, 2022).

Bossu, Wouter et al, 'Legal Aspects of Central Bank Digital Currency: Central Bank and Monetary Law Considerations' (IMF Working Paper No 20/254, 2020).

Buckley, Ross P et al, 'Sovereign Digital Currencies: Reshaping the Design of Money and Payments Systems' (2021) 15(1) *Journal of Payments Strategy and Systems* 7.

Burdon, Mark and Tom Mackie, 'Australia's Consumer Data Right and the Uncertain Role of Information Privacy Law' (2020) 10(3) *International Data Privacy Law* 222.

249 Ibid.

250 Tony Richards, Chris Thompson and Cameron Dark, 'Retail Central Bank Digital Currency: Design Considerations, Rationales and Implications', *RBA Bulletin* (September 2020) <https://www.rba.gov.au/publications/bulletin/2020/sep/retail-central-bank-digital-currency-design-considerations-rationales-and-implications.htm>; Treasury, *Payments System Review 2021* (n 3) 6.

Delivorias, Angelos, 'Central Bank Digital Currencies: Evolution or Revolution?' (Briefing Paper, European Parliament, December 2021) <https://www.europarl.europa.eu/RegData/etudes/BRIE/2021/698804/EPRS_BRI(2021)698804_EN.pdf>.

Didenko, Anton N and Ross P Buckley, 'Central Bank Digital Currencies as a Potential Response to Some Particularly Pacific Problems' (2022) 30(1) *Asia Pacific Law Review* 44.

Farrell, Scott, 'Embedding Open Banking in Banking Law: Responsibilities, Performance, Risk and Trust' (2022) 17(2) *Journal of Business and Technology Law* 265.

Fracassi, Cesare and William Magnuson, 'Data Autonomy' (2021) 74(2) *Vanderbilt Law Review* 327.

Goldbarsht, Doron, Baskaran Balasingham and Jeremy Moller, 'Open Banking in Australia: Competition and Money Laundering, Risks and Benefits' (2021) 32(2) *Journal of Banking and Finance Law and Practice* 1015.

Jeng, Linda (ed), *Open Banking* (Oxford University Press, 2022).

Liu, Han-Wei, 'Two Decades of Laws and Practice around Screen Scraping in the Common Law World and Its Open Banking Watershed Moment' (2020) 30(1) *Washington International Law Journal* 28.

Scott, Susan V and Markos Zachariadis, *The Society for Worldwide Interbank Financial Telecommunication (SWIFT): Cooperative Governance for Network Innovation, Standards, and Community* (Routledge, 2014).

Shen, Wei and Heng Wang, 'Global Stablecoins and China's CBDC: New Moneys with New Impacts on the Financial System?' (2021–2) 41(1) *Review of Banking & Financial Law* 255.

The Treasury, 'Payments System Review: From System to Ecosystem' (June 2021), <https://treasury.gov.au/sites/default/files/2021-08/p2021-198587.pdf>.

Tsang, Cheng-Yun and Ping-Kuei Chen, 'Global Financial Order at a Cross-Road: Do CBDCs Lead to a Balkanisation or Harmonisation? (2023) 59 *Journal of Financial Transformation* (forthcoming).

Tsang, Cheng-Yun and Ping-Kuei Chen, 'Policy Responses to Cross-Border Central Bank Digital Currencies: Assessing the Transborder Effects of Digital Yuan' (2022) 17(2) *Capital Market Law Journal* 237.

Tsang, Cheng-Yun, Alex Yueh-Ping Yang and Ping-Kuei Chen, *Disciplining CBDCs: Addressing the Privacy Aspects and Central Bank Independence* (2022 DC Fintech Week Winning Papers, 20 October 2022).

Wang, Heng, 'China's Approach to Central Bank Digital Currency: Selectively Reshaping International Financial Order?' (2022) 18(1) *University of Pennsylvania Asian Law Review* 77.

Wang, Heng, 'How to Understand China's Approach to Central Bank Digital Currency?' (2023) 50 *Computer Law and Security Review* 1.

Wang, Heng and Ross Buckley, 'The Coming Central Bank Digital Currency Revolution and the E-CNY' (2023) (1) *Singapore Journal of Legal Studies* 145.

Wang, Heng and Simin Gao, 'The Future of the International Financial System: The Emerging CBDC Network and Its Impact on Regulation' (2024) 18(1) *Regulation & Governance* 288.

QUESTIONS

(1) On 15 April 2023, Sarah noticed an unauthorised international transaction of A$3000 dated 1 February 2023 on her credit card statement from Quantum Bank. Sarah brought this to the bank's attention on 16 April 2023. However, Quantum Bank promptly rejected her request for an investigation, citing the credit card's terms and conditions, which state that charge-back requests for unrecognised transactions

must be made within 60 days of the transaction occurring. Feeling frustrated, Sarah is now seeking external advice. Refer to the *ePayments Code* to evaluate the following:

(a) Is Quantum Bank's decision to reject Sarah's request for investigation valid?

(b) If the bank's refusal is not justified, specify the time frame that Quantum Bank must follow upon receiving a report of an unauthorised transaction.

(2) What is a CBDC? How does it differ from Bitcoin or other decentralised cryptocurrencies? Identify two jurisdictions that have already rolled out their CDBCs. Has Australia issued its own CBDC?

(3) In light of Australia's transition to a cashless society – where cash accounted for only 13 per cent of payments in 2022[251] – discuss the challenges and opportunities inherent in this shift. Critically examine the implications for financial inclusion and fairness, particularly for marginalised communities such as people with disabilities, the elderly, and residents of remote areas. If you were a policymaker tasked with designing this new payment ecosystem, what strategies would you employ to ensure these groups are not left behind?

251 Nicola Heath, Lara Heaton and Marc Fennell, 'Australia's Transition to a Cashless Society Raises Concerns about Financial Exclusion, Privacy and Safety', *ABC News* (23 August 2023) <https://www.abc.net.au/news/2023-08-23/cashless-society-financial-exclusion-safety-privacy-concerns/102706718>.

CHAPTER 10

LENDING, SECURED LENDING AND GUARANTEES

10.1 Introduction

In Chapter 2, we examined the role of the *National Consumer Credit Protection Act 2009* (Cth) (the '*NCCPA*') and addressed some regulatory compliance requirements that affect how money can be borrowed. In this chapter, we continue our discussion of lending, focusing on major types of loans and issues that typically arise from the private transactions between borrowers and lenders, with reference made to the *NCCPA* whenever relevant.

Lending often goes hand in hand with some sort of security. Such security serves as legal protection in case of a default. Depending on the nature of the loan, security can take different forms: lenders may take security over a borrower's property, whether real (eg a house) or personal (eg vehicles). Taking security over the real property interests of a borrower enables the lender to exercise certain rights against the property in the event of default. The most usual form of security is a mortgage. Alternatively, guarantees are common in Australia's financing transactions, which will be addressed in Section 10.3. To be sure, lending is a complicated process; creating and registering security interests for financing can be equally, if not more, problematic in practice. The issues discussed herein are, therefore, not exhaustive.

10.2 Lending

Banks make money by borrowing from customers and lending the proceeds to other customers. However, apart from lending via overdraft, banks' lending to customers is not governed by any implied banker–customer contract. One must look to an express (almost always written) contract. Generally speaking (banker's lies aside), bankers have no privileged position as lenders and are in a similar position in general law as any other credit provider. In this chapter, we outline some of the major issues concerning the types of loans most commonly provided by banks.

10.2.1 Types of lending

10.2.1.1 Secured/unsecured loans

An unsecured loan is one under which the lender extends credit, and the borrower agrees to repay the principal with interest and charges. In the event of default, the lender's only remedy is an action for debt/breach of contract. This is only of value if the borrower has funds. On the other hand, a secured loan requires the borrower additionally to provide the lender with some interest in the property, which the lender is able to recover in the event of default.

10.2.1.2 Overdrafts

An overdraft is a current account with a facility that allows the customer to 'overdraw' the account. Generally, the overdrawn amount is repayable on demand. The account is operated like a normal current account, with interest being charged by the bank on the amount of the overdraft. This may be at a higher rate if any agreed overdraft 'limit' is exceeded. It is also common to charge an 'establishment' fee when agreeing to a business overdraft facility.[1]

1 See, eg, 'Business Overdraft', *Commonwealth Bank of Australia* (Web Page, August 2022) <https://www.commbank.com.au/business/loans-and-finance/business-overdraft.html>.

Substantial overdrafts are usually arranged formally ahead of their requirement. However, if the customer writes a cheque that would, if honoured, overdraw their account, the customer may request an overdraft for the same amount, which the bank may or may not approve.[2] Without an agreement to the contrary, the bank may combine the overdraft account with any other current accounts held by the customer with the bank. An agreement precluding the combination of various accounts may be implied but does not follow merely from the fact that the customer opens a new account.

A bank may only exercise its right to repayment on demand by providing the customer reasonable notice. It may not terminate without notice any arrangements made with the customer nor refuse to honour cheques issued before notice is given, as long as the terms of the overdraft are being complied with.[3] Problems arise when the bank repeatedly allows an agreed overdraft limit to be exceeded. May the bank, without notice, refuse to honour a cheque drawn in those circumstances?

Consider *Narni Pty Ltd v National Australia Bank Ltd.*[4] Narni operated an informal overdraft for a year before a formal agreement was put in place. It exceeded the limit and for more than six months the bank honoured cheques in these circumstances. The manager warned Narni on at least three occasions during this time that the bank might refuse to honour these cheques, but nevertheless the cheques continued to be honoured, until one day the bank, without notice, dishonoured one. The Court held that there was no estoppel because the bank had not led Narni to believe that the cheques would continue to be honoured, and indeed the repeated warnings indicated otherwise.

The right of a bank to charge interest on overdrafts – at a variable rate reflecting financial market rates – derives from a term implied by custom and usage.[5] Also, banks may compound interest on overdrafts by adding the interest to the outstanding balance at the end of each interest period. Again, this practice is long recognised. (See *The Maira*[6] and *Bank of New South Wales v Brown*[7].)

The entitlement to charge the customer interest, and to compound it periodically, does not come to an end when the bank demands repayment. It continues until the debt is fully repaid; alternatively, a judgment is obtained (*The Maira*). This can be advantageous to a bank if it is able to invoke escalation clauses that enable it to charge higher rates of interest on default. Such higher rates are usual, but if 'excessive' (ie 'out of all proportion' to a genuine pre-estimate of loss), they are unenforceable as penalties. As the High Court of Australia stated *per curiam* in *Ringrow Pty Ltd v BP Australia Pty Ltd*,[8] 'the propounded penalty must be judged "extravagant and unconscionable in amount". It is not enough that it should be lacking in proportion. It must be "out of all proportion".'[9])

2 *Cuthbert v Robarts, Lubbock & Co* [1909] 2 Ch 226.
3 *Rouse v Bradford Banking Co Ltd* [1894] AC 586.
4 *Narni Pty Ltd v National Australia Bank Ltd* [1998] VSC 146.
5 *Re City and Country Property Bank (in liq)* (1896) 22 VLR 235; *South Australian Banking Co v Horner* (1868) 2 SALR 109.
6 *National Bank of Greece SA v Pinios Shipping Co No 1* [1990] 1 AC 637.
7 *Bank of New South Wales v Brown* (1983) 151 CLR 514.
8 *Ringrow Pty Ltd v BP Australia Pty Ltd* (2005) 224 CLR 656.
9 Ibid 669 [32] (Gleeson CJ, Gummow, Kirby, Hayne, Callinan and Heydon JJ).

A secured overdraft would be considered as being consistent with the customary banker–customer relationship, in which the bank's right to charge and compound interest stands.[10]

10.2.1.3 Term loans

The primary difference between term loans and non-term loans is that the term loan is not repayable on demand; instead, it is repayable at the end of a fixed period. Any demand before this time would be a breach of the contract. These loans are not covered by the implied banker–customer terms (see also Chapter 5 on the banker–customer relationship). Therefore, for instance, there is no implied right of combination. 'Normal' contractual rules apply to the contract.

10.2.1.4 Commercial bills

Recall bills of exchange – in particular, bank bills. In these arrangements, the bank agrees to accept bills drawn on it by the customer up to an agreed limit. (The customer will then discount the bill in the market to obtain funds.) The bank would normally charge an 'acceptance fee' for the provision of the facility.

What about when the acceptor bank is an accommodation party and, thus, bank bills are 'accommodation bills'? An accommodation party is someone who signs a bill without receiving value. Some may argue that the 'acceptance fee' charged by the bank is not a consideration for accepting the bill. If we admit that this is so, merely for the sake of argument, then the bill is discharged if it is paid in due course by the party accommodated[11] – in this case, the customer (and so it need not be paid in due course by the acceptor/drawee for discharge to occur). Thus, for example, customer X draws a bank bill for $500 000, which its bank accepts. Suppose on maturity, for whatever reason, X pays the bill rather than the bank paying it. If the bill is an accommodation bill that discharges the bill, everything is done and dusted, and the customer has no recourse against the bank. This is as it should be.

On the other hand, if the bill is not an accommodation bill, X has recourse against the bank (as acceptor) for $500 000. This surely could not be so, the argument goes. In fact, it likely *is* so, but it is also a term of all bill facilities that the customer will provide the bank with funds to the amount of the bill on its maturity (which also amounts to consideration for the bill). So, if the bill is not an accommodation bill, there is no drama – the customer's claim for $500 000 is cancelled by the bank's contractual right to the same amount. This is a strong argument that bank bill facilities are not accommodation bills. Indeed, the commercial arrangement would make little sense if they were.

Also employing bills of exchange is a so-called discount line under which the bank agrees to discount bills drawn by the customer. For instance, the customer draws a bill on itself to pay the bank $100 000 in 90 days, and the bank provides $98 000 in exchange.

Of rather more interest is the case where the drawer gives security to the acceptor for their promise to put the acceptor in funds at maturity. Does the security 'run with the

10 *National Bank of Australasia v United Hand-in-Hand and Band of Hope Co* (1879) 4 App Cas 391.

11 *Bills of Exchange Act 1909* (Cth) s 64(3).

bill'? It would appear that this is the case. In *Ex parte Waring*,[12] an endorser was forced to pay on a bill where the drawer and acceptor had become insolvent. The drawer had extended security to the acceptor specifically to guarantee payment for the bill. The Court held that the endorser had the right to enforce the security. The subrogation will not, however, apply unless the security was given for the sole purpose of securing payment of the bill.[13]

10.2.1.5 Letters of comfort

Of course, lenders often require guarantees. Under these, the guarantor assumes the indebtedness of the borrower should the borrower default. Loans to proprietary companies almost always require guarantees from the directors. In the case of a loan to one of a group of companies, it is normal to seek guarantees from the other members of the group, or at least from the holding company. These are often resisted as they affect the creditworthiness of the other guarantor companies. A compromise is often struck in the form of a 'letter of comfort'. This is the circumstance of their most common manifestation, although they often appear in relation to international trade. Letters of comfort are rare, and each needs to be interpreted according to its own terms and the usual rules of contractual construction. Sometimes they may have no enforceable content at all. The usual questions arise: whether the statements in the letter are meant to be promissory, and if so, whether they are void for uncertainty. In the more certain cases, the provider of the letter usually undertakes something short of repayment of the debt or indemnification on default, such as maintaining a certain level of investment in the borrower.

Example: *Banque Brussels Lambert SA v Australian National Industries Ltd*[14]

As a condition of a loan, the bank accepted from the defendant, which had a shareholding interest in the borrower, a letter of comfort. The defendant previously refused to enter into a guarantee. The letter consisted of three paragraphs. The first confirmed that the defendant was 'aware' of the loan. It was agreed that this had no promissory effect. (These statements are common in letters of comfort. They appear to be intended to appeal to the 'honour' of the provider of the letter, as a recognition that the provider has some kind of moral obligation with respect to the loan.) The second paragraph consisted of two parts. Under it, the defendant 'stated' the following:

- It was not their intent to reduce their parcel of shareholding in the borrower.
- It 'would' provide the bank with 90 days' notice of any intention to dispose of any shareholding.

The first of these was merely a statement of current intention and so needed only to be true at the time it was made, and was not promissory as to future actions. The Court held that the second was both promissory and certain.

12 *Ex parte Waring* (1815) 34 ER 546.
13 *Scholefield Goodman & Sons Ltd v Zyngier* [1986] VR 311.
14 *Banque Brussels Lambert SA v Australian National Industries Ltd* (1989) 21 NSWLR 502, 504.

The third paragraph read: 'We take this opportunity to confirm that it is our practice to ensure that [the borrower] will at all times be in a position to meet its financial obligations as they fall due.'

In the context of the letter as a whole and the circumstances in which it was provided, the Court held that this statement was promissory not only as to the defendant's policy at the time of the letter but as to its future conduct in respect of the solvency of the borrower.[15]

10.2.2 Types of borrowers

A banker must understand the different legal characteristics of borrowers, as this may affect the types of loans that may be made, the type of security that may be available, and whether guarantees may be taken or be enforceable.

10.2.2.1 Minors

Persons under age 18, of course, do not have full contractual capacity. Beyond that fact, the law is and always has been in a state of confusion. The general rule at common law is that contracts entered into by minors are unenforceable against the minor unless the contract is for a 'necessity' *and* its terms are not so onerous as to render it a contract that effectively gives no benefit to the minor. In New South Wales, the law has been sensibly reformed by the *Minors (Property and Contracts) Act 1970* (NSW) (the '*Minors (P&C) Act*'). In other jurisdictions the common law stands, but is subject to many qualifications and exceptions and minor statutory modifications that are by no means uniform. Banks are as subject to these rules as everyone else. Beyond noting that, primarily because banks are subject to these rules, it is not their normal practice to lend to minors, there are two things to remark on:

(1) The *Minors (P&C) Act* makes an important change in the law in relation to guarantors of loans to minors. Generally, a guarantor cannot be liable unless the principal debtor is liable; hence, a loan that is not recoverable from minors will not be recoverable from their guarantors either. However, the *Minors (P&C) Act* s 47 provides that if the guarantor is of full age, they are bound to the guarantee to the same extent as the minor would be bound to the principal contract were the minor of full age also. (Note also the provisions in the *National Credit Code* s 60(3) in relation to guarantees covered by the Code where the principal debtor is a minor, to the effect that such a guarantee is unenforceable unless a 'prominent' statement is included that the guarantor may not be able to turn to indemnity against the minor.)

(2) It is not unknown for a minor to induce a contract by a representation that they are of full age. In such cases, the other party will not be able to rely on the tort of deceit to recover, because that would amount to indirectly enforcing an unenforceable contract. But equitable relief will be available to the deceived party. For instance, the minor may be required to restore loan funds that remain in their possession.

15 Ibid 525.

10.2.2.2 Unincorporated businesses

Different considerations apply to different types of business organisations when a banker extends credit for the business activities undertaken by the borrower.

- **Sole traders.** There are no special considerations related to lending to sole traders, although (as we will discuss when we look at secured lending in more detail) there may be difficulty in obtaining proper security over stock in trade.
- **Partnerships.** Recall the basic characteristics of a partnership from our discussion in the context of the banker–customer relationship. A partner may bind the partnership, but this is only the case when the purpose is that of the partnership, or apparently that of the partnership. Circumstances such as death, bankruptcy or mental incapacity of a partner will dissolve the partnership. In the event of the death of a partner, for instance, the partner who dies is liable for the debts incurred by the partnership, but the debts of the personal estate would have priority. Since a bank is not generally able to monitor these matters, loans to partnerships usually *expressly* make individual partners jointly and severally liable for the loan. Similarly, joint and several guarantees are normally required from each partner. As noted previously, when discussing the rule in *Clayton's case*,[16] when notified of any change in the composition of the partnership, the bank should cease any activities on any overdraft account. If it is considered desirable to continue dealing with the 'new' partnership, a new account should be opened for that purpose.
- **Limited partnerships.** Each state and territory has legislated to create 'limited partnerships'. These may either be incorporated or unincorporated and are created by registration. The former operates as a separate legal entity. A limited partnership has at least one of each of two types of partners: 'limited partners', whose liability is limited to the amount entered in the register when the partnership is created; and 'general partners', whose liability is similar to that of a partner in a general partnership aforementioned. In dealing with an *incorporated* limited partnership, outsiders are entitled to make certain assumptions (equivalent to those applying to companies under the *Corporations Act 2001* (Cth) ('*Corporations Act*') ss 128, 129).
- **Unincorporated associations.** Recall the previous discussion where we talked about 'special customers' in the context of the banker–customer relationship. Unincorporated associations have no legal identity apart from that of the individuals involved. Any loan is to those individuals.

10.2.2.3 Companies

A company is, of course, a separate legal identity, liable for its own debts. Many proprietary companies are the creatures of their directors, and their primary purpose is to provide those with the advantages of limited liability. As a result, a loan to such a company is almost invariably accompanied by the taking of guarantees from the directors and, where it is available, security over their personal property.

16 *Devaynes v Noble* (1816) 1 Mer 572; 35 ER 781.

All dealings with a company are necessarily through its agents, such as its directors and other executive operatives. Generally, the agents would not have unlimited authority to commit the company by entering into contracts on its behalf. Thus, there is an issue in ascertaining the extent to which a company is bound by an agent who acts beyond its actual or apparent authority. This is the subject of the *Corporations Act* ss 128 and 129, which provide that a person is entitled to make certain assumptions concerning the validity of the agents' acts, and that in the relevant circumstance, the company will be bound by those acts. Again, we discussed this when we looked at the banker–customer relationship with regards to company customers.

A banker should also be aware that there are no statutory limitations on the power of a company to borrow (eg for the purpose of reducing its share capital).[17]

10.2.2.4 Consumers

The *National Credit Code* (the '*NCC*', or the 'Code', sch 1 to the *National Consumer Credit Protection Act 2009* (Cth)), commenced operation on 1 July 2010, replacing the former *Uniform Consumer Credit Code* (the '*UCCC*'), and applies to credit contracts entered into from that date. (Prior contracts, to the extent that they are not continuing credit contracts, remain regulated by the UCCC.)

The *NCC* applies to any credit contract where the debtor is a natural person (or a strata corporation) and the credit is provided wholly or predominately for one of the following reasons:

- for personal, domestic or household purposes
- to purchase, renovate or improve residential property for investment purposes
- to refinance credit provided for the above purposes.[18]

No general exemption is applicable for banks or any other credit providers, but certain types of loans are excluded from the operation of the *NCC*. These include certain kinds of loans traditionally made by banks – for instance:

- where credit is extended without prior agreement (as in an overdraft granted on an overdrawn current account)[19]
- where credit arises out of a bill facility provided by an authorised deposit-taking institution.[20]

The full list of exemptions is set out in the *NCC* s 6.

The *NCC* strictly regulates the form and content of the loan and associated documentation to be provided to a borrower. There must be a pre-contractual statement in the stipulated form setting out matters including:

- the credit provider's name
- the amount of credit

17 See *Corporations Act 2001* (Cth) ch 2J.
18 *National Consumer Credit Code* s 5(1) ('*NCC*').
19 Ibid s 6(4).
20 Ibid s 6(7)(a).

- the interest rate expressed as an annual percentage
- all interest charges.[21]

There are also detailed requirements for copies of credit contract documents to be provided to borrowers, security providers and guarantees.[22] There are no limitations on the type of credit fees and charges imposed, provided complete disclosure is made. However, banks must pass on the exact amount of third-party fees and are not allowed to profit from discounts or commissions on these.

Early termination fees are allowed but are (of course) considered unconscionable if they exceed the genuinely estimated costs and expenses associated with early termination.[23] Victoria implemented 'maximum annual percentage rates' in its enabling legislation.[24] Thus, interest rates exceeding a prescribed amount (48 per cent), calculated by a formula that varies between the jurisdictions, are prohibited. This prohibition applies to credit contracts but not to consumer leases. Additionally, in Victoria, if the credit contract is secured by a mortgage, then the mortgage will be void if the rate exceeds 30 per cent.[25]

Electronic document delivery is allowable under the Code in the event that the consumer makes a positive election to receive electronic communications. In that case, the provisions of the *Electronic Transactions Act 1999* (Cth) apply. The *NCC* installs a regime of civil penalties where a 'key requirement' of the Code is breached (s 111). Key requirements differ according to whether or not the credit contract is continuing. For non-continuing contracts, a civil penalty applies to various non-disclosures. If the contract is a continuing one, penalties may also become applicable where certain information is not disclosed in the periodic statement of account.

Under the Code, a consumer may apply to reopen a contract if it is unjust (s 76). 'Unjust' refers to 'unconscionable, harsh, or oppressive' terms, and courts *must* have regard to the public interest, as well as all the circumstances of the case, in determining the issue of unjustness. They may have regard to the list of matters in the *NCC* s 76(2) to the extent that they are applicable.

The Code also applies to certain guarantees ('related' guarantees) where the credit contract falls under the Code and the guarantor is a natural person (or a strata corporation). These guarantees must be in writing and be signed by the guarantor. The accompanying regulations specify the form and content allowable.[26] Failure to comply renders the guarantee void (s 55). The guarantor must be provided with a copy of the credit contract and a standard-form document explaining their rights and obligations (s 56). These items must be provided to the guarantor before they sign the guarantee. Again, failure renders the guarantee unenforceable (s 55). The guarantor may withdraw at any time

21 Ibid ss 16, 17.
22 Ibid ss 20, 43, 57.
23 Ibid s 76.
24 *Consumer Credit (Victoria) Act 1995* (Vic) s 39.
25 Ibid s 40.
26 *National Consumer Credit Protection Regulations 2010* (Cth) pt 7-3 (related mortgages and guarantees).

prior to the provision of the credit or if the credit contract differs in a material particular from the proposed contract presented to them before signing (s 58). A guarantor may not be liable for more than the amount of the credit contract plus reasonable expenses of enforcement (s 60). The guarantor may, at any time, provided notice is given to the creditor, limit the guarantee; thus, it only applies to the liabilities already accumulated by the debtor (s 60(4)). The provisions relating to reopening unjust transactions also apply to guarantees.

10.3 Secured lending: Real property

10.3.1 Legal and equitable interests

10.3.1.1 Introduction

Proprietary interests may exist either at common law ('legal interests') or in equity ('equitable interests'). This is an artefact of the two court systems that historically operated side by side in England and applied different legal rules to the cases before them. Legal proprietary interests are the creation of the common law courts, while equitable interests are the creation of the competing Court of Chancery.

The common law allowed the creation of a wide range of interests in land: fees simple, life estates, leaseholds, easements, mortgages, and so on. In most instances, the creation and transfer of a legal (ie common law) interest in land must be effected by deed. No other method will do and any defect in the deed will result in the grant failing.

For every legal interest in land, equity recognised a corresponding equitable interest. Thus, for instance, there are not only legal mortgages but equitable mortgages, and so on. Equity, which is concerned less with form and more with intention and good conscience, took a more relaxed approach as to the creation of these equitable estates. It also recognised certain interests in land for which there is no corresponding legal interest (eg restrictive covenants).

10.3.1.2 'Competing interests' – priority rules

The ability to create so many different interests in land leads to the potential for conflict. For example, in a competition between the rights of the holder of a legal mortgage in the land and the holder of an equitable one, whose rights prevail? What is the relative position of first and subsequent mortgagees?

There are four cases to consider:

(1) an earlier legal interest versus a later legal interest
(2) an earlier legal interest versus a later equitable interest
(3) an earlier equitable interest versus a later equitable interest
(4) an earlier equitable interest versus a later legal interest.

In cases (1), (2) and (3), the general rule is that the earlier interest (ie the interest created earlier) takes priority over the later one. The first in time prevails.

However, there are a number of well-established exceptions to the first-in-time principle:

(a) The holder of the prior interest will be postponed if they assist or connive at a fraud which leads the subsequent holder to acquire their interest without notice of the fraud.
(b) The holder of the prior interest will be postponed if they authorise or enable another to create an inconsistent second interest and that person does so but the interest they create exceeds their authority.[27]
(c) The holder of the prior interest will be postponed if they represent that they have no interest and the second person acquires their interest on the faith of that representation.[28]
(d) The holder of the prior interest will be postponed if they are guilty of 'gross negligence' (ie a 'special degree of want of prudence') and the subsequent interest is acquired with due diligence. Typical cases involve either a failure without good reason to take possession of the title documents or a corresponding failure to retain them.[29]

All cases of postponement appear to be based on one or both of two equitable principles, which would mean it would be unfair to advantage the prior interest holder at the expense of the subsequent one:

- An estoppel – the holder of the prior interest is prevented from denying certain facts that they have represented to exist by their words or conduct and which have been relied on by the subsequent interest holder.
- There is some degree of fault (eg fraud or a reprehensible degree of carelessness) on the part of the prior interest holder, and the subsequent interest holder is 'innocent'.

The anomalous case is (4), where the competition is between a prior equitable interest and a subsequent legal one. Here the later legal interest will prevail if it is taken bona fide for value without notice of the prior equitable interest. So, for instance, if M, the holder of a legal fee simple, creates an equitable mortgage in favour of N and then purports to convey the unencumbered fee simple to P, P is not bound by the mortgage as long as P is a bona fide purchaser who has no notice of N's mortgage. Notice is of three kinds: actual, constructive and imputed. The meaning of actual notice is obvious. A person has constructive notice of all facts which they would have discovered had they acted diligently in making all those inquiries which a person would ordinarily be expected to make. And a person has imputed notice of all facts within the actual or constructive notice of their agents for the purpose of acquiring their interest. The time at which the issue notice is determined is the time of the payment of the consideration.

27 *Dickson v Muckleston* (1872) 8 Ch App 155, 160; *Rimmer v Webster* [1902] 2 Ch 163; *Perry-Herrick v Attwood* (1857) 2 De G & J 121; 44 ER 895.
28 *Rice v Rice* (1853) 2 Drew 73; 61 ER 646.
29 *Walker v Linom* [1907] 2 Ch 104, *Clarke v Palmer* (1882) 21 Ch D 124, *Oliver v Hinton* [1899] 2 Ch 264.

In regard to constructive notice, what are the usual and proper inquiries that a person should make? There are at least two fundamental requirements:

(1) To inspect the property. In *Barnhart v Greenshields,*[30] it was held that possession of the land by a person other than the vendor is notice of the interest that the possessor has in the land.
(2) To inspect the title documents.

Note also that a successor in title to a person protected as a bona fide purchaser under this rule is also entitled to priority over earlier equitable interests, and that is so whether or not the successor takes for value or without notice of the prior equitable interest.

10.3.1.3 'Legal' mortgage – general law

At common law, a mortgage consists of the conveyance of the fee simple to the mortgagee with the proviso that the fee simple will be re-conveyed to the mortgagor on repayment of the loan. The mortgagee becomes the legal owner of the fee simple with all associated rights – for instance, possession, right to rents, and so on. Normal terms are, however, that the mortgagor retains possession unless they default. (In effect, the mortgagee lets to the mortgagor as part of the terms.)

The mortgagor's right to have the fee simple restored to them on repayment of the debt is called the 'equity of redemption'. If the mortgagor fails to repay according to the terms, the mortgagee can apply to the court to extinguish the equity of redemption. This is foreclosure. The mortgagor retains their right of redemption until an order for foreclosure is made.

10.3.1.4 Equitable mortgage

Since an 'old-style' legal mortgage conveys the mortgagor's estate to the mortgagee, it must be made by deed to be enforceable at (common) law. But equity recognises a mortgage where, as in *Swiss Bank Corporation Ltd v Lloyd's Bank Ltd,*[31] per Buckley LJ:

> ... the legal owner of property constituting the security enters into some instrument or does some act which, though insufficient to confer a legal estate or title in the subject matter on the mortgagee, nevertheless evidences a contract to do so ...

So, an equitable mortgage exists when the parties act towards each other in a manner consistent with the creation of an agreement to mortgage, or when it can be inferred from their acts that there was a mutual intention to create a mortgage. The following are typical situations:

- Money has been advanced, and either the parties have made a contract to execute a mortgage deed but have not done so, or they have purported to execute a deed but some formality is lacking.[32]

30 *Barnhart v Greenshields* (1853) 9 Moo PC 18; 14 ER 204.
31 *Swiss Bank Corporation Ltd v Lloyds Bank Ltd* [1982] AC 584.
32 *Walsh v Lonsdale* (1882) 21 Ch D 9.

- The lender advances money and the borrower deposits the title documents with the lender as security. Equity sees this as evidencing an agreement to mortgage and deems an equitable mortgage to exist.
- A deed of mortgage is executed, but a prior legal mortgage exists. (As the mortgagor has already conveyed their entire legal interest to the first mortgagee, they have no legal security to give to the second.)

10.3.1.5 Second and subsequent mortgages

For the reason given above, second/subsequent legal mortgages are not possible and attempts to make one will result in an equitable mortgage. An equitable mortgage can also arise in another way. The mortgagor's equity of redemption is an equitable interest that can be made the subject of an equitable mortgage. That is, the mortgagor uses their equity of redemption as security for a loan. As this security is equitable property only, it is correspondingly enforceable only in equity.

10.3.1.6 Remedies on default – general law

The following remedies are implied by law or statute. The mortgage itself may provide for these or other remedies as agreed.

- Sue for the debt.
- Take possession of the property (ie 'enter' it). (A mortgagee that enters does so for the purposes of the security and so has an obligation to account for rents and profits.)
- Lease the property. (Again, there is a duty to account.)
- Appoint a receiver (ie a person to manage the property and devote the income to paying off the mortgage debt). (This remedy is available with respect to legal mortgages only. The right is not exercisable until the mortgagee is entitled to exercise their power of sale, as to which see below. Note also that the receiver is deemed the agent of the mortgagor and so the mortgagee has no liability for rents/profits lost through neglect or wilful acts.)
- Apply to the court for appointment of a receiver (who will act not as an agent for either party but as an officer of the court and will pay the profits of the land into court).
- Apply to the court to foreclose.
- Sell the property. (Again, this applies to legal mortgages only. Equitable mortgagees may apply to the court for an order for sale.)

Note that should the *NCC* apply, there are notice requirements that must be met before enforcement action is taken.[33]

10.3.1.7 The power of sale

This remedy is preferred to foreclosure (which is very rare indeed). It has the advantage that the mortgagor can be pursued for the balance of the debt should the entire debt not be cleared by the sale, whereas foreclosure extinguishes the debt.

33 *NCC* (n 18) s 88(2).

At general law, in the case of a legal mortgage the mortgagee will, of course, have legal title and the sale will pass this to the purchaser; whereas in the case of an equitable mortgage, the mortgagee must first apply to the court for an order vesting legal title in them so that they can then convey this to the purchaser.

The mortgagee is entitled to act in their own interests in selling in order to recover their debt plus interest and costs. However, they are not entitled to disregard the interest of the mortgagor that the best possible price be obtained. The mortgagee must therefore act in good faith and not be 'reckless' (ie indifferent to the interests of the mortgagor) and organise a 'proper' sale and attempt to assure a fair price.[34] In particular, the sale must be to someone other than the mortgagee or their agent.[35]

10.3.1.8 Equitable charges

An equitable charge differs from an equitable mortgage in that there is no intention to grant a right to foreclose. Principal remedies (absent expressly agreed ones) are (court-ordered) sale or receivership (as per equitable mortgages). Where an informal transaction indicates an intention to create a security (eg by deposit of title documents) for repayment of a loan, it is often not obvious whether a charge or mortgage was intended. In such situations, the presumption is that the intention was to create a mortgage unless there is some indication otherwise.

10.3.2 Torrens system

10.3.2.1 Introduction

As noted previously, at common law, legal interests in land could generally only be created/transferred by deed. A seller or mortgagor would therefore attempt to prove their title to the other party's satisfaction by tracing it back through a chain of deeds to an unchallengeable beginning. This 'root of title' was theoretically the original grant by the Crown. Under legislation in most jurisdictions, that root of title now amounts to a deed of transfer of the fee simple that is at least 30 years old and regular on its face. The seller thus produces to the buyer a pile of deeds dating back at least this far and promises that there are no other interests other than those set out in the pile. Locating these deeds can be time consuming, expensive and sometimes impossible. And transferring general law land can, as a result, be both an expensive and uncertain business.

Torrens title is a system of title by registration that seeks to avoid this problem. Land brought under the system is placed on a central government register (the Register of Titles), which shows the boundaries of the land, the name(s) of the registered proprietors and any registered interests affecting their title. A certificate of title (CT) is issued to the holder of the fee simple. Dealings in the land can be registered by presenting the CT to the registrar together with the appropriate document that evidences the dealing. The dealing is then entered on the register and the CT is amended accordingly and reissued.

The Torrens system is implemented in Victoria by the *Transfer of Land Act 1958* (Vic) ('*Transfer of Land Act*'), which allows land to be compulsorily brought under the system.

34 *Pendlebury v Colonial Mutual Life Assurance Society Ltd* (1912) 13 CLR 676.
35 *Farrar v Farrars Ltd* (1880) 40 Ch D 395.

All land in Victoria is now Torrens system land. The other states have similar legislation. New South Wales and Tasmania are the only states with any significant amounts of 'old system' land, and even in those states most land is now under Torrens title.

Registration has three effects:

(1) A registered interest is a valid interest, regardless of any defect in the transaction that led to its creation or in the process of its registration.[36]
(2) Interests – subject to the exceptions discussed below – in land take priority in the order in which they appear on the register (ie in the order that they are registered). In particular, no unregistered interest can have priority over a registered one.
(3) A registered proprietor is not affected by actual or constructive notice of any unregistered interest and is not under any obligation to investigate the circumstances in which previous registered proprietors obtained their title.

This is the principle of indefeasibility of title.[37] Note that the register is a public document that can be searched. The idea is that someone who searches the register and then registers an interest should be assured that only interests already evident on the register will take priority over their interest. There are some exceptions to the indefeasibility principle:

- where the interest was obtained by forgery
- where a person become registered by means of their own fraud or that of their agent,[38]

provided, in both cases, that the title of a registered proprietor who has taken bona fide for valuable consideration, or who has acquired it in good faith for valuable consideration, or of any person bona fide claiming through them, is not affected.

Also, in all states there are specific Acts that charge various rates, taxes and service fees against land (eg in respect of council rates, land taxes, and water, gas and electricity supply charges). These are generally referred to as 'statutory charges'. They are usually to the effect that, if what is owed is not paid, the relevant authority may exercise a power of sale over the land to recover the amount. Generally, the statute that imposes these will override the Torrens legislation, so that even though these interests are not registered they will take priority over a registered interest.

10.3.2.2 Priorities with respect to unregistered interests

As noted, registered interests have priority over all other interests in the order of their registration. (In particular, someone who registers their interest with notice of an unregistered interest will not have their priority affected merely by reason of that notice.) Although there is a deal of academic debate, it is generally accepted in theory (and universally accepted in practice) that registered interests in effect take the place of legal interests and that where an interest would exist at general law, either in law or equity, but is not registered (perhaps, but not necessarily, because it is not registrable), it exists as an 'unregistered' interest under the Torrens system. Further, as between themselves,

36 *Frazer v Walker* [1967] 1 AC 569; *Breskvar v Wall* (1971) 126 CLR 376.
37 *Macquarie Bank Ltd v Sixty-Fourth Throne Pty Ltd* [1998] 3 VR 133.
38 *Russo v Bendigo Bank Ltd* [1999] 3 VR 376.

these unregistered interests behave as if they were equitable interests at general law. So, the priority of unregistered interests as between each other is determined as per the general law relating to priority of competing equitable interests.

10.3.2.3 Mortgages under the Torrens system

Mortgages for land under the Torrens system are created by the registration of a document in the form required by the *Transfer of Land Act* and executed by the mortgagor. (Recall that registered interests take the place of legal interests, and that where equitable interests would exist under the general law they also exist under the Torrens system as unregistered interests.)

Mortgages registered under the Torrens System operate as security and create an interest in the land (by definition as they are registered) but do not transfer the fee simple to the mortgagee. The mortgagor continues to be the owner of the land. Because the mortgage does not transfer title, second and subsequent mortgages can be registered under the Torrens system.

Remedies for default under a registered mortgage

The mortgagee has the right to enter and to let (for no more than one year) on default. However, the mortgagee's principal right, and the one most commonly exercised by banks, is a power of sale. As the mortgagee is not the owner, the Torrens legislation makes provision for the mortgagee to make binding contracts for transfer and to pass title to the purchaser. The purchaser, on registration of the transfer, acquires title free from all interests registered after the mortgage. Once registered, the title attracts the indefeasibility provisions of the legislation.

The mortgagee also has power to appoint a receiver once they become entitled to exercise their power of sale. (It is not necessary that the mortgagee proceed to exercise the power of sale.)

Mortgagees also have a restricted right of foreclosure (ie the right to have the mortgagor's interest transferred to them) on application. However, a strict procedure must be followed, which includes the mortgagee first attempting to clear the debt by exercise of their power of sale at public auction. Foreclosure is rarely exercised.

Discharge

The different types of mortgages are discharged as follows:

- Old system legal mortgages are discharged on re-conveyance of the fee simple to the mortgagor.
- Equitable mortgages are discharged on receipt of payment sufficient to discharge the mortgage obligation.
- Under the Torrens system, a registered mortgage is discharged by registration of a memorandum of discharge, upon which the interest of the mortgagee ceases.

Priority of mortgages

As mortgages take the form of legal/equitable/registered/unregistered interests in land, the normal priority rules discussed previously apply.

Priority of mortgages – tacking

The practice whereby a mortgage is expressed as also securing further future advances not yet made at the time of mortgage is called 'tacking'. The issue arises as to the mortgagee's priority regarding these additional funds where they were lent subsequent to a second mortgage.

Where the first mortgagee advances the additional money with notice of the subsequent mortgage, there is no priority with respect to the additional advance.[39] There is an exception to this rule where the mortgagee is obliged by the terms of the mortgage to advance the money and the mortgagor is likewise obliged to expend it in improvement of the land.[40] Where the mortgagee is merely compelled to make further advances with no obligation on the mortgagor as to how these are used, the right to tack is lost but the granting of the second mortgage relieves the first mortgagee of the obligation to make the further advance.[41]

Mortgage of other interests

The above discussion relates only to mortgages of the fee simple. It is obviously possible to mortgage other interests – for instance, leases, life estates, and so on. The general principles are the same as for the fee simple.

Vitiating factors

Mortgages don't only create property interests; they are also contracts, the validity of which is subject to the general law of contract relating to illegality, capacity, misrepresentation, mistake, undue influence, duress and unconscionability. The applicability of the *Australian Consumer Law*[42] provisions in relation to unconscionability and misleading and deceptive conduct in trade or commerce need to be noted, as do the corresponding provisions relating to misleading and deceptive conduct in the provision of financial services that are contained in the *Australian Securities and Investments Commission Act 2001* (Cth).

The *NCC* makes mortgages that are caught by it unenforceable unless certain disclosure requirements are met by mortgagees. It also restrains a mortgagee from taking any enforcement action without first following the statutorily prescribed procedure giving the mortgagor the opportunity to remedy any default.[43]

10.4 Guarantees

10.4.1 Introduction

10.4.1.1 Parties

There are three parties involved in this context, namely:

39 *Hopkinson v Rolt* (1861) 9 HL Cas 514; 11 ER 829 regarding old system mortgages, and also held to be so with respect to mortgages in *Matzner v Clyde Securities Ltd* [1975] 2 NSWLR 293 and *Mercantile Credits Ltd v Australia and New Zealand Banking Group Ltd* (1988) 48 SASR 407 under the *Real Property Act 1900* (NSW) and the *Real Property Act 1886* (SA), respectively.

40 *Matzner v Clyde Securities Ltd* [1975] 2 NSWLR 293.

41 *West v Williams* [1899] 1 Ch 132, 143–4.

42 *Competition and Consumer Act 2010* (Cth) sch 2.

43 *NCC* (n 18) s 88.

(1) **Principal debtor**: the party contractually bound to do something.
(2) **Creditor**: the party to whom the contractual obligation is made. (Note that the obligation may not necessarily be repayment of money, although it often is. The terms 'debtor' and 'creditor' are used for convenience.)
(3) **Guarantor/surety**: a person undertaking to honour the obligation if the principal debtor does not.

We now consider some of the detailed aspects of how a guarantee operates.

10.4.1.2 Guarantee versus indemnity

A guarantor's liability is co-extensive with, or of the same extent as, the debtor's. If the debtor does not fulfil their obligation, then the guarantor promises that they will. In an indemnity, on the other hand, the promise is to keep the creditor 'harmless against loss' from their transaction with the debtor. Thus, in situations in which the principal transaction is void or unenforceable, or where the debtor has a defence, a guarantor (because of their co-extensive liability) will not be liable, but an indemnifier may be, depending on the terms of the indemnity. Whether a contract is one of guarantee or indemnity is a matter of contractual interpretation, and the use of the words 'guarantee' or 'indemnity' are inconclusive. In all jurisdictions except New South Wales, South Australia and the Australian Capital Territory, there is a statutory requirement that guarantees be evidenced in writing.[44]

10.4.1.3 Consideration

A contract of guarantee (unless under seal) requires consideration. Examples of consideration include:

- provision of credit to the debtor by the creditor at the request of the guarantor
- granting of some indulgence (such as additional time to pay or forgoing legal action) to the debtor at the request of the guarantor
- 'conventional' consideration of some kind, such as payment to the guarantor in exchange for the guarantee.

Where the creditor is a banker, the first two situations are the ones that arise, almost exclusively. Since each of these depends on a request from the guarantor, the bank should be careful to ensure that such a request has actually been made.

10.4.1.4 Continuing guarantees

Guarantees by banks are often of this kind; that is, the guarantee is granted with respect to a series of future dealings or transactions between the creditor and the principal debtor, such as where credit is to be extended to the debtor periodically. A guarantee of an ordinary bank overdraft is considered as a continuing guarantee. Students should revise the various consumer provisions in relation to continuing guarantees.[45]

44 See, eg, *Instruments Act 1958* (Vic) s 126.
45 *NCC* (n 18) div 2.

10.4.1.5 Guarantee not a contract *uberrimae fidei*, but ...

Despite similarities with insurance contracts, guarantees do not involve a duty of positive disclosure. There is no obligation on a creditor, for instance, to inform a prospective guarantor as to the matters that would affect the credit of the debtor. If asked a direct question, then, the banker should, of course, either answer truthfully or decline to answer, citing banker–customer confidentiality if that is applicable. Generally, the normal rules as to misrepresentation and misleading and deceptive conduct apply.

The position is, however, slightly contentious because of remarks made by Lord Campbell in the old (1845) case of *Hamilton v Watson,*[46] which suggest that in some cases there is a duty of positive disclosure. His Lordship said:

> I should think that this might be considered as the criterion whether the disclosure ought to be made voluntarily, namely, whether there is anything that might not naturally be expected to take place between the parties who are concerned in the transaction, that is, whether there be a contract between the debtor and the creditor, to the effect that his position [ie the surety's position] shall be different from that which the surety might naturally expect; and, if so, the surety is to see whether that is disclosed to him. But if there be nothing which might not naturally take place between those parties, then, if the surety would guard against particular perils he must put the question.[47]

The 'rule' in *Hamilton v Watson* is much cited with apparent approval (see, eg, *Goodwin v National Bank of Australasia Ltd,*[48] per Barwick CJ) as a matter of course, but very seldom (if ever) applied. It suffers from the obvious defect that it is not very precisely expressed. One view is that it is best regarded as subsumed/confined by the modern law of mistake (as per *Taylor v Johnson*[49]), and should be taken to express no more than that the guarantee will be voidable for mistake by the surety as to some fact if the mistake was caused by the creditor or the creditor was aware the guarantor was mistaken and took steps to ensure that the guarantor did not become aware of their mistake. A broader interpretation is possible, however, though there is no support for it in decided cases. For example, *Cooper v National Provincial Bank Ltd,*[50] *National Provincial Bank of England Ltd v Glanusk*[51] and *Royal Bank of Scotland v Greenshields*[52] all suggest that unusual circumstances are of themselves insufficient without some element of 'misdirection'.

10.4.2 Liabilities

10.4.2.1 Rights of guarantors

Generally speaking, on default by the debtor, a guarantor stands in place of the debtor concerning the creditor.

46 *Hamilton v Watson* (1845) 8 ER 1339.
47 Ibid 1344.
48 *Goodwin v National Bank of Australasia Ltd* (1968) 117 CLR 173.
49 *Taylor v Johnson* (1983) 151 CLR 422.
50 *Cooper v National Provincial Bank Ltd* [1945] 2 All ER 641.
51 *National Provincial Bank of England Ltd v Glanusk* [1913] 3 KB 335.
52 *Royal Bank of Scotland v Greenshields* [1914] SC 259.

- If the guarantor meets the debtor's obligations, then they have a right to be subrogated to all the creditor's rights against the debtor. Thus, when they have been forced to pay, the guarantor acquires an immediate right of action against the debtor. This means that a guarantor may prove in the debtor's bankruptcy should that occur. Note, however, that standard clauses in guarantees prohibit guarantors from proving in bankruptcy in competition with the creditor.
- The guarantor has an immediate right to have all securities held by the creditor transferred to them. Again, this right is usually circumscribed by a standard clause which provides that this is not to occur until all the debts owed by the debtor (and not just the amount for which the guarantor has agreed to be liable) are discharged.

In relation to this last point, note that where securities are held by the creditor, the creditor is not required to turn to them before resorting to the guarantee provided by the guarantor (*Duncan, Fox & Co v North & South Wales Bank*[53]).

10.4.2.2 Co-guarantors/co-sureties and contribution

Where there is one transaction and multiple guarantors, it would be inequitable if only one of the guarantors were forced to pay the entire debt without any recourse against other guarantors. The rule is as laid down in *Mahoney v McManus*,[54] per Gibbs CJ:

> A surety is entitled to contribution from his co-sureties so that the common burden is borne equally, and so that no surety is required, as between himself and his co-sureties, to pay more than his due share. The right arises whether the sureties are bound jointly, jointly and severally, or severally, and whether by the same or different instruments, and whether or not the sureties knew of each other's existence, provided they are liable in respect of the same debt.[55]

A, B and C are co-sureties for a debt of $120 000 owed by D to E. On default by D, A pays the whole amount to E. A is then entitled to contributions of $40 000 each from B and C. If B is unable to pay at all, then A can claim $60 000 from C. If B is able to pay $20 000 only, then A is entitled to $50 000 from C. Suppose now that A guaranteed the full amount, but that B and C each guaranteed only $60 000. B and C's contribution is then $20 000 each.

The right of contribution arises at common law or equity and does not rely on any contractual agreement, although it can be modified by agreement.

10.4.2.3 Minors

The liability of a guarantor hinges on an existing and enforceable right against the debtor. If there is not one, then the guarantor is not liable. However, note the *Minors (Property and Contracts) Act 1970* (NSW) s 47 and the *Minors Contracts (Miscellaneous Provisions) Act*

53 *Duncan, Fox & Co v North & South Wales Bank* (1879) 11 Ch D 88.
54 *Mahoney v McManus* (1981) 180 CLR 370.
55 Ibid 376.

1979 (SA) s 5, which provide that guarantors will be liable as if the minor debtor was of full age.

Note also again that it is general practice to insert into guarantees a term to the effect that if the debt cannot be recovered from the debtor because of the debtor's contractual incapacity, the guarantor then agrees to be liable for the amount on an indemnity basis. Whether such a clause is enforceable has (strangely) apparently not been tested.

10.4.2.4 *Dobbs* clauses

Evidentiary matters arise where the guarantor disputes that the debtor has defaulted. To smooth the path for the creditor's convenience, standard guarantees thus usually contain a clause providing that the parties agree that some certificate (or similar) signed by an officer of the creditor is 'conclusive evidence' (or similar) of default 'unless there is manifest error'. The High Court in *Dobbs v National Bank of Australasia Ltd*[56] upheld the effectiveness of these clauses. Dobbs was a commercial case, and it is highly likely (though untested) that these clauses are vulnerable to the unconscionability provisions of the *Australian Consumer Law*.

10.4.2.5 Limitation of guarantor's liability

Guarantees may, of course, be limited by amount or by duration. Generally speaking, there is little difficulty here, save for one point. As to limitations on the amount, there are two possible formulas, with different effects.

(1) The surety may guarantee only a certain amount of the debt (eg 'I guarantee $4000 of the amount that you extend to X') ('Form 1').

(2) The surety may guarantee the whole debt but with a limitation on their liability (eg 'I guarantee the whole amount that you extend to X, provided that my liability does not exceed $4000') ('Form 2').

The difference arises because in the event of bankruptcy of the debtor, in Form 2 the guarantor is not permitted to prove in competition with the creditor unless the guarantor has paid the full outstanding amount of the loan (*Re Sass; Ex parte National Provincial Bank of England Ltd*;[57] *Lumley General Insurance Ltd v Oceanfast Marine Pty Ltd*[58]). The situation is the same regarding the surety's ability to turn to any securities given by the debtor in relation to the debt. Under Form 2, the guarantor would have no right against the securities. If Form 1 is used, they have a right to share in the benefit of the securities given by the debtor.

10.4.3 Avoidance

Guarantees are regularly entered into by friends, relations and others at the behest of their friends or relations or others. When these guarantees are called on, as they often are, the warm glow of benevolence felt by the guarantor is frequently replaced by indignant resentment at a wanton abuse of trust, and payment is resisted by appeals

56 *Dobbs v National Bank of Australasia Ltd* (1935) 53 CLR 643.

57 *Re Sass: Ex parte National Provincial Bank of England Ltd* [1896] 2 QB 12.

58 *Lumley General Insurance Ltd v Oceanfast Marine Pty Ltd* [2001] NSWCA 479.

to principles of undue influence, duress and unconscionable behaviour. Judges notably appear to favour the guarantor, rather than the banks. Consequently, the law reports are littered with hundreds of cases where guarantees have been avoided on these grounds. The principles will be familiar to students from contract law. As regards duress and undue influence, the argument goes that the debtor has induced the surety to grant the guarantee by means of duress or (more usually) presumed undue influence, and that the creditor was either aware or should reasonably have been aware of the duress/relationship or (again more likely) was acting as the debtor's agent to procure the guarantee. Alternatively, there is *Commercial Bank of Australia Ltd v Amadio* unconscionability.[59]

Thus, the guarantor is under some disability concerning the creditor (often ignorance of the guarantor's affairs, or of financial affairs) so as to create an inequality to the extent that the guarantor is unable to determine whether the guarantee is in their best interests (which invariably it is not in a non-commercial setting) and the creditor either knew or should reasonably have been aware of the disadvantage and exploited it to obtain the guarantee. Students should revise the general contractual principles in relation to duress, undue influence and unconscionability.[60] However, there is one situation that relates specifically to guarantees that requires particular noting here.

10.4.3.1 Guarantees by married women

For some reason, married women of financial substance are prone casually to guarantee the debts of their ne'er-do-well husbands and require special protection from this defect of character. In *Yerkey v Jones*,[61] Dixon CJ said that if a married woman's consent to become a guarantor for her husband's debt was procured by her husband without her understanding its essential effect, and the creditor accepted the guarantee without taking steps to inform the wife of her obligations, the guarantee could be set aside. The effect of the decision was to place on the creditor an onus to establish that it had taken adequate steps to inform the wife of her obligations *and* was reasonably satisfied that she had a sufficient understanding of these. (Note, by the way, that this is somewhat short of placing the husband–wife relationship into one of the accepted categories of presumed undue influence.)

Yerkey v Jones was decided in 1939. Not only is it arguable that a majority of the Court did not endorse Dixon's statement, but it also might be thought to be inconsistent with contemporary social attitudes and economic reality. (As regards the former, the modern assumption is that women are just as financially capable as men. Regarding the latter, a husband wishing to borrow for business purposes is likely to transfer his non-business assets into his wife's name to avoid risking them.) Nevertheless, the High Court in *Garcia v National Australia Bank Ltd* (1998) affirmed the '*Yerkey* principle' and avoided the guarantee in question.[62] The decision puts Australian law at odds with that in the United

59 *Commercial Bank of Australia Ltd v Amadio* (1983) 151 CLR 447. This was, of course, a guarantee case.

60 See generally Ewan McKendrick, *Contract Law* (Hart Publishing, 15th ed, 2023) ch 17.

61 *Yerkey v Jones* (1939) 63 CLR 649.

62 The surety in question was an experienced businesswoman, but the High Court of Australia declined to overturn the trial judge's finding on the facts that she did not understand her obligations under the guarantee, although clearly Callinan J was tempted. His Honour made the observation that he 'was impressed by the submissions of the respondent that on the evidence the findings of ... want of

Kingdom, where the position is that there is no justification for providing special protection for wives concerning guarantees (See, eg, *Barclays Bank v O'Brien*,[63] a House of Lords decision considered and expressly not followed in *Garcia*.)

The majority judgment also expressed the view that the principle might be extended to 'long term and publicly declared relationships short of marriage between members of the same or opposite sex' where a husband was a guarantor for his wife.[64] However, shortly after, in *State Bank of New South Wales Ltd v Hibbert*,[65] Bryson J declined to extend the principle to de facto wives, and the Australian Capital Territory's Court of Appeal in *Watt v State Bank of New South Wales*[66] likewise declined to do so in the case of guarantees provided by the parents for the debts of their children. Notwithstanding that there has not been a great deal of enthusiasm for *Garcia*,

> ... [t]he result is that a financier taking a guarantee from a married woman must seriously consider the problem of proving that she had sufficient understanding and knowledge of what she was doing. Since it is not at all obvious how this might be done, guarantees from married women must be discounted for the risk that they may be uncollectable if challenged.[67]

It is important to note, though, that the majority in *Garcia* placed considerable emphasis on the fact that the surety was a 'volunteer';[68] that is, that she gained no economic benefit herself from the transaction going ahead. In cases where the wife does obtain such a benefit, the *Yerkey* principle will not apply. (See, eg, *Commonwealth Bank of Australia v Cohen*[69].)

10.4.4 Discharge of the surety

A breach by the creditor of any condition of the guarantee allows termination of the guarantee by the surety.

Subject to contrary provisions in the guarantee contract, a surety will be discharged from its obligations where:

- the debtor pays the debt
- the creditor gives a discharge/release to the debtor
- the creditor amends the original debt agreement in any material manner without the agreement of the surety (eg by granting the debtor additional time)

understanding on the part of the appellant were not open, but not sufficiently so to reach a different conclusion on those basic factual findings' and that 'very rarely will such findings as were made here, be open in the case of a wife with the qualifications, experience and other attributes possessed by this appellant.' See *Garcia v National Australia Bank Ltd* (1998) 194 CLR 395.

63 *Barclays Bank plc v O'Brien* [1994] 1 AC 180.

64 *Garcia v National Australia Bank Ltd* (1998) 194 CLR 395. Of interest is the fact that the dissenting judgment was that of Kirby J. Gaudron, McHugh, Gummow and Hayne JJ delivered a joint judgment in which they sought to ground *Yerkey* in a broader principle relating to 'trust and confidence' between domestic partners that was separate from *Amadio* unconscionability. Callinan J delivered a separate judgment affirming *Yerkey*, but without seeking a broader underlying justification for it.

65 *State Bank of New South Wales Ltd v Hibbert* (2000) 9 BPR 17,543.

66 *Watt v State Bank of New South Wales* [2002] FCA 1184.

67 Alan Tyree, *Banking Law in Australia* (LexisNexis, 9th ed, 2017).

68 *Garcia v National Australia Bank Ltd* (1998) 194 CLR 395, 396.

69 *Commonwealth Bank of Australia v Cohen* (1988) ASC 55-681.

- there is an express or implied term of the guarantee contract leading to the execution of the contract that there is to be a co-surety and that co-surety fails to give their guarantee
- there is an express or implied condition that the guarantee is contingent on the granting or maintenance of specific security and the security is not provided or maintained.

Also:

- Where a creditor relinquishes or losses the benefit of any security held by the creditor, the extent of the guarantor's liability is reduced by the value of the aforementioned security.
- A variation in the constitution of either the debtor or the creditor (eg the constitution of a partnership) terminates the guarantee contract as to any future advances in the absence of further agreement.
- The debtor's death causes the guarantee to 'crystallise', and the guarantor will not be liable for further advances.
- The death of the surety does not necessarily terminate the guarantee. The estate is liable to the extent of past transactions and where the creditor advances further funds, unaware of the death of the surety for those funds. Notice of the death again 'crystallises' the guarantee. (It is usual for guarantees to expressly provide continuing liability until the expiry of three months following receipt in writing from the estate's representatives of intention to determine the guarantee.)

In the case of a continuing guarantee, the surety is entitled to determine the extent of the guarantee as to future advances by giving notice at any time to the creditor. Again, most standard-form guarantees expressly provide that a period of notice is required – usually 90 days or three calendar months.

10.4.5 Statutory provisions affecting guarantees

Students should revise the provisions of the *Australian Consumer Law* and the *National Credit Code*, as they may be relevant to guarantees, and note the role of state-based legislation such as the *Contracts Review Act 1980* (NSW).

10.5 Summary

This chapter discusses various aspects of lending by banks to customers, focusing on different types of lending and different types of borrowers who require different forms of guarantees and loan arrangements. The chapter also discusses secured lending in relation to real property and covers the concept of securities, legal and equitable security interests, priorities when multiple interests exist, and legal implications of the introduction of the Torrens title system. The chapter covers various aspects of guarantees in lending, including legal considerations and the rights and obligations of the parties involved.

A security is an interest in property that allows the creditor to reclaim the debt, or a part of it, from the property under certain circumstances, usually in case of default in repayment. Creditors may prefer taking security along with the borrower's contractual promise to repay.

Before the introduction of the Torrens system of title registration, land conveyance required a complex investigation of ownership, making title uncertain. The old-style mortgages involved conveying the land to the lender with a contractual promise to re-convey upon repayment. However, courts of equity recognised the 'right of redemption', giving borrowers an equitable interest known as the 'equity of redemption'.

With the development of the Torrens system of land registration, indefeasibility of title became crucial. Registration as the owner became conclusive evidence of ownership, subject to limited exceptions related to fraud. The Torrens system issues a certificate of title for each registered parcel of land, serving as important evidence of ownership and historical dealings.

Under the Torrens system, mortgages take a different form. Registered mortgages can be either legal or equitable but have similar rights and obligations implied by the statute. An equitable mortgage could be created by depositing title deeds with the lender. However, registered mortgages offer better protection for both parties. The chapter also discusses priorities among mortgages under the Torrens system.

Guarantors may have little to gain from entering into a guarantee, and therefore, the law tends to be protective of them. Changes in the obligation of the debtor can release the guarantor from their responsibilities. Clauses in guarantees that restrict the rights of guarantors are generally construed strictly against the bank, which is typically responsible for the guarantee's form. The chapter then explores circumstances under which a guarantor may avoid the guarantee contract.

FURTHER READING

Aitken, Lee, '"Agency", Mortgage "Originators", and Loan Enforcement' (2016) 41(3) *Australian Bar Review* 220.

Giancaspro, Mark, '"I Now Pronounce You ... in a State of Uncertainty": Contemporary Treatment of the Wives' Special Equity and a Plan for the Future' (2017) 11(1) *Journal of Equity* 80.

Kokkinis, Andreas and Andrea Miglionico, *Banking Law: Private Transactions and Regulatory Frameworks* (Routledge, 2021) ch 9.

O'Donovan, James, *Lender Liability* (Thomson Reuters, 2nd ed, 2016).

QUESTIONS

(1) David Jones obtained a loan from ABC Bank Ltd, and the bank took a mortgage over a house he owned. During the property market downturn, the value of the house dropped substantially. In January 2022, David's long-time partner, Elise, gave the bank a personal guarantee at the request of the bank. Six months later, David defaulted on the payment of the loan, and the bank attempted to call on the guarantee given by Elise. Advise Elise of her position.

(2) Your friend Lily, who has a 14-year-old child, Lucy, has asked you what she needs to take into account if Lucy is considering borrowing some money from a bank. What is the situation if Lily acts as the guarantor? They both live in New South Wales.

(3) What is the principle underscoring the Torrens system? What are the exceptions to this principle?

INDEX

accounts, 168
  combining accounts
    'exceptions' to *Clayton's* rule, 177–8
    general rules, 175–7
    rule in *Clayton's case*, 177
  dormant accounts, 164–5
  Exchange Settlement Accounts, 251
  freezing the account, 178
    bankruptcy and winding up, *see* bankruptcy and winding up
    death, 178–9
    mental incapacity, 178
  garnishee orders, 184–7
  tracing orders, 187–8
  types of accounts
    current (transaction) accounts, 168
    joint accounts, 172–4
    overdrafts, 170–1
    particular purpose deposits, 170
    savings accounts, 168–9
    statements and passbooks, 174–5
    term deposits, 169–70
    trust accounts, 171–2
APP entities, 134
  access to personal information, 141–2
  adoption, use or disclosure of government related identifiers, 140
  anonymity and pseudonymity, 137
  collection of solicited personal information, 137–8
  correction of personal information, 142
  cross-border disclosure of personal information, 140
  dealing with unsolicited personal information, 138
  direct marketing, 139–40
  notification of the collection of personal information, 138–9
  open and transparent management of personal information, 136–7
  quality of personal information, 141
  security of personal information, 141
  use or disclosure of personal information, 139
Apple Pay, 115, 116, 267–70
APRA–ASIC Committee, 19
AusPayNet, 249–51
  membership types, 249
Australian Competition and Consumer Commission, 28–9, 40, 143, 270, 274
  functional difference to Australian Securities and Investments Commission, 28–9
  primary roles, 28
Australian credit licence, 42, 43, 50, 70, 120
  'best interests' duty, 52–3
  exemptions from licensing requirements, 51
  general conduct obligations of holders, 51–2
  mandatory disclosure requirements, 53
  responsible lending obligation, 54–8
    circumstances where credit contract 'unsuitable', 56–7
    National Consumer Credit Protection Amendment (Supporting Economic Recovery) Bill 2020 (Cth), 57–8
    suitability assessments, 54–5
Australian Financial Complaints Authority, 53, 62, 125
Australian Financial Services Licence, 120, 270
Australian Financial Services Licence licensee's requirements
  'best interests' duty and related obligations, 58–9
    'appropriate advice' duty, 92
    'conflicted remuneration', 98–9
    duty of priority, 92
    duty to warn client advice based on incomplete or inaccurate information, 92
    proposed 'good advice' duty, 96–7
    'safeharbour' conditions, 93–6
  disclosure requirements, 85–6
    Financial Services Guide, 86–7
    Product Disclosure Statement, 88–9
    Statement of Advice, 87–8
  'general advice' versus 'personal advice', 89–90
  general requirements, 85
  representatives, 84–5
  requirements for application, 83

Australian Law Reform Commission
'best interests' duty and, 96–8
Confronting Complexity; Reforming Corporations and Financial Services Legislation, 76–8
Australian Paper Clearing System, 218, 219
Australian Payments Clearing Association Limited, 218
Australian Privacy Principles, 131, 134
APP entities, *see* APP entities
Principle 1: Open and Transparent Management of Personal Information, 136–7
Principle 2: Anonymity and Pseudonymity, 137
Principle 3: Collection of Personal Information, 137–8
Principle 4: Dealing with Unsolicited Personal Information, 138
Principle 5: Notification of the Collection of Personal Information, 138–9
Principle 6: Use or Disclosure of Personal Information, 139
Principle 7: Direct Marketing, 139–40
Principle 8: Cross-border Disclosure of Personal Information, 140
Principle 9: Adoption, Use or Disclosure of Government Related Identifiers, 140
Principle 10: Quality of Personal Information, 141
Principle 11: Security of Personal Information, 141
Principle 12: Access to Personal Information, 141–2, 276–7
Principle 13: Correction of Personal Information, 142
Australian Prudential Regulation Authority, 16, 19, 22–5, 52, 58, 123, 149, 258
areas of focus, 23–4
Council of Financial Regulators membership, 26
enabling legislation, 24–5
Financial Regulator Assessment Authority and, 30–1
key function, 23
mandate, 23
MoU with Australian Securities and Investments Commission, 19–20
primary responsibility, 23
Australian Securities and Investments Commission, 16, 25–6, 40, 55, 58, 60, 68, 69, 110, 257
central role, 25–6
consumer credit protection and, 44–5
consumer protection responsibilities, 26
Council of Financial Regulators membership, 26
digital currencies and, 81
enforcement of *Corporations Act 2001* (Cth), 26
Enhanced Regulatory Sandbox and, 120–2, 125
ePayments Code and, 257–60, 264, 267–8, 283
'factual information', 108
'financial product advice', 108
Financial Regulator Assessment Authority and, 30–1
functional difference to Australian Competition and Consumer Commission, 28–9
granting of Australian Financial Services Licence by, 83
MoU with Australian Prudential Regulation Authority, 19–20
Murray Inquiry recommendations and, 75
National Consumer Credit Protection Act 2009 (Cth) and, 41–2
'personal advice', 108
product intervention power, 100–3
consultation, 102
consumer detriment and, 101–2
duration and amendments to order, 102
examples of interventions, 101
products within scope of, 100–1
publication of order, 102
types of order, 101
regulatory sandbox framework, 119
Australian Securities Commission, 25
Australian Transaction Reports and Analysis Centre, 29–30, 193
international funds transfer instruction, 30
main functions, 29
requirements of reporting entities, 30
suspicious matter report, 30
threshold transaction report, 30
authorised deposit-taking institution licence, 149

authorised deposit-taking institutions, 3, 64, 123, 149
CDR regime and, 275–6
death of depositor and, 179
dormant accounts and, 164–5
as 'financial institution', 212
financial products and, 80
money 'legally payable' to, 165

bailee
bailee for reward, 201
banker's duties as, duties with respect to bailed goods, 200–1
gratuitous bailee, 201
bank cheques, 217
Bank for International Settlements, definition of payment, 250
banker–customer relationship
altering the relationship, 155–7
debtor–creditor relationship, 149–50
implied terms, 151–2
other relationships, 152
special kind of relationship with special terms, 150–1
bank may refuse to make any payments, 151
reasonable care, 151
reasonable notice, 151
terminating the relationship, 154–5
banker's duties
as bailee, duties with respect to bailed goods, 200–1
duty to the enquirer/third parties, 197–9
duty to question a valid mandate, 199–200
Greenwood duty, 191, 204–5, 208, 224
Macmillan duty, 191, 202–4, 208, 224
other possible duties, 205
duty to discover forgeries, 206
duty to organise business, 207–8
duty to prevent forgeries, 206–7
safe custody, 200–2
Tournier duty, 191–7, 208
banking
'business of banking' definition, 149
correspondent banking, 251–2
dormant accounts, 164–5
statutory limitations of actions
general rules, 157–8
limitation and overdrafts, 158–9
who is the customer, 152–4
Banking Code of Practice, 42–4, 58, 131, 152, 156, 165, 176
responsible lending, 54
banking regulation, public interest theory and, 8–9
Banking Royal Commission, 6, 19–20, 30, 31, 70, 95, 99, 100
'best interests' duty and, 58–9
banking sector, grounds for regulation of, 8–9
bankruptcy and winding up
basic terminology, 179
bankruptcy, 179–83
bankruptcy and set-off, 183
winding up, 183–4
banks, 3
nature of the relationship with customers, *see* banker–customer relationship
special customers
companies, 163–4
executors/administrators, 162
incorporated associations, 160
minors, 161–2
partnerships, 160–1
unincorporated associations, 159–60
Basel Committee on Banking Supervision
Core Principles, 34–5
key activities, 35
bills of exchange
acceptance, 237–8
acceptance for honour, 239
dishonored by non-acceptance, 238
dishonoured foreign bills protested, 238–9
general acceptance, 237
partial acceptance, 238
presentment for acceptance, 238
types of qualified acceptance, 237
analysis, 229–32
promissory notes, 232–3
definition
addressed by one person to another, 227–8
bill of exchange, 227
holder in due course, 235
holder of a bill, 233
in writing, 227

bills of exchange (*cont.*)
requiring the drawer to pay at a fixed or determinable future time, 228
requiring the drawer to pay on demand, 228
signed by the person giving it, 228
a sum certain in money, 228–9
to or to the order of a specified person or to bearer, 229
unconditional order, 227
value, 236
discharge, 243
acceptor becoming holder, 244
cancellation, 244
express waiver, 244
material alteration, 244–5
payment in due course, 243–4
liabilities of parties, 240
circuity of action, 242
effect of forgery, 241–2
extent of liability of parties, *see* extent of liability of parties to bills of exchange
inchoate instruments, 242
measure of liability, 243
who may be liable, 240
liability and, 234
holder for value and holder in due course, *see* holder for value and holder in due course
payment, 239–40
transfer/negotiation, 233–4
endorsements, 233–4
restrictive endorsement, 234
Bitcoin, 81, 279
borrowers
types of borrowers
companies, 292–3
consumers, 293–5
minors, 291
unincorporated businesses, 292
BPAY, 131, 256
Brussels Effect, 145
buy now, pay later, 68–70, 101
future regulatory framework, 69–70
regulatory gap, 68–9

central bank digital currency, 279
Australia, 281–3
pilot project, 281–2
China, 280
European Union, 280–1
Singapore, 281
see also digital currencies issued by central banks
cheques, 211–12
bank cheques, 217
crossings
account payee only, 217
definition, 216
effect of crossing, 216
who may cross, 275–6
defences of the paying bank
contractual defences, 224
'equitable defence', 225
statutory defences, 226–7
definition
cheque, 212
date, 215
financial institution, 212–13
no payee, 213
on demand, 214
order and bearer cheques, 215
sum certain, 213
unconditional order, *see* unconditonal order
duty to pay, 219
funds available, 220
legal impediment, 220–1
proper manner, 220
proper presentation, 221–2
meaning of dishonour, 219
payment by cheque, 218–19
prompt payment or dishonour, 222
role of the drawer's signature, 215–16
transfer by negotiation, 215
traveller's cheques, 217–18, 232
wrong amount, 224
wrong person, 224
wrongful dishonour, 222–3
wrongful payment, 224
Clayton's case
exceptions to rule in, 177–8
rule in, 177
commercial bills, 289–90
companies
as borrowers, 292–3
as special bank customers, 163–4
conduct regulation, 13

consumer credit protection, 40–5
  challenges ahead
    payday loans, 65–8
    rise of buy now, pay later, 68–70
  intersection with general law, 42–3
  National Consumer Credit protection Act 2009 (Cth), *see National Consumer Credit Protection Act 2009* (Cth)
  National Credit Code, see National Credit Code
consumer data rights in Australia
  background, 274–5
  Consumer Data Right scheme, 274–5
  data protection/cybersecurity, 277–8
    CDR Privacy Safeguards, 277–8
  data which should be shared, 276–7
    CDR data, 276
  who can participate, 275–6
  who should bear losses and risks, 277
consumers, as borrowers, 293–5
Corporate Law Economic Reform Program, 74–5
correspondent banking, 251–2
Council of Financial Regulators, 26–7, 258
  composition, 26–7
  objective, 27
  soft law and, 27
credit cards, 254–5
credit reporting, *Privacy Act 1988* (Cth) and, 135–6
cryptocurrency, 279
current (transaction) accounts, 168

data protection, 130
  Australia
    common law duties of confidentiality, 132
    equitable duties of confidence, 131–2
    self-regulation, 131
    statutes, 131
  'Brussels Effect', 143
  General Data Protection Regulation (EU), 142–3
debit cards, 255–6
digital advice licensees
  adequate risk management systems, 109
    cyber risks and information security, 109
    monitoring and testing algorithms, 109
  resources, 108–9
digital currencies, Australian Securities and Investments Commission and, 81
digital currencies issued by central banks
  rise of digital currencies, 279
  selected cases
    Australia, 281–3
    China, 280
    European Union, 280–1
    Singapore, 281
  see also central bank digital currency
digital wallet providers, 115, 268
digital wallets, 268–71
  Australian review of role of, 269–70
  functions of, 268
  need for holistic regulatory approach, 270–1
Dobbs clauses, 306
dormant accounts, 164–5
  'unclaimed moneys' definition, 164

e-CNY, 280
efficient capital markets hypothesis, 5–6
electronic banking
  ePayments Code, see ePayments Code
  main payment instruments, 253
    BPAY, 256
    credit cards, 254–5
    debit cards, 255–6
    stored value cards, 256
  Open Banking and, *see* Open Banking
  payment systems, *see* electronic banking payment systems
  regulatory aspects, 247–9
electronic banking payment systems, 247
  components of payment, 250
    correspondent banking, 251–2
    Exchange Settlement Accounts, 251
    funds transfer, 251
    New Payments Platform, 250
    payment orders, 250
    payments clearing, 250–1
    Real-Time Gross Settlement System, 251
  funds transfer system, 247
  payment system definition, 247, 249–50
Enhanced Regulatory Sandbox
  conditions of entry, 121–3
  eligible persons, 121
  other conditions, 125–6

Enhanced Regulatory Sandbox (*cont.*)
premise of, 120
scope of activities, 123–4
testing environment, 120
testing parameters, 120
time frame and exposure limits, 124–5
ePayments Code, 131, 152, 156, 165, 283
emerging challenges, 267
digital wallets, 268–71
fingerprint/facial recognition/biometric authentication, 267–8
screen scraping, 271–2
history, 257
key provisions
allocation of liability for unauthorised transactions, 259–63
complaint process, 266–7
compliance monitoring and data collection, 267
mistaken internet payments, *see* mistaken internet payments
to whom Code applies, 259
types of transactions, 258–9
legal nature of, 257–8
executors/administrators, as special bank customers, 162
extent of liability of parties to bills of exchange
acceptor, 240–1
drawer, 241
endorser, 241
strangers, 241
transferor by delivery, 241
external dispute resolution, 42

Field Services Guide, 86–7
Financial Conduct Authority (UK), regulatory sandbox, 126
financial market governance
global level, 31
Bank for International Settlements, 33–4
Basel Committee on Banking Supervision, 34–6
Financial Stability Board, 31–3
financial products
product design and distribution obligation, 104–7
'issuers' and 'distributors', 104–6
products subject to obligation, 104
product intervention power, 100–3
regulatory framework, 79
Australian Financial Services Licence licensee's requirements, *see* Australian Financial Services Licence licensee's requirements
concept of clients, *see* retail versus wholesale clients
general definition, 80
overriding exclusions, 80–1
specific inclusions, 80
robo-advice, *see* robo-advice
financial products regulation
Australian Law Reform Commission reform recommendations, 76–8
Murray Inquiry, *see* Murray Inquiry
Wallis Inquiry, *see* Wallis Inquiry
Financial Regulator Assessment Authority, 30–1
key functions, 31
financial services
regulatory framework, 78–9
'dealing' definition, 78–9
'financial service' definition, 78
'make a market for a financial product' definition, 79
'registered schemes' definition, 79
Financial Services Guide, 125
Financial Stability Board, 114
financial system
institutions within, 2–3
banks, *see* banks
non-ADI institutions, 3–4
role of, 2
Fintech
definition, 114
as distinct phenomenon, 114–15
'financial disintermediation' and, 115–16
five major categories of, 114
regulatory approach to, 117–18
regulatory sandbox approach, *see* regulatory sandbox
traditional banks and legacy financial institutions and, 116–17
forgeries
banker's duty to discover, 206
banker's duty to prevent, 206–7
bills of exchange and, 241–2
Future of Financial Advice reforms, 90–1, 97

garnishee orders, 184–7
  order *nisi*, 185
General Data Protection Regulation (EU), 142–3, 145
Global Financial Crisis, 3, 36, 54, 58, 115, 117
Global Financial Innovation Network, 129–30
Google Pay, 115, 116, 267, 268
Greenwood duty, 191, 204–5, 208, 224
guarantees
  avoidance, 306–7
    discharge of the surety, 308–9
    guarantees by married women, 307–8
    statutory provisions affecting guarantees, 309
  consideration, 303
  continuing guarantees, 303
  guarantee versus indemnity, 303
  liabilities
    co-guarantors/co-sureties and contribution, 305
    Dobbs clauses, 306
    limitation of guarantor's liability, 306
    minors, 305–6
    rights of guarantors, 304–5
  not a contract *uberrimae fidei*, 304
  parties, 302–3

holder for value and holder in due course, 235
  complete and regular on face, 236–7
  good faith, 236
  notice of defect in title, 237
  overdue, 236
  value, 236

incorporated associations, as special bank customers, 160
insolvency, definition, 179
institutional structure, 13–16
  institutional model, 14–15
  integrated model, 15
  Twin Peaks model, 13–15
    advantages, 15
    disadvantages, 15–16
internet payments, mistaken, *see* mistaken internet payments

joint accounts, 172–4

lender of last resort, 21
lending, 287
  responsible lending obligation, 42, 54–8
  secured lending, real property, *see* real property secured lending
  types of lending
    commercial bills, 289–90
    letters of comfort, 290–1
    overdrafts, 287–9
    secured/unsecured loans, 287
    term loans, 289
letters of comfort, 290–1
limited partnerships, as borrowers, 292

Macmillan duty, 191, 202–4, 208, 224
macro-prudential regulation, 12
minors
  as borrowers, 291
  guarantees and, 305–6
  as special bank customers, 161–2
mistaken internet payments, 263–4
  definition, 263–4
  disclosure, 264
  on-screen warning, 264
  process for handling insufficient funds cases, 266
  process for handling sufficient funds cases, 265–6
  reporting, investigation and recordkeeping, 264–5
mortgage brokers
  'best interests' duty, 58–60
  'conflicted remuneration' restrictions upon, 60–1
mortgages
  equitable mortgage, 297–8
  'legal' mortgage, 297
  second and subsequent mortgages, 298
  Torrens system, *see* Torrens system
Murray Inquiry, 26–7, 31, 75–6, 99–100, 257

National Consumer Credit Protection Act 2009 (Cth)
  Australian Securities and Investments Commission and, 41–2
  covered activities, 46–50
  'credit guide', 53

National Consumer Credit Protection Act 2009 (Cth) (*cont.*)
key categories of credit activity and licensing requirements, 50–3
key features, 45–6
primary consumer credit provisions, 45
primary obligations of the Australian credit licence under
'best interests' duty, 58–61
'conflict priority rule', 60–1
mandatory disclosure requirements, 53
responsible lending obligation, 54–8
National Credit Code, 176
'amount of credit', 47
'charge' made, 49–50
consumers as borrowers and, 293–5
'credit activity', 48
'credit contract', 47–8
credit definition, 47
credit providers and, 45–6
pre-contractual disclosure, 61–4
'hardship notice', 62
'information statement', 61
notice of changes to credit contract, 61–2
'pre-contractual statement', 61
small-amount credit contracts, 64
unjust transactions, 62–4
'predominant purpose', 48
'short term credit', 47
'ultimate purpose' and 'immediate purpose' distinction, 48–9
National Credit Providers Association, 68
nemo dat rule, 216, 232, 235
Notifiable Data Breaches scheme, 133

Office of the Australian Information Commissioner, 132–5, 274
Office of the Privacy Commissioner, 132, 133
Open Banking, 272–4, 283
Australia, 273–4
consumer data rights in Australia, *see* consumer data rights in Australia
European Union model, 272–3
UK model, 273
overdrafts, 170–1, 287–9
informal overdrafts, 170

particular purpose deposits, 170
partnerships
as borrowers, 292
limited partnerships, 292
as special bank customers, 160–1
payday loans, 65–8
'debt spirals' and, 66
predatory marketing and, 66–7
Privacy Act 1988 (Cth)
Australian Privacy Principles, *see* Australian Privacy Principles
background, 132–3
credit reporting, 135–6
review of, 143–5
scope of application and structure, 123–4
APP entities, 134
definition of 'personal information', 133
definition of 'sensitive information', 133–4
private interest theory, 9–10
Product Disclosure Statement, 88–9, 125
Productivity Commission, review of Australian Consumer Policy Framework, major objectives, 41
promissory notes, 232–3
prudential regulation, 11–13
macro-prudential regulation, 12
public interest theory, 8–9
banking regulation and, 8–9

real property secured lending
legal and equitable interests, 295
'competing interests' priority rules, 295–7
equitable charges, 299
equitable mortgage, 297–8
'legal' mortgage general law, 297
power of sale, 298–9
remedies on default, 298
second and subsequent mortgages, 298
Real-Time Gross Settlement System, 251
receivership, 184
function and powers of receiver, 184
regime design strategies, 16
command and control versus self-regulation, 16–17
rules-based versus principles-based regulation, 17–18
regulation
banking, *see* banking regulation
definition, 4–5
financial crises and, 6–7

objectives, 6
conduct regulation, 13
prudential regulation, 11–13
private interest theory, 9–10
public interest theory, 8–9
regime design
institutional structure, *see* institutional structure
strategies, *see* regime design strategies
regulators, 18–20
domestic level
Australian Competition and Consumer Commission, 28–9
Australian Prudential Regulation Authority, 22–5
Australian Securities and Investments Commission, 25–6
Australian Transaction Reports and Analysis Centre, 29–30
Council of Financial Regulators, 26–7
Financial Regulator Assessment Authority, 30–1
Reserve Bank of Australia, 20–2
regulatory sandbox, 118
background, 119–21
Enhanced Regulatory Sandbox, *see* Enhanced Regulatory Sandbox
other jurisdictions
Global Financial Innovation Network, 129–30
United Kingdom, 126
Reserve Bank of Australia, 16, 20–2, 149
authority to designate a payment system, 248–9
central bank digital currency and, 281
Council of Financial Regulators membership, 26
Governor, 22
Payments System Board, 21–2, 247–8
retail versus wholesale clients, 82–3
'business use' test, 82
'client wealth' test, 82
'price or value' test, 82
'professional investor' test, 82
Ripoll Report, 91
robo-advice, 107
adequate risk management systems, 109
cyber risks and information security, 109
monitoring and testing algorithms, 109
compensation arrangements, 110
facts, financial product advice and relevant requirements, 107–8
resources, 108–9
Royal Commission into Misconduct in the Banking, Superannuation and Financial Services Industry, *see* Banking Royal Commission

safe custody, 200–2
sandbox, *see* regulatory sandbox
savings accounts, 168–9
screen scraping, 267, 271–2
secured/unsecured loans, 287
small-amount credit contracts, payday loans, 65, 67–8
sole traders, as borrowers, 292
Statement of Advice, 87–8, 125
statements and passbooks, 174–5
stored value cards, 256

target market determination, 104–5
term deposits, 169–70
term loans, 289
Torrens system, 299–300
mortgages under, 301
discharge, 301
mortgage of other interests, 302
priority of mortgages, 301
remedies for default under a registered mortgage, 301
tacking, 302
vitiating factors, 302
priorities with respect to unregistered interests, 300–1
Tournier duty, 191–7, 208
exceptions to
commercial interest, 194–5
consent, 195–7
legal compulsion, 192–3
public interest, 193–4
tracing orders, 187–8
traveller's cheques, 217–18, 232
trust accounts, 171–2
'knowing assistance', 171, 172
'knowing receipt', 171–2
Twin Peaks model, 13–15
advantages, 15
disadvantages, 15–16

unclaimed moneys, definition, 164
unconditional order, 213–14
  conditional delivery, 214
unincorporated associations
  as borrowers, 292
  as special bank customers, 159–60
unincorporated businesses
  as borrowers, 292
    limited partnerships, 292
    partnerships, 292
    sole traders, 292
    unincorporated associations, 292

voluntary administration, 184

Wallis Inquiry, 14, 18–19, 22, 26, 74–5
WeChat Pay, 268, 270
winding up, *see* bankruptcy and winding up

www.ingramcontent.com/pod-product-compliance
Lightning Source LLC
LaVergne TN
LVHW080019210926
848481LV00011B/3061
9781108999793